Introduction to Early Childhood Education

Sixth Edition

Verna Hildebrand
Michigan State University

Merrill,
an imprint of Prentice Hall
Upper Saddle River, New Jersey   Columbus, Ohio

Library of Congress Cataloging-in-Publication Data

Hildebrand, Verna.
    Introduction to early childhood education / Verna Hildebrand.—6th ed.
        p. cm.
    Includes bibliographical references and index.
    ISBN 0-02-354553-4 (alk. paper)
    1. Early childhood education—United States.   I. Title.
  LB1139.25.H55   1997
372.21'0973—dc20   96-24895
                                              CIP

Cover art: © Kaila Sullivan/Superstock
Editor: Ann Castel Davis
Production Editor: Alexandrina Benedicto Wolf
Design Coordinator: Julia Zonneveld Van Hook
Text Designer: Donna Chernin
Cover Designer: Russ Masseli
Production Manager: Deidra M. Schwartz
Electronic Text Management: Marilyn Wilson Phelps, Matthew Williams, Karen L. Bretz, Tracey B. Ward
Director of Marketing: Kevin Flanagan
Advertising/Marketing Coordinator: Julie Shough

This book was set in Caledonia by Prentice Hall and was printed and bound by R. R. Donnelley & Sons Company. The cover was printed by Phoenix Color Corp.

© 1997 by Prentice-Hall, Inc.
Simon & Schuster/A Viacom Company
Upper Saddle River, New Jersey 07458

Earlier editions © 1991 by Macmillan Publishing Company; 1986, 1981, 1976, and 1971 by Verna Hildebrand.

Printed in the United States of America

10 9 8 7 6 5 4 3 2 1

ISBN: 0-02-354553-4

Prentice-Hall International (UK) Limited, *London*
Prentice-Hall of Australia Pty. Limited, *Sydney*
Prentice-Hall of Canada, Inc., *Toronto*
Prentice-Hall Hispanoamericana, S. A., *Mexico*
Prentice-Hall of India Private Limited, *New Delhi*
Prentice-Hall of Japan, Inc., *Tokyo*
Simon & Schuster Asia Pte. Ltd., *Singapore*
Editora Prentice-Hall do Brasil, Ltda., *Rio de Janeiro*

I wish to dedicate this book to my family—to my husband, John, without whose faith and encouragement this book would never have been written; to my children, Carol and Steve, both of whom weathered the testing of the philosophy presented; to my parents, Carrel and Florence Butcher, who provided encouragement and an opportunity to study; and to Julia, Ellen, and Lisa, three wonderful granddaughters whose joy in living contributed a fresh urgency to the ideas presented.

Preface

Introduction to Early Childhood Education is a textbook written especially for those who are concerned with teaching young children from infancy through age six. It is an introduction to professional preparation for early childhood teachers. Teachers, psychologists, social workers, and administrators concerned with planning sound programs for fostering children's growth and development will find the book relevant. Parents, nurses, librarians, and people associated with various religious programs for young children will find many useful ideas.

Introduction to Early Childhood Education was written from the experience of many years' teaching in the university classroom and in the kindergarten, nursery school, child care center, and university laboratory school. The additional experience of being a parent of a son and daughter has provided incentive for exploring early childhood education from more than the academic vantage point.

The school for young children is approached through the developmental tasks of early childhood. The work of prominent theorists is cited to help students relate theory and practice. The numerous program ideas contained in this book will help with program planning and thus save time and energy for understanding and helping children as individuals. Photographs and incidents involving real children enliven and illustrate points being made.

University students and Head Start teachers provided the initial stimulus for writing this book. Both wanted to help with integrating knowledge about child growth and development into meaningful school programs for young children. In class after class they questioned the curriculum and the techniques observed in early childhood programs. A continuous search was made for improved ideas to use with young children. This book is designed to help students, teachers, and of course ultimately the children they teach.

ORGANIZATION OF THE TEXT

Part I gives an overall view of goals, children, schools, techniques, and curriculum. It is a brief survey designed for initial orientation of the student to the field before the numerous details of a program are presented. This survey will be particularly helpful to the student beginning observation and participation in a group of children as the school term gets underway.

Part II starts with a chapter on how to plan specific learning activities and follows with chapters on all the typical curricular areas, discussing goals and procedures, and making suggestions for a wide variety of learning activities. Guidance suggestions, interpersonal relationships, and parental involvement are stressed in each chapter. Planning is emphasized as teachers and assistants are urged to sit down together to think carefully about the why, what, and how of their teaching. The part ends with a chapter designed to teach the student how to integrate the planning, manage the group of children, and evaluate the results.

Part III discusses the teacher's professional relationship with parents; presents a global view of children's programs; and covers the past, present, and future professional activities.

NEW TO THIS EDITION

Though I was aware of the excellent reception of the first five editions of *Introduction to Early Childhood Education,* I have, during the preparation of this sixth edition, been especially mindful of the need to make improvements. I think no work of this nature is ever really perfected and completed. Unless an author's knowledge and understanding fail to grow, there must be modifications and additions with the passing years. New in this sixth edition, to aid both pre-professional and professional childhood educators, are

- General updating of news about center accreditation, child care legislation, and statistics showing the increasing need for high quality child care.
- New recommendations for additional readings and videos to aid teaching about operating early childhood schools.
- General integration of concepts regarding working with diverse children and families, and applying concepts that are developmentally appropriate to curriculum planning.
- Useful applications of the philosophy of Russian psychologist Lev Vygotsky, whose work complements that of Jean Piaget.
- Fascinating insights from the stimulating program of creative early childhood curriculum development being carried out in Reggio Emilia, Italy, that is creating a flurry of visits and emulations by many early childhood professionals today.

I hope all readers, and especially instructors, student teachers, and teachers of young children, will view this book not as a straitjacket with rigid sequences, answers, and programs but as a flexible aid helping their own creativity and stimulating their minds. Improvements can be made beyond the blueprints frozen into these printed pages. Professionals are expected to modify and improve upon these efforts as experience, reason, and new knowledge guide them—especially if the well-being of our children and of all humankind is to be most effectively served. Without these corrective possibilities, I, as an author, would have some trepidation concerning my impact on future generations.

I have authored or co-authored four related textbooks which may be useful to some readers. *Guiding Young Children, Fifth Edition* (Merrill/Prentice Hall, 1994) focuses on interpersonal relations in children's groups. *Parenting: Rewards and Responsibilities, Fifth Edition* (Glencoe/McGraw-Hill, 1997) is directed toward high school and lower division college classes where students are connecting children's development and parenting. *Management of Child Development Centers, Fourth Edition* (Merrill/Prentice Hall, 1997), co-authored with Patricia Hearron, presents the managerial principles for managers and administrators. *Knowing and Serving Diverse Families* (Merrill/Prentice Hall, 1996), co-authored with Lillian Aotaki Phenice, Mary McPhail Gray, and Rebecca Peña Hines, is useful in your work with parents.

ACKNOWLEDGMENTS

To the many early childhood professionals who have contributed ideas, photos, and feedback over the six editions, to the parents who have permitted their children's photos to appear in the books, to the adopters of the text, and to the students who have used it, I express my thanks.

To the following professional reviewers, many thanks for your efforts: Beverly Brown Dupré, Southern University at New Orleans; Craig H. Hart, Brigham Young University; Jack Mayala, St. Cloud State University; Lillian Oxtoby, Borough of Manhattan Community College; Colleen K. Randel, The University of Texas at Tyler; Deborah J. Smith, Appalachian State University; and Mary Ann Waldon, Texas Southern University.

I also wish to acknowledge the various editors who gave leadership to the development of the text: Ann Davis, my present editor at Merrill/Prentice Hall, Alex Wolf, production editor, and Marilyn Prudente, copy editor.

Verna Hildebrand

Contents

Part 1   1

Teaching in a School for Young Children Today: An Overview

Chapter 1
Introducing Early Childhood Education   2

The Curriculum Is What Happens   4
Current Trends in the Profession   7
Parents Demand Education
    for Young Children   7
Policymakers Take Action   10
Researchers Show Value
    of Early Education   11
Types of Early Childhood Schools   12
Contributions of Professional
    Associations   18
You as an Adult Educator   19
Observing in the Early
    Childhood School   20
Participating in the Early
    Childhood School   22
Student Evaluations   25
Conclusions   26

Chapter 2
Goals for Early Childhood Education   30

Bases for Goals for Early
    Childhood Education   32
Goals for Early Childhood Education   37
Conclusions   44

Chapter 3
Getting to Know Children   43

Characteristics of Children   50
Family Variations   51
Age-Related Characteristics   52
Grouping Children   59
Knowing Children as Individuals   60
Conclusions   61

Chapter 4
Setting the Stage   64

Accreditation of Schools   66
Environment   67
Planning and Organizing   67
Planning for the Opening of School   68
Planning the Arrangement
    of the Facility   68
Planning the Daily Schedule
    or Sequence of Events   71
Additional Tips for the
    First Days of School   78
Conclusions   79

Chapter 5
Teachers and Techniques Used   82

Developing a Unique Teaching Style   84
Using Methods Appropriate
    for Young Children   86
Qualities of a Good Teacher
    of Young Children   86
Guidance and How the
    Teacher Can Use It   87
What Is Guidance?   88
Transitions   95

You as an Adult Educator   95
Conclusions   95

Part 2   99

The Curriculum of the Early Childhood School

Chapter 6
Introduction to Activity Planning   *100*

A Taxonomy of Educational Objectives   102
Planning Is the Key   103
Planning Specific Activities   104
Conclusions   109

Chapter 7
Activities for Infants   *112*

Planning for Infants   114
Environment   114
Goals Based on Child Development
   Research   115
Conclusions   122

Chapter 8
Activities for Toddlers   *126*

Toddler Development as
   the Basis for Planning   129
Themes for Activities   130
Developmental Focus of Activities   131
Contact With Parents   140
Conclusions   140

Chapter 9
Motor Skill Activities   *142*

Motor Skills and Self-efficacy   144
Motor Skill Development   145
Proper Equipment and Support   146
Other Values of Outdoor Activity   155
Requirements of a High-Quality
   Outdoor Program   158
Emergencies   166
Conclusions   166

Chapter 10
Creative Art Activities   *168*

What Is Creativity?   170
Developmental Tasks Fostered
   Through Art Activities   174
Developmental Stages in Children's Art   178
General Classroom Procedures   178
Typical Art Activities for Young Children   182
Helping a New Volunteer   196
Conclusions   197

Chapter 11
Science Activities   *200*

Cognitive Functioning: A Definition   202
Cognitive Development Linked With
   Other Development   202
Goals for Children's Cognitive Growth   203
What Is Science for Young Children?   207
Planning Science Education   209
Suggested Science Experiences   213
Monitoring Science Education   230
Conclusions   230

Chapter 12
Perceptual-Motor Activities   *234*

Value of Perceptual-Motor Activities   236
Premathematics Activities   238
Eye-Hand Coordination Materials   243
Construction Materials   244
Using Microcomputers   249
Conclusions   252

Chapter 13
Language Activities   *254*

Language Definition and Beginnings   256
Relationship of Language Development
   to Total Development   256
Types of Language Development   260
Goals for Language Development   260
How the Teacher Fosters Language
   Development   261
Planning Language Arts Activities   263
Teaching Foreign Language   271

Learning English as a Second Language   272
Dealing With Language Problems   275
Conclusions   277

Chapter 14
Literature Activities and Emerging Literacy   280
The Major Goal: A Lifelong Love of Books   282
Literature Supports All Developmental Tasks   282
The Reading Question   283
Experiencing a Wide Variety of Literature   288
Responding Daily to Literature Experiences   289
Enhancing the Total Program Through Literature   302
Inspiring and Assisting Parents' Participation in Literature Experiences   305
Conclusions   314

Chapter 15
Dramatic Play Activities   316
Dramatic Play: Defined   318
Values of Dramatic Play   318
Planning for Dramatic Play   327
Suggested Props for Dramatic Play Themes   329
Conclusions   336

Chapter 16
Creative Music Activities   338
Enjoying Music: The Major Goal   340
Planning Music Experiences   341
Role of Parents in a Child's Musical Education   358
Conclusions   359

Chapter 17
Field Trips and Special Visitors   364
Planning Field Trips   366
Field Trip Suggestions   369

Special Visitors Invited to the School   374
Conclusions   376

Chapter 18
Food Activities, Meals, and Snacks   378
A Child's Nutrition: Whose Responsibility?   380
Opportunities for Food and Nutrition Education   381
Guides for Food and Nutrition Program Planning   381
Long-Range Goals for Children's Experiences with Food   388
Mealtime in the School for Young Children   394
Communicating With Parents   398
Conclusions   399

Chapter 19
Managing an Early Childhood Group   402
Teachers as Managers   404
Management Tasks
Planning Programs for Young Children   406
Adequate Planning Requires Time   409
Agenda for Planning Conferences   411
Organizing Time, Materials, and Space   416
Staffing   420
Monitoring and Controlling   422
Conclusions   427

Part 3   429

Professional Considerations

Chapter 20
Teacher-Parent Relations   430
A Support System for Families   432
Values of Teacher-Parent Relationships   433
Family Characteristics and Lifestyles   435
Parents' Presence During Beginning Days   435

Types of Contacts Between Parents and
Teachers   436
Experiences for Students and Beginning
Teachers   448
Counseling Help   448
Explaining the Need for Parent Work   448
Conclusions   449

Chapter 21
The World's Children   **452**
Global Interdependence   454
International Year of the Family and the Fourth
World's Women's Conference   454
Multicultural Understanding   455
Child Growth and Development Across
Cultures   457
Early Childhood Education
Around the World   458
Conclusions   477

Chapter 22
The Profession—
Past, Present, and Future   **480**
European Roots   482
Early American Roots   484

The Great Depression Era   486
World War II Era   486
The Early Post–World War II Era   487
The War on Poverty Era: 1960s   490
Early Childhood Education: The 1970s to the
Late 1990s   491
Standards for Child Care   494
The National Association for the Education of
Young Children (NAEYC)   495
The Women's Movement   496
Research Findings   497
Handicapped Young Children   499
Future Trends for Early
Childhood Education   500
Conclusions   501

Glossary   **505**
Name Index   **509**
Subject Index   **513**

PART 1

Teaching in a School for Young Children Today: An Overview

Chapter 1   **Introducing Early Childhood Education**

Chapter 2   **Goals for Early Childhood Education**

Chapter 3   **Getting to Know Children**

Chapter 4   **Setting the Stage**

Chapter 5   **Teachers and Techniques Used**

Introducing Early Childhood Education

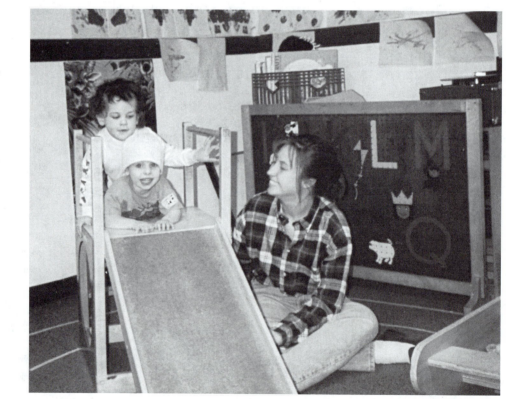

Kansas State University

Objectives

✔ Identify the qualities needed by an early childhood teacher.
✔ Identify different settings where an early childhood teacher works.
✔ Identify current professional efforts to raise standards in early childhood education.
✔ Recognize current demands for the services of early childhood educators.

"Let's build an airport," calls Yolanda as she and Scottie dash into the prekindergarten classroom.

"I'm gonna paint," says Scottie.

Yolanda and Scottie are ready for school. Is school ready for them?

Welcome to the world of early childhood! The early childhood education profession that awaits you can be a creative, challenging, and exciting adventure.

You, as an early childhood teacher, will influence the course of history of the twenty-first century. From moment to moment, each day, you will be putting together what you know about how children grow and develop with appropriate activities and processes, thus creating high-quality programs for children who are in their most formative years. You'll be like the artist who combines the elements of line, color, form, and texture to create a masterpiece. Your "masterpieces" will be the leaders of the twenty-first century. You have an awesome responsibility!

You'll accept all children, whatever their characteristics. You'll delve deeply into your knowledge to understand each one. You'll work hard to prepare a rich, varied, and worthwhile program that meets your own high standards and the high standards of the parents and the community of early childhood scholars whom you have joined. Welcome!

THE CURRICULUM IS WHAT HAPPENS

The curriculum of the early childhood school is the major emphasis in this book. You'll be learning what happens in a school for young children and how to make it happen most effectively. Easels, blocks, and quiet conversations are part of the children's curriculum, just as this course is part of your curriculum in early education. Both are stepping-stones to future skills and knowledge.

You are embarking on one of many interesting courses in the professional field of early childhood education. Your major tasks will focus on young children's learning activities and learning environments. You will be planning, analyzing,

An early childhood school: a place to try out the computer with the help of friends. (Kansas State University)

and evaluating materials, equipment, activities, and approaches used in providing learning experiences for groups of children in infant centers through kindergarten.

This course is full of ideas—utilizing your ideas and those of others. You'll enjoy finding out what children like to do, how to present activities, and why certain equipment is recommended for children. You'll be using all you already know about child development and early childhood education and be adding more information as you read, study, observe, plan for, and interact with children. This field is very dynamic. It is action packed. There is always something new to learn about children and early childhood education.

The terms **early childhood education** and **child development center** will be used to replace the terms *preschool* and *nursery school*. The terms preschool and nursery school seem to downplay the importance of the years of early childhood and the vast amount of significant learning that takes place during this early period in children's lives. This change in terminology represents a professional trend that you can begin incorporating in your own vocabulary.

In this course you'll apply what you have already learned about interacting with young children. Interaction techniques of guidance or discipline are based on theories and research in child development and child psychology. These techniques help you when talking to children, motivating them, and anticipating their next moves or their next level of competence. You'll build on your present base of guidance information and skill and learn more about interpreting children's levels of development, their needs, and behaviors. You'll strive to help children become fully competent individuals.

During this course you'll also apply skills you've learned in cooperating with your class members and the teaching staff of an early childhood center to become a reliable, competent member of the teaching team. The relationships among adults offer opportunities for you to practice job-related skills that are very important to your future success in an early childhood teaching position. For example, in addition to applying knowledge and skills related to children, you'll practice preparing for the teaching role, being on time, shouldering your share of responsibility, assuming increasing levels of responsibility, and being sensitive to the needs, interests, and skills of your co-workers, lead teachers, volunteers, and parents.

An early childhood school: a place to talk things over with the teacher as you work. (Michigan State University)

TALK IT OVER: NO. 1

What are the qualities of a good employee? What is special about being employed to work with young children?

Teaching young children is challenging and rewarding, though at times frustrating. It is an awesome responsibility to influence the lives of children from day to day during their most formative years. This is a profession in the truest sense of the word, and anyone looking for strictly a nine-to-five job should look elsewhere. Your teaching will have long-range implications for the child, the family, the school, the community, and the world. Special preparation is required in order to do well. In fact, you can never stop learning, changing, and updating your knowledge and skill. As in other professions, you must apply ethical procedures in dealing with children, parents, and fellow professionals. You will be on call when needed after hours for a conference or a meeting. Even on vacation you will be a teacher as you see new sights, read new books, or collect objects and ideas that will become learning experiences for your group of children. Teaching young children is one of the helping professions that needs dedicated practitioners.

The foregoing conveys the seriousness of the professional responsibility you are undertaking. Yet there is enjoyment and creativity in it, too. You, as a teacher, will be creative from moment to moment and day to day as you work with a group of young children—each a creative individual in his or her own right. You will create for each child, for each group, for each year, in accordance with needs, goals, plans, and resources of time, money, materials, and available help. No two children will develop in quite the same way. Yes, yours is a creative profession!

Teaching young children will bring enjoyment. If you do not find joy in it, you should look for some other avenue of work, because *work* it surely will be. Young children are spontaneous, loving, curious, and creative. Working with them will keep you young at heart, on your toes, and moving ahead. Children help keep your sense of wonder alive because all things interest them. Little ones express themselves so honestly that it may relieve you to discover a social group so unpretentious.

The early childhood education profession needs happy, intelligent, energetic, and creative teachers to guide it through the years ahead. It is hoped that you will find many satisfactions in the study you have undertaken.

An early childhood school: a place to say "Hi" to the baby. (Children's Center, Denver)

CURRENT TRENDS IN THE PROFESSION

The early childhood education profession has matured a great deal during recent decades. A historical perspective of the profession is available in the final chapter of this book. You might like to read it now and then again later when you have become better acquainted with the issues confronting this field.

In 1980 the Bureau of the Census projected that 6.5 million children ages three to six would be enrolled in early childhood programs in 1990.[1] In 1993 enrollments equalled 7.0 million.[2] With the birthrates staying steady, this indicates that more parents than expected are enrolling their children in early childhood education programs.

In addition to a desire for earlier education, there is also an increasing need for full-day child care services. This demand arises because both parents work outside the home and because single parents rearing their children alone need child care services to supplement the care and attention they can give. There has been a big increase in before- and after-school care.

PARENTS DEMAND EDUCATION FOR YOUNG CHILDREN

Today's parents are increasingly enrolling their young children in early childhood education programs. Figure 1–1 shows the trend line from 1965 to 1993. Today the United States has 96 percent of its five-year-olds in kindergarten and 40 percent of its three- and four-year-olds in prekindergarten programs. Recently, the public consensus has focused on the value to society of these programs. States have been increasing their state funding for prekindergarten programs for four-year-olds as well as giving increased support for kindergartens. Some kindergartens operate full days, equal to the elementary school day.

Many states are mandating support for these early childhood programs through the existing public school system. Unused classroom space is sometimes available at little extra cost beyond that incurred to adapt the rooms for activities appropriate for younger children. Also, a public administrative structure already exists, avoiding the need for a new and costly bureaucracy. In addition, displaced teachers may be available if they are willing to undertake the retraining essential for learning to work appropriately with these younger children.

Many changes have occurred in American families in recent decades. Figure 1–2 shows that the storybook family—father employed while mother stays home with the children—dropped from 43 percent of families in 1976 to 27.5 percent of families in 1987. Couples with children where both parents are employed increased from 33 percent in 1976 to 46 percent in 1987.[3] These dual career couples represent the largest number of households in the United States. Thus, there are numerous children who need child care.

The number of single parents is steadily increasing as one in every two marriages ends in divorce and more single parents never marry or remarry, but rear their children alone. About 900,000 children under age fifteen live with fathers who are single parents. Of these, an estimated 135,000 are age six or below, with about 53,000 of them in organized child care facilities. Single mothers care for 5.6 million children with 539,000 in organized child care facilities.[4] The cost and the hours of operation of these facilities

[1]See U.S. Department of Education, *The Condition of Education, 1980* (Washington, DC: 1980), 197.

[2]Bureau of the Census, *School Enrollment—Social and Economic Characteristics of Students, October 1993* (Washington, DC: 1993).

[3]Bureau of the Census, *Current Population Reports*, Series P-20 (Washington, DC, May 1988), 7.

[4]Bureau of the Census, "Who's Minding the Kids? Child Care Arrangements: Winter 1984–85," in *Current Population Reports* (Washington, DC, 1987), 4.

FIGURE 1–1

Percentage of three- to six-year-olds enrolled in prekindergarten and kindergarten, 1965 and 1971–1993.

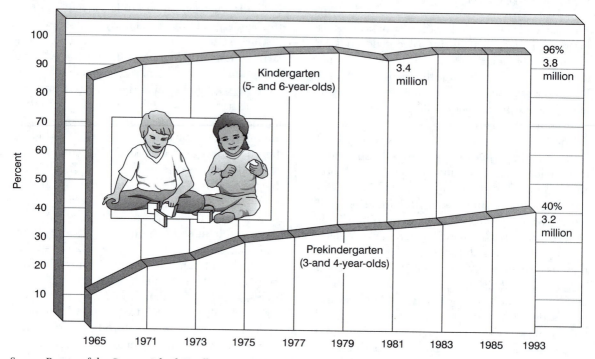

Source: Bureau of the Census, *School Enrollment—Social and Economic Characteristics of Students, October 1993*, (Washington, DC, 1993.)

deter many single parents from using them. They turn to other child care resources—family or friends.

Labor force rates are higher for more educated, older, and first-time mothers, according to U.S. government statistics. See Table 1–1. In 1987, 51 percent of women with newborn infants were in the labor force. This figure was up from 31 percent in 1976. Thus, the demand for more infant and toddler care has increased drastically. The more education the mother has, the more likely that she will return to the labor force after the birth of her first child.[5] Parents with the high-

est educational attainment are also demanding early education for their children.

Another factor has entered the picture, according to the U.S. Bureau of the Census. That factor is job protection while on leave for childbirth. The report states:

A recent Supreme Court decision in *California Federal Savings and Loan Association* v. *Guerra*, has upheld a California law requiring employers to grant up to four-months leave to women medically disabled by pregnancy or childbirth. This ruling, by preserving job retention, may encourage women to return to work shortly after childbirth knowing that a job is still waiting for them without any penalty for taking a leave of absence. This may potentially increase the demand for child care services for

[5]Bureau of the Census, "Fertility of American Women," in *Current Population Reports*, Series P-20 (Washington, DC, May 1988).

FIGURE 1–2
Distribution of married couples, by employment status and fertility.

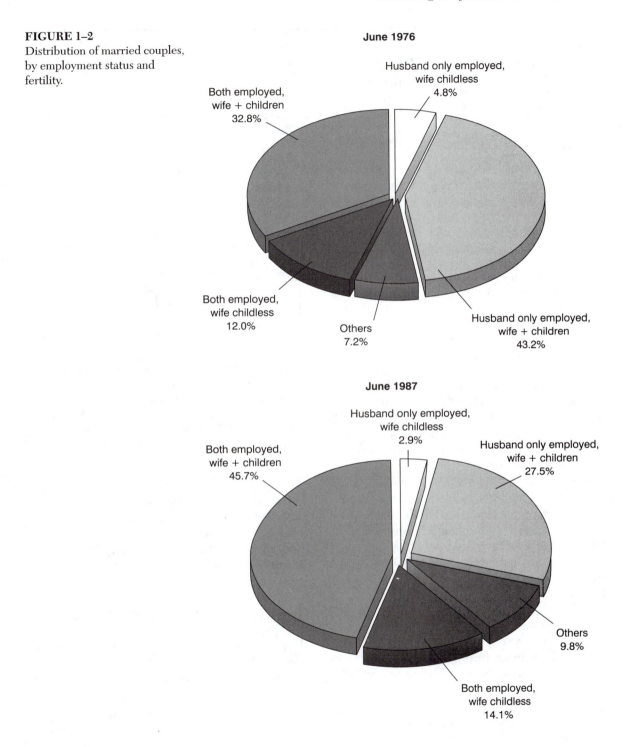

June 1976

Husband only employed, wife childless
4.8%

Both employed, wife + children
32.8%

Both employed, wife childless
12.0%

Others
7.2%

Husband only employed, wife + children
43.2%

June 1987

Husband only employed, wife childless
2.9%

Husband only employed, wife + children
27.5%

Both employed, wife + children
45.7%

Others
9.8%

Both employed, wife childless
14.1%

TABLE 1–1

Women 18 to 44 Years Old Who Had a Birth in the Preceding 12 Months and Their Participation in the Labor Force: Selected Years, 1976 to 1988 (Numbers in Thousands).

Source: Bureau of the Census, June Current Population Surveys of 1976, 1978, and 1980 to 1988; and Bureau of the Census, "Fertility of American Women," in *Current Population Reports*, Series P-20 (Washington, DC, May 1988), 4.

Survey Year	Number of Women	In the Labor Force	
		Number	Percent
1988	3,667	1,866	50.9
1987	3,701	1,881	50.8
1986	3,625	1,805	49.8
1985	3,497	1,691	48.4
1984	3,311	1,547	46.7
1983	3,625	1,563	43.1
1982	3,433	1,508	43.9
1981	3,381	1,411	41.7
1980	3,247	1,233	38.0
1978	3,168	1,120	35.3
1976	2,797	865	31.0

women with infants, thus making child care costs a more integral component of the family budget in the future.[6]

There are numerous messages in the statistics presented. Especially for you, as an early childhood preprofessional, it will be reassuring that you are entering a field that is in increasing demand by parents and by the public at large—both because they want children to have more education and because they want care for children. Also, if you have children, expect to have children, or are a grandparent with interests in children, you can anticipate searching for and paying for early childhood education and/or child care in the future. Certainly the projections indicate that those parents with advanced education desire early childhood education for their children.

Middle-class parents are generally better educated and less tolerant of mediocre child care than are poor parents. Consequently, they are demanding that child care centers provide the same educational opportunities offered in high-quality nursery schools. These parents also expect adequate nurturing and loving for their child. The 1979 National Day Care Study indi-

TALK IT OVER: NO. 2

Discuss with classmates and others the meaning of statistics such as those offered in Table 1–1 and Figures 1–1 and 1–2. What do they mean to the early childhood profession? to you in a given age group? to you as a citizen?

cated that children with more professionally educated teachers showed more advancement than children with less well-educated teachers.[7] Therefore, take your education seriously because it will be of great value to children.

POLICYMAKERS TAKE ACTION

Policymakers in governmental circles at the local, state, and national levels have taken considerable action regarding early childhood education pro-

---

[6]U.S. Bureau of the Census, "Who's Minding the Kids? Child Care Arrangements: Winter 1984–85," in *Current Population Reports*, Series P-70, (Washington, DC, 1987) 12.

[7]Richard Ruopp, *Children at the Center: Final Report of the National Day Care Study* (Cambridge, MA: Abt Associates, 1979), 98.

grams in recent years. The federal government's program, Project Head Start, was initiated in 1965 and continues to the present. Head Start has served over fourteen million children, trained hundreds of teachers and aides, mainstreamed disabled children, and raised program standards to achieve the goals of helping economically poor children get a "head start" on the educational ladder. See Table 1–2 for the numbers of children served by Head Start.

The women's movement since 1970 has pressured policymakers to provide more affordable child care services for mothers who are working or improving themselves by attending school. There are numerous governmental agencies concerned with child care services. The White House Conferences in both 1970 and 1981 cited child care as one of the country's most pressing needs. Recently the plight of "latchkey" children is of increasing concern. These are young elementary-age children who, after school, open their empty house with a key tied to a string around their necks. There is a serious concern about the children's safety and about related fires when children are left unattended. These children's needs have been addressed by increased before- and after-school services, usually on a tuition fee basis. These services have been provided through several programs, including those in the children's school buildings. Preservice students often gain experience through part-time employment in these programs.

RESEARCHERS SHOW VALUE OF EARLY EDUCATION

Researchers have documented the fact that early childhood education pays off well in that these children find more success in later schooling. Many studies accompanied Project Head Start and other innovative programs. (See references to these studies at the end of this chapter.) One prominent study has been carried on since 1962 by David Weikart and others of the High/Scope Foundation of Ypsilanti, Michigan. The study, called the Perry Preschool Project, followed two matched groups of poor black children in the same community. One group received a high-quality preschool experience plus a weekly visit from a teacher in the child's home with the child's mother. The other group did not receive either a preschool experience or a home visit. Both groups attended the public schools of Ypsilanti, Michigan. By adulthood those children with the Perry preschool experience were found to have

1. more success in school, with a larger percentage of high school graduates;
2. more success in obtaining and holding a job, with fewer being unemployed;
3. more success in regular classrooms, with fewer assigned to special education;
4. more success in citizen responsibilities, with fewer becoming delinquent or in conflict with the law.

The study concludes that each dollar spent for preschool education returns four dollars to the community—because of the savings in potential expenditures for special education and delinquency and because the students can contribute economically through their success in school and in holding a job.[8]

---

[8]David P. Weikart et al., *Changed Lives: The Effects of the Perry Preschool Program on Youths Through Age 19* (Ypsilanti, MI: High/Scope Foundation, 1984). Also see Robert E. Slavin, Nancy L. Karweit, and Barbara A. Wasik, "Preventing Early School Failure: What Works?" *Educational Leadership*, 50:4 (December 1992/January 1993), 10–18.

TABLE 1–2
Project Head Start (Summer and Full Year).
Source: Department of Health and Human Services, *Project Head Start Statistical Fact Sheet* (Washington, DC, February 1995).

Fiscal Year	Enrollment* (in 1,000s)	Congressional Appropriation ($ Millions)
1965 (Summer only)	561.0	$ 96.4
1966	733.0	198.9
1967	681.4	349.2
1968	693.9	316.2
1969	663.6	333.9
1970	477.4	325.7
1971	397.5	360.0
1972	379.0	376.3
1973	379.0	400.7
1974	352.8	403.9
1975	349.0	403.9
1976	349.0	441.0
1977	333.0	475.0
1978	391.4	625.0
1979	387.5	680.0
1980	376.3	735.0
1981	387.3	818.7
1982**	395.8	911.7
1983	414.9	912.0
1984	442.1	995.7
1985	452.3	1,075.0
1986	451.7	1,040.3
1987	446.5	1,130.5
1988	448.4	1,206.3
1989	450.9	1,235.0
1990	540.9	1,552.0
1991	583.4	1,951.8
1992	621.0	2,201.8
1993	713.9	2,776.2
1994	740.4	3,325.7

*   A total of 14,594,000 children have been served by the program since it began in 1965.

** Since 1982 only full-year services have been provided.

TYPES OF EARLY CHILDHOOD SCHOOLS

There is an interesting variety of settings where you, as a preservice early childhood teacher, may observe and practice during your college program. Students generally like and are advised to gain experience in different types of schools and with an assortment of ages of children in order to be better prepared for the positions available when they graduate. The variety of early childhood education positions is exciting, especially if, as a graduate, you are free to move about the country or to a foreign country.

Early childhood schools vary as to (1) the ages they serve, (2) the particular services needed by families and the community; (3) their source of funding, and (4) the theoretical approach followed.

TALK IT OVER: NO. 4

Study the yellow pages of the telephone book under "Day Care Centers" and "Schools— Preschool and Kindergarten" to locate some local schools. Talk to parents and teachers and ask, "What types of early childhood education services are available to parents in this community? in nearby smaller or larger communities?" Compare your findings with those of other students.

Ages Served

The particular age or ages served may be a reflection of (1) the legal kindergarten age in the state, (2) parental needs, (3) teachers' or directors' preferences, (4) available facilities or equipment, (5) economic factors, (6) program objectives, and so on. Ages served may range from infants a few weeks old to children around age six. Some centers specialize in certain ages; others offer a comprehensive program for several or all ages. Some place children in single age groups—all threes, for example—whereas others place children of various ages—say three-, four-, and five-year-olds—together. Either type of grouping is acceptable as long as the teachers individualize the program to meet the special needs of each child and the school provides the recommended number of teachers for the number of children being served.

Birth to Three Years

Care for infants and toddlers has received attention since the late 1970s. There are increasing numbers of single-parent families and families where both parents work outside the home who require infant or toddler care. These parents do not have the luxury of staying home to care for their young children. They must work. Career women are returning to their jobs while their babies are still young to keep from giving up needed family income, to keep from losing out on a career already in process, or from fear of being locked out of a job when they are ready to work again. During the peak period of unemployment in the early 1980s, many fathers were laid off, and employed mothers feared that they would be unable to find a job if they did not return to work at the end of their allotted maternity leaves. Thus economic factors have stimulated the growth of infant and toddler care centers.

High-quality infant and toddler care is an expensive enterprise, primarily because one person can care for only three infants or five toddlers, according to many state regulations. Both medical and educational attention has been focused on the standards of quality to be specified for infant and toddler care. The physical and mental health of infants and toddlers is considered extremely vulnerable, requiring strict standards of health and personal attention.[9]

Three- and Four-Year-Olds

Educational programs for three- and four-year-old children have been popular over the past decades. You can see by Figure 1–1 that the number enrolled has increased steadily and that at present about 40 percent of the three- and four-year-olds, or 3.2 million prekindergartners, are enrolled. According to Table 1–2, Project Head Start added large numbers of children to the prekindergarten and kindergarten statistics. There is a movement in some states to bring the four-year-olds into the public school system. Presently most of the four-year-olds being served are considered "at risk" of future failure. James L. Hymes, Jr., a long-time advocate for high-quality early childhood programs, favors this move as long as high standards for four-year-olds' programs are maintained.[10]

---

[9]For a detailed discussion see Bettye Caldwell, "Issues in the Quality of Infant-Toddler Care," *Young Children* 38:5 (July 1983), 48–50.

[10]See James L. Hymes, Jr., "Public School for 4-Year-Olds," *Young Children* 42:2 (January 1987), 51.

Five-Year-Olds

You may wish to become a kindergarten teacher serving five-year-old children. The percentage of children enrolled in kindergarten has been increasing over the years. You can see in Figure 1–1 that 96 percent of five-year-olds in the United States, or 3.8 million, are now enrolled. Kindergartens have traditionally been half-day programs, but some states are now experimenting with making them full-day programs equal to the elementary school day.

Multi-age grouping is one effort to manage developmental differences and prevent kindergarten failure. Multi-age grouping means that children's ages may vary within a class, say, from four years nine months to six years plus. Part of the rationale for this type of grouping states that given a wider age variation, teachers must consciously plan for the least mature and the most mature. For a time many schools were recommending that the immature child be kept home. This procedure was ruled illegal and schools stopped the practice.

The developmental approach advocated in this text suggests that teachers base their expectations on scientific child development information and assessment and not on some artificial measurement handed down by the first grade teachers. Charlesworth emphasizes with the National Association for the Education of Young Children (NAEYC) the concept of "developmentally appropriate practice," which supports the idea that each child can be served within a group based on individual developmental milestones. She does not advocate testing or excluding children as a way to prevent failure.[11] In practice, there is always a range of skills among children in any group. Wise teachers adjust to the children rather than expect the children to do all the adapting. Your task during this course is to learn to plan activities with a range of opportunities

---

[11]See Rosalind Charlesworth, "'Behind' Before They Start: Deciding How to Deal with the Risk of Kindergarten 'Failure,'" *Young Children* 44:3 (March 1989), 5–12.

An early childhood school: a place to climb high.
(S. Russell, photographer)

and skill requirements so that the least skilled and the most skilled child can enjoy them.

Community and Family Needs Determine Types of Schools

Families may seek out the early childhood education they need or the community may decide to provide the services and make them available to families. This section will introduce you to a number of typical early childhood education services and give brief information about their funding.

Kindergartens

Kindergartens have become the most universal early childhood service. Public school boards of education make a decision that children who are five years old will benefit from an early childhood education experience. Taxes support public school kindergartens. Kindergarten is typically not compulsory, but most children attend when it is provided. Privately funded kindergartens collect tuition from parents and generally follow the age guidelines of the public schools.

Laboratory Prekindergarten and Kindergarten Programs

The child development laboratory school may be your first experience with an early childhood education program. Laboratory schools are funded and operated by high schools, vocational technical centers, community colleges, and four-year colleges and universities. Laboratory schools may be organized to serve the needs of the college or secondary school curriculum.

Practicum for Students   Laboratory schools are organized to give practicum experiences to students. A well-educated, experienced lead teacher helps college students learn basic child development and early childhood education principles. The laboratory school is a protected setting for your initial experience. The teacher has time set aside to guide students' learning and is expected to focus on your needs as well as the needs of the young children. Serving as a laboratory teacher is

a complex role, and sometimes you may have to wait for answers to your questions while the teacher cares for children's needs. However, do make notes of your questions because the laboratory teacher will surely expect to answer them at a later time.

One problem with laboratory schools has been that they may demonstrate a program that is very ideal compared to those of the community programs. This may occur because the teachers are well educated, are expected to be innovative, and there are several persons like yourself who can help with the many responsibilities, making the total program more elaborate than would be possible for two teachers alone. While you are in this protected environment, it is important that you take full advantage of its offerings. For example, here you can experiment with a small group or even one child, while others take responsibility for the remainder of the group. Out in the real world you'll be responsible for the whole group and find it hard to spend time alone with one child because you won't have as many helpers. It is also to your advantage if you record the innovative ideas you see demonstrated by your laboratory teachers and others. Such records are valuable resources for your future teaching roles. See the suggestion for your Resource File at the end of this chapter.

Research   Research is often connected with laboratory schools, especially in four-year colleges and universities. Such research strengthens educators' knowledge base for teaching about child development, early childhood education, discipline, parent education, and the like. As you study the research documentation in this book, you can appreciate more fully the soundness of the ideas presented, knowing they are based on research. Later on you may wish to study at the graduate level and carry on research projects. Or, as a classroom teacher, you might suggest projects to researchers as you analyze your work and evaluate children's and parents' progress. Then, as you get feedback from the research, your group of children, and other children as well, can benefit from improved programs.

Experimental Programs   Special experimental or innovative early childhood programs are often tried out in laboratory schools before being advocated for wider use. Such programs may focus on a particular researcher's theory or a particular group of children, such as those who have language delays or those from poor families. Others may test a particular part of the curriculum, such as science, music, motor skill, or social activities. You can check with your institution to learn whether it has been involved with such experimental programs or research.

Child Care Centers

You may take some of your preservice education in and later work in a child care center. These are centers that provide supplemental care for children from infancy through kindergarten ages during the typical working hours of parents. In some localities the hours are from 6:30 A.M. to 6 P.M. Occasionally centers provide twenty-four-hour service. As part of your education it is desirable that you become acquainted with the breadth of services offered by a high-quality child care center in order for you to be able to teach in, or eventually direct, such a center after you graduate.

Child care centers are organized by profit and nonprofit groups. Most charge parents a tuition for sending their child to the center, even if they have a subsidy from a governmental agency, church, or the like. Child care centers are regulated by an agency of your state government, typically the department of social services or health services.

Church-Sponsored Centers   Churches are prime sponsors for both part-day and full-day early childhood education programs. These programs are held in the church-school facilities during the week. Large numbers of churches are

sponsoring these programs.[12] Church leaders are motivated by a desire to provide a needed public service, to make money to help pay for a church-school building, or as a way to attract members to the faith. Some schools located in churches are completely secular, whereas others teach various aspects of the religion. Generally, churches must conform to state licensing standards when providing early childhood education services, with the exception of their short-period Sunday schools.

Employer-Sponsored Child Care   Employer-sponsored child care is currently experiencing a revival, having been pioneered in the United States during World War II when mothers were needed to work in defense plants. Today child care may be provided on the work site for employees' children or an allowance for child care may be part of the employee benefit package, allowing employees to select child care wherever they choose.[13] You'll find these programs in industries, universities, and hospitals.

Family Day Care Homes   Providing family day care is a service that graduates of early childhood education programs sometimes organize in their own homes, especially if the graduate is a parent of young children who would prefer staying home with them, yet wants to apply acquired professional skills. Family day care homes are regulated by a local or state agency. Some states allow family group care that permits the operator to hire an assistant and enroll more children. Family day care is the service of choice for many families. It often provides care for school-age children who attend after school.

---

[12]For a useful report on the extent of church involvement see Eileen W. Lindner, Mary C. Mattis, and June R. Rogers, *When Churches Mind the Children: A Study of Day Care in Local Parishes* (Ypsilanti, MI: The High/Scope Press, 1983).

[13]U.S. Department of Labor, *Child Care: A Workforce Issue* (Washington, DC, April 1988), 125–142.

Drop-In Child Care Drop-in child care services are another type of center where you may find employment. These centers take young children on an hourly basis, usually for an hourly fee, according to the number they are licensed to accept. For instance, churches and community centers may organize "mother's day out" to relieve mothers of child care for a time so they can shop or get medical treatment. Drop-in centers are also located in places such as shopping centers, airports, amusement parks, and ski areas. Drop-in care is sometimes provided in medical centers so that noncontagious children have a child-appropriate environment in which to play while waiting for tests of their siblings.

Some drop-in centers are organized around a child-abuse therapy group to serve parents who may be inclined to abuse their children. Children may be dropped off at the center whenever the parent feels the strain of child care. As a teacher in such a center, you would become an important part of the support team of the mental health agency helping to rehabilitate the abusive parent.

Teaching in a drop-in center requires special preparation. Children are typically strangers with a here-and-now need. The ability to make children feel secure, comfortable, and happy is the primary skill needed. You need a great deal of experience to be most successful in a drop-in center.

Prekindergartens for Three- and Four-Year-Olds

You may gain part of your early childhood education experience in a prekindergarten with a part-day or full-day program. As stated previously, these prekindergartens used to be called preschools or nursery schools, but these terms are being phased out. The schools may be called early childhood education schools or centers or child development centers. Prekindergartens were generally credited with being more educational than child care centers. This difference is being eliminated with increased attention to higher quality in child care.

Many excellent prekindergartens are funded by tuition and have high standards of education. Some schools are operated by nonprofit agencies, whereas others are businesses for profit. The tuition expenses for these schools for some upper-income families can be very high.

There are a few prekindergarten programs for children between eighteen months and three years of age. Generally speaking, however, if one parent is not working outside the home, she or he may prefer to wait a few months before enrolling a child this age. From a student's viewpoint, being able to work with toddlers gives some insight into one of parents' most frustrating periods in their young child's life.

Parent-Cooperative Schools Parent-cooperative schools are typically organized by groups of middle-class families in order to provide a high-quality early childhood educational experience for their children at an affordable price. Because each parent participates as an assistant to the teacher about one-half day each month, the families pay lower tuition rates than they would pay in a typical for-profit school. Parents in cooperatives also contribute labor to build equipment, keep up the facility, and operate the program. One highly valued component of the parent-cooperative is the close link parents feel to their child's education and teacher. Parents learn a great deal about children by helping in their child's group.

Parent-cooperative groups are popular today among families where the mother or father does not hold a full-time job, has flexibility in work hours, or where parents can work out a way to "cooperate." Parent-cooperatives have become less common in recent years due to mothers taking full-time employment. This model of early childhood education is one you should keep in mind as efforts to involve parents are discussed, because parents generally feel involved and satisfied when their children are enrolled in these schools.

Project Head Start   Head Start early childhood centers were first organized under the joint sponsorship of the federal government and a local agency in many American communities in 1965. The program was begun as part of President Lyndon Johnson's War on Poverty. The program brought children of the poor together in groups for educational, medical, and nutritional assistance in hopes of reducing the observed handicap that such children experience when they enter elementary school. Some Head Start programs operated only in the summer and others operated year round. Parent involvement has always been an important part of Head Start programs. As of 1995, thirteen million children have been served by Head Start. For more discussion of Project Head Start see Chapter 22.

Disabled Prekindergartners   The recent trend in education for the disabled is toward integrating these children in regular classrooms if their needs can be met there. This trend began in 1975 with the passage of Public Law 94-142. The federal law provides education for children and mandates an individualized program for each child. Head Start, using federal funds, initiated mainstreaming in Head Start groups. States have passed their own legislation and have provided services to young special needs children in different ways. The 1990 Americans with Disabilities Act extended many benefits to children and to adults. (See Chapter 22.)

Home Start Programs   Home Start programs are usually arranged by the public schools and have four major objectives: (1) to involve parents directly in the educational development of their children, (2) to help strengthen parents' capacity for stimulating their children's development, and (3) to demonstrate and (4) to evaluate methods of delivering services to the parents and children for whom a center-based program is not feasible. The programs are generally federally funded. A trained visitor helps the parents develop an educational program for their children and helps them learn how to carry out the program.

Hospital Schools   Many hospitals are providing an early childhood school for their young patients. Children are brought to a playroom on the children's floor for as much activity as their illness will permit. There is therapeutic value to being with other children, and the children's education also benefits. The teacher may also provide activities in a child's hospital room if the child cannot be moved to the playroom.

This completes a brief discussion of the types of schools where you may practice or finally teach after graduation. You will learn much more about each type as you progress through your studies.

Theoretical Approaches Utilized

The theoretical approach or approaches used by teachers as they plan the goals, activities, modes of interaction, and modes of evaluation in their groups is another possible variation you may encounter in early childhood schools. This book addresses those variations in Chapter 2.

CONTRIBUTIONS OF PROFESSIONAL ASSOCIATIONS

A number of professional organizations are helping the early childhood education profession in many ways. You can join one or more of these organizations and become active with other teachers in your chosen profession. One innovative project is being initiated by the National Association for the Education of Young Children

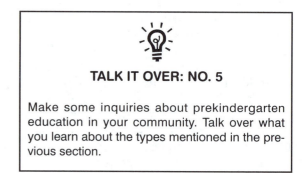

TALK IT OVER: NO. 5

Make some inquiries about prekindergarten education in your community. Talk over what you learn about the types mentioned in the previous section.

(NAEYC). NAEYC is the largest professional organization focusing on the needs of young children. The innovative *Center Accreditation Project* rewards centers with accreditation when they meet standards of high quality. The criteria, agreed upon by a large group of the nation's early childhood educators, parents, and others, are spelled out in *Accreditation Criteria and Procedures of the National Academy of Early Childhood Programs,* first published by NAEYC in 1984.[14] As of late 1995, forty-three hundred centers had been accredited and eight thousand more were doing the self-study in preparation for accreditation.[15]

An account of the first ten years of accreditation experience has been published with details of widespread acceptance and success—and some concerns—in *NAEYC Accreditation: A Decade of Learning and the Years Ahead,* edited by Sue Bredekamp and Barbara Willer (Washington, DC: NAEYC, 1996), or see S. Bredekamp and S. Glowacki, *Young Children* 51:3 (March 1996), 38–44 for the first decade report.

The NAEYC has also worked on criteria for accrediting early childhood teacher education programs for students in four-year colleges and universities. The criteria spell out the areas of knowledge and experience required for a capable, competent teacher of young children. These criteria will be used by the National Council for Accreditation of Teacher Education (NCATE) for accrediting and reaccrediting the early childhood teacher education programs of colleges of teacher education.

The Child Development Associate Consortium (CDAC), through grants from the Office of Health and Human Services, has developed the Child Development Associate (CDA) competencies for child care workers. Competencies are published in a booklet, *CDAC Competency Standards,* which is available from the Council for Early Childhood Professional Recognition, 1341 G St. NW, Suite 400, Washington, DC 20005. A child care worker can follow the self-paced program that leads to CDA certification. Some CDA programs are available in connection with two-year colleges. Head Start centers usually specify CDA or Early Childhood Education certification for teachers they hire.

In addition to these important credentialing tasks, professional organizations publish readable and helpful journals and books and hold local, state, regional, and national meetings where teachers and others can talk over issues they face in serving young children and their families in early childhood centers. You'll surely want to check with your instructor and join a professional organization at your earliest opportunity. It will make a great contribution to your professionalism when you do. See the list of professional organizations at the end of this chapter.

YOU AS AN ADULT EDUCATOR

The role of being an adult educator often sneaks up on teachers of young children. They prepare well for teaching young children, but many do not think about the fact that, as educated professionals, they will soon be responsible for giving leadership to the teaching team of adults. In many cases teachers are responsible for teaching adults how to do what needs to be done in early childhood centers.

As you reflect on the chapter so far and read the following bits of advice for starting your work with young children, begin also to think about ways you could teach these steps to others—co-teachers, parents, volunteers, aides, and so on. As you learn from your instructors in this course and in your school with young children, try to become aware of the process for teaching adults. Reflect on those processes that help you the most and those that are less effective. Thus you will begin to prepare for your role as an adult educator in the field of early childhood education. You

[14]Revised in 1991 and available from NAEYC, 1509 16th St. NW, Washington, DC 20036-1426.

[15]See Marilyn Smith, "NAEYC Annual Report," *Young Children* 51:1 (1995), 45–52.

will feel more skilled when the task presents itself in the future. Some would say that you learn something best when you teach it.

OBSERVING IN THE EARLY CHILDHOOD SCHOOL

Students in early childhood education usually have regular observations scheduled from the beginning of the term. Thus they can see children in action and relate their observations to the theoretical material they are studying in the classroom. Sometimes students may be asked to seek out children to observe. Children may be observed in laboratory schools, in schools not associated with the university, in informal groups, or in a family. In your preparation to become a teacher of young children, it is most helpful to observe situations similar to those in which you may later teach.

The purposes of observation are to help you to relate theory to practice; to understand what it means to be an infant, a toddler, or a three-, four-, or five-year-old; to become acquainted with methods and materials used in the school; and to sense the complications and satisfactions of being a teacher of young children.

To accomplish these purposes you will want to see a typical group of children behaving in typical ways. The following suggestions will help a new observer learn and be welcome.

1. Determine what you expect to see. Your instructor will indicate the points to look for during each observation. You may be given specific questions to answer as you observe.
2. Study the observation assignments for the entire course if they are available. This will help you in observing, understanding, and collecting meaningful examples for assignments.
3. Be sure to read your text, listen to your instructor, and ask questions so that each assignment will be clear. Children are fascinating, and you may enjoy just watching them. However, observation should be done with a purpose if you are to benefit most from it.
4. Take with you an outline of questions you need to answer.

An early childhood school: a place to take notes to learn about children's development. (Michigan State University)

5. Secure or copy a list of names and ages of the children. For easy reference, arrange the list according to chronological age. For some assignments, it is helpful to list the number of months or terms in school and the number and ages of siblings of each child.

6. Generally, it will be necessary to take notes, then write the report of the observation later. A hardback stenographer's notebook is convenient for note taking.

7. An observation booth facilitates observing and makes it easier to watch behavior without affecting it. Safely behind a one-way-vision screen, you can be more objective and will not have to wonder whether you should interact with the child.

8. Be quiet in the booth in order to avoid attracting the children's attention and to avoid disturbing other observers. Sound equipment will, of course, make hearing easier. Video may be available, too.

9. When it is necessary to observe in the room with children, it is important to be as quiet and unobtrusive as possible. You should sit on a low chair, usually along a wall. Children who are accustomed to observers won't pay much attention to you unless you dress in a startling fashion or talk to them.

10. If a child talks to you, answer briefly and return to your writing. If he or she continues to seek your company, you can move to a new location and quietly tell the teacher that this child seems to need someone to talk to. Children have been observed going from observer to observer for short chats. Even though each conversation was short, the total effect was that the child made many contacts with adults but few with children. This situation does not help students to observe child-child interaction. Also, little contribution is made to the goals the teacher has for the child.

11. Unless your presence will interfere, you should move to areas where you can clearly see what the children are doing.

12. Avoid congregating with other adults. This tends to interfere with children's activity and with students' responsibility.

13. Stand near groups of children, or sit on the benches provided, but not on the children's equipment.

14. Identify each set of observation notes by date, time, group, teacher, activity, names, and a description of the setting so that you can recall it later.

15. Include the child's age in your reports because behavior is much more understandable when related to a specific age. For example, use the notation 3–5 to indicate three years five months.

16. If the assignment calls for an **anecdotal record**, record incidents as the child interacts.

17. If the assignment calls for a **diary record**, write down a running account of the behavior of a particular child. Because writing is tiring, diary records may be taken for several minutes followed by a period of rest, then repeated. Write down the time each set of notes was taken.

18. In both anecdotal and diary records quote the exact words of the children and adults and set them off with quotation marks. Exact words are often significant, as we discuss in a later chapter.

19. In reporting either type of observation, carefully separate facts from interpretations. Interpretations include what you think the behavior means and what questions arise in your mind about it. Evaluative words, for example, *good, bad, pretty, ugly, happy, angry,* are part of your interpretation.

20. You may be called on to observe as you work with children. In this case your observation notes will of necessity be brief. Carry a small notebook and pencil in your pocket to be used at these times. A short word or phrase can suffice to help you remember a situation to write about in your reports or to discuss

with the teacher. Such notes should be expanded immediately after the children leave, or the notes will soon be of little help.

21. Do not ask about or make statements about the children in front of children or parents.

22. Discuss your observations with the teacher after the children leave. A teacher is usually too busy to give students' questions sufficient thought while attending the children.

23. No one, on the basis of a short observation, is justified in making sweeping statements about what children "always" or "never" do. Remember, even a full week in school for a child is only a small part of his or her total experience.

24. Ethical treatment of observation data requires that discussions regarding the material be kept within the classroom. Here observations can be discussed in the light of other observers' experience and the knowledge and experience of the course instructor.

PARTICIPATING IN THE EARLY CHILDHOOD SCHOOL

For most students, participating directly with children is a long-awaited and valuable part of preparation to become a teacher. Through participating, you will begin feeling, thinking, and reacting as a teacher. You will be seeing children live and learn together. Not only will you watch teachers, but you will try your own skill and eventually develop a teaching style of your own.

Because students are often scheduled to participate with children at the beginning of a term, before learning the whys and wherefores of school procedures, the following list of participation hints will help during the first confusing weeks. As the course develops, you will gain an understanding of the reasoning contained in these hints.

Hints for New Student Participators

1. Wear clean, comfortable, colorful, washable clothing during your participation. When you are dressed comfortably in washable clothing you need not worry about your clothing and are free to concentrate on the children around you. A wraparound apron is handy to wear around the finger paints.

2. Wear a badge with your name clearly printed on it. Write "student helper" under your name so visitors or parents will know you.

3. Arrive on time at the designated school and check with the teacher for your particular assignments. Note any posted schedules or directions.

4. Attend any conference the teacher holds prior to the arrival of the children or at the end of the day.

5. Ask for advice in handling teaching material with which you are unfamiliar.

6. Avoid making patterns or models in any media for the children.

7. Write the children's names on pictures, starting in the upper left-hand corner and using manuscript writing in uppercase and lowercase letters. See sample manuscript writing in Chapter 13.

John Mary George

8. Sit down to work with the children whenever possible.

9. Talk quietly, using distinct words and short sentences.

10. Sit with the children during group times, for example, storytime, rest, music, and snack.

11. The children will help with cleanup if you make a game of it. Try singing your directions. Try suggesting, "You bring them to me and I'll help you put them on the shelves." Smile and say "Thank you, [child's name]," after each bit of assistance. You'll marvel at how quickly the room or yard gets straightened up.

12. Be an alert observer and you will know when assistance is needed. Move in to help; that's how you learn.

13. Avoid unnecessary conversation with other adults in the room or yard. Save comments for staff meetings.
14. When you have serious doubts about a procedure, say to the children, "Let's ask the teacher."
15. Always keep the children's safety in mind and act to ensure safety.

In the Locker Room

1. Sit on a low chair in a central location so that you'll be at the children's level and can see what help they need. Sitting saves the teacher's back, too!
2. Snowpants usually must be put on before boots. Lay the snowpants out in the correct position in front of the child, who sits on the floor. You can arrange several children around your chair like spokes on a wheel. The same circular arrangement works well for helping with boots, too. A plastic bag over a shoe helps stubborn boots slip on.
3. Give praise generously as you encourage self-help.
4. Give both verbal directions and demonstrations as you help.
5. Jackets can be laid in the open position on a low table. The child turns his or her back to the table and reaches backward, first with one arm and then with the other, to put the arms in the sleeves. Or the jacket can be placed in front of the child with the opening facing upward and the collar closest to the child. The child slips his or her hands into the sleeves, raises the arms, and the coat flips over the head into the correct position. Children enjoy this trick. Zippers and buttons require a number of demonstrations. You may have to fasten them partially to avoid overfrustrating a child who is trying to help him- or herself. Watch closely and help only when a child needs you.
6. For snowy boot removal, sweep snow off the children's boots and snowpants with a small broom while they are still outdoors. Arrange a number of small chairs in a circle around an absorbent rug in the entryway. Preferably, let only a few children enter at a time to avoid congestion. The children sit on the chairs and remove their boots before proceeding to the locker area to remove their other wraps. The rug absorbs moisture and keeps it out of the locker area. An adult can sit in the circle and tug at stubborn boots. Boots may have to be drained and dried before being stored in the lockers. A clothespin with the child's name on it is helpful for clipping pairs of boots together. Boots can be marked with a felt pen.
7. Learn where extra clothes are stored. Most children should have a complete set of extra clothing stored in their lockers for emergency use. Each school needs its own collection of clean "extras" for unusual emergencies. A supply of paper bags should be stored nearby to use for soiled clothes.
8. Kindergartners usually learn to tie their shoes, but younger children as a rule have difficulty with this skill. If you teach kindergartners to call the loops "bunny ears" as you demonstrate tying, they will often become interested in learning.

At Storytime or Singing Time

1. You may be asked to read to a small group. You should read the book to yourself before reading to the children; read several books so some will be familiar to you.
2. Be sure that the children can see the pictures. When the children sit with their backs to the windows, the light is usually best on a book held up for them to see.
3. Give the children opportunities to respond to the story and pictures.
4. If someone else is reading or singing with the group, you should sit with the children. If a child becomes disruptive, quietly suggest appropriate behavior by tapping his or her knee or shoulder. Avoid saying "Shhh" and causing more distraction than the child.
5. Sing along with the children softly so that your voice does not overwhelm their voices.

6. If a child leaves the group, keep an eye on him or her so that the teacher can attend to the total group. If the child does not want to return to the storytime or singing time, help find a quiet activity that does not disturb the other children who are enjoying the group activity. Such a child might enjoy a story alone, so you could try reading, perhaps with the child sitting on your lap.

7. Should a visitor enter when the teacher is conducting storytime or singing time, see if you can assist the visitor until the teacher is free. If the teacher is called out, you should assume responsibility for the group so as to minimize the disruption.

In the Bathroom

1. Certain points in the schedule are usually designated for the toilet routine. At other times, however, keep alert for children who are holding their genitals—usually an indication of a need to urinate.

2. Don't offer children a choice when you are virtually certain they need to urinate. Tell them, "Let's go to the bathroom." Take their hands and guide them quickly to the bathroom.

3. When helping in the bathroom, sit on a low chair in order to be comfortable while assisting children with straps, buttons, zippers, and belts. By sitting nearby you avoid pressuring the child.

4. Boys need to learn to raise the seat, aim accurately as they stand to urinate, then lower the seat. These steps usually require many gentle reminders.

5. Children may worry about the noise of the toilet flushing. If the child hesitates when you suggest that he or she trip the lever, then you flush it until the child gains confidence.

6. Since girls and boys use the same bathroom at the same time, be matter-of-fact and factual when answering questions regarding differences in their bodies. Don't be embarrassed when they look at each other.

7. Toilet accidents are not unusual in groups of three-year-olds. They are less common in older children but still may happen. Wet pants are more common than accidental bowel movements. If Jimmy has an accident, suggest that he try to use the toilet—sometimes he isn't finished and may only wet again as soon as you get the wet pants changed. Get dry clothing from his locker and dress him. Put the soiled clothing in a sack and label it with his name. Be matter-of-fact when other children ask about what has happened. The teacher will report the accident quietly to the parents so that the child doesn't feel betrayed and the parent doesn't feel inclined to punish the child. The teacher might say, "We'll be able to work out this problem. We'll just remember to encourage Jimmy to go to the bathroom right after snack."

8. Children usually enjoy washing their hands. Watch the temperature of the water. Long sessions at the lavatory often indicate that the children would enjoy some water play. Help the children dry their hands well to avoid chapping.

9. Late four-year-olds and fives can usually manage the bathroom routine without much adult help. Sometimes they play. If they spill water, let them mop it up, being matter-of-fact as they do so.

10. Avoid having the children wait in the bathroom. Keep the number entering in accordance with the number of toilets and lavatories available.

11. For infants and toddlers wearing diapers, be sure to follow the approved routine. Wash your hands with soap and water immediately after completing the diaper change.

At Snack Time or Mealtime

1. If you are required to serve the meal, ask for advice on procedures.

2. Sit with the children at the small table.

3. Have a quiet conversation with the children. Avoid intertable conversations.

4. Give quiet directions to aid the children in learning the routine.

5. Tipped-over glasses of beverage are probably the most common mealtime accident. Therefore, encourage the children to keep their glasses positioned toward the center of the table.

6. Use a sponge to wipe the table as you leave. A child might be encouraged to help you.

7. For infant feeding, follow approved practices for clean hands, storing the food, and throwing out food that has been warmed if not eaten.

During Outdoor Activities

1. Dress for the weather from head to toe. Boots, gloves, scarves, and plenty of warm clothing are a must in winter. Comfortable loose clothing is important when it is hot.

2. Go where the children are. Adults should be spaced throughout the yard.

3. Keep off the children's equipment. Children won't use it if adults are sitting on it.

4. Go to a child and get his or her attention before giving directions.

5. Encourage and assist the children in putting things in the storage areas at the end of the period.

6. Tend to children's needs and stay near them. Do not congregate with adults and talk, thus neglecting the children.

7. Regulations require an adult to be in the yard, so do not leave children alone.

At Rest Time

1. Sit by a child who is having difficulty being quiet.

2. Children may quiet down more quickly if they lie on their stomachs. Some like to have their backs massaged.

3. Sing lullabies or say quiet poems to the children.

4. If children need to go to the toilet, help them leave the group quietly. Assist them in the bathroom.

5. Rest time should be a pleasurable experience free of punishing admonitions.

STUDENT EVALUATIONS

Your instructor will discuss with you and your classmates each of the criteria upon which you will be evaluated during this course. Table 1–3 shows a chart of a list of criteria. Your instructor may wish to add others. Duplicate the chart and on your first day start to rate yourself using 5 = highly satisfactory, 4 = satisfactory, 3 = minimum acceptable, 2 = unsatisfactory, 1 = very unsatisfactory, and 0 = not observed or when criteria do not apply. Remember that you are expected to be learning—not to be perfect already—so it is important for you to respond positively to your instructor's suggestions and to discuss ways to improve your performance. Always ask for help when you feel uncertain. When you feel good about an interaction or an activity you've carried out, be sure to let the instructor know.

You can also gain experience in evaluating the center where you are participating. In Chapter 19 you'll find program evaluation discussed. You can develop a form and rate each item on the 5-to-1 scale, as mentioned earlier. The standards will become clearer as you proceed through the course, but it will be good experience for you to begin evaluating early. A few sentences in a diary record will help you recall the events of the day. When you feel there are omissions in the program, be sure to check with others because those events may occur on the hours or days when you are not present.

Evaluation is an essential task of every professional. Certain standards are expected. It will be up to you as a teacher of young children to know when standards are being met and to make corrections when they are not. The best evaluation is self-evaluation and its related self-correction. The early childhood teacher who does well at self-evaluation will seldom be surprised by what an outside evaluator reports.

TABLE 1-3
Student's Self-Evaluation.

	Ratings	
5 = Highly satisfactory	2 = Unsatisfactory	
4 = Satisfactory	1 = Very unsatisfactory	
3 = Minimum acceptable	0 = No opportunity	

					Week					
Criteria	1	2	3	4	5	6	7	8	9	etc.
GENERAL EMPLOYEE BEHAVIOR										
1. Arrives on time										
2. Calls if ill										
3. Makes up excused absences										
4. Dresses appropriately										
5. Prepares for tasks										
6. Attends pre- and post-conferences										
7. Assumes full share of responsibilities during assigned period										
8. Relates to all persons without cultural or gender bias										
PLANNED MICROTEACHING PROJECTS										
1. Presents several ideas for a project										
2. Plans a project in detail and on time										
3. Organizes and presents project										
4. Uses creative techniques or aids										
5. Holds children's interest										
6. Relates to individual children										
7. Questions and comments to children										
8. Sets appropriate limits for children										
9. Solves problems quickly and flexibly										
10. Evaluates outcomes for children										

Conclusions

Early childhood education is an important support service for families and their young children. Through this chapter you have been introduced to a number of types of services available. Each type has some unique characteristics and some common elements. You will learn more about these as your course progresses. Policymakers, professionals, and parents are currently taking serious interest in making early childhood education a high-quality service.

Applications

1. Do the "Talk It Over" activities placed throughout the chapter. If your instructor divides the topics among the class members,

TABLE 1-3
Continued

Criteria	Week 1	2	3	4	5	6	7	8	9	etc.
APPLICATION OF PROFESSIONAL KNOWLEDGE										
1. Relates child development principles to children's behavior										
2. Relates goals of early education to children's needs and interests										
3. Uses approved guidance techniques										
4. Is motivated to perform well										
5. Demonstrates mature, reliable behavior										
6. Relates to staff members										
7. Relates to parents										
8. Evaluates own performance as a means of learning										

Students:
Rate yourself on all applicable criteria on a five-to-one scale. Rate yourself after each day working with children. To receive feedback, discuss your self-ratings with your supervising teacher from time to time.

be sure to listen carefully and participate in discussions as others present their findings.

2. Use Table 1–3 to make your personal evaluation chart. Begin immediately to evaluate your participation with children. Continue to rate yourself throughout the term. Talk your ratings over with your instructor.

3. Begin planning a **Resource File** in which you will collect teaching ideas that you can use with young children. You will see some demonstrated and will read about others. Be sure to record complete detail in order to be able to carry out the activity later. To start your file, label manila file folders with the titles of chapters in this book. When you want to add ideas, type them on file cards and place them in the appropriate folder.

Study Questions

1. List and briefly discuss qualities needed in an early childhood teacher.

2. List and briefly discuss settings where an early childhood teacher may be employed.

3. List and briefly discuss factors affecting current demand for early childhood education services.

4. List and briefly discuss current professional efforts to raise standards in early childhood education.

5. Describe a research study that shows the effectiveness of what the researcher called "high-quality preschool education."

6. Cite a study that showed benefits to children of having professionally prepared teachers.

Videotapes

Career Encounters: Early Childhood Education
    28 minutes

See professionals at work in a variety of early childhood settings. NAEYC Media, 1509 16th St. NW, Washington, DC 20036-1426, 1-800-424-2460.

The Nurturing Community
  30 minutes

Thelma Harms and Debby Cryer explore child-rearing choices and the reasons for the choices parents make. They emphasize that, whatever the child care setting, children's lives should be of a high quality. DC/TATS MEDIA, Frank Porter Graham Child Development Center, University of North Carolina at Chapel Hill CB8040, 300 NCNB Plaza, Chapel Hill, NC 27599-8040.

What Is Quality Child Care?
  53 minutes

Bettye M. Caldwell takes a close look at professional care in this thought-provoking address. NAEYC Media, 1509 16th St. NW, Washington, DC 20036-1426, 1-800-424-2460.

Celebrating Early Childhood Teachers
  22 minutes

An upbeat view of the role of the early childhood professional with a serious side concerning the problems in retaining qualified staff. NAEYC Media, 1509 16th St. NW, Washington, DC 20036-1426, 1-800-424-2460.

Professional Organizations and Their Journals

American Association of Family and Consumer Sciences, 1555 King St., Alexandria, VA 22314. Publishes *Journal of Family and Consumer Sciences.*

Association of Childhood Education International, 11501 Georgia Ave., Suite 315, Wheaton, MD 20902. Publishes *Childhood Education.*

Council for Exceptional Children, 1920 Association Drive, Reston, VA 22091. Publishes *Exceptional Children.*

National Association of Early Childhood Teacher Educators, Dr. Joan Herwig, Pres., Iowa State University, Dept. Child Development, Ames, Iowa 50011-1030. Publishes *The Journal of Early Childhood Teacher Education.*

National Association for the Education of Young Children, 1509 16th St. NW, Washington, DC 20036-1426. Publishes *Young Children.*

National Association for Gifted Children, 4175 Lovell Rd., Suite 140, Circle Pines, MN 55014. Publishes *Gifted Child Quarterly.*

National Council on Family Relations, 1219 University Ave. SE, Minneapolis, MN 55432. Publishes *Family Relationships* and *Journal of Marriage and the Family.*

Organisation Mondiale por L'Education Prescolaire (OMEP), U.S. National Committee, P.O. Box 66, Garrett Park, MD 20896. Publishes *International Journal of Early Childhood.* International President is Dr. Candide Pineault of Québec, Canada, OMEP Secretariat, 1341 G St. NW, Suite 400, Washington, DC 20005.

Additional Journals and Magazines

Child, The New York Times Company Magazine Group, 110 Fifth Ave., New York, NY 10011.

Child and Youth Care Quarterly, Human Sciences Press, 72 Fifth Ave., New York, NY 10011.

Child Care Information Exchange, 17916 NE 103 Ct., Redmond, WA 98052.

Child Development, University of Chicago Press, P.O. Box 37005, Chicago, IL 60637.

Children, Rodale Press, Inc., 33 E. Minor St., Emmaus, PA 18096.

Children Today, Children's Bureau, Office of Child Development, U.S. Department of Health and Human Services, Washington, DC 20201.

Day Care and Early Education, Human Sciences Press, 72 Fifth Ave., New York, NY 10011.

Early Child Development and Care, Roehampton Institute, Southlands College, Wimbledon Parkside, London SW19, England.

Early Education and Development, Psychology Press, Brandon, VT 05733.

Journal of Family Issues, Sage Publications, Inc., 2111 W. Hillcrest Dr., Newbury Park, CA 91320.

Parenting, Parenting Magazine Partners, 301 Howard St., 17th Floor, San Francisco, CA 94105.

Parents Magazine, 685 Third Ave., New York, NY 10017.

Teaching Pre K-8, 40 Richards Ave., Norwalk, CT 06854.

Additional Readings

Alexander, N. P. "School-Age Child Care: Concerns and Challenges." *Young Children* 42:1, 1986, 3–10.

Brand, Susan F. "Undergraduates and Beginning Preschool Teachers Working with Young Children: Educational and Developmental Issues." *Young Children* 45:2, January 1990, 19–24.

Brazelton, T. Berry. *Working and Caring*. Reading, MA: Addison-Wesley, 1983.

Caldwell, Bettye M. *Group Care for Young Children: A Supplement to Parental Care*. Lexington, MA: Lexington Books, 1987.

Casey, M. Beth, and Marjory Lippman. "Learning to Plan Through Play." *Young Children* 46:4, May 1991, 52–57.

Castle, Kathryn. *The Infant & Toddler Handbook: Invitations for Optimum Development*. Atlanta, GA: Humanics Limited, 1983.

Elkind, David. *The Mis-Education of the Preschool Child*. Reading, MA: Addison-Wesley, 1987.

———. "Play." *Young Children* 43:5, July 1988, 2.

Gartrell, Dan. "Punishment or Guidance?" *Young Children* 42:3, March 1987, 55–61.

Hildebrand, Verna. *Guiding Young Children*. Upper Saddle River, NJ: Merrill/Prentice Hall, 1994.

Hildebrand, Verna, and Patricia Hearron. *Management of Child Development Centers*. Upper Saddle River, NJ: Merrill/Prentice Hall, 1997.

Hillman, Carol. *Before the School Bell Rings*. Bloomington, IN: Phi Delta Kappa, 1995.

Honig, Alice Sterling. "Compliance, Control, and Discipline." *Young Children* 40:2, January 1985, 50–58.

Hymes, James L., Jr. "Public School for Four-Year-Olds." *Young Children* 42:2, January 1987, 51–52.

Kostelnik, Marjorie. "Myths Associated with Developmentally Appropriate Programs." *Young Children* 47:4, May 1992, 17–23.

NAEYC. "Child Choice—Another Way to Individualize—Another Form of Preventive Discipline." *Young Children* 43:1, November 1987, 48–54.

———. "NAEYC Position Statement: A Conceptual Framework for Early Childhood Professional Development." *Young Children* 49:3, March 1994, 68–77.

———. "Reaffirming a National Commitment to Children." *Young Children* 50:3, March 1995, 61–63.

National Black Child Development Institute. "Constraints and Opportunities for African American Leadership in Early Childhood Education." *Young Children* 49:4, May 1994, 32–41.

Phillips, Deborah, and Marcy Whitebook. "Who Are Child Care Workers?" *Young Children* 41:4, May 1986, 14–20.

Powell, Douglas R. "After-School Child Care." *Young Children* 42:3, March 1987, 62–70.

Rogers, Cosby S., and Janet K. Sawyers. *Play in the Lives of Children*. Washington, DC: NAEYC, 1991.

Surr, John. "Early Childhood Programs and the Americans with Disabilities Act (ADA)." *Young Children* 47:5, July 1992, 18–21.

Williams, Leslie R., and Doris Pronin Fromberg. *Encyclopedia of Early Childhood Education*. Hamden, CT: Garland Publishing, 1992.

CHAPTER 2

Goals for Early Childhood Education

Baylor University

Objectives

✔ Identify the bases for goals in early childhood education.
✔ Define a theory and identify ways to judge a theory.
✔ Define and identify developmental tasks and what activity is developmentally appropriate as related to early childhood education goals.
✔ State the value of play in early childhood education.

"Why are young children encouraged to throw and catch?"

"Why is a housekeeping corner found in most early childhood rooms?"

"Is it important to read stories to children every day?"

"Should we let a child play alone?"

As you gain experience in early childhood schools you will ask questions such as those just listed. You'll find practices that are similar from classroom to classroom. You'll find many similarities in equipment, supplies, and teaching strategies. However, you'll also find differences, a fact that may at first confuse you. As you gain more knowledge and experience you'll grow to understand that teachers may achieve goals for children through several methods and that some goals may vary according to the teacher's preference and the needs of children in a group. You'll grow to appreciate that being an early childhood teacher requires creativity and professional skills and knowledge and is far from being an assembly-line job where cogs fit perfectly and all the objects come out alike.

BASES FOR GOALS FOR EARLY CHILDHOOD EDUCATION

Goals tell us where we are going—our destination. So where are children going? How far in the future do we want to project them? On what

---

TALK IT OVER: NO. 1

In the long range, how important is what we do with young children in relation to what they eventually become? Discuss.

---

basis do we set our goals? Do we have serious objectives in mind, or do we just want to amuse children?

Selecting goals for an early childhood education center, a classroom, or an individual child will require professional expertise. Dealing with human beings is far different than dealing with mechanical objects. You've already learned in your child development classes that children are unique, with individual needs, interests, and timetables of development. Dr. Bettye Caldwell, a prominent early childhood educator, put it well in a speech to the assembly of the World Organi-

School is a time when you enjoy making new friends. (Pennsylvania State University)

zation for Early Childhood Education when she said, "We can comfortably assert that each child is to some extent like all children, to some extent like some children, and to some extent like no other child."[1] She went on to explain how all children are biological creatures dependent on the same set of conditions to sustain life, that there are similarities among children within certain social and cultural groups, and that each child is unique in temperament, interests, motivation, and so on.

One mother of a painfully shy five-year-old said, "Just once I wish she would stamp her foot and say, 'No I won't!'" Is this mother stating a goal?

Goals Based on Values

Schools for young children, like all American schools, reflect the values enshrined in the U.S. Constitution. A **value** is a concept of the desirable. When you say, "You should _____" or "You ought to _____," you are stating a value. At this point you can draw on your knowledge of or look up the rights stated in the Constitution.

The Constitution and its amendments (new values are added by amendments and interpretations) guarantee certain rights to individuals. In early childhood programs these rights apply to

TALK IT OVER: NO. 3

Brainstorm in your class to develop a list of values you hold regarding education—your own and that of young children. Use words like "should" or "ought" to help designate a value, for example, "Children should go to school." List the values on the board and talk about the action that flows from the value.

Note: To brainstorm, have everyone make contributions to the topic without evaluating their statements. Encourage spontaneity and honor each idea.

children, parents, college students, teachers, and other employees. For example, as a result of interpretations of the Constitution by the Supreme Court, equality of opportunity and treatment should be provided for children of all races.

When you say that teachers ought to be *fair* (or *honest*, or *patient*, or *loyal*), you are saying that being fair (honest, patient, or loyal) is highly valued. When a teacher says that all children should be treated as individuals, this indicates that the value of individual uniqueness is held in high regard by that teacher. Values will be stated throughout this book. You can think about what is written and decide whether you agree or disagree. Values are learned in our homes and schools, in our communities and nation, and through our reading and education. Values are carried into action in homes and schools. Adults teach children values while interacting with them on a daily basis.

Goals Based on Parental Needs

The many types of early childhood schools, as discussed in Chapter 1, suggest that there are needs of parents to be met, especially as early

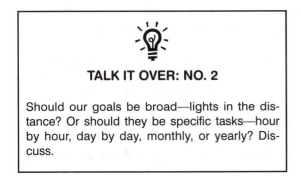

TALK IT OVER: NO. 2

Should our goals be broad—lights in the distance? Or should they be specific tasks—hour by hour, day by day, monthly, or yearly? Discuss.

---

[1]Bettye M. Caldwell, "Child Development and Cultural Diversity," paper presented at the OMEP World Assembly, Geneva, Switzerland, August 1983.

childhood educational services are considered part of a support system for the family. A **support system** complements, augments, or adds to what the family can do for itself. The school, for instance, teaches information the parent may not know or may not know how to teach. Also, the school protects the child and furnishes vital nutrition, rest, and nurturing while the parent works. The school provides parenting information or serves as a referral source to other agencies. The early childhood teacher is often the counselor when the family needs an attentive listener. Developing goals for providing services as needed by parents will be very important.

Given the mandate to serve the needs of parents, one goal we can state is *to provide a safe environment for young children when their parents are not able to be present to protect them.* We also might add *to provide for each child activities that the parents might provide if they could supervise the child during the day.* As you see, many of these goals go unstated, being assumed because the school is designed just for these purposes. Thus, some goals will be part of the chartering process of the school or center.

Goals Based on Children's Needs

Logically, children's programs should be based on children's needs—physical, social, emotional, and cognitive. Or, you might say the needs are health, nutrition, exercise, education, interpersonal relations, self-esteem, language, and so on.

Define Growth, Development, and Maturation

Children are going to grow, develop, and mature while they are in your class and in your care. **Growth** means an increase in weight, height, strength, and so on—measurable attributes. **Development** means that from conception the organism increases in complexity. During infancy, for instance, muscles mature and can hold the child up while she or he sits. Or, an infant's vocal sounds evolve into words, then clusters of words, then whole paragraphs as the child gets older— increasingly complex. Every area of development

School is a time when you enjoy taking responsibility for your own belongings. (Kansas State University)

can offer similar examples. If this more complex behavior does not come about, we know we have a problem. Human children around the world develop in similar ways within a narrow range of timetables.

Of course, growth and development go along together as the child ages and matures. **Maturation** is the natural and orderly sequence of development related to time, culminating in final physical height in the late teens. Mental, emotional, social, and language development keep on increasing in complexity long after mature physical height is achieved. Your senior citizen friends realize that they can still learn far into their later years.

You'll recognize these concepts as topics you studied in your child development course. The information you learned and will use now was discovered by scholars and practitioners over many years, findings that have been checked and refined by practitioners like the teachers and parents you will be working beside. Thus, you might state a broad goal: The children will fulfill their physical, cognitive, emotional, social, and linguistic potential.

Theories of Development

Historically, research in child development, psychology, and early childhood education has advanced theories to help describe and predict human growth, development, and behavior. A **theory** is defined as an organized set of ideas that the theorist formulates about a phenomenon, in this case about children or early childhood education.

You are probably thinking that you'd rather be practical than theoretical when it comes to teaching young children. You may think of theory as boring, scary, or awesome. You may not like learning theorist's names. These feelings are understandable; however, you'll soon see that the theories help draw your attention to details about children that you might miss otherwise. As a teacher, your goal must be to understand children. It will save you lots of time if you take advantage of the insights of other observers of children, including both practitioners and theorists. Knowing the theorists' terms will help you communicate with other professionals. Also, based on your previous experience with children, you may already have a start on formulating your own set of ideas or theories, and you can continue adding new information to your previous information and experience. Before you know it, you'll be handling theoretical ideas with ease.

Qualities of a Useful Theory

For a theory to be useful, the theorist must

1. describe the set of ideas as carefully as possible, defining new terminology and clearly stating the definitions of terms used by others;

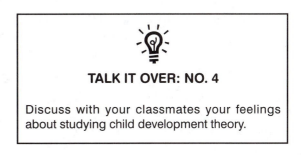

TALK IT OVER: NO. 4

Discuss with your classmates your feelings about studying child development theory.

2. publish the set of ideas in journals that are accessible to researchers, educators, and the public; and
3. welcome tests of the theory by other researchers with results published where all can freely evaluate them.

Gradually a theory either gains support or fades out of the current literature. Educators and researchers keep up on both new and old theories in hopes of finding one, or perhaps a combination, that will do a better job of contributing to the understanding and prediction of growth or behavioral outcomes. Because human beings are so unique, and because ethical considerations prevent experimenting with people in any way that might be harmful, theories about people are difficult to prove. The statistical treatment of data usually hides the details of the individual responses, making it difficult to draw conclusions about an individual with a high degree of certainty. You'll notice that researchers usually say,

TALK IT OVER: NO. 5

Discuss with your classmates what you believe influences the development of a child's (a) personality, (b) ability to learn, and (c) social skills. Summarize your discussion.

"The data indicate _____" not "The data prove _____." If the theory can be proved, it becomes a fact and is no longer a theory. To take a different type of example, you recall that in the pre-Columbus era people held the theory that the world was flat. After the voyage of Columbus and others, the flat-earth theory lost out and the round-earth theory became a fact. Astronauts' trips into outer space have further supported this fact since 1962.

A number of single-domain or more specific theories are available to help you understand single aspects of child development, such as discipline, language, cognition, and social interaction. Single-domain theories help with problems a child may be having. Occasionally, a single-domain theory has been utilized for research purposes wherein a total early childhood program follows one theory to determine whether careful adherence to one approach to education would be best for outcomes for children. To date, the research has been inconclusive regarding any

single theoretical approach. The theory that applies to certain areas of the curriculum will be presented under the most appropriate topic for helping you understand the application of the theory to curriculum. Readings at the end of this chapter will lead you to more in-depth theory.

The most prominent theory used in early childhood education program planning today is called **developmental** because the developmental characteristics and maturational timetables of children are considered the most logical basis for decisions about planning and carrying out educational programs for children. A general holistic approach that can be applied to all ages of children and to all areas of the child's development is needed.

The work of Dr. Robert J. Havighurst will be utilized to help formulate the goals for early childhood education schools. Havighurst's use of the concept of developmental tasks for children of various ages is very helpful to teachers. **Developmental tasks** are defined as "those common

School is a time when you talk new things over with the teacher. (Michigan State University)

tasks each individual of a given age must master within a given society in order to be happy and to master the tasks of the next age."[2] Developmental tasks combine biological, psychological, and sociological aspects of development. Teachers and parents find them useful in planning for a child's next level of development. The developmental tasks cover the whole child from head to toe and also cover all ages from birth to old age. Table 2–1 shows the developmental tasks for infants and young children.

Developmentally Appropriate Practice

The NAEYC has recognized problems practitioners and others have translating developmental information into programs. They have published a booklet titled *Developmentally Appropriate Practice in Early Childhood Programs Serving Children from Birth Through Age 8*.[3] "Developmentally appropriate" is used by Bredekamp in two ways when applying the developmental appropriateness concept to early childhood programs: (1) the developmental research that gives information on typical needs and behaviors of the *age* group and (2) observations showing the developmental level of the *individual* child in a group. That is, when planning activities, teachers will be guided by what a given-age child can typically do, then observe each child in order to individualize the early childhood program for that child. Such a process can make programs fit children, rather than force children to fit programs.

GOALS FOR EARLY CHILDHOOD EDUCATION

Establishing goals must come before attempting to make plans. Your school may have a goal statement agreed upon by parents, teachers, and administrators. A general goal is to help each child live a happy childhood, reach his or her potential, and become a happy, full-functioning adult.

To define goals in terms more helpful to teachers, the concept of developmental tasks as outlined in the work of Carolyn Tryon and J. S. Lilienthal is useful.[4] The developmental tasks are like rungs on a ladder; they are too far apart for the person to scale the wall of maturity without stepping on each rung. Sufficient experience and skill in each task must be achieved before the next task can be reached successfully. When conditions are right, and if the teacher is prepared, children will likely achieve the tasks.

Ten Major Goals

The developmental tasks (left column, Table 2–1) serve as a basis for the ten major goals for infants and young children. Parents and teachers will strive to help children accomplish them. See if there are any you would omit.

Grow in Independence

Children will begin to think of themselves as independent, capable individuals. Adults are responsible for helping each child reach an appropriate level of independence. This goal is always in the teacher's mind when planning the program, equipment, materials, and guidance for children and is remembered when deciding whether or not and how much to help with boots or zippers. The objective is to help each child learn to do things for him- or herself and to make decisions and choices.

Learn to Give and Share, as Well as Receive Affection

From a typical pattern of self-centered affection, children will grow in ability to give and share affection with others their age and with adults

---

[2]Robert J. Havighurst, *Developmental Tasks and Education* (New York: David McKay, 1952), p. 3.
[3]Sue Bredekamp, ed. (Washington, DC: NAEYC, 1991).

[4]Caroline Tryon and J. W. Lilienthal, "Developmental Tasks: The Concept and Its Importance," in *Fostering Mental Health in Our Schools* (ASCD Yearbook) (Washington, DC: ASCD, 1950), 77–128.

TABLE 2–1

Developmental Tasks for Infancy and Early Childhood.

Developmental Tasks	Infancy Birth to 2½	Early Childhood 2½ to 5 Yrs. Old
Growing in independence	A dependent being. Becoming aware.	Needs less private attention. Increases physical independence. Remains emotionally dependent.
Learning to give, share, and receive affection	Developing a feeling for affection. Responding to those who love him/her. Bonding and attachment occur with loved ones.	Developing ability to give affection. Learning to share affection with siblings or others. Responding to acts of affection.
Learning to get along with others	Being aware of others. Developing social interaction. Responding to others.	Beginning to develop ability to interact with agemates. Adjusting to family's expectation of child's role. Enjoys peers.
Developing self-control	Beginning to adjust to expectation of others.	Develops ability to take directions. To be obedient to authority. Growing in ability to control own behavior when authority figures are not present.
Learning human roles	Socialization begins to influence gender role identification.	Learning to identify male and female roles. Experiences and accepts people of many diversities.
Beginning to understand one's own body	Adjusting to adult feeding demand. Adjust to adult cleanliness demand.	Adjusting to expectations resulting from one's improving muscular ability. Developing modesty.
Learning and practicing large and small motor skills	Developing physical equilibrium. Developing eye-hand coordination. Establishing satisfactory rhythms of rest and activity.	Developing large muscle control. Learning to coordinate large and small muscles.

Source: Adapted from Caroline Tryon and J. S. Lilienthal, "Developmental Tasks: The Concept and Its Importance," in *Fostering Mental Health in Our Schools* (ASCD Yearbook) (Washington, DC: ASCD, 1950), 77–128.

both within and outside the family. The teacher helps them to feel secure and loved in their new environment. The teacher makes special plans for working with those children whose home backgrounds have not fostered feelings of love and security and for working with their parents, in hopes of changing some of the negative aspects of the early experience.

Learn to Get Along With Others

As children move out of the social unit of the family into the social unit of the school, the teacher wants their experiences to be positive and happy. Children are protected until they are ready for social relationships. They are helped to learn techniques of interaction that will bring positive responses from others.

TABLE 2–1
Continued

Developmental Tasks	Infancy Birth to 2½	Early Childhood 2½ to 5 Yrs. Old
Beginning to understand and control physical world	Exploring the environment using all five senses.	Meeting adult expectations of restrictive exploration. Manipulating an expanding environment. Satisfying curiosity through exploration.
Learning new words and understanding others	Developing preverbal communication. Developing verbal communication. Beginning concept formation.	Improving one's use of words and understanding of words of others. Improving one's ability to form concepts, reason, describe.
Developing a positive feeling about one's relationship to the world	Developing a sense of trust then a sense of autonomy.	Developing a sense of self as separate from others. Developing a feeling of confidence.

Develop Self-Control

The teacher thinks of discipline as self-control to be developed over time. There are few absolutes. The goal is for each child to become self-disciplined, self-guided, or self-directed. This is in contrast with a child who is only adult controlled or directed. It is desirable for children to learn certain behaviors and the reasons for them. The teacher explains how appropriate responses provide protection for each child as well as for the safety and well-being of others. As children gain understanding, they develop a sound basis for appropriate behavior. Fear of an authoritarian figure does not provide an adequate basis for developing self-control. Experience in making judgments and decisions is provided in order that children will become confident that they can make decisions when the adults are not nearby.

Learn Human Roles

Children will learn various social roles as they mature in a family and within your school or center. They will learn roles related to gender, race, ethnicity, class, religion, families, community, and so on. Today, we are helping children avoid stereotyping as they try out various social roles and learn about others.

Begin to Understand Their Own Bodies

The teacher plans and carries out a program that helps children to understand their bodies and to feed and care for themselves. Health, hygiene, and nutrition are very important.

Learn and Practice Large and Small Motor Skills

A program is designed that challenges each child's small and large muscles. Motor skill practice is encouraged through planning, support, and guidance.

Begin to Understand and Control the Physical World

The teacher helps develop the child's intelligence by encouraging curiosity, thinking, reasoning, and the gathering and using of information. Every effort is made to help children fit together some of the pieces of their world puzzle through careful planning and selection of materials, equipment, and experiences. The teacher expects to provide a background of experiences and atti-

School is a time when you learn to draw and write.
(Michigan State University)

tudes that will make living and learning more meaningful.

Learn New Words and Understand Others

Every opportunity is used by the teacher to foster children's use of language and their understanding when others speak. Concepts develop about everything the children encounter. Teachers help the children use words for new concepts and ideas. Language is strongly emphasized—a rich literacy environment is fostered. Spoken language is encouraged by avoiding the "Shhh." Understanding the child is a goal, as is having one child comprehend another.

Written language abounds in books, displays, and computers. Children are given tools for "reading" and "writing" long before they are expected to read and write English. The pictures they draw, like those of primitive people before them, are their first communications. **Emerging literacy** is the label placed on this goal in many quarters.

Develop a Positive Feeling About Their Relationship to the World

The teacher's and parents' roles are to help children feel good about themselves as they gain experience with the world. A positive self-concept can develop during these early years. The early school experiences, being the child's first, should be happy, positive experiences. An environment that is personally exciting and meaningful will add to the child's drive to learn. It is hoped that children will become self-confident in the school situation. It is highly desirable that school, teachers, friends, experiences, books, and learning be positive experiences from the children's point of view. If children complete early childhood schools with positive views of school, then their motivation should be high for accomplishing the developmental tasks of the elementary school years.

Using the foregoing ten developmental tasks as guides, teachers can plan early childhood programs that foster all areas of a child's development—physical, mental, emotional, social, language, and creative. Each of the ten tasks is important for a balanced program. See how they fit into evaluation of programs in Chapter 19.

How Are Goals Achieved?

The first time you visit an early childhood school, you may wonder how the teacher survives the day or how the children ever learn anything. There is usually a free-flowing informality that is far different from the organization adults are likely to remember in their own schooling.

Planning

Despite the apparent informality and lack of regimentation, a great deal of planning and organizing takes place before, after, and even during the school day. The teacher and assistants meet regularly when the children are not at school to map out the days, weeks, and months ahead. Plans are

School is a place to build something with Legos.
(Kansas State University)

flexible, but a good program for children does not develop haphazardly. The teacher keeps goals for the children firmly in mind. Goals are considered in terms of individual children. The teacher does not lump all children together and say, "All children must learn to _____." There will be a range of skills, behaviors, and competencies in any class. The teacher should expect differences and plan for them.

Learning Centers

The school will generally be arranged in learning centers, sometimes called interest centers or zones. That is, in various parts of the room there will be a place for children to work in art, in science, in music, and so on. They will find zones with blocks, books, and materials for dramatic play. Other zones will display perceptual and number games. In colder climates there may be an indoor zone for vigorous climbing, which substitutes for outdoor activities during bad weather. Though outdoor zones may not be as numerous as those for indoors, the observer will find zones for both quiet and vigorous activity outdoors.

Self-Selected Activity and the Teacher's Role

Finding children talking, laughing, and moving about may be one of the biggest surprises to a new observer. Yet, further observation will reveal that the children are actively learning as they choose their own activities. During the **self-selected activity period** they work individually and in small groups throughout the room or yard. The largest part of the child's day is self-selected. Given a well-designed classroom and play yard equipped with age-appropriate equipment, the major assumption is that in self-selecting activities children will choose what they need most. Whatever they choose to play on or with means they "need" this type of activity for some reason. The assumption is that the environment is a rich one with frivolous and dangerous items omitted.

The informal teaching style may also be a surprise. The teacher's role is to organize the learning centers and see that there is appropriate and sufficient equipment in each for carrying on activities from which the child can choose. Then the teacher relates to each child who is engaged in learning through play. The role is far more than supervisory. The teaching involves moving about, putting in a word here, redirecting there, listening to children's comments and questions.

A teacher may make a note to place in a child's portfolio or evaluation folder or as a reminder to call the child's parents. The teachers have many mental notes accumulating in their heads as they interact with children. There is no time to rest, gossip, or even take care of their own needs.

The assistants and the teacher work as a team. For example, one day the assistant may provide a

School is a place to practice lifting with the crane. (University of New Mexico)

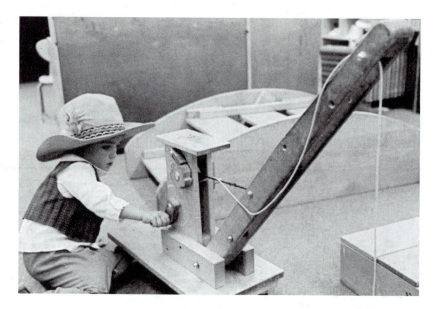

science experiment in one zone that requires close attention. Another day the assistant may keep an eye on all the zones while the teacher concentrates on teaching language arts at the literature table. Through many one-to-one contacts the teachers contribute to the total growth of each child.

Teacher-Structured Activities

Routine activities such as cleanup, storytime, and snack time are also part of the child's day. These are teacher instigated, or teacher structured, requiring some compliance with the teacher's plan. However, they are loosely organized to leave room for individual differences in response. Group activities contribute to the child's learning and develop an esprit de corps in the group.

As a student participator you may be asked to select a zone in which you can begin to develop a relationship with children individually and in small groups. For example, you may sit near the table games or puzzles, observing and helping where needed. The teacher may brief you on procedures, schedules, and the like, or may offer advice when it seems warranted. For the most

part, though, you will be left to handle your assignment as well as you can—applying your knowledge from readings and other sources. After you are acquainted with the children, you may move into situations in which you work with larger numbers of children. Each day after the children have gone, you will have an opportunity to question the teacher and seek recommendations for handling special problems you've encountered.

How Does Organization Facilitate Goals?

Do children really learn anything worthwhile in such a free setting? This may be the student's first reaction and question. Doubt also is usually common among teachers who are already experienced in teaching upper elementary and secondary grades.

Almost inevitably problems arise in groups of small children when an adult tries to get all the children doing the same thing at the same time. Young children are not accustomed to sitting still. Their attention spans may be short. However, the

TALK IT OVER: NO. 6

Consider the spatial arrangement of an early childhood classroom. What learning centers did you see? What equipment and supplies were present? How were boundaries defined? What did children do? Discuss.

learning experiences with a variety of enticing equipment that openly invites the child's use.

The teacher plans learning experiences that permit children to educate themselves. As they make discoveries through their senses—sight, touch, taste, smell, and hearing—they will communicate with other children and teachers, developing language vital to all learning. Also they will concentrate because they are doing something that interests them. They will investigate, manipulate, and create, thereby contributing to their intelligence and storehouse of knowledge.

Through individual, small-group, and whole-group activities, the teacher structures a flexible, individualized, and academically sound program. To observe or participate in an early childhood school where children are dynamically involved in their own learning is to become convinced that much worthwhile learning is taking place.

To the casual observer, children who are exercising their free choice during the self-selected activity periods are "just playing." Some may advocate reducing the amount of self-directed play activity by focusing upon academic objec-

attention span of many children is longer when they are involved in a self-chosen activity, not an adult-initiated one.

Children have a natural inclination to explore and manipulate. This inclination is to be exploited when planning the educational environment for the young child. Put a puzzle on the table so that the child can see it. Usually the child can't resist taking the puzzle apart. And when successful at working it, the child has developed both physically and mentally. The effective school setting provides for numerous

School is a time when you can get someone to read you a book. (San Antonio College)

tives and relegating all nonacademic objectives to a secondary position. However, Lawrence K. Frank, a distinguished scholar of child growth and development, would not consider the self-directed activity previously described as "nonacademic." He wrote, "Hence through play the child continually rehearses, practices, and endlessly explores and manipulates whatever he can manage to transfer imaginatively into equivalents of the adult world. He experiments with and tries to establish the meaning and use of a variety of symbols, especially language, as he tries to cope with this often perplexing grown-up world."[5] Today Frank's words are accepted by both teachers and parents.

Indeed, play is very valuable. Frank and Theresa Caplan, writing *The Power of Play*, discuss the following sixteen values of play.[6]

1. Play aids growth.
2. Play is a voluntary activity.
3. Play offers a child freedom of action.
4. Play provides an imaginary world a child can master.
5. Play has elements of adventure in it.
6. Play provides a base for language building.
7. Play has unique power for building interpersonal relations.
8. Play offers opportunities for mastery of the physical self.
9. Play furthers interest and concentration.
10. Play is the way children investigate the material world.
11. Play is a way of learning adult roles.
12. Play is always a dynamic way of learning.
13. Play refines a child's judgments.
14. Play can be academically structured.
15. Play is vitalizing.
16. Play is essential to the survival of humans.

The advocates of less play and more academic activities are really suggesting more teacher instigated or structured activities. As a future professional leader and educator of your staff and parents, reflect on ways you might discuss issues of values, goals, and teaching strategies with adults involved in your program. Play initiated by the children is academic and social. Children use their language, their hands, and their legs to play, thus enhancing every area of their bodies.

Conclusions

A developmental philosophy of early childhood education has been described. Teachers establish goals before planning programs. Developmentally appropriate goals for the young child have been stated in terms of the developmental tasks of early childhood. Goals are achieved through careful planning and through arranging centers in which children can learn as they use the materials and equipment of their choice. Routine activities are organized in a way that leaves room for individual differences.

As you read, observe, participate, and plan for a career in teaching, you must judge the merits of various teaching approaches. In what sort of school atmosphere does a child best learn academically significant concepts? What teaching methods are most appropriate to the philosophy, ideals, and needs of a democratic society?

The teacher is of utmost significance. Perhaps you can sense through your observation and participation what Moustakas calls "the bond" between teacher and child from which "opportunities and resources emerge which enable both child and teacher to realize hidden potential, to release creative capacities, and to stretch to new horizons of experience, together and alone, where learning has an impact on total being and where life has a passionate, enduring character."[7]

Applications

1. Do the "Talk It Over" activities placed throughout the chapter.

[5]Lawrence K. Frank, "Play and Child Development," in *Play—Children's Business, Guide to Selection of Toys and Games: Infants to Twelve-Year-Olds* (Washington, DC: Association for Childhood Education International, 1963), 4–5.
[6]Frank and Theresa Caplan, *The Power of Play* (Garden City, NY: Anchor Press, Doubleday, 1973), xii-xvii.
[7]Clark Moustakas, *The Authentic Teacher* (Cambridge, MA: Howard A. Doyle, 1967), 58.

2. List the ten developmental tasks down one side of a paper. After each one write one or more behaviors that you at your present age are doing to prepare yourself for your next level of developmental tasks. What conclusions do you reach about yourself?
3. Using your chart evaluate your participation with children. (See Application 2, Chapter 1, for details.)

Study Questions

1. Define *values*.
2. Explain how values affect (a) education and (b) early childhood education.
3. Define a *support system*. Explain how early childhood education services are part of a family support system.
4. Define a *theory*.
5. State three qualities of a useful theory. Explain how a theory differs from a fact.
6. How does Dr. Robert J. Havighurst define *developmental tasks*?
7. List the ten developmental tasks.
8. Define the two major characteristics of an activity that would be called developmentally appropriate. Contrast this activity with one that is developmentally inappropriate.
9. List one or more behaviors under each developmental task that a young child who is working on that task will do or learn. What difference will the child's age make?
10. List and explain four ways that goals are achieved in early childhood education centers.
11. List the values children derive from playing. Write your answer to a parent who says, "All they do is play."

Videotapes

Play and Learning
    18 minutes

A discussion with Dr. Barbara Biber. Why is play important? What do children learn when they play? NAEYC Media, 1509 16th St. NW, Washington, DC 20036-1426, 1-800-424-2460.

Environments for Young Children
    18 minutes

A discussion with Elizabeth Prescott and Elizabeth Jones answering the question, "How do the materials and arrangement of the environment help meet your goals for children?" NAEYC Media, 1509 16th St. NW, Washington, DC 20036-1426, 1-800-424-2460.

Playing and Learning
    30 minutes

Explains stages of preschool play as the natural way to learn from infancy through kindergarten. DC/TATS MEDIA, Frank Porter Graham Child Development Center, University of North Carolina at Chapel Hill CB8040, 300 NCNB Plaza, Chapel Hill, NC 27599-8040.

What Is Quality Child Care?
    57 minutes

Why isn't our society child oriented? An inspiring keynote address by Asa G. Hilliard, III. NAEYC Media, 1509 16th St. NW, Washington, DC 20036-1426, 1-800-424-2460.

Additional Readings

Blank, Helen. "Early Childhood and the Public Schools: An Essential Partnership." *Young Children* 40:4, May 1985, 52–55.

Brazelton, T. Berry. *To Listen to a Child: Understanding the Normal Problems of Growing Up.* Reading, MA: Addison-Wesley, 1984.

Bredekamp, Sue, ed. *Developmentally Appropriate Practice in Early Childhood Programs Serving Children from Birth Through Age 8.* Washington, DC: NAEYC, 1987.

———. *Accreditation Criteria and Procedures of the National Academy of Early Childhood Programs.* Washington, DC: NAEYC, 1991.

Coleman, Mick. "Planning for the Changing Nature of Family Life in Schools for Young Children." *Young Children* 46:4, May 1991, 15–20.

Curry, Nancy E., and Cal N. Johnson. *Beyond Self-Esteem: Developing a Genuine Sense of Human Value.* Washington, DC: NAEYC, 1994.

Department of Health and Human Services Advisory Committee on Head Start Quality and Expansion. "Creating a 21st Century Head Start." *Young Children* 49:1, March 1994, 65–67.

Ford, Sylvia A. "The Facilitator's Role in Children's Play." *Young Children* 48:6, September 1993, 66–69.

Greenberg, Polly. "Why Not Academic Preschool? (Part 1)." *Young Children* 45:2, January 1990, 70–80.

———. "Why Not Academic Preschool? (Part 2) Autocracy or Democracy in the Classroom." *Young Children* 47:3, March 1992, 54–64.

Hildebrand, Verna. *Fundamentos de Educación Infantil: Jardín de Niños y Preprimaria.* Mexico, DF: Editorial Limusa, 1992.

Levine, James A., Dennis T. Murphy, and Sherrill Wilson. *Getting Men Involved: Strategies for Early Childhood Programs.* New York: Scholastic, 1993.

McBride, Brent A. "Interaction, Accessibility, and Responsibility: A View of Father Involvement and How to Encourage It." *Young Children* 49:5, July 1989, 13–19.

Morris, Sandra L. "Supporting the Breastfeeding Relationship During Child Care: Why Is It Important?" *Young Children* 50:2, January 1995, 59–66.

NAEYC. "Guidelines for Appropriate Curriculum Content and Assessment in Programs Serving Children Ages 3 Through 8." *Young Children* 46:3, March 1991, 21–38.

———. "Using NAEYC's Code of Ethics: A Tool for Real Life." *Young Children* 50:1, November 1994, 62–63.

Sawyers, Janet K., and Cosby S. Rogers. *Helping Young Children Develop Through Play: A Practical Guide for Parents, Caregivers, and Teachers.* Washington, DC: NAEYC, 1990.

Sulzby, Elizabeth. "I Can Write! Encouraging Emergent Writers." *Scholastic Pre-K Today,* January 1993, 30–33.

Theillheimer, Rachel. "Something for Everyone: Benefits of Mixed-Age Grouping for Children, Parents, and Teachers." *Young Children* 48:5, July 1993, 82–87.

Thorne, Barrie. *Gender Play: Girls and Boys in School.* New Brunswick, NJ: Rutgers University Press, 1993.

CHAPTER 3

Getting to Know Children

Southeast Oakland Vocational Technical Center

Objectives

✔ Describe characteristics of children of each age from infancy through age five.
✔ Identify factors in decisions regarding group size and age range within early childhood groups.
✔ Identify measures taken to acquaint the child and parents with the staff and facility of a school.
✔ State the obligation to protect the privacy of families.

"We get to help more with the three-year-olds than we did with the fives."

"Whew! There is never a dull moment in here with these four-year-olds!"

"I feel useless. These fives don't need our help."

S uch comments are common when early childhood education students talk about their observing and participating assignments in groups of young children. When given an opportunity to see different age groups, students discover common characteristics of an age. They may also note wide differences between children who are the same age.

The following discussion of children's characteristics may be a review for you. However, curriculum for early childhood depends on understanding the developmental ages and stages children are in. Thus, you can use this chapter to understand the basic concepts of children's development as the various curricular ideas are offered.

CHARACTERISTICS OF CHILDREN

Children are unique. You can spend your lifetime career learning in increasing depth about one or more aspects of how children grow and develop.

A toddler likes to investigate things through touching and tasting. (V. Hildebrand, photographer)

Most researchers specialize in one or only a few related aspects of development, for example, in language or in motor development. Most of this chapter focuses primarily on age-related characteristics of children. Age related to development is believed to be the major criterion for decisions you will confront during your course. However, as you study further and take increasing responsibility in early childhood programs, you will observe continuously and grow in your ability to consider other characteristics of children and of their parents as you endeavor to meet their needs.

Sociocultural Characteristics

Children are a blend of racial, ethnic, socioeconomic class, and religious and cultural heritage characteristics that helps make each child unique. Sometimes disabling conditions also prevail. You, of course, have a similar variety of characteristics.

Just as you would like to be accepted fully, regardless of your sociocultural characteristics, so, too, do children and their parents want to be accepted fully. Throughout your study of early childhood education and your observation of children, you will learn to accept all children without wanting to change them into your own image.

Children of each gender and all cultural and racial groups will be fully accepted. You will plan equally for them and encourage all to participate fully in your program and its parts. Goals for each child's total development will be paramount.

As you become acquainted with children and others with sociocultural characteristics unfamiliar to you, make efforts to read widely about the people of the various cultures.[1] Try to learn what researchers who have studied that culture have discovered that could help you better understand a child or parent from that group. You will grow in your appreciation and understanding of those individuals. For example, when you learn that

---

[1] A recommended reading for all early childhood students to help you understand children who differ from you is *Knowing and Serving Diverse Families* by V. Hildebrand, L. Phenice, M. Gray, and R. Hines (Upper Saddle River, NJ: Merrill/Prentice-Hall, 1996).

children in Asian cultures are typically taught to be very deferential to adults and to show this deference by lowering their eyes when addressed, you will understand why looking directly at a teacher is difficult for some children. Imagine yourself in their culture, not knowing how to show deference to individuals. See Chapter 21 for further discussion of children in various cultures and Chapter 20 for additional information on parents.

Some children will be from various language groups or from a section of the United States where English is spoken with a different accent or dialect. You'll be challenged as you make efforts to understand each child's body language and his or her other efforts to communicate. Always help children and their parents to know that you appreciate their unique characteristics. In a number of chapters suggestions have been made for involving parents in teaching other children to appreciate the similarities and differences arising from various cultures—perhaps through music or storytelling. See in Chapter 17 the section on special visitors.

During some eras in the United States, children of foreign-born parents were made to feel that they had to be assimilated immediately. They denied every aspect of their heritage. For example, children in families where they might have become bilingual were only taught English. Today we as a profession are encouraging full acceptance of the heritage of each child and family. We welcome all to full citizenship. We encourage them to maintain a language and an identity with their cultural characteristics while participating fully in the offerings of their new culture in America. According to researchers, "Young children who receive natural exposure to a second language are likely to eventually achieve higher levels of second language proficiency than adults."[2]

Whatever you do, learn to accept and to enjoy the diversity of people and especially to recog-

nize the common bond of humanity in people of all cultures—undoubtedly a basic requirement for a more harmonious world.

FAMILY VARIATIONS

You will also encounter children from families with problems or families living in varied structural groups, some very different from your own. There are family and personal travails that affect children, but that children have no power to change. A child's family situation may change or be affected due to conditions such as single parenthood, divorce, remarriage, blended families, or joint custody. Children's lives change when a parent loses a job; when a grandparent or foster parent becomes the child's guardian; when there is child abuse or neglect; when family members are ill, die, or become disabled; when a family has refugee or immigrant status; or when there is parental absence, either permanent or resulting from work-force assignments such as the military.

When these conditions arise for children in your group, your patience and understanding will be essential. You will be tested at times beyond your present knowledge or experience. However, it is important to remember that the children are being tested even more as they struggle to survive and thrive. Parents need stable, dedicated, nonjudgmental, and helpful teachers during stressful times. Ask your lead teacher if there are any details about the families that would help you understand the children better.

There are support groups dedicated to helping people in some of these family conditions. You may wish to contact support groups or social agencies for information that would help you to understand the child better, to learn how you might help the adults, or to discover referral sources. Read articles in newspapers, magazines, and professional journals to help you, as a teacher, learn more about helping children living in varied families. As you study you will grow in empathy and understanding.

[2]Lourdes Diaz Soto, "Understanding Bilingual/Bicultural Young Children," *Young Children* 46:2 (January 1991), 32.

A five-year-old may be able to tie her shoes after a nap, yet other fives may not tie their shoes yet. (Children's Center, Denver)

AGE-RELATED CHARACTERISTICS

Children of each age have characteristics that distinguish them from children who are older and younger. These characteristics have been described in numerous books, articles, and bulletins published by researchers over many years. Studies continue by child development researchers. There are still gaps in our knowledge, and there are always possibilities for describing in greater detail the ways children grow and develop.

This chapter summarizes briefly some of the most salient characteristics of children of each age involved in early childhood programs. It is recommended that you refer to a child development or child psychology text to increase your depth of understanding. Always keep such a reference handy.

In addition, the NAEYC has published a booklet based on developmental research that details for practitioners developmental characteristics and the typical strategies for working with chil-

dren of each age. This booklet is edited by Sue Bredekamp and titled, *Developmentally Appropriate Practice in Early Childhood Programs Serving Children from Birth Through Age 8.*[3]

Before you begin working with children, try to review the characteristics of children of the age you expect to teach. Then upon arrival in your assigned center, you can concentrate on observing the specific children in your group to see how those general characteristics do or do not fit particular children. If you wonder about a behavior, always ask your instructor or the child's teacher about it. As you begin planning learning activities for children, you will keep clearly in mind the typical characteristics of the age you are teaching.

Infants and Toddlers

You may be assigned to work with infants or toddlers as part of your practical experience in early childhood education courses. Babies will seem to spend a lot of time eating, sleeping, and being

---

[3]Washington, DC: NAEYC, 1987.

changed, but they are learning, and there is a great deal for you to learn. They will need lots of cuddling and gentle handling. Please refer to Chapters 7 and 8 for general characteristics of infants and toddlers as applied to planning for and interacting with them in a center.

Late Two-Year-Olds and Young Threes

If you observe a group of late twos and young three-year-olds, you may find there is very little conversation. Most children's vocabularies are limited at this age. They often get what they want by physical rather than verbal means. Children may be playing quite far apart, yet never seem to feel left out. Even if they are playing close together, each will be playing his or her own game. This is called **parallel play**. You will see little interaction between the children.

Physical skills interest twos and threes. They may seek compliments on how high they are on the slide or jungle gym. They may need encouragement, help, and reassurance the first few times they use a piece of equipment. Twos may

prefer to push a kiddie car, but the tricycle usually attracts the threes. Twos look clumsy and precarious to many visitors, who worry that they will fall. However, they generally won't fall if they climb from their own motivation. If they are encouraged by another child or an adult to go beyond what they personally feel is a safe height, then the teacher should be nearby to avoid accidents.

For most twos and young threes, the school is their first group experience away from home. This age group should have a sufficient number of adults ready to provide individualized attention. The ability to play a nurturing role when necessary is a characteristic of a good teacher for this age group. Introduction to group living may be painful for some of the children. It may be difficult for the child's parents, too! Children enter prekindergarten with differing amounts of experience outside the home. One child may readily accept a teacher because of pleasant experiences with baby-sitters, relatives, or religious school teachers. If previous experience has been

A toddler likes to try to dress himself, so a dad who has patience to wait is important. (Kansas State University)

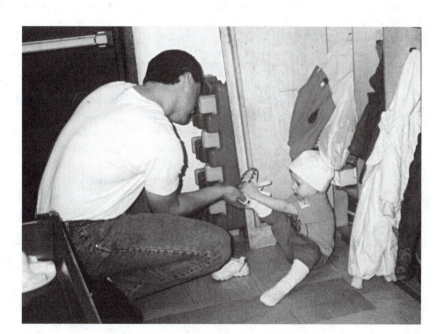

unpleasant, however, the teacher may be in for a difficult time. Many young children will have had virtually no experience away from home. When they arrive at school among strange adults and children, they are overcome with fear. Adults must learn to console them.

Teachers of twos and young threes must be on the alert for signs indicating a child's need to use the toilet. The child may fidget restlessly, or become unusually quiet, or hold a hand pressing the genitals. As soon as the signs are noticed, the wise teacher heads straight for the bathroom with the child in hand. Young children can't wait! The teacher talks in a quiet voice while leading the child to the bathroom. Although schools generally prefer to enroll children who are toilet trained, every teacher of two- and three-year-olds knows that bladder control is frequently not well established. The teacher is alert to prevent accidents. The teacher's guidance will vary from child to child as efforts are made to understand each one. Some may need a helping hand, others may need only a reminder. A mature child will go to the toilet when necessary without attention. Some may fear the noise of the flushing water. If this is true, do not require the child to flush the toilet until greater maturity overcomes this fear.

Lunch or snack with twos and young threes is a serious business. They eat well and talk little. Often they spill food and milk. Fingers are the popular eating tool.

Resting time should provide a closeness to the teacher or other adults. In groups that meet only a few hours, children may not be required to lie down to rest. However, in child care centers where children stay a full day, nap time is essential. These youngsters may be exhausted because of the amount of stimulation they receive in the group and because most arrive at school quite early. Bedtime has many associations for children. They may be weepy because parents are not there. Many hands and much patience are required to get a happy, restful nap time under way.

Comparing the teaching in a group of young children with the teaching in an older group, you will note that the younger child gets more help, more demonstration, more reassurance, and more assistance while trying a new skill. The teacher uses words, gestures, and actions because the young child's verbal understandings are being developed. Action cues help the child to understand.

Late Threes and Fours

Three-and-a-half and four-year-olds have many characteristics in common. During their first days in school they may have anxiety periods, just as do the two-year-olds and young threes. Generally, anxiety periods will be of short duration because the child has had more occasions to leave home and enter into groups, knowing parents always return. Being more experienced, this child will be more curious about what the other children are doing and will move in the direction of the action. The parent who remains at school will probably find he or she is not needed.

Children of this age ask many questions. They ask some questions because they really want to know the answer. They ask some simply because they want attention. Others they ask because they wish someone would ask them that question—they know the answer and enjoy a chance to show off. Verbally they have developed by leaps and bounds from the younger age discussed previously. They understand more vocabulary than they are able to use.

At this period there is a rapid increase in reasoning and concept building. Late threes and four-year-olds want to know about everything and to experiment with any material provided for them. Interest is maintained over a longer period of time than in younger children.

These children are more active. They run faster, climb more easily, and swing higher. Many can now pump the swing. They ride their tricycles fast, bumping into things and people, and even upsetting the tricycles deliberately.

Socially, late three- and four-year-olds play closer together, sometimes sharing toys. The more mature will make suggestions for the others. This is parallel play, showing the beginning of **cooperative play**. Cooperative play occurs between two or more children. They evolve a theme, actively arrange their environment, use language extensively, and share social give-and-take. Increased verbal and motor abilities seem to be facilitating factors.

During the fourth year boys often choose activities traditionally thought of as masculine. For example, they select big blocks and cars. Girls often like the housekeeping area or other so-called more feminine activities. However, there is still a great deal of interaction between boys and girls as they play in the learning areas. Imaginative themes develop in the group.

Teachers can help avoid gender segregation by encouraging all children to participate in all activities. For example, with our newer understanding of the impact of socialization and gender stereotyping, the teacher may not only permit but encourage girls to be more rambunctious, physical, and loud in their play and boys to be more loving, helping, and aesthetic. Societal gains from removing gender, racial, and ethnic stereotypes can be substantial.

Four-year-olds vacillate between wanting to be big and enjoying being little. One day they can do something for themselves; the next day they would like you to do it for them—or at least give a little help.

The late threes and four-year-olds may be picky eaters. They may indicate their likes and dislikes strongly, thus asserting themselves. Their growth rate has slowed down and they require less food. Therefore, avoid pressuring children to eat.

Toileting is generally quite routine in these groups. A wise teacher is quick to note indications of a child's need and will remind him or her to go. Most four-year-olds prefer to take care of toileting without help.

At this age children usually think they're too old to rest. Rest time is therefore better received if it is called quiet time. However, three- or four-year-olds still need to slow down or they may become exhausted, hyperactive, or grouchy. In child care centers adjustments may have to be made for older children who aren't sleepy. Sometimes they can be given resting and reading privileges in a room away from the sleepers.

Three-year-olds are known for their negativism. Wording questions and requests to avoid that "No" seems to be the key to living harmoniously with threes. Fours, instead of saying "No," typically find other ways (dawdling or talking) to resist what adults want them to do. Almost all have difficulty waiting for their turn.

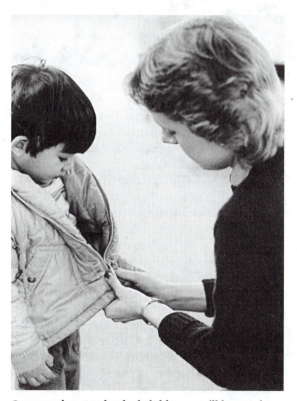

Once you know individual children, you'll know when a little help is needed. (Kansas State University)

Every experience you have with children helps you understand them better. (V. Hildebrand, photographer)

TALK IT OVER: NO. 1

Discuss experiences you've had with three- and four-year-olds. State each child's age and describe his or her behavior.

Fives and Young Sixes

The fives and young six-year-olds found in kindergartens are different from the groups we have been discussing. They are much easier to organize into a group because of their increased use and understanding of words. They seem more patient and can wait for their turn—though not indefinitely. They seem to have a genuine interest in pleasing their teachers, their parents, and anyone else who shows interest in them. Many will have had prekindergarten experience.

In addition to increased verbal skills, fives and sixes are highly curious about everything they see and hear. They want to know. They like to experiment. They often wonder how something works and will take it apart in an effort to find out. They are highly creative if their previous experience has stimulated their imagination. They will be creative in every aspect of their learning if the atmosphere is conducive to experimentation.

Socially these children enjoy each other. Cooperation on intricate projects may last several days. Each group usually has a number of strong leaders with creative ideas for projects or dramatic play. Boys and girls often play together. However, girls tend to choose a "best friend"— often resulting in easily hurt feelings if the friend finds someone else. Boys are less inclined toward a single friend and usually enjoy activities that incorporate a large group of boys at a time. All activity is not cooperative, however. Because of a longer attention span, a child may work on a pro-

Knowing children's parents helps as you guide each child's adjustment and learning. (Mieko Kosobayashi, photographer)

ject alone while others do something else. This type of independent activity frequently occurs with the more socially secure children.

A charming characteristic of children of this age is their growing sense of humor. At the younger ages children are too literal to appreciate a joke. Now they enjoy jokes, riddles, and nonsense songs and poems. They like to rhyme words and may taunt their friends verbally.

Motor coordination is generally well developed. Kindergartners enjoy learning new skills. Chinning, skating, and riding a two-wheel bike are challenges they appreciate. Small motor coordination is also developing, so that a crayon marks where the child wants it to mark. More complicated puzzles and building toys are enjoyed.

With so much growth in all areas of development, the teacher's role is to provide a wide variety of activities. Activities must be constantly new, different, and appealing. When a teacher knows that children have not learned something thoroughly, concepts must be presented in fresh ways; otherwise the group will show that they are bored. Because of the wider variety of interests, the teacher must plan to have many activities going on in a group at once. When kindergartners have had previous prekindergarten experience or are from advantaged homes, an even wider variety of challenging activities is crucial. There is so much in this world to learn that it is a severe indictment of the teacher if a group of kindergartners becomes bored.

Some typical behaviors and other characteristics of children found in early childhood programs have been described. Each child differs regarding these characteristics. When it is said that two-year-olds are typically negative, it means that most, but not necessarily all, two-year-olds are negative. The same is true of the other behaviors described. Normative data only indicate typical characteristics and therefore are not really an evaluation of behavior.

Any plan for learning to be developmentally appropriate must take into consideration the ages and stages of the children in the group. To master advanced skills, the child must first succeed in the more elementary ones. This fact is important in all areas of learning and must be taken into account as teachers provide experiences and set expectations for individual children. A three-year-old may advance along the developmental continuum and master some skills that are typical of five-year-olds. A five-year-old may have a slower rate of development and be like three-year-olds in some skills. Both new skills and new knowledge build on past knowledge and skills.

It is important for teachers to become knowledgeable about child growth and development, to learn to assess accurately a child's level of development, and to incorporate this knowledge into planning for children at school.

Special Children

Children with special needs or disabling conditions may be found in early childhood classrooms under a program called **mainstreaming**. States differ as to the age when state funds may be used to help pay for a disabled child's care and education. Some funds may be available for consultants to help plan and carry out programs for children with special needs. Head Start has pioneered integration of special children in its groups.

Your child development knowledge will serve you well as you learn to plan for young special needs children. It is important to remember that they are children and that most have a majority of characteristics that are normal and similar to those of other children. Due to their disability, they may go through the normal stages at a slower pace. Thus techniques for working with chronologically younger children may be called for.

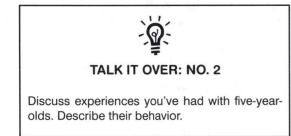

TALK IT OVER: NO. 2

Discuss experiences you've had with five-year-olds. Describe their behavior.

TALK IT OVER: NO. 3

Discuss any experience you've had with special needs children. What questions concerned you the most?

Teachers must apply the developmental tasks discussed in Chapter 2 to the needs of these children and help them progress little by little—cheering each child and parents as new stages are reached. With a developmental approach one is likely to pace the child properly—knowing that there will be a developmental range in any classroom. Many of the activities suggested for the typical early childhood curriculum will be appropriate at some level for the child with special needs.

Teachers must be willing to read books and articles and attend workshops addressing specific disabilities. For example, learning to do sign language for the deaf is required, and learning to keep the environment clear of hazards is essential for blind children. Teachers should feel free to ask a lot of questions. Consultants should be available at some level to consult with parents and teachers; and both should take full advantage of consultants' expertise.

Students who participate in programs with special children should ask for specific suggestions for dealing with the special child. Sometimes students feel they are the only inexperienced person, when in reality most of the staff may be exploring and learning with the new challenge.

Each child has strengths he or she can use to compensate or deal with the disability. Identifying those strengths may be a first task. For example, a child may enjoy being in the presence of others, or have a sunny disposition that makes others like him or her, or have strong persistence for completing a task. These are strengths that can contribute to overcoming or adjusting to the disability.

Working with parents is particularly essential with special children. Parents learn techniques for handling the child that can help the school staff. Parents also can learn from the teachers who may discover a new approach for helping their child. Thus, close communication is essential.

There is a growing demand for early childhood professionals who have had experience and training with special children. Thus your initiation to them through your participation could help you decide whether you might like to become specialized in educating special needs children.

Age for Entering School

Using the developmentally appropriate approach enables the teacher to enroll and plan for children with a wide range of developmental levels. Although a child is three, or four, or five, his or her performance might be that of a chronologically younger child. Teachers always plan a wide array of activities that can be completed at various skill or complexity levels—the appropriate level for each individual child is what is expected and rewarded.

The beauty of the approach suggested is that the more skilled children tutor the less experienced children and serve as motivating role models for less skilled children to emulate. This fits psychologist Vygotsky's concept of scaffolding and social interaction in learning. It happens frequently in the relaxed self-directed atmosphere in our programs. More about Vygotsky is discussed later.

Recently there has been a very considerable discussion regarding the appropriate curriculum for five-year-olds. Teachers have been pressured to make the curriculum more difficult regardless of studies that indicate that development cannot be rushed. Tests used to pigeonhole children have been highly criticized, and NAEYC has published the *NAEYC Position Statement on Developmentally Appropriate Practice in the Primary Grades, Serving 5- Through 8-Year-Olds.* (Washington, DC: NAEYC, 1987).

Most teachers who are well prepared in early childhood development and education know how to tailor a program to build on a child's strengths and make the school fit individual children in a class that has a range of skills and abilities. Children do not "fail sandbox," as the comment goes, when they are given developmentally appropriate activities. They achieve happily.

GROUPING CHILDREN

Schools vary in their policy of grouping children. A single group may range from ages two to six. In other schools separate, more homogeneous age groups of threes, fours, and fives exist. Licensing standards are one determinant. Flexible grouping is followed in some programs. For example, a physically skillful late three-year-old may be allowed some time with the four-year-old group. The teacher may even transfer the child if all areas of development justify it.

A case can be made for nearly any age combination. Some teachers like to have older children with the younger. They reason that it is more like a family as older children learn to help out the younger ones. In a classroom with a wide age range an immature older child can find a playmate with similar skills. In a single-age classroom this child may feel inferior.

Some teachers object to a wide-age-range classroom because the great differences make it difficult to plan activities with sufficient challenge for the most mature children. Frequently a teacher has little to say about the ages of the children in the group. Enrollment lists are often simply handed to the teacher. A public school usually enrolls any child who registers. Sometimes children are recruited with little regard for age. But even if the children were all the same age, teachers would find wide variations in development. With a mixture of ages the range of differences is still greater. Teachers must plan a variety of activities for self-selection—some to challenge the most skillful child and others to encourage the least skillful.

Size of Group

Fewer than eighteen children per group is best from the viewpoint of both the children and the teachers, according to studies. A small group permits the teachers to know the children and the parents better. Children, too, get better acquainted with their teachers and each other if the group is small. Also, it is easier to avoid overstimulation and fatigue. Every group should have a minimum of two adults in order to cope with emergencies. A ratio of one adult per five children is suggested, especially in groups of special needs children, where individualized teaching is of special importance. Research indicates that the larger the group, the more authoritarian the leadership becomes in order to maintain control. A small group is more conducive to a democratic arrangement.

NAEYC recommends the following maximum staff-child ratios and group sizes:[4]

Age	Ratio	Maximum Group Size
Birth–12 mo.	1:4	8
24–36 mo.	1:5	10
36 mo.	1:10	20
48 mo.	1:10	20
60 mo.	1:10	20

KNOWING CHILDREN AS INDIVIDUALS

Classroom Observation

Teachers begin accumulating information about the children from the first moment they know which children will be in their group. Because each child is unique, understanding each one is a difficult task. The teacher makes a systematic effort to learn about each child by carrying a notebook in which information is recorded. Periodically a progress report is made for each child. An observer may be assigned to take diary records of

[4]Sue Bredekamp, ed., *Accreditation Criteria and Procedures of the National Academy of Early Childhood Programs* (Washington, DC: NAEYC, 1991), 24.

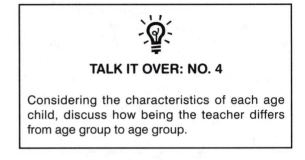

TALK IT OVER: NO. 4

Considering the characteristics of each age child, discuss how being the teacher differs from age group to age group.

each child's activity and manner of response. Combining observations and information from various sources, the teacher plans a program to fulfill each child's needs. Students will benefit from the teacher's careful study as they are provided with background information for understanding more about the children. Refer to Chapter 1 for information on being a good observer.

Home Visits

Besides working with the children at school, most teachers make periodic visits to the home in order to get better acquainted with the child and the family. You, as a participating student, may be invited to accompany the teacher on a home visit. Students, and even some teachers, are often hesitant about making home visits. Once they have made a few visits, however, they realize their value in developing understanding, appreciation, and rapport. For details on making home visits, please turn to Chapter 20, Teacher-Parent Relations.

Family Visits to the School

During the home visit a time can be agreed upon for the family to see the school facilities. These family visits to the school afford university students who may be assigned to that laboratory an excellent opportunity to get acquainted with children.

As a result of the home visit, the teacher and family now greet each other as old friends. Student helpers can be available to help quietly as the child looks around. The child usually explores quickly, finding the locker with his or her name on it, the bathroom, the various learning centers, and the playground. Sometimes the child meets new classmates because several families (including siblings) may drop in for their visits at the same time. If a child had any worries, they are usually allayed by now. The child is ready to enter school.

Teachers' Files

Teachers will keep files for each child containing various types of information. Since dealing with a family results in a highly personal relationship, professional standards and adherence to ethical procedures require that personal information revealed by parents be kept strictly confidential. For this reason, teachers are not at liberty to open all files to the students or to tell them all they know about a child's family. Some teachers keep two separate files: one containing objective data, to which the students have access; the other containing more subjective notes and evaluations that are not open to the students.

Students also may have occasion to obtain very personal information about a family. They too must treat the information as confidential. It is sound policy for a school to ask students to discuss the child only with the child's teacher or in the theory class that accompanies the course. Using anecdotal material for coffee-house conversation is a sure way to embarrass the student, the teacher, and the parents. In a social situation, information becomes gossip. Parents can quickly lose confidence in the school if they feel their personal lives are not being protected. Imagine the teacher's chagrin when a mother reported that her husband had learned from one of his students that their son was "the holy terror of the nursery school." Even if the story were true, the teacher should be the one to bring the child's conduct to the parents' attention and to discuss the problem in the light of possible remedies. Health forms, questionnaires, and tests are objective data that may be open to students.

Conclusions

Getting to know children is a continuing process. Real understanding requires a depth of percep-

tion that comes with training and experience and, of course, may never really be completely achieved. Information regarding children can be obtained from research, from parents, and from previous experience with children. Each child has characteristics that are similar to those of other children of that age. Each child also has unique characteristics. The similarities enable the teacher to work with children in a group. A range of interests and abilities will exist in every age group. The teacher and the student of early childhood education are challenged to learn to gauge the level of a child's development and to plan a program that meets the developmental needs of individual children.

Continuing to grow in your own understanding of human development and behavior and helping all adults involved in your program—parents, aides, principals, and volunteers—to understand development and behavior will be essential tasks for you as a professional teacher. Think about the educational processes that are effective for this learning. Learning about human development is essential and should be ongoing and dynamic for all concerned.

Applications

1. Do the "Talk It Over" activities suggested in the chapter.
2. Make a chart for identifying characteristics of each child. List the ten developmental tasks (see Chapter 2) down one side of a paper. Across the top make column headings for each age. Fill in characteristic behavior for each task under each age group.
3. Watch a film showing young children of different ages. Make notes on the characteristic behavior of each age child.
4. Test your ability to observe a child, analyze his or her characteristics, make a guess as to the child's age, and check the correctness of your estimate. (This activity could take place in a supermarket or through use of a film.)
5. Add notes to your Resource File on children's characteristics.

Study Questions

1. Describe typical behaviors of each age child from infancy through kindergarten.
2. Explain (a) solitary play, (b) parallel play, (c) cooperative play, and (d) why these concepts are relevant to early childhood teachers.
3. Explain factors affecting a decision on group size and age range within a group in an early childhood center.

Videotapes

Developmentally Appropriate Practice: Birth Through Age 5
    27 minutes

Shows teachers and children in developmentally appropriate programs. Shows inappropriate practices. NAEYC Media, 1509 16th St. NW, Washington, DC 20036-1426, 1-800-424-2460.

Meeting Special Needs
    30 minutes

Focuses on the alternatives parents have for the care and education of young children with special needs. Describes home, mainstreamed, and specialized programs, along with parent and professional comments. Work of Thelma Harms and Debby Cryer. DC/TATS MEDIA, Frank Porter Graham Child Development Center, University of North Carolina at Chapel Hill CB8040, 300 NCNB Plaza, Chapel Hill, NC 27599-8040.

Using the Early Childhood Classroom Observation
    26 minutes

How to use the observation scale that is part of the self-study package for NAEYC accreditation. NAEYC Media, 1509 16th St. NW, Washington, DC 20036-1426, 1-800-424-2460.

Curriculum for Preschool and Kindergarten
    16 minutes

A discussion with Lillian Katz. What is appropriate for four- and five-year-olds? NAEYC Media, 1509 16th St. NW, Washington, DC 20036-1426, 1-800-424-2460.

Additional Readings

Abbott, Carol F., and Susan Gold. "Conferring with Parents When You're Concerned That Their Child Needs Special Services." *Young Children* 46:4, May 1991, 10–14.

Allen, K. E. *Mainstreaming in Early Childhood Education*. Albany, NY: Delmar, 1980.

Atkins, Cammie. "Writing: Doing Something Constructive." *Young Children* 40:1, November 1984, 3–7.

Balaban, Nancy. "The Role of the Child Care Professional in Caring for Infants, Toddlers, and Their Families." *Young Children* 47:5, July 1992, 66–71.

Berk, Laura. "Why Children Talk to Themselves." *Young Children* 40:5, July 1985, 46–52.

Brazelton, T. Berry. *Infants and Mothers*. New York: Dell, 1986.

———. *Toddlers and Parents: A Declaration of Independence*. New York: Dell, 1986.

Brazelton, T. Berry, and Michael Yogman. *Affective Development in Infancy*. New York: Ablex, 1986.

Bredekamp, Sue, ed. *Developmentally Appropriate Practice in Early Childhood Programs Serving Children From Birth Through Age 8*. Washington, DC: NAEYC, 1987.

Bullock, Janis R. "Lonely Children." *Young Children* 48:6, September 1993, 53–57.

Elkind, David. *The Hurried Child*. Reading MA: Addison-Wesley, 1981.

———. "The Child Yesterday, Today, and Tomorrow." *Young Children* 42:4, May 1987, 6–11.

———. *The Mis-education of the Preschool Child*. Reading, MA: Addison-Wesley, 1987.

Fauvre, Mary. "Including Young Children with 'New' Chronic Illnesses in an Early Childhood Education Setting." *Young Children* 43:6, September 1988, 71–77.

Feeney, Stephanie. "The Aggressive Child." *Young Children* 43:2, January 1988, 48–51.

Froschl, Merle, et al. *Including All of Us: An Early Childhood Curriculum about Disability*. New York: Educational Equity Concepts, 1984.

Gage, Jim, and Susan Workman. "Creating Family Support Systems: In Head Start and Beyond." *Young Children* 50:1, November 1994, 74–77.

Hale, Janice. "The Transmission of Cultural Values to Young African American Children." *Young Children* 46:6, September 1991, 7–15.

Hanline, Mary Frances. "Integrating Disabled Children." *Young Children* 40:2, January 1985, 45–48.

Hatch, Thomas C. "Looking at Hank, Looking at Ira: Looking at Individual Four-Year-Olds, Especially Their Leadership Styles." *Young Children* 45:5, July 1990, 11–17.

Hildebrand, Verna. *Parenting: Rewards and Responsibilities.* New York: McGraw-Hill, 1994.

Hillman, Carol. *Teaching Four-Year-Olds, A Personal Journey.* Bloomington, IN: Phi Delta Kappa, 1992.

Honig, Alice Sterling. "Stress and Coping in Children (Part 1)." *Young Children* 41:4, May 1986, 50–63.

———. "Stress and Coping in Children (Part 2)." *Young Children* 41:5, July 1986, 47–59.

———. "The Shy Child." *Young Children* 42:4, May 1987, 54–64.

Javernick, Ellen. "Johnny's Not Jumping: Can We Help Obese Children?" *Young Children* 43:2, January 1988, 18–23.

Maker, C. June, Aleene B. Nelson, and Judith A. Rogers. "Giftedness, Diversity, and Problem-Solving." In *Early Childhood Education 95/96.* eds. Karen M. Paciorek and Joyce H. Monro. Guilford, CT: Dushkin, 1995, 174–182.

Manfredi/Petitt, Lynn A. "Multicultural Sensitivity: It's More than Skin Deep!" *Young Children* 50:1, November 1994, 72–73.

Meddin, Barbara J., and Anita L. Rosen. "Child Abuse and Neglect: Prevention and Reporting." *Young Children* 41:4, July 1986, 26–30.

Melson, Gail F., and Alan Fogel. "The Development of Nurturance in Young Children." *Young Children* 43:3, March 1988, 57–65.

NAEYC. "The Difficult Child." *Young Children* 43:5, July 1988, 60–68.

———. "Discipline: Are Tantrums Normal?" *Young Children* 43:6, September 1988, 35–40.

Nourot, Patricia Monighan, and Judith L. Van Hoorn. "Symbolic Play in Preschool and Primary Settings." *Young Children* 46:6, September 1991, 40–49.

Pellegrini, A. D., and Jane C. Perlmutter. "Rough-and-Tumble Play on the Elementary School Playground." *Young Children* 43:2, January 1988, 14–17.

Phillips, Carol Brunson. "Nurturing Diversity For Today's Children and Tomorrow's Leaders." *Young Children* 43:2, January 1988, 42–47, 59–63.

Schiamberg, Lawrence. *Child and Adolescent Development.* New York: Macmillan, 1988.

Schweinhart, Lawrence J. "Observing Young Children in Action." *Young Children* 48:5, July 1993, 29–33.

Seefeldt, Carol, and Sallie Tinney. "Dinosaurs: The Past Is Present." *Young Children* 40:4, May 1985, 20–24.

Soderman, Anne. "Dealing with Difficult Young Children." *Young Children* 40:5, July 1985, 15–20.

Soto, Lourdes Diaz. "Understanding Bilingual/Bicultural Young Children." *Young Children* 46:2, January 1991, 30–35.

Spock, Benjamin, and Michael Rothenberg. *Dr. Spock's Baby and Child Care.* New York: Pocket Books, 1985.

Wardle, Francis. "Are You Sensitive to Interracial Children's Special Identity Needs?" *Young Children* 42:2, January 1987, 53–59.

———. "Endorsing Children's Differences: Meeting the Needs of Adopted Minority Children." *Young Children* 45:5, July 1990, 44–46.

Wolfson, Evelyn. "American Indian Culture." *Young Children* 48:2, January 1993, 79–80.

Zill, Nicholas, Mary Collins, Jerry West, and Elvie Hausken. "Approaching Kindergarten: A Look at Preschoolers in the United States." *Young Children* 51:1, November 1995, 35–38.

CHAPTER 4

Setting the Stage

University of Illinois

Objectives

✔ Define center accreditation.
✔ Explain factors considered in planning and organizing the environment of the early childhood program.

"How does accreditation work?"

"How did you get your group started?"

"How do you plan for the first day at school?"

Questions such as those preceding are often asked by students who watch a smoothly functioning early childhood group during the latter part of a school year. These students are experienced enough to realize that the smooth operation does not happen by accident.

Some early childhood education students have the opportunity to help the teacher make the necessary preparations for the beginning of school. They see exactly what is required for starting a new group.

ACCREDITATION OF SCHOOLS

Accreditation is a distinction awarded to early childhood schools and child care centers for having met the standards for high quality and completed the procedures for outside validation of that high quality in a process supervised by the National Academy of Early Childhood Programs, a division of the National Association for the Education of Young Children (NAEYC).

The criteria for high quality are defined in a booklet, *Accreditation Criteria and Procedures of the National Academy of Early Childhood Programs.*[1] The standards were agreed on by early childhood professionals and parents from across the nation before they were accepted by NAEYC. In 1996 there were over forty-three hundred centers accredited and nearly eight thousand in the process of becoming accredited. This is considered excellent progress in a program that was initiated only in 1984. The accreditation process has been recognized by many as a measure of the high quality care and attention that American children should receive. A U.S. General Accounting Office publication states, "NAEYC provides the only national voluntary accreditation system for early childhood education centers and schools."[2]

---

[1]Sue Bredekamp, ed. (Washington, DC: NAEYC, 1996).
[2]U.S. General Accounting Office, *Early Childhood Education: Information on Costs and Services at High-Quality Centers* (Washington, DC: GPO, July 1989), p. 5.

Adequate planning means that adults have time to speak with a child until he has received the information needed. (University of Illinois)

ENVIRONMENT

As you begin your quest to learn how programs are developed for young children, one of the first things you will notice is the setting in which early childhood education takes place. This chapter will help you appreciate the many details that teachers plan and organize in order to ensure that children are safe, comfortable, and able to learn as they come to school each day.

The criteria for center accreditation spell out specific detail for standards for safety for children and for arrangements that facilitate the constructive play that is the basis of young children's learning.

PLANNING AND ORGANIZING

Setting the stage for a high-quality program for young children requires teachers to perform two activities well—planning and organizing. **Planning** means setting objectives and prearranging the details of the early childhood education program in order to achieve the objectives for individuals and the group. Planning requires time for studious, thoughtful, quiet work. Plans are made daily, weekly, and yearly. They focus on individual children and their parents, on the group as a whole, on standards and goals, and on the interests and talents of the teachers. Most plans are written out in detail and are evaluated daily as feedback is received from the children and parents.

Organizing means putting in readiness the facility, equipment, materials, strategies, and procedures for coherent and cooperative action with

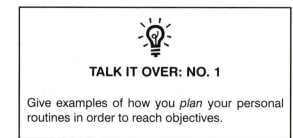

TALK IT OVER: NO. 1

Give examples of how you *plan* your personal routines in order to reach objectives.

TALK IT OVER: NO. 2

Give examples of how you *organize* your personal living space, materials, and procedures to reach your objectives.

the goal of producing a high-quality early childhood program. Organizing requires "getting busy" after the quiet planning sessions. Organizing requires time, energy, and creativity of the staff.

Both planning and organizing require that teachers have knowledge of goals for young chil-

Adequate planning means it is easy for each child to place her belongings where they can be found when needed. (Children's Center, Denver)

dren (Chapter 2), a philosophical base and standards for the curriculum choices (Chapter 2), knowledge of the particular age of children being taught (Chapter 3), and information about individual children and their families (Chapter 3). Teachers' experience and ability to evaluate previous planning and organizing—that is, learning from the past—lead to better performance in the future.

The objective of this chapter is to highlight planning and organizing so that you will begin to appreciate the time the teacher devotes to these responsibilities. By observing closely, questioning the teacher, and assisting wherever you can, you, as a future teacher, can begin to learn to plan and organize. Be particularly observant when the teacher's original plans aren't working out and alterations or substitutions are needed. Often these are the occasions when the teacher's experience shines through.

You can give feedback to the staff that will help in future planning. For example, one student reported that when managing the finger painting table there had been too many children for each child to work comfortably. The next time they planned finger painting, the staff planned another interesting activity that attracted some children. Thus congestion was reduced. Also the space was arranged with one less chair, which suggested the number of children who could use that learning center comfortably. Teachers appreciate such feedback from student helpers.

This chapter is designed to help you begin to appreciate the extent of the teacher's planning and organizing. In Chapter 6 you will be given specific help for planning specific curricular activities, and each subsequent chapter will give you details regarding each type of activity. Finally, in Chapter 19 you will be ready to integrate all you've learned into planning a total program. If you have questions along the way, feel free to turn to Chapter 6 or 19 for help in planning and organizing a program. In addition, for a discussion of the manager's role in planning and organizing on a centerwide basis, you may wish

TALK IT OVER: NO. 3

Give examples of how planning and organizing reduce stress on children, teachers, and parents. Show how planning and organizing facilitate reaching objectives.

to refer to the book by Hildebrand and Hearron, *Management of Child Development Centers* (Prentice Hall, 1997).

PLANNING FOR THE OPENING OF SCHOOL

Before the children arrive, the teacher should (1) arrange the facility where school is held, (2) plan the daily schedule, and (3) choose the learning experiences for the children. Arranging the facility and organizing a workable schedule are covered in this chapter. Learning experiences are referred to only briefly in this chapter but are discussed in detail in Part 2.

PLANNING THE ARRANGEMENT OF THE FACILITY

Equipping and arranging the schoolroom and yard are similar to furnishing and arranging a house or an apartment. The teacher takes inventory of the functions that must be performed and plans for the most efficient use of the space available. Everyone knows that it is exciting to plan new space before it is built. Using old space may be a greater challenge. More creativity is often required on the part of those planning to operate in old space designed for other purposes.

Careful planning of room arrangement, storage spaces, and equipment can facilitate the teacher's handling of the children. There are many functions the children can perform for themselves. They can help with others if the facilities are carefully arranged. Children learn favorable attitudes toward helping, care of equipment, and cooperation when they are expected to help and are taught to help. For example, older children can wash the easel and the paintbrushes if the cleanup sink is at their height and sponges are provided. When children put away their own toys, they learn responsibility and the teacher's time and energy can be used for other educational purposes.

A large rectangular playroom containing about fifty square feet per child is usually satisfactory. More space is desirable in colder climates where longer periods of the day are spent indoors. Where weather permits extensive use of outdoor space, less indoor space might suffice. Space should be allowed for the number of adults in the program. One large room is superior to several small ones in terms of supervising and teaching.

The room is divided into learning centers or zones. **Learning centers** are areas of the larger playroom or yard that are partially enclosed, perhaps by low storage shelves, and contain the needed materials and equipment for a certain type of learning activity. There are centers for (1) art activities, (2) science activities, (3) literature-language activities, (4) music activities, (5) dramatic play, (6) blockbuilding activities, (7) manipulative toys and games, and (8) carpentry or sand activities when space permits. Also, provision must be made for eating, toileting, resting, and storing each child's belongings. Shelves and other storage facilities can serve as low dividers between learning centers while they hold the equipment and materials needed in those centers. Care should be taken to keep the storage facilities low so that the teacher can observe the action in each center. Also, child-height shelves encourage children to get out and put away materials and thus develop independence. In some climates it is necessary to have a large-muscle activity center indoors.

The rooms should have a light, airy, warm look and be friendly and inviting. An artistic use of color—such as subdued walls with color supplied by equipment and children's art products—is aesthetically pleasing and gives a feeling of happiness without being overstimulating. Soft light and enough electrical outlets with safety features are important. There are many new materials with washable, durable finishes that are useful for decorating and equipping rooms housing young children.

Every effort should be made to reduce the noise level in the rooms by the use of draperies, carpeting, acoustical tile, and other soundproofing. Carpeting is particularly desirable in block, dress-up, and story areas. Flooring that can be readily mopped should be used in painting, eating, and water-play areas until carpeting proves itself and janitorial services are equipped to cope with carpet cleaning. One corner can be used for quiet activities and the opposite corner for active and noisy events.

Traffic Patterns

The teachers visualize how the children will move through the room. Where do they enter and leave the school? Where will they store their wraps? Where do they go to get to the bathroom? Which entrance will they use going to and coming from outside activities? Where will the snack be served? Where will the children rest? The best arrangement will require a minimum amount of reminding children what to do next. The teacher will study traffic patterns and organize the room to minimize children getting in each other's way.

Locker Spaces

Locker spaces should be close to the door where parents will enter and call for their child. If lockers are in out-of-the-way places, reminders will be required to get coats into the lockers. This little space, sometimes simply a modest hook, becomes a child's place to call his or her own.

Adequate planning makes an infant's mother comfortable when the caregiver takes over. (Cloud County, Kansas Community College)

Parents, teachers, and child will know where to look for belongings. It is convenient if a cubicle or locker is included where the child's treasures can be placed. Names clearly printed in capital and small letters should be placed above the locker. A symbol or picture is used by some teachers to help children identify their lockers. However, most will quickly learn to locate the locker by its position in the room—or by the name above it.

Bathroom

The toilet often requires rapid entry and should be readily accessible. Toilets and sinks should be at the children's height. A minimum of two toilets and two lavatories for each group of children is recommended. Boys and girls both use toilets in the same room. Doors are not needed on toilets

for children up to five years old. The absence of doors facilitates supervision. Five-year-olds usually are beginning to appreciate privacy, so shutter-type doors that spring closed can be installed. Even for five-year-olds there is no need for separate bathrooms for boys and girls.

Low Sinks

Bathroom lavatories should be about 22 inches high. Faucets that work by pressing a lever with the knee or by a foot lever will eliminate running water in an empty bathroom. A low sink in the creative arts center is convenient; here paints can be mixed, paper and sponges moistened, and children and supplies washed without the art cleanup interfering with the bathroom routine. A low drinking fountain both indoors and out permits children to help themselves to a drink—a frequently neglected need.

Resting Space

A quiet time of songs and stories will rest children; hence a space should be designated for quiet-time activity. Ideally this space should be located away from distracting toys. Short rest periods can take place without formal stretching out. If the room is carpeted, the children may stretch out without being told. Where there is no carpeting, a few throw rugs or carpet squares will cushion the children lying down or sitting. It should be noted that severe efforts to get everyone lying down often yield negative results and negative attitudes toward sleep.

In full-day groups, where napping is essential, cots with sheets and blankets will be required. Sufficient storage space and space to place the cots will be necessary. When you are putting a number of children together for sleeping, it is urgent that the utmost care be taken to ensure that fire exits are accessible.

Eating Space

Snack or lunch is most conveniently served near the kitchen area. Serving carts or trays can be used if food must be carried some distance. Lists of required utensils should be attached to the cart to prevent forgetting needed items. Sanitary and aesthetic aspects must be kept in mind. Small tables and chairs are required for serving lunch. Some teachers prefer that all children sit down at the same time for midmorning and midafternoon snack. Others serve snacks in a come-and-go fashion as the children sit on the floor or the grass, and fewer chairs and tables are needed.

Space for Learning Centers and Storage

Each learning center should have open storage space available for the materials and equipment that the children will use in the center. Closed storage space is best for materials and equipment that are seasonal or that are brought into the room only occasionally. Thought should be given to where the children will use a toy. Toys should be stored close to where they will be used. For example, puzzles are best used on tables, so the storage should be near the tables. Blocks require open space for building and should be stored and used in an out-of-the-way area so that other children who are merely passing by will not interfere with block building. Toys, such as cars, that are used with blocks should be on open shelves near the blocks.

The housekeeping corner and dress-up clothes suggesting dramatic play should have sufficient storage space so that the children can constructively select materials for their dramatic games. If possible, the teacher should keep all materials available so that the children can readily get them. When space is limited, the children should know what materials are available and feel free to ask for them to supplement any idea they may have. If props are stored close by, the teacher too will be able to add them quickly to support dramatic play that is developing.

A literature-language arts area should be located in a quiet nook with a low table and with books on an open shelf so that children can use them freely as they are interested. The teacher will also use this learning center for planned language experiences for small groups of children. A collection of science books should be kept as a permanent resource so that the children, assistants, and teachers can develop the habit of looking things up whenever an occasion arises.

A music area can consist of a simple record player for children to operate and a few suitable records in a rack. If it is located adjacent to open space, the children may respond with a dance or organize a band from instruments stored nearby.

The creative arts center needs natural lighting, a close water supply, and materials for artistic endeavors. The following should be easily accessible to the children: drawing paper, crayons, glue, scissors, stapler, string, masking tape, and paper punch. These supplies will be incorporated into many kinds of play if available on a low, open shelf. Art materials that the teachers feel need closer supervision can be stored near the art area sink.

A science center is best located near a window because sunlight is helpful in many experiments. A small table or shelf will encourage children to display their specimens for others to see and handle. Room should be available to seat several children so that planned discussions can take place in this area.

Arranging learning centers and areas for quiet activity is as important outdoors as indoors. Water available for drinking, for wetting sand, and for mixing and cleaning up paints increases the ease with which the yard functions for the total program. Proper storage is essential for outdoor equipment. Children can be taught proper care of the equipment if storage is designed so that they can easily remove and return equipment.

PLANNING THE DAILY SCHEDULE OR SEQUENCE OF EVENTS

Choosing a schedule is another requirement before the first day of school begins. A schedule becomes the structure within which the teacher and the children work. To an outsider it may appear as if there is no structure at all—the children seem to be doing just what they want to do. Yet it *is* in fact a framework or structure, with flexibility and room for individuality. When you have planned a sequence of events, the children will soon learn to guide themselves. If you implement the plan in a flexible manner, interpreting the needs of individuals in your group, the activity will move with ease. There will be a maximum of learning, a minimum of teacher direction, and a minimum of child tension.

The following is an example of a child whose behavior was entirely self-directed because of his awareness of the planned sequence of events: Mike noticed the children entering the kindergarten room as he slid down the slide. Finishing the ride, he ran to the door, which was being held open by the teacher. Mike smiled at the teacher, entered, and ran up the stairs. After putting his hat and coat in his locker, Mike went directly to the bathroom. Here he urinated, flushed the toilet, and washed his hands. He went to the snack table and found the place marked with his place card and sat down. He visited with his friends as they too found their places and sat down for a snack.

This short episode occurred without the teacher telling Mike any of the steps he was to take. The routine was the same every day, and Mike was happy knowing and doing what was expected of him. The routine seemed to fit his needs because there was no looking back at the slide or detouring to other areas as he progressed through the procedure.

The teacher had planned carefully from the beginning to develop the sequence that fitted the children's needs. The children were reminded of that sequence for a few days. Most learned quickly. Some children reminded those who forgot, until eventually all the children mastered the routine without reminders.

If the routine had not fitted the group, the teacher might have observed resistance, such as

children taking one more slide or otherwise not being ready to go indoors. If lockers had been in an out-of-the-way place, Mike might have dropped his coat on a chair and needed a reminder to put it in the locker.

The teacher plans the schedule or the sequence of events by designating big blocks of time that will constitute the framework for fitting in the learning opportunities, which will be discussed in detail in Part 2. The half-day program typically has three large blocks of time; the full-day center, six. See Figures 4–1 and 4–2.

The major considerations for scheduling activities are (1) goals for the group, (2) special needs of the group, (3) time of day the children arrive, (4) how long the children stay at school, (5) what happens at home before the child goes to school, and (6) season of the year.

Time Block I

A block of about 60 minutes for self-selected activity—either indoors or outdoors—is a good way to start the day. As children arrive, they find an activity that interests them. If they are slow starters, nobody rushes them to socialize; they are free to choose a puzzle and be alone. If they want to socialize, they can approach a friend in the housekeeping corner or one using the slide. Latecomers need not feel unduly uncomfortable, as they may when a group assembly occurs first. Beginning with a self-directed activity period enables teachers to talk to parents and also to give each child a little attention as he or she enters the school. Children should never feel as one little girl put it to her mother after school, "I don't know if my teacher even knew I was there. She never called my name once."

The first large block of time might vary from 30 to 90 minutes, depending on all the factors just mentioned and the number of special learning experiences the teacher may have planned for the day. There should always be provision within each time block for both quiet and vigorous activity to take care of the differing needs and interests of the children.

FIGURE 4–1
Sample of a daily schedule.

DAILY SCHEDULE FOR SHORT-DAY GROUPS		
A.M.	P.M.	
9:00–10:00	1:00–2:00	Self-selected activity indoors
10:00	2:00	Cleanup time (can vary a few minutes either way). As the children finish helping with cleanup, they go to the toilet if necessary, and wash their hands.
10:15–10:25	2:15–2:25	Snack. With older children, sharing time* goes on at the same time as snack.
10:25–10:45	2:25–2:45	The children move to a story group or groups. They sit on the floor. They select a book for "reading" as they pass the shelf. They look at the book or just talk quietly. The teacher finishes the period with some songs, a special story, planning, or discussion.
10:45–11:30	2:45–3:30	Outdoor self-selected activity
11:30–11:40	3:30–3:40	Cleanup time. Preparation to go home.
11:45	3:45	Dismissal

*Sharing time is a period when children are called on to share some article or news they have brought from home. Discussed in detail in the chapter on language arts.

Time Block II

The second block of time is more teacher structured or directed. It includes a period of cleaning up, washing hands, toileting, serving snack, singing, and listening to a story. It is a slowing down and relaxing time of day. This period could last from 30 to 45 minutes. There is some movement between the various activities. The story and singing groups, especially for younger children, contain four or five children at most, rather than the entire group.

This quiet group time provides for rest without being called that, because the words *sleep* and *rest* may create strongly negative feelings in some children. As the teacher considers the needs of the children, a decision can be made about how much rest the children require. What time do they go to bed? What time do they get up? It is unrealistic to assume that a healthy child who has had 12 hours of sleep and barely gets up in time to reach the early childhood center by 9 A.M. will need to rest on a cot at 10 or 10:30 A.M. As one child said, "I thought we came here to learn stuff. I already know how to sleep!" However, rest routines can provide positive learning experiences. Individual needs should be met. Younger children and those arriving very early may need some real rest.

Time Block III

The third block of time will be another self-selected activity period. If the first one was

FIGURE 4–2
Sample of a time block plan.

TIME BLOCK PLAN*

Time Block I   Self-Selected Activity (Indoors)

Art   Music
Science   Dramatic play
Table games   Small, wheeled objects
Blocks   Language arts
Books

Time Block II   Teacher-Structured Activity

Cleanup
Toileting, washing hands
Snack
Quiet time:
    looking at books
    music
    storytime and discussions

Time Block III   Self-Selected Activity (Outdoors)

Climbing   Riding tricycles
Swinging   Sand play
Running   Science

Time Block IV   Lunch Period

Washing hands, toileting
Resting prior to lunch
Eating
Washing hands
Going home or preparing for nap

Time Block V   Nap Time

Dressing for bed   Toileting
Sleeping   Dressing

Time Block VI   Self-Selected Activity

New activities
Snack
Outdoor play

*Blocks I, II, and III are typical of half-day programs where lunch is not
served. The six blocks are more typical of full-day centers. Blocks I and
III may be interchanged for variation and for meeting the needs of the
children as discussed elsewhere.

Adequate planning makes routines such as washing unhurried and interesting to children. (Kansas State University)

indoors, then the second one will be outdoors, and vice versa. Again there will be a variety of activities so that children can choose or be guided into quiet or active play as seems to fit their needs. Every school should provide outdoor activities daily.

Time Block IV

If the program calls for lunch, another block of time will be used in preparing for and in eating lunch. Many people feel that a quiet time just prior to lunch rests the children and helps them eat better. Considerable time is required to move the children from their learning activities to toileting, washing, resting, and finally to eating.

The schedule after lunch is also important, and a definite plan for this next step is crucial. Is it time for the children to go home? Or take a nap? Or go outdoors to play? Or begin their school

day? Some afternoon groups may begin with lunch as some morning groups may begin with breakfast. Having next steps clearly in mind helps the teacher guide children in the routine. Some children will need to wash again after lunch and frequently will need to use the toilet. In order that all adults are not distracted from attending the children left at the lunch tables, it is usually best to have one adult assigned to supervise the children after they leave the lunch table.

Time Block V

Where naps are given, they usually follow the lunch hour immediately. The sleeping area should be prepared while the children are having lunch. After a busy morning that starts early for many, the subdued light, soft music, and comfortable bed should be welcome. Efforts to keep the voices low, the pace slow, and a positive attitude toward the nap period will pay dividends. Because excessively long naps may interfere with the home bedtime schedules, it is well to confer with parents regarding a reasonable length of the nap period for their children.

There may be a few children who won't sleep. Some children get adequate rest at night. Provision can be made to keep nonsleepers from interfering with the sleeping children. Usually the older children do not need sleep. They can rest in an adjacent room while "reading" a book. Some children who seem to need sleep but are alert to all movement can be encouraged to sleep face down. Sometimes if the teacher gently massages the shoulders, the child will relax and go to sleep. Children have varying feelings about bedtime and may become lonesome for their parents. At no time should bedtime become a period for harsh discipline or punishment.

Time Block VI

Following nap time, toileting, dressing, and self-selected activity can again take place. In full-day centers there may be a new shift of personnel because the morning staff comes to work early. For insecure children the new shift may present problems that teachers should be prepared to handle. The new teachers with their different ways will add variety for the children. New materials should be offered that were not available in the morning. Some find this time useful for having children help prepare materials for the next day's activity, for example, filling trays with materials to use for collage or mixing new paints. Outdoor play is usually enjoyed by children after a nap. Working parents coming home to family responsibilities may not have time to supervise their children outdoors and are happy that the school provides outdoor play. However, every effort should be made to avoid exhausting these children physically. Tired children will be cranky. Cranky children are not pleasant for parents who are tired themselves after a full day's work. For this reason a quiet group for listening to stories and singing songs is popular in late afternoon.

Departure Time

Before it is going-home time, children's belongings, art products, and so forth should be checked to see that all are ready to be sent home. Having everything ready avoids the strain of looking for things that cannot be found and paves the way for a smooth and happy departure of the children with their parents.

Transition Times

Transition points between activities and big blocks of time should be planned carefully. The teacher plans just what the children are to do and then states the directions clearly. If planning is adequate, the children will move with ease through the routines, will not be running into each other, will know what comes next, and will not have to wait. To young children, waiting is tedious and probably just as uninteresting as it is for adults; therefore it should be avoided. It may help to have one teacher start an activity while another teacher brings up the stragglers or forms a new group. For more detailed suggestions see Chapters 5 and 14.

Providing for Flexibility

The sample schedule shown in Figure 4–1 is a flexible guide. Each period of time can be shortened or lengthened as needs warrant. If children are just beginning to use something they have spent all hour building, then an additional 10 or 15 minutes will give them a feeling of greater satisfaction. Advising the children a few minutes ahead that there will be a change in activities enables the children to terminate projects to their satisfaction. If presented in a positive manner, cleanup time can be fun for the children—especially if the teacher is assisting. It can also be a learning experience for children and a big help to the teachers.

Providing for Weather Changes

Any plan must be judged against how well it adapts to days of inclement weather. Ideally, the teacher hopes to disturb the routine as little as possible on bad days, knowing that changes tend to confuse young children. On a rainy day the first self-selected activity period can be extended about 30 minutes and other routines can occur in sequence until after the story period. Then if the teacher plans some singing games, tumbling activities, or the like instead of the outdoor activity, the children will probably move through a rainy day without realizing a difference in schedule until the teacher announces the time to go home. They may then ask, "Well, aren't we going to play outside?" If a rainy-day room or a protected porch or patio is provided, only minor schedule adjustments need to be made on a rainy day. A walk in the rain with boots and umbrellas can provide learning opportunities and can also provide the energy release ordinarily gained in outdoor activities.

The teacher makes the schedule to fit the needs of the particular group of children. A plan is required that takes care of all needs. The plan must be one in which the teacher has confidence and with which he or she feels comfortable working. Morning groups in early fall or late spring or summer may be anxious to have outdoor activities when they arrive. In that case, the teacher may choose a self-selected outdoor activity period as the first large time block.

In cold seasons or wet climates the early morning may be too cold or wet for outdoor activities. The outdoor period would then be postponed until late morning, when the dew is off the grass and the sun has warmed the air. In snowsuit climates the schedule may be adjusted to minimize dressing and undressing. For example, in an afternoon group, parents were asked to send the children to school already dressed in snowsuits for outdoor activity. Outdoor self-selected activities were scheduled for the first part of the afternoon at school. This schedule had additional merit because these children were staying indoors during their mornings at home. Their exuberance during the outdoor period, even in very cold weather, indicated that a need was being met.

Children who were not interested in outdoor activity were allowed to enter the indoor play area when they chose. This suggests another alternative a teacher may use. Indoor and outdoor activities may take place at the same time when the spaces are adjacent or when there are enough adults to supervise activities going on in both places.

During warm weather it is possible to provide almost the entire program outside if the teacher moves some activities out that are normally done indoors. A shaded area is essential in many regions during hot weather. Teachers note that when the weather turns warm the children will begin playing outside in their neighborhoods during the morning. If the children are playing vigorously in the morning, the afternoon program should be restful to avoid excessive fatigue.

Staff Assignments

Staff assignments are important every day, but especially on opening days. Students or other assistants who have accompanied the teacher on the home visits or have helped when the family visited the school will know the children. The staff should get together and pool their guesses regarding individual children's needs. Staff cooperation is important. Team teaching has always been common in prekindergartens and is increasingly common in kindergartens. No one will be able to predict with much accuracy how these first days will go. Brief daily discussion of goals, children, routines, and procedures will give teachers confidence in each other as unpredictable situations arise.

A democratic plan of operation enables all teachers, student teachers, parent assistants, and volunteers to be on an equal plane. The head teacher, who in the final analysis is responsible, must assume the lead. However, more creative teaching will develop within the staff if adults feel that their contributions are significant and that they can follow their own creative teaching ideas without unnecessary interference. Teachers often vary in their teaching styles. Differences need not confuse the children if all adults are working toward common goals.

A head teacher needs at least one assistant, no matter how small the school. If each person is to gain personal satisfaction when working with young children, all responsibilities—the good and bad, the hard and easy, the clean and dirty, and the pleasant and unpleasant—should be shared fairly. The children are the winners when adults work together, the losers when they don't.

Just as each child is unique, so is each adult. Each person has strengths and weaknesses. The individual's strength should be capitalized upon and the weak areas overcome. As one assistant said during a planning session, "I'm not as good as Betty Kay in music, but I'd love to try leading the singing." Another said, "Could I be responsible for the finger painting? I've never supervised that before." The assistants were volunteering to learn. Learning means growing and becoming a better teacher. The stage must be set so that each adult can make a satisfying contribution. Planning and posting of responsibilities help achieve the goals of the center.

Before long in your student teaching course and in your first teaching position, you will be in charge of setting the stage not only for a group of children, but also for one or more adult assistants. Therefore, during this course, while you are planning and organizing for children, be sure you give some thought to how adults work together cooperatively. Remember the steps you are learning now are steps you may very soon be helping other adults learn.

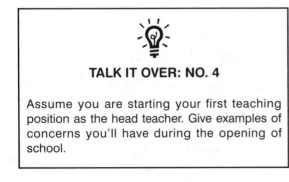

TALK IT OVER: NO. 4

Assume you are starting your first teaching position as the head teacher. Give examples of concerns you'll have during the opening of school.

ADDITIONAL TIPS FOR THE FIRST DAYS OF SCHOOL

Introducing a Few Children Each Day

When a teacher is starting a new group of children, she or he can ensure time to give attention to each child's needs by dividing the group and introducing only a few new children each day. Perhaps by the fifth or sixth day all the children can be attending. If such a staggered opening plan is not feasible, a number of assistants or volunteers should be available to handle routines while the teacher is kept free to work with children who are uneasy about being at school. First days make a lasting impression on the child. Every effort should be made to ensure that every child has a happy time.

Beginning With Easily Supervised Activities

The activities offered the first day or two should be ones that are very easily supervised. For example, crayons are likely to be familiar to the children and thus require no special help or encouragement for the children to use. Getting involved in finger painting will be fine later on. These first days the teacher may be needed other places on short notice and would not want to be delayed while washing off finger paints.

Name Tags

The teacher should prepare name tags for everyone for the first day of school. Convention badges work fine for adults. For children excellent name tags can be made from two layers of art sponge or felt glued with a piece of muslin between them and trimmed with pinking shears. Sponge and felt come in pretty colors and might be coordinated into a color scheme or a teaching plan. Tags can be about 2 inches wide and cut to fit each name. Names are lettered in manuscript printing with a marking pen. Name tags that are made of colored paper and laminated with a plastic film are also satisfactory if laminating equipment is available.

Most teachers prefer to pin the name tag to the front of the child's shirt with a large safety pin. Some prefer pinning the name tags on the child's back to discourage children from pinning their own, thus extending the life of the name tags. However, if the tags are pinned in front, the children will feel great satisfaction when they are able to open and close that pin! A new style convention badge with a swivel clip on a pocket of plastic is well worth the cost.

Health Measures

Health inspection has not been mentioned so far. This does not mean that the child's health is not an important concern. Far from it. Parents should be urged to send only healthy children to school. They should be advised to look at their child and say, "If Doug were someone else's child, would I want my child exposed to him?" Parents should know that if a child becomes ill, they will be called. Parents who are working are urged to leave telephone numbers of neighbors or relatives who would care for their sick child in case the parent could not be found. Actually, all children's records should carry a second telephone number because parents often run errands during a child's hours in school and might not be available immediately.

Parents' cooperation on health matters is probably more effective than having an inspection. Persons without training will see very little in the throats of young children. Even registered nurses will miss significant symptoms. Children who attend morning schools may not seem ill at nine o'clock but may be quite ill by eleven. Teachers must always be alert for signs of illness. They should isolate the sick child under proper supervision and call the parents.

In afternoon groups parents are advised that if children have symptoms in the morning, they will be much better off taking a rest at home in the afternoon than going to school, where they might get overtired and might also expose friends to a communicable disease. Attention to vaccinations must be given in admission procedures.

With good vaccination programs some communicable diseases can be nearly eliminated.

If a child gets a communicable disease, the parents of children who, according to school records, have not had the disease are notified. Parents may then be on the lookout for symptoms and avoid sending their children to school on days they might expose the entire group to a disease.

When inspections are necessary, the nurse should wear regular street clothes to avoid arousing the anxiety that a uniform often creates. Frequent hand washing with soap for both children and adults is an excellent health measure.

Conclusions

Setting the stage for the opening of school focuses on accreditation criteria and on the important functions of planning and organizing—especially arranging the facility, planning the daily schedule, choosing the learning experiences for the children, and making staff assignments. The teacher takes an inventory of the functions that must be performed and plans the most efficient use of the space available. Learning centers are arranged along with storage for the needed equipment and supplies. Traffic patterns are a consideration. The schedule or sequence of events is the structure within which the teacher and children work. All planning is of a tentative nature until the teacher becomes acquainted with a particular group of children. Definite planning is required as the teacher sets the stage for the children's behavior and learning.

Applications

1. Define accreditation. Tell who sponsors it and how it can improve quality for young children's programs.
2. Study the learning centers in your early childhood school.
   a. Label each center using labels found in the chapter.
   b. List the equipment and supplies found in each learning center.
   c. Indicate how many children can comfortably work in each learning center at a time.

d. Tally the total learning spaces for the classroom and play yard.

Discuss your findings with your classmates.

3. Evaluate your participation using the evaluation form prepared in Chapter 1. Discuss your progress with your supervising teacher.

4. Add information on room arrangements to your Resource File.

Study Questions

1. Define *planning* and *organizing* in an early childhood setting.
2. Give examples of building materials and procedures that will help reduce noise levels in a center.
3. List characteristics of good locker space.
4. List characteristics of good resting space.
5. List characteristics of good eating space.
6. List characteristics of good bathroom space.
7. Define and describe a *learning center*.
8. Explain the concept of time blocks in planning schedules.
9. List and describe procedures teachers find especially helpful during the first days of school when introducing a new group of young children to the school.

Additional Readings

Bredekamp, Sue, ed. *Developmentally Appropriate Practice in Early Childhood Programs Serving Children from Birth Through Age 8.* Washington, DC: NAEYC, 1987.

———. *Accreditation Criteria and Procedures of the National Academy of Early Childhood Programs.* Washington, DC: NAEYC, 1991.

Galvin, Emily Sedgwick. "The Joy of Seasons: With the Children, Discover the Joys of Nature." *Young Children* 49:4, May 1994, 4–9.

Hildebrand, Verna. *Guiding Young Children,* Upper Saddle River, NJ: Merrill/Prentice Hall, 1994.

Hildebrand, Verna, and Patricia Hearron. *Management of Child Development Centers.* Upper Saddle River, NJ: Merrill/Prentice Hall, 1997.

Jalongo, Mary Renek. "Teaching Young Children to Become Better Listeners." *Young Children* 51:2, January 1996, 21–26.

Meyerhoff, Michael K. "Of Baseball and Babies: Are You Unconsciously Discouraging Father Involvement in Infant Care?" *Young Children* 49:4, May 1994, 17–19.

NAEYC. "Good Discipline Is, in Large Part, the Result of a Fantastic Curriculum." *Young Children* 42:3, March 1987, 49–51.

Rivkin, Mary. "Science Is a Way of Life." *Young Children* 47:4, May 1992, 4–8.

Weiser, Margaret. *Group Care and Education of Infants and Toddlers.* Upper Saddle River, NJ: Merrill/Prentice Hall, 1986.

CHAPTER 5

Teachers and Techniques Used

McQueen Preschool, Howard University

Objectives

✔ Define a teaching style.
✔ Define guidance and its goal.
✔ Define and give examples of indirect guidance.
✔ Define and give examples of direct guidance.

"How do you stay so calm?"

"Do you always remember to be positive?"

"Why do personal messages work?"

You may ask the teacher questions like these as you work together guiding young children. You may feel that because the teacher's guidance works so well that there is a magic formula. What is it that makes guidance effective? Is the success due to the methods or due to the teacher?

Each teacher is unique, just as each child is unique. Good teachers develop a teaching style all their own. Each teacher's style will be different from all other teaching styles encountered either during your education or in a teaching position.

DEVELOPING A UNIQUE TEACHING STYLE

A teaching style is the teacher's manner and method of teaching. Individual personality is an important factor in determining a teaching style. As each teacher develops a program and builds a relationship with children, conscious and unconscious integration of all she or he knows and feels

occurs, and a personal teaching style evolves. The teacher's self-knowledge and knowledge of the children and their families will affect teaching style. The teacher's philosophy of education and political and moral value systems will also influence personal teaching style.

Goals call for influencing positively children's inborn creative potential—their potential for uniqueness. Teaching skills and attitudes should be directed toward allowing children to try out their own ideas in the protected environments of both school and home.

Tegano, Moran, and Sawyers[1] use information from their studies of children's creativity to describe effective ways for adults to foster creative behavior in young children. They emphasize taking time to "respond," versus "reacting" quickly. A thoughtful response means that adults think through the effect their words and deeds

---

[1]Tegano, Deborah W., James D. Moran, III, and Janet K. Sawyers, *Creativity in Early Childhood Classrooms* (Washington, DC: National Education Association, 1991), pp. 87–109.

Teachers can observe closely, be verbally supportive, and encourage the child's creativity by saying, "What else might you do with this toy?" (Kansas State University)

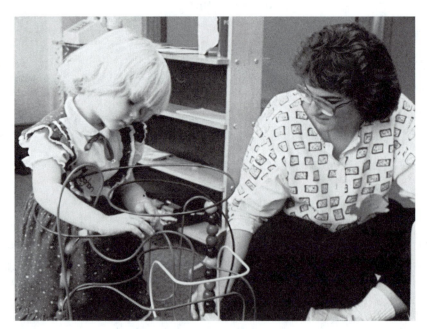

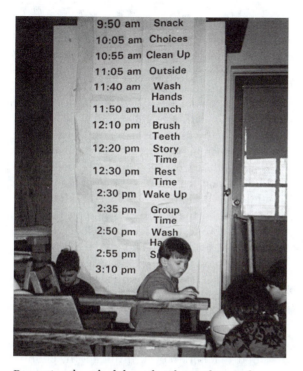

9:50 am	Snack
10:05 am	Choices
10:55 am	Clean Up
11:05 am	Outside
11:40 am	Wash Hands
11:50 am	Lunch
12:10 pm	Brush Teeth
12:20 pm	Story Time
12:30 pm	Rest Time
2:30 pm	Wake Up
2:35 pm	Group Time
2:50 pm	Wash Ha...
2:55 pm	S...
3:10 pm	

By posting the schedule so that the teachers and helpers can see it, the children will also learn to recognize the sequence of events and perhaps even read some of the items. (University of Illinois)

will have on the child or children—both in the present situation and in the future as well—before interacting with the child. These authors present a sound argument for a **developmental ecological** approach that "mediates the biological and cultural influences and the influence of the individual child's cognitive and personality traits." In other words, taking time to think through a number of factors is the best way to ensure future creative behavior in children.

Teaching styles may be placed on continuums ranging between democratic and authoritarian, organized and haphazard, passive and active, formal and informal, person-centered and subject-matter-centered. Students in training are often frustrated by the differing teaching styles they observe among demonstration teachers. Universities deliberately assign students to a variety of early childhood groups to give them opportunities to see different teachers in action. This practice should assure students that no one teaching style is the "correct way." For those who still insist on a "right way," this practice may create confusion. Yet if demonstration teachers can use differing teaching styles while achieving similar goals for young children, students should reason that they too will be free to develop their own style of teaching.

Demonstration teachers worthy of their positions are creative, innovative, and inquisitive. They experiment and evaluate continuously. They relate differently to both children and university students from class to class. Teaching is looked upon as a creative profession, and teachers never expect the factors to be enough alike for everything to remain the same. Neither would they expect student teachers to duplicate their style of teaching.

Students should be encouraged to go forth and develop their own teaching styles in light of their own personalities, their own experiences, the age they teach, and related research. It is of crucial importance that the professionals in early childhood education keep a questioning attitude and endeavor to make improvements. Each teacher who works with young children should feel this challenge.

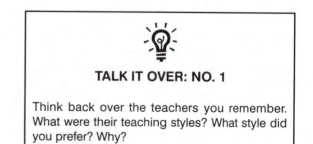

TALK IT OVER: NO. 1

Think back over the teachers you remember. What were their teaching styles? What style did you prefer? Why?

USING METHODS APPROPRIATE FOR YOUNG CHILDREN

Methods of teaching include lecturing, recitation, discussion, laboratory experiments, demonstrations, field trips, and audiovisual aids. Every teacher uses each of these methods within a personal teaching style. However, because of the way the young child learns, certain methods are more appropriate than others. For example, teachers rarely lecture to young children. One quickly discovers that lecturing is ineffective. Methods that allow one-to-one contacts with the child are far more in keeping with the needs and interests of young children.

Identification is also an important component of a teaching style. James Hymes, Jr., describes it as a process of silent teaching. He says that the child feels in tune with the teacher, likes her, and wants to be like her. The teacher is the heroine. (Hymes spoke primarily of female teachers in his discussion, although he was a well known professional leader.) Through this intimate relationship teachers have a potent educative force. Identification works only when relationships are close, warm, and friendly.[2]

The student is challenged to observe experienced teachers using various teaching methods with young children. Students should question the use of each method and continue to question as they establish their own groups and incorporate teaching methods into a unique teaching style.

QUALITIES OF A GOOD TEACHER OF YOUNG CHILDREN

A good teacher makes a significant contribution to society. The contribution cannot be measured, but it will affect the present generation and, through them, the generations to come. The good teacher likes children and is dedicated to instilling in children a desire to learn and to become independent learners. Children are encouraged to express themselves. Their curiosity is aroused, and the teacher gives them understanding, affection, and support when needed; yet they are encouraged to grow up.

Good teachers have self-confidence and are ready to cope with responsibility. They believe that the job is important and that teaching will make a significant contribution to the lives of the children. Good teachers feel accepted and liked by children, parents, and colleagues. They are able to bridge the diversities among families, making each one feel accepted. Good teachers are happy individuals on and off the job. Though serious at times, they enjoy life, can laugh and be happy, and can encourage others' sense of humor and laughter. Good teachers find some fulfillment outside of their work with children and thus avoid the crippling effect that results when teachers gratify all their needs through work.

Good teachers have confidence in people, believing that both children and parents are basically good. Recognizing that behavior has meaning, teachers seek to discover the meaning. Good teachers believe that children *can* learn and that through the efforts of all the children *will* learn. They are deeply committed to seeking a new and deeper understanding of individuals and families in every walk of like. Good teachers can empathize with the parents and children.

Effective teachers can adapt information to the young child's level. The university curriculum can become the curriculum of the school for young children. For example, a university freshman wrote to her younger brother, "I am taking botany. We put a plant in dye to watch the vascular tissue carrying it up through the leaves. You did that in kindergarten with celery, remember?"

Good teachers' scholarship should go beyond what they expect to teach. Their obvious enthusiasm for understanding the political, social, scientific, and aesthetic world will infect young learners. Beauty has priority in the classroom—in arrangements and relationships. Good teachers

---

[2]James Hymes, Jr., *Teaching the Child Under Six* (Upper Saddle River, NJ: Merrill/Prentice Hall, 1974), pp. 107–109.

understand not only the implications of educating a child in a democracy as opposed to education in an authoritarian society but also the application of the scientific method in social as well as physical science.

Good teachers are well informed about human growth and development. They know what to expect from children and how to plan for and assist growth, development, and maturation. They also have the knowledge and skill to interpret this information for parents.

Good teachers of young children work constantly to improve their ability to guide children's learning. Parents are helped to learn to contribute effectively to their child's education. The teachers make a serious effort to discover effective methods of working with children and parents individually and in groups.

Good teachers strive to mold all skills and knowledge into a teaching style that is comfortable and unique. With each new experience the student who is preparing to teach moves a step forward in developing a personal teaching style.

The NAEYC has emphasized techniques for working with young children in a publication titled *Developmentally Appropriate Practice in Early Childhood Programs Serving Children from Birth Through Age 8.*[3] The popularity of the booklet is evidence of the critical importance of thinking through the guidance techniques used. Guidance techniques also are important criteria in the evaluation of centers for accreditation. For more information on accreditation see Chapter 4 or the booklet setting forth the criteria for accreditation.[4]

GUIDANCE AND HOW THE TEACHER CAN USE IT

Many students can accept the philosophy of a democratic, child-centered early childhood edu-

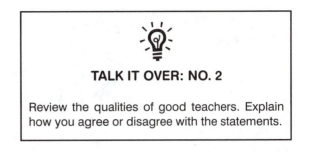

TALK IT OVER: NO. 2

Review the qualities of good teachers. Explain how you agree or disagree with the statements.

cation program. They can also accept the rationale for an individualized, self-selected learning environment for the young child. Students are often baffled, however, when confronted with the problem of operating a classroom and relating to children within such a framework.

Most students remember their elementary and secondary classrooms. They may even recall their first grade, when they had 15 minutes of morning news followed by reading circles or seatwork, then 15 minutes of recess followed by science. Teachers who try to organize young children in such a rigid fashion court disaster. Trying to get everyone to do the same thing at one time is virtually impossible. A contest results between the teacher and the children. When silence is highly valued, as it is in some classes, the only way silence can be maintained is through coercion, punishment, and threats.

Order can be maintained within the framework of an individualized, self-directed learning environment. The teacher should feel sure that the activities of individuals and groups of children can be stopped when necessary and that the children will listen and respond. Limits that protect each child, the property, and the learning environment should be set. The teacher should exercise the obligation to set limits (make rules) so that the group can learn together harmoniously. There is no place in early childhood education for a total free-for-all.

Democratic living can begin with very young children. They will learn and respond to rules that keep the group functioning on an even keel. They cannot be expected to learn all the rules

---

[3]Sue Bredekamp, ed. (Washington, DC: NAEYC, 1987.)
[4]Sue Bredekamp, ed., *Accreditation Criteria and Procedures of the National Academy of Early Childhood Programs* (Washington, DC: NAEYC, 1991).

Planning for a spontaneous storytime during playtime
means that those who are really interested will stay.
(Mount St. Vincent's Child Study Center, Halifax,
Nova Scotia)

overnight. Transgressions are often due to forgetting or misunderstanding and normally occur
with only a few children at a time.

Some prefer to use the word *discipline* when
discussing helping children learn to accept societal standards of behavior. However, *discipline*
frequently carries the connotation of punishment,
which makes the word less desirable in our educational setting. That is, the question, How do
you discipline your child? usually translates into,

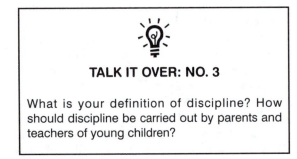

TALK IT OVER: NO. 3

What is your definition of discipline? How
should discipline be carried out by parents and
teachers of young children?

How do you punish your child? In the educational setting and with a developmental philosophy of early childhood education, the word *guidance* is more appropriate. Punishment is unsuited
to early childhood centers.

WHAT IS GUIDANCE?[5]

The term **guidance** is defined as everything
adults deliberately do and say, either directly or
indirectly, to influence a child's behavior. A self-
guided or self-disciplined child is the goal. The
teacher manages the group of young children
through carefully conceived teaching techniques
and the special personal relationship being
developed with the class. The teacher wants children to assume as much responsibility for conducting themselves as they are ready to assume.
The teacher helps children to grow in ability
until they can assume the responsibility for conducting themselves when teachers, parents,
police, or other authority figures are not present
to enforce correct behavior. The teacher does not
want the children to be like Janet, who wanted to
jump over a bonfire and kept saying, "My mother
didn't tell me *not* to!" The teacher knows parents
will not always be present to say "no." All children must learn to make decisions that affect
their personal safety—perhaps their very lives.
One of the developmental tasks for the young
child is to develop self-control.

Guidance can be either *indirect* or *direct*.
Indirect guidance includes all the teacher's
behind-the-scenes work, including that discussed
in Chapter 4, which sets the stage for the behavior the teacher expects. Through **direct guidance**
the teacher deals directly with the child.

Indirect Guidance

The teacher guides the child indirectly through
the arrangement of learning centers in the room

---

[5]For a more extensive discussion of guidance in all aspects of
an early childhood center, see Verna Hildebrand, *Guiding
Young Children* (Upper Saddle River, NJ: Merrill/Prentice
Hall, 1994).

and the yard, through the daily schedule, and through work with parents. The type of equipment selected and the richness of the curriculum of learning experiences provided indirectly affect the ease with which children do what is expected. Hymes says, "Bored children will be bad."[6] Keeping that in mind, the teacher will provide plenty of learning experiences that are neither too hard nor too easy. The youngsters will be so actively involved in learning that they will have little time for misbehavior. Detailed procedures for enriching the curriculum follow in Part 2.

An example of indirect guidance would be when the teacher alters the physical environment and thereby influences the children's behavior. To illustrate: The teacher sees a large group of children having a lively game on top of a large packing box. The teacher is foresighted, knowing from experience that this type of setting often creates difficulty. Falling or pushing may occur. The teacher quietly moves another packing box near and, using a walking plank, makes a bridge between the boxes. The children move to include the second box. The game takes on new dimensions with the additional space. Through quietly changing the physical environment, the teacher averts a possible conflict or danger.

As another example, the teacher may note that a number of children are waiting for a turn to swing. Knowing how hard it is for them to wait, the teacher thinks of an activity that might attract the swingers, or at least give the waiters an interesting diversion while they wait. One teacher lines up a few tricycles and gets out the traffic signs. In a moment there is a line of traffic and a police officer directing it. As anticipated, the swingers leave their swings, and no longer is there a line at the swing set. The teacher has not only extended the play of the children but has averted what might have become a difficult problem of sharing the swings.

---

[6]James Hymes, Jr., *Behavior and Misbehavior* (Upper Saddle River, NJ: Prentice Hall, 1955), p. 57.

TALK IT OVER: NO. 4

Record two examples of a teacher altering the environment to improve interaction among the children. Discuss the outcomes with your classmates. Note how your example fits the definition of indirect guidance.

The teacher can use indirect guidance by taking care of the children's needs for stretching, shifting position, and getting attention during a group activity. For example, during group time the teacher notes that the children are being distracted by a child who is kicking a neighbor's foot. Rather than call further attention to the fidgeting child, a decision is made to teach a new singing game that requires everyone to stand up. The teacher regains the attention of all the children, and the group time proceeds smoothly.

Indirect guidance is a very effective tool for the teacher to use in managing a group of children. If it is used well, many observers will remark that the children seem to be doing just what they want to do. The teacher can smile, knowing that the stage was set for the behavior being observed. Indirect guidance provides greater success than if the teacher were to spend hours lecturing the children on how to behave.

Direct Guidance

Direct guidance includes all of the *physical, verbal,* and *affective* means the teacher uses to influence the child's behavior. It includes speaking, teaching, demonstrating, helping, leading, loving, approving, disapproving, compelling, restraining, punishing, and even ignoring. The good teacher uses the positive methods in this list far more than the negative. The positive methods contribute more to the goal of the child becoming self-directed. Frequent use of compelling,

Some children appreciate a supportive adult's presence and conversation as they play alone. (Kansas State University)

restraining, or punishing should serve as a warning that the teacher's guidance leaves something to be desired. There is no place in teaching for physical or mental punishment. Punishment produces feelings that may not be conducive to learning, creates negative attitudes toward school and teachers, and does little to help the child develop self-direction. If you feel like punishing a child, go immediately to your supervising teacher for assistance.

Verbal Guidance

Verbal guidance is a form of direct guidance. In guiding a child, the teacher gets the child's attention and speaks to him or her in words easily understood. The teacher stoops or sits at the child's level facing the child. If the words aren't fully understood, the child can interpret the meaning from facial expressions and gestures. The teacher speaks quietly to individual children, seldom to the whole group. Verbal statements may be accompanied by action such as leading, helping, or demonstrating—whichever seems to

be required for fuller understanding. Experience shows that shouting across the room or yard seldom brings forth the desired behavior, and directions given on a to-whom-it-may-concern basis are seldom heeded. Some verbal techniques the teacher will find helpful follow.

Using Voice Effectively The teacher's voice is a teaching tool. How guidance is said as well as what is said will guide the children's response. They will know by the firmness in the voice and their previous experience with the teacher's guidance that they are expected to comply. For example, children generally respond willingly to the teacher calling, "Time to go inside," while standing at the door waiting for them to come. They learn the first day that if they linger, the teacher reinforces the statement by taking their hand and leading them indoors.

Intonation can be used effectively in telling stories, reciting poetry, and singing. However, some individuals have harsh, raspy, or otherwise unpleasant voices that can be hard to listen to for several hours a day. Teachers and teachers-to-be with such voices can often benefit from voice modulation lessons from a speech therapist or coach. Therapists have measuring tools to help give objective data on voice quality. One such teacher said she hated the sound of her voice on her answering machine so much that she turned it off. Then she got help from a speech coach and softened the tones of her voice.

Speaking Slowly and Calmly   The teacher generally speaks in a slow, calm, quiet manner with eyes on the listener. On rare occasions she or he might speak with obvious alarm if the situation warrants it and calls for quick compliance; for example, if a serious danger arises. The latter technique will be used sparingly so that the children will not get accustomed to it and fail to respond when there is real reason for quick action.

Using Few Directions   The teacher gives a minimum number of directions. However, those directions that are given are reinforced if necessary, and the teacher sees to it that the directions are carried out. Reinforcing or following through simply means that the teacher leads the child to do what is asked. The number of direct commands is limited and appropriate for the children. Split-second responses are not expected, however. Children are given some leeway in the time allowed to carry out a direction. For

instance, before giving direction to children to go indoors, the teacher will first remind them that they will be going in soon. This practice helps children bring to a close any activity they have started. When given a little time to terminate their activity, children are likely to comply and are less likely to feel the teacher's decision is unfair.

Some children are taught not to look directly at adults when they speak. This is true of several cultural groups. You can imagine such a child's dismay at having a teacher demand eye-to-eye contact. These children need sympathetic understanding, never criticism.[7]

The teacher should avoid giving several directions at a time. Often teachers forget that children's attention spans are short and give a long series of unrelated directions that may be confusing to young children. If directions are given one at a time, children are more likely to remember the requests until the tasks are accomplished.

Giving Clear, Short, Positive Directions   The teacher remembers to be clear in giving directions. Reasons are given for requests. Direct positive statements are best. They tell the child what *to* do instead of only what *not* to do. A "don't" command leaves a child uncertain as to how to proceed. The first part of the statement should contain the action clause. Reasons are then added. For example, "Walk around the blocks, Peter. John isn't ready to have his building knocked down yet." "Mary, hold your glass up straight. The milk will spill." In each example, the child knows immediately what to do and why.

Giving Choices   The teacher guides children by helping them make choices. She or he wants them to have experience in making up their own minds and deciding things for themselves. The

---

[7]You might like to refer to V. Hildebrand, L. Phenice, M. Gray, and R. Hines, *Knowing and Serving Diverse Families* (Upper Saddle River, NJ: Prentice Hall, 1996) for related information about several cultural groups that you may encounter in your early childhood classes.

teacher may offer a child a choice between playing indoors or out, between listening to a story now or later, between painting or drawing. When giving a choice, one should leave the choice up to the child. It is easy to use the phrase, "Would you like _____," when one really intends the child to do something specific. A teacher uses this phrase only when willing to accept the choice the child makes. The teacher can narrow down choices in order to give the child experience in decision making. Instead of asking a new child, "What would you like to play?" one might say, "You could paint or play with blocks. Which would you like?"

Personalizing Messages A **personal message** consists of three parts:

1. a reflection of the child's point of view,
2. a statement of the adult's emotions about the child's behavior, and
3. a description of an alternate behavior for the child to pursue.

Personal messages can tell children what they are doing right. Also, in problem situations, personal messages set the stage either for children to comply on their own or for the adult to impose consequences when children fail to obey. The adult says, "You're angry. It upsets me when you hit. Hitting hurts. Tell John what he did that made you so angry." This is a personal message, according to Kostelnik et al.[8]

Redirecting Effectively Detouring or redirecting children from unsafe or unsociable behavior requires imagination. When children are doing something unacceptable, the teacher's task is to think of an activity that requires behavior of about the same type that *is* acceptable. For example, if the children holding their fire hoses are climbing on a storage shed that is too steep for safety, the suggestion to move to the packing

boxes for their house-on-fire will be acceptable to the teacher and the children.

There are many examples of detouring or redirecting children's behavior. One day three children were piling up locust beans that had fallen from the trees. Two children began pelting the third with the beans. The teacher knew this type of play would not be fun for the third child for long and suggested, "Let's see if we can throw the beans over this packing box." They responded to the suggestion, and a probable crisis was averted. Distraction works well with toddlers but is less effective as the child matures. The teacher simply redirects the child's attention to a new object or situation.

Using Words to Motivate Motivating the child is a common use of verbal guidance. Self-motivation is by far the most desirable type of motivator. The children should develop plenty of self-confidence. They need to feel competent and important. If the learning environment is set up so that natural curiosity is aroused, then little has to be said to motivate children. As they see others involved in an activity, they usually want to observe and to try it.

Care should be taken to keep competition to a minimum. Avoid motivating by asking who is best, fastest, or tallest. It should be remembered that children who are highly competitive are seldom friends. Failing in competition contributes to a lack of self-confidence. A better method is to motivate according to the child's own record. For example, "You are swinging higher than you did yesterday."

Embarrassing the child is also a poor motivating technique. Calling a child a "baby" or "naughty" or drawing attention to a difficulty such as wet pants in no way contributes to the happy self-confidence for which teachers strive.

Physical Guidance
Physical guidance is the second form of direct guidance. When the teacher uses techniques such as helping, demonstrating, leading, restraining, removing, ignoring, and punishing, this is physical guidance.

---

[8]M. Kostelnik, Laura Stein, Alice Whiren, and Anne Soderman, *Guiding Children's Social Development* (Albany, NY: Delmar, 1993), pp. 201–202.

Demonstrating is effective with young learners because their language development may be too inadequate for them to learn only through words. Nearly anyone learning a new skill is helped by watching a demonstration. It is even more helpful if the person demonstrating goes slowly enough so that the learner can concurrently copy the motions. Consider this example: The four-year-olds were having difficulty opening the door to the school. Telling them to hold down the thumb lever, then push, was ineffective. However, when the teacher took time to show each child how to open the door and supervised the practice for a few minutes, many were able to accomplish the task.

The teacher of younger children frequently has to give a supporting hand to encourage them and help them feel safe while trying a new activity. For example, some children were climbing the newly cut log left in their yard. The most skillful children climbed up quickly, walked along the trunk, and jumped off the end. Though more cautious and hesitant, the less agile children still wanted to try. The teacher offered a steadying hand until they had practiced enough to increase their confidence.

The teacher faces many decisions about whether to help children. The goal is for children to grow in independence. Persistence or sticking to a task is also valued. Children vary as to how much frustration they can tolerate. Some children react to frustration by giving up or getting angry. The teacher must decide when and how much to help. Sometimes the teacher helps the child get beyond an obstacle so that he or she can complete the task. For example, Jamie had unzipped his boots and he was struggling to get them off. The teacher watched his effort, reached over, and showed him how to slip the boot an inch or two beyond the heel. Jamie was elated as the boot yielded to his final tug. Soon he could do the task alone.

Teachers may have to restrain children to prevent them from hurting others or damaging property. The teacher must protect the entire group.

It is much better to stop a child than to allow one to harm others. Efforts should then be made to help the aggressive child reduce angry feelings. Often such activities as hammering nails, pounding clay, or punching the punching bag will help. When restraint is needed frequently with the same child, the teacher must ask what this behavior means to the child and what circumstances prompt it. With close study of the child, the teacher may develop more appropriate guidance.

Removing a child from the group is another way of guiding a child who is having difficulty in the group. Difficulties that arise when a child loses control are often due to overfatigue. For example, when Carlos cannot cope with a situation, the teacher may choose to remove him completely, lead him to a quiet nook, and then talk, read, or sing with him for a while. It also is possible to look for the playdough or some favorite toy. By involving Carlos in a way that will relax him, the teacher averts problems. If a firm, loving, nonpunishing attitude is maintained, the child will welcome the respite and may even seek help another time when he feels his control slipping.

Affective Guidance

Affective guidance is the third form of direct guidance. Affective, of course, refers to feelings. Affective guidance may simply be a smile directed across the room. Words may accompany the recognition on the teacher's part that the child feels satisfied, such as, "You feel really good about your building, don't you, Jake?" Sadness or negative feelings may also be recognized by saying, "You feel upset when Penny grabs your mittens, don't you, Sue?" Statements can be somewhat tentative, leaving children opportunity to tell you that you've misunderstood their feeling.

Approval and disapproval and positive and negative feedback are forms of direct guidance. Verbally labeling behavior helps the child learn. In the following example, John knows the teacher will approve if he repeats the behavior. "John, I like the way you shared the cars with Mark," said the teacher. "When you let Mark use your car, you are sharing." Sharing is one of those vague attributes that most adults wish for in children and one that is very difficult to explain to the child. Sharing should be labeled so that children can begin to recognize it and know what the teacher means when saying, "We are learning to share our toys."

The use of praise should be sincere and given for merit—even if small. When a child makes a number of paintings, the teacher need not praise them all, but can say, "You have been working hard. Which painting do you think is the prettiest?" Insincere praise will be suspect even to children. Children should not need praise for all good behavior. That is, in the long run, they should find satisfaction in their behavior and not just the praise received for doing the appropriate act.

Praise and approval should come to children for jobs well done. Likewise, disapproval should focus on the child's act, not the child. "We don't like spitting, Brad. When we need to spit, we spit in the toilet." In this example no accusation is made that Brad is "bad" when he spits.

A silent smile from across the room or a pat on the head conveys approval. Privately bestowed verbal praise avoids confusing the other children and discourages competition. For example, Peter heard the teacher exclaiming over David's art project. Peter looked at the praised art product and immediately rearranged his own project to fit the praised model. Peter's self-confidence and creativity were unwittingly undermined by the praise for David's picture. No amount of persuasion would convince Peter that the teacher also liked the way he had first made his picture.

Ignoring some behavior is appropriate, depending on the individual and his or her age. Hymes advises teachers not to make an issue over every little fall from grace and says it is often helpful to be half deaf and nearsighted.[9] Surely transgressions may actually be progress

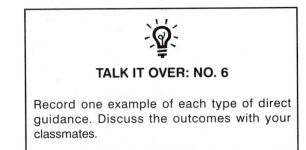

TALK IT OVER: NO. 6

Record one example of each type of direct guidance. Discuss the outcomes with your classmates.

for certain children. For example, Mary never did anything "wrong" and never said "no" to anyone. She was painfully shy and always proper. The teacher's rule was that children stay out of certain pieces of the housekeeping equipment. However, one day when Mary was seen in the dollhouse kitchen climbing up through the opening left for the dishpan sink, the teacher turned her back and allowed Mary to go ahead without the customary disapproval.

The teacher's interaction with a young child should help keep communication open and help the child feel better about him- or herself. Teachers should be aware that because children are immature and inexperienced they do not see a situation in the same way that teachers do. Before we judge a situation or react strongly or drastically, we should try to get the child's view. Thomas Gordon, in his book *T.E.T.: Teacher Effectiveness Training*,[10] gives teachers a framework for practicing interactional skills with their students that are positive and growth producing. He calls it a "no-lose method." Based on humanistic psychology, Gordon's method allows both children and adults to feel good about the methods used.[11]

---

[9]Hymes, *Behavior and Misbehavior*, p. 29.

[10]New York: Peter H. Wyden, 1974.
[11]Thomas Gordon's method was used successfully for staff evaluations, as reported by Carol E. Caltron and Earline D. Kendall, "Staff Evaluation That Promotes Growth and Problem Solving," *Young Children* 39:6 (September 1984), 61–64.

TRANSITIONS

The daily schedule is planned in blocks of time. The children gain a sense of security when they begin to know what happens in each time block. It helps them too if they know what happens between time blocks. That's where the plans for transitions come in.

How do you move children comfortably from indoors to out-of-doors or vice versa without causing mass confusion? How do you prevent waiting in lines, pushing, and crowding, which may trigger harsh words or harsh fists? The answer is to plan for transitions.

To plan transitions, teachers must consider the space and paths available, where children will be congregated, and where they'll need to move for the next activities. Then think about how to get the children to the next activity in the space and time available.

Usually a direct path is needed; otherwise you lose some children en route. Having only a few children moving at once also helps. As an example, let's say children's storytime is over and it is time for snacks. Warning, "Don't everyone go at once," won't do. In planning sessions you might color-code name tags; then it is easy to say, "Those with brown tags go to table number one. Those with red tags go to table number two," and so on. If prior arrangements weren't made, then say, "All children with red shoes go to table number one," then choose brown, black, and so on. Another day choose other criteria to keep it a surprise. Adapting a song to include the names of different children in each verse can signal them when it is their turn to move. For example, to the tune of "The More We Get Together" the teacher and children can sing:

The more we get together,
Together, together,
The more we get together
The happier we'll be.
We're ready for Becky, and Jimmy,

And Susie, and Milton.
The more we get together
The happier we'll be.

If you are taking a field trip, some prior planning and list making are quite essential. Make lists of children who are compatible and give them to the driver. Call out the names of the children in each group and ask them to meet their driver in the block corner, for example. Then when all are together, that driver can move the group to the car to be buckled properly in restraint belts.

There are numerous transitions to be planned for in every childhood school. Some specific helps are offered for storytime in Chapter 14. Your creativity should be operating to think of new ways to make the transitions go smoothly. To be most helpful, staff members all need to be aware of the transition techniques you plan to use.

YOU AS AN ADULT EDUCATOR

The teaching techniques suggested in this chapter will be among the early lessons you, as lead teacher, will need to teach helpers who are new to working with young children in a center. Adults, like children, take time to get adjusted. Your patience will be required as you help beginners learn the techniques for interacting with young children. Time and again you will give a new person a hint to try out. Then later in staff conferences you will discuss further the reasons for using the suggested technique. You can suggest that they read about discipline.

Of course, allowances must be made for individuality. However, as lead teacher—and therefore the responsible adult—you must require that staff members meet certain standards. If one is punitive or shouts at children, for example, this behavior is intolerable and the individual would have to change or be dismissed.

Conclusions

A distinct manner and method of teaching make up each teacher's teaching style. Good teachers develop a unique teaching style as guidance is used to influence the behavior of the children. Guidance can be thought of as either indirect or direct. Children are guided indirectly as the teacher arranges the learning centers, plans the daily schedule, and works with parents. Verbal, physical, and affective guidance make up direct guidance techniques.

Good teachers relax and enjoy the children, yet they are ready to use the guidance techniques described previously while supervising the group. At times teachers may appear to have eyes in the back of their heads, perhaps giving attention to a single child, and yet responding readily to a difficulty in the far corner of the room or yard. In some ways teachers are like the cowboys of the Old West who rode with the herds. According to the historian J. Frank Dobie, they "knew how to linger; they had 'ample time'; but their repose was the repose of strength, capable of steel-spring action and not that of constitutional lethargy."[12]

After teaching in an early childhood school, you may feel certain that Frank Dobie was describing you. Teaching young children requires almost instantaneous response to situations. The response that contributes to goals for educating children so that they can reach their highest potential demands insight, knowledge, and empathy from teachers.

Applications

1. Discuss the "Talk It Over" items suggested in the chapter. Summarize your conclusions.
2. Get permission, then rearrange a piece or two of the children's equipment. Record what happens when the children notice the change. Explain how your experience relates to the discussion of indirect guidance.
3. Rate your participation on the evaluation form developed in Chapter 1. Think about how you feel about your learning.

---

[12]J. Frank Dobie, *The Longhorns* (New York: Bramhall House, 1961), p. xix.

4. Add ideas about guiding children to your Resource File.

Study Questions

1. Define *teaching styles*. Discuss different styles.
2. Define *guidance* and state the goal of guidance.
3. Define and give examples of *indirect guidance*.
4. Define and give examples of *direct guidance*: (a) physical, (b) verbal, and (c) affective.
5. Write five examples of positive guidance statements you might use with young children.
6. Assume children are playing at the water table. They excitedly splash water. The teacher says, "If you splash water you'll get the floor all wet. People will get their jeans wet and they won't like you if you get them wet." Shorten the teacher's statement to make it follow the rules stated in the chapter. Discuss what you would change and why.
7. Explain how ignoring a child's misbehavior can be appropriate guidance at times.
8. Discuss when giving a choice is appropriate.
9. Discuss punishment as a method of guidance.

Videotapes

Building Self-Confidence
   30 minutes

Explores how parents and caregivers can develop self-confidence and a positive self-concept in young children. Thelma Harms and Debby Cryer. DC/TATS MEDIA, Frank Porter Graham Child Development Center, University of North Carolina at Chapel Hill CB8040, 300 NCNB Plaza, Chapel Hill, NC 27599-8040.

Discipline: Appropriate Guidance of Young Children
   28 minutes

Illustrates how positive guidance of young children toward healthy development is the foundation of a good early childhood program. It shows ways to handle hitting, tattling, taking turns, temper tantrums. From South Carolina Educational Television, NAEYC Media, 1509 16th St. NW, Washington, DC 20036-1426, 1-800-424-2460.

Relating to Others
17 minutes

A discussion with Dr. James Hymes, Jr. How do adults help children become self-disciplined? NAEYC Media, 1509 16th St. NW, Washington, DC 20036-1426, 1-800-424-2460.

Relating to Others
30 minutes

Examines positive ways that adults can help children develop age-appropriate skills such as sharing and empathy. Thelma Harms and Debby Cryer. DC/TATS MEDIA. Frank Porter Graham Child Development Center, University of North Carolina at Chapel Hill CB8040, 300 NCNB Plaza, Chapel Hill, NC 27599-8040.

Appropriate Curriculum for Young Children: The Role of the Teacher
28 minutes

NAEYC Media, 1509 16th St. NW, Washington, DC 20036-1426, 1-800-424-2460.

Building Quality Child Care: Independence
20 minutes

NAEYC Media, 1509 16th St. NW, Washington, DC 20036-1426, 1-800-424-2460.

Celebrating Early Childhood Teachers
22 minutes

A view of the role of the early childhood education professional. NAEYC Media, 1509 16th St. NW, Washington, DC 20036-1426, 1-800-424-2460.

Discipline: Appropriate Guidance of Young Children
28 minutes

Positive guidance of young children toward healthy social and emotional development. Handling difficult situations. NAEYC Media, 1509 16th St. NW, Washington, DC 20036-1426, 1-800-424-2460.

Additional Readings

Betz, Carl. "Beyond Time-Out: Tips for a Teacher." *Young Children* 49:3, March 1994, 10–14.

Daniel, Jerlean. "New Beginnings: Transitions for Difficult Children." *Young Children* 50:3, March 1995, 17–23.

Dinkmeyer, Don. "Teaching Responsibility: Developing Personal Accountability Through Natural and Logical Consequences." In *Experts Advise Parents*, ed. Eileen Shiff. New York: Delcorte Press, 1987, 173–199.

Dinkmeyer, Don, and Rudolph Dreikurs. *Encouraging Children to Learn: The Encouragement Process.* Upper Saddle River, NJ: Prentice Hall, 1979.

Elicker, James, and Cheryl Forner Wood. "Adult-Child Relationships in Early Childhood Programs." *Young Children* 51:1, November 1995, 69–78.

Goffin, Stacie G. "Cooperative Behaviors: They Need Our Support." *Young Children* 42:2, January 1987, 75–81.

Hildebrand, Verna. *Guiding Young Children.* Upper Saddle River, NJ: Merrill/Prentice Hall, 1994.

Hildebrand, Verna, and Patricia Hearron. *Management of Child Development Centers.* Upper Saddle River, NJ: Merrill/Prentice Hall, 1997.

Hitz, Randy, and Amy Driscoll. "Praise or Encouragement?" *Young Children* 43:5, July 1988, 6–13.

Honig, Alice Sterling. "Compliance, Control, and Discipline." *Young Children* 40:2, January 1985, 50–58, and *Young Children* 40:3, March 1985, 47–52.

Lasky, Lila, and Rose Mukerji. *Art: Basic for Young Children.* Washington, DC: NAEYC, 1995.

Marshall, Hermine H. "Beyond, 'I like the Way. . . .'" *Young Children* 50:2, January 1995, 26–28.

Miller, Cheri S. "Building Self-Control: Discipline for Young Children." *Young Children* 40:1, November 1984, 15–25.

NAEYC. "Discipline: Are Tantrums Normal?" *Young Children* 43:6, September 1988, 35–40.

———. "Child Choice—Another Way to Individualize—Another Form of Preventive Discipline." *Young Children* 43:1, November 1987, 48–54.

Perry, Gail, and Mary Rivkin. "Teachers and Science." *Young Children* 47:4, May 1992, 9–16.

Rogers, Dwight L., and Dorene D. Ross. "Encouraging Positive Social Interaction Among Young Children." *Young Children* 41:3, March 1986, 12–17.

Weber-Schwartz, Nancy. "Patience or Understanding?" *Young Children* 42:3, March 1987, 52–54.

PART 2

The Curriculum of the Early Childhood School

Chapter 6   Introduction to Activity Planning

Chapter 7   Activities for Infants

Chapter 8   Activities for Toddlers

Chapter 9   Motor Skill Activities

Chapter 10   Creative Art Activities

Chapter 11   Science Activities

Chapter 12   Perceptual-Motor Activities

Chapter 13   Language Activities

Chapter 14   Literature Activities and Emerging Literacy

Chapter 15   Dramatic Play Activities

Chapter 16   Creative Music Activities

Chapter 17   Field Trips and Special Visitors

Chapter 18   Food Activities, Meals, and Snacks

Chapter 19   Managing an Early Childhood Group

CHAPTER 6

Introduction to Activity Planning

Southeast Oakland Vocational Technical School

Objectives

✔ Know the stages in planning educational objectives as identified in the Bloom Taxonomy of Educational Objectives.

✔ Know the basic components of planning an activity to be carried out in the early childhood school.

✔ Define Vygotsky's idea about scaffolding.

"I just had a super time with the children doing finger painting," reported Roger.

"My! the children were really active in my high-jump activity!" exclaimed Mary.

Mary and Roger are college students who are meeting with the teacher of the children's group where they are doing their practicum for their early childhood education course. The teacher and students will be evaluating where they have been and where they are going. The teacher, in consultation with the instructor of the course, and the students have agreed on some goals and ground rules for the students' participation. The supervising teacher meets with the students to iron out details for their work with the young children. Step by step, Mary and Roger are gaining the experience needed for planning an integrated curriculum and managing a whole group. These tasks are discussed further in Chapter 19.

A TAXONOMY OF EDUCATIONAL OBJECTIVES

A useful guide to activity planning or planning a course for students was devised by Dr. Benjamin Bloom, an educational researcher, with the help of many others. They developed the *Taxonomy of Educational Objectives: The Cognitive Domain*, which is summarized in Figure 6–1. The classification is often referred to as the Bloom Taxonomy. Bloom believes that educators must be aware of these levels when planning educational experiences.[1]

By studying Figure 6–1 you can think about yourself and your level of knowledge. On some subjects you may find yourself at Level 6, ready to do an evaluation and, perhaps, make recommendations to others in this subject area. You may also be at Level 1 (knowledge) on some topic that is new to you when you hear about it on the evening news. Take the subject of early childhood education; where are you, your instructors, and the general population on that subject?

A plan for personalizing the program can focus on the children's birthdays. What would you do with this arrangement? (Children's Center, Denver)

Children are also at different points in their level of information as well as in their level of development. Each child has unique interests and needs. When you plan an activity you'll try to learn where the children are in their knowledge, then start from there to build. You can use the Bloom Taxonomy to help you tailor your objectives and plans to the appropriate level. You'll refer back to the developmental tasks in Chapter 2 as you plan various activities.

Bloom's work is a developmental sequence for cognitive learning. Of course, there are similar sequences for other areas of children's learning—large- and small-muscle motor skills, language skills, and social skills. If you think about it for a while, in addition to cognitive skills, based on your knowledge of child development, you could

---

[1]Benjamin S. Bloom, ed., *Taxonomy of Educational Objectives, Handbook I: The Cognitive Domain* (New York: David McKay, 1956), pp. 62–168.

FIGURE 6–1

Taxonomy of educational objectives in the cognitive domain.

Source: Adapted from Benjamin S. Bloom, ed., *Taxonomy of Educational Objectives, Handbook I: Cognitive Domain* (New York: David McKay, 1956), pp. 62–168.

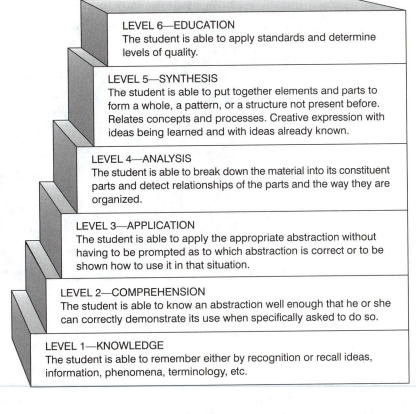

LEVEL 6—EDUCATION
The student is able to apply standards and determine levels of quality.

LEVEL 5—SYNTHESIS
The student is able to put together elements and parts to form a whole, a pattern, or a structure not present before. Relates concepts and processes. Creative expression with ideas being learned and with ideas already known.

LEVEL 4—ANALYSIS
The student is able to break down the material into its constituent parts and detect relationships of the parts and the way they are organized.

LEVEL 3—APPLICATION
The student is able to apply the appropriate abstraction without having to be prompted as to which abstraction is correct or to be shown how to use it in that situation.

LEVEL 2—COMPREHENSION
The student is able to know an abstraction well enough that he or she can correctly demonstrate its use when specifically asked to do so.

LEVEL 1—KNOWLEDGE
The student is able to remember either by recognition or recall ideas, information, phenomena, terminology, etc.

develop a stair-step plan for acquisition of skills in many areas of learning.

In this chapter, Bloom's work is simply illustrative. Throughout the following twelve chapters, works by other researchers will be cited.

Their research has been published and enables practitioners, such as teachers, to make use of the findings as they plan for and work with children.[2]

PLANNING IS THE KEY

Positive outcomes for children happen by design, not by accident. Planning is the key to designing a high-quality early childhood program that fos-

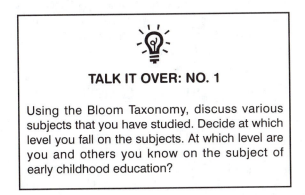

TALK IT OVER: NO. 1

Using the Bloom Taxonomy, discuss various subjects that you have studied. Decide at which level you fall on the subjects. At which level are you and others you know on the subject of early childhood education?

---

[2]You may also want to use NAEYC's booklet, *Guidelines for Appropriate Curriculum Content and Assessment in Programs Serving Children 3 Through 8 Years of Age,* Sue Bredekamp, ed. (Washington, DC: NAEYC, 1992). Also, two other NAEYC booklets edited by Sue Bredekamp will be useful. They are *Accreditation Criteria and Procedures of the National Academy of Early Childhood Programs* (Washington, DC: NAEYC, 1991) and *Developmentally Appropriate Practice in Early Childhood Programs Serving Children from Birth Through Age 8* (Washington, DC: NAEYC, 1987).

Plants give life to the room and children learn interesting concepts. What do you know that you might teach children in a plant activity? (Children's Center, Denver)

ters the accomplishment of the developmental tasks that were discussed in Chapter 2. A rich, viable program takes lots of planning, organizing, and coordinating. Teachers, assistants, and students who participate in the classroom should become involved in the planning and evaluating functions. It takes time to sit together to assess children's needs and interests, to evaluate previous plans, and to propose the activities that will meet children's needs and interests. As students, you should avail yourself of every opportunity to participate in planning sessions with experienced teachers.

Writing down plans is essential to ensure high-quality programs. The less experience the staff member has, the more detailed the written plans must be. It will save precious minutes if recipes and procedures are written on cards or on lesson plan forms and filed in a convenient book or file enabling future use without additional search. You will find good use for the Resource File suggested in Chapter 1. The computer is a great help in making planning easier.

Organizing

Organizing the materials and equipment in a manner that will facilitate children's use of them follows decisions in the planning session. You may be designated as the one to set up a certain area. When you plan your special activity, you will be fully in charge of organizing the area where the activity will be presented and of cleaning up the area afterward.

PLANNING SPECIFIC ACTIVITIES

A typical procedure early in teacher education programs is for students to carry out one special activity each time they come to the school. That activity is selected from each curricular area offered in the school—art, literature, science, and so on. Later, during the practice teaching phase, the student coordinates all the curricular activities and helpers, building on the earlier experience of carrying out one activity at a time. The opportunity to do one activity at a time without being totally in charge gives you a chance to learn in more depth and to get your feet wet gradually. Some students are both excited about and a little frightened by their new opportunities. If you are well prepared, however, it will be "a piece of cake."

Choice of Activity

The selection of a particular activity should be made in consultation with your supervising teacher in the children's school. After you observe the children and read your text for ideas, you can make a list of several activities that you'd like to try out. You will want your activity to fit in with the theme the teacher has set for the week during which you'll be carrying out your activity. You'll need to be planning far in advance, so begin early.

Confer with the teacher so you both can come to an agreement as to what activity would best fit into the overall plan and when the activity should be carried out within the schedule. Once the written plan is complete, show it to the teacher for approval. Then move ahead getting everything ready. Remember that the materials you prepare can often be used again and again—in student teaching and in future teaching. They can become part of your Resource File. Thus, the time spent on this one activity will have many payoffs for you.

Activity Plan

An **activity plan** could be made for every learning experience offered in the school. It is a challenging exercise to look at each piece of equipment or learning episode in the school and attempt to make an activity plan. Each of the ideas offered in Part 2 of this book will help with this thinking. Figure 6–2 is an example of a completed plan for using one type of equipment. The items entered under each heading on this sample activity plan will vary depending on the activity you select. For many activities, you can refer to the curriculum chapters to help you formulate relevant and rather complete entries fitting the requirements of each heading. It is important to think through each step in the activity plan. Unless you are highly experienced with children and with the activity, you will readily cope with the variety of children's responses and behaviors only if you are super prepared.

In planning a finger painting project, for example, you will find in Chapter 10 all the information for your activity plan. You will discover that this medium gives children an opportunity to practice small motor skills and to create their own designs. These could be your *Developmental Goals* for a particular day. Your *Objective* for children on a particular day could be to manipulate the finger paints with fingers, hands, and arms and create a design of their own choosing. Likewise, *Materials Needed*, *Procedures*, and *Guidance Suggestions* can be found in each chapter where a particular activity is discussed.

Small Group

It is suggested that the first activity you plan be presented to a few children at a time. The major reason for this suggestion is that it will enable you to be more firmly in control and not overwhelmed. Also, you can often repeat an activity several times in a given class period and thus refine your procedure and learn from your mistakes. Children are usually more satisfied with a small group, too, because you are less familiar to them than their teacher and it takes time to get acquainted with you and your ideas. Do try to insist that you work with only a few children, even if teachers will "let" you work with more. If you do the activity for the whole group, always try it out on a few children first.

Talking Children Through Your Activity

You're planning an activity that you believe is appropriate for the children in your group and

FIGURE 6–2
Activity plan form.

SAMPLE ACTIVITY PLAN
(with sample plan)

Name of Activity: *Parquetry blocks*

Developmental Goal:
1. Vocabulary development
2. Perceptual development

Objectives: Given a set of parquetry blocks with matching forms the child will, each time,
1. match colors,
2. match shapes,
3. name colors,
4. name shapes.

Materials Needed: *3 parquetry sets*

Procedure:
Place parquetry sets in an inviting location in the room.
Sit with children. Observe their use of the sets.
Let them discover and teach each other.
Answer any questions. Note their use of vocabulary.
Encourage naming of shapes and colors.

Guidance Suggestions Including Limits:
Play a game: "Show me the *(red square)."*
Encourage them to make their own designs after they accomplish matching.

Special Objectives:
To see if Amanda is able to name colors.
To see if John can count to four. Encourage his practice.

Evaluation:
Hide shape and/or color—ask child to name it when it is uncovered.
Check chart to see which ones child knows.

Suggestions for Future Use:

that they will enjoy. You've thought about your goals and have assembled the materials and set the stage for a few children at a time to try out your activity—let's say it is an art project with three colors and new style brushes to use for painting. Your activity takes place during self-selected play time when children have many choices of play activities.

The ideas of Lev Vygotsky will be useful to you as you talk to and interact with the children

A balloon-batting activity requires equipment, procedures, and rules. Why do you think the carpet squares are helpful? What developmental processes are stimulated? (Kansas State University)

TALK IT OVER: NO. 2

Discuss the procedure for overall planning in the school where you participate. Who does it? How much time is allowed for planning? How much is written down? How is evaluation done? Make inquiries if you can't answer these questions.

as they try your new activity and relate it to art activities they've been having all along. You may be asking who Vygotsky is. He was a Russian psychologist who believed "that all uniquely human, higher forms of mental activity are jointly constructed and transferred to children through dialogues with other people"[3]

According to Berk, Vygotsky believed "early childhood teachers and peers can 'scaffold' young children's play, nurturing the transition to make believe and its elaboration throughout the preschool years." As you know, a scaffold is an adjustable supporting framework around a building that is being built or repaired. So "scaffold" to Vygotsky is the support or interaction of the adults and somewhat older peers with the young child as he or she reaches each new height in thought and action.

Parents and caregivers can help children learn to pretend at a young age as they talk with and show make-believe feeding of a doll, for example, or pretend to feed the infant with a make-believe spoon. What might the children pretend with the paints that you are providing?

All the while, your running conversation engages the child and responds to the child's cues and actions. Where the conversation and action goes is unpredictable, yet fun for the child. Your careful listening and eye-to-eye contact in social interaction with the child during any play activity will make that play more advanced than one observes when the child plays alone, says Berk. Also, in the presence of other children the

[3]Laura E. Berk, "Vygotsky's Theory: The Importance of Make-Believe Play," *Young Children* 50:1(November 1994), 30–39.

A sand or sawdust multipurpose tray or table can give children a quiet place for symbolic farm play. Notice the large throw rug under the table. Why do you think the teachers placed the rug there? (University of Illinois)

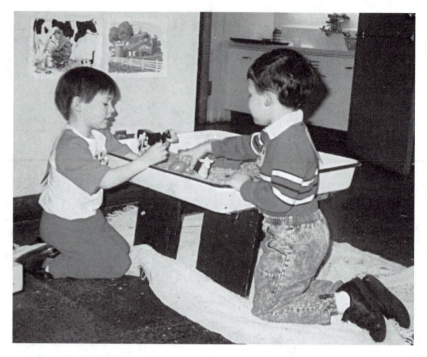

conversation may include them in surprising ways when the adult stays close and involved.

This doesn't mean for you to dominate the activity or be overly enthusiastic or loud, but to be a very close observer and quiet conversationalist responding to each child's cues. You will indeed talk the children through your activity as they participate in what you have planned for them.

Thus, in your painting project you'll watch closely and respond verbally as often as you can as you pick up on the child's words or actions. Keep your eyes on the children so you can read the meanings on each one's face. Later on, try to write down some of the interesting tangents the work and conversation took. Keep such a record with all the activities you plan.

Vygotsky's work has found enthusiastic responses among early childhood educators partly because he seems to be labeling actions within play that many educators have discovered

on their own. Vygotsky's work is contrasted with Piaget's, who was writing about the same time. The Russian's works were not translated until much later, however, probably due to the world wars and the complexity of making Russian translations. Piaget implies that the stages he found will evolve with maturation. See Chapter 11.

Observing

To be constantly alert to all that goes on in your school should be one of your goals. This is a big order, especially when you are new.

You will have an assignment. Be sure to do that assignment well. While doing it, observe and make mental or actual notes of which children are in your area and what they do. Eventually you will know such details as which children are left-handed, which ones need reminding to go to the bathroom, and which ones need help putting on their shoes. In addition, keep an eye on the rest of the room or play yard. What activities are the other adults carrying out? How do they handle problems? If you haven't carried out an activity like the one they are doing, ask them later about it. You can learn a great deal from watching others, especially as you have standards for high-quality teaching drawn to your attention in your classes.

Keeping a log or diary of your day in the early childhood school will provide you with a valuable resource for later use when you will be in charge of a group. With a few personal notes on your reactions, you'll be able to recall your day in that school quite vividly. You can also use a diary in an evaluation of the program. At the end of the term or year you can tally the various curricular activities you've observed.

Evaluating

Evaluating must be part of every teaching and every planning session. All staff members can contribute to information on how individual children are progressing and provide ideas for activities suggested by children's interests. Sharing information in a conference should help the staff move toward a professional consultative level where some philosophical ideas about children and early childhood education can be discussed along with the "nuts and bolts" of the operation.

An important characteristic of the best demonstration teachers is their ability to involve others in planning, preparation, and evaluation. As a student, you can take careful note and learn from the teacher's leadership style, because in a very short time you'll be the lead teacher with responsibility for a whole group of children and a number of adult helpers besides.

Conclusions

The work of Benjamin Bloom and others has been utilized as a basis for planning a curriculum. The opportunity for students to plan and carry out specific learning activities for the children in an early childhood school is a special learning tool. You are building your expertise little by little. By following the suggestions given, the children, supervising teacher, and college students will all have a pleasant experience in the early childhood school.

Even sandbox play requires a plan. What developmental differences will you anticipate among the children? What tools are needed? Are tools all in good condition? Who will take them to the sandbox? Who will supervise the sandbox? Who will return the equipment at the end of the day? (Kansas State University)

Applications

1. Do the "Talk It Over" items in the chapter. Can you draw conclusions about how planning is done in your school?
2. Discuss with your instructors the desired format of activity plans and evaluations.
3. Evaluate your own participation on your evaluation form.
4. Add sample plans for activities to your Resource File.

Study Questions

1. Identify the six levels of the Bloom Taxonomy of Educational Objectives. Describe each level. Give examples from adult subject matter and from children's subject matter.
2. Identify and give examples of the basic components of an activity plan.

Videotapes

Culture and Education of Young Children
    16 minutes

Carol Philips shows how respect for our cultural diversity and recognition of its richness can enhance children's learning. NAEYC Media, 1509 16th St. NW, Washington, DC 20036-1426, 1-800-424-2460.

Additional Readings

Berk, Laura E., and Adam Winsler. *Scaffolding Children's Learning: Vygotsky and Early Childhood Education*. Washington, DC: NAEYC, 1995.

Bowman, Barbara, and Elizabeth Beyer. "Young Children: Thoughts on Technology and Early Childhood Education." In *Early Childhood Education 95/96*, eds. Karen M. Paciorek and Joyce H. Monro. Guilford, CT: Dushkin, 1995, 192–198.

Henniger, Michael L. "Planning for Outdoor Play." *Young Children* 49:4, May 1994, 10–15.

Kostelnik, Marjorie, ed. *Teaching Young Children Using Themes*. Chicago, IL: Scott Foresman, 1991.

Vygotsky, Lev. *Mind in Society: The Development of Higher Psychological Processes*, eds. M. Cole, V. John-Steiner, S. Scribner, and E. Souberman. Cambridge, MA: Harvard University Press, 1978.

Wheat, Rebecca. "Help Children Work Through Emotional Difficulties—Sand Trays Are Great." *Young Children* 51:1, November 1995, 82–83.

CHAPTER 7

Activities for Infants

V. Hildebrand

Objectives

✔ Identify developmental goals for infants.
✔ Identify activities appropriate for infants.
✔ Identify strategies for working with infants.

Paul, age six months, was sitting on the floor focusing attention on a rag doll. Grasping the doll by the leg he began shaking it vigorously. Glancing up, he caught his caregiver's eye. The caregiver smiled and, pointing, said, "Doll. Doll. Paul has a doll."

PLANNING FOR INFANTS

The first principle to remember in planning learning opportunities for infants is that everything the child does offers a learning opportunity. In one way or another the routine care, the nurturing, and the playing contribute to physical-motor development, social-emotional development, and cognitive and language development.

The second principle is that typical infants from the earliest months are motivated to grow and develop optimally in all areas. They have an innate drive to learn and to develop. When infants are healthy, parental and caregiver's efforts need to be directed primarily toward making the environment safe while the infants strive toward becoming the complex individuals they will eventually grow to be.

A third principle is that there are individual differences among infants. Each day will bring new growth and behavior, with each infant reaching the benchmarks of development at slightly different times. On the whole, girls reach most milestones somewhat ahead of boys. Remembering this principle helps one appreciate each child as an individual, and keeps adults from inappropriately comparing one child with another.

These three principles are supported by worthwhile publications of the NAEYC. These booklets should be part of each center's library. They give a detailed description of high-quality infant/toddler care.[1]

Dr. Alice Honig has directed an infant/toddler center at Syracuse University for thirteen years and is considered an authority on infant/toddler care. She suggests that the ingredients of high-quality infant/toddler caregiving are

1. maintaining highest standards for feeding and health care practices,

2. giving individualized attentive loving,
3. respecting individual tempos and exploration needs,
4. enriching language experiences,
5. promoting social experiences including altruism, and
6. facilitating cognitive development.[2]

ENVIRONMENT

An environment that promotes growth, development, and learning must be arranged by the adults who are responsible for the infants. Having each set of caregivers decide on a theme for the week helps encourage individuality, creativity, and helpful interaction. For example, the theme can be babies. To support this theme the teachers can use photos of babies to decorate their bulletin boards, use books and puzzles with baby pictures, and add baby pictures to the mobile in the middle of the room. Care must be taken to keep themes uncomplicated. They should be simple, single concepts with simple, generic labels. Wait till much later to teach about baby animals, which, as a concept, will build on the concept of human babies. Labeling a concept is the beginning level for infants who are just starting to learn that objects have names. Other themes can follow: cats, dogs, rabbits, birds, trucks, cars, bicycles, trees, flowers, and so on.

Responsible teachers and directors will pay careful attention to hygienic conditions of care in order to keep infants physically healthy. You must wash your hands after every diaper change *and* after wiping runny noses to keep down infections. Your careful attention to following health regulations must be emphasized repeatedly to protect infants and caregivers and even the parents and siblings of the infants. Some infections, such as hepatitis, are more harmful to the latter than to the infants.

---

[1]Sue Bredekamp, ed., *Accreditation Criteria and Procedures of the National Academy of Early Childhood Programs* (Washington, DC: NAEYC, 1991) and *Developmentally Appropriate Practice in Early Childhood Programs Serving Children from Birth Through Age 8* (Washington, DC: NAEYC, 1987).

[2]Alice Sterling Honig, "Quality Infant/Toddler Caregiving: Are There Magic Recipes?" *Young Children* 44:4 (May 1989), 4–10.

While caring for infants, you'll witness activities that only an infant can do—like sucking her toe! (V. Hildebrand, photographer)

The infant center will be providing a support service to the families. While you, as a preservice student, may not be fully responsible for the environment, you should evaluate what you see, contribute ideas when feasible, and help establish the best conditions possible for the infants with whom you are working.

GOALS BASED ON CHILD DEVELOPMENT RESEARCH

Goals for an infant center program will be based on knowledge of how infants grow and develop. In addition, through observation of individual infants, goals for each child will be determined. Thus, you, as a preservice teacher, have an opportunity to apply in very specific ways the information on child development and child psychology that you have learned in previous courses. You will refer to basic texts in child development frequently, as will the caregivers and teachers of infants with whom you work, in order to apply developmental information as individually as possible.

In the following section four major goals are outlined and ways caregivers can help fulfill each goal during the day-to-day interaction with infants are discussed. The four main goals are

1. building a sense of trust,
2. encouraging social skill development,
3. stimulating language and cognitive development, and
4. promoting physical-motor development.

Building a Sense of Trust

Building a sense of trust within the infant is one of the earliest goals of the early infancy period. Psychologist Erik Erikson emphasizes building trust in his theory of psychosocial development.[3] Infants learn to trust when their parents and caregivers respond to them warmly and consistently, and when they are handled gently and in a timely manner, not left to wait to have needs taken care of. During this early period bonding is taking place between the infant and his or her parents and perhaps siblings. In the infant care situation bonding can also occur with caregivers. This is a major reason why experts recommend that caregivers must be responsible for only three infants and that the same caregiver stay with the infants over time to add to the infants' sense of security, trust, and bondedness.

As a caregiver, you will promote bonding between parents and infants. For example, you will facilitate a mother breast-feeding her infant, if that can be scheduled, or the bottle-feeding by either parent if one can take the time to come at feeding time. In some of our on-site corporate child care centers, bonding relationships with both mothers and fathers are encouraged

---

[3]Lawrence Schiamberg, *Child and Adolescent Development* (New York: Macmillan, 1988), p. 45.

because parents work only a short distance from the infant center and can visit during the workday.

Each day you will report to parents significant milestones their infant has reached, even as you report any problems that arise. You will help these parents appreciate their infant by letting them know how much you appreciate the child. A word of caution is essential—avoid feeling and implying to parents that you are more concerned about the child than they are. Your role is to build up the parental relationship and never to undermine it. Parents often feel guilt when they have an infant in an infant center. If your center is a really great place to be, with high standards of quality, then there should be little basis for their guilt feelings. Infants in high-quality care centers will fare better than children in many other care arrangements. High-quality caregivers and programs are the key factors.

A sense of trust develops as infants are held warmly and close to the chest while feeding. Qui-etly talking or singing to infants, with eye-to-eye contact, as they are diapered or dressed is a must. A rocking chair for this close cuddling time should be available. The baby's name must be used frequently.

In addition, you will observe each infant in your care to understand as fully as possible how to meet each one's individual needs. You will carry out the unique role you can play in promoting each infant's sense of trust. When other staff or substitutes are needed to care for "your" infants, you will give detailed directions in order that routines the infants have learned to depend on are carried out as nearly as possible the way they are when you are there. Of course, in centers where infants attend more than 8 hours there will be more than one caregiver. It is essential that these individuals work together for the good of the infants.

Developing a positive self-concept in each infant is a major objective in high-quality programs. Feeling positive about one's self comes

Infant care must give both infant and parent time to continue bonding. Caregivers can learn techniques of care from parents. (Youb Kim, photographer)

from having one's needs met by friendly, loving people. Thus, you should look directly into each baby's eyes with patience, a smile, and a quiet comment of endearment. Your handling should be gentle, showing your sense of caring.

Encouraging Social Skill Development

Humans are social beings; thus the infant is interested in watching others in the family or in the infant center. Caregivers in centers facilitate socialization by speaking to individual infants frequently and helping them enjoy the other babies. Though infants will play alone with their toys throughout this period because they are in a stage of solitary play, it does not mean that they will not enjoy the presence of other children. They like to see what others are doing. They might like for the older prekindergartners to say "hi" as they pass by on the playground. They will be over a year old when they first realize that people who are out of sight still exist. That's one reason babies can be so easily distracted—in their thinking the person or thing they want no longer exists once their attention is drawn to something else. Psychologist Jean Piaget called this concept **object permanence**.[4]

Your role as a beginning caregiver is to keep the social environment uncrowded so that infants cannot hurt each other inadvertently. Be sure there are enough balls, rings, or cuddly toys so sharing is not a problem. Infants, of course, do not understand ownership or sharing of a toy, so lectures on the topics will fall on deaf ears.

You will be responsible for keeping the social environment safe so each infant can enjoy the presence of the others. However, hunger, fatigue, and overstimulation caused by too many people or too much activity can give the infant too much to cope with and could harm social skill development. When infants become hungry or tired, their need for food and rest should be taken care of immediately. This is part of individualizing the program.

4Ibid., pp. 244–245.

TALK IT OVER

What are some ways you have observed the experienced caregivers and parents using distraction to help calm a baby?

You are modeling social skills when you greet babies, respond to their cues, and take care of their needs. Many babies and others learn best from watching role models.

Stimulating Language and Cognitive Development

From the time infants first hear human voices, they are building their abilities for speaking. First come months of listening, cooing, and babbling. Hearing is essential to language development, and each newborn's hearing is typically tested in the hospital's newborn nursery. Hearing aids are fitted on nonhearing infants, for without perceiving speech the child will not be able to develop speech. Thus, if you notice that an infant doesn't seem to hear, be sure to bring this observation to the attention of the center's director, who would likely observe the baby before talking to the parents about having the infant's hearing checked by a physician.

As Mary spoke to Paul in our opening anecdote, "Doll. Doll. Paul has a doll," she was using words that Paul could soon begin to identify and understand. Many call these utterances *telegraphic*, due to their unelaborated quality as in a telegram. Many such instances of conversation take place between parents or caregivers and infants. The adults model language, and each is encouraged to talk to the infant with eye-to-eye contact.

By watching closely, adults recognize that infants' early movements signal communication.

What difference would it make if you knew that an infant's grandfather was a major caregiver in his life? (Cloud County, Kansas Community College)

For example, infants often lean forward toward a speaker, have heightened animation in their voices, and mimic words or intonations, as they "talk" to others. Of course, speech is not conversation without someone bouncing back the ideas, so adults need to provide "answers" to infants, responding numerous times a day with a few words that show that others are interested in talking to them.[5]

As you recall from your previous study, Dr. Jean Piaget, the noted psychologist, labeled the earliest stage of the development of reasoning, occurring during approximately the first two years of life, the **sensorimotor** stage.[6] Sensorimotor is a two-part word, giving clues to Piaget's

observation that sensory perceptions, reasoning, and motor response are linked. Infants learn everything through one of the five senses (hearing, seeing, touching, tasting, and smelling) and act on their perceptions through movement. That is, you can tell when a baby recognizes a person or object by the motor behavior he or she performs, such as smiling or reaching out.

For fun, and to learn how much a baby is observing and thinking about what he or she sees, hide a toy under a diaper. Wait to see what the baby does. If nothing happens, say, "Where is it?" then show the baby where the toy went. Smile and say, "Here it is!" Try the game on future days. Eventually the infant will follow your movement, until one day he or she will actually move toward the hidden toy and pull the diaper off. What excitement will result! This little game is further evidence of the baby's understanding that objects, though out of sight, still exist—are permanent. *Object permanence* was mentioned earlier in relation to people. Understanding object permanence is a big step in infants' cognitive development.

Soon after the infant can sit up, a picture book can be introduced, enabling the child to respond to the pictures. Usually the best books have colorful pictures of familiar objects such as a glass of milk, a toy, or baby shoes. You can state the concept name such as, "Milk, glass of milk," as you turn the pages. Before long the child will reciprocate, "Milk," when that page is turned. Thus, literacy education begins in a natural, warm, positive setting with the baby's interest being the guide.

Throughout all the routines, your conversations with the infants include labeling objects in the environment. You can tell infants some details just for the fun of it and to have something sensible to say; however, expecting them to remember from one day to the next is premature. For instance, while diapering an infant the caregiver told the baby how they were going to the park to pick autumn leaves and bring them back to decorate the center. The baby responded by

---

[5]See T. Berry Brazelton, *Infants and Mothers* (New York: Dell, 1983).
[6]See L. Schiamberg, op. cit., or other child development text for more detail on Piaget's work.

It is stimulating for infants to be in the presence of other infants and to be able to look in a mirror. (Kadena Air Force Child Care Center, Okinawa)

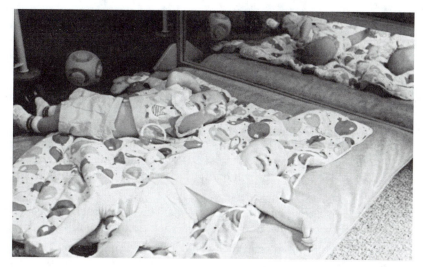

cooing and kicking happily—enjoying the contact and attention—but couldn't understand or remember the story.

You can sing songs or recite poetry with infants to direct attention or to stimulate the child to look at something, such as a bird outside the window. Recite the poem "Little birdie with a yellow bill, hopped upon my window sill" when you see a bird you want the infant to notice.

Infant's rooms should be decorated with interesting and colorful pictures and mobiles to stimulate the child to observe, point out, ask questions, and make comments about. These objects should be renewed from week to week so there are new things to look at and talk about. As suggested earlier, the objects, books, and toys can be selected to fit a theme each week.

The busy interpersonal social interaction suggested in these examples supports psychologist Lev Vygotsky's contention (discussed in Chapter 6) that adults help children learn through social interaction and through building a "scaffold" toward information the child is learning.

Promoting Physical-Motor Development

Before the infants can roll over on their own, they need adults to roll them over. This makes their muscles feel good and gives them new vistas to see. Even very young babies will be able to move their head from side to side. Eventually the infants can roll over in the crib alone—a first stage of motor liberation. It is only a few months before an infant is so very active physically that being left unguarded on a bed or table is inviting disaster. Be sure a baby is safe from falls before leaving him or her unattended.

Sitting in an inclined seat or a special baby's swing offers the infant further liberation. The child can see what goes on in the room and can also attend to auditory stimuli. You'll notice infants who hear the cart with trays look toward the door in anticipation, for example. This behavior is evidence of their learning.

Sitting on the floor is pleasant for infants. Several interesting toys should be placed nearby. These toys may stimulate the child to crawl to retrieve them. Keep babies sitting far enough apart that they will not hurt each other if they move quickly with a toy. Caregivers often join the infants on the floor.

Remember, the natural movement for an infant is to pick up an object and immediately put it to the mouth. Thus, the toys chosen must be appropriate for mouthing and must be kept washed and disinfected to avoid sharing germs in

TEN MINUTES IN AN INFANT TEACHER'S LIFE

Student observations of a teacher called T in an infant group. Three infants were T's responsibility. Lauren was twelve months; Ricky, nine months; and Kurt, eight months of age. The following notes depict 10 consecutive minutes selected from hours of direct observations.*

11:05 A.M.

T goes into the playroom. Ricky arriving with his mother is handed over to T, who reaches for him. He embraces her. T says warmly, "Well, hi, Ricky. You came in late today. We missed you." To Ricky's mother T says, "He's got a little bit of milk left in the bottle. Why don't you take it? We'll keep the full ones." T carries the bottles to the refrigerator while also carrying Ricky.

Lauren is sitting on the carpet crying. The other teacher asks about putting Lauren to bed. "No. I'll wait awhile. She gets her medicine about noon. We'll put her to bed after that."

T holds both Lauren and Ricky on her lap and sings a song—

> "Trot, Trot to Boston.
> Trot, Trot to Maine.
> Trot, Trot to Providence,
> And b—a—ck (leans children back) again."

T bounces both children on her knee. "Whoopee!" T claps after singing. Andrew joins in the clapping. "You're a good clapper, Andrew," says T.

Kurt pulls to his knees in the highchair. T says, "Sit down, Kurt. Kurt sit. Kurt sit." Kurt sits back down.

T says to Lauren, who is still on T's knee, "Are you getting tired, Lauren?" She cradles Lauren in her arm and rocks her a little.

so far as is practical. Infants when teething need a firm rubber object to gnaw on.

A practical health hint is to remove the mouthed object for later disinfecting to keep germs from spreading. Some centers keep a special container in each room where such "used" toys are stashed to be disinfected at the end of the day. Thus, the toys are out of sight and not a temptation to the child anymore.

It is important that caregivers all keep their hands clean. A box of premoistened wipes should be on each shelf to use for quick cleanups for adults and for children. Plenty of tissues should

also be available so the caregivers do not have to leave the room to find one when a little nose needs wiping. Be sure to clean your hands with the wipes after helping a child blow his or her nose. You'll be surprised at how many colds you might cut short with this routine attention to germ removal.

Allow crawling babies to roam in an enclosed area. They should be able to pull up to a sturdy chair or shelf. They will enjoy pulling up to a mirror and patting the baby they see there. A small carpeted platform for crawling up on and over will be of interest, though infants may get

Ricky falls while moving. "Ricky, what was that about?" asks T. Ricky gets up.

Kurt is kneeling on the chair again. T, holding Lauren, stands and says to Lauren, "Let's go talk to Kurt. Kurt, I know you want to see the people over there, but you need to sit on your bottom." She takes Kurt out of the highchair and sits him on the floor.

11:10 A.M.

T says, "Let's get some toys out." She sits Lauren down on the floor and takes a box of musical pull toys from the shelf. T says, "Here we go. Let's make pretty sounds." T demonstrates pulling the musical toy. T says, "Try that, Lauren. Here's the handle. You're going to make some music."

T pulls a small wagon that also has a musical sound and a toy Snoopy dog riding in it. T says, "Ricky, we can take Snoopy for a ride. He's in the wagon." Ricky brings an elephant to the wagon. "Oh, you want the elephant in, too. You're going to give elephant a good ride, Ricky." T holds Ricky's hand while they pull the wagon a few steps.

T smiles as Lauren makes music by shaking the toy. T imitates Lauren shaking the toy. "Is that fun? You've got both hands filled." Lauren gives T one of her toys. T shakes it. They both shake their toy simultaneously. Lauren smiles. "This is fun, Lauren," says T. The other infants watch.

11:15 A.M.

*Briget Blaszczynski, a Michigan State University senior honors student in the child development and teaching major, made a series of observations focusing on the role of teachers of infants. Observations were made in an NAEYC-accredited child care center in February. The observations show a teacher (1) who was constantly alert, (2) used infant's names, (3) gave affection and reassurance, (4) used language though the infants' responses were through body language, (5) calmly redirected behavior, (6) was prepared for typical infant behavior, (7) recognized when another activity was needed, and (8) was very busy (this being only 10 minutes of an 8-hour day). Used with permission of Briget Blaszczynski, a Mary Foley Fellowship recipient, 1988–89.

up on top and need help getting down. Babies who are beginning to let loose from their support (the chair or wall) to start walking may be dangerous to themselves or others if they are carrying objects. Watch carefully for objects that are hard enough to hurt if the baby hits them as he or she falls down. You will enjoy giving an adventuring near-walker your hand so he or she can try to walk. What an exciting day to report to the parents! Always remember to report to them.

Do not worry about babies' frequent falls as they start walking. With a layer of diaper and with their short legs and flexible joints, they seldom hurt themselves. Avoid verbal exclamations that might cause an infant to be fearful. Of course, keep them from heights where falls would hurt.

The infant's grasp is a whole-fist grasp. Even so, the baby may like to use a crayon for marking on a large sheet of paper while sitting at a table. It is good to use a seat fastened to the table. The infants usually explore with the large size crayon, and follow the line with interest. During the first attempts, the lines will be undirected and randomly placed on the page. Remember, the baby may want to chew the crayon. Tell the infant,

Safety-type cribs wheel right out the safety door in case of fire, make a safe environment, and contribute to the baby's developing sense of trust. (U.S. Army Child Development Services, Baumholder, Germany)

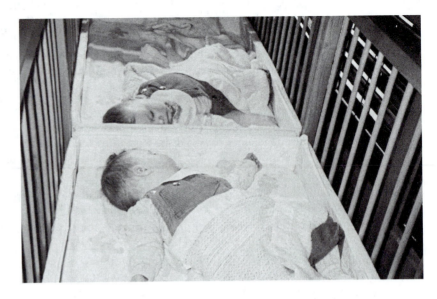

"Mark here," as you point to the paper. Put the crayons out of sight when the infant finishes because crayons should be used in a specific place when you have time to supervise.

Conclusions

Activities for infants are planned based on what research reveals about typical development of infants and on the individual child's developmental level as observed in the center. One caregiver can typically handle only three or four babies in groups of no more than eight babies. Caregivers give infants full care and carry out all activities with them. Because bonding is so important, the fewer caregivers who handle the babies, the more secure the infants will be. Efforts to support the parents in bonding with their infant are highly desirable.

Planning for the infants requires a stimulating environment that gives babies something to look at and respond to. Each area of an infant's development is considered in planning. Communication with parents is vital, such as giving them information on new milestones the baby has reached and on any problems that may have arisen during the day.

Applications

1. Do the "Talk It Over" activity.
2. List the four development areas and under each one list five ideas suggested for stimulating that area of development in infants.
3. Define *bonding* and think of the ways your center is fostering bonding (a) with parents and (b) with staff.
4. Work with an experienced caregiver or parent. Record details of what you did and what the baby did. What items fit with what you have read in this chapter? What items do you need more information on?
5. Make a detailed written observation for 5 to 10 minutes of a teacher or caregiver working in an infant care center. Summarize your conclusions.

Study Questions

1. State the three main principles of planning for infants.
2. State goals for infants. State the basis for these goals.
3. List the names of researchers cited in the chapter. Look each person up in a child

development text and write a paragraph on what each contributed to child development knowledge.

4. State the developmental areas discussed and list activities under each area that would help an infant develop further.

5. List the activities suggested for involving parents in the infant's development and education.

6. List the characteristics of high-quality infant caregivers.

Videotapes

Caring for Infants and Toddlers
17 minutes

Dr. Bettye M. Caldwell discusses how the unique needs of infants and toddlers are met in group care. NAEYC Media, 1509 16th St. NW, Washington, DC 20036-1426, 1-800-424-2460.

A Secure Beginning
30 minutes

Follows the development of children's relationships to others, examining attachment, dependence, and independence. Based on work of Dr. Thelma Harms and Debby Cryer. DC/TATS MEDIA, Frank Porter Graham Child Development Center, University of North Carolina at Chapel Hill CB8040, 300 NCNB Plaza, Chapel Hill, NC 27599-8040.

Training System for Caregivers
30 minutes

California Department of Education, Child Development Division, 560 J Street, Suite 220, Sacramento, CA 95814.

Seeing Infants With New Eyes
26 minutes

Work of Magda Gerber who shows how adult interactions make a difference with infants. NAEYC Media, 1509 16th St. NW, Washington, DC 20036-1426, 1-800-424-2460.

Caring for Our Children
30 minutes each

Part 1. Standards and You
Part 2. Basic Caregiving
Part 3. Ready for Anything
Part 4. Setting Up for Health and Safe Care
Part 5. Keeping It in Shape
Part 6. When Children Are Ill

American Academy of Pediatrics and NAEYC produced videos to support high-quality infant care. Set of six. NAEYC Media, 1509 16th St. NW, Washington, DC: 20036-1426, 1-800-424-2460.

Infant Curriculum: Great Explorations
20 minutes

Exploration is essential in infancy. Focuses on stages of development from birth through 15 months. Uses routines to support an infant's explorations. NAEYC Media, 1509 16th St. NW, Washington, DC 20036-1426, 1-800-424-2460.

Additional Readings

Brazelton, T. Berry. *On Becoming a Family: The Growth of Attachment.* New York: Dell, 1981.

——. *Infants and Mothers.* New York: Dell, 1983.

——. *To Listen to a Child: Understanding the Normal Problems of Growing Up.* Boston: Addison-Wesley, 1984.

——. *What Every Baby Knows.* Boston: Addison-Wesley, 1987.

Caruso, David A. "Infants' Exploratory Play: Implications for Child Care." *Young Children* 40:1, November 1984, 27–30.

——. "Play and Learning in Infancy: Research and Implications." *Young Children* 43:6, September 1988, 63–70.

Castle, Kathryn. *The Infant & Toddler Handbook: Invitations for Optimum Development.* Atlanta, GA: Humanics Limited, 1983.

Dittmann, Laura L. "Finding the Best Care for Your Infant or Toddler." *Young Children* 41:3, March 1986, 43–46.

Eheart, Brenda K., and Robin Lynn Leavitt. "Supporting Toddler Play." *Young Children* 40:3, March 1985, 18–22.

Greenberg, Polly. *Character Development: Encouraging Self-Esteem & Self-Discipline in Infants, Toddlers, & Two-Year-Olds.* Washington, DC: NAEYC, 1995.

Honig, Alice Sterling. "Risk Factors in Infants and Young Children." *Young Children* 39:4, May 1984, 60–73.

Hughes, Fergus P., James Elicker, and Linn C. Veen. "A Program of Play for Infants and Their Caregivers." *Young Children* 50:2, January 1995, 52–58.

Jalongo, Mary Renck. "Do Security Blankets Belong in Preschool?" *Young Children* 42:3, March 1987, 3–8.

Lally, J. Ronald. "The Impact of Child Care Policies and Practices on Infant/Toddler Identity Formation." *Young Children* 51:1, November 1995, 58–67.

NAEYC. "What Is Curriculum for Infants in Family Day Care (or Elsewhere)?" *Young Children* 42:5, July 1987, 58–62.

Pizzo, Peggy Daly. "Family-Centered Head Start for Infants and Toddlers: A Renewed Direction for Project Head Start." *Young Children* 45:6, September 1990, 30–35.

Reinsberg, Judy. "Reflections on Quality Infant Care." *Young Children* 50:6, September 1995, 23–25.

Ross, Helen Warren. "Integrating Infants With Disabilities? Can 'Ordinary' Caregivers Do It?" *Young Children* 47:3, March 1992, 65–71.

Weiser, Margaret G. *Group Care and Education of Infants and Toddlers.* Upper Saddle River, NJ: Merrill/Prentice Hall, 1986.

White, Burton. *The First Three Years of Life.* Upper Saddle River, NJ: Prentice Hall, 1984.

Wilson, LaVisa C. *Infants & Toddlers: Curriculum and Teaching.* Albany, NY: Delmar, 1990.

CHAPTER 8

Activities for Toddlers

S. Masud

Objectives

✔ Identify developmental goals for toddlers.
✔ Identify activities appropriate for toddlers.
✔ Identify strategies for working with toddlers.

Carol and Susan were together at Carol's house to celebrate their second birthdays, which fell two days apart. While their mothers were fixing dinner, the two toddlers went to Carol's room to play. They found the open vaseline jar on the diapering table. They touched it, smelled it, then began using it to finger paint on the bedroom wall. They were playing very quietly as they explored the greasy medium as it slid over the wallpaper.

These two children had been toddlers for a year. They played together frequently and enjoyed each other's company. Their parents also enjoyed being together and frequently arranged outings so the girls could play together and the parents could visit.

Infants turn into toddlers by virtue of learning to walk. For some, walking comes at eight months, whereas for others it may come as late as eighteen months. On the average, walking begins at twelve months of age. The toddler period lasts from about age one to around two-and-a-half years of age.

A toddler's walk or toddle is different from the walk of an older child. The baby's legs are short relative to the length of the trunk. The bones are cushioned with cartilage, creating a flexible resiliency when the toddler falls. The diaper makes the pelvic region appear far bigger than it really is and also provides a protective padding for the numerous falls that the toddler will take. The toddle is a side-to-side walk with legs at first somewhat rigid compared to the heel-to-toe walk with forward momentum of the child after age three.

Once infants walk they are far more vulnerable to accidents. They can move very quickly when they want to. Their motor skill development has far outstripped their reasoning capacity, so they cannot foresee the dangers into which their motor skills can place them, for example, behind a car in the driveway or up on the kitchen cabinet. Being the parent or caregiver for a toddler requires additional vigilance and precaution compared to caring for an infant.

Toddlers are said to have short attention spans—unless they are doing something they particularly want to do. When the toddler gets quiet is the time for the parent to get going and check up on the toddler. This is a simple rule for parents and caregivers to follow. For example, the two toddlers in the anecdote that opened this chapter were celebrating their second birthdays together. They "finger painted" with vaseline on the bedroom wall. Their mothers, fixing dinner in an adjoining room, wondered why things had gotten so quiet—then they found out!

The vaseline anecdote also points out that toddlers can get into household supplies that could

Teaching toddlers calls for staying close by and giving each individual encouragement. (Kansas State University)

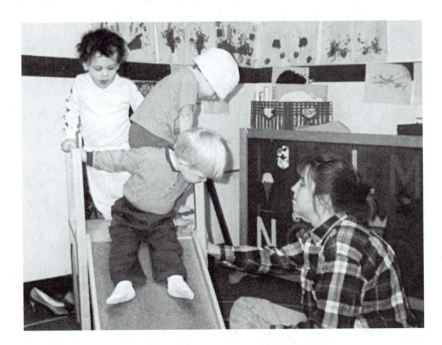

A toddler has a long attention span when she follows her own interests, like exploring a leaf she picks up in her forefinger grasp. (Rebecca Peña Hines, photographer)

be dangerous to them. In this case, the vaseline was not harmful to them, but cleaning supplies found under a sink are dangerous, often poisonous, and thousands of young children are harmed by such materials every year.

TODDLER DEVELOPMENT AS THE BASIS FOR PLANNING

The developmental characteristics of toddlers determine the goals and strategies for working with them. As with infants, teachers and caregivers study carefully the research for the general characteristics of toddlers. This information provides the usual stages of development and tells the range in months when certain milestones are typically achieved by children.

After understanding developmental information, each teacher must study the particular children in the group to assess where individual children are developmentally and plan strategies, activities, and expectations accordingly. Children generally need to follow every step in a sequence of development, though one can expect individual differences in how long a child stays at any given stage. The booklet edited by Sue Bredekamp, *Developmentally Appropriate Practice in Early Childhood Programs Serving Children from Birth Through Age 8,*[1] is a consensus of members of the NAEYC of ways to apply developmental characteristics to strategies for planning for and working with children of various age groups from birth through age eight.

The term "developmentally appropriate" in the booklet's title has been discussed at length by the members of NAEYC. **Developmentally**

---

[1]Washington, DC: NAEYC, 1987.

Soft balls are enjoyed by toddlers as they roll them on the floor or in the grass outdoors. Don't expect them to play ball as you might a few years later on. (Ishien Li, photographer)

appropriate refers to both the age appropriateness and the individual appropriateness of the program. For example, the appropriate goals for the toddler stage come from child development research. These goals are combined with the strategies that generally work with toddlers; then, goals and strategies are linked with the individual characteristics of each child to arrive at plans that are considered developmentally appropriate for a given child in a toddler center.

The number of toddlers in each group is kept at ten or fewer, with two adult caregivers to each group, or a ratio of 1:5. One important reason two adults are needed in every room is to ensure adequate safety in the group if one caregiver must do something special for one child in an emergency situation.[2]

THEMES FOR ACTIVITIES

It helps most teachers to decide on a theme for a one- to two-week period. From this theme the

pictures are selected for the bulletin boards. Puzzles and books are selected according to the theme. Toys that contribute to the theme may be placed on the shelves, as well as scientific artifacts and the like. Themes selected should be based on the toddlers' interests and the environment that is near at hand. That is, in a rural area a farming theme might cover many items and be offered frequently, whereas in a seaside school there would be more emphasis on boats and fish than the rural school would offer. Themes are a framework or focus for many learning activities. Many routine activities remain the same for toddlers, even when using themes. Themes serve the purpose of furnishing inspiration and stimulation not only to toddlers but to the teachers for whom life could become rather mundane if they planned the same activities every day.

Some schools overemphasize holiday themes to the neglect of other information and boredom for the children may set in after a while. High-quality schools try to use more developmentally suitable themes, leaving holiday information to take its place within the framework of other concepts a child must learn. Most holiday concepts are very abstract and far beyond the real under-

---

[2]For details regarding NAEYC consensus on staff-child ratios see Sue Bredekamp, ed., *Accreditation Criteria and Procedures of the National Academy of Early Childhood Programs* (Washington, DC: NAEYC, 1984).

Toddlers usually play side by side in *parallel play*, enjoying the company of others but keeping to their own toy and using little conversation. (Pennsylvania State University)

standing of toddlers. Much holiday activity is overstimulating and thus tiring to toddlers.

DEVELOPMENTAL FOCUS OF ACTIVITIES

A discussion follows that focuses on strategies for teachers and activities appropriate for toddlers to fulfill the following developmental goals:

1. building a sense of autonomy and self-efficacy,
2. encouraging social skill development,
3. stimulating language and cognitive development, and
4. stimulating physical-motor development.

Building a Sense of Autonomy and Self-efficacy

Autonomy
Building a sense of **autonomy** is proposed by psychologist Erik Erikson for the child's second and third year of life.[3] This stage builds on the

---

[3]Lawrence Schiamberg, *Child and Adolescent Development* (New York: Macmillan, 1988), p. 45.

sense of trust that developed during the first year. You have studied Erikson's theory in your previous courses in child development. Now you will see autonomy expressed before your very eyes. The children want to use all their powers to move, to talk, to reason, and to learn. During this period toddlers learn they can make things happen by deciding. They start saying "no" when people begin asking them to do things. Though this stage is frequently frustrating to parents, it is one of progress for the toddlers.

The stage of autonomy frustrates parents frequently because they now have to cope with the child's blossoming individuality, whereas the infant had not challenged parental authority. Often toddlers actually say "no" to something they'd really like. Thus, adults learn to avoid asking, "Would you like _____?" Rather, they present a situation in an interesting way, and the child's natural motivation to explore supersedes the recently found freedom of saying "no."

You will deal with toddlers in many routine situations. Learn to state your guidance in positive form. For example, say, "Use your fork for the meat," rather than "Don't use your fingers." Realize that the child can refuse to eat or sleep

Toddlers can reach objects by standing on tiptoes. Remember they can reach dangerous heights, too, so keep your eyes on them. (Cloud County, Kansas Community College)

and that you'll have to respect the child's decision. Avoid getting into power struggles with toddlers. They often win!

Self-efficacy

Self-efficacy, one aspect of autonomy, is the child's feeling of self-confidence that is so evident in the early days of toddlerhood. Albert Bandura, a prominent social psychologist, writes that **self-efficacy** means the individual's belief in his or her own ability to perform a behavior. Toddlers, it seems, believe they can do anything—at least they want to try. So, why not? Self-efficacy is an attitude that adults in children's lives should want to preserve in them forever. Throughout life there will always be new things to learn, and an attitude of "of course I can learn that" will be a marvelous asset!

Bandura finds that self-efficacy comes from the following four sources:[4]

1. Personal accomplishment. Success encourages the individual to repeat the behavior. Success with one task tends to generalize to other tasks.
2. Vicarious experience. Seeing others successfully do a task and enjoying a behavior encourages a new learner to try it.
3. Verbal persuasion. Verbal prompting and reassurance may encourage a small child to make efforts to try various tasks. "You can do it," is said hundreds of times by parents and caregivers. Bandura's studies suggest that verbal persuasion is weak if a history of failure is present.[5]
4. Emotional arousal. Good feelings result from success, and fear and anxiety often accompany failure. According to Bandura, people with high self-efficacy are spurred to greater efforts when confronted by obstacles. Those who perceive themselves as inefficacious dwell on their personal deficiencies and experience stress and ineffectiveness.[6]

According to Bandura's studies, personal accomplishment is the most powerful source of information about one's self-efficacy. Thus, the earliest experiences of infants and toddlers are laying the foundation for the child's future.[7]

Individuality

We give toddlers recognition of their individuality by frequently calling them by their names. One's name is part of his or her self-concept. We talk to

[4]Albert Bandura, *Social Foundations of Thought and Action: A Social Cognitive Theory* (Upper Saddle River, NJ: Prentice Hall, 1986), pp. 399–401.
[5]Albert Bandura, *Social Learning Theory* (Upper Saddle River, NJ: Prentice Hall, 1977), p. 82.
[6]Bandura, *Social Foundations*, p. 394.
[7]For more on the application of Bandura's work, see Verna Hildebrand, "Young Children's Self-Care and Independence Tasks: Applying Self-Efficacy Theory," *Early Child Development and Care* 30 (1988), 199–204.

toddlers individually about something, perhaps their pet or sibling, that is different for each child. These conversations go on while other children are playing. Because of toddlers' egocentrism, don't expect them to be interested in hearing very much about each other in a group time.

Toddlers love to see themselves in photos and announce, "That's me." Therefore, the center displays photos liberally. Teachers frequently take photos on a home visit and use the photos for display in the classroom or to make a storybook about children in the group. If they do, it often becomes the favorite book and may be used every day. Many teachers keep a camera handy to record current moments at the center that the children would surely like to remember.

With all activities that give toddlers a sense of autonomy and self-efficacy comes the positive self-esteem for which everyone strives. Careful attention to developmental characteristics will prevent teachers from pressing children to achieve tasks beyond their developmental means. Tasks beyond their developmental means could be such demands as making children sit still for a long time, or telling them to be quiet, or forcing them to share a toy, or making them listen to a very long story when two short ones would be better.

The toddlers' parents will be guided by teachers to understand and appreciate their child in terms of the appropriate developmental level. Discussions, readings, films, and other means are employed by capable teachers to help parents appreciate more fully their children's accomplishments. However, some parents will argue that when children reach elementary school (or high school, or college) they are going to have to do what everyone else does, or wait their turn, or in some ways conform and that, therefore, they should have to conform in a toddler center to get ready for the next level. The professional answer, understanding the developmental point of view, is that if parents and teachers allow the children to develop fully and fulfill the developmental tasks of the early ages, they will be ready for the tasks of the next age. (Review the developmental

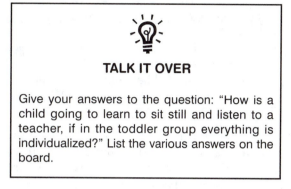

TALK IT OVER

Give your answers to the question: "How is a child going to learn to sit still and listen to a teacher, if in the toddler group everything is individualized?" List the various answers on the board.

tasks that were presented in Chapter 2 as the basis for goals for early childhood programs.)

Recall some instances in your own schooling where you were very happy and satisfied or were dissatisfied. Speculate on what made the difference. Share experiences with classmates.

Encouraging Social Skill Development

Two-year-old Ellen asked, "Can I help?" when her grandmother was setting the table for supper. Her grandmother asked, "How did you learn to put on the silverware like this?" Ellen quickly and proudly replied, "At my Children's Center."

Ellen's teacher encouraged helping skills in the young toddlers by letting them help serve their snack and clean up after their lunch. She did not involve the children because they were already competent, for of course they dropped things and spilled things. The teacher's goal was one of increasing the children's competence. In other words, it takes time, probably more time, to involve children in the routine tasks of a center, but their competency improves when teachers do involve them. The same can be said if parents involve children at home.

There are many, many opportunities in a center for children to help themselves, help other children, and help the teachers. Adults serve children well when they encourage that helping. An older toddler can hold the book and "read" a story to a younger one. Children like the respon-

TEN MINUTES IN A TODDLER TEACHER'S LIFE

Student observations in a toddler group, of a teacher called T. Four children were T's primary responsibility in a group of eight toddlers. All are about eighteen months of age. The group has been divided between two teachers. The following notes depict 10 consecutive minutes selected from several hours of direct observations.*

10:10 A.M.

T goes into the kitchen and brings out two dishpans full of warm, sudsy water. The dishpans are set on a platform about 6 inches high made by laying two large 12-by-18-inch wooden blocks side by side on the floor. Cotton rugs are placed on the blocks and on the floor to absorb anticipated spills. Sponges and washcloths are nearby. Small terry towels are hung on the back of a chair. The toddlers gather around the dishpans, anticipating the water play.

T says, "We will wash the babies." She puts four small rubber dolls on the floor nearby.

Chris cries. T comforts her and says, "Chris, what happened?" Chris quits crying. T pushes up Chris's sleeves. Chris puts a doll in the water.

T rolls up Dave's sleeves before he reaches in the water. "Here, Dave, wash the baby." (To tune, Mulberry Bush) T sings, "This is the way we wash our babies . . . early in the morning."

T directs each toddler, "Josh, here's a baby. Logan, wash the baby. Here, Dave, here's a baby. Wash his tummy. That's the way." T repeats the song, "This is the way we wash our babies. . . . "

When Dave squeezes the sponge outside the dishpan, T says, "Dave, keep the water in the dishpan."

When Logan lifts his doll out and starts to carry it away, T asks, "Here, Logan, do you want to dry the baby?" T hands Logan a towel. "That's it, dry the baby with the towel." Logan smiles and dries the doll, then drops it as a final gesture. He claps. T says, "Good!" Logan goes to a toy shelf nearby.

10:15 A.M.

T gives a sponge to Chris and says, "Chris, you can wash the baby." Chris washes the doll and plays in the suds.

Dave turns aside to squeeze the sponge on the floor. "Dave, keep your sponge over the dishpan. Wash the baby," says T.

---

sibility of running an errand for the teacher. Each can take a turn at a cleanup time job.

At times we can teach toddlers how to be gentle so they can help a friend. For instance, Jed was crying bitterly on his first day at school. Michael gently reached out to caress Jed's chin as though to say, "Cheer up, old chap." Jed calmed down and nestled into the teacher's arms. Michael, even at a tender age, had helped one

who later became a friend. An expression of empathy is surprising in one as young as Michael. "That's nice," said the teacher. "You want Jed to like school, don't you Michael?"

Parallel Play Stage

Toddlers may still play at the **solitary** play stage, playing alone with a toy without regard for others present. However, with some social experience

T winds up a musical toy Logan brings to her. "Make it go, Logan," she says.

T says, "Josh, you are washing the baby's face. Good."

T says, "Dave, squeeze it over the dishpan; you'll get all wet. Over the dishpan. Over the dishpan, Dave," as she places her hands on his shoulders and turns him around to the dishpan. "There you go. Good."

T pushes up Chris's sleeves again. "We want you to stay dry, Chris."

Jack, who belongs in the other group, passes by and gives T a hug. T returns the hug and says, "Hi, Jack."

T says to Dave again, "Dave, the water needs to stay in the dishpan. Do you want to dry your baby? Here's a towel, Dave. Want to dry the baby?"

Dave shakes his head, "No."

T echo's Dave's "No. You aren't finished yet?"

Dave squeezes water on the floor again with the sponge. T reminds him, "Over the dishpan, Dave, over the dishpan."

Chris looks at the sponge, then puts it in her mouth. T says, "Chris, you won't like that. Wash the baby with it. Wash the baby."

Logan cries, unable to get on a chair. T says, "Here Logan," and turns a chair so Logan can get up on it.

Chris moves her leg as if she intends to get in the dishpan of water. T lifts Chris away from the dishpan, saying, "This water is for the babies. Give your baby a bath, Chris." Chris smacks her lips looking at T. T smacks her lips as though giving a kiss, and smiles at Chris.

10:20 A.M.

*Briget Blaszczynski, a Michigan State University senior honors student in the child development and teaching major, made a series of observations focusing on the role of teachers of toddlers. Observations were made in an NAEYC-accredited child care center in February. The observations show a teacher (1) who was constantly alert, (2) used toddler's names, (3) gave affection and reassurance, (4) used language and responded to nonverbal cues of children, (5) calmly redirected behavior, (6) was prepared for typical toddler behavior, and (7) was very busy (this being only 10 minutes of an 8-hour day). Used with permission of Briget Blaszczynski, a Mary Foley Fellowship recipient, 1988–89.

they will move to the **parallel** play stage. In this stage a child plays alongside other children. You'll frequently see toddlers, each with a toy car or truck, scooting along on the floor and making sound effects as they go. They may talk about what they are doing or where they are going; however, the theme is still individualistic. The pretend play, often called dramatic play, is beginning to develop as language develops. Toddlers do enjoy the presence of the other children.

At the parallel play stage the teacher's role is to provide sufficient similar toys to give each child one. A new or shy child may observe for a period of time, biding his or her time before taking part. After a quiet invitation to join, after providing a suitable toy nearby, the adult should let the child take it from there. A new child may take several days to integrate into a group.

Sharing and Taking Turns
It helps social interaction if groups are small—three or four children. Adults should be nearby to guide children who have problems taking turns and sharing. For example, Kim, a toddler,

wants to join others playing with cars and trucks. It is best to help Kim find a suitable substitute, say another car or truck like the other children have. If there are no more cars or trucks, you might help Kim build a hangar nearby for airplanes. With the presence of airplanes, a hangar might be equally as interesting and perhaps even attract the interest of the children with the cars and trucks. Taking turns and sharing will come more spontaneously in older ages.

Parents should be encouraged to help their toddlers' social development by letting them play with one other child at a time. In one-to-one situations they will readily learn to use their language skills to solve social problems. Language skills are developing simultaneously with other skills. We turn now to elaborate on the connections between language and cognitive development.

Stimulating Language and Cognitive Development

Toddlers are very interested in learning new things (cognitive development) and they are simultaneously learning the language that labels new concepts. To learn to speak one must be encouraged and allowed to speak. A quiet classroom is seldom a goal in an early childhood center. A hum of spontaneous conversations is music to the ears of early childhood teachers.

The small groups of toddlers, as required for licensing, is designed to facilitate one-to-one interaction. This fits well with Lev Vygotsky's theory that social interactions are essential for children to learn language and the roles of society. In our 10 minutes with a toddler teacher, you can readily appreciate how much interpersonal conversation this busy teacher produced. Using names of children and objects, helping children focus and repeat, giving positive praise, and responding to each child's movements are all part of the social interaction Vygotsky believes is essential for language and learning, according to Berk.[8]

---

[8]Laura E. Berk, "Vygotsky's Theory: The Importance of Make-Believe Play," *Young Children* 50:1 (November 1994), 30–39.

Free to Speak

High-quality standards for early childhood schools and centers specify that there shall be several teachers with each group of children, so parents will be assured that every child will be listened to, and that someone will have time for each child. Keeping the groups small enables each child to have ample opportunity for self-expression. No child should go unnoticed like one kindergartner who said sadly, "The teacher didn't call my name once today."

Books

Offering books early in children's lives sows the seeds of literacy. Books offer boundless opportunity to learn information about topics within the children's lives and beyond. Toddlers learn words for the new concepts presented. They learn to question and comment on the stories and ideas. As they relate illustrations to the topic, they are, in fact, learning to "read." They may make up their own stories and hear them read. An early clue to whether a child has had books read to him or her before is whether the child turns the book right side up when it is presented upside down.

Books are essential in classrooms. By using the public library, teachers can extend the offerings in literature. Special stories can be developed for telling. Poetry can be read or recited. Children will join in the repeat refrain when there is one in a poem, just as they join in the chorus of a song.

Books should be read to individual toddlers or to groups of no larger than four or five. It is far better to let each teacher manage a small group of children for a story that all five will listen to attentively than try to manage a large group, with the period spent admonishing children on how to behave. After some months of having stories in small groups, the children can have a larger group for a storytime occasionally—perhaps also for a slide show, film strip, or video story.

Some teachers argue that they need to hold "large group time" because children will eventually have to behave appropriately in a much larger group. However, toddlers come from homes where, if they have had stories, their storytime has been one-to-one on a parent's lap. Including four other children in storytime is a big leap forward, but not the giant step that meeting with ten other children would be. For children from disadvantaged homes, who may be having their first exposure to books, the small group and one-to-one format is essential. By individualizing the approach to literature, the teacher can excite children about the wonderful world of picture books. Parents can be encouraged to contribute to the child's developing literacy by borrowing library books to read at home.

Songs

Songs also give toddlers opportunities to practice their vocabularies and their listening and expressive language skills. It is delightful to watch and listen to toddlers singing the songs they have learned. One gets a firm sense of the strength of their memories. Some may sing at home, yet not at school, so don't be discouraged if they appear to be observers.

Many songs that toddlers will enjoy are listed in Chapter 16 on music. First, you must enjoy the songs because enjoyment is catching. Prepare a few simple songs ahead of time and jot down the words even if you think you know them well. Keep the verses short, the rhythm strong, and the repeat obvious, and children will soon be singing along with you. Make a set of song cards to carry in your pocket, so you'll learn the old standbys of the early childhood teachers. Think up new words for old tunes as you help children put toys away or wash up for snack. They will enjoy this game and join in with you. They will be practicing language and cognitive skills in the process.

Cognitive development is fostered by all the language activities suggested. Informational concepts are selected from the toddlers' closest environments, the home and family and the school and classmates.

Hands-on Activities

Hands-on activity is the rule for early childhood cognitive experiences, and it is especially important in toddler groups. Never expect to tell toddlers much in a "lecture" type presentation. Rather, let them handle objects, talk about them, label them, and relate them to things they've seen before. One teacher should be close by to listen and respond to children's comments.

Perceptual-Motor Toys

Perceptual-motor toys such as puzzles, simple puzzle or form boards, and nested boxes are taken apart and put together repeatedly by toddlers. They feel a great sense of accomplishment when their puzzle is back together again. They gain perceptions of parts and wholes. Such toys are self-correcting, because children can see immediately what they have done correctly or incorrectly.

Art Activities

Art materials give toddlers opportunities to learn their colors and to use tools of writing and drawing. As you will read in the chapter on art (Chapter 10), the child will scribble during the first experiences with a drawing tool. Scribbling is characteristic of children even into their fourth year as they await maturation of small muscles and eye-hand coordination.

Provide bits of colored and textured materials the children can glue in random designs of their own choice. To help instill creativity—a highly prized possession—no patterns or models are offered. Simply supply large sheets of plain paper on which the child can create a drawing or collage of interest to him or her.

Craft-type activities like making a caterpillar out of an egg carton or a flowerpot out of a cottage cheese carton are avoided because they do not contribute to expressions of individual creativity. They often require extensive adult directions to which the toddler is totally unable to respond. Teachers who attempt these projects end up doing the vast majority of the work for the child, which, of course, obviates the goals of self-expression completely.

Stimulating Physical-Motor Development

The newfound freedom to move is a primary characteristic of the toddler period. What fun they have toddling to and fro and finally running! They will generally move without encouragement. In fact, most activities designed for cognitive, social, or language development succeed best if toddlers can move while doing them—and often fail if the requirement is to sit still while doing them. Most toddlers get plenty of exercise. Exercise, of course, is essential for the development and maintenance of a healthy body.

Being outdoors is highly desirable and toddlers should be taken outdoors every day. Outdoor play requires that a system be developed to get the toddlers dressed and outside quickly to avoid overheating from the warm outdoor clothing they wear. Getting outside can be a big motivator for children to learn to help dress themselves. Teachers must work with parents to be sure the clothing provided is easy to take off and put on.

The period from age one to age six is a critical period for the development of locomotor skills, according to motor skill research being done at Michigan State University by Vern Seefeldt and John Haubenstricker. Their findings are derived from analyzing miles of movie film taken of children being tested on various skills. They have been able to describe the stages of motor skill development. Several photos from this study and stages the researchers have described are included in Chapter 9 of this book. The proficiency barrier arises at kindergarten age, wherein children need to have achieved the fundamental locomotion skills before age five or they will have difficulty later on with the skills required of youngsters in elementary school. The studies also show that elementary children referred to them with learning disabilities frequently have poorly developed motor skills and low levels of self-esteem.[9]

New snow is fascinating to toddlers as they make tracks. Be sure they are properly attired before allowing them to enjoy the snow. (C. Hildebrand, photographer)

Seefeldt and Haubenstricker encourage early childhood educators to practice motor skills deliberately with children rather than leave this important learning to chance. Their studies show that with instruction children can achieve desired motor skills and that children enjoy this instruction when it is matched with activities just right for their level of motor skill development. Their studies support including instruction and practice on motor skills in any program for young children.

Toddlers enjoy using their newfound motor skills. They quickly dress for outdoor play when they realize they can go outdoors. Their throwing and catching skills are in early formative stages. Therefore, they do not make good partners for each other, but need adult partners who can adjust to the throwing or catching needs fitting the children's skill level. For example, stage-one

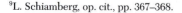

[9]L. Schiamberg, op. cit., pp. 367–368.

catchers stand facing a throwing partner without ability to move in the direction of the ball when it is thrown. Their arms encircle the ball, which typically falls through their arms before their arms close on it—even when large size balls are used.

Stage-one throwers, on the other hand, throw a ball with a back-to-front lob without moving the feet forward or aiming at the partner who is waiting for it. Young children will enjoy throwing with adults who will throw small balls that fit their small hands. Sponge balls (like Nerf) are excellent for practicing these skills. Hard balls will hurt and should be avoided.

A flopsy doodle, made of a skein of yarn tied in the middle and cut at the loops, makes a good catching object for young children, as does a crocheted ball that is soft when it hits the chest of the receiving child.

Climbing and running skills should be practiced on a regular basis. Teachers can help with this practice by participating with other children. Some teachers make obstacle courses around the yard with items to jump over, steps to climb up and down, and zigzags to follow in a path. Running will warm up children (and teachers) on a cold day.

Music

Many music activities invite the use of large muscles, and toddlers are very receptive to doing free movement activities in response to music. Here the key word is *free* because they will often resist organized activities that would require them to hold hands or do the same activity as everyone else. They will have trouble doing more than one thing at a time, for instance, doing hand movements to songs while they sing. Usually they will stop one while they concentrate on the other.

Aerobics

Aerobics have become the vogue for adults; many people use this means of exercise to stay in shape. Aerobic exercise can also be used with young children. They enjoy the rhythm of the music and the chance to move. For toddlers the instruction must be drastically simplified. Enjoyment will come from doing the exercise with others who are interested, but not from following every direction the leader gives.

Small Motor Skills

Small motor skill practice is of increasing interest to toddlers. Their pincer grasp has recently developed, which makes them able to pick up small items to pop into their mouths. They will enjoy pasting, drawing, and painting. Stringing beads may be of interest if the strings have good tips and the holes aren't too small. Dressing skills are beginning to be of interest. A toddler can unzip a coat, untie shoes, and undress dolls before being able to do the opposite action. Feeding skills are developing as the child uses the spoon and fingers to get most of a meal eaten. Encouraging the practice of all these skills adds to the child's growing independence and self-efficacy. Individual praise for a job well done is desirable.

Toilet Training

Toilet training will typically not be started before age two or even age three, depending on the child's level of maturity and interest. The muscles that control the opening to the bladder and rectum need sufficient time to mature before any control is possible. Then the child must begin to understand what the purpose is. Girls are typically toilet trained before boys the same age.

Because disposable diapers are increasingly comfortable and feel dry even when they are wet, extra time is needed to teach some children to use the toilet. In the toddler group some children will want to use the toilet, or at least to try. Teachers simply must individualize toileting. Once the child begins to be able to go to the toilet, adults must be alert to the child's need and help him or her get there before an accident takes place. Children should never be blamed or shamed for toilet accidents. Be sure to wash your hands after helping with a child's diaper or toileting, as is required in regulations for controlling diseases.

High-quality toddler care supplements the nurturing that good parents give their child. (M. Kummerow, photographer)

CONTACT WITH PARENTS

Very close cooperation must be developed between the parents and the toddlers' teachers. The toddler center is a supplement to the home. Parents should expect to learn about their toddler, and teachers should expect parents to share information that will help the child's day at the center. Systems must be in place to ensure this cooperation. As a future teacher you should be aware of your responsibility to foster this two-way street of communication for the welfare of the toddlers whom you serve.

Conclusions

Details of planning for and working with toddlers are presented in recognition of a growing responsibility for teaching rapidly increasing numbers of toddlers within the field of early childhood education. All developmental areas must be considered in planning to achieve a goal of a well-developed individual. The ratio of children to adults should be five to one, with group size kept at ten or fewer.

Toddlers have strong needs for developing autonomy and self-efficacy. Work with them should be individualized by making the offerings of the school fit the toddler, rather than trying to mold the toddler to fit the school. If parents and teachers are wise enough to recognize toddlers' developmental characteristics and are also wise enough to flow with, rather than against, these characteristics, they will find toddlers have special charm and warmth and are delightful little people with whom to work.

Applications

1. Do the "Talk It Over" activity in the chapter.
2. List the four developmental areas. Under each area write at least five ideas suggested for stimulating that area of development in toddlers.
3. Work with an experienced toddler teacher in a toddler care center or with a parent of a toddler. Record details of what you do and what the toddler does. Reread this chapter and note what items you've listed were discussed in the chapter and what items were

not. On what items do you need more information?

4. Brainstorm some themes that would be appropriate to use with a group of toddlers in your town.

Study Questions

1. Discuss the term *developmentally appropriate* and tell how it is applied in program planning.
2. What is the meaning of *autonomy*? Who wrote about autonomy? What does autonomy mean to the parent or teacher of a toddler?
3. What is the meaning of *self-efficacy*? Who wrote about self-efficacy? What does self-efficacy mean to a parent or teacher of a toddler?
4. What are some strategies for helping a toddler express individuality?
5. Describe the parallel play stage and tell how you could foster parallel play in the toddler center.

Videotapes

Developmentally Appropriate Practice: Birth Through Age 5
   27 minutes

Shows teachers and children in developmentally appropriate programs. Shows inappropriate practices. NAEYC Media, 1509 16th St. NW, Washington, DC 20036-1426, 1-800-424-2460.

Toddler Curriculum: Making Connections
   20 minutes

Shows how toddlers develop and learn in a developmentally appropriate environment. NAEYC Media, 1509 16th St. NW, Washington, DC: 20036-1426, 1-800-424-2460.

Additional Readings

Brazelton, T. Berry. *To Listen to a Child: Understanding the Normal Problems of Growing Up.* Boston: Addison-Wesley, 1984.

Da Ros, Denise, and Angela Wong. "Naptime: A Transition With Ease." *Young Children* 50:1, November 1994, 69.

Dittman, Laura L. "Finding the Best Care for Your Infant or Toddler." *Young Children* 41:3, March 1986, 43–46.

Eheart, Brenda K., and Robin Lynn Leavitt. "Supporting Toddler Play." *Young Children* 40:3, March 1985, 18–22.

French, Lucia. "Two-Year-Olds and Learning Through Language." *Young Children* 51:2, January 1996, 17–20.

Gowen, Jean W. "The Early Development of Symbolic Play." *Young Children* 50:3, March 1995, 74–84.

Honig, Alice Sterling. "Risk Factors in Infants and Young Children." *Young Children* 39:4, May 1984, 60–73.

———. "Quality Infant/Toddler Caregiving: Are There Magic Recipes?" *Young Children* 44:4, May 1989, 4–10.

Jalongo, Mary Renck. "Do Security Blankets Belong in Preschool?" *Young Children* 42:3, March 1987, 3–8.

NAEYC. "What Is Curriculum for Infants in Family Day Care (or Elsewhere)?" *Young Children* 42:5, July 1987, 58–62.

Pizzo, Peggy Daly. "Family-Centered Head Start for Infants and Toddlers: A Renewed Direction for Project Head Start." *Young Children* 45:6, September 1990, 30–35.

Schiamberg, Lawrence. *Child and Adolescent Development.* New York: Macmillan, 1988.

Stonehouse, Ann. *Trusting Toddlers: Planning for One- to Three-Year-Olds in Child Care Centers.* St. Paul, MN: Toys N Things Press, 1990.

Weiser, Margaret G. *Group Care and Education of Infants and Toddlers.* Upper Saddle River, NJ: Merrill/Prentice Hall, 1986.

White, Burton. *The First Three Years of Life.* Upper Saddle River, NJ: Prentice Hall, 1984.

Wilson, LaVisa G. *Infants & Toddlers: Curriculum and Teaching.* Albany, NY: Delmar, 1990.

CHAPTER 9

Motor Skill Activities

Kansas State University

Objectives

✔ Identify motor skill stages discovered by researchers studying the development of young children.

✔ Explain the rationale for utilizing certain procedures and equipment to foster motor skill development in children.

✔ Plan and evaluate outdoor activities involving large motor skills and other abilities.

✔ Identify and evaluate the use of space, equipment, and guidance for developing large motor skills in children.

"Hi! I'm way up here!"

"I can climb up there all by myself."

"I'm going down BACKWARDS!"

"Catch me. Okay?"

Vigorous motor skill activity is part of every high-quality early childhood program every day. You'll hear happy, exuberant exclamations like these anytime you enter a children's outdoor play yard. "Let's go bye-bye," excites the baby at home or in an infant school. Prekindergarten and kindergarten children run for their coats when their teacher says, "Time to go outside." Older children's eyes sparkle and books get shoved into desks when the recess bell rings. Even some elders are happy when friends invite them to go jogging.

Vigorous outdoor activity appeals to the young and to many oldsters as well. Exercise is essential for good health, according to authorities. Attitudes toward exercise are formed in the early years, and competencies are developing that will remain with individuals throughout their lifetimes.

Learning and practicing large and small motor skills are among the important developmental tasks (see Chapter 2). Children make progress on these and other tasks in the outdoor program of a high-quality early childhood education program.

University students are called upon to observe and help in the outdoor program. The first chapter of this section on curriculum is devoted to children's learning activities that typically take place out-of-doors. Students who appreciate these activities will be able to make meaningful contributions when they are outdoors with children during the term. So, get into your weather-suitable comfortable clothing and enjoy being in this special learning environment that most children dearly love. Be prepared to state what children learn as they play vigorously. You will have responsibility for safety, so learn the rules immediately. Stay close to the larger groups of children and ignore any adults who just wish to enjoy the sunshine and think, erroneously, that this time period isn't important.

MOTOR SKILLS AND SELF-EFFICACY

Self-efficacy refers to the individual's belief in his or her own ability to perform a behavior. Self-efficacy is a term introduced earlier when toddlers were discussed. Identified by Albert Bandura, a social psychologist, the concept of self-efficacy applies to all areas of the early childhood program. In brief, you'll recognize children's self-efficacy in their willingness and eagerness to try new things.

Bandura believes that there are four sources of self-efficacy: (1) personal accomplishment, (2) vicarious experience, (3) verbal persuasion, and (4) emotional arousal.[1]

Practicing motor-skill activities with appropriate equipment in a high-quality early childhood program offers numerous opportunities for children to maintain their self-efficacy, or feelings of self-confidence. By setting expectations at levels

Early childhood is a time to practice motor skills like jumping. (Michigan State University)

---

[1]Albert Bandura, *Social Foundations of Thought and Action: A Social Cognitive Theory* (Upper Saddle River, NJ: Prentice Hall, 1986), pp. 399–401.

where each child experiences personal accomplishment, teachers and parents contribute to the child's self-efficacy. Self-efficacy can be expressed in every area of individual expression within the program, from arrival to departure throughout the day.

You can think about your own self-efficacy. Think of something new a person like you might learn—perhaps to operate a computer or to water-ski—assuming you have not already learned those skills. The speed at which you would take up an offer to be tutored in these skills might be considered a measure of your self-confidence or self-efficacy. Would you say, "I can learn to do it!"? As an adult, you can surely recall numerous times when it was important to have confidence in learning something new. Self-efficacy is an important characteristic of each child to preserve and foster in all early childhood programs and beyond.

MOTOR SKILL DEVELOPMENT[2]

Motor skills are required to control the body. When skills for moving the body such as running, jumping, or climbing are discussed, they are called **large motor** or **gross muscular skills**. When skills such as writing, tying, or using scissors are discussed, they are called **small motor** or **fine motor skills**. According to developmental studies the pattern of motor development is predictable in its broader aspects with individual differences occurring in the timetable.[3]

Motor skill development is usually the first value of outdoor play activity that comes to mind. Large motor skills are critical to each individual's development and to the enjoyment of life. The

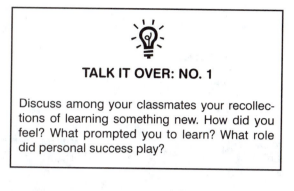

TALK IT OVER: NO. 1

Discuss among your classmates your recollections of learning something new. How did you feel? What prompted you to learn? What role did personal success play?

long lives that today's children can be expected to live make it even more critical that their physical bodies and motor skills be developed adequately.

In the typical indoor classroom, vigorous activity is not encouraged, and children may not be allowed to run, jump, climb, or catch. Although such restrictions might be expected indoors, often these large motor skills are also being curtailed outdoors. Teachers may excuse this lack of large motor skill practice by indicating that they are afraid for the children's safety, that there is little or no equipment, or that they place priority on mental tasks. However, research findings indicate that children need teachers who will plan opportunities for them to practice needed large motor skills. Wisely, many schools and centers where winter lasts many months are arranging space and schedules to allow for vigorous motor skill activity inside. This comes with the knowledge that large motor skills should not wait until spring.

At Michigan State University Drs. Vern Seefeldt, John Haubenstricker, and Crystal Branta have been engaged in a longitudinal research program designed to examine small children's physical growth, motor maturity, and motor development. The research team observed the same children every month over a period of years. They found that "rudimentary stages of the fundamental motor skills which include walking, running, hopping, jumping, skipping, leaping, throwing, catching, etc., must be established very

---

[2]The author is indebted to Dr. Vern Seefeldt and Dr. John Haubenstricker of Michigan State University for permission to use research results, descriptions of sequential stages of motor skill development, and photographs, and for consultations on the content of this section of this chapter.

[3]Lawrence Schiamberg, *Human Development* (New York: Macmillan, 1988), pp. 305–315.

When executing a Stage 3 punt, the performer steps forward with the supporting limb as the ball is released in a forward, downward direction. The striking leg then swings forward as the ball descends toward the surface.

146

Striking a ball from a tee, using a Stage 4 pattern. Striking at the Stage 4 developmental level involves a shift of the body weight to the rear or right foot of a right-handed batter. As the bat moves forward the weight is transferred to the forward or left foot. At the point of contact the body weight has rotated so that it is over the left foot, with the right foot in position to provide stability during the follow-through phase.

early in life if a child is to advance to more mature stages."[4]

In addition to this research, Seefeldt and his co-workers have organized remedial groups for children referred to them for the assessment of physical motor skills. Seefeldt says, "The children who come to us at age five with poorly established preliminary stages in fundamental motor skills are unlikely to become highly skilled, even though we provide additional sessions with a one-to-one teacher-pupil ratio."[5] As a result of their work, these researchers have grown increasingly convinced that parents and early childhood teachers must engage children in practicing these skills.

The Seefeldt team has been able to analyze the sequential stages children go through in learning many of the fundamental motor skills. They have grouped the skills as follows:

Locomotor skills—moving from place to place

walk	jump	hop	stop	fall
run	gallop	skip	start	dodge
leap	slide	roll		

Nonlocomotor skills—moving body parts, with child stationary

swing	stretch	turn	lift
sway	curl	bend	pull
rock	twist	push	

Projection and reception skills—propelling and catching objects

| catch | punt | dribble | trap |
| throw | strike | kick | bounce |

---

[4]For a detailed review of the scientific literature and a report of the Michigan State University Motor Performance Study, see Crystal Branta, John Haubenstricker, and Vern Seefeldt's chapter, "Age Changes in Motor Skills During Childhood and Adolescence," in *Exercise and Sport Sciences Review*, R. L. Terjung, ed., vol. 12 (Lexington, MA: Collamore Press, D. C. Heath, 1984), pp. 467–521.

[5]Vern Seefeldt, "The Role of Motor Skills in the Lives of Children with Learning Disabilities," paper presented at the Conference of the Association for Children with Learning Disabilities, Detroit, Michigan, March 1973.

If you have compared the way a toddler and an older sibling throw a ball, you know there are differences in their manner of handling the ball and of managing their body during the throw. Through the use of film records Seefeldt's team has been able to describe in detail the developmental sequence of many of these motor skills. Seefeldt believes that knowing these stages of development will assist parents and teachers, and later on coaches, in providing appropriate experiences for individual children. The young child should be helped to the next stage in the hierarchy rather than encouraged or pressed to skip a stage or two. For example, a child should master catching a large ball before being expected to use a baseball and glove.

Seefeldt and Haubenstricker have identified, described, and made available the developmental sequences for catching, kicking, throwing, and the standing long jump. See Figure 9–1. They have analyzed additional skills and their findings will be available in their forthcoming publications.

Figures 9–1 through 9–4 give details of the stages for four skills. With practice you can easily recognize each child's level with respect to each skill and thus make plans for activities to stimulate development toward the next stage. Records of children's stages can be recorded on charts and kept in their personal files.

PROPER EQUIPMENT AND SUPPORT

Parents and teachers can make an important contribution to children's motor skill development through providing proper equipment, sequencing the tasks to encourage the children to practice comfortably rather than competitively, and giving each some one-to-one attention. For throwing, the child should have a small ball that fits the small hand—usually a tennis ball, sponge ball, or beanbag. A patient adult should play ball with the child, because if two unskilled children attempt to play together, they won't be able to make many adjustments necessary for a successful experience for each one.

For catching, a soccer-size ball made of a soft material—rubber, sponge, or polyester fill—is needed. If you notice in the last photo on page 151, the child hugs the ball when catching it. Obviously, a tennis ball would fall through the hug. Also, the ball hits the chest and at times bumps the face, hence the ball's softness makes it less of a threat. Children in Stages 1, 2, or 3 need a patient adult to help them practice catching. Their same-stage friends will be unable to accommodate their needs.

A flopsy doodle, made with a skein of yarn tied in the middle and cut at the loops, makes a good throwing and catching object. It can be used in a room at school or home, and the yarn ends make catching it easier for some. The flopsy doodle can be carried on the head or shoulder and contribute to games the children find fun.

Skills are not specifically related to chronological age, size, or gender, but are a result of a combination of maturation and experience. Teachers and parents must remember that grouping children by chronological age, body size, or gender will still leave a wide variation in stages of motor skill development. You have heard the derogatory comment, "He throws like a girl." Generally, it means the child is stuck on Stage 2 or 3 of the throwing sequence. That is, he is stepping off on the foot that is on the same side as the throwing arm, and thus is unable to produce adequate velocity or distance on the ball. With only a little attention an adult can help a boy or girl practice stepping off with the foot that is opposite to the throwing arm, turning that side of the body toward the target, and winding up low past the hip and up. (See Stage 4 description in Figure 9-2.)

The stereotypic throws-like-a-girl comment would not be true of girls if they were given adequate practice. The study shows that there are no significant differences in boys and girls in motor skill stages initially. Differences occur only as socialization and differential practice and training take place.

TALK IT OVER: NO. 2

Discuss some games or techniques you might use that would encourage children to practice fundamental motor skills. Be creative. What are some novel ways?

For some disabled children gloves with Velcro palms will help them catch a flopsy doodle or a crocheted or knitted ball. They can feel successful in catching this way. For batting practice, a whiffle ball—a lightweight, hollow, molded polyethylene ball—may be tied to an elastic rope and suspended from a tree limb at the right height to allow children to practice batting with a plastic bat. Because the ball is attached, the child can practice alone without having to chase the ball each time after hitting it. A ball may also be placed on a rubber cone (the type used to mark a street) or on a tee to enable the young batter to practice striking a ball that is stationary. (See the photos on p.147.)

Young "round-ballers" can throw balls into wastebaskets, or hoops can be lowered to encourage their practice. A sponge ball (a Nerf ball or the like) or a crocheted or knitted ball stuffed with polyester is harmless to people and furnishings it might hit while the young child practices throwing, catching, punting, and batting. The child will not fear being hit by such a ball. Proper equipment helps young children to reach goals, and parents should be encouraged to use such equipment.

Keeping an inflated beach ball, sponge ball, or balloon in the air encourages children to stand on tiptoe and to stretch and leap. Balls and beanbags encourage the practice of projection and reception skills. Children may like to throw the balls against a wall or into a large receptacle, such as a

FIGURE 9–1

Developmental sequence of catching.

Stage 1	The arms of the performer are directly in front of the body, with the elbows extended and the palms facing upward or inward. As the ball contacts the hands or arms the elbows flex and the arms and hands attempt to secure the ball by holding it against the chest.
Stage 2	The child prepares to receive the object with the arms in front of the body, the elbows extended or slightly flexed. Upon presentation of the ball the arms begin an encircling motion that ends when the ball is secured against the chest. The arm action in Stage 2 begins before the ball contacts the body.
Stage 3	The child prepares to receive the ball with arms that are slightly flexed and extended forward at the shoulder.
	Substage 1 The child uses the chest as the first point of contact with the ball and attempts to secure the ball by holding it to the chest with the hands and arms.
	Substage 2 The child attempts to catch the ball with the hands. Failure to hold it securely results in an attempt to guide the ball to the chest, where it is controlled by the hands and arms.
Stage 4	The child prepares to receive the ball by flexing the elbows and presenting the arms toward the approaching ball. Skillful performers may keep the elbows at the sides and flex the arms simultaneously as they bring them forward to meet the ball. The ball is caught with the hands and does not contact any other body part.
Stage 5	The upper body movement is identical to that of Stage 4. In addition, the child is required to change the stationary base in order to receive the ball. Stage 5 is apparently difficult for many children when they are required to move in relation to an approaching ball.

Source: The sequences of the four motor skills described in Figures 9–1—9–4 were provided by John Haubenstricker and Vern Seefeldt from their Motor Performance Study at Michigan State University.

packing box. The smaller the child, the larger the ball required. Dribbling has been successfully taught by some teachers who had a standard gymnasium for practice. A regulation basketball is desirable for this activity. Both girls and boys enjoyed doing the skill.

An obstacle course may be set up with various pieces of equipment, and the children may be required to climb up on a packing box, jump across a plank held up by sawhorses, climb through the rungs on the jungle gym, and run down an inclined plane attached to the jungle

A three-year-old child catching a ball with a Stage 2 pattern. Catching a ball at the second development level involves placing the arms in front of the body in preparation to receive the ball. The arms begin moving toward the body while the ball is still airborne. The first point of contact occurs when the ball strikes the chest. At that instant the arms and hands encircle the ball and secure it by pressing it next to the body in a bear hug movement.

FIGURE 9–2
Developmental sequence of throwing.

Stage 1	The motion is essentially in a back-to-front or posterior-anterior direction. The feet remain fixed with little or no trunk rotation. The force of movement comes from hip flexion, moving the shoulder forward, and extending the elbow.
Stage 2	The feet gradually remain stationary with a wide base of support, but a step with the right or the left foot in the direction of the throw may be taken. The force is directed more toward a direction parallel to the floor, with the hips and trunk moving as one unit. The motion may resemble a "sling" as the body and extended arm rotate as if around a vertical axis.
Stage 3	The primary change from Stage 2 is that the movement of the foot on the same side as the throwing arm is a stride in the direction of the throw. The trunk rotation may be decreased in relation to Stage, 2, but the hip flexion is increased.
Stage 4	The movement is contralateral, with the leg opposite the throwing arm striding forward as the throwing arm moves during the "windup" phase. The stride forward with the contralateral leg provides a wide base of support and greater stability during the force production phase of the throw.
Stage 5	The windup phase begins with the throwing hand moving in a downward arc and then backward as the opposite leg moves forward. This concurrent action rotates the hip and spine into position for forceful derotation. As the contralateral foot strikes the surface, the hips, spine, and shoulders begin derotating in sequence. The contralateral leg begins to extend at the knee, providing an equal and opposite reaction to the throwing arm. The arm opposite the throwing limb also moves forcefully toward the body to assist in the "equal and opposite" reaction.

gym. Such a game gives children the opportunity to practice several fundamental skills.

The teacher can encourage jumping by placing one end of a bamboo fishing pole on the ground and the other end on a sawhorse or jungle gym for the children to jump over. The fishing pole should be loosely held, so that if the child hits the pole while jumping, the pole will fall easily and the child will not be hurt. The angle of the pole allows the children to jump where they are ready—high or low. This exercise requires propelling the body up and over. The teacher can encourage the long jump by marking a V shape on the grass or tumbling mat and encouraging the children to jump where they can make it across. Children typically fall after a jump, making the softer surface important. Avoidance of failure is important, and competition between children should also be avoided. Games of hopscotch give good hopping and jumping practice. Boys and girls should be equally encouraged to practice all skills.

Nonlocomotor skills can be combined with locomotor skills through music and rhythm activ-

Throwing a ball with a Stage 4 pattern. The throw at a Stage 4 developmental level involves opposition of movement between the arms and the feet; as the throwing arm (right) moves backward in the preparatory phase, the left foot moves forward to receive the weight as the arm moves forward to release the ball. The force of the throw is shifted to the left foot as the body "follows through" its motion after the throw.

FIGURE 9–3

Developmental sequence of kicking.

Stage 1	The performer is usually stationary and positioned near the ball. Knee joint extension occurs after contacting the ball, resulting in a pushing rather than a striking action. The knee of the kicking leg continues to extend. If the trunk is inclined forward, the performer will step forward to gain balance. If the trunk is leaning backward, the kicking leg will move backward to achieve body balance after the kick.
Stage 2	The performer is stationary. The kicking leg moves forward with the knee joint in a flexed position. Knee joint extension begins just prior to foot contact with the ball. Arm-leg opposition occurs during the kick. Knee extension continues after the ball leaves the foot, but the force is usually not sufficient to move the body forward. Instead, the performer usually steps sideward or backward.
Stage 3	The performer takes one or more deliberate steps to approach the ball. The kicking foot stays near the surface as it approaches the ball, resulting in less flexion than in Stage 2. The trunk remains nearly upright, preventing maximum force production. The knee begins to extend prior to contact. The force of the kick may carry the performer past the point of contact if the approach was vigorous.
Stage 4	The approach involves one or more steps with the final "step" being an airborne run or leap providing hyperextension of the hip and flexion of the knee. The shoulders are retracted and the trunk is inclined backward as the supporting leg begins to move forward. The movement of the thigh nearly stops as the knee joint begins to extend rapidly just prior to contact with the ball. In the follow-through, if the forward momentum of the kick is sufficient, the performer either hops on the support leg or scissors the legs while airborne in order to land on the kicking foot.

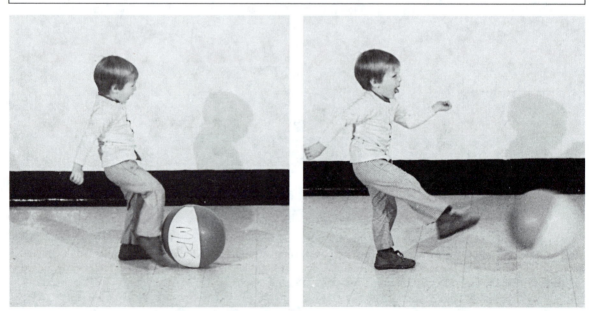

Kicking a ball with a Stage 2 pattern. Kicking involves striking a stationary ball with the foot. Kicking is learned with less difficulty than punting because the former eliminates the need to relate to an approaching object during the performance. The body remains stationary during the contact phase, but the performer generally steps backward after the kick to regain the balance that was lost momentarily during the contact phase. Note that there is cross-body opposition of movement in the arms and feet after the ball is contacted.

FIGURE 9–4
Developmental sequence of the standing long jump.

Stage 1	The child bends the knees and moves the arms backward in preparation for jumping. The vertical component of force may be greater than the horizontal, resulting in a jump that is upward rather than forward. Arms move backward, acting as brakes to stop the momentum of the trunk as the legs extend in front of the center of mass.
Stage 2	The arms move in a front-to-back direction during the preparatory phase, but move sideward (winging action) during the "in-flight" phase. The knees and hips flex and extend more fully than in Stage 1. The landing is made with the center of gravity above the base of support, with the thighs perpendicular to the floor rather than parallel as in the "reaching" position of Stage 4.
Stage 3	The arms swing backward and then move forward vigorously during the preparatory phase. Upon takeoff the arms extend and move forward to approximately the height of the head. The arms remain in this position during the first half of the jump and then move down and backward in preparation for landing. The knee extension at the takeoff is nearly complete, but the angle of the jump still exceeds 45 degrees.
Stage 4	The arms extend vigorously forward and upward upon takeoff, reaching full extension above the head at "lift-off." The hips and knees are extended fully, with the takeoff angle at 45 degrees or less. In preparation for landing the arms are brought downward and the legs are thrust forward until the thighs are parallel to the surface. The center of gravity is far behind the base of support upon landing, but at the moment of contact the knees are flexed and the arms are thrust forward in order to keep the body from falling backward.

ities. A tom-tom, a tambourine, maracas, or recorded music may accompany the activity. The teacher should draw the children's attention to or get them to suggest different ways of using the body. Carrying ribbons or scarves or wearing full skirts encourages using the body to sway, twist, and bend. The hula hoop also encourages body movement.

OTHER VALUES OF OUTDOOR ACTIVITY

Mental, Social, and Emotional Development

Outdoor activity makes outstanding contributions to young children's lives. The goals for motor skill development are interrelated with goals for mental, social, and emotional development.

The reason outdoor activity is so popular with every age is that it honestly meets the needs of the individuals. Why do elementary children answer, "Recess," when asked, "What do you like best at school?" Recess is popular because it is freer of adult interferences—interferences that must at times be frustrating and stifling to children. A time for outdoor activity provides a release from tensions that build up from prolonged sitting, thinking, creating, being quiet, and trying to be "good."

The outdoor period provides the child additional stimuli to meet friends and talk over mutual interests. Children talk, shout, laugh, and

Jumping at Stage 1. The preparatory phases of jumping are essentially the same for all developmental levels of jumping. However, the force-production phases—especially those actions that occur immediately before, during, and after the point at which the feet leave the surface—distinguishes the various levels of performance. The performer moves the arms backward immediately upon takeoff in an attempt to restrict the forward movement of the trunk. In Stage 1 jumping behavior the arms act as "brakes" to forward momentum.

sing outdoors with less restraint than may occur in classrooms. Language flows naturally. Children use their outdoor period to make plans and do things together. Sharing and other social skills develop. Outdoor activity may provide social acceptance and leadership for those children who have difficulty with more formal activities.

Individual motor skills, such as pulling, pushing, lifting, balancing, running, climbing, pedaling, steering, riding, jumping, throwing, and swinging, are practiced. These skills contribute to children's self-assurance, making them more confident when facing new experiences. Interaction with people of all ages is facilitated through motor skills. Skill in swimming dramatizes this fact. Once young children swim with confidence, they can swim with adults and teenagers as well as with children their own age. Until they develop swimming skills, they are relegated to the shallow pool and their fellow nonswimmers. Or five-year-olds who have graduated to a two-wheel bicycle are not only kings in their own crowd, but are also admitted to the school-age set and are ready for family rides.

Negative and hostile feelings can be drained off through the activities the out-of-doors provides. Throwing balls and beanbags, punching the punching bag, or pounding nails are examples of acceptable outlets for "bad" feelings. Vigorous running and riding also provide release for pent-up feelings.

Of course, the mind continues to develop out-of-doors as well. In fact, the new environment will stimulate curiosity and exploration in children. They can make many observations on their own. They can test out their ideas and come to many conclusions. Children may seem to be only exercising their legs or vocal chords, but their minds are also developing. Physical and mental development are closely related. For example, such concepts as fast and slow, high and low, long and short, and hard and easy are readily experienced. The child expresses intellectual understanding through motor skills. Adults make inferences about intellectual growth through observing a child involved with activities.

Learning to dribble proved interesting to the four-year-olds when the gymnasium was used for exercise. (Children's Center, Denver)

Developing large muscle coordination during vigorous play leads to improved small muscle coordination. Small muscle coordination is required in order to write, draw, cut, tie, or manipulate such things as puzzles and equipment.

The imaginative games and dramatic play observed during children's outdoor activity challenge the child's creativity, concepts, and memory. All are part of the child's mental development.

Vigorous physical activity stimulates all vital processes, such as circulation, respiration, and elimination. Eating habits improve, and rest is more welcome.

Dr. Jean Mayer, professor of nutrition at the Harvard School of Public Health, states that physical activity is the most important environmental variable affecting obesity in children. Obese children exercise less than lean children, yet often eat the same amounts. In diet therapy a long-term regimen of increased exercise is needed.[6]

Additional values of the outdoor self-selected activity period are the opportunities it affords children to feel free and to enjoy fresh air and sunshine. Children's happiness in outdoor activities is clearly expressed in their laughter, squeals, and shouts. Where harsh weather is frequent, suitable substitutes for outdoor play must be available.

REQUIREMENTS OF A HIGH-QUALITY OUTDOOR PROGRAM

A high-quality early childhood education program includes plans for a daily outdoor self-selected activity period. It is possible in some climates to hold virtually the entire school day outdoors. If the outdoor period is to make the maximum contribution to the development of the child, the following are required: (1) careful planning, (2) adequate space, (3) appropriate equipment, (4) sufficient time, and (5) appropriate guidance.[7]

Careful Planning

Teachers should plan outdoor and large motor activities as thoughtfully as they do indoor activities. Too many teachers simply turn children loose in the outdoor play yard with little or no thought about variety, sequencing, or challenging activities. Children should have an opportunity for outdoor activities every day. During severe weather, gymnasium activities may be substi-

tuted. Typically, children desire lively action and need little urging to participate.

Referring to the list of fundamental motor skills, the teacher will plan to involve each child in these activities regularly. The teacher individualizes planning and evaluating of motor skills by (1) observing each child, (2) checking and recording skill mastery, (3) planning and encouraging each child to practice each skill, and (4) encouraging the child to try the next stage in the motor sequence when he or she seems ready.

Locomotor skills can be practiced through such games as follow-the-leader, with a few children at a time following an adult through several skills on the list. For example, the leader could move from running, to jumping, to galloping, to leaping, as the group of children is led around the play yard. Another day several of the other skills can be practiced. Such games are helpful on cold days to get children moving, warmed up, and having a good time. The activities serve similar ends for teachers and help them release the energy and tension that inevitably build up.

Moveable equipment should be regrouped from time to time to stimulate new use of it. Close observation of the children's interests will guide the teacher in planning activities and arranging equipment. Children will gladly give advice and assistance. For example, when cowboy play is popular, the packing boxes are called "barns," and a corral is needed for the cowboy's

[6]Myron Winick, "Childhood Obesity," *Nutrition Today* 9:3 (May/June 1974), 9. Also see "Childhood Obesity: Prevention and Treatment," by Phillip M. Wishon, Robert Bower, and Ben Eller, *Young Children* 39:1 (November 1983), 21–27.
[7]For a helpful rating scale for playgrounds see "How Can Playgrounds Be Improved?" by Penny Lovell and Thelma Harms, *Young Children* 40:3 (March 1985), 3–8.

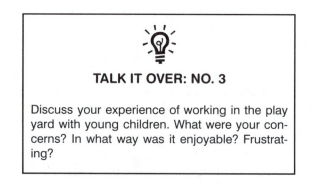

TALK IT OVER: NO. 3

Discuss your experience of working in the play yard with young children. What were your concerns? In what way was it enjoyable? Frustrating?

tricycle "horses." The teacher assists the cowboys in getting the barn in the correct position.

The teacher should make plans to stimulate children's mental development while they are out-of-doors. Many indoor experiments, such as those using inclines or balances, can be repeated outdoors. Spontaneous learning about weather, plants, insects, and animals is natural for the yard. Specimens can be observed, discussed, classified, labeled, imitated, and taken indoors. It is helpful to have science books, specimen jars, butterfly nets, and magnifying glasses available to use in extending the learning. Through close involvement in children's learning, the teacher will be able to ask questions that help children see relationships and make comparisons between their discoveries and the adult world. Planned experiences are initiated for children who don't seem to have questions.

Quiet activities have a definite place outdoors. Children should always be able to choose between active and less active outdoor activity. Music, perhaps with guitar or Autoharp, is delightful. Stories told or read to small groups are pleasant. Children enjoy a period of looking at books alone, so books should be available. Even resting takes on positive dimensions when a blanket is spread under a tree.

Plans for social and emotional growth should also be on the outdoor agenda. Planning for small-group projects is an excellent time for children to practice sharing, taking turns, persisting toward a goal, and responding to frustration.

The teacher's attitude toward the outdoors is quickly indicated by what is planned and what children are permitted to do outdoors. Teachers who don't particularly enjoy the outdoors should make an effort to learn to enjoy it. They should dress appropriately for the weather. With proper attire from head to toe, the teacher will begin to appreciate the exhilarating freshness of a winter day or the peaceful sunshine of a spring afternoon just as much as the children enjoy the out-of-doors.

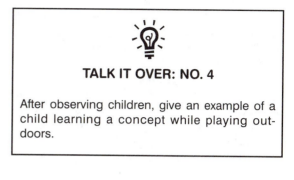

TALK IT OVER: NO. 4

After observing children, give an example of a child learning a concept while playing outdoors.

Adequate Space[8]

Children probably often feel cooped up. They need the outdoor space that a good school affords. At home their living space may be shared with a number of siblings. Their playground may be the city streets and sidewalks. Even where parks and playgrounds are available, the parent may curtail the child's use of them. When playgrounds are overcrowded, the young child may feel insecure among the many strangers.

Children who live in economically advantaged homes with plenty of room both indoors and out may also need the outdoor activities offered at school. These children may have few friends their age to share their elaborate home setting or to offer stimulation. They may stay indoors to have the companionship of a parent or household employee.

In the microscopic yards of some hillside slums and suburbs children are unable to use a ball or bike. Even a good run is impossible because the terrain is too steep, and gravity is against them.

Space, then, becomes a cherished item in the modern world. Early childhood education pro-

[8]For a comprehensive analysis and recommendations regarding amounts and use of space, see Sybil Kritchevsky, Elizabeth Prescott, and Less Walling, *Planning Environments for Young Children: Physical Space* (Washington, DC: NAEYC, 1977).

grams should endeavor to provide 75 to 200 square feet of outdoor space for each child. Careful planning is required to see that all space is used judiciously.

The outdoor space should be safe from traffic so that the children can use it without fear and without constant reminders to protect themselves. The fence should permit children to see the outside world, yet be high enough for security and designed to discourage climbing. Gates with secure latches are needed. One important practical aspect to consider when planning the fence is to provide some way for trucks with sand and equipment to make deliveries.

The space should be large enough for the number of children who may use it at any given time. When space must be shared with other groups, it is well to agree on a time schedule to avoid conflict from overcrowding. In schools housing older children it is wise to take prekindergarten children and kindergartners outdoors when older children are at work in the building. Thus the fear and confusion younger children feel when older children play at the same time may be avoided.

The best outdoor space is adjacent to and on the same level as the indoor room. The toilet must be near the entrance. Time and energy for both teachers and children are used more effectively when indoor and outdoor spaces are adjacent. Materials can be easily moved in and out. Supervision is simpler. Children's needs can best be met if the whole group is not required to be outside or inside at a given time.

Good playground space provides a variety of levels and challenges to the children. There should be knolls and flat surfaces, grassy expanses and hard-surfaced areas. Open space is necessary for exuberant play. A quiet nook for resting and reflecting is just as important. There should be protected areas so that the benefits of the outdoors can be enjoyed when the rains come. Shade is pleasantly cooling when the sunshine is very hot. Protection from prevailing winds makes space usable on wintry days. The space should be located where children can be allowed to be noisy.

Phyllis Lueck designed a creative outdoor learning environment. The tricycle paths had various textures and finishes—pebbly, smooth, gravel, asphalt, and cement ridged like a washboard. A bridge across a little gully required careful driving, for it had narrow tracks that just fit the tricycle tires. In addition, various types of wind chimes gave the children an opportunity to hear variations in sounds when they rang the chimes.[9]

Adequate drainage is important. A sloping yard of slightly sandy soil dries off quickly after a shower. Wood chips, gravel, and other materials can be used to weatherize the surface and keep the children out of the mud. When planning a riding lane for wheel toys, one should remember that a ribbon of hard surface encircling the play area simplifies driving rules. Ramps, inclines, or knolls add interest and challenge young riders.

The play yard should be designed to facilitate teaching. Out-of-the-way corners, equipment, and foliage that block the teacher's view prevent good teaching and supervision.

The space should be attractive. A variety of plantings can provide interesting natural science experiences as well as beauty. Special attention to finishes and colors will make the yard more inviting to all.

In some schools there is space to house several animal pets, which provide learning experiences for the children. In other schools the yard might be used for a day to house someone's pet rabbit or a lamb borrowed from a farmer friend. From watching a wriggling worm or a soaring bird the children can be stimulated to observe and learn about living creatures.

Children may not get enough vigorous outdoor exercise in climates that are extremely hot or cold. In such situations protected space for large motor activities—climbing, sliding, run-

---

[9]Phyllis Lueck, "Planning an Outdoor Learning Environment," *Theory into Practice* 12:2 (April 1973), 121–127.

ning, and riding—should be located elsewhere. For example, a protected patio, a rainy-day room, or a gymnasium can serve this purpose if it is carefully planned and equipped.

Appropriate Equipment

Equipping the schoolyard is a major endeavor. A knowledge of children's needs, interests, and abilities is required for choosing appropriate equipment. Money, planning, and imagination are also required.

There should be equipment for climbing, swinging, balancing, pulling, lifting, chinning, sliding, riding, building, and pounding. Some large boxes or structures are needed that lend themselves to imaginative games for children to develop. Sand, mud, and water are essentials.

There must be enough equipment so that all children using the yard at one time may find a suitable activity. If there is a shortage of equipment, then children direct their energy against each other and toward climbing on gates and fences. Ample equipment is essential if the outdoor program is to make its rightful contribution to the child's overall development.

The equipment should contain a few pieces that the children will find somewhat difficult to master at the beginning of the school year. For example, only one five-year-old was able to use the trapeze in September. However, during the final weeks of school almost every child went hand over hand on that trapeze.

Trees and Garden

Live trees in the yard can provide challenging climbing experiences, refreshing shade, and outstanding opportunities to watch nature's sequences. A fallen tree trimmed down to two or three major forks provides children a gnarled surface for climbing, sitting, and jumping. As the bark loosens the children will enjoy helping to remove it. With years of use the surface will become shiny. The tree trunk will contribute to imaginative play, serving as a spaceship, an airplane, or a train, depending on the idea of the moment.

When an area in the yard is set aside for the spring garden or the fall bulb planting, sturdy short-handled garden tools are useful. Quality tools should be purchased to encourage a young gardener. A corner can be reserved for "just digging."

Water play is delightful outdoors when the weather is warm. Plastic aprons are essential to keep clothes dry. A specially made portable water table with a galvanized lining that makes a 10-inch deep sink is convenient for both indoor and outdoor water play. Children, however, will enjoy even a dishpan or a bucket of water. When children are furnished soap, they will happily wash the doll clothes or tricycles. A wading pool is popular in summer. Of course, for safety, utmost care must be taken to have the water play supervised at all times.

When given a can of water and a small paintbrush, the young child likes to "paint" the side of the storage shed or the jungle gym—painting as carefully as any painter. A paper cup of water with detergent suds and a drinking straw make bubble blowing easy. Both activities are fun on warm sunny days.

Wintertime, with its snow and ice, provides children water in another form. When dressed properly, children enjoy the snow. Children often lie in the snow making snow angels, like Peter in Ezra Jack Keats's *A Snowy Day*, and gaining information about their body shapes and sizes. Sleds are standard equipment in schools in snowy climates. Only a small knoll is necessary to bring joy to young sledders. Pans of snow can be taken indoors for measurement or experimentation.

Imaginative Play

A playhouse structure—which can double as a storage room—stimulates children's dramatic play. When it is designed with a variety of stairs and ladders, the child's climbing skills are developed. A firepole, a rope ladder, or a metal slide can be built into the structure for the child's quick "escape." Doll carriages and dress-up clothes contribute to imaginative outdoor play.

The jungle gym offers a challenge to children's climbing muscles and their imagination. It should be sturdy. Though a steel gym is cold to the touch, it does not become as dangerously deteriorated as a wooden one. A jungle gym is best located on a grassy surface or over tanbark or wood chips so that falls will be cushioned.

A slide should be low enough that the teacher can reach the child at the top. This is important for a young group. Also, the slide should be flat enough at the bottom so children will not shoot out into the dirt from a fast ride. Popular slides in some schools are those built into tree houses or other structures. Children can then incorporate the slide into imaginary play more readily than when it is a single, isolated piece of equipment.

Old cars, trucks, boats, and even airplanes have been used in school yards to stimulate imaginary games. Usually these are mere skeletons with doors, windows, and all loose gadgets removed. They should be colorfully painted to avoid giving the area a junkyard appearance.

Large packing boxes of varying sizes and colors can become the center for dramatic play. To imaginative children a large box can be a "barn" for tricycle "horses" or the "living room" of the little "house." Several boxes built from sturdy pine lumber ranging down from 54″ × 54″ × 54″ and painted with high-quality outdoor paint will be invaluable in the outdoor program.

Other accessory pieces such as barrels, ladders, sawhorses, and planks have many uses. Planks can become bridges between packing boxes. A jumping board can be made from low blocks or sawhorses placed under each end of a plank. A sliding board can be made from a plank with one end resting on the jungle gym.

A collection of large hollow blocks painted or varnished for use out-of-doors adds to the quality of the play. Corrals, roads, bridges, and houses are designed by young "engineers" when they are provided with an adequate supply of blocks. Out-of-the-weather storage is required for most blocks. Block storage and movement will be facilitated if blocks are stored on a wheeled dolly that is easily rolled in and out.

A sufficient number of sturdy wheel toys should be available so the children can perfect their cycling skills. Wheeled equipment is also useful in dramatic play. In a group of twenty children about ten wheel toys—tricycles of various sizes, wagons, tractors, and the like—should be available.

Rocking-boat-type equipment, either to stand or to sit on, provides pleasant opportunities for developing arm and leg muscle coordination.

Swings

A good choice of swing is the glider type requiring two children to face each other and cooperate in a push-pull motion. With this type of swing, goals for self-help, cooperation, and socialization are fostered in ways not achieved with traditional swings.

For younger children traditional swings should have strap seats. This seat, which resembles a horse saddle cinch, does not harm the child as a hard seat may if the child gets hit with it. The seat curves to fit the child's body so that falling is less likely. Because children cannot stand up easily in strap seats, they will be less popular with older children. For older children the swing should have a rigid seat made of lightweight plastic material.

The tire swing is the favorite swing in many yards. It is simply a tire hung from a tree limb with a chain. The tire may be suspended in only one place or anchored with three chains that hold the tire parallel to the ground, making room for three children.

Sand

A sandpile provides a quiet, restful area and an inexpensive medium for children. A good-quality sand can be purchased. A wood-frame box with a 10-inch ledge provides a seat for the children when the sand is wet. Children will use the ledge as a "table" as they turn out their "cakes." A lid for the sandbox is essential in neighborhoods where cats might contaminate the sand. The lid can be hinged along the edges in such a way that it becomes a seat when opened.

Sand should be kept moist. Dry sand gets in hair and eyes more readily than damp sand. Moist sand is more easily molded into cakes or tunnels. Numerous containers should be provided. Kitchen castoffs are excellent: juice cans, old pots and pans, plastic milk cartons, and funnels made from the tops of plastic bottles are all suitable sand toys. The teacher should examine the collection from time to time and replace broken items. A large number of metal shovels makes sharing less difficult. The sandbox with numerous containers of various sizes gives children opportunities to measure, count, and label the products they are making so carefully. The sandbox affords a place to rest, yet keep busy and in touch with friends.

Carpentry

Young carpenters will enjoy pounding and sawing in the play yard. Carpenter's benches, old worktables, and packing boxes can provide space on which to work. Real tools should be purchased and kept in good working condition. Separate clamps or vises attached to the tables are handy for helping the child hold the wood. Water paints can be made available so that little carpenters can finish up their projects in style. Nuts and bolts make interesting manipulative and sorting experiences and may be used in wood projects. Wrenches may be needed for some projects.

Cabinetmakers will usually give teachers the scraps of wood from their scrap bin. Sometimes the teacher is able to interest them in the children's projects, and they will save unusual shapes as they cut them out. Under saws, planes, and drills the teacher will find sawdust and shavings of various sizes that are useful in numerous art projects.

Table Toys and Snacks

Various table toys from inside can be used outside also. Finger painting and clay take on new possibilities when used outdoors. Easels can be set up outside for painting.

Children get thirsty when they are very active. Drinking water should be available, from either a drinking fountain or a pitcher of water brought outside. It is very convenient to have weatherproofed tables so that an outdoor snack or lunch can be served.

Storage and Maintenance

Storage for all outdoor equipment should be designed to encourage the children to help put things away. Proper storage of toys teaches children desirable habits. At the same time children can be very helpful to the teacher. Most equipment deteriorates in wet weather; therefore proper storage is essential.

An adequate budget is needed to keep equipment properly maintained. Equipment with pieces that are loose or missing is often frustrating and unsafe for children's use. Equipment represents a substantial investment in time and money.

Sufficient Time

The time block set aside for outdoor, self-selected motor skill activity should be at least 30 minutes long. Thirty minutes or more are needed to encourage the children to go beyond the level of just letting off steam. With a large block of time children will engage in constructive, thoughtful activity. Teachers may observe that the first few minutes outdoors children often seem compulsive in activity. They may grab at the first toy they see, or monopolize the tricycle, or hold a swing with an I-got-here-first attitude. After 10 to 15 minutes, when they realize they will have time left over for additional play, they begin to plan activities. When children accustom themselves to long outdoor periods, many satisfying learning experiences take place.

In warm climates virtually the entire school day and most of the school's learning centers can be carried on out-of-doors. Care should be taken to avoid overtiring those children who use the large muscle equipment extensively in an effort to keep up with a special friend. It is essential to include routine quiet times in the planning for outdoor activities. Shade is important, too.

Sufficient time outdoors should be considered a must for large motor activities, fresh air, and sunshine. With modern clothing even snowy and rainy days can be enjoyed by children and teachers. Teachers in full-day programs must realize that when children are kept indoors in the center for 8 to 10 hours, there will be little or no daylight hours left for outdoor activity when the children get home—even assuming they have a productive learning environment in which to play at home. The school's outdoor activities become essential in these cases and appreciated by parents.

Appropriate Guidance

Applying the principles of guidance learned in Chapter 5, indirect and direct guidance and affective guidance are all required. Also the principles learned in Chapter 4 regarding setting the stage will be useful in planning for and interacting with children in activities out-of-doors.

Teachers will enjoy guiding children's learning outdoors if they understand the stages of physical and motor development. This understanding will help adults overcome excessive concern that children will hurt themselves, provide clues to when children's safety requires the teacher to stop an activity, and preclude unnecessary labeling of activities as "dangerous."

Many adults are fearful when children climb. A general rule followed by most experienced teachers is that children will climb only as high as they feel safe. If they are overencouraged by adults or other children to go beyond the point where they feel safe, or if they appear to be showing off, then the teacher should stay close by to prevent accidents.

Teachers must be willing to set limits that protect the safety of the children, protect the learning environment, and protect property. The teacher will define and give reasons for the limitations set—"Your sand is for digging. Sand hurts Jane's eyes." Removing a child from the sandbox or other equipment if the child does not abide by the rules may be necessary at times.

When a teacher sees only one or two children on a piece of high equipment, there may be no need to worry. However, if more than two chil-

dren are climbing on a slide, a jungle gym, or a packing box, it is a situation to watch. Crowding invites pushing. The teacher can first move closer to the group. If all is peaceful, there may be no need to say anything. The teacher is close enough to know when guidance is needed to ensure safety.

In practice the mere movement of the teacher close to a play group is a reminder to the children to play according to the established rules. Therefore, without saying anything, the teacher will influence the behavior of the children. In addition, if the group is too large for the equipment, the teacher can directly or indirectly extend the play to a larger area. Setting up an enticing new climbing arrangement nearby that will attract some children and thus reduce the size of the first group to a safe number may be desirable.

Using traditional swings, a child consciously or unconsciously may isolate himself or herself from the group. Guidance may help a child who swings alone all the time to feel confident enough to try other activities. Some will try new things if there is no one to push the swing.

Certain children monopolize a teacher by repeatedly requesting a push in the swing. If the school has a traditional swing, the teacher will want the children to learn to pump the swing themselves. The following is one way to help children learn to pump. When Carla seems eager to learn, the teacher places a plank directly behind the swing, extending back from the spot where Carla's feet rest. The far end is elevated with a large hollow block or sawhorse, making an

TALK IT OVER: NO. 5

Discuss safety measures for children in the play yard.

inclined plane. Holding the swing chains tight with the seat under her, Carla then walks backward up the plank. As she sits down on the seat, her feet go up in the air and she "takes off." She will be thrilled at the newfound independence in being able to make herself go in the swing and will practice the feat over and over again. In some schools the incline is built as a ramp under the swings used by the younger children.

Another useful method to encourage pumping is to pull the child forward in the swing, grasping the feet instead of pushing from behind. For example, the teacher warns Tony what to expect, then gives both his feet a slight tug. She encourages him as he swings forward, to reach with his feet for her hands, which are held up higher and higher. This reaching gets his feet up, and eventually he feels secure enough to relax and let his shoulders and torso move with the swing. Verbal encouragement and the accompanying words, "bending and stretching," will label the action of his legs and help him get the rhythm. Children enjoy the socializing with the teacher that this technique encourages.

Sharing is one of those elusive qualities that adults would have all children develop. The teacher's guidance is often required in problems of sharing. In addition to social learning, sharing affords children concrete experience with quantity, number, and division—all mathematical concepts. Sharing toys is easier when there is a sufficient quantity, because a child does not like to wait indefinitely for a desired toy. A new toy may have to be rationed so that each child can have a turn. Rationing and sharing are different. With rationing one hopes to ensure equal use of a given supply. With sharing one finds joy and satisfaction in mutual or partial use of a thing.

There is a feeling that goes with sharing that comes from having "enough." Adults may tell Abe that he has had the toy long enough, but only Abe really knows. How would you react if someone told you that you had had enough to eat? You'd probably think, "How does she know I've had enough?"

People share voluntarily, willingly, happily, and frequently when they feel that the decision is theirs. Children who feel loved and self-confident are more willing to share. Usually only those who know each other very well share voluntarily. Significant sharing can be observed when two children are having a happy time together. There will be mutual give-and-take that is the real essence of sharing. Statements like "We share in this school" or "You've got to learn to share" do not really help the child learn. Children interpret these statements to mean you expect them to divide up the goods and will force them to do so if they refuse.

It is helpful to identify activity verbally as "sharing" so that the child will grasp what is meant by the expression. For example, Jack arrived in the kindergarten and observed the children petting some new guinea pigs. He walked up and immediately said, "You've got to share." His behavior indicated that he expected everyone to step aside and give him a guinea pig. When at last he got his turn, he quickly forgot his admonition to the other children. "Sharing" was in Jack's vocabulary but not in his repertoire of behaviors and feelings. The next time the teacher sees Jack share, a helpful statement would be, "There, Jack, you shared with Bill." To promote sharing the teacher provides a sufficient number of toys, then works to establish a climate of mutual love and respect that brings sharing about voluntarily.

A new toy in a school may need to be rationed, but the sooner it can become "yours while you are using it," the better. This yours-while-you-are-using-it policy allows a child to use equipment until there is a feeling of "enough." Then the child will be able to share. The policy also avoids having the teacher become a timekeeper.

Teachers often have difficulty with some children monopolizing certain equipment. Monopolizing may occur because children are unable to think of anything else to do. For example, the boys in one group monopolized the tricycles. The teachers decided to give the girls a chance at the tricycles by dismissing them to the yard first for a few days. Another day everyone wearing red was chosen to go to the yard first. Such procedures gave others a chance to use the tricycles. Guidance in helping the boys find suitable alternatives to tricycle riding was called for. Teachers should be observant and prevent the practice of one child or clique tyrannizing the others in order to get certain equipment.

Toys brought from home handicap the teacher in a yours-while-you-are-using-it policy. Personal toys are usually unsuited for use by a group. Some are so fragile that they may get broken if they are shared. It is well to discourage children from bringing personal toys to school, although there are cases in which children need their own toys for personal security. This, of course, will be an exception. In these cases a frank explanation to the other children that "Jill feels better today with her own doll; perhaps tomorrow she will enjoy our dolls" is sufficient.

The teacher's guidance is often required to keep children from getting overheated outdoors or in. Many wraps that are appropriate when the child is moving slowly in the early morning are unnecessary when going full speed in the sunshine later on. A good rule, of course, is to encourage the children to decide for themselves when they need to shed their wraps. The teacher should err on the side of letting the children take off coats if they wish. It is hard for adults to realize how hot children get from their vigorous activity.

In some climates boots are kept in the locker all the time because of the prevailing wet grass in the yard. Extra boots, mittens, and hats stored in the school closet can supply children who do not have their own. Parents often need suggestions as to appropriate clothing to send and even to purchase.

EMERGENCIES

If a child falls while playing, it is better for the teacher to comfort the child on the ground for a few minutes while trying to determine how serious the injury is. For the teacher to jerk the child up to standing or into the arms will certainly be frightening and may do serious damage to a limb if one is broken. In time of emergency a teacher's calmness can relax the hurt child, reassure the other children, and guide the assistants' efforts to be helpful. A coherent report of the mishap must be given to the parents or the doctor if either must be called.

In case of a serious accident a full account should be typed immediately to ensure recall of all details. Reports should be filed with appropriate authorities. If the school is covered by insurance, this report will be required by the insurance company.

Conclusions

A high-quality early childhood program includes adequate motor skill practice and healthful exercise for each child each day. Children's motor development during the early years provides the foundation for their future skill level. Skills can be fostered by adults who analyze the child's development level and give the child proper equipment and guidance.

Teachers need to realize the value of offering a rich motor-skill program to young children. Adequate plans ensure that goals are achieved for each child. Teachers can make wise use of space and be creative in selection and arrangement of equipment. In addition, appropriate guidance and teaching techniques ensure meaningful outdoor learning experiences for all the children.

Applications

1. Discuss the "Talk It Over" items in the chapter.
2. Write an activity plan for a motor skill or outdoor activity for a few children using information and the sample (Figure 6-2) in Chapter 6. Secure approval, carry out the plan, and evaluate the results from the children's point of view and from your viewpoint. Prepare a report and hand it in along with your approved activity plan.

3. Evaluate your total participation performance on your evaluation form developed in Chapter 1.
4. Add ideas and plans for motor skills and outdoor activities to your Resource File.

Study Questions

1. Explain the major finding of the Seefeldt and Haubenstricker study of young children's motor skills.
2. Describe the stages of catching. Describe the type of ball to use to play catch with a young child.
3. Describe the stages of throwing. Describe the type of ball to use to practice throwing with a young child.
4. Define *self-efficacy*. Tell how it applies to outdoor play activity.
5. Discuss the role of planning in the outdoor play program.
6. Discuss the use of space in the outdoor play program.
7. Discuss the allocation of time in the outdoor play program.
8. Discuss guidance measures for outdoor play activities.
9. Discuss safety in the play yard.
10. Classify play activity for the play yard, and list several specific activities for each classification.

Videotapes

Fundamental Object Control Skills
    60 minutes

Developmental patterns for throwing, catching, kicking, punting, and striking skills. Vern Seefeldt and John Haubenstricker, Michigan State University Motor Performance Study, IMC 134, East Lansing, Michigan 48824-1030, 517-355-4741.

Fundamental Locomotor Skills
    60 minutes

Developmental patterns for running, galloping, hopping, skipping, and jumping skills. John Haubenstricker and Vern Seefeldt, Michigan State University Motor Performance Study, IMC 134, East Lansing, Michigan 48824-1030, 517-355-4741.

Additional Readings

Branta, Crystal. "Motoric and Fitness Assessment of Young Children." In *Young Children on the Grow: Health, Activity, and Education in the Preschool Setting*, ed. Charlotte M. Hendricks. Washington, DC: ERIC Clearinghouse on Teacher Education, 1992, 89–107.

Bredekamp, Sue, ed. *Developmentally Appropriate Practice in Early Childhood Programs Serving Children from Birth Through Age 8*. Washington, DC: NAEYC, 1987.

Corbin, Charles. *A Textbook of Motor Development*. Dubuque, IA: W. C. Brown, 1980.

Cratty, Bryant J. *Perceptual and Motor Development in Infants and Young Children*. Upper Saddle River, NJ: Prentice Hall, 1986.

Esbensen, S. B. *The Early Childhood Playground: An Outdoor Classroom*. Ypsilanti, MI: High/Scope Press, 1987.

Frost, Joe L., and Sue C. Wortham. "The Evolution of American Playgrounds." *Young Children* 43:5, July 1988, 19–28.

Hildebrand, Verna. *Guiding Young Children*. Upper Saddle River, NJ: Merrill/Prentice Hall, 1994.

Poest, Catherine A., Jean R. Williams, David D. Witt, and Mary Ellen Atwood. "Challenge Me to Move: Large Muscle Development in Young Children." *Young Children* 45:5, July 1990, 4–10.

Sullivan, Molly. *Feeling Strong, Feeling Free: Movement Exploration for Young Children*. Washington, DC: NAEYC, 1995.

Wardle, Francis. "Alternatives . . . Bruderhof Education: Outdoor School." *Young Children* 50:1, March 1995, 68–73.

CHAPTER 10

Creative Art Activities

Children's Center, Denver

Objectives

✔ Define *creativity* and identify ways creativity is fostered in the Reggio Emilia and other schools.

✔ Explain how *developmentally appropriate* applies during use of art materials.

✔ Identify the developmental stages found by researchers studying children's use of art materials.

✔ Explain how the use of art materials offers children early literacy experiences.

✔ Describe and evaluate the use of space, supplies, equipment, and guidance for developing children's creativity.

"I'm makin' a picture for my Mommy," says four-year-old Pete.

"This is me with my sister. She is bigger than me," volunteers Janet, as she hangs up her painting.

"I like to finger paint. I go around and around," says three-year-old Alonzo.

These children are expressing their ideas through art media available in their early childhood schools. As they paint they provide observers insights into their skills, concepts, and relationships with people in their lives.

Children enjoy the many and varied art experiences offered in good schools for young children. Through these activities children integrate all areas of their growth—creative, physical, mental, language, social, and emotional. Teachers at all levels are accepting the importance of encouraging the inventive, original, self-initiated, and self-motivated behavior that is the creative potential in each child.

WHAT IS CREATIVITY?

Creativity is the individual's original, unique, different, personalized, inventive approach to people, language, activities, and problem solving. Creativity is the principle focus of an early childhood school founded in Reggio Emilia, Italy, in 1945. Evidence has been accumulating in recent years that shows the school's special integrated approach is fostering many expressions of chil-

dren's creativity, which have come to be called "the hundred languages of children." Americans have been visiting Italy's Reggio Emilia School, listening to and reading reports, and viewing exhibits and videos of Reggio Emilia's work. Many are discussing Reggio Emilia's total approach to education and how it might be emulated for stimulating more creative action within American early childhood programs.

According to Loris Malaguzzi, the founder of the Reggio Emilia School:[1]

> We can sum up our beliefs as follows:
> 1. Creativity should not be considered a separate mental faculty but a characteristic of our way of thinking, knowing, and making choices;
> 2. Creativity seems to emerge from multiple experiences, coupled with a well-supported development of personal resources, including a sense of freedom to venture beyond the known;
> 3. Creativity seems to express itself through cognitive, affective, and imaginative processes.

[1]Carolyn Edwards, Lella Gandini, and George Forman, eds., *The Hundred Languages of Children: The Reggio Emilia Approach to Early Childhood Education* (Norwood, NJ: Ablex, 1993), pp. 70–71.

Easel painting provides many opportunities for children to express their creativity. Twin boys created these paintings without watching each other. (Southeast Oakland Vocational Technical Center)

These come together and support the skills for predicting and arriving at unexpected solutions;

4. The most favorable situation for creativity seems to be interpersonal exchange, with negotiation of conflicts and comparison of ideas and actions being the decisive elements;

5. Creativity seems to find its power when adults are less tied to prescriptive teaching methods, but instead become observers and interpreters of problematic situations;

6. Creativity seems to be favored or disfavored according to the expectations of teachers, schools, families, and communities as well as society at large, according to the ways children perceive these expectations;

7. Creativity becomes more visible when adults try to be more attentive to the cognitive processes of children than to the results they achieve in various fields of doing and understanding;

8. The more teachers are convinced that intellectual and expressive activities have both multiplying and unifying possibilities, the more creativity favors friendly exchanges with imagination and fantasy;

9. Creativity requires that the *school of knowing* finds connections with the *school of expressing,* opening the doors (this is our slogan) to the hundred languages of children.

Malaguzzi goes on to state that "the spirit of play can pervade also the formation and construction of thought. . . . Our task, regarding creativity, is to help children climb their own mountains, as high as possible."

Malaguzzi attributes Reggio Emilia's theoretical base as being stimulated by readings from J. P. Guilford, Paul Torrance, Jerome Bruner, Jean Piaget, Kurt Lewin, Carl Rogers, and Abraham Maslow. These psychologists are familiar to you as you've read about their work in child development and child psychology texts. Applications of their works are suggested in this book and in other early childhood literature.

The project approach is the primary method used in the Reggio Emilia school. Teachers, parents, and children are working together in exciting broad-based projects that integrate the desired learning experiences with all aspects of the program. Discussion is a high-priority activity. Projects grow out of children's interests and questions. More time is allocated for extensions of projects to allow for the depth needed. Many records are kept by teachers in order to know where a given child is in developmental thinking, reasoning, and expression. Keep this approach in mind as you plan for children's activities.

Howard Gardner, author of *Multiple Intelligences: The Theory in Practice,*[2] has stimulated teachers to move beyond a simple definition of cognition to one where planning takes place in seven domains: (1) linguistic, (2) logical-mathematical, (3) spatial, (4) musical, (5) bodily-kinesthetic, (6) interpersonal, and (7) intrapersonal. He finds that the Reggio Emilia School's approach "challenges so many false dichotomies . . . by achieving a unique harmony that spans those contrasts, it reconfigures our sclerotic categorical systems." Gardner concludes by saying that Reggio Emilia "epitomizes education that is effective and humane; its students undergo a sustained apprenticeship in humanity, one which may last a lifetime."[3]

According to Lowenfeld and Brittain, specialists in creativity and children's art, creativity is exhibited by people who have the motivation, curiosity, and imagination

1. to search for and discover answers;
2. to question existing solutions to problems;
3. to rethink, restructure, and find new relationships;
4. to be open toward the unknown or new;
5. to be flexible, nonconforming, and nondogmatic;
6. to be self-expressive and original;
7. to use divergent thinking.[4]

---

[2]New York: Harper Collins, 1993.
[3]Gardner, Howard, "Forward: Complementary Perspectives on Reggio Emilia," in *The Hundred Languages of Children,* ed. Carolyn Edwards et al., pp. xi, xiii.
[4]Viktor Lowenfeld and W. Lambert Brittain, *Creative and Mental Growth* (New York: Macmillan, 1982), pp. 69–93.

Creativity is a state of mind that carries over into all kinds of behavior. Human beings are all creative with language because to speak one must create new sentences each time one makes an utterance. Creativity is demanded in social situations, in physical-motor activities as one adjusts to the environment, and in cognitive activities. Children are all born with creativity.

Adults are often confused about creativity. Rigid, stifling, or unsupported early experience may have made them doubt their own creativity. They may think that only artists are creative. It sometimes helps to think of creativity as a personal resource that is part of everyday decision making. Each person has some unique ways of applying knowledge to the tasks of everyday living. That's creativity in operation.

Creative potential gives people the motivation to change, to shift gears in a rapidly changing society. From a very practical point of view, it is extremely important that a person's creativity be fostered to its fullest extent. Village blacksmiths of great-grandfather's day may have lamented that there were no more horses to be shod, but they turned to repairing the wheels of the tractors that replaced the horses and used many of the same materials and skills. They saw the possibilities and learned new ways of using their resources. They didn't let the need to change throw them into psychological or economic despair.

A walk down any street on any day reveals how someone's creativity has made life easier:

The window washer uses a rubber blade on a long stick; the painter uses a roller instead of a brush; the street sweeper now drives a big machine instead of carrying a broom and a pail; the businessperson has a choice of computer software; office forces have automatic machines; the bus driver serves customers faster because buses have two doors to speed the process of moving people on and off. All these improvements are the result of someone's creativity. Industry often encourages creative suggestions from employees through incentive payments.

A look in the household section of a historical museum shows how pioneers used their creative ingenuity to lighten household tasks. The pioneer housewife must have said, "I wish there was a better way to peel these apples besides sitting here with this knife." Having made the complaint, she set not only her own creative thoughts in operation but perhaps those of others who eventually came up with a gadget for peeling and coring apples.

Modern society needs people who will ask important questions and seek solutions. When people are encouraged to question and are encouraged to engage in creative thought and experimentation, problem solving and progress will come more rapidly. The questioning attitude will contribute to creative thinking whether the question deals with a household task or problems of world peace. Progress can take place only if individuals ask the question, "Couldn't we do this a better way?"

The aesthetic aspects of creativity are available to all. Individuals live more fully when they appreciate beauty, whether in nature, in work, or in human relationships.

Brain Functions and Creative Expression

Supporting the concept that intellect is the critical, creative, and contemplative side of the mind is recent research into mapping the various functions of the brain. You may be aware that your

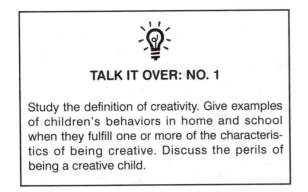

TALK IT OVER: NO. 1

Study the definition of creativity. Give examples of children's behaviors in home and school when they fulfill one or more of the characteristics of being creative. Discuss the perils of being a creative child.

Finger painting is an interesting and creative experience for young children. (Kansas State University)

brain's left hemisphere controls the motor functions of the right side of your body, while the right hemisphere of the brain controls the left side of your body. According to Dr. David Galin, M.D., "the specialization of the right hemisphere has only recently been widely recognized: it is very good at perceiving and expressing novel and complex visual, spatial, and musical patterns." The right hemisphere is said to function in a *holistic mode,* according to Galin, while the left hemisphere functions in an *"analytic, logical mode,* for which words are an excellent tool." Based on this work it is Galin's conclusion that "if we want to cultivate creativity, it appears that we must first develop each mode, both the rational-analytic and the intuitive-holistic; second, we must develop the ability to inhibit either one when it is inappropriate to the task at hand; and finally we must be able to operate in both modes in a complementary fashion."[5]

"Integration of the brain's two thinking systems has also been suggested as a model of creativity," according to Languis and others. They write that

creative productivity involves both the intuitive sensing of patterns and the analytic organization of ideas into propositions, thus tapping the high-level cognitive capabilities of both hemispheres. Moreover, access to and communication between the hemispheres may be the key to expanding creative potential. Therefore, an appropriate program goal might be to facilitate in children the ability to shift flexibly between both modes of thinking and to use, value, and trust ideas derived equally from both strategies.[6]

The research in brain hemispheres is giving support to educators who have long advocated lots of hands-on activities and the use of art materials as vital to children's learning. Hands-on activities, pictorial figures, and three-dimensional figures, called **analog** in the new computer language, are processed in the right side of the brain. Such right-brain activities can also aid in the learning of **digital** information such as numbers, letters, and words, which is a left-brain activity. Raising the issue of computers in this context suggests that caution must be taken that

---

[5]David Galin, M.D., "Educating Both Halves of the Brain," *Childhood Education* 53:1 (October 1979), 18.

[6]Marlin Languis, Tobie Sanders, and Steven Tipps, *Brain and Learning: Directions in Early Childhood Education* (Washington, DC: NAEYC, 1980), p. 49.

the left brain is not the only hemisphere stimulated in the new computer age.

Children have differing learning styles. Some learn the analytic-logical types of information quickly, whereas others need pictures and function well with objects in space. The first style is referred to as left-brained, the second as right-brained. What is needed to utilize most fully the marvelous resources of the child's brain is a combination of learning activities presented in a variety of modes. The process of using art materials and tools is extremely important to children's learning.

DEVELOPMENTAL TASKS FOSTERED THROUGH ART ACTIVITIES

The developmental tasks of each child are fostered through use of art materials. By reviewing those tasks in Chapter 2 and relating them to the discussion that follows, you will be able to see how each task is touched in some way when the child uses art materials and participates in creative activity.

Fostering Creativity Through the Arts

"The goal for art education is to use the creative process to make people more creative regardless of where their creativeness will be applied," wrote Viktor Lowenfeld in *Creative and Mental Growth*.[7] Lowenfeld and Brittain, in a later edition of that book, wrote, "Child art is highly individual. No two children express themselves entirely alike." One of the vital aims of art education is to bring out the individual differences that make up each child's personality. To suppress these individual differences, to emphasize the final product, to reward one youngster over another, goes against the basic premises of creative expression.[8]

In high-quality early childhood programs opportunities abound for children's creativity and divergent thinking to find expression. In every segment of the curriculum there is room for children to "put it together" in new ways. The teacher values the unique, spontaneous, fresh, and imaginative manner with which the child faces the challenge of learning. The child's use of art materials is a regularly offered part of the program.

The end products of the creative process, such as paintings, collages, and other works of art, may have little value in the marketplace, yet the creative process involved is of great value to the developing child. Patterns are not used to get products that look "just so." Coloring-book-type line drawings to fill in are not provided. The teacher has faith in the child and often tells the child so. The teacher refrains from helping the child outright. Confidence in the child is stated time and time again. Bolstering self-confidence, the teacher encourages experimentation and commends the unique way in which the child solves a problem.

If the teacher loses faith in the child's creative ability or falls victim to pressures to produce products, it will hurt the child and his or her future creativity. Henceforth, the child will wait for the teacher's idea, or "correct" way, before beginning. The child won't enjoy the products or the process.

Max is an example of a child whose creativity suffered when products were emphasized. He was a child who had creative teachers during prekindergarten and kindergarten years. He used new materials with great confidence. In the first grade Max was told that Christmas drawings would be selected for a display in an uptown department store. Max became anxious and practiced diligently so that his drawing might be chosen. It was selected.

Upon seeing the picture, his kindergarten teacher felt something was amiss. She later commented to Max, "Max, I saw your picture in the exhibit uptown." Max responded, "Did you see

---

[7]New York: Macmillan, 1957, p. 5.
[8]Lowenfeld and Brittain, op. cit., p. 167.

```
    ╭─────────────────────────────────╮
    │              ☀☀☀               │
    │               -◯-              │
    │                                 │
    │       TALK IT OVER: NO. 2       │
    │                                 │
    │  Discuss the meaning of the     │
    │  statement, "It is the          │
    │  process not the product that   │
    │  is important to the            │
    │  young child." Tell how you     │
    │  can incorporate this           │
    │  finding in your work with      │
    │  young children.                │
    ╰─────────────────────────────────╯
```

those angels? My teacher did those and she ruined it." Max had enjoyed neither the process nor the product. He did not enjoy winning with help. The first-grade teacher surely got little satisfaction from displaying her work as child's art.

Fostering Perceptual-Motor Skills Through the Arts

Creativity should be reason enough for offering children a wide array of art media and for helping them find one that especially allows expression of their feelings, moods, and ideas. However, other important reasons are apparent. The skills developed through using the art materials are both prewriting and prereading skills, sometimes called *emerging literacy*. Clearly, the small motor skills are being developed. One has only to watch a class of three-year-olds as the children draw and cut, then move on to a class of four- or five-year-olds to see how much skill the threes can be expected to develop in the next year or two.

Eye–hand coordination is continuously practiced as the hand draws a head in the "right" place or puts a wheel on a "car" in the customary spot. Picking up and placing the collage materials require eye–hand coordination, as does squeezing the glue bottle to drop the glue in the right spot. Using scissors to cut on a line is a complicated coordination task to master.

Through art activities children learn to concentrate their attention on the figures or designs they place on the page or background, helping them

develop figure and ground concepts. Later, in writing, a child must concentrate on the black squiggles, not on the white space surrounding them.

Fostering Cognitive Growth Through the Arts

According to Brittain's research in children's art, "The production of art provides one of the best ways for a preschool child to understand, organize, and utilize concepts."[9] Brittain finds that when adults serve as a sounding board for children as they paint and draw, the children put more details in their pictures. Children are constantly translating ideas into various media, showing their awareness of the world around them.

Experience with colors and their various shades and hues is provided in most of the activities. Children easily learn the names and discover the combinations of primary colors that make secondary colors and so on. Watch them at the finger painting table, for example, as they combine blue and yellow. "Look! Teacher! Teacher! I made green!" shouts Cindy.

Through art media children also gain experience putting pieces together to make a whole, learning whole-part relationships. For example, when children add eyes, ears, nose, and mouth to a circle to make a face, they are learning with some precision the parts of the body. One five-year-old, Steve, looked at a picture he had drawn of himself a few months earlier. The picture had six fingers on the hands. "Hum," he laughed, "I put six fingers on my hand." In only a few brief months Steve had become more discriminating. Now he would add the correct number of parts to his figure.

Early Writing and Reading
The art table is usually the site of the child's first attempts to write his or her name, which must be

---

[9]W. Lambert Brittain, *Creativity, Art, and the Young Child* (New York: Macmillan, 1979), p. 18. In this book Brittain reports on research conducted with young children using art media. There are many points that will interest early childhood educators.

FIGURE 10-1

Drawings provide information about each child's level of representation. This array, done in private sessions, is typical of a four-year-old group near the end of the school year. The numbers refer to the child's age in years and months. Drawings range from the scribble stage to the preschematic stage including a base line. (See Brittain's stages in this chapter.) The children were directed to "draw a man, the best man you know how."

from left to right in our language. The teacher teaches the child to use manuscript printing and to start in the left-hand corner of the page in order to avoid scrambling and crowding letters, as will happen when starting too far over to the right. Forming those letters is clearly an early reading experience as well as a writing experience.

The typical first writing is called **manuscript**, or *Palmer,* and is characterized by straight lines and circles. Recently a form called **D'Nealian** (from the name of the inventor, D. Neal Thurber) has been introduced; it is characterized by slanting the letters, which makes them adaptable to cursive writing later on. You should consult with your teacher in order to follow a consistent form for the children to learn to write and to read. See Chapter 13, Figures 13–1 and 13–2, showing the format of letters and the direction the pencil moves in both Palmer and D'Nealian styles of writing.

Concepts of shape are also required in reading and are common among the art materials. Shapes are cut out, drawn, compared, and named. Likenesses and differences in shapes are frequently discussed. "I want some shiny squares like yours," said Jack. "Here," said Todd, handing him a piece. "No, I want gold shiny squares, not silver shiny squares." said Jack.

Letters from cereal boxes and other publications can be added to the collage materials. These encourage children to form their names and other words. Carol Seefeldt strongly advocates building curricular activities around the child's name because each has a strong identification with this symbol.[10]

Fostering Social-Emotional Growth Through the Arts

The child's personality often shines through loud and clear when he or she draws or paints, for example, the little redheaded boy who drew red-haired boys in striped T-shirts. No one doubted who the drawings represented. Drawings by young children are typically egocentric. Brittain says that "Art activities not only reflect a child's inner self: they help form it."[11]

Family members are frequently represented in children's drawings. Feelings for others may be reflected in the drawings or through conversations while drawing or painting. However, Brittain cautions against deriving conclusions about a child's emotional state from too little evidence. He says, "It is ridiculous to arrive at conclusions about a child's mental health by diagnosing drawings or paintings we have not seen him creating."[12] Brittain concludes, "Unless the setting is carefully controlled with a good deal of information other than drawings available, interpretations of scribbles and early representations by children provide no insight and are of no clinical value to a teacher in a normal school situation."[13]

Arlie, for example, worried many observers because he painted a solid sheet of black. However, the teacher was not alarmed because Arlie often talked about the fire that burned the garage next door to his home. The teacher knew that the fire had been an alarming event in the neighborhood. Arlie was allowed to paint as he wished. Finally, one day Arlie painted his paper yellow. He reported that the painters had used yellow paint to paint the neighbor's garage. Arlie's opportunity to paint as he chose for all those days perhaps relieved him of tensions associated with the fire.

Pete's mother worried because her five-year-old was drawing armless human figures. In a discussion with the teacher the mother realized that she had seen only a couple of pictures in which he had tried to draw human figures. The teacher also explained to Pete's mother that it was not

---

[10]Carol Seefeldt, "What's in a Name? Lots to Learn!" *Young Children* 39:5 (July 1984), 24–30. Also see Carol Vukelich and Joanne Golden's article, "Early Writing: Development and Teaching Strategies," *Young Children* 39:2 (January 1984), 3–8.

[11]Brittain, op. cit., p. 184.
[12]Ibid., p. 121.
[13]Ibid., p. 127.

unusual for Pete to be enticed away from the drawing table by another child or by another activity before his drawing was finished. The teacher might discuss the armless drawings with Pete, asking, "What is the man doing?" "What does your man need to throw a ball?" Such questions would help him think of the relationship between activities and body parts.

Considering armless human figures, Jacqueline Goodnow, who has made numerous studies of children's drawings, indicates that "armless humans reflect no strange perception on the part of a child; instead they may often simply reflect the sense of having finished by the time one reaches the bottom." Goodnow reports that children draw from the top of the page to the bottom. Children fall in two groups, those who finish details as they go and those who go back to finish details. The latter are most likely to leave off arms. She said of the seventy-nine children in one study only forty included arms, and for those forty children twenty-eight drew the arms on last.[14]

DEVELOPMENTAL STAGES IN CHILDREN'S ART

Creative development, as with other areas of development, has its typical ages and stages. When the teacher and parent understand the various levels, they can help, not hinder, the child's creative growth. Brittain describes several stages of particular importance to teachers of young children. Knowing these developmental stages will help teachers (1) plan art activities at an appropriate level, (2) set an appropriate level of expectations for children, (3) appreciate children's drawings and art projects, and (4) have an appropriate basis for discussing children's art with parents.

Children's creative growth can be inferred from the number of independent themes they

---

[14]Jacqueline Goodnow, *Children Drawing* (Cambridge, MA: Harvard University Press, 1977), p. 56.

TALK IT OVER: NO. 3

Observe a child using an art material. Make a 5-minute diary record of what you observe the child doing and saying. Share observations among your classmates. What conclusions can you draw?

---

produce and whether or not they seem to be imitating other children. Physical growth may be indicated by their skill with tools and by exaggeration of some body part and the vigorousness of their participation.

Children may occasionally regress to previous levels of artistic behavior just as they may regress emotionally. When attempting to understand or to explain a child's art products, one should be careful not to draw conclusions from an inadequate sample of a child's work or from scanty knowledge about the child's experience.

GENERAL CLASSROOM PROCEDURES

Atmosphere

An atmosphere of freedom is important if the child is to develop creative potential. Children who feel free to try new ways of using materials will be more creative than children who are taught there is only one right way to do everything. From the very first day, the teacher must allow children to be experimental. "I know you have ideas. Let's see how many different pictures we can make," says the teacher to the children. If this faith falters or if patterns are given, then the children will wait for the teacher's intervention every day.

An uncritical atmosphere will help the child feel safe, secure, and unthreatened by the

STAGES IN YOUNG CHILDREN'S ART

W. Lambert Brittain

Stage one—Random Scribbling—age one to two or two and a half

The drawing tool is held tightly and is rarely taken from the paper. It may be held as a hammer at times. Lines are made with simple arm movements, the swing of the arm back and forth determining the direction and length of the lines. The child watches what he or she is doing, watching to follow and enjoy the lines rather than control them.

Stage two—Controlled Scribbling—age two or three or three and a half

The wrist is more flexible than in stage one. There is a wider range of scribbles and more intricate patterns of loops. The child makes the tool go across the page as desired.

Stage three—Named Scribbling—age three and a half to four or four and a half

The naming of scribbles illustrates an important step toward the development of abstract thought. Lines become symbols that stand for things.

Stage four—Early Representational—age four years plus

The child can reproduce a symbol for an object though not a likeness. Representations have little in common with what adults consider the real world. The child does not seem to be attempting a photographic likeness. What adults see as distortions are not distortions to the child.

Stage five—Preschematic Drawing—age five years plus

Now there is a right-side up and a line for the sky and ground. Relative sizes of objects begin to be portrayed. Objects and people are painted.[15]

---

teacher, peers, or family. Expectations are kept at a reasonable level so that each child can hope to succeed. Children will set their own pace. In any class there will be a wide range of abilities; therefore, materials must be suited to this wide range. For example, in a three- or four-year-old group the stages will range from scribbling to preschematic. Measures should be taken to protect the child's right to "just paint."

Children who feel skillful and self-confident will make the most effort to be creative. Therefore, teachers plan to give children opportunities to practice skills. They create an environment in which the child feels safe to practice a new skill. Children receive instruction when they ask or seem mature enough to benefit from it. Such skills as holding a crayon, cutting with scissors, using the stapler, tying a bow, or squeezing the glue bottle may profitably be demonstrated to a child who is ready to learn them. Most small motor skills contribute eventually to writing skill. Self-confidence is fostered through the mastery of skills.

The teacher should feel obligated to provide painting aprons that help protect children's clothing. The parents' complaints at home about messy clothing will adversely affect the child's creative expression. The wise teacher will guide parents in choosing appropriate clothing for their children to wear to school in order that they can participate fully in all activities.

In case of an unusual amount of spilling, the teacher can advise parents about helpful laundry procedures. When sending home children's painted or glued products, the teacher should take care that smearing of clothes and cars en route home is avoided. Ideally, the child's creations should be dry before they're sent home.

---

[15]Brittain, op. cit., pp. 28–40.

Dry chalk still smears, however. Some products can be sent in paper bags and others rolled together and held by a rubber band. Such measures may sound overprotective of parents; however, some empathy on the teacher's part results in better cooperation from parents.

To say there is freedom does not mean the teacher does not have established rules. Logically, messy activity is located where it can be cleaned up readily. Rules are set about splashing paints, dropping clay, and washing hands.

Appropriate Comments

When commenting to a child, it is best to say, "Would you like to tell me about your picture?" rather than to guess what the child is painting. Avoid saying the same comment to every child, such as, "That's wonderful!" or "That's nice." Instead, pick out some element in the art work—line, form, color, texture, or use of space—and discuss it with the child. For example, you might say, "You used triangles in interesting ways. Can you tell me how you happened to use triangles?"

Too many questions may invite casual naming that may not have much relationship to the original ideas. For example, Doug alarmed his father because he always reported having painted a "monster." The father asked the teacher about the paintings, and she recalled quite a different theme during Doug's time at the easel. Apparently Doug was pleased with the increased attention this picture title drew from his father.

The teacher protects the child from the criticism of peers. Verbally the stage is set for acceptance of all children's creations. "You each can paint what you are thinking" and "Each of you sees an object a little differently" are examples of comments one can make to set the stage for individuality. The teacher displays something from everyone. As some children do like to take art products home, it is well for the teacher to ask permission to keep a painting for display. The teacher refrains from choosing only the "best" for exhibit. It is important to avoid arousing compe-

Toddler art starts with a loosely held crayon, a scribbling motion, and a smile of satisfaction. (F. Kertez, photographer)

tition between children. Hands are kept off children's products no matter how much the teacher might think the picture could be improved.

Parental criticism of a child's art can be devastating. Therefore, the teacher makes efforts to communicate to parents the expected standards and the level of their child's creative development. For example, reassuring parents that scribbling is typical of their Johnny's age group and that other children in the group are scribbling, too, helps the parents become more accepting of Johnny's scribbling. Parents may have to be alerted so that they can curb older siblings' criticisms or efforts to improve a young child's products.

Not infrequently a young child competes with a school-age sibling. One young child, Linda, carelessly splashed paint on many pages to have as many products to show her parents as her school-age sibling brought home. When this happens, parents may then be counseled to lay out the array of paintings and let their child choose a favorite. This technique can help steer the child away from mass production and back onto a track of self-expression. However, the problem of sibling rivalry is also one the parent may need help with. Some young children react to home competition by refusing to create any product the teacher might encourage them to take home. Parents may pressure the child to bring something home. When a child spends the day playing with blocks or cooperating in the doll house, there is nothing to take home. Parents need this other behavioral information so that they do not overvalue art products.

Organizing the Art Centers

Most art materials are presented in the early childhood school during the indoor self-selected activity period. In mild climates art materials should be moved outdoors. Having a smorgasbord of art materials available along with other activities enables a child to create when he or she wants to and enables the teacher to work with small groups of children. With a wide variety of materials no one activity attracts all the children at one time. They naturally move to learning centers that draw their attention. After satisfying their need, they move to another center. They may be stimulated by the attractiveness of the center per se or to a valued friend who happens to be interested in that activity. The wise teacher will make the art centers as much self-service from the children's standpoint as possible. Children enjoy independence. When not tied too closely to one center, the teacher is freer to assist in other centers as needed.

The activities of the art center often require using water and washing hands. The logical location of the art center is near the water supply. An ideal situation is to have a low sink in the art center in order to keep the children from running to the bathroom with paint-covered hands and aprons. A dishpan or a bucket of water can substitute for some of the needed water if a sink is not available. Remember to bring along the paper towels.

An area for drying products is required—preferably one that the children can use themselves. Newspapers under drying racks or shelves can eliminate difficult cleanup problems later on.

Planning so that the art center is efficiently arranged encourages the children's use of the center and facilitates the teacher's supervision. If supplies are carefully stored and labeled, the teacher can get needed items in a hurry. The stage can be set so that the children can help with cleaning up the art center. They wash easels, brushes, and tables with as much enthusiasm as they paint—sometimes with more enthusiasm.

Children will use art materials spontaneously and incorporate them into other play if they are stored on an open shelf where they can reach them without asking for assistance. Newsprint, colored copier paper, crayons, markers, scissors, bottles of glue, stapler, paper punch, felt pens, masking tape, and string are items children use frequently.

Two examples support this idea. The five-year-olds had just returned from a trip to a farm. They were getting their drinks and discussing all they had seen. Sherry quietly walked to the art center, found materials, and created a pig in a basket. Both were made from paper in three dimensions. Sherry used the scissors and stapler. Her spontaneous creation showed clearly what she had liked best about the trip. The second example involves four-year-olds playing store. A child expressed a need for money in the cash register. One enterprising young man hastened to the art center, cut green paper into squares, and returned to set himself up as banker, giving money to the customers who were shopping at the store.

Places to display children's art products should be available throughout the room. Art gives the room a personal, colorful appearance.

Creativity is expressed when art materials are plentiful and directions minimal. (Bethany Weekday School, Houston)

The objects should be changed frequently to keep the interest high. Children lose interest in their own products quickly and may not even want to claim them a day or so after working on them. When children seem to have a special need to take a product home, the teacher can ask if they would like to make something special to put up in the display. If they indicate they would not, then of course it isn't important to them.

Although the following pages contain suggestions for numerous art activities, the teacher who wants depth of expression to develop in children will give them repeated opportunities to use basic paint, clay, and crayons rather than continuously changing materials. Lowenfeld and Brittain say of schools where materials continuously change, "The danger is that students may begin to feel that art is nothing more than a series of little projects or a series of experimentations with materials, bearing little relationship to expression or creativity."[16]

---

[16]Lowenfeld and Brittain, op. cit., p. 88.

TYPICAL ART ACTIVITIES FOR YOUNG CHILDREN

Painting

Easel Painting

Easel painting is an enjoyable activity for young children, and most teachers feel it should be available every day. Painting helps children develop their motor skills and express concepts and feelings. They learn to judge space size and to fill the space. They learn about colors and lines.

Tempera paints in either liquid or powdered form are available from art shops and school supply stores. A cup of liquid starch mixed in a quart of water used to mix dry tempera will prevent the watery consistency caused by the settling out of the paint. Watery paint is unpopular with children. About a quart of each color should be mixed and stored to be ready when needed. For very young children one primary color at the easel at a time is sufficient. As they gain skill and show interest in more color, then all of the primary colors are added. Older children will enjoy variety in the paint, including brown and black. Pastel colors delight children and are made by the addition of color to white. White paint is popular when colored paper is available. Jars of disposable plastic or styrofoam cups may be used for paints. Disposables save a tedious washing chore. (Recyclable disposables are a good choice.)

Brushes   Brushes to use at the easel are usually the long-handled (12-inch) variety that allows a full shoulder stroke. A stiff bristle is best. A variety of brush sizes is appreciated by older children. Foam brushes found in a paint store offer variety, are inexpensive, and come in several widths.

Mixing or stirring paint with brushes breaks off the bristles. To avoid damaging brushes, care should be exercised when washing and drying the brushes. A useful aid in washing and drying brushes can be made from the bottom half of a plastic milk bottle. Puncture the bottom with holes so that water will run through, then place the brushes in the container and set it under running water for a few minutes. The paint on the brushes will soak loose. Place the brushes to dry, handles down, in a storage container. Washing the easel brushes is a popular activity with children. Perhaps it runs a close second to clapping the erasers!

Easels   Several styles of easels are available commercially. Excellent ones can also be homemade. A wide board can be hung along a wall to be used for an easel. A 4-inch wedge behind and at the bottom of the board will hold it out from the wall and give it an appropriate angle. Or two Masonite boards can be hinged and held folded as a triangle with a metal strap. This easel can be used at the table. You can also make easels from large cardboard boxes by cutting through them diagonally. Paper is held with large tack pins. Painting paper can be placed on the wall, the table, the floor, or the sidewalk. The easels used should be the correct height for young children. Easel legs can be sawed off to an appropriate height.

Paper   Painting on large sheets of newsprint with large brushes is suggested for young children. Large materials encourage the use of their large muscles and accommodate their large designs. A minimum size of 20-by-27 inches is suggested. Paper cut to size is available from school supply stores. Some newspaper shops will cut newsprint for the school. Other publishers may donate roll ends to the school. If donations are common at the school, a paper cutter like that used for cutting wrapping paper in stores might be a good investment. A cutter speeds the preparation of the paper.

Manila paper 12-by-18 inches is appropriate for some painting. Colored paper is available and is especially delightful with white paints on a snowy day. For variety, textured paper such as the back of embossed wallpaper is interesting. Outdated wallpaper sample books can be secured from wallpaper companies. Printed newspaper can be used occasionally. Large shapes like pumpkins or hearts can be cut out and used for painting to add further variety.

Attention must be given to attaching the easel paper to the easel. The common manner of using clamps or clothespins is not satisfactory because young children can't operate the clamps without dropping the paper. Some easels have two smooth-headed nails placed about 24 inches apart at the top of the easel. The newsprint is then punched with a paper punch so that the holes match the nails. A day's supply of paper can be hung on the easel. Children can then easily remove their paper when finished and hang the painting to dry. They become more self-sufficient, taking care of the job themselves. The busy teacher is helped at the same time. Paper supplies should be stored close by the painting area.

Easel painting is very popular and is commonly planned on a daily basis. A stampede of painters results when easel painting is offered infrequently. Regular usage helps avoid complicated problems of sharing. Children who desire to produce a detailed painting or several paintings need not be rushed to finish. Closure or completion is an important aspect to encourage in creative people. Thus allowing children to finish a product to their satisfaction is important if we are to foster a habit of becoming finishers as well as starters. The child who wants to paint and is required to wait can be reassured that paints will be available the next school day.

There is good reason to place easels side by side so that children can socialize as they paint. They may share both paints and ideas. If easels are available daily, two easels are usually sufficient for a group of twenty children. More places to paint will be necessary if painting is planned only occasionally.

Guidance may be required to encourage children to squeeze their brushes against the side of the jar—especially if the teacher notes that the child is disturbed by the drips. Teachers can encourage the use of the same brush for each color by saying, "Keep the red brush in the red paint." Children's names are printed at the top left-hand corner of the painting in manuscript letters to help identify paintings, to stress the importance of the child's name, and to teach recognition of names.

Custodians will appreciate the use of a speckled throw rug under the easels to catch the occasional drips. Throw rugs are easily washed and are more aesthetically pleasing than newspapers.

It is well to pour only a small amount of paint in the paint jars for a class of young painters. With close observation for a few days, teachers can judge the approximate amount of paint needed for a session. Children normally overlay one color on the others when making their paintings. Overlaying is not to be discouraged, because children learn about the mixing of colors this way. They frequently forget, or as yet don't understand, about matching up the brush in hand with the color from which it came, so that further mixing results. Mixing and matching are, of course, two of the important learnings from the painting experience. Even though the teacher knows paints will get mixed up, it is best to start with clear colors each day. By starting with a

---

TALK IT OVER: NO. 4

Discuss among your classmates the outcomes of your planned art activity with young children. What did you learn that might help others? What did you discover about children? Yourself?

---

small amount of paint and replenishing as needed, the wasting of paint is avoided and clear colors are more likely.

If children are painting a mural on the floor, the wall, or a table, or if makeshift easels do not have the usual tray for holding paint jars, then some arrangement should be made to prevent paint jars from tipping over. Muffin tins can be used to hold jars containing paint. A cardboard serving tray from the drive-in hamburger stand is just right to hold paint jars. Simply place the paint jars where the soft drinks are usually set. A similar holder can be cut from a cardboard box.

String Painting
The same mixture of tempera paint as discussed for easel painting is used for string painting. The child holds one end of a 15-inch string, such as twine, yarn, or thread, and drops the string into the paint. Slowly the child pulls out the string and lets the paint drip off. The wet string is moved around on the paper to make various patterns. Several colors can be available with different strings in each color.

For variation children may pull the string through folded paper. For example, they arrange the paint-covered strings on one half of the paper and fold the other half over onto the strings. Holding the folded paper together, they pull the dry end of each string with their free hand. Interesting variations in designs result. The child observes the shading and blending of colors.

Block Printing

The same mixture of tempera paint is used for block printing. A shallow pan is used to arrange stamp pads of various colors. Pads are cut from several layers of paper towel, cheesecloth, or thin sponge and saturated with color. There should be only enough paint to leave color on the object without dripping. Prints can be made from a variety of objects, such as clothespins, a potato masher, a sponge, vegetables, toys, pieces of wood, and spools. Children enjoy making prints from designs cut in potato halves.

You can make rollers by dipping heavy strings in glue and wrapping them around tubes from paper towels. When the glue is dry, roll the roller on a paint pad, then roll it across the paper. Fingers also make interesting designs. In fact, children may see any painting activity as an opportunity for finger painting—a response that teachers should be prepared to accept.

Squeeze-Bottle Painting

All sorts of products, from soap to mustard, are sold in squeeze bottles with small openings. Teachers save such bottles to fill with tempera paint. Using the bottle tip as a painting tool makes an acceptable substitute for dribbling the white glue that children seem inclined to do. Practice in using the squeeze bottle helps the child control the amount of paint applied to the paper. Tempera is used with manila or construction paper. The children use the bottle tip to draw their design. They also may like to place drips of color on the paper, then fold the paper. Unusual designs are discovered as they unfold the paper. Shoe polish bottles and roll-on deodorant bottles can be used in a similar fashion.

Splatter Painting

Splatter painting is done by brushing a paint-filled toothbrush across a wire screen. A kitchen strainer works fine for a screen. You can also make a screen by attaching a square of window screening to a wooden frame of about 6 inches to 8 inches square. The children place their paper on the table. Then they place an object such as a leaf or a key on the paper. Over this goes the screen. The child brushes the paint-filled toothbrush back and forth, getting the splatter effect around the outline of the object. A similar finished product is accomplished when a small sponge dipped in paint is used to stipple around the object.

Blot Painting

Blot painting is the result when paper is folded in half, reopened, and the child then brushes, squeezes, or strings paint on one side of the fold. The paper is then folded back over the painted side, and the palm of the hand is rubbed across the paper. Children enjoy the surprise of the blending and duplicating effect.

Sand or Sawdust Painting

Sand or sawdust is mixed with moist tempera. A shaker with large holes is used to shake the mixture onto paper covered with glue or paste. Sand painting is best done out-of-doors to avoid difficult cleaning problems. Glitter can be used in place of sand or sawdust. Always cover the table with newspaper first to make cleaning up easier.

Object Painting

Using the tempera to paint wood and box collages and carpentry projects is a worthwhile conclusion to three-dimensional projects. Children enjoy painting props for their dramatic play, such as a cardboard train or a valentine mailbox.

Color Absorption

A thin solution of tempera or vegetable coloring is placed in a small dish. Several colors are provided. The child folds paper towels or squares of old sheeting and dips corners into the various colors. Children will be fascinated by the blending and shading of colors. A surface well padded with newspaper is necessary for drying these drippy products.

Finger Painting

Finger painting provides both an outlet for children's creativity and a medium for messing. This latter objective is important because modern

Children have long attention spans when painting their box creations using sponge brushes from a hardware store. (Oregon State University)

children are often under a great deal of parental pressure to stay clean. Designs with finger paint can be made, erased, and made again. Personal problem areas can be expressed, then obliterated with one stroke—a behavior that gives evidence that finger painting has therapeutic value. The medium is highly relaxing for children. Children learn concepts through their experimentation with the mixing and blending of colors. Pictures are rarely a pure color because children can't resist trying to find out what happens if they add a little blue here or a little yellow there. Teachers and parents should not be disturbed that paintings turn out a uniform muddy color. The only way to obtain pictures of pure color is to limit the choice to one color. If the children know there are several colors available, they will certainly feel deprived if not allowed to choose from all of them and mix them together.

The majority of children will enjoy finger painting. The teacher may encourage the children to participate by sitting with them and actually manipulating the paint while talking to them. Seeing the teacher's hands in the paint will reassure the doubters that she or he really means that it is all right to get messy. The teacher may involve a hesitant child by permitting him or her to help mix the paint with a beater or a spoon. However, some children prefer to watch for a long time and may never feel comfortable with finger paints. They should, of course, not be forced to finger paint.

If finger paints are provided frequently, there is less necessity for the teacher to permit large numbers of children to finger paint on a given day—which would make supervision difficult. From the practical side it is much easier to have five children painting on four different days than to try to manage finger painting for twenty on one day. It is well to limit the number of painters to a number the teacher can supervise and still keep an eye on the other activities in the room. Some teachers prefer to store the finger paints where children can help themselves whenever they desire to paint. The less pressure there is to give many people turns, the more satisfying the experience will be for the individual child.

Of course, the only tool needed for finger painting is the child's hands. The child gets full shoulder and arm movement from a standing position. Hands, knuckles, fingernails, and even the whole lower arm produce various effects. Questions like "How does it look if you use the side of your hand?" will encourage the child to experiment.

Music with soothing rhythms is especially appropriate while the children are finger painting. If the teacher plays staccato music, one shouldn't be surprised that the children splash the paint all around.

There are five necessities for finger painting—finger paints, a place to paint, aprons, a place to wash up, and a place to dry paintings.

Materials   Finger paints can be obtained commercially or mixed in the school. Two types are available commercially: one is the consistency of a thick paste, the other is a powder that the child shakes onto the wet paper from a shaker-type container. The young child likes lots of paint per picture and enjoys making many pictures. Commercial finger paints are quite expensive when provided in the amount that is necessary in the average class. Therefore a less expensive material is usually essential. Homemade products fulfill all the objectives of the medium. However, the exception is the quality of the finished picture. If a finger painting is desired for a place mat or a book cover, the teacher can use the commercial paint on that occasion.

Finger painting may be done on paper, on trays, or directly on the table. Suitable paper is of a glossy variety available in 20-by-24-inch sizes from school supply companies. Shelf paper and pages from glossy magazines can be substituted. Painting directly on wet trays, heavy plastic, oilcloth, or a wet table is practical because young children gain much of their satisfaction from the finger painting process and little from the resulting picture. Some parents have reported allowing their child to use a soap-base finger paint on the tile wall around the bathtub. The tub and the child are quickly cleaned when the shower is turned on. These latter suggestions do save the cost of the paper and the problems of wetting the paper and drying the paintings. A suggested variation is to let the child paint on the table or tray and then make a print of the final design by covering the painted surface with a sheet of paper and smoothing the paper with the palm of the hand. As the paper is peeled back, the transferred design is revealed. Printed newspaper gives an interesting effect when used for these prints.

Aprons and Washing

Aprons are essential if the children are to participate freely and not receive criticism at home for soiled clothing. Suitable paint aprons can be made from cotton-backed plastic. (See Figure 10–2.) The edges need no finishing. The neck strap of elastic and ties of cotton tape are quickly attached by sewing machine. Teachers can instruct the children to push up their sleeves. When the children wear their paint-splattered aprons as they go to wash their hands, paint will rub off on the edge of the sink as they reach forward to turn on the water. The teacher can remind the children to use the sponge to wash off the front of the sink so that the next child using it won't get the paint on clothes. Children frequently enjoy the cleanup as much as or more than the painting activity. Some schools use adult shirts for painting smocks rather than aprons. Older siblings' shirts are a better size for children under six than are adult sizes.

Drying Space and Cleanup

Drying space for finger paintings is a problem in nearly every school. A folding wooden rack (a clotheshorse) such as that used in the home for drying clothes and household linen may be satisfactory, or a clothesline, a shelf, a table, or the floor can be used. The children will use a great deal of paint if the amount is not limited by the

FIGURE 10-2
An easy-to-make painting apron
is made from cotton-backed
plastic with an elastic neck strap
and cotton tape ties.

teacher. The paintings will be excessively wet and may need to be laid flat to dry. Drying areas should be protected by a layer of newspaper because the starch material used to make finger paints sticks like glue and is therefore difficult to clean up. When the teacher plans ahead, cleaning up after finger painting is not difficult.

If the children paint on trays or on the table, a container to hold the used paint may be necessary. A rubber spatula or a wooden tongue blade from the nurse's station is useful for scraping up paint. Trays and plastic table coverings are readily washed under the faucet.

When the teacher establishes a routine and has everything ready before the children arrive, the finger paint project will go smoothly. Materials can be organized in an assembly-line fashion. For example, a table should contain a stack of glossy paper stacked upside down so that names can be written on the back, a dark crayon for writing names, a dishpan with enough water for wetting the paper, sponges, and a bucket of water for cleaning up. With guidance from the teacher the children can learn to handle the preparation and drying of their finger painting paper themselves.

RECIPES FOR HOMEMADE FINGER PAINT

Wheat-Paste or Wallpaper-Paste Uncooked Method
(Time: 3 minutes)

Mix in a large bowl:

1 pint water

1 ¼ cups dry wallpaper paste

Put the water in the bowl. Using a quick stirring motion with one hand, pour in dry wallpaper paste with the other. Keep stirring and adding paste until the proper thickness is achieved. Pour into jars and stir in tempera paint for color. A drop or two of wintergreen (purchased in a drugstore) will disguise the odor of the mixture if it seems unpleasant. *Caution:* Some wallpaper pastes contain a chemical mouse deterrent. Teachers should read the labels of all materials used to ensure that they do not contain chemicals harmful to children.

Cooked-Starch Method
(Time: 10 minutes plus cooling time)

Mix in a large bowl:

1 cup laundry starch or cornstarch dissolved in a small amount of cold water

5 cups boiling water added slowly to dissolved starch

Cook the mixture until it is thick and glossy. Add 1 cup mild soap flakes. Add color in separate containers. Cool before using.

Liquid-Starch Method
(Time: none)

Give the children a tablespoon of liquid starch. Let them shake tempera on with a salt shaker. (If you feel this is wasteful of the paint supply, then mix the color in the starch before presenting it to the children.)

Soap-Flaked Method
(Time: 10 minutes)

Mix in a small bowl:

Soap flakes

A small amount of water

Beat until stiff with an eggbeater. Use white soap on dark paper, or add color to the soap and use it on light-colored paper. Gives a slight three-dimensional effect.

Teachers commonly complain that finger paints are "too messy" or that children or furnishings get paint all over them. Careful organization eliminates some of these complaints. To minimize messy problems, it helps to cover the table with several layers of newspaper; then when one child uses a large amount of paint that oozes over the side of the paper, you can easily prepare the place for the next child by peeling off a layer of newspaper. Also, less mess results if the children stand up to paint. Without thinking, children will handle chairs with paint-covered hands, so chairs should be removed. The teacher may choose to wear a long apron to eliminate concern over getting paint on clothing.

Foot Painting

Foot painting is a variation of finger painting that you might like to try on a warm spring or summer day when the children are wearing light shoes and shorts and you can work outside without shoes. The children will have the unusual experience of seeing their footprints and perhaps creating designs on a paper or on the sidewalks. This project might create real havoc inside a classroom unless many adults are present to help with shoes and other problems that do not occur outdoors on warm days. Outdoors the garden hose can be of great help in cleaning up the painters' feet and the painting area.

Drawing

Drawing offers children a prewriting experience. Using a tool, they gain experience making lines and filling in the spaces, developing small muscle coordination in order to control the tool. The stages discussed earlier also apply to this technique. Drawing is likely to be more familiar than other techniques when children enter school.

Crayons

Crayons are probably the art medium most familiar to children. If a child has any art material at home, surely it will be crayons. Crayons give children a medium that expresses their creativity and permits them to see clearly the results of the movement of the tool. In comparison with other media crayons make it harder for a small child to obtain depth of color without prolonged effort and are therefore somewhat unsatisfactory. By unwrapping the paper from the crayon, the child can use the side as well as the tip of the crayon. Some new types of crayons are softer and make it easier for the child to obtain color intensity. Children enjoy the type of crayon that is dipped in water as it is used.

Because crayons are likely to be familiar, the teacher often plans the use of this medium during the first days of school. The teacher wants the children to feel at home and begin participating freely. They are more likely to do so upon seeing materials they know.

Children should be allowed to create their own designs on newsprint, manila paper, or colored copier paper. Coloring-book-type material tends to stifle the child's creativity and is not recommended. A teacher should have confidence in the child's ability to create designs—and to fill in the color within the borders. The teacher can encourage exploration with various types of lines and shapes. Crayon prints can be made if a flat object—a leaf, a penny, or a piece of lace—is placed under the paper, which the child covers with color, using the side of the crayon.

Crayon Resist

Crayon resist is a technique that involves making a drawing in crayon, then painting over the design with a thin wash of watercolor. Especially effective is a white wash on black or blue paper or a black wash over Halloween pumpkins. This technique works best with fives and sixes, who will be willing to overlay their drawings with several more layers of crayon. Without the thick layer of wax the resist effect doesn't work. The wash is a thinned tempera paint. The teacher should experiment with the materials before presenting them to the children.

Felt Pens or Markers

Felt pens come in many colors and some have washable ink, making them appropriate for use with young children. Though these are a more expensive medium, they may well encourage learning activity by some children who are not happy with other media. The colors are intense and transfer easily to paper. Teaching children to cap their pens tightly after use will help make the ink last longer.

Chalk

Using chalk on the chalkboard gives the child another drawing medium. It, too, is a worthwhile prewriting experience. A chalkboard can be made from a piece of wallboard, plywood, or heavy cardboard painted with blackboard paint. (It need not be black.) Chalks in many colors are available. Children will enjoy the large soft chalk called *pastels* because the color transfers readily. Pastels come in bright colors and are about 4 inches long and an inch thick. Blackboard chalk is much harder.

Wet chalk can provide a creative experience wherein pastel chalks are used on wet manila construction paper. Large wrapping-paper murals are interesting when done with wet chalk. The chalk is dipped in water, then the child draws with the chalk. A starchy water (see the section on tempera paint) is sometimes used to moisten the paper and gives a shiny effect when dry. Because of the size of the chalk, the children are able to make large motions and large objects in their drawings. Children like this medium because they get deep color quickly. Pastels also work well for making murals using large paper tacked to the wall or spread on the floor or a table.

The children will need aprons. They occasionally see wet chalk as another finger paint. The table is more easily cleaned up if it is covered with newspaper. A drying area is required. Care should be taken when you are sending chalk drawings home because chalk will rub off on clothing and car upholstery, making parents unhappy. It is sometimes convenient to roll the drawings and secure them with a rubber band.

Gluing, Cutting, and Tearing

A *collage* is an artistic composition of fragments of paper and other material. The word comes from a French word meaning *gluing*. The opportunity to be creative with odds and ends of "junk" is very popular with young children. They develop skills while using the scissors, glue sticks, glue bottles, and paste brushes. They develop eye–hand coordination; a sense of balance, size, color, and proportion; and a sense of the third dimension (depth).

The collage invites creativity even by adults because they acquire a habit of seeing a creative use for many things one might throw away. What

As children use tools for drawing, name writing begins. Name writing is one of the early literacy experiences. (Michigan State University)

can be done with those colorful bags that department stores put your purchases in? those perfume and makeup boxes? or the towel and toilet paper rolls? Your roommate or spouse will probably be dismayed as you hoard such junk for creative art activities, so plan early to organize the materials and minimize the fire hazard and the clutter. In a time of high costs and pollution, recycling is of increasing importance—and you get fine materials for children's art activities without cost. Friends and parents will save things for you, too.

Art made by using clean, edible food can be costly and wasteful. In one child care center the children who were pasting pieces of breakfast cereal on collages might have been better off if the cereal had been served to them with milk. Far preferable for use on collages are scraps waiting to be given a new use, so look for them.

Tearing and Cutting

Tearing and cutting are two methods of preparing material for the collage. Young children simply enjoy an opportunity to tear and cut. Well before children can manipulate the scissors, they are able to tear paper into bits. Parents probably remember a time when their child tore up the unread newspaper or ripped a favorite magazine. Children can be encouraged to tear paper for their artwork. Even after they can use the scissors, they may like to use the tearing method to obtain certain effects. Cutting with scissors requires finer eye–hand coordination and more mature motor skills than does tearing. Older children who have not had experience with scissors will pass through a stage of awkwardness in using them. Older children benefit from suggestions as to how to use scissors more than do younger children. Both groups seem to need ample time to experiment with scissors until they discover a satisfactory way to hold and use them.

Blunt-end scissors should be provided. They should be kept free of paste and glue and in good operating condition. Nothing is so frustrating as scissors that do not cut. The teacher should try scissors out occasionally to be sure they are usable.

Left-handed scissors should be purchased for the left-handed children. This fact seems to surprise some people, but a right-handed teacher need only try to use right-handed scissors in the left hand to see why left-handed children have difficulty cutting with them. They can't see the line that they are trying to cut unless they hold their work far to the right so they can see over the blade of the scissors. Some left-handed scissors come with colored handles to aid children in distinguishing them from right-handed ones. If they are not clearly marked, the teacher may tie colored yarn to the handles of the left-handed scissors.

If a child has difficulty learning to cut with scissors, a teacher may want to try double-ring training scissors. This scissors has an extra set of rings that allow the teacher's hand to fit over the child's hand to help the child develop the cutting technique.

It is interesting for children to experiment with cutting different lines—jagged, wavy, straight, fringed, or some combination of these. Kindergartners will enjoy cutting strips of lightweight paper and curling them with the edge of the scissors' blade. These curls may be used to decorate various objects. Old magazines provide a stimulus to the young cutters. They can choose one type of object to look for—e.g., cars, food for Thanksgiving dinner, toys, animals, or babies. However, adults should not be surprised when children get sidetracked and cut out other interesting objects.

The light weight of colored typing or copier paper makes it especially useful for free cutting by young children. Lightweight paper is easier to fold and cut than construction paper. Also, five sheets of typing paper cost the same as one sheet of construction paper. Scraps of leftover paper can be prepared for collage work. When the teacher plans to let the children practice cutting—say, hearts—squares of paper can be prepared ahead of time to enable the children to cut out several objects per page. When it is left up to the children, they will cut their object out of the center of the large sheet, leaving the remainder for scrap.

Gluing or Pasting

Gluing or pasting is a skill children learn to help them complete their collages. Children may at first manipulate the paste or glue much as they do finger paint. They use excessive amounts when judged by adult standards. Using white glue in squeeze bottles is very interesting to children. They often use this glue as a white paint, making designs on their paper. To curb this use of glue, the teacher can give the children white tempera paint in plastic squeeze bottles to be used for making designs. Occasionally the teacher can demonstrate the amount of glue required by saying, "The white glue is very strong. See, it takes only a tiny spot to hold this big piece of paper." Sometimes such a demonstration helps reduce the amount of glue children use. Because white glue holds more securely than paste, it is better to give children white glue for structures that have considerable weight or strain. When cherished objects fall apart, it is very frustrating to children. White glue can be purchased in gallon bottles, then transferred first to a squeeze bottle with a large opening, such as those used for mustard, and next transferred to the small bottles that children can handle. For some projects white glue can be diluted with water and brushed with paste brushes or foam brushes. Some white glues wash out of clothing. For applying a material such as Miracle Muck over large areas, small (3" wide) paint rollers with foam rollers (rather than the pile-on-cardboard rollers) work great for spreading the muck quickly enough that none of it has a chance to dry before laying fabric over it. This same technique would work great with the white glue. These rollers also work well for painting any large areas. The foam rollers are easy to wash and can be reused.

Paste can be made from flour and water. It can also be bought in quantity. Since paste dries quickly, it should be kept covered as much as possible. Children may like brushes or sticks to use with paste. Newer glue sticks are convenient. They must be capped when not in use.

The variety of materials for collage is limited only by the imagination of the teacher and the children. The home, the yard, the workshop, the park, and construction sites are places to look for castoff materials suitable for three-dimensional art projects. The teacher's role is to provide an interesting assortment of materials, and the children's creativity will do the rest. Most of the materials can be castoffs—helping ease the strain on the center's budget. Labeled shoe boxes or coffee cans containing collage materials help keep cupboards tidy and materials easily obtainable.

Suggested materials for collage are

- acorns
- bird gravel
- boxes, tubes, and egg cartons from the kitchen
- cellophane and tissue paper
- confetti
- corn (Start with dry corn on the cob. Let the children shell it.)
- cotton, fabric, wool, yard, and fur
- cupcake papers and paper candy cups from boxed candy
- doilies (paper or foil)
- eggshells (colored or white) to cover collages or to be glued to bottles for vases
- excelsior or other packing material
- feathers
- glitter
- grass, twigs, leaves, flowers
- gummed paper, stamps, and holiday stickers
- magazines and catalogs
- matchsticks, toothpicks, popsicle sticks, and tongue blades
- paper cups (the cone-shaped cups are especially interesting)
- paper scraps, construction paper, wrapping paper, holiday cards, foils, wallpaper, corrugated paper
- nutshells
- precut shapes (hearts, diamonds, squares, triangles, and circles)

- sawdust and wood shavings
- salt or sand colored with tempera
- spools and wood pieces
- straws (drinking) or wheat straw
- strips of newspaper or magazines
- Styrofoam curls and pieces
- wire and pipe cleaners

Three-Dimensional Art

Sculptures made with three-dimensional materials form another type of collage. Box art is one form in which the children create their structures from an assortment of disposable containers, such as boxes and tubes. Scraps of wood offer another texture and can be glued together to form sculptures. Wood scraps can be obtained from carpentry and cabinet shops. White glue is essential for these structures. After drying, these art objects can be painted.

Modeling

Plastic modeling materials give children another medium for creative self-expression. The form changes as the child uses the material. Material such as ceramic clay, playdough, Plasticene, salt ceramic, Silly Putty, sawdust with wheat paste, and sand are common materials for modeling. Children enjoy the opportunity to be messy with these materials. Children can change the material and can add or subtract from the amount. They can experiment with shapes—forming the same piece first into a long worm, then into a flat pancake. There is opportunity to pound and squeeze, which may help a child work out hostile or aggressive feelings. Children imitate and socialize during the activity. While enjoying the "gushy" mixture of clay and water, Kim said, "I'm making chocolate soup."

The products will be quite primitive. The same developmental stages apply in modeling as in drawing. The teacher and the parents will have to be content with simple products. Most teachers of young children make no attempt to save the products. Firing of young children's clay products is usually disappointing.

Ceramic Clay

Ceramic clay—sometimes called mud clay—will attract children, especially if the teacher works at the table with them. A visit to an art center to see a potter at work offers an opportunity to observe the relationship of the potter's work to familiar vases, pitchers, and plates. Such a visit will encourage many nonparticipators to use this "messy" medium.

The teacher should provide modeling materials in good condition. It helps for adults to manipulate the clay beforehand to be sure that it is soft enough for the children to use. Sitting with the children and manipulating the clay in the manner that they are using it is best. Avoid making models for children, for this invites them to become spectators and does not fulfill goals for individual development.

Ceramic clay may be purchased ready to use or in a powdered form that must be mixed with water. Your local potters' guild may sell you clay or allow you to prepare it in their facilities. The clay can be used and reused. If it becomes dry, the clay is reclaimed by adding water. If the clay dries in large lumps, it can be placed in a cloth bag and pounded to a powdery consistency, then moistened again. Children can be taught to leave the clay molded in large balls with a big thumb hole in the side; then water can be added to the thumb hole to help keep the clay at a proper consistency. The storage container should be covered tightly. Boards for use on the table where the children will use the clay may be made of Masonite and should be about 15 inches square. Cotton-backed plastic with the plastic side down on the table makes a good working surface. The covering is simply hung to dry until the next clay experience. The children need no tools. A tongue blade from the nurse's station is useful for scraping clay from the board. Aprons for the children are important.

Playdough

Playdough provides many of the same experiences as clay. However, most children do not think of dough as being dirty, as they do clay. Therefore they do not have the inhibitions they may have in working with clay. They are inclined to play at being cooks, saying, "I'm making cookies." If cookies or pancakes have been recent group projects, this experience may be played out with the playdough.

The playdough can be made with little difficulty. The homemade varieties are usually superior to commercial doughs and are, of course, cheaper. Teachers should test the consistency of the doughs they give the children. Playdough should be soft and moist enough so that the child can readily manipulate it. The salt content should be low, so that the dough does not dry out the child's hands. Additional flour may be required if the dough is sticky. Cutters, rolling pins, and plates may add to the child's enjoyment. Parents appreciate playdough recipes because playdough is a good home activity. Playdough is easily cleaned up and makes a good gift.

Plasticene

Plasticene is a commercial plastic medium. It is less useful for young children than the materials previously discussed. However, it introduces some variety for the children if offered occasionally. The Plasticene must be warm to be malleable for small hands. The teacher may set it near a radiator or work it in her or his own hands before offering it to the children. Variety and art stores sell Plasticene.

Sand

Sand can be provided indoors in a sand table or outdoors in the yard. It lends itself to quiet, individual creative play or to creative group interaction. Older children develop themes and carry them out cooperatively. Sand should be of beach quality and clean. It should be kept moist so the children can pack it tightly into molds or tunnels and so it won't fly into hair and eyes. Plenty of shovels should be available. Sifters and containers to fill are popular. Kitchen castoffs, such as pans and cans, encourage the playing of home-

maker roles. Small cars or trucks or chunks of wood to substitute for cars will stimulate road building. When used indoors, sand may damage floor coverings and finishes. The sand table can be located on a cement floor if available. Firm rules (limits) regarding proper conduct around the sand should be established from the beginning. Avoid overcrowding.

Blocks

Blocks are mentioned here because of the creative opportunities they offer children. They will be discussed in other chapters because of their contribution to outdoor play, to concept building, and to dramatic play—all interrelated. The "whole child" learns when playing with blocks. Gross motor skills and minute small motor coordinations will be challenged by blocks. Some children who are not attracted to other creative media are happy using blocks. Parents may need to be reassured that the child who uses blocks is indeed creative. Because the child's creativity is expressed with the school's blocks, there are no products to take home for parental approval.

Carpentry

Carpentry is a creative medium that offers emotional release and opportunities to develop large and small muscle skills. A table with vises and clamps to hold the wood for sawing or hammering is a big help to young children. Real tools that work well should be purchased. Scrap lumber can usually be obtained from cabinet shops or lumberyards. Bottle caps and spools make wheels for objects.

The safe use of tools is a major item to learn. Rules for using tools must be carefully set by the teacher. Supervising and limiting the number of children at work around the carpentry table are important safety precautions.

The use of glue in place of hammering can satisfy children who like to use wood but don't like to hammer. Paints can be available to paint the products. Of course, outdoors is the best place for this noisy activity. A separate indoor space

RECIPES FOR PLAYDOUGH

Uncooked Playdough

Mix in a large bowl:

2 cups flour

1 cup salt

6 teaspoons alum (from grocery store)

2 tablespoons salad oil

1 cup water plus desired color (vegetable color or tempera paint)

This recipe is simple enough that a group of children can help the teacher make it. Of course, let them use the dough immediately. If stored in a plastic bag, it will keep several weeks.

Cooked Playdough

1. Mix in a large bowl:

   1 cup flour

   $\frac{1}{2}$ cup cornstarch

   1 cup water

2. Boil in a pan:

   4 cups water

   1 cup salt

3. Slowly pour the boiling water into the bowl mixture until they are mixed thoroughly. The mixture will have a white-sauce appearance. Then put this mixture back in the pan, cook it over low heat, stirring constantly until it is thickened and stands stiff. Cooking time: 10–15 minutes.

4. Cool.

5. Stir in 4 to 5 cups of flour until a dough consistency is obtained. More flour may have to be added to make the dough workable.

6. Then knead in as much flour as is required to obtain a good, pliable, soft, but not sticky, consistency. Makes fifteen to twenty medium-sized balls.

7. Store the dough in a plastic bag. Refrigerate it for best keeping. Allow it to warm to room temperature before using it. If it becomes sticky, add flour. Children enjoy working in flour.

with acoustical tile can be prepared for young carpenters, however, and other quiet activities can still be enjoyed in the playroom.

HELPING A NEW VOLUNTEER

When you are the lead teacher, you will frequently be called on to orient new volunteers, assistants, and even parents who assist in the art area. Actually, considerable inservice education should occur before people are assigned to help with children. Because of the sensitive nature of creative expression, children should have teachers who know and understand them well. However, a new person may need assistance in setting up the area efficiently to help eliminate problems that often occur with poor arrangements. You will want to state your policy about freedom of

"Silly Putty"

Mix in a large bowl:

2 cups white glue

1 ¾ cups liquid starch or cornstarch

Add desired vegetable coloring.

Salt Ceramic

1. Heat in a saucepan until boiling:

   2 cups salt

   ⅔ cup water

2. Add while stirring quickly:

   1 cup cornstarch dissolved in ½ cup cold water

3. Mix with the hands. The mixture may need a few more drops of water to make pliable dough. Use it to make a child's handprint, tree decorations, or beads. Hardens at room temperature in two days. Can be painted.

Sawdust Dough

Mix in a large bowl:

Wallpaper paste with only enough water to make a paste

Add sawdust until dough consistency is produced.

Let figures dry thoroughly for several days. Paint or shellac.

---

expression and creativity and advise specifically against modeling figures or helping the child draw or paint. Help arrange the area so the individual will have only a few children at work in the area at a time. Give constructive positive feedback as the period progresses.

Conclusions

Creativity is a human potential that integrates physical, mental, social, and emotional growth. Creativity is fostered in good schools for young children by a free, flexible, accepting, and open environment and by teachers who are openly discovering, inventing, and creating. Many activities have been suggested to help start the teacher toward creative teaching. For neither the children nor the teacher are patterns presented—

only raw materials have been suggested and the reassurance that "you can do it."

In addition to the opportunity for creative self-expression, the child is practicing many small motor skills, eye-hand coordination, left-to-right progression, and whole-part relationships, all of which are foundations for later reading and writing. The opportunity for self-expression should be enough to sell an art program, but the additional benefits further strengthen the reasons for providing art activities.

The approach of the Reggio Emilia schools in Italy has been described. Creativity abounds in this program that is stimulating the interest of both theoreticians and practitioners. Through gaining knowledge of Reggio Emilia you can further your appreciation of the possibilities for integrating creativity into various aspects of the curriculum.

Applications

1. Do the "Talk It Over" activities suggested in the chapter.
2. Write an activity plan for an art activity for a few children using information and the sample (Figure 6–2) in Chapter 6. Secure approval, carry out the plan, and evaluate the results from the children's point of view and from your viewpoint. Prepare a report and hand it in along with your approved activity plan.
3. Evaluate your total participation performance on your evaluation form developed in Chapter 1.
4. Add ideas and plans for art activities to your Resource File.

Study Questions

1. Define *creativity*.
2. Identify ways creativity is fostered in early childhood schools.
3. Describe Reggio Emilia schools.
4. Refer to the developmental tasks in Chapter 2. Make notes on how art activity can contribute to each developmental task for a child.
5. Name and illustrate with a drawing the developmental stages of children's art as described by Brittain.
6. Discuss the findings on right- and left-brain research and the implications for art education.
7. Explain how writing and reading are fostered by art activities.
8. Make a chart showing each category of art activity—painting, drawing, building, modeling, and cutting and gluing. Outline appropriate space recommendations, supplies, equipment, and guidance for each one.

Videotapes

Thinking and Creativity
30 minutes
Thelma Harms and Debby Cryer explore the differences between adults' and children's thinking and describe the function of creative experiences as a unique way of learning through discovery. Explores the concept of giftedness. DC/TATS MEDIA, Frank Porter Graham Child Development Center, University of North Carolina at Chapel Hill CB8040, 300 NCNB Plaza, Chapel Hill, NC 27599-8040.

Additional Readings

Brittain, W. Lambert. *Creativity, Art, and the Young Child.* New York: Macmillan, 1979.

Cartwright, Sally. "Learning with Large Blocks." *Young Children* 45:3, March 1990, 38–41.

Cole, Elizabeth, and Claire Schaefer. "Can Young Children Be Art Critics?" *Young Children* 45:2, January 1990, 33–38.

de la Roche, Elisa. "Snowflakes: Developing Meaningful Art Experiences for Young Children." *Young Children* 51:2, January 1996, 82–83.

Edwards, Linda C. *Affective Development and the Creative Arts.* Upper Saddle River, NJ: Merrill/Prentice Hall, 1990.

Feeney, Stephanie, and Eva Moravcik. "A Thing of Beauty: Aesthetic Development in Young Children." *Young Children* 42:6, September 1987, 7–15.

Goodnow, Jacqueline. *Children's Drawings.* Cambridge, MA: Harvard University Press, 1977.

Gowan, J. C., J. Khatena, and E. Paul Torrance. *Creativity: Its Educational Implications.* Dubuque, IA: Kendall/Hunt, 1981.

Harms, T., and R. M. Clifford. *Early Childhood Environment Rating Scale.* New York: Teachers College Press, 1980.

Hayes, Linda F. "From Scribbling to Writing: Smooth the Way." *Young Children* 45:3, March 1990, 62–68.

Katz, Lilian G. "Impressions of Reggio Emilia Preschools." *Young Children* 45:6, September 1990, 11–12.

New, Rebecca. "Excellent Early Education: A City in Italy Has It." *Young Children* 45:6, September 1990, 4–10.

Ornstein, R. "The Split and Whole Brain." *Human Nature* 1:5, 1978, 76–83.

Reifel, Stuart. "Block Construction: Children's Developmental Landmarks in Representation of Space." *Young Children* 40:1, November 1984, 61–67.

Schirrmacher, Robert. "Talking with Young Children About Their Art." *Young Children* 41:5, July 1986, 3–7.

Seefeldt, Carol. "Art—A Serious Work." *Young Children* 50:3, March 1995, 39–45.

Smith, N. R. *Experience and Art: Teaching Children to Paint.* New York: Teachers College Press, 1983.

Torrance, E. Paul. *Guiding Creative Talent.* Huntington, NY: Robert Krieger, 1976.

Wolf, Aline D. "Art Postcards—Another Aspect of Your Aesthetics Program." *Young Children* 45:2, January 1990, 39–43.

CHAPTER 11

Science Activities

Southeast Oakland Vocational Technical Center

Objectives

✔ Identify stages of children's cognitive development according to several research theories.

✔ Define science and the scientific method.

✔ Identify the factors that influence planning of children's science activities.

✔ Identify and give a rationale for a cumulative plan.

✔ Identify and evaluate activities that give children insights into the biological, physical, and social sciences.

"How do you tell which one is mine, if you put them all together?" asked four-year-old Sandra as she helped her teacher arrange the cups of newly planted seeds in the sun on the window ledge.

"If all the people in the state lived in one house, it would have to be BIG," exclaimed five-year-old Miguel.

Questions and comments like these flow naturally in high-quality early childhood centers. Sandra and Miguel are using their reasoning ability. They are growing cognitively. Their teachers are setting the stage for this learning to occur.

COGNITIVE FUNCTIONING: A DEFINITION

The word **cognitive** comes from the Latin word *cognoscere*, which means *to know*. Cognitive functioning can be thought of as the act or process of knowing, including awareness and judgment. Some call cognitive functioning mental or intellectual functioning. **Cognitive development** refers to the increased depth and breadth of intellectual or mental functioning that occurs as the individual matures. The brain is the center for cognitive functioning, storing and utilizing information gained through the five sensory modes—seeing, hearing, touching, tasting,

and smelling. Some researchers describe the brain as functioning like a giant computer, yet the brain performs feats that computers are not now capable of.

COGNITIVE DEVELOPMENT LINKED WITH OTHER DEVELOPMENT

Physiological conditions, including genetic inheritance, affect the development of the brain from the moment of conception. Adequate nutrition, both prenatally and postnatally, restricted or no drug use, and the absence of disease or damage to mother and child set the stage for the healthy child with a well-developed brain.

As the infant matures, learning takes place following sensory stimulation from people, things, and activity in the environment. Interpersonal aspects influence the infant's cognitive functioning. The loving and supportive interaction the child experiences with parents and caregivers

Listening to a seashell is a typical science activity for children, especially those living close to the ocean. (Rebecca Peña Hines, photographer)

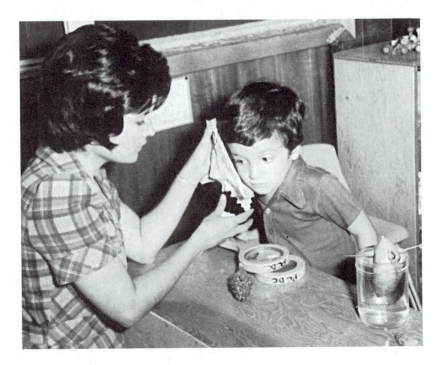

Discovering a shadow, an early science activity for a toddler. (J. Page, photographer)

influences the child's level of autonomy and developing concept of self. Information is perceived through the senses and is stored in the brain.

The brain is intricately involved with the development of motor skills also. Moving the body involves many levels of knowing and functioning by the brain. The right hemisphere of the brain controls the left side of the body, and the left hemisphere of the brain controls the right side of the body.

During the years before school "the connection between the two hemispheres of the brain is less complete than it will be after 7 or 8 years of age. In order to develop both sides of the brain fully during the time before much intercommunication occurs, it is recommended that children have abundant music, rhythmic exercises, movement exploration, art materials, and other right-hemisphere-related experiences, as well as those

more pertinent to the left hemisphere, such as speaking, reading, and counting."[1]

Other aspects of brain development and functioning are discussed in Chapters 10 and 13. The left-dominant functioning is called **verbal-analytical** because the person operating in the left hemisphere is effective in dealing with the object world, is analytical, rational, and abstract in cognitive style. The cognitive style of the right-hemisphere-oriented person is described as **holistic**, meaning that the individual tends to use imagination, creativity, and intuition and is able to see a situation or picture as a whole.[2]

The research into—and suggested applications of—brain mapping are still in the formative stage, yet they seem to have implications for parents and teachers of young children. One thing experienced early childhood educators can readily appreciate is the variety of cognitive styles in young children. They've usually called it individuality. Every day a teacher sees children like Tina, who say, "We have these kinds of flowers in our backyard," and who are operating in a left-hemisphere or analytical mode. Teachers also have children like Miguel, who appears to get the whole picture when he says, "If all the people in the state lived in one house it would have to be BIG!" The challenge is to stimulate both hemispheres of each child's brain and help each child use the style appropriate for each new situation.

GOALS FOR CHILDREN'S COGNITIVE GROWTH

Fostering children's cognitive growth in the early years is very important. By reviewing the developmental tasks in Chapter 2 you will note the cognitive component in each one. Developing

---

[1]Laura E. Berk, *Child Development* (Boston: Allyn and Bacon, 1991), pp. 192–194.
[2]For an interesting analysis see Thomas Banville, "Brain 'Hemisphericity': A High Voltage Topic," *Early Years* 10:2 (September 1979), 51–53, and continued in 10:2 (October 1979), 38–41.

and utilizing children's curiosity are prime objectives. Encouraging children to think, reason, infer, and generalize is desirable. Briefly, the children are learning

1. to understand the world around them,
2. to understand people and things,
3. to understand their bodies and feelings and how to care for themselves,
4. to symbolize—using language and forms to communicate,
5. to make choices and decisions and grow in independence,
6. to do what is right according to values of the local, national, and global community.

Types of Intellectual Operations

According to psychologist Guilford, children may be capable of five different types of intellectual operations:

1. They may perceive or recognize a problem: **cognition**.
2. They may be able to retain what is recognized and recall it: **memory**.
3. They may use the information perceived and retained to find the one right answer: **convergent thinking**.
4. They may take off from information already processed, seeking a novel, a different kind of answer: **divergent thinking**.
5. They may evaluate critically the solution hit upon, perhaps sensing a deficiency in their problem solving and trying to correct it: **evaluative thinking**.[3]

The teacher will plan learning experiences to foster each of these five operations.

If teachers and parents hope to stimulate learning meaningfully they must help the child organize knowledge in meaningful ways. Children are accepted and not ridiculed for their lack of knowledge. They are supported in their need to learn from firsthand experience. Selecting and planning experiences to satisfy children's mental needs are important in both the home and the school.

Piaget's Stages of Mental Growth

In recent years the work of Jean Piaget, the Swiss child psychologist, has received considerable attention from early childhood educators and psychologists. Many of Piaget's observations began as he watched the development of his own three youngsters. Piaget made his observations and carried on research for many years and contemporary researchers are continuing his work. Piaget described four stages of cognitive or intellectual development.[4] Two of these stages are of major interest to those who are caring for and teaching young children in homes and in all types of early childhood education programs.

Figure 11–1 is a conceptualization of Piaget's stages. It indicates a few important characteristics of each stage and helps you think of each stage as an undergirding support for the next and ensuing stages, an important concept in human development. For progression from infancy upward, read the table from bottom to top.

Sensorimotor

Piaget called the earliest stage **sensorimotor**. This label and stage link movement with stimuli perceived through the senses. The stage includes the months from birth to age two. This period is one in which the child learns to control the body in space. It is a period of reflexes and a period when intelligence exists without language or symbols. During these first two years the infant or toddler learns by exploring space bodily and

---

[3]J. P. Guilford, *Personality* (New York: McGraw-Hill, 1959), pp. 359–394. Also see J. P. Guilford, "The Structure-of-Intellect Model," in *Handbook of Intelligence*, ed. B. B. Wolman (New York: Wiley, 1985), pp. 225–266.

[4]See Jean Piaget, *The Psychology of Intelligence* (London: Routledge and Kegan Paul, 1950) for additional details of Piaget's theory. For easy-to-understand applications of Piaget's theory see *Cognition in Early Childhood* by Janie Dyson Osborn and D. Keith Osborn (Athens, GA: Education Associates, 1983).

FIGURE 11–1
Summary of Piaget's stages of
cognitive development.

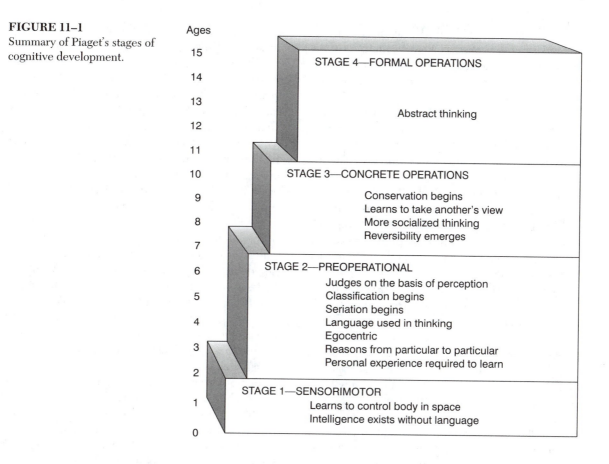

Ages

15

14

13

12

11

10

9

8

7

6

5

4

3

2

1

0

STAGE 4—FORMAL OPERATIONS

Abstract thinking

STAGE 3—CONCRETE OPERATIONS
Conservation begins
Learns to take another's view
More socialized thinking
Reversibility emerges

STAGE 2—PREOPERATIONAL
Judges on the basis of perception
Classification begins
Seriation begins
Language used in thinking
Egocentric
Reasons from particular to particular
Personal experience required to learn

STAGE 1—SENSORIMOTOR
Learns to control body in space
Intelligence exists without language

by handling objects and exploring them through touching, tasting, seeing, hearing, and smelling.

Preoperational

The **preoperational** stage, Piaget's second stage, follows the sensorimotor stage. As the label implies, it is the period prior to logical thinking or operations. The preoperational stage is one of "here and now." It lasts approximately from ages two years to seven years.

The preoperational is a self-centered or ego-centered stage during which children view their surroundings primarily in terms of themselves. Their learning requires experiences with real objects and things as opposed to being told about things. The child now begins to think of things

that are not present. You can observe examples of this as you watch children play family, pet, or worker roles in dramatic play.

Piaget said a child receives stimuli from the environment and acts on the stimuli with whatever prior experience he or she has in a process called **assimilation**. For example, toddlers flail their spindle toys the same way they learned to shake their rattles. This, of course, creates a problem because the former are heavier and more harmful to themselves and others. Therefore, they must learn some new behavior, for example, putting the discs over the spindle instead of shaking the toy vigorously. They thus **accommodate** to the new toy by learning new behaviors.

The preoperational child reasons from the particular to the particular. Piaget called this type of reasoning **transductive**. The child erroneously puts objects and events together that don't logically go together.

In this stage young children begin to classify objects according to some criterion. After sorting objects according to one criterion, they become focused or **centered** and cannot shift and classify according to another. For example, after sorting beads according to color, they will not be able to cancel that perception and re-sort the beads according to shape. According to this finding, we would only confuse children by presenting them with multifaceted problems when they are in this stage of development.

Young children between two and seven think very differently than older children and adults. It will be a challenge for you to listen as children reveal their mode of thinking through their language and behavior. Children need to discover knowledge for themselves. It is of no use to teach them to parrot the right answers before they have any basis for understanding the concepts. Kamii, a researcher studying applications of Piaget's theories writes, "Children can be taught to give correct answers to 2 + 3, but they cannot be taught directly the relationships underlying this addition."[5]

Concrete Operations

The third stage in Piaget's scheme is called **concrete operations**. Now the child can reason logically about things and ideas. This stage occurs from the seventh to the eleventh year. In this stage the school-age child learns to take another's view. He or she learns that substance, weight, length, area, and numbers remain the same regardless of changes in position. Piaget called this process **conservation**. The classic experiment that is simple for anyone to try is to show the child liquid in a tall glass, then pour it into a

squat one, and ask the child which glass has the most liquid. During the years from two through six the child says the tall one has the most, whereas during the period of seven to eleven years the child is said to "conserve" when reasoning that changing the size of the container doesn't change the amount of liquid.

Piaget discusses the aspect of **reversibility** in flexible and controlled thought, which he says emerges when the child is from seven to eleven years old. Now the child can think of an act and think it undone. For example, Juanita can stand in the kitchen door in her muddy boots and think of the muddy tracks she'll make if she enters and walks across the floor. She can mentally think of her deed undone (tracks removed). During her first six years she couldn't do this much reasoning. If you had asked her after she walked across the floor, "Did you make those tracks on the floor?" she may have denied it. She was honestly unable to reverse her thoughts or think about the floor when it was clean. By placing reversibility in this older age bracket, Piaget helps us understand that our young children are generally unable to do the mental scheming that sometimes is attributed to them. For example, when three-year-old Billy's mother says, "He's flattering me so I'll let him play with his battery car," it is highly improbable that Billy is sophisticated enough to have schemed in that way.

Formal Operations

Piaget's fourth stage is called **formal operations**. This stage begins around the eleventh year and continues through maturity. Now adolescents can think about their own thinking. They can think about what could be as well as what is, something they could not do earlier. They can now think about and deal with concepts in the abstract. At a personal level, for example, they can understand their bank account and the amount of money they have available. They do not need to have their bankbook in their pocket to know when they have funds for a certain need. A young child whose favorite toy or security blanket is left at

---

[5]Constance Kamii, *Number in Preschool & Kindergarten* (Washington, DC: NAEYC, 1982), p. 15.

grandmother's can't reason that it is safe. He or she must have it in hand to be sure.

Clearly stages three and four are far out of the range of early childhood education, but they are presented here because our understanding and design of programs for the development and education of young children will be aided. The sensorimotor and preoperational stages are of concern to us in our planning. Being familiar with the more advanced stages helps us know what is too complicated for our young children. Piaget's work is helpful to teachers because it serves as a guide for setting expectations for children. Teachers understand that the child is the center of his or her reasoning universe. They realize that they should not be critical of the child for being self-centered; it is simply part of being a young child. Knowing future stages helps adults provide experiences that will help the child move comfortably into advanced stages when he or she is ready.

Piaget, like most researchers, set age brackets cautiously, knowing that many deviations from what appears "normal" in research are still normal for any particular child. Because no child is 100 percent consistent in a behavior, it is unwise to say, "Johnny always does _____." It is even more unwise to say, "All children do _____."

Piaget himself suggested that it is foolish to set out deliberately to "teach" these stages. He thought they evolved from children's step-by-step development as they use things and socialize in their environment. When he was asked whether teachers should present the same types of tasks to children that he did in his research, Piaget replied, "If the aim is to accelerate the development of these operations, it is idiotic."[6]

Kamii, after many experiments and attempts to build a Piaget-type curriculum for nursery school, has said, "I found in Piaget's theory many reasons why dramatic play, painting, block building, paper folding, Jell-O-making, etc., were so relevant to education. The more I studied Piaget's theory, the more I came to respect the intuitive wisdom of the traditional nursery school."[7]

Vygotsky's Scaffolding

Psychologist Lev Vygotsky was introduced in Chapter 6 with the suggestion that his work is useful with many curriculum activities for early childhood schools. This will be true of your science activities. Remember his idea about "scaffolding" children's learning?[8]

Let's assume you've planned a science activity with magnets. Remember to try to listen closely enough to understand what each child knows about the magnets you have assembled. Then tailor your social and verbal interaction with each child who participates in your activity to help develop the "scaffold" to new learning that Vygotsky proposes. For example, note what the child says when trying to pick up paper, paper clips, pennies, brass buttons, and pins. Can the child generalize anything discovered? Take time, stay as relaxed and unrushed as you can so you can encourage the talking, exploring, and concluding. Thus, feel happy if only a few children attend your activity, especially if they take time to explore and talk about their knowledge—what they already seem to understand and the questions they are asking as they learn more. Remember the verbal give-and-take is very important for children's learning—and for you to learn how to do. Write down some things you observe and learn to remember yourself and to share with others.

WHAT IS SCIENCE FOR YOUNG CHILDREN?

Science can be defined as *systematized knowledge*. In the adult world, knowledge is grouped

---

[6]Eleanore Duckworth, "Piaget Takes a Teacher's Look," *Learning* 2:2 (October 1973), 22.

[7]Constance Kamii, "An Application of Piaget's Theory to the Conceptualization of a Preschool Curriculum," *The Preschool in Action*, ed. Ronald K. Parker (Boston: Allyn & Bacon, 1972), p. 119.

[8]See Laura E. Berk, "Vygotsky's Theory: The Importance of Make-Believe Play," *Young Children* 50:1, November 1994, 30–39.

TALK IT OVER: NO. 1

Study the previous section on brain development, cognitive development, and intellectual
operations. What common factors do the three
theories contain? Discuss.

into the physical, natural, biological, and social
sciences, literature, music, mathematics, and the
arts. These are human-made systems. All have
important concepts for young children.

It has been said that the university curriculum
can become the curriculum for the early childhood school. The teacher needs a liberal education
to teach the concepts and to appreciate the meaning of those concepts for the child and the society.
No matter how extensive a teacher's education,
children will raise questions to which a teacher
will answer, "Let's find out," or "Let's go and look

that up." There will be surprises. Today's children
have amazing bits and pieces of information they
are trying to fit into meaningful packages.

Using the **scientific method** requires one to
observe, make inquiries, seek reasons, and experiment. Answers today may be inadequate or
become fallacies tomorrow. Thus, all "truths" are
held in a tentative mode. The process of the scientific method is important, especially in early
childhood schools. Teachers' efforts should go
into keeping children's curiosity alive, rather
than teaching specific facts.

Teachers may be surprised at the amount of
information known by some children in their
groups. Educated parents, television, and travel
are all factors contributing to the breadth of a
child's knowledge. One boy's "I'm going to be an
ichthyologist" sent the teacher scurrying to a dic-
tionary. Many teachers have drawn on concepts
from biology class to respond to "Was I in my
mommy's stomach before I got borned?" "Today
is Hanukkah" need not embarrass a teacher who
has studied the world's great religions in humani-
ties classes.

A window garden is a fine science activity, especially during
winter when children can't
enjoy plant life outdoors.
(Children's Center, Denver)

PLANNING SCIENCE EDUCATION

If teachers are convinced of the importance of children using the scientific method to gain information about their world, and if teachers are aware of how children learn cognitive information, what further considerations are relevant in curriculum planning?

Planning science activities is being introduced in this chapter. However, additional information and ideas follow in Chapters 12 (Perceptual-Motor Activities), 17 (Field Trips and Special Visitors), and 18 (Food Activities), with connections to language, literature, music, and dramatic play activities emphasized in other chapters. Each curriculum activity is really part of a whole picture teachers are putting together in a manner appropriate to the age, interests, and abilities of children in this group.

Children's Needs and Interests

The teacher begins with the children, assessing continuously what they know and what they want and need to know. Linking new knowledge to prior knowledge is an important psychological principle to follow. At first, plans are based on general knowledge of young children. As the teacher gets to know the group personally, plans are individualized.

Within any early childhood classroom, teachers should expect and plan for a range of interests and abilities among children. Children can individually sample from the science menu according to their own desires of the moment. The format is hands-on, individual, and discovery learning, not lecturing. Themes or concepts will appear and reappear from time to time throughout the early childhood period, enabling children to learn more and more as their experience and interests develop.

A building-block approach is used that lays a firm foundation, then continues building, one block at a time. No chimneys are built before the basement is dug. The children become personally and actively involved in their own education.

They are helped to find concrete ways of relating new knowledge to what they already know. Learning takes time and lots of repetition. This is a trying-it-out experimental laboratory approach. Children are more likely to understand and remember information that they discover themselves.

Teachers plan a rich curriculum of science activities to stimulate children's five senses. Spontaneous events are valued and utilized for their scientific teaching whenever they arise. For example, the children find a caterpillar. While other plans wait, this furry creature becomes the focus of learning for several days. The children observe how the caterpillar moves, how it eats, and finally how it spins a cocoon. The teacher tells about the stages of metamorphosis. Good teaching results when a teacher is able to capitalize on a spontaneous interest such as this one. It is also true, however, that children who do not happen to discover a caterpillar may benefit from being introduced to one by the teacher. The motivation may not be as high as when they discover something themselves, but if they are allowed to watch and hold the caterpillar the teacher brings to them, their knowledge will be enhanced. Later, when they find a caterpillar, they may recognize it and learn new facts. Knowledge is seldom a once-over-all-is-learned event. Each time a person confronts a concept his or her previous experience helps add to its meaning, a fact that should be taken into consideration in planning. Concepts worth learning should be introduced numerous times and in a variety of ways. Each time children will add new information to their storehouse of knowledge. It will help you plan educational objectives for science to refer to the Bloom Taxonomy discussed in Chapter 6.

Cumulative Plan

A **cumulative plan** is the name given to this building-block approach just described. This plan is continuous, starting with a simple concept at the beginning of the year and adding experiences throughout the year. As each new experience is added, the children are helped to reflect back to the related experiences they have had. Six broad themes are suggested to run concurrently as cumulative plans. The themes are

1. the child—his or her name, gender, health, safety, and relationship to the family, the school, the community, and the world;
2. the community—its people, workers, institutions, and traditional festivals;
3. the world of plants—especially those the child sees every day and those that provide food;
4. the world of animals—especially those the child sees every day and those that provide food;
5. the world of machines—including vehicles and other large and small machines;
6. the physical forces in the world.

Selecting a Theme for the Week

Within each general theme teachers will develop a specific theme or a focus for the week to be used as a guide for planning and for selection of books, puzzles, songs, stories, room decorations, and field trips. It should be a loose framework, allowing for flexibility to repeat interesting themes from a prior week or to eliminate an activity if children's interests suggest something more appropriate at the moment. As was discussed in Chapter 8, holidays are a very small part of planning when thematic planning is utilized.

Following is a brief example of a cumulative plan as it develops in relation to plants in the child's world (item 3 in the preceding list). In September and October the children pick fall crops—corn, apples, and pumpkins. They collect leaves and make a book of them. They plant crocuses and tulip bulbs in the yard and pot geraniums for their classroom. In November and December they make pumpkin custard and pumpkin bread and talk about the leaves in their

book as they observe the bare branches of the trees. New plants are brought into the classroom to brighten it up, and they are compared to the geraniums. Applesauce is made in February, and the children discover crocuses peeking out of the snow and recall having planted them in the fall. They plant seeds in the window box in March and plan to transplant the seedlings to the play yard or to their homes in the spring. Trees and shrubs are observed as they bloom and get their new leaves. The geraniums are reset in the garden. The children plant lettuce, anticipating a salad later on. They watch a farmer planting corn and recall the corn they picked in the fall. From these activities the children begin to understand the interrelatedness of their learning.

Each of the six themes suggested, and perhaps others, can be developed as a cumulative plan. Teachers in different localities would develop the sequence differently.

Environment

The school environment is the second major consideration when the teacher is planning science education. The total learning environment can stimulate the young child to want to learn. An intriguing array of challenging activities, many displays to look at, and materials available for experimenting will stimulate curiosity. Readily available reference books will promote questions and provide answers. A science table or corner can be arranged where new science projects begin and ongoing projects continue. A special table or shelf can hold treasures children bring from their homes or yards. They can share and discuss discoveries with friends.

A want-to-know attitude permeates the atmosphere. No shame follows a mistake, as it is safe for a child to admit not knowing. Experimenting is encouraged. If some idea fails to work, there is always something else to try. The teacher encourages exchanging ideas and helping others answer questions. Alert teachers note questions children ask and plan experiences to answer those ques-

Introducing the concept of temperature is appropriate for older prekindergarteners. (Michigan State University)

tions. The self-selection-type organization in the classroom facilitates an individual or small-group lesson. Small group learning is more meaningful than large-group lectures at this age.

Teachers work with parents and encourage their participation in their child's learning. Open communication invites teachers and parents to share the learning experiences that are available to the children. This information better enables both teacher and parent to understand the child and helps parents supplement the school activities. Teachers may need to discuss levels of expectation with parents. The teacher may help one family enrich the child's experience, while encouraging another family to let up on the pressure.

Questioning the Children

Questions have an important place in schools for young children. The children's questions, as well as the teacher's, must be held in high regard. A child's curious questioning must be encouraged. These questions may often be answered by peers, or after the child explores the environment, they may be answered by the child. Often a child's questions require the teacher to encourage further exploration rather than to answer immediately. Normally children are more enthusiastic about seeking answers to questions that they themselves are asking. Therefore, we should encourage children to ask their own questions and seek answers.

Questioning children skillfully is an essential technique for teachers. It is important for the teacher to establish communication with each child and to indicate recognition of each child. Teachers use questioning to stimulate the child's awareness of new information. Questioning signals the child that it is his or her turn to speak and to display knowledge, thoughts, and feelings verbally.

In planning learning activities for children, the teacher must give attention to and plan questioning. Many un-thought-out questions lead only to a "yes" or "no" answer and not at all to the goal the teacher had in mind.

Types of teachers' questions were the subject of a research project by Zimmerman and

Bergan.[9] These researchers identified the following seven categories of questions based on the intellectual operations required by the questions. Note the similarity of these categories with the types of intellectual operations identified by Guilford cited earlier.

1. Perceptual—questions concerning the characteristics of objects; e.g., "What (shape, color, size) is your name tag?"
2. Cognitive—questions about comprehension or knowledge; e.g., "What's wrong with this (picture, wagon, shoestring)?"
3. Memory—questions asking for the recall of information that was received earlier; e.g., "What did the man say he fed the (cows, horses, ducks, pigs)?"
4. Divergent—questions asking for several student ideas regarding the presented stimulus; e.g., "What other ways can you put these (materials, colors, shapes) together?"
5. Convergent—questions asking for a single correct response from the child from a field of alternatives; e.g., "How many (mittens, children, shoes, fingers) do we have?"
6. Evaluative—questions asking for student responses concerning the extent to which information matches criteria; e.g., "Which car went (faster, slower, farther)?"
7. Other—questions that do not fit the above categories; e.g., "Would you like to bring the (book, puzzle, chair)?"

The researchers found that first-grade teachers placed an unusual amount of emphasis on factual knowledge, thereby largely omitting other critical intellectual operations. Teachers who had experience and training in question asking gave more emphasis to teaching those intellectual skills stimulated by divergent and evaluative questions. The researchers said that questions guiding children to perceive and process relevant stimuli would help them become aware of the subtle sensory discriminations they can make in the environment. Increased motivation is an expected result.

Teachers should become aware of the type of intellectual operation they have in mind as a learning goal and develop questioning that helps reveal how the child arrived at the conclusion. Caution is suggested to teachers to avoid overzealous concern for emphasizing every aspect of a learning activity in a single learning episode. Learning is never a one-session experience. We must realize that there will be other days to add new information and learning.

Eric Berne, in the book *Games People Play*, wrote the following about awareness, giving food for thought to questioners, whether parents or teachers.

> Awareness means the capacity to see a coffee pot and hear the birds sing in one's own way, and not the way one was taught. It may be assumed on good grounds that seeing and hearing have a different quality for infants than for grownups, and that they are more aesthetic and less intellectual in the first years of life. A little boy sees and hears birds with delight. Then the "good father" comes along and feels he should "share" the experience and help his son "develop." He says: "That's a jay, and this is a sparrow." The moment the little boy is concerned with which is a jay and which is a sparrow, he can no longer see the birds or hear them sing. He has to see and hear them the way his father wants him to. Father has good reasons on his side, since few people can afford to go through life listening to the birds sing, and the sooner the little boy starts his "education" the better. Maybe he will be an ornithologist when he grows up. A few people, however, can still see and hear in the old way. But most of the members of the human race have lost the capacity to be painters, poets, or musicians, and are not left the option of seeing and hearing directly even if they can afford to; they must get it second hand. The recovery of this ability is called here "awareness."[10]

[9]Barry J. Zimmerman and John R. Bergan, "Intellectual Operations in Teacher Question-Asking Behavior," *Merrill-Palmer Quarterly* 17:1 (January 1971), 19–26.

[10]Eric Berne, *Games People Play* (London: Andre Deutch Ltd., 1966), p. 178.

In our eagerness for children to become well informed, let us grant them their right to learn in their own way, giving attention to the birds' songs on one day and to the differentiation of species of birds at a later date. Motivation for learning is within the child.

SUGGESTED SCIENCE EXPERIENCES

Understanding Oneself and Others

A number of the development tasks (discussed in Chapter 2) that serve as the basis for goals in the early childhood curriculum relate to helping children understand themselves and others. Developing understanding of oneself and others involves intellectual, social, physical, and emotional learning that must receive prime time in schools. Feelings of self-worth are invariably linked to the individuals' success in school and throughout life. The school should seek to build children's feelings of self-importance, their feelings of autonomy, their skills in dealing with the expectations of home and school, and their abilities to express themselves through words and deeds. Teachers should think of the child's self-concept as a subject for study throughout the school years.

The total environment of the school should be designed to offer children a maximum of success and minimum of frustration. Equipment is child-sized and it works. Little is off limits or has to be protected. The teacher-pupil ratio ensures each child a teacher who has time for him or her as an individual. The expectations of the school are individually based and developmentally sound.

The Psychological Self

"That means me!" exclaimed five-year-old Anna as she found her name on a list. The answer to the question of "Who am I?" begins when Anna knows her name. The school helps children learn their personal symbol by using names in conversation, by making children name tags, and by writing their names on their products and on their lockers.

Children's self-images are formed largely from how they think others feel toward them. In the free-flowing small groups that are typical in schools for young children the teacher can help each child learn that he or she is a creative, intelligent, important member of the group. "Mary is smiling, she is glad you gave her some clay, Ted." The teacher's comment helps Ted learn that he can make changes in situations—that he can act as well as be acted upon. "Just tell Jack you aren't through" helps a shy child, Sara, defend her rights and moves her a step toward self-confidence in dealing with peers.

Teachers can become effective listeners, and through their responses to children's conversation they can help children understand their own feelings. The teacher frequently hears a child's opinion about how other significant people (parents, siblings, children, teachers) feel toward him. If Leo says, "My daddy hates me," the typical adult wants to say quickly, "Oh, all daddies love their little boys," and change the subject to something more pleasant. The child notes at once that the teacher doesn't want to hear about his feelings. However, the teacher could respond to "My daddy hates me" with "Tell me about it." If the teacher could use the tone of voice that he or she would use if Leo had said, "My daddy has red hair," then Leo might feel free to discuss his thoughts and feelings. Through a discussion he would become more able to cope with his situation. When teachers serve as a sounding board without taking sides or making judgments, they may discover that they need to work more closely with families or make referrals.

The Physical Self

"How do I look?" is a question regarding the physical self that can best be answered by a look in the mirror. Each classroom should have a high-quality, full-length mirror placed in a strategic spot. Many homes do not have a low mirror and some have no mirrors at all. Children may literally not have seen themselves. With a good mirror children can admire the way they look, see smudges on their faces, straighten the firefighter's hats they're wearing, or adjust dress-up clothes before beginning a dance. Mirrors over lavatories are useful but show only the face.

Photographs, too, make significant contributions to the child's understanding of physical appearance. A child's picture can be used over his or her locker to identify personal space. Group photos hung at the children's eye level can be used to decorate the room. *Our Very Own Story Book* can be made using individual photos on 10-by-12-inch tagboard pages put together with notebook rings. Exclamations such as "That's you!" and "That's me!" will continue throughout the year and show the continued satisfaction the children receive from having pictures of themselves continuously available to them.

Attendance charts can become more graphically symbolic and meaningful for the children. Figure 11–2 is an example of a chart that shows the names of the children present. The children learn the concepts of present and absent. They often learn to read the names and count the number of children.

Children talk freely about their ages. They are proud to become four, or five, or six. However, they may worry about their size. One petite five-year-old girl began quizzing her mother at length about midgets. The mother learned through their discussion that her daughter believed she might never grow up because she was the smallest in her class. An observant five-year-old boy was heard to say as he stood beside a three-year-old playmate, "Well, you're taller but I'm older." Occasionally, being the tallest or the smallest in a group is cause for deep concern to a child. Teachers should sense whether it bothers a tall child to be chosen frequently to reach something "because you are tallest." Teachers can likewise observe a child's reaction to being chosen to ride in the baby carriage "because you're the smallest." The child's size may be a fact the child would like to discuss but might not enjoy having group attention focused upon. Any comparisons that unnecessarily cause one child to feel inferior

to another should be avoided. To help a child build a positive self-image, teachers should avoid comparing children on the basis of tallest-shortest, biggest-smallest, oldest-youngest, fastest-slowest, best-worst, or prettiest-ugliest.

Many opportunities arise to teach about growing. Children get new shoes because their old ones are too small. New teeth replace baby teeth. Hair and fingernails require cutting. Because children seem to want to grow, teachers should use any cue to enlighten or reassure children about growing.

The child's actual motor skills are an important part of the self-concept. Also the way a child compares his or her motor capabilities to those of peers is important. Development of large and small motor skills is fostered in good schools for children under six. For example, Jeff was the oldest and tallest child in a four-year-old group. He was one of several children trying a new rope swing that required standing on the packing box, holding on to the rope, swinging away from the box, and dropping to the ground. Jeff hesitated, obviously afraid but wanting to try it. By explaining the sequential steps and protecting him while practicing, the teacher helped Jeff constructively solve the dilemma. He grew in self-confidence as he practiced the new skill.

Gender Role Identification

Sex   Generally the word **sex** refers to biology and anatomy. People are said to be of the male sex or the female sex as determined by (1) external sex organs, (2) internal sex organs, and (3) secondary sexual development at puberty—breasts, beards, and the like.

Gender   The word **gender** refers to a set of qualities and behavior expected from a female or male by society. A person's gender behavior is believed to be affected by social or cultural expectations that come from the idea that certain qualities and therefore certain roles are "natural" for men or women. These roles are learned, change over time, and vary widely within and among cultures.

FIGURE 11–2

A chart placed on a low bulletin board will encourage children to count, to read names, to differentiate between symbols, and to understand the concept of being absent or present. The dolls are made of a double thickness of colored paper. A thumbtack inserted between the layers before the two layers are glued together makes the dolls easy to move on the board. A piece of masking tape under the tack makes the dolls more durable. Laminating or covering them with clear contact paper will also increase their durability.

Another important aspect of the child's self-concept is gender role identification. Most children are happy with their own gender, and the teacher should help a child understand the concept of maleness and femaleness. Feelings regarding gender are laid in the early years. Occasionally teachers need to work with parents who seem to be unaccepting of the child's gender

so that parents' negative attitudes will not harm the child's self-concept.

Some cultural groups have such a strong preference for boys that it pervades their lives even in the United States where more equality is expected. Such parents may need help to understand teaching that emphasizes equality and may disagree with the teachers who expect and state such a value. Thus, teachers must be prepared to discuss their views objectively.[11]

In early childhood schools all activities and equipment are available for use equally by boys and girls. Teachers should evaluate books and activities critically to see whether they arbitrarily assign gender roles. Often teachers themselves must broaden their ideas of male and female roles, both in society and in the family. Modern thinking has merged the roles into more of a single, humanistic one.

Boys and girls under six typically share the same bathroom at school. Such an arrangement provides a healthy environment for learning valuable information about their bodies. Children will look at each other's bodies during the toileting. They will ask questions that can be answered factually. Their concerns over being made differently can be recognized and discussed. Correct terms are used in discussions. Children may seek clarification of information they are receiving at home or elsewhere. It is therefore necessary for the teachers and the parents to compare notes in order that the child is not left more confused than enlightened.

The handling of the genitals, or masturbation, is generally a harmless activity and is often observed among young children. Masturbation may have various meanings, so a child must be observed individually so that the purpose of masturbation for a given child can be discovered. Of course, masturbation can mean that the child is insecure and unhappy. However, it can also mean that the child is bored and needs more active play, that clothing is too tight, that there is a rash on the genitals, or that there is a need to urinate. Teachers must have an enlightened attitude and avoid shaming the child—a technique that would harm the child's positive self-image. Teachers may also need to assist parents in their understanding and handling of this behavior.

In light of current concern for reported sexual abuse of young children by a few parents, others, and even caregivers, some teachers are teaching children that they should tell their parents or teachers if anyone touches their private genitalia. Such teaching should be carefully planned with parents and the early childhood staff. Every effort must be made to make the discussion developmentally appropriate to help children understand, rather than become fearful. One should realize that strangers are seldom the culprits in sexual abuse cases. Of course, teachers have a legal obligation to report to authorities evidence of child abuse, including sexual abuse.

Caring for the Self

Caring for the self is an important part of the learning of a child under six. The routines related to eating, eliminating, resting, and bathing will require many reminders before they become comfortable routines. Each routine invites many questions before the child fully understands. School and home supplement each other. Efforts should be made to keep the expectations in line with the child's developmental level and to help the child understand the reasons for learning these routines. Children feel grown-up when taking care of their own needs. It is during routines that children may first show that they have a concept of "self" as a separate entity. They may refuse to eat, to sleep, or to eliminate as prescribed.

The teacher uses the lunch or snack period to help children think about foods and learn how foods make them grow. Food preparation projects may serve to interest children in their nutrition. For details on food projects see Chapter 18. Teachers may wish to check their local office of the National Dairy Council and the local Cooperative Extension Expanded Nutrition office for aids for teaching nutrition to children.

Caring for teeth, nails, and hair can be brought to children's attention. Some local dental associations have excellent materials available for teachers to use when teaching dental hygiene.

---

[11]The reader can explore gender preference in a number of cultures in more detail in V. Hildebrand, L. Phenice, M. Gray, and R. Hines, *Knowing and Serving Diverse Families* (Upper Saddle River, NJ: Merrill/Prentice Hall, 1996), Chapters 4–9.

Teachers demonstrate their interest in good grooming by helping children comb their hair after napping or by helping them find a fresh outfit when one gets soiled or damaged. In centers a special holder is made for each child's comb and toothbrush.

The parents' cooperation can be solicited so that they too will encourage and teach the children to help themselves. Figure 11–3 is a visual aid that can be duplicated and sent home with children to encourage and remind them to become more independent. In a note to parents the teacher suggests that the chart be attached to the wall with plastic tape and that parents say to the child, "Have you checked your chart?" Avoid nagging about specifics. This is an effort to get the child to take responsibility for routines. The chart helps some parents realize how capable their child can be.

Safety is an obvious area of study. No one is as vulnerable to accidental death as the child under six. For the first two to three years adults assume total responsibility for a child's safety. After that the child must be relied upon to take more and more responsibility for safety. The teacher's role is to develop an understanding of safety in the home, school, play yard, street, and family car. Some state automobile clubs have had excellent materials prepared for teachers to use on safety in the car and on streets. The use of seatbelts is a good topic to focus on with both children and parents. Developing an understanding of the rules for personal self-preservation is important. The child's conscience must be encouraged to function. Developing inner control with an understanding of rules, not blind adherence to them, can be a major accomplishment of the young child's life.

Young children are at first basically egocentric. They develop into social beings who want to know about and to relate to others in their environment. They will eventually want to know about people far away in time and place. A great number of meaningful learning experiences can stem from a continuing emphasis on helping children to understand themselves and others. Learning experiences, both planned and incidental, must be related personally to the children. The learnings will "take" only if the children are personally involved.

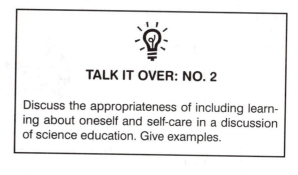

TALK IT OVER: NO. 2

Discuss the appropriateness of including learning about oneself and self-care in a discussion of science education. Give examples.

The Family—A Part of the Self

The family constellation can be the subject of a great deal of learning. Each teacher of young children hears examples of children's confusion about kinship. "Is that your daddy?" is the usual question when children see the teacher with any man. Youthful aunts or uncles were called "my grandma's kids" by one five-year-old.

Children's literature typically shows a family with one boy and one girl, both about the same age. A discussion can help children talk about their families and begin to understand the variations existing among families. Foster children and grandparents may be part of the family. The teacher may have most uncertainties with those children who have no parents or only one parent. If a recent divorce or death has occurred, the child may need someone who will listen to talk about the event without prying for more information than the child is ready to give. Teachers should know their children's families well in order to avoid creating unnecessary heartaches for already troubled children. For example, the kindergarten teacher who directed her class to mold ashtrays from ceramic clay for "your father's Christmas present" should have remembered that one child's father had died only days before school started in the fall. Thus, the project

FIGURE 11–3
A reminder chart to help children become independent.

was one this child could not do with pleasure, and likewise such a specific assignment probably would not be suitable for a child from a non-smoking family.

When one child's mother has had a new baby, the interest in the event can be used to help the children verbalize questions and seek answers regarding human reproduction, which they may not have had occasion to discuss before. All children enjoy hearing about when they were babies. Teachers can involve children in discussions that will bring out both information and feelings about babyhood. A recognition of family differences and an open discussion of the feelings children have toward their younger siblings or how they, as younger siblings, are treated by their older brothers or sisters can help children work through their jealous or ambivalent feelings.

Fascinating studies about race, language, and culture can be developed from a child's experience in a family. A teacher must first seek to understand and appreciate children and families, including those who differ from him- or herself. Striving for mutual understanding and greater appreciation for all racial and ethnic groups is essential.

Understanding the Community

The local and world community are of interest to children. The study can start with the neighborhood and community, its people, their houses and jobs, community helpers, and institutions. Traditional festivals and holidays can be studied under this theme. Field trips and special visitors are methods often used for this social science education.

A study of the community is relevant to children. Learning about the houses people live in helps to orient children to the world outside their families. Walks can be taken from neighborhood schools to see houses, yards, and pets belonging to members of the class. Occasionally children feel different because they live in a mobile home

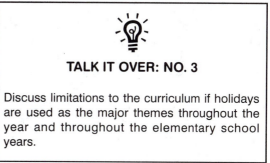

TALK IT OVER: NO. 3

Discuss limitations to the curriculum if holidays are used as the major themes throughout the year and throughout the elementary school years.

or an apartment, while others live in single-family dwellings. A suitable study can help each gain some appreciation of his or her own home and more understanding of those of friends.

The whole subject of the world of work can be approached from where "my mother or daddy works." The study takes on added meaning when John's dad is the highway patrolman who shows the class his patrol car. Or they'll look at buses with increased interest after Bettie's mom arranges for the bus to take the class on a tour of the city when she has a day off from her job as a driver. The police station loses its fearsome aspects when the police officer is Cathy's daddy, whom the children have met at school in his sport shirt. They listen attentively as the police officer tells them how to be safe on city streets. They'll like to look at the officer's badge.

The first and most obvious place to look for learning resources is among the parents of the children in the group. Parents can be encouraged to suggest the names of members of their family and friends who may also be called on to help. There is no particular list of people young children must know, so the enthusiastic cooperation of their families is a worthwhile place to start. Any community helper—firefighter, grocer, filling station operator, or mechanic—could be studied.

The search for people with special talents, hobbies, exhibits, and the like that can be shared with the group of children is well worth the teacher's effort. It may be a father who comes to school to twang his banjo, a retired railroader who displays his electric train hobby, or a mother who has the lead in the civic theater. When a child's parent is a learning resource, the child, of course, gets special recognition through the experience and other children gain understanding of the diversity among people. The people themselves learn something of the value of educating children under six.

Kindergarten children can begin learning concepts of democracy, government, and voting. Decisions can be arrived at by voting. Leaders can be elected for a day or a special event. Important state or national events can be discussed at school. One inauguration day the teacher said, "Here is a picture of our new president. Tonight when your parents listen to the news, watch to see if you can see our new president." A week later one of the shyest boys in the group led the teacher to the picture on the bulletin board and reported, "I saw him (the president) on TV."

The World—A Part of the Self

Older children are often fascinated by people and customs from faraway countries. This is true especially if they have occasion to know someone from far away, or if the teacher or a child has had some foreign experience. Parents or grandparents of children may make valuable contributions.

In one group a student from India observed the kindergarten children once each week. They were curious and asked her many questions. She talked with them about school, food, and children in India and showed them pictures and souvenirs. She danced and sang songs from her country. The children were entranced as she demonstrated how her sari was wrapped. The warmth and understanding that developed between the Indian girl and the kindergarten children were heartening to see.

In another instance, some Vietnamese students let kindergarten children try on their rice-straw hats when they came to dance. They

Hooking up those bells and lights is a fascinating science activity. (Michigan State University)

invited the children to dance and sing. The next time the Vietnamese girls were to visit, the children suggested that they would like to make hats so that they could dance "better." Before the day of the return visit the children each made a paper Vietnamese hat. They enjoyed the music and their dancing.

A parent's business trip or the teacher's vacation can stimulate interest in travel, maps, and faraway places. Discussion and role-playing of travel experiences by the children can follow. A teacher may initiate such study by sending children postcards when away on a trip.

Outer space intrigues young children just as it does their elders. Children can imagine making a trip in a spacecraft. Television adventures, space museums, and news programs help children learn concepts and vocabulary so they can talk about and play out the roles of space explorers. Teachers will search for ways to answer their questions.

Understanding the Physical World

Understanding the physical world is a lifelong pursuit that begins in early childhood. The child picks up a piece of ice covering a puddle in the play yard, plucks a dandelion, or buttons a coat against the chilly winds. Each time the child is responding to the physical world. Each response contains some learning experience and motivation that will serve the teacher as the incidents are used to help children understand what is taking place in their world.

Weather and Seasonal Changes

Weather and seasonal changes are worthy subjects for children's science lessons. Weather limits what the children can do and determines their dress; they hear it discussed frequently among adults. There will be numerous opportunities for the teacher to include concepts about the weather, the seasons, and atmospheric changes in the planned experiences for the young children.

A school for young children should use opportunities to observe and discuss all weather conditions—sun, rain, clouds, wind, snow, even hurricanes and tornadoes if the children are interested. Personal experiences reinforce weather concepts. For example, children who take a walk in the rain wearing boots and carrying umbrellas have a chance to see, hear, smell, and feel the effects of the rain. Through questions the teacher can help alert the children to the logic for wearing appropriate clothing. The children eventually learn to choose clothing that is appropriate for the weather. The teacher can ask: "You wore your raincoat today. Can you tell me why?" "If you go outdoors today, what will you need on your hands?" "Why?" "How does it happen we aren't wearing our coats today?"

When studying the seasons, teachers should remember that the child's frame of reference is not well developed. If a child is three years old in the spring of the year, for example, the teacher should remember that a year earlier in the spring this child was only a two-year-old. It is unlikely that anyone spent much time then discussing the seasonal changes that were taking place or that it would be remembered if someone had. Parents, commenting on a child's increased knowledge, often say, "This year spring means something to my daughters."

The secrets of nature are awe-inspiring. Yes, nature may be overlooked in our busy, technically oriented world, unless thoughtful teachers keep youngsters tuned in on it. Having a sense of wonder that is alive is surely a prime requisite for teachers of young children. Children will enjoy the tiniest dandelion that "nobody cares if you pick." They will be joyous when they find the crocus they planted in the fall. A spring walk to see, hear, feel, and smell the evidences of spring is surely a delight to all, especially if the children are permitted to bring back a few sprigs of blossoms to decorate the room. A fall walk has equal beauty, with its glorious colors. In fall there are leaves to push into a pile and jump into, and perhaps apples or cotton to pick.

Beauty, too, is the morning after a snow. Adults so often ruin such days by complaining about the traffic snarls and the problems with shoveling. Snow is no problem to children. They'll shovel if someone will just let them have a snow shovel. They'll roll in the snow, taste it, and jump into any "mountain" of snow they see.

Some teachers really have to force themselves to enjoy nature. It may take effort to awaken the senses so that one can appreciate how fresh and exciting all nature is for small children. Once awakened, teachers won't be able to pass a fallen hedge apple, a dandelion seed, or a budding shrub without thinking, "Oh, I must let the children see this." Reading Henry David Thoreau's *Walden*, Rachel Carson's *The Sense of Wonder*, or Anne Morrow Lindberg's *Gift from the Sea* may help a teacher appreciate nature after facing the city's gray walls and streets too long.

According to Fenton, an outdoor educator, "I made one rule for myself: 'Outside and unarmed!' That meant the only teaching materials used were found outdoors. The only concepts I would teach would be those the children could experience directly. We used ourselves: the children's sense of nature and my own skills."[12]

Growing Plants

Window Gardens   Classroom projects can involve children in planting, watering, and observing. Plants also add a cheery note to the room. An indoor window box containing a variety of plants with room for adding new ones from time to time is worthwhile. Geraniums, petunias, ivy, philodendrons, tomatoes, and beans are all grown with relative ease.

An attractive indoor plant can be grown from a sweet potato placed in water. Because growers dry sweet potatoes artificially to keep them from sprouting, a teacher may have difficulty finding one with a few purple eyes that will sprout. Sweet potatoes may require several weeks to sprout. It helps to use warm water and to keep the container in a warm place. Tops from carrots, beets, turnips, and pineapples can be planted in water or wet sand. The top should include about one inch of the vegetable or fruit. The children will watch the new shoots grow.

Onions or garlic can be suspended with toothpicks, about half immersed in water. The children will watch new green shoots and roots grow. Parents can snip the young onion and garlic blades for salads when this project is carried on at home.

Watching the plant "drink" is a favorite experiment. If celery, a white carnation, or an iris is placed in colored water, the leaves and petals will become tinged with color overnight. The children can observe that the vascular tissue carried the water to the leaves.

Seeds   Study of the seeds of various plants and observation of their travel by wind and water are interesting to children. One group of children who had been alerted to notice tree seeds in the spring called the maple seed the "helicopter blade" and delighted in tossing them up to watch them twirl to the ground. Such labeling is an example of the child's attempt to relate new concepts to those already known.

When seeds are planted in clear plastic cups, the children can see the root systems develop. Learning is also facilitated if some seeds are kept damp on a wet sponge wrapped in a damp cloth. Each day the children can unroll the cloth to see if the seeds are sprouting. They can use the magnifying glass to examine the sprouts. This observation can be related to the seed they have planted under the soil. You can imagine the interest children will have in eating alfalfa sprouts or bean sprouts for lunch or snack during the time of the seed-sprouting experiments. Sometimes the teacher may like each child to have his or her own plant to care for. Beans, pumpkins, and tomatoes can be planted in milk cartons or styrofoam cups; then when the danger of frost is past, the children can transplant each plant outside, either at home or at school. They can then continue to watch their plant develop. One child's pumpkin vined into the family's cherry tree. The child thought it was a big joke to tell people that "my cherry tree has pumpkins in it"—and it did!

An outdoor garden is popular in many schools where space permits. Some children planted Kentucky Wonder beans along their kindergarten fence. The vines grew to cover the fence. Imagine the fun they had picking and tasting their own beans!

The plant's need for sunlight, soil, and moisture can be studied. One experimental plant can be kept without light and another can be kept without water, so that the children can learn what happens if the plant does not have these necessities.

Bulbs   Tulips, hyacinths, and daffodils can be planted in pots in the fall, stored outdoors during the winter, then brought indoors to force early spring blooms. Pussy willows and forsythia will bloom if cut in the bud stage and brought indoors. Early spring bouquets are especially welcome after long cold winters. In some localities fall is the time to plant bulbs outdoors so that children can discover their blooms in the spring.

---

[12]Gail McClelland Fenton, "Back to Our Roots in Nature's Classroom," *Young Children* 51:3, March 1996, 8–11.

Plants in the Fall In the fall Indian corn, pumpkins, and bouquets of dry seeds and beans can add color to the room. A mobile of colored leaves is very effective. Coat leaves with wax by pressing them between layers of wax paper with a hot iron before arranging them. The wax helps keep leaves from curling up as they dry.

Tree leaves, buds, cones, fruits, and bark can be collected by the children during various seasons to help increase their awareness of trees. Trees' value for lumber and papermaking should not be overlooked. Leaf collections can be pressed between layers of clear plastic adhesive and kept in a book.

Projects such as picking fruits for eating or making jelly, picking pumpkins for the classroom jack-o'-lantern, or cutting an evergreen tree at the tree farm add to children's information regarding plants.

A study of local crops that contribute both to the nation's food and fiber and to the livelihood of families in a community can offer numerous learning experiences for young children. Several field trips a year may be possible to follow a crop from planting to harvesting. Even in a farming community where a particular crop is the mainstay of the economy, the teacher will have some children who have no contact with its production. All children will profit from observing and discussing the growing and harvesting process in relation to finished products. The farm children who already know about the crop can be the teacher's outstanding information source. The farm child's own farm and parents may contribute to the learning.

A Texas child, Berta, invited her class to her cotton farm during harvest time. The children ran among the rows of cotton plucking white bolls for a "bouquet." They watched the cotton-picking machine, called the cotton stripper, pick the bolls and fill huge wagons with them. En route back to school the group stopped at the cotton gin and saw farmers bringing in wagons piled high with cotton. On the other side of the gin they watched huge trucks being loaded with five-hundred-pound bales of cotton. A few weeks later the children excitedly reported that cotton bales had been placed along the street in the downtown area. (It was cotton promotion week.) They knew where those bales had come from. They felt very knowledgeable. Further discussion and recall of their trip followed. The total experience increased their understanding of cotton as a plant. The study was related to the children personally through the clothing they were wearing and alerted them to the community in which they lived. They appreciated more fully the jobs of their families and friends.

A teacher is encouraged to find resources in the local community that can provide highly relevant learning experiences for children studying the world of growing things. An action program of planting, watering, harvesting, and using plants should be included. Local farmers and others involved always seem to enjoy having children show an interest in their work.

A supply of reference books to supplement discussion and experiments is essential. The more the teacher knows about the subject, the more the children can learn. The children will learn to refer to books for information, a good habit to cultivate.

The Animal World

The world of animals offers almost unlimited opportunities for enriching children's experience. The teacher must search for worthwhile experiences for the group. The teacher seeks accurate information and uses correct terms. Although an encyclopedia is helpful, one may wish to call specialists, such as those in the Cooperative Extension service, for localized information. Sufficient time is given the children to observe and to verbalize their findings. The teacher carefully indicates points for observation and tells about relationships that may not have been discovered by the children. Preparations are made to answer such questions as the following:

What is it called?

How and what does it eat?

How does it move?

How does it reproduce?

Where does it live?

What sounds does it make?

How does it see, smell, and hear?

How does the animal protect itself?

How do humans use the animal?

In the Classroom Rabbits, gerbils, guinea pigs, white rats or mice, turtles, and fish are common animals that may be kept for a time in the classroom. Horned toads also are harmless pets. They are common in arid regions, where children frequently bring them to school. They may also be purchased from pet stores. Advice concerning the health, safety, temperature, feeding, watering, and exercising of the animals kept in the classroom may be needed from a specialist. The animals must be treated kindly and not overhandled or used as toys. Children can be taught how to

care for the animal properly. If adequate care or housing is not available for an animal in the classroom, the teacher should consider keeping the animal for only a few hours so that the children can have some experience with it.

Children learn from sharing their new pups or kittens with their classmates. Pets can be brought to school while they are still young enough to remain in a box or a basket. The teacher can arrange a tour to children's homes to see their mature pets. Pictures of pets and their owners can be taken on a home visit. Children who have pets can tell the non-pet-owners practical pointers on pet care. A visit to a local pet shop can be arranged to increase the children's knowledge of the animals for pets. Here the children will find some of the more unusual pets, too.

Earthworms are favorites of children, but may be far down the list for some teachers. Nonetheless, children learn many things from observing and handling earthworms, and teachers should

Animals are popular visitors with many things to learn about them.

lay aside their prejudices and learn to tolerate worms. Worms can be collected in dirt and kept in a container for some time. If children have a spot for digging in their yard, they may collect worms for a "fishing trip."

Animal Sources of Food and Fiber Animals as a source of food and fiber will provide valuable learning experiences for children. The sources of familiar foods will interest the children. Teachers should be alert to the specialized nature of modern agriculture. The storybook farmer who owns every kind of animal is a rarity today. To avoid the teaching of misconceptions, up-to-date ideas of farming and farm equipment should be understood by teachers. Watch especially the accuracy of some of the storybooks you choose to use with farm studies.

A visit to a dairy to see cows being milked is very worthwhile because milk is a familiar food. Visits to farms where pigs, sheep, beef cattle, turkeys, or chickens are raised help children learn about the sources of common foods. The sight, sound, smell, and touch experiences can be related to taste experiences they have at home and school. Farm visits during the spring months show children the mother animals and their young—a subject of high interest to young children. Parents can be encouraged to visit dairies and farms.

Animals at the Park, Zoo, and Museum Ducks, geese, and swans may be available for the children to visit and feed in a public pond. Dry bread crumbs offered by the child will encourage the ducks to come close. Children seem to be especially attracted to ducks. Robert McCloskey's book, *Make Way for Ducklings*, is both a delightful story and a help to the teacher who is teaching the ways of the duck world. One mother reports that when they lived near Boston, her youngest daughter's kindergarten class followed the path of the ducks in the story. The children were absolutely delighted. The children will learn from having a duck visit their classroom and swim in their water table. The teacher should be prepared for the fluttering of wet wings, puddles on the floor or grass, and excited children. This close-up view will help the children see the use the duck makes of its webbed feet.

Studying the familiar animals first is best in a class of young children. Parents who take their children to a zoo consistently report that the favorite exhibits are ducks and other farm animals. These are the animals most frequently seen and most often pictured in children's books. Exotic animals from far away and prehistoric animals are for the older under-six children.

Marine Life Schools located within travel distance of the sea, lakes, or rivers will give children a special opportunity to learn about animals that make their homes in water. When the families of the children vacation near the water or make their living through fishing or a related industry, marine life is a significant subject for children to study. Some marine animals can be brought into the classroom. Visits can be made to public displays.

Watching tadpoles develop into frogs intrigues nearly everyone. Tadpoles can be secured from ponds. They can be kept in an aquarium until the legs form. The children can use the magnifying glass to observe the leg buds appearing.

The care and feeding of fish make another worthwhile classroom project. A teacher can choose a single bowl with one goldfish or a sophisticated, balanced aquarium with collections of tropical fish. If she or he has the knowledge to build an aquarium or is willing to learn, young children will be eager helpers.

Bird Life An egg-hatching experience can help children learn answers to some of their questions regarding reproduction. However, incubating the fertile eggs and waiting the twenty-one days required for a chicken to hatch may be too tedious for young children. It may be more feasible to obtain eggs from a hatchery that have been incubated for nineteen or twenty days. A warm box can be arranged with an electric light for heat. If the teacher secures about a dozen eggs, it is probable that a few will hatch during the day. Children and adults alike will watch breathlessly as chicks peck their way out of the shells.

The box should be large enough so that the hatched chicks can move away from the light if they are too warm. Chicks will move closer to the light if they are chilled. Chicks might be kept in the classroom for several days. The teacher should seek advice from a hatchery regarding the proper care and feeding of the chicks. Some hatcheries and museums have exhibits in which the hatching process and day-old chicks can be observed. Teachers can advise parents of the value of taking their children to see such exhibits.

Bird life will interest the children. A small bird such as a parakeet or a canary can be enjoyed in the classroom. The children can learn a great deal from the care and feeding of the bird. Some teachers may prefer having the bird visit school for only a few days or weeks.

Birds in their natural habitat can be observed with interest. Children can learn the names of birds and their housing and eating habits. Children can be encouraged to listen to the birds' songs and may learn to recognize some songs. Children will like to discuss information about reproduction. Birdhouses and feeders can be made from plastic milk bottles or cartons. Ready-cut wooden birdhouses are available in variety stores. Bird feeders can be made to attract birds to the school yard. Advice regarding the appropriate food to attract local species of birds is available from the wildlife service in each state. Drinking water may be provided for birds in cold climates where water sources freeze up. A birdbath will attract birds. A collection of strings, yarn, and bits of cotton or hair for birds to use in building nests will also attract them and give children an incentive to watch birds closely and quietly.

Insect Life   The world of insects offers children opportunities to discover, to observe, to question, to classify, and to relate. A butterfly net and a collecting jar may be enough to encourage an interest in entomology. One goal is to develop curiosity, teach safety, and avoid screeching every time an insect appears.

Ant farms are easily made. Clean and dry a large glass jar and make a lid from a double layer of nylon net held with a rubber band across the top. Scoop up an anthill—sand, dirt, and ants—filling the jar and covering it with the nylon net. A queen ant (winged) should be included. Wrap a dark paper around the jar for a number of days. The ants will restore order to their empire. The darkness will encourage the ants to redig their tunnels close to the glass. Once the ants feel at home, they will go about their business. The children can provide bits of various foods to see what foods the ants like best and what they do with it. A tablespoon of honey or overripe fruit will be popular. A flashlight and a magnifying glass will help the child follow the ants in the trails. There is a great deal for teachers and children to learn about ants. The children can be taught some safety precautions regarding them. Ant farms are also available through school supply houses.

Butterflies, moths, beetles, and even spiders will be interesting to children. Discovering a spider's web and using a magnifying glass to watch the spider work can be very educational. A class collection of insects can be started. Collections can sometimes be borrowed from libraries or science departments.

Concept of Death   The concept of death frequently comes up during incidental or planned studies of animals. The presence of a pet may encourage children to talk about the death of their own pets. In one five-year-old group the children began telling stories about how their pets had died. The children listened politely to each other and vied for a chance to tell their story. When a lull came in the discussion, the teacher thought it might be time for a pet story with a happy ending, and told one. Again they listened attentively. However, the second the story was over another child had a story of a pet's death. The teacher concluded that the talk of death was meeting a need for these children and took a cue from them as to when to terminate the discussion.

Physical Forces and Their Interaction

The following suggestions will give teachers a few ideas for helping children learn how physical

---

☼💡

TALK IT OVER: NO. 4

Give an example of a planned science activity you've observed in an early childhood school. What happened? What equipment was used? What do you think children learn?

---

forces interact in their world. Most of the following suggestions are very abstract. Young children may learn a little at Level 1 on the Bloom Taxonomy (see Chapter 6). That is, they may learn a word for the force and begin to realize that it exists. Remember to plan many hands-on experiences and to relate the concepts to children's interests and questions. For example, if you want to present batteries and circuits to light a bulb or ring a bell, help children to relate the new experience with the batteries they use to run a toy.

Electricity

Electricity is used to produce light, heat, and energy. Dry cell batteries can be used to ring bells and to light bulbs. Children can learn to complete the circuit to make it work. Show the children the electric element on the hot plate or the electric frying pan used for cooking projects. They can learn such words as *battery, circuit, outlets, plugs, bulbs,* and *switches.* Static electricity is produced as children walk across the carpet or rub balloons on slacks. Children enjoy the game of shocking their friends.

Magnetism

Children learn that only certain objects are attracted to magnets. Avoid overgeneralizing that all metals are attracted to a magnet because some metals are not, for example, copper and brass. Make a fishing game using a stick with a magnet on the string and a paper clip on paper fish, numbers, colors, or letters. The children can be encouraged to talk about their catch.

Temperature

Temperature can be related to the children, the room, water, or the outdoors. Temperatures can be compared by the use of two thermometers. A cardboard thermometer can be made so that the child can duplicate the reading of the real thermometer. Children can observe whether the real thermometer goes up or down. Teachers can provide experiences with steam, with freezing foods, or with drying clothes. The children can set water outside to freeze on a very cold day or bring ice or snow indoors to melt. Gelatin dessert cooled outdoors helps children conclude that the air outside is as "cold as the refrigerator." Thus children learn about materials that are solid at one temperature and liquid at another.

Air

Provide opportunities to show that air is all around. Make or buy pinwheels to watch in the breeze. Build and fly a kite. Fill balloons with air. Have the children hold their nose and mouth to see how long they can go without breathing. Place a glass over a lighted candle to demonstrate that fire needs air to burn. Have the children learn words like *air, wind, breeze, oxygen,* and *movement.*

Volume

Volume can be studied at the water table as the child pours from one container to another. A number of containers of various sizes should be provided. Funnels, cups, sieves, and a toy waterwheel all can provide interesting experiments. Volume is experienced at the snack table as children pour beverages, or during cooking projects as they measure ingredients. You might try out Piaget's experiment on conservation of volume, using liquid in a tall and a squat glass and seeing what happens.

Length and Distance

Length and distance can be learned by comparisons of the length of pencils, nails, pegs, or blocks. The teacher uses "shortest" or "longest" to designate the plank or table being sought. Con-

Blowing bubbles holds a considerable amount of fascination for young children. (University of Illinois)

cepts of length and distance can be experienced in the room or the yard or around the block.

Size, Shape, and Weight
As children use blocks and packing boxes of various sizes, they learn about size, shape, and weight. Concepts such as big-little, large-small, high-low, wide-narrow, and long-short are learned through the motor activities involved in building. Learning names for geometric shapes and relating the concept of shape to toys and materials in the environment are important. Children may use functional labels such as *window* for a square. At that point they are ready to learn to label it a *square*.

Balance
Balancing is needed on teeter-totters, walking planks, and rocking boats and to walk on a railing or wall. During block play this concept can be demonstrated if the children fail to grasp it themselves. Use the word "balance" to help children label the concept.

Speed
Opportunities to learn concepts of fast and slow are developed through the use of wheel toys and swings or through rolling objects of different sizes and weights down an inclined plane.

Gravity
Children experience the effects of gravity when rolling down a hill, sliding down the slide, flying paper airplanes, and throwing handkerchief parachutes. The teacher can teach this concept when cautioning children about taking heavy objects into high places.

Machines and Tools
Americans are gadget-minded, and the typical child today has had more experience with large and small machines than many adults of other generations. Machines and tools make work easier. The children help the teacher hammer nails in a favorite packing box. The children use carpenter's tools. The teacher asks them how they would hammer or saw if there were no tools. They help the teacher use pliers to tighten a bolt on a tricycle handlebar. Could they do this with their fingers? When a wheel comes off a toy, there may be an opportunity to examine the axle and perhaps the ball bearing. An inclined plane can help the group move a heavy object up on a packing box. A pulley can be fashioned with a rope and a box to show that through the use of the pulley the child can lift an object impossible to lift outright. It is an interesting game. A collection of bolts and nuts of varying sizes provides a sorting and matching experience related to the world of machines. Small motor skills are practiced as the children screw the nuts on the bolts. Tools and other construction toys give children opportunities to become inventors—discovering new combinations each time.

Large machines are of particular interest to children. They like to get close to, even on the machines if safety precautions permit. As various community helpers are studied throughout the year, the children can see a fire truck, police car, cement mixer, road grader, delivery truck, tractor, or wheat combine. During studies of transportation they can visit a plane, train, or bus.

Sounds

Sounds are of interest to children. Most young children learn such parlor tricks as "What does a dog say?" Teachers know that children run to the window or become fearful when a siren is heard near the school. Because children are usually alert to fine differences in sounds, they are good imitators. Their attention may have to be directed so that they learn to identify new sounds. On a walk in the woods they can be encouraged to "listen to the quiet," as one child put it.

A study of sounds can include the sounds of toys; the sounds of household machines, such as a mixer, a sewing machine, a telephone, or a clock; the sounds of people laughing, crying, or scolding; and the sounds of animals. Attention can be drawn to pitch, rhythm, and volume.

Concepts of sound will be better learned if one has real-life experiences with the sounds. Though children learn to answer "moo" when asked "What does the cow say?" they really understand after a visit to the dairy. "She *does* say moo!" confirmed a five-year-old.

Vibrations produce sounds. Children learn from making, feeling, and hearing vibrations. They discover they can stop vibrations with their hands. Musical instruments of various kinds offer numerous possibilities. Tapping various materials to hear the sound differences allows children to experiment with sound production. A tuning fork can provide the opportunity for additional exploration of vibrations. Further suggestions will be included in the music and rhythm chapter.

Listening to sound is, of course, one way the child develops language in the first place. Promoting listening as well as talking is important in all communication. Suggestions to help foster language development will be included in the chapter on language experiences.

Many children are concerned by night sounds. Some children have deep fears regarding sounds they hear when they awake at night. Experience identifying sounds can help them realize how the sound is being made so that it will not be frightening.

Chemistry in Cooking and Cleaning

The kitchen is one of the best chemistry laboratories. With the teachers' assistance children can stir up food mixtures of various types. The children can discover the effects of heating and cooling. For details related to cooking projects see Chapter 18.

Using solvents to clean up various substances also teaches children the nature of chemicals. For example, waxed crayon stuck to table tops is impossible to clean up with water, yet comes off readily when liquid wax is used. (Teachers should remember this and avoid using harsh cleansers on smooth finishes.) Children can learn that the use of detergent or soap makes the water more effective for removing the dirt from their hands.

Colors

Concepts of color develop during the years before age six. Color is closely related to the creative art materials discussed in Chapter 8. Discussion of color should be included in any experience in which it is relevant. The use of a prism to refract the light and show the colors of the rainbow gives children a pleasant way to discover color. Children learn the names for common colors.

Time

Americans, more so than people of many other cultures, are time oriented. Children become time conscious early partly due to their TV programs. A phrase like "after *Sesame Street*" is a common time-orienting phrase used by adults. American children learn early that it is important to be on time for an appointment.

Teachers help children's time orientation by developing regular routines; for example, juice is served about 10 A.M. A cardboard clock placed under or beside a real clock can be set with the time for an anticipated event. Children will keep their eye on the real clock with hands to see when it moves to the set time. They are learning to tell time. Children can read digital clocks before they understand clocks with hands.

The calendar may interest some young children. Little by little they learn the days of the week—that Monday is the first day of school in the week and Friday the last. They will be able to remember some of the names of the months. A class calendar can be marked with special dates—holidays and birthdays. Some teachers like to permit one child to mark the day's weather on the calendar each day. Both calendars and clocks give children experience with numbers. Much of this is very abstract, with depth of understanding to be developed in the children's later years.

As children begin to gain an understanding of time, they are also learning the routine of seasonal changes, the sequence of the sun rising and setting, and their own routine during the day.

Historical time is a difficult concept for young children. When visiting a historical train exhibit, a four-year-old said, "It was an old-old train, and an old-old man showed it to us. He was fifteen or sixteen." The phrases "olden days" and "when you were a little girl" are often used by children to designate times long gone.

Geology

Mike, a five-year-old, showed a favorite rock at show-and-tell saying, "This is a quartz crystal. My brother's Scout leader gave it to me." With Mike's enthusiasm as a starter, the entire class became immersed in a study of rocks that was carried on throughout the school year. The children brought rocks and fossils found along streets and alleys in their neighborhoods. The teacher too brought rocks—pumice that floats, obsidian used by the Indians for scrapers, and lava collected from lava beds in Central America. The lava led naturally to a discussion of volcanoes. The teacher brought slides and set up a viewing area where some children looked again and again at color photos taken of an erupting volcano. The

children pored over the encyclopedia—"the important books," as they called them—looking for pictures of volcanoes. Some volcanoes were pictured with prehistoric animals. This fact led them into a study of dinosaurs. Combining the two interests led naturally to the museum to see minerals under ultraviolet light and to see dinosaur skeletons.

A few rocks and a magnifying glass can start the study of rocks. Purchasing a labeled collection can encourage a beginner, whether teacher or child, to identify, classify, and label. Nearly every locality has its rock hounds (collectors) who are usually eager to share their hobbies with children.

In mining communities and oil-producing areas special emphasis can be placed on the local minerals. Children can learn something of the formations, the method of extracting, and the economic importance of the mines or wells—especially the energy resources used by a family.

MONITORING SCIENCE EDUCATION

Teachers should spend some time with each child to learn how the science education is being received. During some of the activities the teacher should question the child to learn how he or she reasons out problems. Listen carefully as a child explains an experiment. It helps if the teacher uses an attendance list to be sure to talk to or watch each and every child. If it is discovered that a few are not participating in science, then wondering why not is in order. Perhaps activities are wrong, unattractive, or geared to an improper pace. Notes on children's interests can be made and placed in a file for use with parents in conferences.

Conclusions

Stimulating the child's cognitive growth is of foremost importance during the years before age six. Brain research and the work by Guilford, Bloom, Piaget, Vygotsky, and Kamii suggest how this growth takes place. Children make serious attempts to make sense out of the world they live in. Early education can offer many projects and experiences through which children can discover concepts and build on the concepts they already have. A creative teacher, who has a well-developed sense of wonder and curiosity, will encourage children to discover, think, reason, make inferences, and generalize.

The cumulative plan or building-block approach is suggested; each concept should be firmly based on what the child already knows. Experiences the teacher plans should remain highly relevant to the child's here-and-now experience throughout the early years. Many experiences can be repeated frequently, with children learning something each time. The teacher's role is one of being certain that there is a wealth of things to learn throughout the program and that the children feel free to experiment, question, and discover new ideas. The science curriculum for the early childhood school should be planned carefully and concretely. It is well to build on spontaneous experience of the children, but a program that relies wholly on such experiences will be cheating the children. Children want to learn and they can learn. Teachers must have faith in each child's ability. Learning science need not be a grim business but a really satisfying, invigorating experience that brings joy to lips and smiles to faces. Should a child turn away and show no interest, the behavior suggests that the teacher must search elsewhere for a meaningful experience for that particular child. It is a teacher's obligation to do this searching.

Applications

1. Discuss the "Talk It Over" items found in the chapter.
2. Write an activity plan for a science activity for a few children using information and the sample plan (Figure 6–2) in Chapter 6. Secure approval, carry out the plan, and evaluate the results from the children's point of view and from your viewpoint. Prepare a report and hand it in along with your approved activity plan.
3. Evaluate your total participation performance on your evaluation form developed in Chapter 1.
4. Add ideas and plans for science activities to your Resource File.

Study Questions

1. Define *science, the scientific method, cumulative plan,* and *resource unit.*
2. Explain the four stages of cognitive development according to Piaget. Give examples of reasoning at each stage.
3. Identify the intellectual operations as defined by Guilford.
4. Discuss findings in right- and left-brain research and the implications for early childhood education.
5. List and discuss the factors teachers consider in planning science education.
6. List each category of science activity presented and suggest activities for young children for each category.
7. Describe a high-quality environment in a school that best facilitates children's learning science.

Videotapes

How Young Children Learn to Think
   19 minutes

A discussion with Constance Kamii giving a clear, concrete explanation of Piaget's theory of how children acquire knowledge. NAEYC Media, 1509 16th St., NW, Washington, DC 20036-1426, 1-800-424-2460.

Kids Construction Video
   60 minutes

Gives children insights into many real pieces of large construction equipment in action. Hard Hat Harry Videos, Box 4174, Dept. HA46-CH, Huntington Station, NY 11746, 1-800-346-6100.

Sensory Play: Constructing Realities
18 minutes
Children's first-hand experiences with sensory exploration contribute to overall development. NAEYC Media, 1509 16th St., NW, Washington, DC 20036-1426, 1-800-424-2460.

Sharing Nature with Young Children
18 minutes
Working with young children's natural curiosity turns commonplace natural phenomena into exciting learning experiences. NAEYC Media, 1509 16th St. NW, Washington, DC 20036-1426, 1-800-424-2460.

Additional Readings

Berk, Laura E., and Adam Winsler. *Scaffolding Children's Learning: Vygotsky and Early Childhood Education.* Washington, DC: NAEYC, 1994.

Borden, Esta J. "The Community Connection—It Works!" *Young Children* 42:4, May 1987, 14–23.

Charlesworth, R., and K. K. Lind. *Math and Sciences for Young Children.* Albany, NY: Delmar, 1990.

Cohen, Stewart. "Fostering Shared Learning Among Children and Adults: The Children's Museum." *Young Children* 44:4, May 1989, 21–24.

DeVries, Rheta, and Betty Zan. "Creating a Constructivist Classroom Atmosphere." *Young Children* 51:1, November 1995, 4–13.

Flemming, B., et al. *Resources for Creative Teaching in Early Childhood Education.* New York: Harcourt Brace Jovanovich, 1977.

Forman, G., and D. S. Kuschner. *The Child's Construction of Knowledge: Piaget for Teaching Children.* Washington, DC: NAEYC, 1984.

Goffin, Stacie G. "Problem Solving: Encouraging Active Learning." *Young Children* 40:3, March 1985, 28–32.

Harlan, Jean D. *Science Experiences for the Early Childhood Years.* Upper Saddle River, NJ: Merrill/Prentice Hall, 1988.

Holt, Bess-Gene. *Science with Young Children.* Washington, DC: NAEYC, 1989.

Kamii, Constance. *Numbers in Preschool and Kindergarten: Educational Implications of Piaget's Theory.* Washington, DC: NAEYC, 1982.

Kitano, Margie K. "The K-3 Teacher's Role in Recognizing and Supporting Young Gifted Children." *Young Children* 44:3, March 1989, 57–64.

Mills, Heidi. "Teaching Math Concepts in a K-1 Class Doesn't Have to Be Like Pulling Teeth." *Young Children* 48:2, January 1993, 17–20.

NAEYC. "Promoting Science in Your Program: Use Outstanding Science Books." *Young Children* 44:1, November 1988, 72–73.

Ranger Rick's Nature Magazine. Washington, DC: National Wildlife Federation.

Riley, Sue Spayth. "Pilgrimage to Elmwood Cemetery." *Young Children* 44:2, January 1989, 33–36.

Smith, Robert. "Theoretical Framework for Preschool Science Experiences." *Young Children* 42:2, January 1987, 34–40.

Sprung, Barbara. *Perspectives on Non-sexist Early Childhood Education.* New York: Teachers College Press, 1978.

Ziemer, Maryann. "Science and the Early Childhood Curriculum: One Thing Leads to Another." *Young Children* 42:6, January 1987, 44–51.

Your Big Backyard. Washington, DC: National Wildlife Federation.

CHAPTER 12

Perceptual-Motor Activities

F. Kertez

Objectives

✔ Relate perceptual-motor materials to stages of cognitive and small-motor development.

✔ Identify premathematics activities and relate them to Piaget's research in cognitive development.

✔ Identify and evaluate perceptual-motor activities offered in early childhood schools.

✔ Identify factors related to using microcomputers for perceptual-motor and other learning.

"I can help you do that fire truck puzzle," volunteered Pete.

"I like the fire truck puzzle. We went to see fire trucks," said Kerry.

Puzzles are just one of a number of perceptual-motor materials called **structured** because their form or composition does not change with use. Structured learning materials have size, shape, weight, color, and texture that remain constant. Many manipulative toys of the early childhood classroom contribute to children learning from play materials that challenge their perceptual-motor abilities and contribute to their cognitive skills in the process.

Children can become intensely involved when using these materials. For example, Maria, standing at a small table, firmly dumped the six-piece wooden puzzle out on the table. She immediately began replacing the pieces in the frame, one at a time. The largest piece went in first. It was the duck's body. Next, in went the head, followed by the bill and the feet. Maria was deeply absorbed in the task and did not notice what others were doing nearby. As the last piece dropped in place, Maria, looking up from her task, clapped her hands joyfully and smiled with self-satisfaction. Something about doing the puzzle must have given Maria some reward; no one was near who acknowledged her success, yet she flipped the puzzle over and began to work it again.

Completing a puzzle gives this child an immediate sense of satisfaction. She knows when it is complete and correct. (National Institute of Education, Child Study Center, U.S. Office of Education)

VALUE OF PERCEPTUAL-MOTOR ACTIVITIES

Young children learn about their world through perceiving stimuli from their five senses and reacting to the stimuli motorically with hands, feet, tongue, and body. They engage in perceptual-motor behavior as a result of things they see, touch, taste, smell, and hear. Many perceptual-motor behaviors are related to routines of home and school, such as eating and dressing. Over time a large number of play materials have been developed to help children learn characteristics and abstractions in the world. These are structured materials such as puzzles, form boards, and various games and manipulatives.

This chapter can be considered an extension of Chapter 11 on science activities. The activities and materials to be discussed are designed to help children further understand their world and to discover new relationships.

To help understand the rationale for presenting perceptual-motor activities to children, you should review the developmental tasks in Chapter 2, Bloom's Taxonomy of Educational Objectives and Vygotsky's theory in Chapter 6, the right-left brain research in Chapters 10 and 11, and Piaget's developmental stages and Guilford's intellectual operations in Chapter 11. These theoretical frameworks will help you think about children's learning as you observe and plan perceptual-motor activities for them.

For example, perceptual-motor materials contribute to all five of Guilford's intellectual operations discussed in Chapter 11. When children recognize the problem or task suggested by the toy, they are using **cognition**. In the puzzle example, Maria knew the task required putting the pieces back in the frame. **Memory** was used when Maria recalled other puzzles, recalled the picture, or remembered from previous experience where each of the pieces belonged. It is clear from her speed that she was using little trial and error as she may have during her first use of the puzzle. **Convergent thinking** was being used, for in this type of material there tends to be one right answer or use, as contrasted with art materials, previously discussed, which encourage wide variation in use. However, **divergent thinking** or novel use or response is possible with many structured materials, if the adults will permit novel uses. The puzzle Maria worked, for example, might have been put together on the table without the use of the frame, or upside down without the clues derived from the painted designs on the pieces. Or Maria might have traced around the pieces and made a drawing of a duck, a somewhat unusual use for puzzle pieces. **Evaluation** occurred when Maria put a piece in the wrong place and, realizing her error, retrieved the piece and placed it correctly. Many structured learning materials are self-correcting. That is, they won't work or be complete unless everything is in its correct place.[1]

Sensorimotor experience is derived through structured learning materials. The children use their senses and small muscles to explore the materials. They learn most from having ample time to explore the materials—building, arranging, dismantling, and redoing. Having adults ask questions about the characteristics of the material or what they are doing with it is generally considered to be important but is secondary to exploration in the learning process for young children.

Eye–hand coordination is developed with many of the materials because they require seeing the pieces and manipulating them in specific ways. Puzzle pieces are arranged in the frame, beads are strung, pegs are placed perpendicularly in the holes of a pegboard. Many of the materials require small muscle coordination, but large muscles and eyes are also coordinated when planks and packing boxes are manipulated on the playground or in the block corner.

Concepts of many kinds develop through the use of structured learning materials. Size, shape, weight, color, and texture are experienced. Spatial concepts—large, small, thick, thin, up, over, around, under, beside, and so on—become clearer as the child uses these toys. The mathematical concepts of number, quantity, and equivalence are experienced as children count, exchange, measure, and balance with these materials.

Perception of whole-part relationships is gained with many of these materials. In Maria's puzzle, for example, she recognized the parts (feet, bill) and their relationship to the rest of the duck. You may observe children who do not recognize the pieces that are eyes or hands, for example, and watch them try to fit them into what may appear to you to be illogical places. If so, they may need your help or verbal guidance. Attention can be directed to likenesses and differences. Perhaps in the duck puzzle the two feet are alike and interchangeable, but perhaps not, and the children then learn to note the difference between them. Color is also an important characteristic of many of these toys. Children learn to label and differentiate colors while enjoying puzzles.

Figure–ground perception is experienced through some of the toys. That is, one child may concentrate on the puzzle frame whereas another concentrates on the picture design of the pieces. Thus each child would be perceiving the task of the puzzle differently. The child's perception, then, influences how the adult offers help.

---

[1] J. P. Guilford, *Personality* (New York: McGraw-Hill, 1959), pp. 359–394, or see Guilford's "Structure-of-Intellect" model in Laura E. Berk, *Child Development* (Boston: Allyn and Bacon, 1991), pp. 301–304.

Matching colors is the task of this game. The teacher talks over choices in the beginning. (McQueen Preschool, Howard University)

Vocabulary is continuously growing as children talk about what they are doing, labeling the objects, the parts, and the process they are involved in. Some social conversation arises naturally as children share materials, cooperate on building or putting toys together, or have disputes over prior rights to a toy or a learning space. Such behavior fits Vygotsky's theory of learning through social discourse.

Curiosity is developed and satisfied through the use of these structured materials. Motivation is high because children are generally attracted to things that come apart, things that move, and things that they can handle without admonishment. A sense of accomplishment is quickly achieved, and the child can select another toy or repeat the use of the original one. Certain of these materials reward persistence, as children easily note when the puzzle is worked or the lotto board is filled up.

Inventiveness and creativity are fostered by some of these structured learning materials. Structured materials may attract children who shy away from the messy, nonstructured art media. These children are finding an avenue of

creative expression that is valid and comfortable for them.

Many premathematics, prereading, and prewriting skills are developed through these materials, for example, handedness, left-to-right progression, symbol correspondence, and observation. Ascertaining likenesses, differences, and whole-part relationships, which are inherent in many of these toys, contributes to these academic skills.

The self-pacing quality and generally individual use of the structured learning materials give children a chance to explore, correct, test, and retest by themselves while remaining more free of competition than they may with some other materials or activities found in the early childhood center.

PREMATHEMATICS ACTIVITIES

There are many premathematics activities that children engage in before they are ready for full-blown mathematical problems. Premathematics experiences, like prereading and prewriting, have an important place in the early childhood program.

Construction toys provide creative experiences for young children. (S. Russell, photographer)

Recall that in the summary of Piaget's research in Chapter 11 it was indicated that children under seven are in the sensorimotor and preoperational stages of development. This means that children need to act on real objects in real situations for their logical reasoning to develop. Children of these ages do not reason abstractly as do older children and adults.

Constance Kamii, a researcher of Piaget's theories, says that "construction of number" is the principal objective for arithmetic in preschool and kindergarten. She writes, "The construction of number exists in the child's head and is, therefore, unobservable. The quantification of objects is partly observable." Kamii goes on to suggest activities of quantification, saying she is "hypoth-

esizing that the thinking involved in the child's attempt to quantify objects must help the child construct number, if he is already at a relatively high level of constructing it."[2] The reader will remember that when a researcher is testing hypotheses about phenomena, information is being sought to confirm or reject the hypotheses. In this case, research so far does not really convince Kamii that quantification of objects (counting) will help children's "construction of number" in their heads. However, she is suggesting that teachers go ahead and help children learn to count because it may help.

To teach number, Kamii advises teachers to remember that the real objective must be an emphasis on the thinking that takes place in the child's head and not on the observable behavior of quantifying objects correctly.[3] In good Piaget fashion, teachers should question the child to discover how the child arrived at the answer. Just getting the right answer is not sufficient. This requires one-to-one teacher–child sessions that are fun—not work.

The activities that follow are to be offered to young children in an open, free, and comfortable atmosphere with emphasis on the process rather than the product. Some children will be obviously excited about working with numbers in many contexts. Others may show little or no interest and should be given time to become interested. As one teacher says of her plans, "We start early with premathematics and expect mature reasoning to occur late."

Incidental Experiences With Number

"How old are you, little girl?" asks a kindly lady in the grocery store. Little Mary shyly puts up three fingers. She may say, "Three." Chances are that Mary couldn't do this old parlor trick at two, and after five she'll probably just give a verbal answer. Mathematical learning begins at a young

---

[2]Constance Kamii, *Number in Preschool and Kindergarten* (Washington, DC: NAEYC, 1982), p. 24.
[3]Ibid., p. 25.

Large wooden blocks are an outstanding perceptual-motor resource. (Metropolitan State University)

age, especially when concepts are closely related to the child. Mary is beginning to learn mathematics.

Numbers surround us. In fact, with the advent of the computer many people feel that they are being dehumanized by being assigned numbers that can be fed into machines. The child may have a social security number at a young age, a phone number, a house number, a number of brothers and sisters, one tricycle, many books, a few dolls, or so many pennies. Children see their mother using money or measuring a cup of sugar and two eggs for a cake; she divides the candy bar in half or fills the glass half full of their favorite soft drink. Children hear about a TV program on Channel 2 at eight o'clock. They see parents scurrying around to keep an appointment at a certain hour, or they go for a visit on a given date and hear of plans for next year.

Incidental happenings such as the preceding may constitute the children's mathematical experience as they enter school. The teacher's role is one of clarifying present concepts and adding new concepts in a meaningful way. Numbers can continue to be introduced to children in natural ways as they come up incidentally during school activities.

Quantification

Children can count any object from the pegs on the pegboard to the tricycles in the play yard. They won't know at first that every object needs a number. They often skip over some numbers, saying "1, 2, 3, 14, 17." They like to sing counting songs, which helps them develop the proper vocabulary when they want to count. It is considerable time before they know that the last number is the total.

One-to-One Correspondence

Matching the number of painters to the number of chairs at the painting table is a lesson in one-to-one correspondence. Teachers can involve the children in problem solving by getting them to help with the counting. Many experiences at the school can help with one-to-one correspondence.

Measurements

"How tall are you today, Jeff?" asks the teacher as she proceeds to measure and record the height of each child. She tells Jeff, "You are 44 inches. Last fall you were 43 inches. You've grown 1 inch. An inch is this much." The teacher shows the child an inch on the measuring device. She can continue the measurements with weights and add both figures to a chart with the children's names. She labels the tools used to make the measurements.

In food experiences other tools are used and other measurements are important. The temperature of the oven is a large number. The use of a thermometer in the classroom gives an opportunity for children to see and "read" other numbers. Taking the thermometer outdoors on a cold day will help children become acquainted with the concept of measuring the temperature of the air.

Seriation

Seriation is another perceptual activity described by Piaget. The child looks at at least three objects, determines whether they are the same, and then arranges them in a series, perhaps according to size. Maria Montessori, a pioneer early childhood educator, also felt that seriation was important. She presented children with numerous graduated cylinders that fit in matching holes in a long bar. This matching game was self-correcting; that is, the child knew the correct arrangement by the way the cylinders fitted the spaces.

Nested boxes or cans are examples of seriation toys. Another is the Montessori "pink tower," built from graduated boxes stacked to make a tower. This toy has been replicated by numerous manufacturers since Montessori's day. Teachers can prepare tin cans of various sizes in the same way.

The stacking disc toy, consisting of a single spindle over which the child slips colored discs, is familiar to most. Graduated from the large base to a screw-on top, the toy is a challenge to perceptual, coordination, and seriation skills. When this toy is given to toddlers before the "age of accountability," they frequently use the spindle part for a hammer, much to the dismay of their educationally helpful parents.

To learn discrimination of relative size, the child may line up objects in order. Many common objects found in the home and school—such as balls, pop bottles, and cold cream jars—can be used for this purpose. In guiding the child's participation, be sure that you offer appropriate word pairs for the comparisons—tallest-shortest, biggest-smallest, longest-shortest, and so on.

Children can also practice seriation in arranging chairs or tricycles in the room or yard. "Let's put all the large ones in the back," suggests the teacher. The children may need help with the labels describing these perceptual tasks.

Classification

Classification means grouping items on the basis of some characteristic. Be sure to give children only one variable at a time; that is, if you ask the child to classify according to color, then save classifying according to shape for another day. Piaget's work suggests that children become "centered" on one characteristic and cannot "decenter" to classify according to another criterion.

The imaginative teacher can make a classifying experience out of numerous common objects. Helping sort the plastic spoons and forks in the housekeeping corner is a classifying experience. The block corner, with its shelf of squares, triangles, cylinders, and so on, is a classification opportunity. With this perception, teachers realize that putting away the blocks is a valuable learning experience for children. This holds true in most areas of school; for example, the crayons all go together in one basket and the scissors in another, and the tricycles are all grouped in one storage closet.

Cubes, beads, pegs, buttons, bolts and nuts, bottle caps, and other objects can be used for sorting (classifying) experiences. In classifying you simply group things together that are alike in some way. Egg cartons or muffin tins are handy for separating small objects. Boxes can be divided into sections to accommodate larger objects. You might have little cars in several colors. You can work with a child, saying, "Give me one like mine." If the child is learning colors, say, "Give me a red one." After the group has been sorted you can ask, "What color are these cars?" After they are mixed up again you might say, "Put your finger on the red block," helping the child learn the color labels.

Following classification activities, the children can count the various groups of objects. They can lay them out in one-to-one correspondence. Talking about the process helps the children learn.

Making Sets

Making sets of items helps develop number skills. "Put your blocks in sets of two," or, "See how many sets you can make with your pile of blocks." It is important that children be allowed to move their objects around in a spontaneous fashion and discover sets themselves. Making sets can often flow from a classification experience. Playing dominoes provides great experience with sets.

Geometric forms in many sizes help children learn whole and part concepts. (Oregon State University)

Reading Numbers

Being able to read a number is not equivalent to understanding what it means. Reading the clock, the calendar, thermometer, TV dial, prices on items, speed limit signs, and so on is very interesting to some children. They may soon try writing the numbers and should be helped when they desire to learn.

Games

Uncle Wiggily, Candyland, and similar games require the ability to match, count, and take turns with peers. Delbert, Jamie, and the teacher, Sue Smith, were about to begin another game of Candyland. As happens from time to time with some structured learning activities, a dispute developed. Both boys were yelling, "I wanna be first! Let me go first." Sue Smith picked up a red token, placed her hands behind her back, and said, "Whoever picks the hand with the red token goes first." Both boys were satisfied. Sue, like many good teachers, knows and utilizes various successful methods for settling disputes quickly—methods that avoid harsh discipline and that promote good relationships and facilitate a continuation of the desired learning activities.

When using the board games children often devise their own rules. It is interesting to observe a game when they use their own rules. Quietly observe what happens, instead of getting upset that they aren't following the rules.

Some children play dominoes—even double nines—and appear to be reading the designs of dots more than they are counting them. Nonetheless dominoes are very good practice with numbers, especially if played simply as a matching game.

Card games such as "concentration" and "fish" can be enjoyed by some children in older groups. Some games require collecting cards that are alike. A simple way to use the cards with younger children is to let them sort the cards into their various categories.[4]

Attendance Charts

Attendance charts and other records can be posted and will give children some counting and

---

[4]For a helpful discussion and description of numerous games, see Constance Kamii and Rheta DeVries, *Group Games in Early Education: Implications of Piaget's Theory* (Washington, DC: NAEYC, 1980).

reading experience. See Figure 11–2 for an example of an interesting attendance chart.

Evaluate Children's Number Concepts

The teacher can test an individual child's concepts by using ten cubes or pennies. If the child is momentarily unoccupied or stops for a chat, the teacher initiates a game of hiding the cubes or pennies, brings out a given number and asks, "How many are there?" The teacher can continue the game, arranging items in various sets until getting a clear idea of the child's ability. By keeping a chart the teacher can record concepts each child understands. This study can guide the planning of further number experience.

EYE–HAND COORDINATION MATERIALS

Perception materials help the child learn through the senses—touching, seeing, hearing, smelling, and tasting. The perceptual process includes judgment and subtle discrimination.

One group of materials helps the child to learn small motor coordination and to practice these motor skills until they become automatic. You, for example, once had to look at and think consciously about tying your shoelace; now you do it automatically.

Small motor coordination plays an important role in reading and writing, which are in their preliminary stages during the early years. Lugo and Hershey suggest four steps in the sequence of mastering a fine motor skill: (1) the needed maturation of the visual and hand muscles must be present, (2) the child notes the problem or task and is motivated to try to do it, (3) the child tries out the task, and (4) the child practices until mastery is achieved.[5] Children in our early childhood centers may be at any stage of this four-step sequence.

---

[5]James O. Lugo and Gerald L. Hershey, *Human Development* (New York: Macmillan, 1974), pp. 365–366.

TALK IT OVER: NO. 1

Discuss the issues involved as children learn mathematics.

Eye–hand coordination is practiced in many situations in school. Using writing and drawing tools and scissors, tearing paper, and squeezing glue bottles are examples. Turning pages of books, and buttoning and zipping clothing all contribute to coordination practice.

Coordination skills are preliminary to many other motor skills, and teachers can encourage their practice by setting expectations that are individual. Age is not the best criterion, and some three-year-olds excel some fives. A child may be more advanced in some skills than in others. Competitive situations should be avoided, for when a child fails, he or she may grow tense and begin to avoid the practice that is needed. Our task is to present the children with interesting materials and with support while they develop and practice these skills.

Bead or Ring Stringing

Manipulative skills develop as the child strings beads or rings. Special laces with metal tips are available, making the task easier when the holes are small. In an emergency a piece of masking tape rolled securely around the end of a lace will make the tip firm and enable the child to get it through the bead. At a beginning level the child will mostly be concerned with transferring beads to string. Later the child will become selective, perhaps choosing red beads, or square ones, or even alternating the beads to form a pattern.

Another lacing task is tying shoelaces. This is a practical task, and parents will be happy if their children learn to do it. There are several shoelacing toys available, but the inventive teacher can merely provide a discarded shoe for children to practice lacing and tying. However, both teachers and parents should remember that tying shoelaces is generally learned when the child is five or six years old. Also in the clothing line are items used to practice buttoning, zipping, and snapping. Though these, too, are available commercially, they can be made by anyone with some time, materials, and elementary sewing skills.

Lacing string or yarn in sewing cards and special lacing cards gives good practice. One drawback is that the teachers generally must unlace the cards to prepare them for reuse, a task that becomes time-consuming and tedious. Sewing on burlap with yarn using large blunt plastic needles is a similar task, and the child is allowed to keep his or her creation. The teacher will want a needle threader to help with keeping the children's needles threaded. It is wise to start the day with a number of needles already threaded. Tacking burlap to wooden frames helps the children use it more successfully.

Pegboards

Pegboards and a basket of colorful pegs especially intrigue the youngest children. First they select pegs at random and concentrate on fitting them in the holes. Later, children may create designs or follow a friend's pattern or the teacher's. Squares of ceiling tile with holes or pieces of packing foam can be used for pegboards, thus providing children another sensory experience.

Sorting Shapes

Parquetry blocks require the child to organize basic geometric-shaped blocks according to designs in the bottom of the box. In helping a child new to parquetry, you can say, "Which block looks like this one?" as you point to a geometric shape. Children enjoy sorting the parquetry blocks into piles of "look-alikes" on the table and even like to arrange their own designs

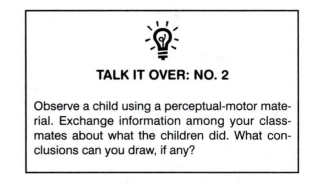

TALK IT OVER: NO. 2

Observe a child using a perceptual-motor material. Exchange information among your classmates about what the children did. What conclusions can you draw, if any?

without the aid of the printed designs. This is a creative use of the toy that should be encouraged. Various other games encourage children to classify shapes. Teachers should go a step further and call the children's attention to shapes in their classroom and in the play yard. Even snacks come in various sizes and interesting shapes, from triangle sandwiches to round cookies.

CONSTRUCTION MATERIALS

Several types of construction materials allow children to build, thus helping them discover balance, weight, height, and depth. Some materials are quite small and can be used most comfortably on a table, whereas others are large and are used on the floor or in the play yard.

Blocks[6]

Blocks are probably one of the most important types of equipment supplied by a high-quality early childhood education center. They give children an opportunity to express their ideas, interpret what they observe, and express their feelings. The shelves of blocks may be the first equipment that impresses a visitor, because blocks are displayed in a prominent place and there are many of

---

[6]For in-depth information on current use as well as the history of using blocks in the nursery school and kindergarten see *The Block Book* edited by Elizabeth S. Hirsch (Washington, DC: NAEYC, 1984). Chapters are written by early childhood educators who have studied children's use of blocks.

One-to-one correspondence helps a child learn mathematical concepts. (Oregon State University)

them. This arrangement encourages the children to incorporate them into many types of play. Children discover height, balance, and directionality as they use blocks. They learn to judge the amount of space required to enclose themselves or a toy animal or car. They experience distance as they select a block to make a bridge over their road. Ideas, information, and creativity are coordinated as children use blocks. They recall a house and build one for a doll family. A bridge or overpass is recalled and built over a road. Gravity is experienced as blocks topple down or the small toy car runs down the ramps the children build. Note the involvement of the children in the following incident.

Steve and Eddie were using the large hollow wooden blocks. Using the ramp, they found some excitement in running their cars down the ramp and seeing them shoot rapidly off to one side. They noted other ramps in the corner of the room and brought them to add to their ramp. It didn't work, they discovered, to lay the ramps together on the same level. Steve and Eddie sur-

veyed their problem, then brought a large block to put under one ramp, creating excitement for all when their cars swooshed down the two-ramp run. Now they added two big blocks and a third ramp to make a three-ramp run. "Wow!" exclaimed Eddie, "Everybody stand back. This is really going to be a race now!" The downhill run proved interesting not only to Steve and Eddie but to other children who were attracted by the excitement, until numerous races developed out of the two boys' initial idea. Gravity had been discovered that afternoon, and it was a simple matter for the teacher to give the boys and the others a label for it as the activity came to a close that day.

Large Blocks
Large blocks come in several varieties. The largest are usually about 22-by-11-by-5½ inches, with the smaller ones being half or one-fourth the large size. Hollow wooden blocks have been available for many years and are extremely popular in early childhood groups. Hollow blocks are

large enough for children to use in dramatic play that incorporates them as actors. Though expensive, the large blocks are very durable, making them an almost permanent investment for the school. Large blocks are now being made of polyethylene and other synthetic materials. These blocks have the advantage of being weatherproof and not splitting or peeling in moist climates. Auxiliary pieces, such as planks and ramps, greatly increase versatility. A set of sixty large blocks for twenty prekindergarten children and a set of seventy-five for twenty kindergarten children are recommended.

Large packing boxes used in the play yard may contribute the same kind of learning as blocks and they possess the additional virtue of allowing the child to get inside them. When large wooden boxes are made specifically for school use, they should be made in several sizes. Children will learn that one size may be more useful for one activity than another. Hollow blocks and packing boxes can be combined in interesting and productive play. It is convenient to have a push truck in the play yard to encourage children to take the blocks where they see a use for them. Also, when the play is finished, the blocks are easily loaded on the truck and returned to storage.

Foam and cardboard blocks are an outstanding and less expensive substitute for wooden blocks. These approximately shoe-box-sized blocks are colorful, and they are made with an inside support that reinforces them, making them stronger than they appear at first glance. Surprisingly, even adults won't squash them if they stand on them. Parents who purchased a dozen cardboard blocks when their children were small say these blocks represent their best-spent toy dollars because their children have used them extensively for many years. Five dozen will serve a classroom for a number of years for indoor block play. They are not appropriate for damp play yards.

Unit Blocks

Unit blocks are all multiples or divisions of the basic unit, which measures $1\frac{3}{8}$-by-$2\frac{3}{4}$-by-$5\frac{1}{2}$

inches. All are made of hardwoods and are carefully sanded. Besides squares and rectangles there are columns, arches, triangles, quarter circles, and numerous other shapes. All fit together precisely. About five hundred pieces are needed in a typical early childhood classroom. Storage for unit blocks should include enough shelf space to accommodate each shape and size of block without crowding. These shapes can be marked on the back of the shelves with a drawing to help children and adults find where the different blocks go at cleanup time. Obviously sorting and classifying are important opportunities for cognitive learning. Small trucks stored near the blocks encourage children to load and unload blocks as well as to build roads for the vehicles.

Small Blocks

Small blocks are much smaller even than unit blocks and contribute especially to small muscle dexterity. These blocks are made of either wood or plastic. Many are very small, and though interlocking, they make somewhat fragile and unstable buildings; therefore, using them on a table is usually preferred. The older four- and five-year-old children generally have the muscle coordination and patience to enjoy these small blocks, whereas younger children find them frustrating. Some sets are profitably kept in the "rainy-day closet" to be brought out only rarely when a new activity is needed to replace rained-out activities.

Block Substitutes

Block substitutes are made by some inventive teachers and parents. They stuff one cardboard milk carton with newspaper; then as it stands upright, a second milk carton opened at the top is forced down over the first carton. The edges can be taped with plastic or masking tape.

Guiding Block Play

Guiding block play presents many opportunities for creative teaching. Children will use many blocks and build magnificent structures if the schedule is open enough to allow sufficient time and if adults encourage creativity. With all blocks

Unit blocks are carefully engineered, matching precisely so ends match. Storage is facilitated with designs on the shelves. (Child Study Center, Institute of Education, U.S. Department of Education)

the teacher's role is to provide an adequate number for the group of children and to store them where the children have ample building space away from generally used traffic lanes. Auxiliary figures and toys stored nearby make outstanding contributions to block play. Carpeting on the block-playing area will absorb the noise made by falling blocks and the children's exuberant play.

Block structures are often knocked down by the builder. This is quite acceptable when it is the child's own structure, but the teacher can also encourage children to use their creativity in taking down their block structure piece by piece. Sorting and categorizing skills can be learned while the blocks are being placed on the shelves. If the teacher works with the children as they put blocks away saying, "You bring them to me, and I'll help put them on the shelves," the resulting cooperation may be surprising. With a cooperative air the children will help and others will join in the fun, even though they may not have used the blocks. If the teacher says "Thank you" or "What a big load!" these rewards will usually be sufficient to get the children's happy cooperation.

Singing a song, like "Pickin' up blocks and puttin' 'em on the shelf" to the tune of "Pawpaw Patch," helps, too. By all means avoid having a curse placed on using the blocks by assistants too lazy to help with putting them away. All should avoid the admonition, "*You* got the blocks out, *you* put them away," which is sometimes heard. Such a technique discourages the children's use of this valuable educational resource.

Children should be warned that cleanup time is approaching, so that they can finish their building project and the imaginative play that accompanies it. The teacher may extend the play period to allow the children who have worked diligently to construct something to have a few minutes to use it. In this way the teacher avoids frustrating the children and shows understanding of the children's need to use a building they have constructed.

Sometimes the teacher may permit the children to leave their block structures set up so that they can add to them from day to day. This practice is most feasible when a single group uses the room. With care, it can be allowed when one teacher has two groups using a room or even when two teachers share a room—if good cooperation exists between the teachers.

Other Construction Toys

In addition to blocks there are many other interesting construction toys. Some are plastic and some are wooden. Some pop together over a plastic bubble or knob; some fit together in precut grooves or join with snaps like the grippers on a child's pajamas. Like blocks, these toys give the child an opportunity to build in three dimensions and to use imagination. They also give practice in small muscle coordination. Some can be frustrating to young children who are not coordinated enough to handle them. Some come with patterns to copy, which are generally too difficult for young children and may inhibit creativity. Therefore extensive use of patterns should be avoided. Children should have ample opportunity to create their own designs and structures.

Puzzles

Puzzles are popular construction toys, as indicated in the opening anecdote of this chapter. Puzzles differ from other construction toys, however, for the task calls for the child to assemble pieces in a specific and preconceived way to make a picture in its original form. This is a clear example of a convergent task—one calling for one right answer.

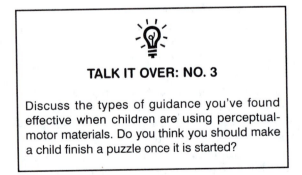

TALK IT OVER: NO. 3

Discuss the types of guidance you've found effective when children are using perceptual-motor materials. Do you think you should make a child finish a puzzle once it is started?

There are a number of different kinds of puzzles. The most popular for children under six are those made of wood. Recently some have been made from colorful rubber, which adds an interesting textural experience. Puzzles are very durable, withstanding years of use by classes of children if care is taken not to lose pieces. Choices of puzzles include such things as animals, vehicles, and familiar scenes from children's lives and from books they know. Usually each piece is an object, a part, or a body, enabling children to think about replacing a head, a foot, or a wheel. This arrangement helps the child grasp the concepts of whole and part. Another type of puzzle provides inlays of whole objects grouped with related objects—such as five fruits, five vegetables, or five objects to wear when it rains. Some puzzles have knobs for removing the pieces, but although knobs do give the child experience in grasping, they seem unessential to puzzles and are easily broken off. Puzzles can be stored in specially built racks, which aids their care and protection. Knob puzzles require special racks.

Puzzles must be selected according to the number of pieces with which the child is ready to cope. Development and experience are more important than chronological age; however, four to six pieces are usually appropriate for three-year-olds and up to thirty for advanced kindergartners. Some kindergartners may even be ready for the United States map puzzle.

Guiding a child's use of puzzles begins with selecting the level of puzzle the child is ready for—not too hard, not too easy. Sometimes a child gains confidence from putting together a simple, familiar puzzle before going on to harder ones. Sometimes suggesting removing one piece, then replacing it, helps a child who is having trouble proceeding. You can offer a little help and encouragement if a child seems ready to give up, though you should avoid compelling a child to complete a puzzle. However, a common situation is for the child to help the adult, for there is nothing so sobering as to be left to work a child's puzzle that you haven't seen whole! Jim, a graduate student, had this happen to him the first day he worked with a four-year-old group. He picked up the jumbled mass in honest embarrassment, asking himself out loud, "Now, how in the world do you do this?" Whereupon a child, Sara, volunteered, "Here, I'll help you." And she did, with the eternal thanks of the young man.

Arranging the puzzle storage adjacent to tables encourages children to use puzzles and other structured learning materials on the tables, helps keep pieces from being mislaid, and helps keep the distractions of other tasks from interfering with the child's work. If a teacher checks the toys after each self-selected activity period, the children can be asked to help look for any missing pieces before the pieces are lost for good. Sometimes children absentmindedly place pieces in their pockets, so simply say, "Children, check your pockets to see if our missing puzzle piece is hiding there." Seek the cooperation of the custodians too, so they won't sweep out your precious pieces. Once a puzzle piece is missing the puzzle should be retired for repair. One method of repairing a puzzle is to line the hole with plastic wrap and fill it with wood filler, letting it set. After it is set it can be painted, hopefully to match the rest of the puzzle.

Puzzles are a long-range investment. Some puzzles should be stored away to rotate as "new" from time to time. They are an activity that children can usually manage without much help or supervision, leaving teachers free to handle more complicated learning centers.

Children can occasionally make their own puzzles by selecting a magazine picture and gluing it to cardboard—men's shirt boards work well. Put the glued picture flat under books to dry, with wax paper on top of the picture. Wax paper does not adhere to white glue. After the glue is dry, the pieces can be cut. A paper cutter is helpful for this task. Remember to make the pieces simple at first; then they can be cut further if the child is ready.

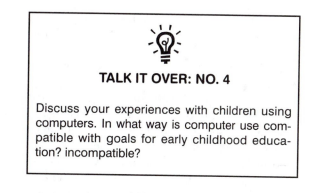

TALK IT OVER: NO. 4

Discuss your experiences with children using computers. In what way is computer use compatible with goals for early childhood education? incompatible?

USING MICROCOMPUTERS

Early childhood schools are beginning to try out computers with young children. In recent years microcomputers have become more affordable to individuals and schools. Elementary and secondary schools have introduced them for instructional purposes. Early childhood teachers are curious about whether computers will be useful in helping children learn what they want and need to learn at this young age. Mathematics, reading, and perceptual tasks are typical subjects addressed in computer software programs.

Knowing Piaget's, Kamii's, and others' concern for children needing experiences with real objects in real situations for learning, teachers are wondering if the abstract pictures on the computer screen and the oral instructions (when available) are within young children's level of understanding. As discussed earlier under premathematics activities, research indicates that a child's ability to give a correct answer does not necessarily mean that the child has internalized a "construction of number."

Definitive research studies supporting the use of microcomputers, as part of the early childhood curriculum, are yet to be done. L. Goodwin, W. Goodwin, and Garel surveyed the research associated with young children and computer use and found that studies were not decisive because of methodological difficulties. In a study of their own, these researchers found the control group demonstrated significantly higher interest in microcomputers than did adult-assisted and adult-unassisted three- and four-year-olds. No significant cognitive differences were found in the three groups.[7]

David Elkind, a prominent child psychologist and past president of NAEYC, is concerned about the "mis-education of the preschool child." Elkind writes, "There is no evidence that early exposure to a technology in any way accelerates mental development. . . . A computer does not alter our ability to remember any more than a lever alters our muscles."[8]

Parental Reaction

Many parents are enthusiastic about their child's learning about and using computers in the early childhood school. Many of today's adults have had to overcome some anxiety in using computers and believe that if children grow up with them, they will not suffer such discomfort. Many parents in high-technology areas have their own computers at home. Some parents are working at home at a computer that is networked to their office and other computers. Children in such homes probably have opportunities to use computers. Some parents interpret the installation of a computer for the children to use in a school as a measure of high quality in the school. Clearly this could be as much of an erroneous criterion of quality as is having a minibus that picks up and delivers children. Computer companies have been using hard-sell advertising on parents to get them to buy home computers to "ensure your child's future success."

One early childhood specialist said his own four-year-old son was interested in the computer as long as they worked together on a program, but he lost interest if Dad was not there. This suggests that having Dad's attention was the important part, rather than the computer.

Teachers' Reactions

Early childhood teachers are proceeding cautiously. They want early childhood education to remain a particularly humanistic experience. They worry that sitting at a machine for long periods could dehumanize education. Even though microcomputers are cheaper than previously, they still require a sizable budget to purchase and equip with software programs. Teachers question allocating such a proportion of the budget to this use. In other words, "What will children have to do without if we provide computers?"

Both teachers and parents have questioned the values introduced in some computer programs when the correct answers are shot down with bullets or arrows. These individuals feel that learning should not be associated with tools of violence.

Some teachers who have experimented with teaching reading by computer have felt that the negative feedback from the machine was very harsh. They indicated that early childhood programs had other effective ways of teaching the same thing. Teachers who used the computer to teach *under, over, into,* and *behind* felt the same way. The word-processing component was of interest to some children. As with using the typewriter, children like seeing numbers, letters, and words appear on the screen and then moving them around or making them disappear. Some saw an analogy with playing the piano and experimenting with a melody. The important factor seemed to be allowing the child to explore the machine in his or her own way.

Most of the computer programs require an adult to read and explain the instructions. Thus it is essential for adults to be thoroughly familiar with the computer and the software and take time to work with individual children. Space

---

[7]L. D. Goodwin, W. L. Goodwin, and M. B. Garel, "Use of Microcomputers with Preschoolers: A Review of the Literature," reprinted in M. Jensen and Z. Chevalier, eds., *Issues and Advocacy in Early Education* (Boston: Allyn and Bacon, 1990), pp. 248–259.

[8]David Elkind, "Mis-education," reprinted in Judy McKee and Karen Paciorek, eds., *Annual Editions: Early Childhood Education 89/90* (Guilford, CN: Dushkin, 1989), pp. 160–163.

The computer offers many matching games. Many prekindergarten children can play solitaire faster than adults can. (Kansas State University)

around the computer is needed for several people. Teachers like to plan for at least three children working together. Some use chairs; others have experimented with having the computer on a counter at children's height. It is reported that both boys and girls are equally interested in computers. It is important that a gender bias not be introduced into computer usage, that is, making the computer more a boy's than girl's machine.

Practically speaking, packages of software, or programs, are needed in order for the computer to know what to do when certain keys are pressed. Software has come a long way in a few years, but still has far to go. Companies selling software will allow teachers to sample software packages and try them out in their own schools before buying them. Teachers recommend careful assessment before purchasing the computer as well as after. The type of software available may determine the choice of computer in the first place.

In a report that summarizes research on children's use of computers and reviews many aspects, Clements, Nastasi, and Swaminathan say that "computers can accentuate, rather than attenuate, existing social patterns; for example, children's cooperative interactions increase, they seek and receive more help from each other and the teacher, they form new friendships because of shared interests, and they identify new leaders known as 'the computer experts'" (p. 63). In conclusion the authors state that "well-planned, integrated computer activities can increase achievement in cost-effective ways." Also, "for many teachers, a variety of experiences leads them to reflect and reorganize their thinking about young children's learning."[9]

---

[9]Douglas H. Clements, Bonnie K. Nastasi, and Sudha Swaminathan, "Young Children and Computers: Crossroads and Directions From Research," *Young Children* 48:2 (January 1993), 56–63.

One problem indicated by many who are using computers is that the teachers are often unfamiliar with, even afraid of, the computer and thus cannot help children appreciate it. In the computer age, it is quite essential that you, a preservice teacher, gain computer skills. Then as improved software programs for children are developed, you will be able to use them comfortably. In the meantime, the computer will be a tremendous help to you in doing your own work and perhaps in getting a job, because job applications now often ask for the various kinds of software programs candidates can use.

Conclusions

Perceptual-motor activities are called structured because their size, shape, color, and texture do not change as children use them. Children's cognitive, motor, and social development is stimulated through the use of perceptual-motor activities. Premathematics concepts are often part of perceptual-motor activities. According to Kamii's research, the goal for premathematics activities for young children is to help them learn a construction of number in their heads, and not to parrot the right answers.

Many perceptual-motor activities are manipulated individually and are self-paced and self-correcting. Inventiveness and creativity are fostered by many of the structured materials and may be an important avenue of expression for those children who do not enjoy nonstructured activities. Early literacy skills are being developed through the use of structured learning materials, for example, left-to-right progressions, handedness, and symbol comparisons.

The pros and cons of the use of microcomputers were discussed. Use of computers is expected to develop as research and experience give teachers information about what children can appropriately gain by using them. Today most schools have at least one computer.

Applications

1. Discuss the "Talk It Over" items found in the chapter.
2. Write an activity plan for a perceptual-motor activity for a few children, using information and the sample plan (Figure 6–2) in Chapter 6. Secure approval, carry out the plan, and evaluate the results from the children's point of view and from your viewpoint. Prepare a report and hand it in along with your approved activity plan.
3. Evaluate your total participation performance on your evaluation form developed in Chapter 1.
4. Add ideas and plans for perceptual-motor activities to your Resource File.

Study Questions

1. Define *perceptual-motor activities*. State their value to children's education.
2. Explain the major objective in premathematics activities.
3. Identify Constance Kamii's research and her conclusions regarding children's "construction of number."
4. Define and explain (a) *quantification*, (b) *one-to-one correspondence*, (c) *centered* and *decentered*, (d) *classification*, (e) *seriation*, and (f) *making sets*.
5. Describe coordination materials.
6. Describe construction materials.
7. Describe the different types of blocks and the value of each type in early childhood schools.
8. Discuss the pros and cons of computer use in early childhood schools.

Videotapes

The Adventure Begins: Preschool and Technology
   10 minutes

Shows how computers can become an integral part of enhancing learning in developmentally appropriate programs for young children. NAEYC Media, 1509 16th St. NW, Washington DC 20036-1426, 1-800-424-2460.

Block Play: Constructing Realities
  20 minutes

Shows how children acquire knowledge through block play, stages in block play, and skills they practice. NAEYC Media, 1509 16th St. NW, Washington DC 20036-1426, 1-800-424-2460.

A Classroom With Blocks
  13 minutes

Video helps teachers tap the potential for learning found in blocks. NAEYC Media, 1509 16th St. NW, Washington DC 20036-1426, 1-800-424-2460.

Additional Readings

Burns, M. Susan, Laura Goin, and Jan Tribble Donion. "A Computer in My Room." *Young Children* 45:2, January 1990, 62–67.

Cartwright, Sally. "Learning with Large Blocks." *Young Children* 45:3, March 1990, 38–41.

Clements, D. H. "Computers and Young Children: A Review of Research." *Young Children* 43:1, November 1987, 34–44.

Clements, Douglas H., Bonnie Nastasi, and Sudha Swaminathan. "Young Children and Computers." *Young Children* 48:2, January 1993, 56–63.

Forman, George E., and David S. Kuschner. *The Child's Construction of Knowledge: Piaget for Teaching Children.* Washington, DC: NAEYC, 1984.

Hirsch, Elizabeth S., ed. *The Block Book.* Washington, DC: NAEYC, 1995.

Kamii, Constance. *Number in Preschool and Kindergarten: Educational Implications of Piaget's Theory.* Washington, DC: NAEYC, 1982.

Kamii, Constance, and Rheta DeVries. *Piaget, Children, and Number.* Washington, DC: NAEYC, 1976.

————. *Group Games in Early Education.* Washington, DC: NAEYC, 1980.

Leithead, Marion. "Happy Hammering . . . A Hammering Activity Center with Built-In Success." *Young Children* 51:3, March 1996, 12.

Osborn, Janie D., and Keith Osborn. *Cognition in Early Childhood.* Athens, GA: Education Associates, 1983.

Reifel, Stuart. "Block Construction: Children's Developmental Landmarks in Representation of Space." *Young Children* 40:1, November 1984, 61–67.

Skeen, P., A. P. Garner, and S. Cartwright. *Woodworking for Young Children.* Washington, DC: NAEYC, 1984.

CHAPTER 13

Language Activities

U.S. Army Child Development Services, Baumholder, Germany

Objectives

✔ Relate developmental tasks and language development.
✔ Identify major goals and state how early childhood teachers foster language development and emerging literacy.
✔ Suggest ways to help children learning English as a second language and children with language problems.
✔ Identify and evaluate language activities offered in early childhood schools.

"I feel like I've had a bath in lollipop suds," said four-year-old Julia, wiping her sweaty brow after running and climbing on a hot humid day.

Julia's comment is one of many examples of creative speech you might hear as you listen carefully to children. The out-of-the-mouths-of-babes stories told by proud parents and doting grandparents focus on the unique word combinations children invent. Children enjoy coining new words, rhyming words, and experimenting with words. Unhampered by knowing the "right" way to say something, children's expressions are often colorful and original. Kornei Chukovsky, a famous linguist who collects examples of children's creative language, says, "Beginning with the age of two, every child becomes for a short period of time a linguistic genius."[1]

Children's strengths shine through in their early efforts to communicate. They learn first in the family, acquiring their native tongue there. Chukovsky believes they work hard and says, "In truth, the young child is the hardest mental toiler on the planet. Fortunately he does not even suspect this."[2]

LANGUAGE DEFINITION AND BEGINNINGS

Language is a symbol system wherein things and ideas are represented by spoken and written words. Language has an enduring quality, representing the past, present, and future. Language enriches our present human exchanges and connects us with past and future generations of other humans. Historically, this connection was once in the form of pictures on cave walls, then later of words in books, then of disk and film. Today, words and ideas will be preserved electronically on tape and video as well as in printed forms for generations to come.

Self-efficacy is the child's own assessment of his or her ability to perform a behavior. Self-efficacy in learning language is evident in the examples from Chukovsky's work mentioned in the opening paragraphs. Children do not suffer from lack of confidence when they begin to learn. However, self-efficacy is affected most by personal accomplishment, according to studies by social psychologist Albert Bandura.[3] A critical question to keep in mind is, How can parents and teachers preserve the child's high level of motivation and self-efficacy for language learning?

RELATIONSHIP OF LANGUAGE DEVELOPMENT TO TOTAL DEVELOPMENT

Language development influences and is influenced by all other areas of development. One look at the developmental tasks discussed in Chapter 2 shows that one task in particular deals directly with language—learning new words and understanding the language of others. Other tasks, such as developing independence, giving affection, getting along with others, understanding one's body and the physical world, and developing a positive feeling about oneself, all have language components or, at higher levels, are expressed by language. Understanding the linkages between language development and other areas of development will help parents and teachers plan most effectively for children.

Physical Development

Biological factors affect the child's speaking and hearing ability. In the mid-1960s a worldwide epidemic of *rubella* (also called German measles or three-day-measles) caused large numbers of genetic defects, depending on the critical period in which the mother-to-be had the disease. Over twenty thousand pregnant American women had the disease with severe consequences for many babies. Among the infants 20 percent died and many others suffered heart defects; eye cataracts;

---

[1] K. Chukovsky, *From Two to Five* (Berkeley: University of California Press, 1968), p. 7.
[2] Ibid., p. 10.

[3] A. Bandura, *Social Foundations of Thought and Action* (Upper Saddle River, NJ: Prentice Hall, 1986), p. 391. His work was also discussed in Chapters 9 and 10 in reference to other skills.

With language skills children organize their play. (University of Illinois)

deafness; genital, urinary, and gastrointestinal anomalies; and mental retardation.[4] Today, thanks to a public health effort, a vaccine can prevent women from contracting *rubella.*

Birth injuries may impair the child's ability to speak and hear. Brain damage or injury to the speaking and hearing organs in childhood may be equally disabling.[5] Also, adenoids may grow into a child's ear and nose passages, interfering with hearing and breath control.

Teachers should be certain that children are hearing. A section toward the end of this chapter focuses on hearing problems. Briefly, children may give evidence of poor hearing by lack of attention, by not following directions, or by disinterest in listening-type activities. A child who eats noisily may have a problem with adenoids. Parents should be alerted to the need for a medical checkup.

Physical development affects the organs of hearing and speech. A malfunction in any organ can create language handicaps. Newborn infants are now tested for hearing in the hospital nursery. Hearing aids are fitted to the infant when a hearing loss is discovered. A hearing aid helps the infant hear all the prelanguage sounds commonly heard by hearing infants.[6] A child whose speech and hearing therapy is left until later childhood may first require training in the infant languages of babbling, lolling, and gibberish. Finally, words are introduced.

Social Development

Of course, the child's first social environment is the family. A child's language is influenced by relationships with family members. If a good verbal relationship exists, children have more advanced language skills than others in their age

[4]Laura E. Berk, *Child Development* (Boston, MA: Allyn and Bacon, 1991), pp. 94–95.
[5]L. Fisch, "Causes of Congenital Deafness," *International Audiology* 8:1 (1969), 85–89.

[6]Marion P. Downs and W. G. Hemenway, "Report of the Hearing Screening of 17,000 Neonates," *International Audiology* 8:1 (1969), 72–76.

group. Stimulation from parents, siblings, and playmates is extremely significant. Children want to communicate. Since birth they have been learning to interpret the words and actions of family and friends and, in turn, they learn the words and actions that these people will understand. Communication is a two-way street—individuals try to let others know their thoughts and feelings while the recipients try to decode the messages. This is a marvelous human capacity, and we want the child to continue to grow in both the production and the comprehension of language.

Social development is fostered when children have language skills. Language skill encourages a child to make social contacts. The solitary play of a two-year-old develops into cooperative play as the child matures in ability to communicate. Then the child can approach another child verbally as well as physically. Children with the most advanced language skills make the most social contacts, lead others in activities, and organize cooperative play.

The social environment of the child is always within a cultural context. Children will learn to speak the language of their family and neighborhood. When they arrive in early childhood programs they will broaden their culture and begin learning to communicate with other children and teachers. The attitudes of the adults will be significant in this new learning. Whether it is a rural child learning new urban expressions and accents or one who speaks the language of another country, each child's language deserves respect and serious effort on the part of all to understand the child and help the child in learning to communicate and to understand the communication of others.

To the credit of the marvelous human mind, these transitions occur quite rapidly. For example, if you have three Korean children in your school, before long those children will be trying English with all others except their Korean friends. This cognitive exception occurs at younger years than some theorists would have us believe and is delightful to observe. Other children may simplify their English for a little while to help the second-language learner understand. Warmth and acceptance of each individual child is probably the key that fosters children's effort, as Chukovsky's quote in this chapter's opening pages indicates, the young child is a hard mental toiler!

The NAEYC's position on linguistic and cultural diversity codifies what has been this author's philosophy expressed in this textbook since its inception. The NAEYC position statement logically deals with four aspects of early education: children, parents, personnel, and programs.[7]

Emotional Development

Emotional development is also fostered when the child has language skills. Both good and bad feelings can be expressed verbally. The child is able to protest when things go against his or her wishes. The total emotional climate of the child's environment will affect the child's speech progress. Being very shy or insecure will negatively affect the ability to express oneself. Language skill affects the child's self-efficacy. Positive feelings accompany successful communication.

Cognitive Development

The brain is the center of both cognitive and language development. Recent work in mapping the

TALK IT OVER: NO. 1

Write down what a child says while speaking. Also write down what another child answers. Share the example with your class, giving the children's ages as you begin. What seems characteristic of the children's language?

---

[7]NAEYC, "NAEYC Position Statement Responding to Linguistic and Cultural Diversity—Recommendations for Effective Early Childhood Education," *Young Children* 51:2 (January 1996), 4–12.

Once children understand language they can take directions. (University of South Carolina)

functions of the brain indicates the left hemisphere controls both language and analytical thinking. Healthy people use both sides. Because of individual differences in dominance, however, one person may have a cognitive style that is **verbal-analytical** if he or she operates primarily in the left hemisphere and another a **holistic** style if operating primarily in the right hemisphere.[8] The first type might be said to see the trees while the second sees the forest. According to Banville, "The kinds of functions involved in recognizing colors and the shapes of letters and words is right-brained; the association of the spoken word with the shapes and colors is a left-brained process (occurring in the language areas of the left hemisphere)."[9]

This research helps one appreciate the complexity of language learning. It may help teachers understand, too, why numerous methods of teaching are required when working with young children. Pictures, which are perceived primarily by the right brain, present an experience different from auditory stimuli. One child may learn better from one than from another. Between ages two and eight is said to be the period of greatest linguistic abilities.

Second Language Acquisition

According to some research the necessity of coping with more than one language may, for some children, hamper the development of skill in a single language. It is necessary for them to learn two words for each concept. Other research suggests the opposite. As the global economy grows more important, it becomes increasingly more desirable for children to speak more than one language. In an earlier era it was thought to be disadvantageous for a preschool child to learn a second language. Current research suggests the very opposite, that the best time to learn is early and the best way to learn is from a person who speaks that language as a mother tongue, that is, a native speaker. Advantages are in terms of ease of learning sounds, flexibility of brain function, and related cognitive development.[10]

Wagman, studying the effect on children of learning two languages, writes, "A social environment in which the child is positively motivated to learn two languages is hard to find naturally; more frequently it has to be consciously created by the strenuous efforts of schools and social agencies." She then reports on a study where English-speaking children learned French in Montreal and one where Cuban children, whose first language was Spanish, learned English in Miami. The studies show the interdependence of language education, parental and teacher attitudes, and sociocultural environment. Wagman

---

[8]David Galin, M.D., "Educating Both Halves of the Brain," *Childhood Education* 53:1 (1976), 18.
[9]Thomas Banville, "Brain Hemisphericity: A High Voltage Topic," *Early Years* 10:1 (January 1979), 53.

[10] See bilingualism in Berk, op. cit., pp. 378–380.

concludes that second language acquisition is stronger where parents are supportive of it.[11]

Bilingual three- to six-year-old children, or those who are becoming bilingual, readily differentiate which language to use with a specific child or teacher. You will observe them in play situations when, unselfconsciously and with ease, they flip from one language to the other, based on the language of the person they are speaking to at the moment. This finding is counter to Piaget's belief that taking the perspective of the other is not characteristic of young children.

In many foreign capitals where American diplomats' children enroll in school side by side with national children, children are taught in both languages. Starting in prekindergarten, classes are typically in English for half the day and in the national language the other half. Children will use both languages in their informal play as well as in their schoolwork. Thus, in order to facilitate both bilingual exchange and facility in the mother tongue, teachers need to be sure to group a few language-alike children together with others. Without a friend with whom to speak, let's say Thai, a child may lose interest in speaking Thai. Also, frequently stating the value of using both languages will give both languages prestige in children's eyes.

TYPES OF LANGUAGE DEVELOPMENT

There are basically two types of language development. First, there is aural or **receptive language**—hearing and comprehending the language of others. Body language, though without sound, is part of receptive language. Second, there is oral or **productive language**, sometimes called **expressive language**, which is the formation of words, thoughts, and ideas in overt utterances. Both types of language must figure prominently in early childhood schools and in the programs that are presented to children. The following goals include activities to enhance both receptive and productive language.

GOALS FOR LANGUAGE DEVELOPMENT

Young children's language achievements should be appreciated. Most children learn sufficient language to communicate with very few problems. When problems do arise, the teacher should make a careful analysis before intervening. In planning language activities for children and interacting with them, consider the following goals.

1. *Producing Verbal Sounds* The ability to hear and make verbal sounds is essential to speech production. Most babies produce verbal sounds effectively at birth. Verbal sound production is rarely a problem, and hearing difficulty occurs in only a small number of children. Once heard, the verbal sounds must be decoded into meaning for the individual. Newborn infants respond differently to sounds of high and low intensity. Infants especially respond to human voices. A parent or caregiver who talks to the baby begins to receive positive responses as the baby babbles—often with inflections that parallel those used by the parent. The baby's alert eyes follow the speaking parents' eyes. Long before being able to speak, the toddler can respond accurately to commands such as "Bring me the ball," "Wave bye-bye," or "Give mommy the spoon." Throughout childhood and even in adulthood people can comprehend language that they may not be able to duplicate.

2. *Speaking in Distinct Syllables, Articulating Clearly* Articulation is an important factor in both speaking and comprehension. There are numerous sounds for the English vowels. Consonants such as s, v, r, t, and l and blends of two or three consonants are frequently not learned completely until children are seven or eight years

[11]Anita Wagman, "Language Experiences in Bilingualism," *Childhood Education* 58:1 (September/October 1981), 14–19.

old. More discussion of articulation problems comes in a later section of this chapter.

3. *Formulating New Words, New Word Combinations, and Eventually Statements and Questions* Eventually the child puts sounds together that make words. Language is a two-way street—listening and speaking. Here language, creativity, and the thinking process are combined. Children are often heard verbalizing as they go about an activity such as climbing, cutting, or dressing. This may serve as a private rehearsal. Even adults sometimes verbalize the directions for an activity that is new or difficult for them. Children work hard yet enthusiastically at this task of communicating through language. Every sentence is a fresh new creation.

4. *Learning a Vocabulary* Labels for objects, ideas, actions, and descriptors of many kinds are needed. New experiences enrich the child's vocabulary. In addition, many opportunities to express thoughts out loud, to be talked to, and read to are needed.

5. *Using Standard Rules of Grammar* The child gradually begins to sense the rules of grammar for the language by experimenting with it daily. Each language has specific rules. English has irregular verbs that may cause children considerable difficulty. There is a customary placement of pronouns, articles, prepositions, adjectives, and adverbs for children to learn. The young child will not be able to state grammar rules. Communication can and does take place without perfect grammar.

6. *Developing a Voice of Culturally Appropriate Quality, Pitch, Intensity, and Timbre* Voice, in this context, is culturally approved, being pitched higher in Chinese, for example, than in English. Certain stress, intonation, and pauses are all to be learned.

7. *Developing Fluency of Speech* Fluency refers to the person's ability to choose words quickly and to speak in a smooth effortless manner. Fluency is a long-range goal, as are most of the goals for language development.

TALK IT OVER: NO. 2

Describe the language of a child who you'd say is fluent. Give the child's age and relate prior experiences at home and school to the child's present language level. What conclusions can you draw?

---

8. *Developing an Ability to Read and Write Language* Literacy is emerging through many of the children's activities. Eventually the child will begin to write his or her name, a caption on a painting, and eventually paragraphs. Along with writing comes reading. With writing skills the child can share ideas with others not present. With reading skills children can learn from people of previous generations and from far away places. Children can leave their own thoughts for others to read. The first seven goals provide a foundation for this last goal. The basics of language development are accomplished in only five or so years. For the individual, language continues to increase in its complexity throughout life.

HOW THE TEACHER FOSTERS LANGUAGE DEVELOPMENT

What does the early childhood teacher do to foster language development? A number of suggestions follow.

1. *The teacher establishes a comfortably relaxed atmosphere.* The teacher stimulates the children to talk freely with everyone. Children are encouraged to exchange ideas, share information, and ask questions. Though teachers may make an effort to encourage "indoor voices" in the classroom, they appreciate children who are happy, lively, and talkative. Silence is not a sacred

commodity. In fact, the young child's classroom or play yard is almost never quiet. Teachers may at times have to interpret the "noisy classroom" to other teachers, administrators, janitors, cooks, and parents. As Landreth says, "How can a child learn he has views if he is never permitted to express them?"[12]

2. *The teacher values each child and finds time to let each talk.* Each adult serves as a model for the child's speech, speaking clearly and correctly, and using words, gestures, and examples to help the child understand. Teachers quietly seek out children who are less assured and help them feel at ease when talking with them and others. They visit children at home and talk with their parents to learn the personal interests of each child. When teachers know about family events, pets, siblings, or toys, they can engage a child in conversation on personally interesting subjects. A teacher may discover a subject that a child likes to discuss and reserve that topic for their private conversations. One child goes skiing; another goes fishing; another raises rabbits. One teacher learned a few words of Russian to be able to say good-bye to a child who spoke Russian.

3. *The teacher capitalizes on every opportunity to extend a child's vocabulary, to increase his or her ability to formulate sentences, and to describe an event in a sequence.* Every learning experience is considered for its language possibilities. For example, following a cooking experience, the teacher asks questions to enable the children to practice the new words the experience has introduced. A few days later the children recall the cooking experience and relate it to another project that has been planned for them. The teacher may ask the children to tell what they plan to tell their parents about the activities of their day in school. When children have been personally involved in activities, they

The teacher's guidance and consolation can be understood through spoken and body language. (Michigan State University)

can talk more easily. Verbalizing helps them remember. The teacher may send home materials that encourage children to speak. Their products give something to show and to explain to their parents.

4. *The teacher gives clear directions.* When giving directions, she or he demonstrates as well as talks in order to give the children clues to the meaning of what is said. The teacher also avoids putting too many ideas in a single sentence. She or he gets the children's attention and speaks clearly.

5. *The teacher makes plans for the children's language development.* Both talking and listening experiences are planned. The teacher assesses the needs of individual children to determine the activities that are most appropriate for each. A variety of activities is planned in order to interest the children and keep them eager to learn. Inter-

---

[12]Catherine Landreth, *Early Childhood Behavior and Learning* (New York: Knopf, 1967), p. 199.

esting displays of pictures and objects in the classroom are planned to stimulate conversation.

6. *The teacher allows a child to finish a statement or question.* Believing that incorrect speech is better than no speech, children are never interrupted to correct grammar or pronunciation. All teachers should be aware that though there is considerable uniformity in language in the country, there are regional accents and dialects that make it difficult even for educated people to communicate. Teachers must be most sensitive when helping children who are new in the community and children from various ethnic groups. The teacher's language is not "better" than such a child's, just as a New Yorker's language is not "better" than a Southerner's. With conscientious effort, they can all communicate.

7. *The teacher uses open-ended questions that encourage the children to elaborate on their ideas, information, and feelings—to use their skills in thinking and putting it all together.* For example, the teacher says, "What do you think the boy will do now?" instead of "Did you take a trip?" The second question in these two examples can be answered with a yes or a no and does not call for further elaboration. The teacher might say, "Would you tell me about _____?" or, "I'm interested in where you found the _____."

8. *The teacher strives to be the kind of person the children want to identify with.* Identification is a powerful force in language acquisition. Children try to act and talk like people they identify with.

9. *The teacher accepts the children as they are and avoids moralizing.* To keep communication channels open, the teacher avoids telling them how they "ought" to act, think, or feel.

10. *The teacher pays attention to the children, and reflects their words and body language back to them to let them know their communication is heard and understood.* For example, if Ken bites his nails and looks fearful, the teacher recognizes his state—he's scared. She says, "It's scary to get so close to the train, isn't it?" When the teacher is competent at interpreting the meaning beyond the children's words, she or he is really tuned in to children.

11. *The teacher has fun with language.* Having fun includes picking up on the children's verbal horseplay, chanting as they chant, rhyming as they rhyme, laughing as they laugh, and enjoying their fun with language and all communication.

12. *The teacher avoids being fussy about names and titles.* Such fussiness can stifle the children's conversation. Surely a wise principal would not want to hear the teacher say, "Stop chattering and speak to our principal, Mr. Smith, correctly and with respect, Jonathan."

13. *The teacher watches for evidence that a child does not hear.* Evidence includes children who don't speak, those who don't appear to hear, those who don't respond to directions until after the other children start, and those who talk with a nasal twang or who eat unusually noisily. Such symptoms suggest to the teacher the need for medical referrals, hearing and speech assessment, and possible therapy. It is important to take care of problems before the child develops habits that are difficult to change.

14. *The teacher shows that language is valued.* A teacher who values language writes down stories, songs, poems, and sayings a child expresses, and reads them back to the child, showing that language is valued and teaching that there is a relationship between spoken language and the written words found in books.

PLANNING LANGUAGE ARTS ACTIVITIES

Language is a two-way street—listening and speaking. Listening may be as important as speaking itself. Listening must be done with comprehension. Active thinking should accompany listening. Teachers can't be sure that a child sitting quietly is listening. The entire program, both indoors and out, affords numerous opportunities for involving children with language.

Every experience with books contributes to greater language facility and literacy. (Kansas State University)

When the teacher starts a new project or a learning experience, techniques are used to quiet the children and gain their attention. Groups are kept to four or five children. A song, a poem, a fingerplay, a puppet, or a new picture can serve this purpose. The teacher will want them to follow the discussion, think critically about what is said, be stimulated to further interest, and react with new behavior or new understanding. All children will not respond to all projects. Therefore other activities are kept available for those with different interests. As each activity is planned, teachers should note new words and phrases that the children can learn. Plenty of time should be allowed for children's comments and questions as an activity progresses.

Games

Games such as Simon Says can be played with small groups to encourage listening and learning new vocabulary. The common "Simon says, 'Stand up'" can be altered to "Simon says, 'Put your hands *above* your heads' or 'Put your hands *below* your chair.'" Such a game can be played at the snack table while the children are waiting for the snack to come, or at the gate when they are waiting for their parents or a bus.

Guessing games can be created by the teacher as the characteristics of familiar objects for children to guess are described. At first, the objects should be near at hand. Later, out-of-sight objects at home and at school can be described. After some experience the children can take turns describing objects.

The teacher can say, "I'm thinking of something that is—HOT. What could it be?" When the children catch on, a child can be invited to choose the object and the adjective, whisper the choice in the teacher's ear, and then tell the others whether they are correct as they guess.

A box or a bag with several objects for children to feel, describe, and name invites conversation. They can learn to use such words as *rough, smooth, large, small, hard,* and *soft* as they try to identify the object. The teacher can select familiar items. *Large* and *small* can be learned more readily by using two sizes of the same objects—buttons, Jell-O boxes, milk cartons, and so on.

Jokes

Fives begin understanding humor—puns, riddles, and jokes. Five-year-olds enjoy correcting the teacher who says absurd things like "Shall we wait until the streetlight turns purple?" Children like to play tricks on others, too, once their concepts are well-enough formed so that they can recognize the absurdities.

Records, Films, Audio- and Videotapes

Records and tapes are outstanding aids that encourage listening. A record player that is simple enough for the children to operate will encourage voluntary listening. The collection of records should be changed frequently. A quiet nook that is free of distractions is a good location for the record player.

Tape recordings of the children's conversations, stories, and songs encourage the children to listen for their own voices. Stories the children record can be typed and placed in a book, or they can be sent home. Thus their value is enhanced, and the children begin to see a relationship between spoken and written words.

Headsets for a record player or a tape recorder are valuable additions to equipment. Occasionally a child wants to hear a record that interferes with another child's activity, or a child may want to hear the same record over and over. Using the headset avoids disturbing others. Teachers can record stories for children to use with books, saving many dollars over commercial tape costs. One teacher sets up the video camera in the yard and records stories for children. Such recordings could be used on days a teacher cannot be at school.

Music

Teachers can hum or play a tune or a rhythm for the children to guess. Children can learn to lead this listening game too. Children need opportunities both to listen to music and to participate. Songs help children add new words to their vocabularies. Further discussion of music and rhythm follows in Chapter 16.

Literature

The use of good literature contributes to language. Poetry challenges children's listening. Children can help the teacher rhyme words. With only a little experience children will know that the word in a poem to rhyme with *ice* is *slice* or *mice*. Many good poems are available for children that, when presented enthusiastically, will interest them. Suggestions for books, poems, and finger plays are given in Chapter 14.

Writing

Spoken language precedes written language. However, three- to five-year-olds often have a fascination for people's names and want to write friends' names or their names on their products. They may begin writing phonetically, printing words the best they can while they sound them out orally. They may ask adults to spell names and other words for them. Dictating stories and letters for adults to write down is interesting to some children. A free-flowing oral vocabulary can lead to free-flowing writing. All of these are early steps in writing and reading that alert early childhood teachers can encourage.

When writing children's names on name tags, bulletin boards, and lists, you should use a consistent format for the letters to enable the children to learn how their names look in print and for them to be able to duplicate the format when they become interested in writing. See Figures 13–1 and 13–2 for typical formats for traditional Palmer manuscript and for D'Nealian manuscript writing. Be sure to label letters in names as you write them, saying for example, "C-A-T-R-I-N-A, that spells Catrina."

Left-Handers

Teachers should carefully study the best way to help the young left-handed child place the page at the appropriate angle before him or her on the table and use the writing tool correctly. Without help, some left-handers develop their own methods and may criticize throughout their life their teachers who failed to help them when they were in a formative stage of learning to write.

Parent Help

Parents may want advice as to how they can help their child. Early in the year you can share with parents a format chart, such as shown in Figures 13–1 and 13–2, as a way of encouraging them to use your choice of writing style.

However, don't be surprised if children learn a style of letters at home that differs from the school's style. Rather than make an issue of the fact, remember that the young child's writing style is still very fluid, with years before a particular style is learned. Considering your goals for both child and parent, therefore, it is generally

FIGURE 13–1

The typical Palmer manuscript printing (the stick and O style) with arrows for appropriate direction of the pencil. This style has been prominent in kindergartens and first grades for nearly one hundred years.

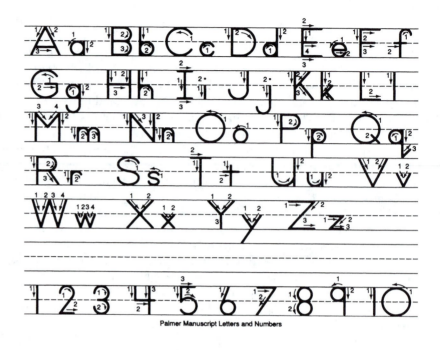

Palmer Manuscript Letters and Numbers

better to let the child continue experimenting enthusiastically with writing, and to express pleasure with parents who help their child.

Typewriter or Computer

Children have long enjoyed the opportunity to use a typewriter if someone would allow them to use one. (See Dramatic Play, Chapter 15.) Children like to see letters appear on a page. Of course, the typewriter keys often become jammed. Now children are enjoying computers that enable them to play with letters on the screen. The delete button is so much easier to use than the eraser! Four- and five-year-olds become interested in typing their friends' names and names of family members. If children freely elect to type on the typewriter or the computer and to leave when they are tired, it will predictably be a positive experience. In fact, many believe the computer may, indeed, contribute immeasurably to the improvement of skills in writing composition for this new generation of

children as they become liberated from the tedious small-motor writing tasks (and erasers!) suggested when the child uses one of the format choices illustrated in Figures 13–1 and 13–2. Many college students remember that a "messy" paper placed their composition in a lower grade category. With the use of computers and printers, judgment of a child's composition will in the future rest on what is written, rather than on its appearance.

Emerging Literacy

The whole-language approach suggested throughout this book combines speaking, understanding spoken words, writing, and reading, and leads children gradually to writing and reading. Through many prewriting and prereading opportunities children become literate.

A whole-language approach is advocated when considering young children's writing, instead of isolating words as a separate concept to learn. When children show an interest in writing,

FIGURE 13–2
The D'Nealian style letters and numbers with arrows showing the direction of the pencil. The D'Nealian writing style is characterized by slanted letters made in one continuous motion with a small upward curl at the end of the letters. The form facilitates connections with other letters when the child moves into cursive writing later on.[13]

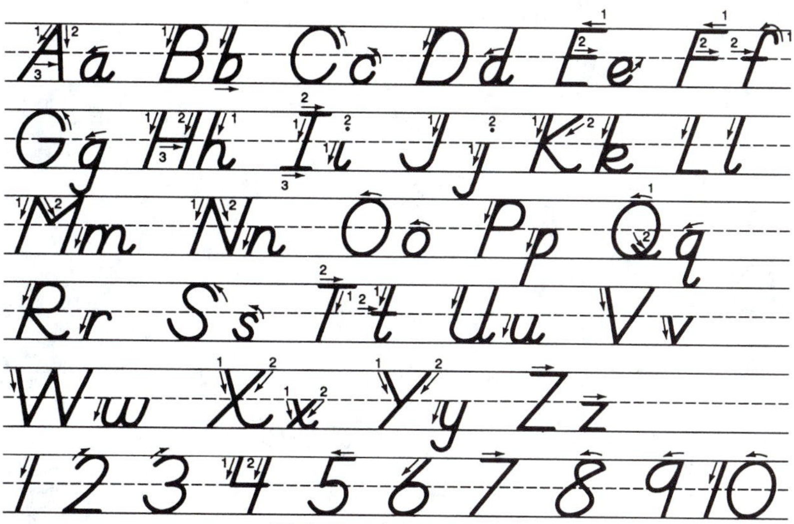

D'Nealian Manuscript Letters and Numbers

we let them write. Figures 13–3 and 13–4 are examples of three-year-old Ellen's early writing. Figures 13–5 and 13–6 are her older sister's examples of invented spelling. Julia sounds out words as she goes. Her ideas flow quickly to the page. She uses invented spelling (some call it "kid" spelling) to write paragraphs, to label pictures, and to write notes to her grandparents. Her oral fluency contributes to fluency in writing. She writes on topics of interest to her.

Your children, too, will be motivated to try to write when they are doing interesting things and want to tell someone about them, perhaps their parents at home. Whatever you do, restrain your impulse to drill or become an automatic spelling machine, telling them how words are spelled. From names and familiar words they'll know how

certain consonants sound. Let them start there. Just encourage children to communicate ideas through their drawings and their invented language. Rather than help too much, tell them to write like it sounds, helping with consonants' sounds when they need it. Both you and they will be glad you did.

Dramatic Play

Imaginative role-playing, so popular with young children, contributes to their language development. Children need to talk to make their wants known, they have concrete objects to discuss as they play, and they enact roles they have observed. All these conditions contribute to learning. Dramatic play is discussed further in Chapter 15.

Puppets and flannel-board figures are useful aids for encouraging children to speak. Shy children find that speaking through a puppet or a figure is easier. Torrance, who has done notable

---

[13]The term D'Nealian is derived from the founder's name, D. Neal Thurber. For more information see D. Neal Thurber, *D'Nealian Manuscript: A Continuous Approach to Handwriting* (Novato, CA: Academic Therapy Publications, 1984).

FIGURE 13–3

Shows Ellen (age 3-3) places **E**, **L**, and **N** in lines across her page. She earlier made what looked like lowercase **e**'s across pages.

work in children's creative language expression, gives children a "magic net," under which they imaginatively become whatever they wish. They wear the magic net and stand, walk, talk, or dance like the person, animal, or object they wish to become. Torrance used colored netting 36-by-72 inches and gave about ten children "magic nets" at one time.[14]

Telephones

Telephones are extremely useful for encouraging conversation, and every school should have several phones for children to play with. The children will often talk to each other, and the teacher

FIGURE 13–4

Shows Ellen's (age 3-9) capital **E**'s and **L**'s at the top of her drawing. In typical prekindergarten fashion, Ellen made the **ELL** too far to the right and ran out of room. She then carried the end of the word, **EN**, to the left side of the page where there was room. She made an error when it came to making the **N** and marked it out. This drawing indicates Ellen is beginning to get the letters for her name in proper order.

can talk to a child in casual conversation or ask for information such as, "What is your telephone number?" "What is your home address?".

Field Trips

Field trips and other special events will help extend the child's language. From firsthand experiences the child builds a frame of reference with which to compare new information, whether it comes through reading, listening, or experimenting.

---

[14]E. Paul Torrance, *Encouraging Creativity in the Classroom* (Dubuque, IA: Brown, 1970), pp. 3–5.

FIGURE 13–5

Shows the work of Ellen's sister, Julia. At age 6, Julia made human figures and labeled each one. In this period, she often made pictures of her family in this fashion. She asked those around her to spell the noun she wanted to write.

Children learn early to screen out some of the sound in the modern, mechanistic, and sound-bombarding environment. As noise, excess sound makes individuals tired and confused. Children's perception of the sound environment can be enhanced if teachers take time to show an interest when a child indicates hearing an unusual sound—say, a bird's song. Also, teachers can take children on walks and focus on listening to the many sounds in the environment that one often screens out, such as the screech of car brakes, the toot of a train whistle in the distance, or of the songs of birds drifting among the branches. Details for planning field trips are given in Chapter 17.

Sharing Time

Sharing time, or show-and-tell, is a popular activity in the kindergarten. This is an organized time when an individual child shows the group some-

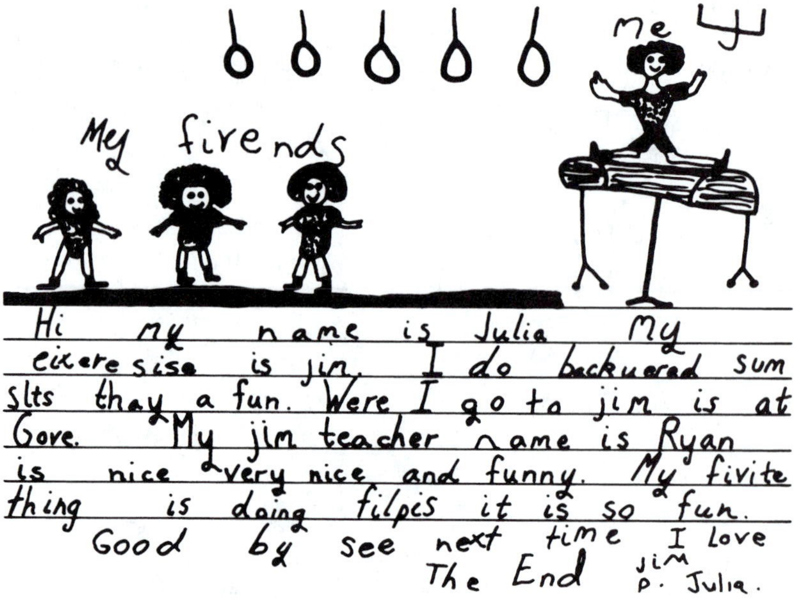

FIGURE 13–6

Shows Julia's school paper at age 7-5 years. She has used "invented spelling," having sounded out each word. The words *backuered* (backward) and *filpis* (flips) are typical examples of a child overgeneralizing on vowel sounds. She is learning phonics in a very practical way. (Figure 13–6 translation: Hi, my name is Julia. My exercise is gym. I do backward somersaults. They are fun. Where I go to gym is at Gove [the community center]. My gym teacher's name is Ryan. He is nice, very nice and funny. My favorite thing is doing flips. It is so fun. Good-bye. See [you] next time. I love gym. The end. Julia)

thing brought from home or tells about some event. The activity gives the child an opportunity to speak before the group. The child is encouraged to develop the discussion in logical sequence. Children learn to listen and then ask the speaker questions. They all learn to take turns.

Parents should be enlisted to help the children select worthwhile things or ideas to share during show-and-tell. They can help the children plan what they will tell. Parents can help their children keep track of which day of the week is their sharing day, for once the show-and-tell idea becomes popular in a class, it is seldom feasible to let everyone speak each day. In a class of fifteen or more children the sharing time could take an hour—much too long to expect active listening. Overlong periods rob other meaningful activities of their rightful time in the schedule. A calendar can be arranged designating a certain day for each child to bring or tell something. Exceptions are made, of course, when a child has

something very special for show-and-tell: A new baby sister or the first flower of spring qualifies.

In some groups sharing time is held during snack time. When only a portion of the group is slated to speak, daily sharing time requires only a few minutes. Table conversation, a valued language experience, is also encouraged.

The key to success is the teacher, who must develop skill in directing sharing time in order to make it a pleasant learning experience for both the speaker and the group. Skill is needed in drawing out the shy speaker and limiting the verbose one. Also, the teacher will preserve the child's dignity and allow for individual differences in ability to participate. Learning can be increased if the teacher judiciously raises questions and directs the children's attention. Occasionally a teacher may designate certain things as being good for sharing time, such as fall seeds or leaves.

A "sharing table" can be set up for children to display their specimens and treasures. The self-selected activity time can be used for individual discussion of these objects. Because many three- and four-year-old children are not ready for an organized sharing time, a sharing table may be substituted. Always remember that the goal is positive language experiences.

TEACHING FOREIGN LANGUAGE

"Why doesn't the school teach a foreign language?" "Are there advantages to teaching a second language to young children living in an English-speaking environment?" These questions are often raised by parents. There is a difference of opinion with regard to the optimum time to introduce a foreign language. Some authorities believe that the training should begin early. Others do not believe that all research supports early foreign language instruction. However, linguist Anita Wagman concludes that studies, especially of Canadian children who enter second-language study in either French or English, "consistently demonstrate that two linguistic perspectives open the child's mind to greater nonverbal, mathematical, and conceptual flexibility."[15]

In some situations the child must learn a second language. Many disadvantaged children are, in effect, learning a second language.[16] The school starts with whatever language skill children have and teaches them English much as a foreign language is taught.[17, 18]

A five-year study of the effects of teaching Spanish to kindergarten children was carried on at Texas Tech University. The classes were made up of middle-class five-year-olds in the laboratory kindergarten. During the five years five groups received Spanish lessons. Lessons lasted from 10 to 15 minutes per day and varied from one to two semesters' duration. The study was designed to find

- whether five-year-olds could be motivated to learn Spanish,
- what could be taught to them,
- what methods could be used effectively.

Lessons were carefully outlined with the Spanish staff of the Department of Foreign Languages. Spanish professors and students in language "methods" classes taught the children for three years. The kindergarten teacher and Spanish-speaking child development majors taught the last two. The kindergarten teacher and college students had considerable enthusiasm for the language. Incidental events often became language lessons. For example, during snack time, the teacher would ask, «¿Quién quiere más leche?» The children learned to hold up their hands and respond, «Más leche, por favor.» ("Who wants more milk?" "More milk, please.")

The cooperation of the kindergarten teacher and the language instructors was important to the success of the project. The new language was never an isolated experience. Using trained language teachers gave the children good models to imitate. The kindergarten teacher's active participation protected the children from teaching methods that did not consider their individual needs and development. Because of the teacher's participation, the language and related experiences permeated the entire program.

Lessons were planned to focus on familiar objects, expressions, and situations at home and school. A single concept was presented in various interesting ways to keep the interest high. For example, when the children were learning to count, they counted the number of children, the number of girls, and the number of chairs. They also sang "Ten Little Indians" in Spanish and took

[15]Anita Wagman, op. cit., p. 19.
[16]Joan C. Baratz, "Language in the Economically Disadvantaged Child," *Journal of American Speech and Hearing Research* 10:4 (1968), 142–145.
[17]Berk, op. cit., pp. 378–380.
[18]George I. Sanchez, "Significance of Language Handicap," in *Learning a New Language*, ed. Margaret Rasmussen (Washington, DC: Association for Childhood Education International, 1958), pp. 25–32. See also Luis M. Laosa, "Socialization, Education, and Continuity: The Importance of Sociocultural Context," reprinted in Mary Jensen and Zelda Chevalier, eds., *Issues and Advocacy in Early Education* (Boston: Allyn and Bacon, 1990), pp. 306–311.

turns counting individually. Counting was interwoven with other concepts that were being learned. Teaching aids of all kinds were used to present real things and models for the children to talk about. The lessons were short and they were fun.

The outcome seemed positive in most respects. The children leaped the language barrier with grace. Spanish was a natural choice for that community, which had a 20 percent Mexican-American population and a natural relationship to Mexico. The children learned about some of the festivals that are part of Mexican tradition. They were interested in learning the new language. Often they reported having heard Spanish on the radio (not uncommon in that part of Texas), or someone speaking it while they were shopping downtown, or at home where older brothers and sisters were studying Spanish for school.

The games and songs particularly appealed to the children. They liked being called on to participate individually, although they were never forced to respond until they indicated their readiness. Children who had trouble articulating English sounds were actually helped by saying the sound in Spanish. The boy who spoke German was given private help in English during the Spanish lessons. However, he had so much facility with languages that he learned a number of Spanish expressions from the children who were using them in their play.

The staff, the students, and the parents gleaned valuable information during these sessions. It was interesting to all to observe the children learning a subject about which one could assume no prior knowledge or home practice. Many early childhood education students expected to teach Spanish-speaking children in Head Start and felt they had learned teaching methods that would help them.

The importance of planning was clear. Deciding the concepts to teach, planning the sequence for teaching, and preparing the teaching aids took considerable time and thought. Concepts related closely to children were the best choices.

Better pronunciation resulted from individual participation than from group recitation. The teacher's verbal approval was of greatest importance. Approval was given both to the group and to individuals.

Whereas teachers with much teaching experience could keep a large group interested, beginning teachers were more successful with small groups. All planned activities were fun. Involving children in a variety of songs, games, pictures, toys, stories, and role-playing contributed to the success of the lessons. Teachers frequently shifted from one teaching method to another to maintain high interest.

LEARNING ENGLISH AS A SECOND LANGUAGE

During a teacher's visit to the home of a family with children in prekindergarten, the two daughters, one age three and the other age four-and-a-half, spoke fluently in English without a hint of accent. These children had spent about two years in United States child care centers. Their teachers and the children spoke only English. Their parents, much shyer, spoke hesitatingly with accents carried over from their Hungarian upbringing. The family speaks Hungarian at home to ensure the ability to communicate with relatives when visiting in the "old country." These children are becoming truly bilingual, developing fluency in both languages.

In some sections of the United States numerous language groups are represented among the children found in early childhood schools. The Bilingual Education Act of 1967–68 requires teaching children in their native language until their English develops. Unfortunately, the United States has few elementary teachers trained in foreign languages and funding has been minimal for preparing teachers.

Learning something about the particular foreign language that children in your group speak is helpful. You can learn at least a few words, just to be friendly. Find out if there are particular difficulties that persons learning English from that foreign language typically have. You may find such information in a textbook for a course in English as a second language. If you can't locate a book, question an adult who is a native speaker of that language who has learned English. For example, you'll learn that Spanish-speaking people often have trouble with their *i* sound because every *i* in Spanish has an *e* sound. They will say "beel" for *bill* or "heel" for *hill.* Such a habit requires lots of patience, numerous word games, and a long time to correct. There are other examples, like adjectives being added to or placed after nouns, and words with gender-specific endings that may be confusing to a child in your group. You'll know better how to help when you understand the nature of the confusion the child confronts.

In an effort to improve the situation for non-English-speaking children, Head Start and many other early childhood education centers have hired aides with the same language backgrounds as the children. They help ease the transition for children into the English-speaking world. Developing fluency in English is usually the primary goal of most groups, rather than parallel development of two languages. Goals for bilingualism could help English learning.

The greatest improvement in the last decade is the increased respect for other languages and cultures among early childhood educators. Many are going beyond teaching respect for the child's home language to teaching all children about customs, dress, foods, and so on from other cultures. Global education has become a popular innovation in the elementary schools' social studies curriculum.

Children's lives are enriched when they associate with children from other countries and cultures. For example, in one group the five-year-olds were especially interested in their new German classmate, Franz. They wanted to know where he had come from, how he had traveled, and if he had gone to school in Germany. The teacher introduced a world map to locate Germany and taught the group a few German words. The new child was delighted. He soon felt at ease and spoke to the children in German. The unfamiliar sound awed the children, and the teacher had to reassure them that it was all right to speak to him in English, explaining that he could tell by their gestures some of the things they wanted him to do. In a short time he learned some English phrases that helped his social relations.

In the case of the German boy the parents were strongly in favor of the child's learning English. Occasionally the families speaking a foreign language do not readily accept their child's learning English. In this case the school must build a bridge of friendship and respect to the other culture to help the family accept and encourage their child learning the new language.

Teachers who work with young children from ethnic or language groups different from their own sometimes erroneously judge or downgrade the children's language abilities or may fail to have positive expectations for such children. Such judgments are unfair to these children and their parents. Children from such groups are often unusually quiet as new students in a strange school situation, just as vivacious adults often become tongue-tied when they venture into a new country, where the language and the customs are different from their own.

We must remember that the young children entering early childhood schools generally have very few experiences outside their home and neighborhood, regardless of their socioeconomic background. When they are confronted with a school situation in which the setting, adults, language, and ethnic mix are new, different, and perhaps incomprehensible, it is not surprising that these children appear frightened, shy, and quiet.

Working With Spanish-Speaking Children

Rebecca Peña Hines is a noted early childhood educator who grew up speaking Spanish at home

TALK IT OVER: NO. 3

Describe a child you know who has learned or is learning a second language. What is the child's age? What are the child's language characteristics? How do adults help the child?

and learning English at school. She has been associated with the Parent-Child Development Center in Houston, Texas, and she expresses many concerns about the situation facing the Spanish-speaking child.[19]

Hines indicated that Mexican-American parents, and especially grandparents, are usually deeply interested in their children's maintaining their Spanish language. Their attitude, is, of course, defensible, because it is their language and the language of their ancestors—a beautiful language with a body of great literature. A large portion of the Western Hemisphere speaks Spanish. Some Mexican-American parents who want their child to function in the English-speaking world sometimes go to the extreme of speaking only English at home, creating some raised eyebrows among friends and neighbors, who may look upon that family as "putting on airs." However, with the recent Chicano movement, the younger generation of parents and soon-to-be parents has revived an interest and a pride in maintaining the Spanish language, along with the other rich and positive aspects of the Mexican-American culture.

---

[19]In making the following suggestions for working with children from Mexican-American homes I have drawn upon discussions with Rebecca Peña Hines and upon materials she presented at the annual meeting workshops of the NAEYC. For more of Hines's work on the bilingual child and family see V. Hildebrand, L. Phenice, M. Gray, and R. Hines, *Knowing and Serving Diverse Families* (Upper Saddle River, NJ: Merrill/Prentice Hall, 1996), Chapter 5.

Chicano children (and any non-English-speaking children) may have an uphill language struggle in typical schools. English should be taught in a manner that builds on a Spanish-speaking child's already-developed language foundation. Chicano children are often erroneously considered by observers to be "nonverbal" or "slow" when, in fact, these outsiders are merely observing the child's reaction to strangers and to a largely different environment.

Young Chicano children are generally friendly, open, and verbal if they have a teacher or an aide who speaks Spanish and who can build warm communication with the children and their parents through appreciation of their unique background and culture. Hines points out that bilingual-bicultural aides and teachers are needed for young Chicano children. Bilingual adults will teach Spanish to these children, adding to their vocabulary for expressing their needs and concepts. Gradually English is introduced to the children on an individual and small-group basis—thus building a bilingual base for the children. They eventually learn two words for each concept and expression, and at times they integrate the two languages in interesting and unique ways. Reinforcement of the cultural strengths in the children's background, such as Spanish music, literature, and festivals, serves to enhance further the children's feeling of who they are.

Hines, whose work has been concentrated in Texas, California, and Washington, believes that English-speaking teachers can learn to communicate with Spanish-speaking children. The teachers can learn some key words and phrases in Spanish in order to understand and to respond, just as a teacher of a deaf child can learn to communicate with a few hand symbols. Spanish songs like those included in this book (Chapter 16) can be learned rather easily and sung with the children. The child's parents might be enlisted to help with pronunciation. Pictures including Chicano children and their families can be displayed and used for learning activities within the classroom. Curriculum plans can introduce cultural objects—piñatas, books, and foods—that are familiar to Mexican-American children, helping them with adjustment and with enhancing their self-concepts.

Even when the class includes only one or two Spanish-speaking children, these steps are important to those individuals and also to the other children, who will learn much from an introduction to different cultures such as the Mexican-American culture.

Teachers are advised to continue talking to the child in English even though they believe the child does not understand. Children frequently can understand much more than they can speak. Eventually the words will take on meaning. The tone of voice and the body language accompanying the words give clues to the child concerning meaning and also communicate warmth and interest. Likewise, English-speaking children in the class should be encouraged to talk with non-English-speaking children in order to develop peer relationships and provide models. Both groups will benefit as the children learn language expressions from each other. Important learning flows in both directions.

All children have a right to expect teachers to respect their culture. If teachers have an attitude of respect and positive expectation, the children and the parents will be responsive to the teachers and the school. The children will then have a firm foundation for climbing up the educational ladder.

Working With Children With Nonstandard English

Some young black children and others who come with a nonstandard English dialect present certain challenges for teachers. Researchers who have studied the linguistic components of the black dialect find it simply different and not deficient. The dialect is usually well developed and expressive and serves useful purposes in the exchange of ideas, information, and feelings. There are numerous debates as to whether or not children should be taught standard English. A

TALK IT OVER: NO. 4

Describe a child you know who is or was having speech therapy. What was the problem? How was the child helped? Did the teacher play a role in the speech therapy?

---

casual survey of black public figures—educators, politicians, artists, writers, and television commentators—generally reveals a high proficiency in standard English.

Researchers Cullinan, Jagger, and Strickland have concluded that it is a defensible objective to expand the language of black children with dialects to include standard English without reducing the proficiency in their native black English.[20] Children who speak black English must be fully accepted as equals, be encouraged to talk using their own language traditions, and be helped to develop new language forms through such opportunities for speaking and comprehending as have been suggested in this chapter and throughout the text.[21]

DEALING WITH LANGUAGE PROBLEMS

Articulation

It is too much to expect children in early childhood schools to make all sounds correctly. For example, in a study of 308 first-grade children, Roe and Milisen found that 88 percent had trouble with *z*, 69 percent with *g*, 45.7 percent with *t*,

---

[20]Bernice E. Cullinan, Angela M. Jagger, and Dorothy Strickland, "Language for Black Children in the Primary Grades: A Research Report," *Young Children* 29:2 (January 1974), 98–112.

[21]A helpful discussion of the characteristics of black English is found in Berk, op. cit., pp. 326–329

and 17.6 percent with *r*. Blends such as *st* and *dr* were easier than either *s* or *d* followed by a vowel for most of the children.[22] Many articulation errors are common and are eliminated without therapy as the child matures.[23] Templin's studies indicate that on the basis of cross-sectional data fewer children than anticipated had achieved adequate articulation at the beginning of the second grade. She found that boys were about one year slower than girls.[24]

How does a teacher help children with obvious language deficiencies? The teacher cannot be a speech therapist. Children with severe problems should be under the care of a trained professional. The therapist can help the teacher choose activities that will be beneficial for a child with problems. Help at this young age includes games that might be played with children with normal speech so that attention need not be focused on the child with a deficiency.

The teacher may need to help interpret a child's comment as in the following example. On a trip to a farm four-year-old Michael said excitedly, "The 'ticky 'tepped on it!" Five-year-old Angella replied, "Michael, I can't hear you." Michael, raising his voice repeated, "The 'ticky 'tepped on it." Angella raised her voice and shouted, "Michael, I can't hear you!" Michael, now quite exasperated, started to shout his statement when the teacher stepped up. "Angella, Michael is telling you that the chicken stepped on the egg." Both children seemed relieved that the teacher had aided their efforts to communicate.

Only one teacher, not the whole staff, should focus on a child's speech problems. Excessive pressure may add complications and lead the child to feel that no one is pleased. The teacher who has the best rapport with the child should be the one to intervene actively. Other helpers may correctly restate words misused so that the child can hear them, but they should leave the actual intervention to that one designated teacher. The total staff, including bus drivers and cooks, should be advised of the procedure because they, too, have an opportunity to help.

One helpful procedure is for adults simply to restate a child's mispronounced words or ungrammatical phrases in a corrected form so that the child may begin to hear the correct pattern. Asking the child to repeat specific words or phrases often produces tension that causes further problems. Van Riper says that it is frequently ear training that is needed rather than mouth training. He suggests that only one sound be worked on at a time.[25] If a child says "wed" for "red," the child may not be hearing the *r*. Speech therapists would not practice with the child on the word *red* but on a completely unfamiliar word, such as *rebel* or *referee*. Therapists use nonsense words to advantage when helping a child relearn a sound.[26] The sounds can be practiced in isolation, in games or singing, and in mimicking animals or machines.

Hearing

Children with hearing difficulties can be mainstreamed into a regular classroom if they wear hearing aids and if they have had enough experience to make their wants known.[27] Sufficient assistance for the teacher is essential. An assistant can work with the child when the teacher is in charge of activities in which the child cannot or does not want to participate. The teachers can learn many of the signs that deaf children are

---

[22]Vivian Roe and R. Milisen, "The Effects of Maturation upon Defective Articulation in Elementary Grades," *Journal of Speech Disorders* 7:1 (March 1942), 42.

[23]Anne S. Morency, Joseph M. Wepman, and Paul S. Weiner, "Studies in Speech: Developmental Articulation Inaccuracy," *Elementary School Journal* (1967), 329–337.

[24]Mildred C. Templin, "Research on Articulation Development," in *The Young Child*, ed. Willard W. Hartrup and Nancy L. Smothergill (Washington, DC: NAEYC, 1967), pp. 109–124.

[25]Charles Van Riper, *Speech Correction Principles and Methods* (Upper Saddle River, NJ: Prentice-Hall, 1963), pp. 248–249.

[26]Ibid., p. 279.

[27]Vivian W. Stern, "Fingerpaint on the Hearing Aid," *The Volta Review* 71:3 (1969), 149–154.

taught and increase communication greatly. The advice and assistance of a specialist should now be available in all communities. Assistance is provided through Public Law 94-142, the Education for All Handicapped Children Act. Early childhood educators should seek out this assistance for themselves and for the parents of the child.

Conclusions

A whole-language approach can permeate the entire early childhood curriculum. A classroom alive with happy conversations is indicative of an environment that is helping children learn language. Steps in language development are considered to indicate areas of growth expected of the young child. Goals are helpful when considering problem areas and bilingualism. They can be most helpful in planning formal and informal interaction with young children. Suggestions have been included to help teachers enhance the child's listening and speaking skills. Early writing is highlighted. Teachers set the stage for the children to exchange ideas, share information, and ask questions. Teaching a foreign language and English as a second language were discussed.

Applications

1. Discuss the "Talk It Over" items found in the chapter.
2. Write an activity plan for a language activity for a few children using information and the sample plan (Figure 6–2) in Chapter 6. Secure approval, carry out the plan, and evaluate the results from the children's point of view and from your viewpoint. Prepare a report and hand it in along with your approved activity plan.
3. Evaluate your total participation performance on your evaluation form developed in Chapter 1. Discuss your progress with your supervising teacher.
4. Add ideas and plans for language activities to your Resource File.

Study Questions

1. Discuss how language development relates to social, emotional, cognitive, and physical development. What role does creativity play?
2. State and explain the eight major goals for language development.
3. Explain the differences between oral and aural language.
4. List and explain steps teachers can take to foster children's language development, emerging literacy, or learning a second language.
5. What conclusion does Anita Wagman draw from studies of children learning two languages?
6. State some conclusions about working with Spanish-speaking children and those speaking black English.
7. List some conclusions regarding helping children with articulation and hearing problems.
8. Describe a high-quality environment in a school that best facilitates children's language development. What activities can be planned?

Videotapes

Listening and Talking
   30 minutes

Thelma Harms and Debby Cryer explain how language develops as a medium for communication and thinking. DC/TATS MEDIA, Frank Porter Graham Child Development Center, University of North Carolina at Chapel Hill CB8040, 300 NCNB Plaza, Chapel Hill, NC 27599-8040.

Whole-Language Learning
   20 minutes

Provides classroom examples of whole-language learning. Shows teacher and parent roles in whole-language activities. NAEYC Media, 1509 16th St. NW, Washington, DC 20036-1426, 1-800-424-2460.

Additional Readings

Atkins, Cammie. "Writing: Doing Something Constructive." *Young Children* 40:1, November 1984, 3–7.

Barbour, Nita, et al. "Sand: A Resource for the Language Arts." *Young Children* 42:2, January 1987, 20–25.

Bayman, Aroti G. "An Example of a Small Project for Kindergartners That Includes Some 3R's Learning." *Young Children* 50:6, September 1995, 27–31.

Berk, Laura. "Why Children Talk to Themselves: Research in Review." *Young Children* 40:5, July 1985, 46–52.

———. *Child Development.* Boston: Allyn and Bacon, 1991.

Brock, Dana R., and Elizabeth L. Dodd. "A Family Lending Library: Promoting Early Literacy Development." *Young Children* 49:3, March 1994, 16–21.

Cazdon, Courtney B. *Language Experience in Early Childhood Education.* Washington, DC: NAEYC, 1981.

Chukovsky, Kornei. *From Two to Five.* Berkeley: University of California Press, 1968.

Crinklaw-Kiser, Donna. "Integrating Music With Whole Language Through the Orff-Schulwerk Process." *Young Children* 51:5, July 1996, 15–21.

Dumtschin, Joyce U. "Recognize Language Development and Delay in Early Childhood." *Young Children* 43:3, March 1988, 16–24.

Dyson, Anne Haas. "Symbol Makers, Symbol Weavers: How Children Link Play, Pictures, and Print." *Young Children* 45:2, January 1990, 50–57.

Garcia, Eugene E. "Bilingualism in Early Childhood." *Young Children* 35:4, May 1980, 52–66.

Genishi, Celia. "Children's Language: Learning Words from Experience." *Young Children* 44:1, November 1988, 16–23.

George, Felicia. "Checklist for a Non-sexist Classroom." *Young Children* 45:2, January 1990, 10–11.

Hayes, Linda F. "From Scribbling to Writing: Smooth the Way." *Young Children* 45:3, March 1990, 62–68.

Honig, Alice S. "Language Environments for Young Children." *Young Children* 38:1, November 1982, 56–67.

Hough, Ruth A., Joanne R. Nurss, and Dolores Wood. "Tell Me a Story: Making Opportunities for Elaborated Languages in Early Childhood Classrooms." *Young Children* 43:1, November 1987, 6–12.

International Reading Association. "Literacy Development and Pre-First Grade." *Young Children* 41:4, May 1986, 10–13.

Juliebö, Moira, and Joyce Edwards. "Encouraging Meaning Making in Young Writers." *Young Children* 44:2, January 1989, 22–33.

Manning, Maryann, Gary Manning, and Gayle Morrison. "Letter-Writing Connections: A Teacher, First-Graders, and Their Parents." *Young Children* 50:6, September 1995, 34–38.

Moore, Shirley F., and Catherine R. Cooper, eds. *The Young Child: Review of Research.* Vol. 3. Washington, DC: NAEYC, 1982.

Morrow, Lesley M., and Jeffrey K. Smith. *Assessment for Instruction in Early Literacy.* Upper Saddle River, NJ: Prentice-Hall, 1990.

NAEYC. "NAEYC Position Statement Responding to Linguistic and Cultural Diversity—Recommendations for Effective Early Childhood Education." *Young Children* 51:2, January 1996, 4–12.

Schon, Isabel. "Noteworthy Books in Spanish for Young Children." *Young Children* 46:4, May 1991, 65.

Sheldon, Amy. "'Kings Are Royaler Than Queens': Language and Socialization." *Young Children* 45:2, January 1990, 4–9.

Sholtys, Katherine C. "A New Language, A New Life." *Young Children* 44:3, March 1989, 76–77.

Walton, Sherry. "Katy Learns to Read and Write." *Young Children* 44:5, July 1989, 52–57.

CHAPTER 14

Literature Activities and Emerging Literacy

Kansas State University

Objectives

✔ Relate literature activities to the developmental tasks and to learning to read.
✔ Identify the opportunities teachers and parents have for introducing young children to literature.
✔ Identify guides for selecting literature for children under six.
✔ Identify reasons for introducing young children to poetry.
✔ Identify and evaluate literature activities offered in early childhood schools.

"My Mommy got this book from the library and I love, love, love it!" exclaimed five-year-old Peter as he turned the pages of a picture book he had selected from the fresh supply neatly arranged in his kindergarten room.

P eter's teacher often said, "Being part of the wonderful way children respond to good books is one of teaching's greatest rewards."

Through literature children find the history of the human race, the hopes of the future, and the record of happiness and pathos. Between the covers of a book children find the mechanical, the artistic, the beautiful, and the ugly.

THE MAJOR GOAL: A LIFELONG LOVE OF BOOKS

The teacher and parent who want children to live full lives will help them learn to love books. The teacher is, of course, especially concerned with children's emerging literacy skills and will enrich

Toddlers are ready for sustained interest in books both individually and in groups of one or two more children. (C. Hildebrand, photographer)

children's lives with literature in a variety of ways in order to create in them a strong desire to learn to read. Thus the teacher's main goal when offering literature to young children in the early childhood school is to initiate for each child a romance with books that will continue throughout a lifetime.

Teachers will use five important avenues for achieving a lifelong love of books:

1. Provide early literacy experiences that will stimulate children's desire to learn to read.
2. Provide opportunities for children to get acquainted with, handle, and "read" a wide variety of high-quality children's literature.
3. Provide daily opportunities for each child to see, hear, and respond to well-prepared literature experiences.
4. Provide books and other written materials to enhance all components of the young children's program.
5. Provide inspiration and assistance to parents in order to involve them in their children's literature experience.

LITERATURE SUPPORTS ALL DEVELOPMENTAL TASKS

It is worthwhile to realize that through literature activities all the developmental tasks are supported. Of course, through literature the oral symbols of the language become the written symbols of the language; and culture can be passed on through written means. Children's vocabularies are increased through exposure to literature.

Other developmental tasks are frequently highlighted through literature, such as achieving independence, giving affection, getting along with others, understanding right and wrong, and being self-confident. Information books help the children grow in understanding, such as books about human roles, the human body, motor skills, and the world. As children's small muscles develop, they handle books more carefully.

TALK IT OVER: NO. 1

Explain what you have heard parents say about children learning to read. What are their concerns?

THE READING QUESTION

"When will my child begin to read?" is a question parents often ask the early childhood teacher. No one skill that children learn receives as much attention as reading. A number of writers have instilled fear and guilt feelings in parents and teachers whose children aren't reading by nursery school age. Of course, all adults want children to learn to read. Reading skills are basic in modern society. However, no one has yet found thorough reliable research that early readers read with more comprehension or, as adults, are more devoted to literature than children who learn later.

What Is Reading?

Reading can be defined as making sense out of letters or symbols. Note the requirement is *making sense*, not merely pronouncing the symbols. To make sense means to comprehend or understand. In reading one must understand the concepts symbolized by the letters.

An example may help clarify this definition. Any adult with reasonable reading skills could probably read a book on nuclear physics—to choose one of the highly technical sciences—using "read" in the sense of pronouncing the words. Yet would the person be able to comprehend the content just because it could be read? Would motivation be high for reading such a book if one did not understand it? The answer is no to both questions. Without experiences and back-

Children's spontaneous use of books is desirable in the early childhood school. (Michigan State University)

ground information that provide a frame of reference, the words would be meaningless. Motivation for reading them would be low. Therefore, it seems logical that the young child needs experiences to support the words he or she reads.

Emerging Literacy

Literacy has taken on increased urgency in recent years as citizens realize how vital literacy is for living and working in a twenty-first century society. As early childhood teachers, you are on the frontline for starting children on the road to literacy. In many of the things you do, you not only deal directly with children but will be connected with the children's parents. Parental cooperation, modeling, and encouragement are ingredients that are vitally important in each child's eventual competency in reading.

Reading acquisition follows a developmental sequence. Mason's work on the early steps of reading is highlighted in Figure 14–1, along with activities that contribute to the goal for each level. The stair-step conceptualization helps you visualize how Levels 2 and 3 build on the Level 1 foundation. One notes that learning to read is more than memorization of the ABC's. The researcher specifically recognizes the early experience at home with parents as a primary source of young children's information and experience at Levels 1 and 2.[1]

Self-efficacy

A discussion of learning to read and of the child's eventual use of literature as a source of information and pleasure has many connections with an individual's feelings of self-efficacy. Self-efficacy has been discussed in relation to other areas of development and means *the child's feelings of confidence in his or her ability to perform a task.* Self-efficacy has relevance for developing literacy. Sources of self-efficacy, according to Bandura, are (1) personal accomplishment, (2) vicarious experience, (3) verbal persuasion, and (4) emotional arousal.[2] To keep children feeling successful, it is very important to present prereading activities that children can accomplish successfully. This means that both parents and teachers build a firm foundation of early prereading activities at which each child can be successful before more advanced and abstract activities are presented. As for emotional arousal, teachers should be sure that reading books, telling stories, and other related literacy activities are enjoyable so that, like Peter in the opening anecdote, each will "love, love, love" books.

---

[1]Jana Mason, "When Do Children Begin to Read: An Exploration of Four-year-old Children's Letter and Word Reading Competencies," *Reading Research Quarterly* 2 (1980), 203–227. Also see Susan Kontos, "What Preschool Children Know About Reading and How They Learn It," *Young Children* 42:1 (November 1986), 58–66.

[2]Albert Bandura, *Social Foundations of Thought and Action: A Social Cognitive Theory* (Upper Saddle River, NJ: Prentice-Hall, 1986), p. 394.

Prereading Experiences

What are the experiences that prepare the child to read? Is the school entirely responsible for prereading experiences?

Learning to read has two levels. The first is having the desire or motivation to read and an insatiable curiosity about what a word, page, or volume says. Bright, enthusiastic children often teach themselves to read without lessons. The second level is more mechanical, using methods, procedures, and analytical skills to decipher words or a narrative. This level is laborious, often dull, but worth the effort if the first level of motivation for understanding the printed page is in place.

Reading may be somewhat like driving a car. A driver can drive fluidly—skillfully park, reverse, and travel far—without understanding the inner mechanisms of the car or being able to analyze and repair the vehicle. Being interested in driving may precede strong interest in the mechanics of cars, but being interested in mechanics probably does not create the motivation to drive. Thus it is with reading. Developing the motivation for reading precedes tackling the mechanics of reading; however, starting with the mechanics of reading may interfere with the motivation to read.

Prereading experiences are those events that occur before the child begins to read. These experiences give the child a background for understanding what is read. Such experiences begin at birth and continue throughout the individual's life. For a child they are the home, the family, the school, the neighborhood, the television, and life's events wherever they occur. Prereading experiences link speaking, comprehension, writing, drawing, and reading from the early years on.

Simply handling lots of books, turning pages, analyzing the drawings, and discussing them with friends as well as having books read aloud provide children with substantial prereading experiences. The notion that symbols on the page represent people, places, things, and actions develops in the child's mind as books are used

FIGURE 14–1
DEVELOPMENTAL LEV-
ELS OF EMERGING LITER-
ACY.

Source: Adapted from Jana Mason,
"When Do Children Begin to Read:
An Exploration of Four-year-old
Children's Letter and Word Read-
ing Competencies," *Reading
Research Quarterly* 2 (1980),
203–227.

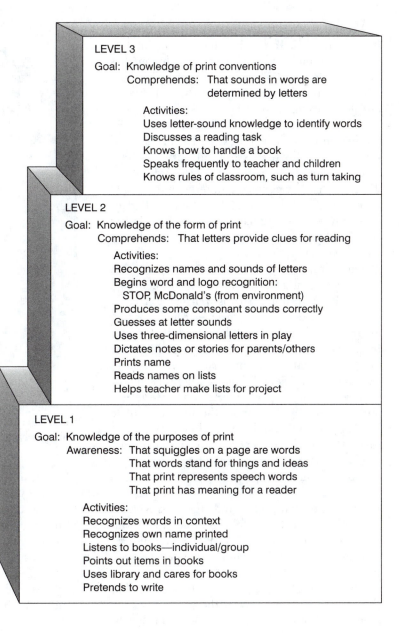

LEVEL 3

Goal: Knowledge of print conventions
      Comprehends: That sounds in words are
                    determined by letters

      Activities:
      Uses letter-sound knowledge to identify words
      Discusses a reading task
      Knows how to handle a book
      Speaks frequently to teacher and children
      Knows rules of classroom, such as turn taking

LEVEL 2

Goal: Knowledge of the form of print
      Comprehends: That letters provide clues for reading

      Activities:
      Recognizes names and sounds of letters
      Begins word and logo recognition:
       STOP, McDonald's (from environment)
      Produces some consonant sounds correctly
      Guesses at letter sounds
      Uses three-dimensional letters in play
      Dictates notes or stories for parents/others
      Prints name
      Reads names on lists
      Helps teacher make lists for project

LEVEL 1

Goal: Knowledge of the purposes of print
      Awareness: That squiggles on a page are words
                 That words stand for things and ideas
                 That print represents speech words
                 That print has meaning for a reader

      Activities:
      Recognizes words in context
      Recognizes own name printed
      Listens to books—individual/group
      Points out items in books
      Uses library and cares for books
      Pretends to write

during these early years. The concept of left-to-right progression begins to be understood as the child turns page after page and notices that the teachers start at the left each time the page turns. The child realizes, too, that the artist's drawings are associated with the printed words, and before long the child begins to sequence the story from memory while looking at the pictures. One frequently notices a child "reading" to friends if an adult is not available.

Vocabulary-building experiences are prereading experiences. In several chapters of this text the opportunity for vocabulary enrichment has been pointed out. The opportunity to practice letter sounds, blend sounds, words, and rhymes are all prereading experiences.

The child who learns to differentiate between largest and smallest, tallest and shortest, and longest and shortest is helped with reading. These concepts help the child to understand when the teacher points out differences in capital letters and small letters. Making lines and forms in art projects, seeing names written from left to right, and learning to write from left to right are all prereading experiences.

One of the first things a child must learn is that little black squiggles (symbols) have meaning. "This label says 'John.' That is your name. Here it is on your locker," says the teacher. She helps him begin to learn that the symbols *J-o-h-n* stand for him. Over and over he sees *John*—on his name tag, on his paintings, on his coat, on his treasures from home. His friend Bill has a different symbol.

Teachers label many objects and write letters and stories, which support the idea that little black marks tell something and convey a message. The child must even learn to concentrate on the black marks—not on the white space surrounding them on the page.

Many parents supplement the labeling that teachers are doing. "The red sign says *STOP*," says John's dad. Later, John reminds dad, "But you were supposed to S-T-O-P and you didn't." This indicates an understanding of both the symbol and the meaning.

Differentiating puzzle pieces; fitting together the parquetry blocks, with their squares, diamonds, and triangles; choosing pegs and beads; arranging the block-city; aligning toys; and choosing blocks of a correct size and shape are all prereading experiences with structured media.

Games such as Candyland, Merry Milkman, Uncle Wiggily, dominoes, playing cards, and the various lotto games all require prereading skills. Such games contribute to number concepts.

Children's customary home literature experience is close and personal. A teacher's goal is to encourage parents to read to their children frequently. (L. Schiamberg, photographer)

These games are especially useful in the kindergarten, where cooperative verbal skills and longer attention spans make sustained interest in games possible.

The children's experiences of assuming various roles in spontaneous dramatic play gives them a feeling for the characters in the books they read. The outdoor program, with its opportunities to extend the children's perceptions of nature and with its outlets for energy and imagination, also makes contributions to children's reading background.

The rich curriculum offered by the good early childhood school is full of prereading experiences. These experiences help children develop a frame of reference for relating what is being read and what they will later read.

Will You Teach Reading?

Teachers should anticipate and plan how they will answer parents' questions about teaching reading if they should ask. If you take a positive stance, you'll reassure parents that you've seriously considered the issue. Parents want to know, the community wants to know, and even children want to know. Are you going to teach reading?

An honest answer is probably, "No, not in the same way that you expect the first-grade teacher to teach reading." Then go on to explain, "However, every experience the school offers will be a prereading and prewriting experience. Day after day a rich curriculum in science, language, art, music, and literature will be providing the frame of reference so basic to recognizing symbols and understanding what is read."

Further than this, a policy can be stated that on an individual basis children will be encouraged to learn to read. If Johnny wants to read to the teacher or an assistant, he will find a ready helper. When Jane points to a word and wants to know what the word is, someone will tell her. If a child volunteers to read to the children, he or she will be encouraged—yet the staff will avoid making others feel left out because they haven't learned yet. If a child memorizes a favorite story, it is fine if the child wants to "read" it to some friends. When the child corrects a teacher for omitting or changing a phrase in a favorite story, the teacher can take this in stride, knowing the child's memory for detail is a plus on the reading ledger.

The emphasis on learning to read will be entirely individually focused. For the group as a whole the teaching of reading will be left to the first-grade teacher, who has special visual aids, and special techniques that the child will find fresh and exciting if they aren't usurped by the early childhood teacher and labored over prematurely.

Stimulating a Desire to Read

The years before six are important years for developing children's romance with books. This is a period for the adults in children's lives to help them catch the enthusiasm for books. The best word is "catch" rather than "teach" because contagion is far more effective than teaching. Attitudes at home and school affect children's attitudes toward books. Loving books makes using them for learning and enjoyment much easier. Many people have lost or never have had a really good feeling associated with books. They may be college students who dread the thought of a library assignment, adults who seldom read, and families who are lost when the television is broken. Or, they may be people who, as children or youths, were accused of being "lazy" when they spent time reading. And to avoid this criticism, they spent time at household chores or other "worthwhile" work instead of reading.

When children have a happy introduction to books, they discover in them fun, laughter, adventure, romance, information, and enlightenment. They want more. They feel that books are their friends. They may want to carry them around or take them to bed. They like the sharing with parent, teacher, friend, grandparent, or sibling that books invite. Children, like adults who love books, will turn to books for solace in lonely moments or for a laugh when in a happy mood. Once a child like Peter in our opening story is "hooked on books," so to speak, he or she will want to learn to read. In fact, motivation is high. Given a rich menu of books in the earliest years, a child will develop ideas, vocabulary, and grammar. The child will discriminate between sounds and begin to differentiate the symbols on the printed page. Reading will come easily.

Some parents and teachers push children into the mechanics of reading before the children have been convinced that books really offer them something. Children have to feel that the task of learning to read is worth the effort.

Neither a teacher nor a parent who lacks enthusiasm can infect a child with enthusiasm for reading. But many parents and teachers have overcome this handicap by working hard to learn about children's books in order to help their own children. In the process they have been inspired to capture the romance with books they missed in their own growing up. It is never too late. Two books from the public library by Annis Duff, *Bequest of Wings*,[3] and *Longer Flight*,[4] will help adults who want to get acquainted with children's books. Anne Eaton's *Reading With Children*[5] and Nancy Larrick's *A Parent's Guide to Children's Reading*[6] will offer stimulation. Remember to ask for books through library loan if they can't be found on the shelves.

EXPERIENCING A WIDE VARIETY OF LITERATURE

A well-chosen collection of good books will await all children whose parents and teachers are working to develop in them a love of books. The opportunity to browse for enjoyment and to use books personally and voluntarily helps a child develop a love of books. The school will of necessity budget considerable funds for purchasing the book collection, for keeping it up to date, and for repair and replacement. The collection can be supplemented by the community library collections.

The Book Corner

The book corner should be separated from the other play areas by dividers to provide a quiet, undisturbed atmosphere that encourages concentration. Carpeting will improve the atmosphere. A table will help the children handle books more carefully. Books should be invitingly displayed on a rack that allows the cover of the book to show. Because the book corner is available during the self-selected activity period, the children will browse on their own. Teachers will usually find several eager listeners if they will take time to

read a story. A child who wants a story should be able to find someone to read it. This area is often popular with new aides, volunteers, or college students who are getting acquainted with the children.

A fresh supply of books should be selected regularly. Certain favorites can remain available for a few weeks. Books can be selected to give information related to concepts being developed or to stimulate questions and observations regarding concepts the teacher anticipates emphasizing in the future. Books "just for fun" should always be available. Here on the shelf can be displayed books that may meet the needs of certain children, such as books on hospitalization, death, or divorce. Such books are used on a one-to-one basis with a child when the teacher feels the child is ready to discuss his or her troubling situation. These books probably would not be selected for a large-group storytime.

To ensure a wider selection of books in the book corner and to give children experience in the public library, a kindergarten teacher developed the custom of allowing a committee of three children to accompany an assistant to the library once every two weeks. They chose one book for each child in the class. Often the class made suggestions to the committee about books they'd like. The children became comfortable in the library, chatting with the librarians and looking over the exhibits. The names of the books were recorded and date-due cards removed as precautions against their loss before the books were displayed in the classroom.

If children are given opportunity and encouragement to use them, books can be taken outdoors during nice weather for a pleasant small-group story or individual reading. In climates where a major part of the school day is spent outdoors, a book rack can become standard outdoor equipment.

Puppets, flannel board, and flannel-board figures, if stored in the book corner, can readily contribute to literature and language experiences. A place to plug in the record player or tape

---

[3]Annis Duff, *Bequest of Wings* (New York: Viking, 1944).
[4]Annis Duff, *Longer Flight* (New York: Viking, 1955).
[5]Anne Eaton, *Reading With Children* (New York: Viking, 1957).
[6]Nancy Larrick, *A Parent's Guide to Children's Reading* (New York: Bantam, 1982).

recorder is also an asset, because these devices are used to advantage here. Recorded stories can be commercial products or recorded by a teacher or parent. The child may look at the book as the record or tape plays.

Illustrations in Books

Teachers should learn to appreciate the art in children's picture books. Much beauty, strength, and feeling are seen in some picture books. Once acquainted with an artist's work, the teacher's enjoyment of picture books will be enhanced. Pictures contribute a great deal to children's enjoyment of books.

The Caldecott Medal is given yearly to honor one of the earliest picture book artists, Randolph Caldecott. Caldecott, an Englishman, lived from 1846 to 1886. His children's books were illustrated after 1878.[7] It is interesting to study the evolution of children's books over the years. One method of study is to seek out the Caldecott Medal winners.

As one studies picture books, it is easy to become impressed with the wide variation in technique and medium that is used by artists. There are many outstanding picture book artists. You'll enjoy learning to recognize their work.

Illustrations in books help children understand what is happening in the story even if they don't hear or understand the words. Pictures should leave accurate concepts. Children are less confused if objects appear whole. Some books have small or abstract pictures that are difficult to see from a distance. Teachers should place the books they expect to use for group storytime across the room and judge whether the children will be able to see the pictures. When the children can't see the picture, they can be expected to lose interest and perhaps to misbehave. Books with pictures that are difficult to see can be used for individual reading. If the story is especially strong, the teacher can tell it, using other visual aids such as puppets or flannel-board figures.

_____

[7]*Encyclopedia Britannica*, 1969, s.v. "Caldecott, Randolph."

One of the teacher's difficulties in choosing books will come when trying to find books that tell stories of people of various races, colors, and creeds in this country and the world. For example, the total list of books with black children that are suitable in content and illustration to read to three-year-olds is quite limited. For four- and five-year-olds the list doesn't grow by many items. The list is just as meager for the Mexican-American, native American, Arab-American, or Asian-American child.

Not only do children need books picturing faces the same color as theirs for identification purposes, but all children at some point will benefit from books with faces, homes, families, and customs different from their own; such books expand their knowledge of the world's peoples. Global or multicultural education is now a popular part of the curriculum.

What, then, can teachers do to remedy the lack of multicultural picture books? First, they should keep asking bookstores, librarians, publishers, and writers for such books. Second, they may have to make their own. Teachers have always been self-reliant. If they need something they can't buy, they make a substitute. Teachers can illustrate homemade books or provide visual aids for storytime by taking photographs; finding paper dolls; using magazine, newspaper, or catalog pictures; or using some of the interracial teaching aids on the market. Homemade books will be discussed in a later section. Of course, it is worthwhile for children to watch puppets and flannel-board figures that represent minority children even when no children from that group are in the class.

RESPONDING DAILY TO LITERATURE EXPERIENCES

Stories and poetry presented in a regular storytime attract and hold children's attention when presentations are well prepared by teachers. Storytime is one of the times in the early childhood

The teacher role-plays a library experience, making children comfortable when they visit the library, because they know what to expect. (Kansas State University)

school when the children come together in either a large group or several small groups for stories. Small groups with four to five children are recommended for three-year-olds and young fours. Planning a storytime for an individual child may be needed for a child who is not ready for a group experience. The children will sense that storytime is an important time of day if the teacher (1) chooses a good story and prepares it well, (2) sets the stage for quiet listening-responding behavior, (3) plans some soothing activities, and (4) plans a smooth transition so that the children know what to expect. If, on the other hand, the teacher haphazardly plucks a book from the shelf and sandwiches storytime between snack time and going outdoors, or if the assistants are running around cleaning up the room while the story is in progress, the children can be expected to feel that storytime is rather unimportant.

Choosing a Story

Choosing an appropriate story and deciding on a technique for its presentation are two of the most important aspects of the teacher's planning. Teachers should choose literature that they themselves like. It is not likely they will put their best effort into a story they don't enjoy. The story must be right for the children. They should be able to understand it. The story should be chosen with the children's ages, interests, and previous experience in mind. Teachers must look hard and long to find suitable stories for the youngest children. It is far better to present two short stories that will hold the children's attention than to select a longer story and lose their interest before it ends. However, when the teacher misjudges the children's interest and selects a story that fails to appeal, it is wise to skip hastily through the pages, telling salient parts, and conclude the storytime with something that does appeal to the group. Never admonish children to be quiet when it is your problem for choosing the wrong story.

The following are general guides for selecting children's literature. Stories and books should

- be about young children and familiar people, animals, and activities;

- contain about one sentence per page for three-year-olds or up to three sentences for five-year-olds;
- have a vocabulary the child can be expected to understand or to learn;
- be illustrated with clear, whole pictures that depict the action taking place;
- be selected both for fun and for information;
- be fantasies that do not harm children if chosen for fun;
- provide accurate information about the real world if chosen for information.

Teachers should become familiar with their school library and with a selected group of outstanding books in order to be able to find a story that will appeal to their children even on a moment's notice. It often happens that emergencies arise—schedules don't work out, special performers are late, or rain pours just when an outdoor activity is planned. If the teacher can reach for a book with knowledge of its special appeal, holding the group together and avoiding the disruptive behavior that emergencies often trigger in children will not be difficult.

Listed below are books that are predictable winners for each age listed. These books incorporate the characteristics of content, illustrations, length of sentences, and number of pages typically enjoyed by children of each age. Of course many other books could have been listed. However, it is each teacher's responsibility to learn to choose the right books for the children in a particular group. New students should study these suggested books, compare other books to them, and try out various books with children in order to learn to select books wisely.

For Infants

Select cardboard books with 1 colorful illustration per page. Encourage child to say, "Ball, cup, shoe," as represented.

For Toddlers

Brown, M. W., *Goodnight Moon*
Flack, M., *Ask Mr. Bear*

Jackson, Kathryn, *Busy Timmy*
Keats, Ezra Jack, *Peter's Chair*

For Three-Year-Olds

Omerod, J., *Moonlight*
Omerod, J., *Sunshine*
Gipson, Morrell, *Hello Peter*
Jackson, Kathryn, *Busy Timmy*
Keats, Ezra Jack, *The Snowy Day*
Lenski, Lois, *Big Little Davy*

For Four-Year-Olds

Brown, Margaret W., *The Noisy Book*
Flack, Marjorie, *Tim Tadpole and the Great Bullfrog*
McCloskey, Robert, *Blueberries for Sal*
McCloskey, Robert, *Make Way for Ducklings*
Rey, H. A., *Curious George*

For Five-Year-Olds

Burton, Virginia Lee, *Mike Mulligan and His Steam Shovel*
Daugherty, James, *Andy and the Lion*
Gag, Wanda, *Millions of Cats*
McCloskey, Robert, *One Morning in Maine*
Petersham, Maud and Miska, *The Circus Baby*
Zion, Gene, *Harry the Dirty Dog*

Late in the kindergarten year, when the teacher is sure of the sophistication of the group, more fanciful stories and those with some distance in time and place might be selected.

Choosing Poetry[8]

Poetry, like good books and music, offers children an avenue of feeling, of expressing, and of learn-

---

[8]The author is indebted to Rebecca Peña Hines, who helped formulate the section on children's poetry, which was given as a joint workshop at the National Association for the Education of Young Children. Originally illustrations of Spanish poetry were also included. An article, "The Pied Pipers of Poetry," was published in *Young Children* 36:2 (January 1981), 12–17.

ing. Poetry is artistic. It is creative. Poetry can be polite, pompous, pitiful, pretty, and witty. It is, as Josephine Jacobsen, a consultant to the Library of Congress says, "those certain words in a certain cadence that makes poetry different from other literature forms." There are many reasons why poetry can make a valuable contribution to the early childhood curriculum.

Enjoyment

Enjoyment is the number one reason for using poetry with young children. They have a natural affinity for poetry, for they dearly love playing with words, with funny sounds, with repeats and rhymes. Using a wide selection of poems in order to tap the children's many interests is important. Also, to help keep enjoyment in poetry, do not belabor or dissect poems—as you may have had to do in high school. If children do not immediately enjoy a poem, then save it for a time when you may find them ready to like it.

Listening

Listening is a second reason for using poetry. To get the meaning from spoken communication, a child must listen to what the other person is saying and then decode it. Poetry helps sharpen listening skills. Poems such as "I Want a Rabbit" and "Missing" by A. A. Milne[9] are readily listened to by children. A wintertime favorite is

Once There Was a Snowman

Once there was a snowman
Stood outside the door
Thought he'd like to come inside
And dance around the floor.

Thought he'd like to warm himself
By the firelight red.
Thought he'd like to climb
Upon the big white bed.

So he called the North Wind,
"Help me now I pray.
I'm completely frozen,
Standing here all day."

So the North Wind came along
And blew him in the door,
And now there's nothing left of him
But a puddle on the floor.

author unknown

Attention

A perfect attention-getter is the poem "I'm Hiding," by Dorothy Aldis from her collection *All Together*.[10] Every child stops what he or she is doing to find out where the child in the poem is hiding. It works like magic every time. "This Little Boy" is another poem that catches children's attention.

This Little Boy

This little boy is ready for bed
Low on his pillow he lays his head
Pulls up the covers so warm and tight
And there he sleeps all through the night.

Morning comes! His eyes open wide!
Quickly he throws the covers aside!
Jumps out of bed, puts on his clothes,
And off to nursery school he goes.

author unknown

Creative Language Expression

Another reason for including poetry in children's programs is the development of creative language expression. Good poets are masters at the art of using language creatively and expressively. Poets may use few words, but cause your mind and heart to know and to feel what they have known and felt. They write of ordinary things like

---

[9]A. A. Milne, *When We Were Very Young* (New York: E. P. Dutton, 1924).

[10]Dorothy Aldis, *All Together* (Putnam, 1952), pp. 71–72.

Polly Chase Boyden's poem, "Mud," which starts "Mud is very nice to feel," and children gain a new perception of something they know.

Children, too, are often poetic. Consider the poetry in this exchange between two four-year-olds.

My name is Michael
I love to recycle.

My name is Sandy
I love candy.

Another little boy sang as he swung in a blooming mimosa tree and watched the bees flitting among the flowers,

I love to sing, sing, sing.
A bee likes to sting, sting, sting.
Ping-a-ty Ping!

Special recognition can be given to a child's original poem by writing it down and letting the child take the poem home. Or, the poem could be posted or placed in a class book. Care must be taken to avoid competition.

Teachers and parents, too, can also be creative poets. Here is a poem a teacher wrote for a child on her birthday.

Glenda's Birthday

Today is Glenda's birthday.
She is four-years-old you see,
She'll paint with paints,
Play with clay,
And maybe climb a tree.

Today is Glenda's birthday.
Now we are here to say
"Happy birthday, Glenda"
In a very special way.

"Happy Birthday!"

V. Hildebrand

Guidance

Another use of poems is to help guide a child into desired behavior. You may be familiar with using the fingerplay "Grandma's glasses" when you want to get little hands to relax for storytime. "The Mitten Song" by Mary Louise Allen[11] is useful for helping children to remember to put their "thumbs in the thumb-place and fingers all together" when putting on their winter mittens.

Concepts

Concepts can be introduced, explained, and expanded through poetry. To learn a concept well, a child must meet it numerous times in numerous ways, and poetry can be very helpful. Here's one about a squirrel.

The Squirrel

Whiskey, frisky
Hippity hop.
Up he goes
To the tree top;

Whirly, twirly,
Round and round,
Down he scampers
To the ground.

Furly, curly,
What a tail;
Tall as a feather
Broad as a sail!

Where's his supper?
In the shell.
Snappity, crakity,
Out it fell!

author unknown

Concepts of cultural heritage, holidays, peace, love, numbers, and the like all can be found in poetry. Many are in books that are illustrated

---

[11]Mary Louise Allen, *A Pocket Full of Poems* (New York: Harper & Row, 1957).

with delightful drawings. Aileen Fisher is an author-artist who has many beautiful poetry-stories about nature, such as *Cricket in a Thicket*,[12] *Feathered Ones and Furry*,[13] and *Listen Rabbit*.[14]

Vocabulary

Gradual building of vocabulary also comes with the use of poetry. New concepts call for new words. Poetry helps children practice these words. When we show young children pussy willows in the spring, for example, they are usually new to them—or they don't remember them from last spring. They probably know the word *pussy* from another context. The poem called "Catkin" is chanted going up the scale, with the "Meow meows" going quickly down the scale.

Catkin

I have a little pussy,

Her coat is warm and grey,

She lives out in the meadow,

Not very far away.

Now she's a little pussy,

She'll never be a cat,

For she's a pussy willow,

Now what do you think of that?

Meow, meow, meow, meow

SCAT!

author unknown

Reading Readiness

The use of poetry enhances reading readiness. A careful reading of only a few poems makes this quality of poetry clear. For example, rhyming and listening to rhyming are good phonics practice.

TALK IT OVER: NO. 2

Recall a poem or nursery rhyme you learned early in your life. In what circumstances was it taught? Share with your classmates.

Try Maurice Sendak's *Chicken Soup With Rice*.[15] The greatest contribution to reading readiness, however, is the love of fine literature that is taught and caught.

Memory

Memory is an important intellectual operation that is enhanced through use of poetry. The little poems and songs give children something to remember. Parents and teachers can evaluate the child's learning as they notice how well he or she recalls poems.

Humor

Humor often is appreciated in poems, the punch line or pun tickling the funny bones of the later four- and five-year-olds. Try "Eletelephony" by Laura I. Richards[16] for a humorous play on words, or "I Know an Old Lady," by Rose Bonne and Allan Mills.[17]

Teachers and parents should practice reading poetry aloud so that the cadence, rhyme, and message are heard clearly by the children. Puppets and flannel boards may be helpful. Collections of poetry may have few or only small illustrations. You can reproduce these using an overhead projector or simply show the tiny picture so the children will realize that listening is

---

[12]Aileen Fisher, *Cricket in a Thicket* (New York: Charles Scribner's Sons, 1963).

[13]Aileen Fisher, *Feathered Ones and Furry* (New York: Thomas Y. Crowell, 1971).

[14]Aileen Fisher, *Listen Rabbit* (New York: Thomas Y. Crowell, 1964).

[15]Maurice Sendak, *Chicken Soup With Rice* (New York: Harper & Row, 1962).

[16]Laura E. Richards, in *Poems Children Will Sit Still For*, ed. Beatrice S. de Regniers et al. (New York: Scholastic Book Services, 1969), p. 92.

[17]Rose Bonne and Allan Mills, *I Know an Old Lady* (New York: Rand McNally, 1961).

needed to get the message. If you transcribe the poem on a card, children won't demand to "see the picture" as they may when you hold a book. Be sure to use your voice well. Separating conversations in the poem from the narrative aids the hearer in getting the message. Keep your eyes on children's faces, then you'll know how well they are comprehending.

In addition to books of poems mentioned in the footnotes, a few important poetry books are listed here.

- Ciardi, John. *Fast and Slow* (Boston: Houghton Mifflin, 1975).
- Holman, Felice. *I Hear You Smiling and Other Poems* (New York: Charles Scribner's Sons, 1973).
- Keats, Ezra Jack. *Over in the Meadow* (New York: Four Winds Press, 1971).
- Lee, Dennis. *Alligator Pie* (Boston: Houghton Mifflin, 1975).
- Mizumura, Kazue. *If I Were a Cricket . . .* (New York: Thomas Y. Crowell, 1973).
- Ness, Evaline. *Amelia Mixed the Mustard and Other Poems* (New York: Charles Scribner's Sons, 1975).
- Talbot, Toby. *Coplas—Folkpoems in Spanish and English* (New York: Four Winds Press, 1972).
- Whiteside, Karen. *Lullaby of the Wind* (New York: Harper & Row, 1984).
- Zolotow, Charlotte. *Summer Is . . .* (New York: Thomas Y. Crowell, 1983).
- Zolotow, Charlotte. *Some Things Go Together* (New York: Thomas Y. Crowell, 1983).

Choosing a Storytime Technique

Every effort should be made to make storytime a vibrant, interesting, and unique experience for children. Storytime should never become the same old thing. The teacher can develop a number of techniques that will make it an event that is looked forward to. What are some of these techniques?

The teacher inserts a little game into literature experience time by carrying poem, story, or fingerplay titles in her pockets. Children select, then may choose to recite alone or to have everyone join in. (Savannah, Georgia, prekindergarten)

Read Directly From a Book

This technique is best when you have outstanding poetry or prose with large outstanding illustrations. Certainly when the author and the artist provide a well-integrated piece of literature, it is well to let it carry the children along.

Big books are one of the literature innovations of recent years. Big books originated in New Zealand as part of the whole-language approach to teaching reading. They are typically 15-by-18 inches in size, in full color, and come with an easel for displaying them. Many of the Caldecott

Medal picture books have been selected for big book publication. Some publishers have a coordinated package, which is composed of a big book, six matching paperback books, and a matching cassette tape, allowing individual use of the small books and/or cassette tape after a major presentation using the big book. These are available for purchase and in some resource libraries. They add an interesting variation to storytime and help alleviate a problem because children are able to see clearly the big book illustrations from a distance. Given the extra cost, most teachers will evaluate carefully before investing in big books.

Use the Illustrations of a Book While Paraphrasing the Story

This technique works well with informational material that is too long and detailed for the children, yet has illustrations related to their interests.

Tell the Story

Storytelling is one of the oldest arts. It certainly should not become a lost art in the early childhood school just because publishers have given us many good books. Listening to a story without the aid of pictures requires more attention from children than listening to stories from picture books. A good storyteller needs preparation and practice.

The storyteller can use various props to invite attention and set the mood for the story, such as wearing an apron when reading *Apron On, Apron Off* by Helen Kay,[18] or an old straw hat during *Who Took the Farmer's Hat?* by Joan Nodset,[19] or a pretty rose for *No Roses for Harry* by Gene Zion.[20] A collection of hats can illustrate *Caps for Sale* by Esphyr Slobodkina.[21] A plush bunny or doggy can sit beside the teacher during a pet story and tell the teacher "when everyone is ready to listen."

---

[18]Helen Kay, *Apron On, Apron Off* (Upper Saddle River, NJ: Scholastic Book Services, 1968).
[19]Joan Nodset, *Who Took the Farmer's Hat?* (New York: Harper & Row, 1963).
[20]Gene Zion, *No Roses for Harry* (New York: Harper & Row, 1958).
[21]Esphyr Slobodkina, *Caps for Sale* (New York: Scott, 1947).

The teacher chooses a good story and learns to tell it. For a new story it helps to make notes on index cards until one becomes familiar with the story. It is important to do the story well. The teacher should use vocal inflections to create the various characters and help the children differentiate between them. Eye contact with each listener will help hold attention and help the teacher feel the impact the story is making. The teacher may move the head, body, or arms to help dramatize the story. However, teachers are cautioned not to select frightening stories or to build up unnecessary suspense or fear through their dramatizations.

The teacher can help children realize that they too are storytellers. Type, write, or tape-record a child as he or she tells an exciting event. Read this back to the child to help him or her realize the words really did tell a story.

Tell a Story With Flannel Board

You can make a flannel board by covering a large piece of cardboard with a piece of outing flannel. A neutral gray is a satisfactory color. An easel or some other stand for holding the board will be convenient. You can make another type of flannel board by covering the bottom of a large cardboard box; then cut the sides diagonally to support the flannel board at a 45-degree angle.

Figures that represent the characters in the story are cut out of felt, pelon, flannel, or paper. A small piece of Velcro, sandpaper, or masking tape attached to the back of the figure makes it adhere to the flannel. Figures are available commercially that represent community helpers, family members, and some traditional stories. Such items can be used in many stories. All the characters in a story need not be made. Sometimes a single figure or picture will provide the children a focus for their attention as they listen.

Children will enjoy and learn from using the flannel-board figures. They will not only tell the story the teacher tells but will create their own stories. Such use can take place during the self-selected activity period. However, during the storytime the teacher may or may not let the children handle the figures. The decision will depend on goals. If the teacher wants the children to hear a meaningful story in sequence, then handling the figures personally may be best, keeping them out of sight until time for them to appear. However, if encouraging individual participation is more important than story sequence, the teacher may give each child a figure to place on the board when it is called for. This technique does detract from the story and may be hard on the figures. It is true that teachers may spend a great deal of time making these figures and often prefer that they remain "special" to add spice at storytime.

The true-to-life stories of Martin and Judy in *Martin and Judy* by Verna Hills Bayley[22] lend themselves to adaptation for the flannel board. This three-volume series has the advantage of featuring the same little boy and girl, with whom children readily identify. *Ask Mr. Bear* by Marjorie Flack,[23] *The City Noisy Book* by Margaret Wise Brown,[24] and *I Can Count* by Carl Memling[25] are examples of stories that are readily illustrated on the flannel board.

Tell a Story With Puppets

Puppets often inspire quiet children to talk. Children may appear tense during a story until they have an opportunity to be one of the characters through a puppet. Depending on the objective, the teacher will vary the decision as to who will speak for the puppets. The choice of stories and the use of puppets will depend on the age and experience of the children.

Homemade hand puppets can be made of paper sacks, socks, vegetables, or cutouts on a stick. Finger puppets can be made of decorated Styrofoam balls or of construction paper attached to the finger by a paper ring. Many commercial puppets are available. A worthwhile addition to the school is a set of family puppets made of molded plastic. These family puppets are available in several diverse cultural selections. By purchasing several sets, the teacher can enlarge the family. Extra adults can be grandparents or other relatives. Delightful for animal stories are plush bunny, dog, and lion puppets.

To encourage puppetry during the self-selected activity period, a cardboard box can be cut to resemble a television set, or a table can be turned on its side to make a stage. The children will conceal themselves behind the "TV" or "stage," holding up the puppets for manipulation or speaking. If a few chairs are arranged for the "audience," the listeners will come and go as interested.

Role-Play a Story

Children can become involved in a story through creative dramatics. The teacher may tell or read a story, then let the children present their version. Care should be taken to avoid indicating that there are certain words that must be said. The children may be encouraged to play various roles without attaching them to a story. The teacher might say, "Who would like to be the mother calling the children to come to breakfast?" Who will be the father? or the children? A drama suitable for Broadway may result.

Make Up a Magazine Picture Story

The teacher selects a number of pictures saved from magazines and stacks the pictures in an order that might suggest a story sequence. For example, picture number one is a girl, number two is a dog, number three is a girl and a dog running, and number four is a dog doing tricks or eating. The teacher may start with the phrase, "Once upon a time there was a _____," then let the children take it from there. The first few sessions may produce very short stories, so the teacher should prepare several sets. However, once the idea catches on, the children will enjoy

[22]Verna Hills Bayley, *Martin and Judy*, 3 vols. (Boston: Beacon Press, 1959).

[23]Marjorie Flack, *Ask Mr. Bear* (New York: Macmillan, 1932).

[24]Margaret Wise Brown, *The City Noisy Book* (New York: Harper & Row, 1939).

[25]Carl Memling, *I Can Count* (New York: Western, 1963).

Dramatizing a book can start simply, perhaps by wearing hats to listen to *Caps for Sale*. (Southeast Oakland Vocational Technical Center)

elaborating on the details in the pictures and the action they can imagine.

This same storytelling technique is used to tell the stories with the pictures in *My Weekly Surprise*, a newspaper published for kindergartners but usable with many fours.[26] The cover picture invariably is a good story starter. The children's imaginations do the rest.

Use Filmstrip Stories and Videotapes

Some filmstrip and videotape stories have been made from outstanding picture books. To see the enlargement of the drawings from such books as Robert McCloskey's *Make Way for Ducklings*[27] is to appreciate anew the great care he took in illustrating the book. One drawback of these stories is that they are used frequently on television and may not be new to the children. This may not lessen the enjoyment of them, of course, but teachers should realize this fact and not be too disappointed if the children say, "We've seen that."

---

[26]*My Weekly Surprise* (American Education Publications, Education Center, Columbus, OH 43216).
[27]Robert McCloskey, *Make Way for Ducklings* (New York: Viking, 1941).

Provide Story Recordings

Story recordings are popular with children. Stories usually include some music and sound effects that would be difficult for the teacher to add. Therefore the recording offers the child a variation. Outstanding stories should be used for group time. The record jacket or a picture related to the story can be attached to the flannel board for a focus of attention.

Recordings of published books are now available, so the book can be held for viewing while the record plays. Some recordings have both book and filmstrip available. Recorded stories will provide important listening opportunities for individual children during the self-selected activity period. Using home recording equipment, many teachers now make their own story tapes for children to use independently.

The following recorded stories are particularly popular with children. Picture books are available for the stories.

Muffin in the City	*Blueberries for Sal*
Muffin in the Country	*Madeline's Rescue*
The Little Firemen	*Make Way for Ducklings*

The Carrot Seed   *Georgie the*
Andy and the Lion   *Friendly Ghost*
Story About Ping

Sing a Story Song

A number of children's songs are complete with plot, suspense, and climax. Teachers will find eager listeners if they occasionally sing a story to the group. They may accompany themselves on an instrument—guitar, Autoharp, or piano. Also, they may illustrate the song at the flannel board while singing. "Mary Had a Little Lamb," "John Henry," "Eency Weency Spider," and "Hush, Little Baby"—all familiar songs for young children—can be thought of as stories the first time they are introduced. "I Know an Old Lady," a humorous, fanciful story by Rose Bonne and Allan Mills, is delightful to sing in kindergarten.[28] Younger children, however, take the song too literally. Of course, the children will want to sing along, so let them!

Size of Story Groups

Small groups of four or five children make more effective story groups, particularly for younger children. The youngest children like to feel close to the teacher and to be able to respond to the book individually—verbally and physically—which is sometimes difficult to permit in a large group. Gradually, as children mature, the groups can be combined. When there are a number of assistants in a group—aides, volunteers, cooperating parents, or students—it is especially sensible to use their help in order to divide the group for storytime. Even when the group remains together, the assistants should join the storytime. Their interest will encourage children's interest, and the assistants will become familiar with a situation they may be called on to take over in the future.

When the teacher really believes that there are books for every child, she or he will seek to interest every child in books. For one or two in the group it may mean an almost private story session.

---

[28]Rose Bonne and Allan Mills, *I Know an Old Lady* (Englewood Cliffs, NJ: Scholastic Book Services, 1961).

Patty and Martha were examples of three-year-olds who could not tolerate a group story-time even in groups of four or five children. Patty was easily distracted. Martha wanted to sit directly in front of the book, which blocked others' view. These two found joy in books, however, when read to together. Sometimes they asked to hear several books that they had selected. Finally, at age four, they decided they would like to hear the story with the other children.

Patty and Martha could easily have become storytime distractors in the playhouse or at the puzzle shelf. But the teacher felt storytime too important to give up and sought a combination that would interest them. The tiny group was the solution. In thinking of Patty and Martha, one must note that they were three-year-olds. Their experience with storytime before coming to school had been of a warm sitting-on-the-lap variety with their parents. Teachers may have to carry some of this practice into the school. Even in an understaffed school, a nonteaching staff member might have been enlisted to read to Patty and Martha or to supervise as they listened to a story record. Community or student volunteers could provide valuable assistance with such children. When children cannot be enticed to participate in storytime, their activity elsewhere should not be distracting to the children who do want to take part. Time during the self-selected activity period can be used to encourage children like Patty and Martha to become interested in books.

Chairs or Floor for Storytime?

The choice between having children sit on chairs or the floor will be a personal one of the teacher's. Some like chairs because each child has a place and one does not block the view of another so easily. Others say chairs can become a distracting element—rocking back and forth—or that children on the ends of the circle may be slighted because they can't see the book and therefore lose interest.

Some teachers like to group the children on the floor, especially if it is carpeted. They feel this arrangement promotes a cozier, more restful atmosphere. Rug sample "sit-upons" can provide individual places. Children should be able to relax and not be unduly cramped together.

The book or flannel board should be in good light so that the children can see the pictures. Pictures must be large enough to be seen by those in the back of the group. Some books are inappropriate for groups because the illustrations aren't clear from a distance. Children will readily become disinterested if they cannot see the pictures. Teachers should arrange the group so that the children don't face the glare of the windows. The teacher can sit on the floor or on a low chair, whichever makes it easier for all the children to see. It takes practice to hold a book so children can see and you can still read at the same time. That's only one reason why advance planning and careful reading of the book prior to storytime are so essential.

Transition to Storytime

Transitions or changes in activity can be made smoothly and with a minimum of fuss. When the children are expected to make such shifts in their routine, the teacher must first decide what behavior is desirable and plan accordingly. Where do the children go first? Which paths do they use? Is the path clear of obstructions? Will the children have room or will they run into each other? Are there distracting elements on the way? Having studied the plan through, the teacher explains it to the children and helps them learn to follow it. A regular routine should be worked out so that the children can predict what will take place and what their role is. Given a general routine with room for individual differences, children will behave in appropriate ways with only a little practice. Other transition suggestions are presented in Chapter 5.

Each teacher will work out the transition to fit the group and room. To shift from snack to story-time, for example, it is common in some groups to have the children deposit snack dishes on a tray, then walk past a book rack and select books. They take the books to the corner of the room reserved for storytime. They relax and "read" their books to themselves, share them with a child sitting nearby, exchange them with others, or visit quietly until most of the group has arrived.

The teacher, too, relaxes while talking with children informally, commenting on pictures they are enjoying in their books, encouraging a child to find a picture of special interest, or just listening attentively.

When it appears that most children are through looking at their books, the teacher sings a song, which is the cue to pass the books to an assistant. The teacher immediately begins a series of fingerplays, poems, and songs. These activities are valuable for their literary and musical qualities and because they encourage children's attention and participation and help develop cohesiveness within the group. A discussion related to experiences that took place earlier in the day or about tomorrow's projects may be worked in around a wide selection of songs, poems, and fingerplays. A fingerplay will quiet a group of fidgeting children quicker than nearly any technique, especially if the verse begins in a quiet voice that makes children wonder what is taking place. Teachers can often use fingerplays in place of saying "Shh!".

Fingerplays are short poems with actions for the child to do while saying the words. The actions seem to help hold the child's attention. Teachers can encourage children to use fingerplays creatively by adding new verses and motions. Hundreds of fingerplays have been published in a variety of books, so the teacher has only to select those preferred and to memorize and use them frequently. *Let's Do Fingerplays* by Grayson[29] and *Wee Sing: Children's Songs and*

---

[29]Marion F. Grayson, *Let's Do Fingerplays* (Washington, DC: Robert B. Luce, 1962).

Fingerplays by Beall and Nipp[30] are examples of books of fingerplays available. A few fingerplays with suggested actions are provided at the end of this chapter.

Fingerplays can be soothing or they can be rollicking. The teacher learns to sense which type is needed to set the mood. For example, if the children are getting ready to listen to a story, the choice would be a quiet fingerplay—not one that would cause the children to get up and clap. Clapping behavior would dispel the mood the teacher is trying to establish for the story. On the other hand, if the children have been listening quietly to a story, the teacher might choose a lively fingerplay to give them the cue that it is time for them to get up and become active again.

It is helpful to arrange new fingerplays on index cards and carry them in a pocket in order to have them handy for these moments. Fingerplays are simple enough so that children can be encouraged to "Remember to say this at home tonight." Parents enjoy such samples of their child's learning.

Additional Tips for Storytime

The teacher who chooses a good story, perfects a technique, and plans a smooth transition between other activities and storytime still has some steps to take before completing a satisfactory group literature experience.

Once the group is ready, the teacher should proceed directly to the first sentence of the story. To tell young children about an author or discuss why the story is appropriate that day invites disruption of the listening mood the teacher has worked to establish. After a few pages it is sometimes possible to ask children why they think this story was chosen today. As for the author, after the book becomes a favorite—after many readings—the group might be interested in some interesting fact about the author.

Children will not automatically know what behavior is expected at storytime unless the teacher teaches them gently and firmly. A good story experience will be sufficient reward. Eye contact with each child throughout the story helps each feel that the teacher is talking directly to him or her. The teacher's eyes keep moving from child to child. If a child appears to become distracted, the teacher's eyes resting on the child for a moment often is enough to draw attention back to the story. If a child seems about to become disruptive one can say, for example, "John, do you know what the old man said?" The child who is easily distracted can be invited to "Sit up here close to me, and I'll help you remember to be a good listener." Then touching a knee or shoulder can be a gentle reminder. Care should be taken to be sure the children understand that the place by the teacher is not a punishing seat—the offer is to "help," not punish. Also, a second adult who sits with the children is a great help in handling special problems that may arise. The teacher who is reading may then concentrate on holding the attention of the group.

Teachers develop skill in acknowledging a child's verbal contribution during storytime. One of the teacher's reasons for the choice of story is that it will have special meaning for the children. When this goal is successful, the children will be bubbling over with personal references stimulated by the story. This is good—just what the teacher wants. Yet only a limited number of children can be listened to before the group becomes impatient. They are egocentric. If they can't talk, too, and can't have the story, then they take things into their own hands. They may talk or even poke their neighbors. Sometimes the teacher's nod or smile will be sufficient recognition of a child's comment. Sometimes the teacher may pause to listen, then grasp the lead when the child pauses. Using a "secret sign" such as a nod, a wink, or a wave of the index finger that means

---

[30]Pamela Conn Beall and Susan Hagen Nipp, *Wee Sing: Children's Songs and Fingerplays* (Los Angeles: Price/Stern/Sloan, 1984).

"Let's wait until we finish the story" will help quiet children. Of course, when the story is complete, the teacher must then hold a discussion, permitting the children to talk about the ideas in the story. Discussion, besides being excellent for language development, helps the teacher correct misconceptions. Discussions help the teacher gain more understanding of individual children.

The Martin and Judy stories[31] are examples of stories that encourage personal identification. In such stories the teacher may read or tell awhile, then let the children talk about their experience, and finally say, "Let's see how Martin and Judy worked it out." This statement helps regain their attention, and the storytime can go on.

An old farmer said of the movies, "You gotta go to know if you shoulda gone." And so it is with storytime. The teacher's role is to lead children into an avenue of enjoyment. Then they will be happy to go to storytime each day.

ENHANCING THE TOTAL PROGRAM THROUGH LITERATURE

Providing books to help answer questions children ask is an important way of fulfilling our major goal of helping children learn to love books. Information from books can be used to support a new concept in music as well as in science, sports, or geography. Some of the materials may have to be adapted by the teacher if they are prepared for adults or older children. "Let's look it up" can become an important attitude for young children to develop.

Reference books such as *The New Grolier Student Encyclopedia*,[32] *The Random House Children's Encyclopedia*,[33] and others will help

answer some of the children's questions. They should have a permanent place in the room. One group called such a collection "the important books."

Children's books may become obsolete, depicting technical or social concepts that are outdated. For example, unless specifically designed to depict the historical, books about transportation and farming should be relatively new. Also, books indicating roles of boys and girls and men and women need careful scrutiny for gender-role stereotyping. Recent research indicates that many picture books and other books used in early elementary schools depict girls as weak characters in observer, nonaggressive roles, and boys are pictured as leaders and as characters having the most fun and curiosity.[34] Similarly, books showing children of ethnic groups other than white have been quite rare until recently. Also, a variety of family forms is beginning to appear in children's literature—divorced families, multiracial families, and extended families. Such books help children understand aspects of life that may at times be puzzling to them.

Teachers must put extra effort into selecting books with new information. In the interim they can develop some homemade books for their groups. For example, with the aid of magazine illustrations and photographs, books can be made from heavy tagboard and notebook rings. Books with children from various ethnic groups can be made. There are several magazines devoted to black culture, and magazines from Mexico might be a source of pictures of persons of Hispanic heritage. Ethnic stereotypes should be avoided, such as depicting native Americans only in headdresses. It is important for a child of an ethnic group to have some literature depicting his or

---

[31]Bayley, op. cit.

[32]*The New Grolier Student Encyclopedia* (Danbury, CT: Grolier Educational Corp., 1991).

[33]Ann Kramer, ed., *The Random House Children's Encyclopedia* (New York: Random House, 1991).

[34]For advice on choosing literature sensitive to gender roles, see Karyn Wellhousen, "Girls Can Be Bull Riders, Too! Supporting Children's Understanding of Gender Roles Through Children's Literature," *Young Children* 51:5 (July 1996), 79–83.

her group, and it is also important that the children of each group learn about children who have different cultural and ethnic backgrounds.[35]

We all must understand that "difference" in culture of language does not mean "deficient." For instance, just because the teacher cannot understand the child's Chinese expressions does not mean that those expressions are not clear to one who does understand Chinese. The NAEYC, recognizing the growing interest in serving the children from many cultural and language groups more effectively, after intense study produced and adopted a position statement on this topic. It makes recommendations in four areas of early childhood education: (1) working with children, (2) working with families, (3) working with professionals, and (4) developing programs.[36] The conclusions are in agreement with those recommended in this text and in the text recommended in other chapters, *Knowing and Serving Diverse Families.*[37]

Children's Own Stories

Children can learn that their own words make stories and even books. A trip or an interesting discovery can prompt a story. The children dictate, the teacher writes. Dictation can be done individually during the self-selected activity period or with the group during storytime. Sometimes the class can be divided into groups to write several stories.

Young children won't have patience enough for the teacher to print carefully as they dictate their story, so the teacher might take the dictation on a lined tablet and transcribe it later. Some version of shorthand to keep up with the flow of ideas may be needed. If two adults can work together, one can write while the other keeps the ideas coming and helps a child hold on to a thought until the writer gets it down. A tape recorder is very useful in these instances. When a lull comes in the contributions, the transcriber can read "the story so far." Then the children can be asked if they had other thoughts as they listened to their story. The story can be typed, posted on the bulletin board, and read at storytime the next day. A copy can be sent home to parents in a special booklet. The children will relive the event each time they hear the story.

Four-year-olds dictated the following story after a trip to see the train engine that is on exhibit on the Michigan State campus.

THE TRAIN

Monday we went to explore the M.S.U. train.

It was as high as the ceiling. No! It was high like a house. There were big, big wheels. Everything was black.

We climbed tall stairs to get to the top.

We got to pull the train whistle rope. It was an old, old train and there was an old, old man. He helped us ring the bell. He was sixteen or seventeen.

It had a dark scary coal car behind it. It was a coal engine. I think it was a steam engine.

We sat in the driver's chair. We found where the brakes were.

We pulled the track switch thing. It was broke. The train was on tracks—that's how it goes.

It was fun to visit that train!

---

[35]See L. Derman-Sparks and the A.B.C. Task Force, *Anti-bias Curriculum: Tools for Empowering Young Children* (Washington, DC: NAEYC, 1989). Also see Olivia Saracho and Bernard Spodek, *Understanding the Multicultural Experience* (Washington, DC: NAEYC, 1983) for suggestions for increasing the cultural richness of your curriculum.

[36]NAEYC, "NAEYC Position Statement Responding to Linguistic and Cultural Diversity—Recommendations for Effective Early Childhood Education," *Young Children* 51:2 (January 1996), 4–12.

[37]V. Hildebrand, L. A. Phenice, M. M. Gray, and R. P. Hines, *Knowing and Serving Diverse Families* (Upper Saddle River, NJ: Merrill/Prentice Hall, 1996).

The five-year-olds dictated "The Turkey Farm" after a Thanksgiving trip to a local turkey farm. The story was duplicated and placed in their class booklet and later shared with their parents.

THE TURKEY FARM

At the turkey farm there were 5,000 turkeys. They were white turkeys and black turkeys. The girl turkeys were white and the boy turkeys were black. All the sick turkeys were in the back pens. Mary found a feather that was both black and white.

They fed the turkeys grain—it was maize.

The turkeys make loud noises—it was gobble, gobble.

One was following me. Some got out. One of them flied! The teachers caught a turkey and let us pet him. It didn't scare me.

It smelled awful. It smelled like bacon. It smelled like chicken do-do-do—ugh!

It was fun to go to the turkey farm.

A picture book can be made of the story. Pages can be cut from cardboard and fastened with notebook rings. A few lines from the story can be lettered on each page. It can be illustrated with drawings, with magazine pictures, with pictures copied from books on a photocopier, or with photographs if available. Because the children are the authors, the book will be one of the most popular in the school.

Sometimes in place of a story the group dictates a thank-you letter to someone who has made a special event possible. An example follows. Mr. Caldwell is a police officer and Prince is his trained police dog.

Dictating a letter or a story is a creative literature and language experience. Each child derives satisfaction from his or her contribution and will remember that contribution as the story is read and reread.

Dear Mr. Caldwell,

We liked your dog, Prince. Thank you for bringing him. We liked to see him climb up the slide and slide down it and climb over the boxes. We liked the commands you gave the dog. We liked to see him jump through the swing. His name sounds like "Prince Charming." We liked him to do everything. We liked to see you slide down the big slide. We liked to see him go up and down on the seesaw. We didn't know policemen and dogs went around at night playing on our seesaw!

Love,
The Kindergarten Kids

By recording children's expressions, one is readily impressed with the effects children achieve with language. When dictation is taken from children, care should be used to preserve their original and often charming phrases.

The Library

The school's book collection should be given continuous attention. A sizable budget for new books should be available yearly to add new issues and replace worn-out books. Teachers should keep abreast of the new books coming out by reading reviews in *The Horn Book Magazine*,[38] *Childhood Education*,[39] *Young Children*,[40] and *Parents' Magazine*.[41] Booklets such as *Recommended Children's Books*, published by the *School Library Journal*,[42] and *Bibliography of Books for Children*,

---

[38]*The Horn Book Magazine* (The Horn Book, Inc., 585 Boylston St., Boston, MA 02110).

[39]*Childhood Education* (journal of The Association for Childhood Education International, 11501 Georgia Ave., Suite 315, Wheaton, MD 20902).

[40]*Young Children* (journal of the NAEYC, 1509 16th St. NW, Washington, DC 20036-1426).

[41]*Parents' Magazine* (Parents' Magazine Enterprises, 52 Vanderbilt Ave., New York, NY 10017).

[42]*School Library Journal* (R. R. Bowker Co., 1180 Avenue of the Americas, New York, NY 1

published by the Association for Childhood Education International,[43] provide information on both new and old recommended books.

Filing

A system of filing books in the school library should be developed. Some teachers like to color-code the binding of each book with colored plastic tape to designate the subject matter of the book. Books might be grouped according to interests, such as children, animals, transportation, and plants. Books also can be filed according to author. This method encourages the staff to become aware of the names of authors. In either case a cross-listing in an up-to-date card file will help new users find the books they seek. The microcomputer greatly facilitates keeping the booklist up-to-date.

Books should be removed when they become unrepairable. Out-of-date books should be filed in a separate section to be referred to when they are needed for studies of "the olden days." Many picture books related to farming, housing, and transportation fall into this category now.

Repair

Books should be kept in good repair. If pages are torn, they encourage children's misuse. If pages are missing, the book should be replaced or discarded. Pictures from old books can be salvaged to make illustrations for flannel-board stories or homemade books. For the best book-mending materials, check with your local bookstore or librarian.

INSPIRING AND ASSISTING PARENTS' PARTICIPATION IN LITERATURE EXPERIENCES

It is important for teachers to encourage parents to make contributions to children's literature

[43]Association for Childhood Education International, 11501 Georgia Ave., Suite 315, Wheaton, MD 20902.

experiences. The school cannot assume the total responsibility if maximum learning is desired. Even highly educated parents often need guidance in helping their children.

Teachers can help parents become enthusiastic about children's books. The reading attitudes of the adults in children's lives—whether parents, teachers, siblings, grandparents, babysitters, or librarians—will influence children's literature experiences and the pleasure they derive from them.

Whenever an opportunity arises, teachers can promptly suggest titles and authors of books on subjects of interest to parents. Suggestions on how books can be secured at the library or borrowed from the school's collection will be welcomed. Some parents need to know where the library is and how to get there, how many books they can check out, and how much the service costs.

Get Books Into the Home

Without books at home the child cannot look at books as desired and, of course, parents cannot read to a child. The school can operate a lending library if it has the resources. For example, in one school paperback picture books were secured, covered with clear plastic adhesive to increase durability, and loaned to the children. A large mailing envelope was labeled with each child's name to provide a safe place for carrying and storing the book. A 5-by-7-inch card was made for each child and carried the name of the books

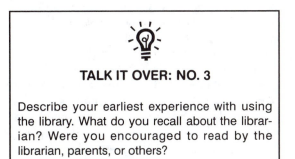

TALK IT OVER: NO. 3

Describe your earliest experience with using the library. What do you recall about the librarian? Were you encouraged to read by the librarian, parents, or others?

checked out. At a glance the teacher had an indication of a child's interest in books. Each time the child returned a book, another was chosen. The staff felt that because paperback books were relatively inexpensive, the cost of lost books would not be formidable. In practice, no books were lost.

The teacher plans ways to encourage parents to use the public library with their children. The library habit is a good family habit even for families who buy books. Of course, no family can buy the wealth of books available there. The library should become an enjoyable place to go. Then research assignments in later years won't hold so much dread for children.

If the school can introduce children to the library, they in turn can encourage reluctant parents to take them there. Many public libraries have a story hour to which young children are invited. The teacher can give this information to parents, along with a personal endorsement. Parents can be encouraged to use the story hour as an opportunity to check out books for home use.

Both parents and children will find the children's librarians very hospitable. Their goal is to make people feel at home in the library and to make every effort to bring children and books together. One may notice that librarians often know children's names and their reading interests. The librarian will help search for whatever subject the child wants to read about.

Buying Books

Buying books is another way for children to have them at home. Parents can be reassured that picture books can be enjoyed over and over, that they start the literary process, and will eventually serve as practice reading material. Therefore the money used for books is well spent. Some schools purchase paperback books in quantity and maintain a bookstore where children can spend their allowance. Buying books is, of course, a good way for the child to spend his or her money.

Teachers can help parents buy books by ordering them through the school. Of course, handling

---

TALK IT OVER: NO. 4

Display, if available, and discuss books designed to help children understand topics such as divorce, adoption, new family styles, and so on. Identify characteristics and evaluate.

---

money is not one of the teachers' favorite tasks, but the responsibility is sometimes assumed when it means getting books into the homes of children.

There are a number of book clubs that parents may ask about. Parents also seek advice when buying an encyclopedia. Teachers can help children by helping parents make the best decision regarding books to purchase.

Encourage Parents to Read to Children

It is enjoyable for the child if several family members take an interest in his or her picture books. Grandparents and siblings as well as parents can read to the child. Choices of books should include old favorites as well as new books that extend the child's knowledge.

Whoever reads should encourage the child to talk about the book. They can ask: "What was the dog's name? Who took the farmer's hat? How was Martin feeling? Why did the father say that?" Such conversation helps the child think about what is heard and gives language practice. It strengthens the child's understanding and helps remembering, too. However, avoid questions to the point that pure enjoyment of the story is lost.

During the latter months of kindergarten, parents may express the feeling that picture books are "old hat." This may be their impatience over wanting the child to begin reading. The teacher can suggest series books such as *"B" Is for Betsy* by Carolyn Haywood[44] or *Henry Huggins* by Beverly Cleary,[45] to be read on a chapter-a-night basis. Such books carry children into the school age and extend their experience with books.

Parents can be advised to continue to read to their child a year or more after he or she starts reading. Many parents say their children enjoyed reading aloud together through fourth grade. The mechanics of learning to read are laborious and often discouraging even to children who have enjoyed a rich background of literature and are highly motivated to learn to read. Of course, the beginning reader needs time to practice reading at home, but the parents can continue a diet of stimulating, exciting books until the laborious read-aloud stage is passed. Hearing books that are advanced beyond those the child can read will motivate the child laboring over those first primers. The parent can let the child gradually assume the reading role—perhaps at first on pages containing illustrations. Or, the parent may read the narrative parts while the child reads the conversation. Such reading is also good practice for vocal inflections. Any method that gives the child reading practice, yet keeps the story moving, will help keep reading motivation high. Be sure to take time to laugh at funny parts and appreciate the artist's illustrations.

---

[44]Carolyn Haywood, *"B" Is for Betsy* (New York: Harcourt, Brace & World, 1939).
[45]Beverly Cleary, *Henry Huggins* (New York: Morrow, 1953).

FINGERPLAYS AND BODY ACTION POEMS
Quiet Fingerplays

Bunny	Finger Actions
There's nothing as soft as a bunny,	(One hand is an imaginary bunny being petted by the other hand.)
A wee little, soft little bunny.	
He can hop on his toes,	(Fingers hop.)
And wiggle his nose.	(Hand on nose, wiggle it.)
And his powder puff tail	(Move hand to rear to indicate tail.)
Is quite funny.	

Grandma's Glasses	
Here are grandma's glasses.	(Fingers make glasses over eyes.)
Here is grandma's hat.	(Two index fingers make pointed hat.)
Here's the way she folds her hands	(Fold hands and lay in lap.)
And lays them in her lap.	

Grandpa's Glasses	
Grandpa lost his glasses,	(Fingers make glasses over eyes.)
Before he went to bed,	
Guess where grandma found them?	
Right on top of grandpa's head!	(Move glasses on top of head.)

Three Balls	
Here's a ball.	(Make round shape with thumb and index finger.)
Here's a ball.	(Make round shape with two thumbs and two index fingers.)
Here's a great big ball.	(Make third ball with both arms.)
Let's count them.	(Repeat for the count.)
One, two, three.	

Ten Fingers

I have ten little fingers,	(Extend fingers of both hands.)
And they all belong to me.	(Point to self.)
I can make them do things.	
Would you like to see?	
I can shut them up tight	(Make fists.)
And open them wide.	(Spread fingers open.)
I can put them together	(Clasp hands together.)
Or make them hide.	(Put hands behind back.)
I can make them jump high.	(Raise hands high.)
I can make them jump low.	(Reach low.)
I can fold them quietly.	(Fold and lay hands in lap.)
And hold them just so.	

My Turtle

This is my turtle.	(Make fist and extend thumb.)
He lives in a shell.	(Indicate fist as shell.)
He likes his home very well.	
He pokes his head out when he wants to eat,	(Extend thumb and wiggle.)
And pulls it back in when he wants to sleep.	(Hide thumb in fist.)

My Eye and Ear

This is my eye.	(Cover one eye.)
This is my ear.	(Cover one ear.)
This is to see.	(Look around.)
And this is to hear.	(Cup hand around ear.)

Boisterous Fingerplays

Mr. Bullfrog

Mr. Bullfrog sat on a big old rock.	(Fist with thumb up.)
Along came a little boy.	(Left hand walk.)
Mr. Bullfrog KERPLOP!	(Both hands slap knee.)

Pig

I had a little pig	(Fist with thumb up.)
And I fed it in a trough,	(Make cup of left hand.)
He got so big and fat,	(Make circle of arms.)
That his tail popped off!	(Clap both hands on knees.)
So, I got me a hammer	(One hand is hammer.)
And I got me a nail	(Hammer on thumb of other hand.)
And I made that pig	(Continue to hammer.)
A wooden tail!	

Five Little Astronauts

Five little astronauts	(Hold up fingers of one hand.)
Ready for outer-space.	
The first one said,	(Hold up one finger.)
"Let's have a race."	
The second one said,	(Hold up two fingers.)
"The weather's too rough."	
The third one said,	(Hold up three fingers.)
"Oh don't be gruff."	
The fourth one said,	(Hold up four fingers.)
"I'm ready enough."	
The fifth one said,	(Hold up five fingers.)
"Let's Blast Off!"	
10, 9, 8, 7, 6, 5, 4, 3, 2, 1.	(Start with ten fingers and put one down with each number.)
BLAST OFF!!!	(Clap loudly with "Blast Off!")

Firefighters

Ten little firefighters	(Lay all fingers out straight on knees or floor.)
Sleeping in a row.	
Ding-dong goes the bell	(Pretend to ring bell.)
Down the pole they go.	(Pretend to be sliding down pole.)
Jumping on the engine	
EE—RR—OOO	(Make siren noise.)
Putting out the fire.	(Pretend to use fire hoses.)
Then home so slow.	
And back to bed again	(Lay all fingers in a row again.)
All in a row.	

Little Bunny

There was a little bunny	(Make ears over head with fingers.)
Who lived in the wood.	
He wiggled his ears	(Wiggle fingers.)
As a good bunny should.	
He hopped by a squirrel,	(Fingers hop along arm or on floor.)
He hopped by a tree,	
He stared at the squirrel,	(Cock head and look.)
He stared at the tree,	
But he made faces at me!	(Wiggle nose.)

Counting

One, two, three, four,	(Extend fingers one at a time.)
Mary at the cottage door.	
Five, six, seven, eight,	(Change to say "cookies," "celery," or whatever the child is eating.)
Eating (cherries) off her plate.	

Five Little Birds

Five little birds, high in a tree,	(Extend five fingers.)
The first one says, "What do I see?"	(Extend one finger.)
The second one says, "I see a street."	(Extend two fingers.)
The third one says, "I see seeds to eat."	(Extend three fingers.)
The fourth one says, "The seeds are wheat."	(Extend four fingers.)
The fifth one says, "Tweet, tweet, tweet."	(Extend five fingers.)

I'm the Little Hot Dog

My father owns the butcher shop.	(Clap on "Hot Dog.")
My mother cuts the meat.	
And I'm the little Hot Dog	
That runs around the street.	

Five Little Hot Dogs

Five little hot dogs frying in a pan,	(Extend five fingers.)
The grease got hot and one went Bam!	(Clap.)
Four little hot dogs frying in a pan,	(Extend four fingers.)
The grease got hot and another went Bam!	(Clap.)
Three little hot dogs frying in a pan.	(Extend three fingers.)
The grease got hot and another went Bam!	(Clap.)
Two little hot dogs frying in a pan,	(Extend two fingers.)
The grease got hot and another went Bam!	(Clap.)
One little hot dog frying in a pan,	(Extend one finger.)
The grease got hot and another went Bam!	(Clap.)
No little hot dogs frying in the pan,	(Make fist.)
The grease got hot and the pan went BAM!	(Clap loudly.)

Baby Bumblebee

I'm bringing home a baby bumblebee.	(Cup hand pretending to hold bee.)
Oh, won't my mommy be so proud of me?	
I'm bringing home a baby bumblebee.	
Oops! He stung me!	(Toss hand excitedly.)

Moderately Active Fingerplays

Five Little Rabbits

Five little rabbits	(Show five fingers.)
Under a log.	(Cover with other hand.)
One says, "Hark, I hear a dog!"	(Show one finger. Hand behind ear.)
One says, "Look, I see a man!"	(Point indicating eye.)
One says, "Run, as fast as you can."	(Make fingers run.)
One says, "Pooh, I'm not afraid."	(Thumbs in armpits.)
One says, "Shh, keep in the shade."	(Finger to lips.)
So they all lay still	(Five fingers under hand.)

Under a log,
And the man passed by
And so did the dog.

Here Is a Bunny

Here is a bunny   (Fist with two fingers extended.)
With ears so funny,
And here is his hole in the ground.   (Thumb and index finger form circle.)
When a noise he hears,
He pricks up his ears   (Extend fingers quickly.)
And jumps in his hole in the ground.   (Pretend to put bunny in hole.)

Five Little Pumpkins

Five little pumpkins,   (Show five fingers.)
Sitting on a gate.
The first one said,   (Show one finger.)
"It's getting late."
The second one said,   (Show two fingers.)
"There are witches in the air."
The third one said, "We don't care."   (Show three fingers.)
The fourth one said,   (Show four fingers.)
"Let's run, run, run."
The fifth one said,   (Show five fingers.)
"Isn't Halloween fun?"
"OOOOOOW" went the wind,
And OUT went the light.   (Clap on "OUT.")
Those five little pumpkins   (Five fingers roll behind child.)
Rolled fast out of sight.

Touch Game

Touch your nose.   (Finger on nose.)
Touch your chin.   (Finger on chin.)
That's the way this game begins.
Touch your eyes.   (Fingers on eyes.)
Touch your knees.   (Fingers on knees.)
Now pretend you're going to sneeze.   (Cover mouth with hand.)
Touch one ear.   (Finger on ear.)
Touch two lips right here.   (Finger on lips.)
Touch your elbows where they bend.   (Fingers on elbows—cross hands.)
That's the way this touch game ends.

Robin Redbreast

Little Robin Redbreast   (Thumb and little finger extended.)
Sat upon a rail,   (Move thumb.)
Niddle, noddle went his head   (Move little finger.)
And wiggle, waggle went his tail.

Body Action Poems

Whirling Top

I am a top, all wound up tight.	(Loop arms around knees while sitting.)
I whirl and whirl with all my might.	(Whirl around fast.)
And now the whirls are out of me,	(Whirl slowly.)
So I will rest as still as can be.	(Come to rest.)

Dressing Warmly

Let's put on our mittens	(Pretend to pull on mittens.)
And button up our coat.	(Pretend to button coat.)
Wrap a scarf snugly	(Pretend to tie scarf around neck.)
Around our throat.	
Pull on our boots,	(Pretend to pull up boots.)
Fasten the straps,	(Pretend to tighten straps on boots.)
And tie on tightly	(Pretend to tie bow under chin.)
Our warm winter caps.	
Then open the door	(Pretend to turn knob on door.)
And out we go	(Make fingers walk on floor if sitting, or walk out door if standing.)
Into the soft and feathery snow.	

Keeping Dry

Put up your umbrella	(Pretend to extend umbrella.)
To keep yourself dry;	
Put up your umbrella,	
There's rain in the sky.	
Pitter, patter, pitter, patter,	(Make fingers tap on floor.)
Softly it falls.	
Hurry home quickly	
Before Mother calls.	

Bounce Like Ball

I'm bouncing, bouncing everywhere.	(Children standing.)
I bounce and bounce into the air.	(Jump up and down with rhythm.)
I'm bouncing like a great big ball.	(Fall down in place.)
I bounce and bounce, then down I fall.	

The Elephant

The elephant is so big and fat.	(Circle arms.)
He walks like this, he walks like that.	(Walk.)
He has no fingers, he has no toes,	(Point.)
But, oh my goodness, what a nose!	(Swing arm low for trunk.)

My Rabbit

My rabbit has two big ears   (Extend two fingers for bunny ears.)
And a funny little nose.   (Pat nose.)
He likes to nibble carrots   (Pretend to nibble.)
And he hops where'er he goes.   (Move hand, making fingers "hop," or if standing,
                                          hops on tiptoes.)

Gardening

This is the way I plant my garden—   (Bend down and dig.)
Digging, digging in the ground.
The sun shines warm and bright above it; (Make circle with arms overhead.)
Gently the rain comes falling down.   (Tap like rain on hard surface.)
This is the way the small seeds open.   (Open hands slowly.)
Slowly the shoots begin to grow.   (Bending down, put up arm.)
These are my pretty garden flowers,
Standing, standing in a row.   (Stand proudly and smiling.)

My Garden

I dig, dig, dig,   (Pretend to dig in standing position.)
And I plant some seeds.   (Pretend to drop seeds in row.)
I rake, rake, rake.   (Pretend to rake.)
I pull some weeds.   (Pretend to pull weeds.)
I wait and watch,   (Look at ground.)
And soon I know
I'll be here to watch
My garden grow.

Hammering

Johnny pounds with one hammer,   (Pound palm with fist of other hand.)
One hammer, one hammer,   (Have one finger extended.)
Johnny pounds with one hammer,   (Have two fingers extended.)
But Jimmy pounds with two.   (Continue pounding palm.)
Jimmy pounds with two hammers,
Two hammers, two hammers,
Jimmy pounds with two hammers,
But Betty pounds with three.   (Have three fingers extended.)

(Use children's names and continue up to five hammers.)

Note: All these fingerplays and poems are by unknown authors.

Conclusions

The most important goal for parents and teachers of young children is to start children on the road to a lifelong love of books. Teachers will use five important avenues for achieving this goal by providing

1. early prereading experiences that will stimulate children's emerging literacy;
2. opportunities for children to get acquainted with, handle, and "read" a wide variety of high-quality children's literature;
3. daily opportunities for each child to see, hear, and respond to well-prepared literature experiences;
4. books and other written materials to enhance all components of the program; and
5. inspiration and assistance to parents in order to involve them in their children's literature experiences.

Applications

1. Discuss the "Talk It Over" items found in the chapter.
2. Write an activity plan for a literature activity for a few children, using the sample plan in Chapter 6 (Figure 6-2). Develop special aids for your story. (Be sure to try the plan out with only a few children before using it for a larger group.) Secure approval, carry out the plan, and evaluate the results from the children's point of view and your viewpoint. Prepare a report and hand it in along with your approved activity plan.
3. Evaluate your total participation on your evaluation form developed in Chapter 1.
4. Add ideas and plans for literature activities to your Resource File.

Study Questions

1. Discuss literature activities and the associated developmental tasks.
2. Assume you are the lead teacher in a group of three- to six-year-olds. Write a two-page

statement for the children's parents stating your school's philosophy about teaching reading. Discuss your statement with other classmates.
3. State and explain the general guides for selecting literature for young children.
4. State and explain the value of using poetry with young children.
5. Describe storytime techniques and the purpose of using a number of different techniques.
6. Discuss the pros and cons of large and small group size for storytime, seating arrangement, placement of lighting, requiring each child to have a storytime experience, and using the library.
7. Suggest several ways to encourage library use by families in your group.
8. Suggest several ways to encourage parental involvement with children and literature.

Videotapes

Reading and Young Children
    15 minutes

Dr. Jan McCarthy tells teachers what they can say to parents who think their children should learn formal reading in preschool. NAEYC Media, 1509 16th St. NW, Washington, DC 20036-1426, 1-800-424-2460.

Sharing Books With Young Children
    26 minutes

Betsy Hearne gives an enthusiastic presentation showing new picture books for young children. ALAVIDEO, 50 East Huron St., Chicago, IL 60611.

Additional Readings

Bader, Lois. *Reading and Language Inventory.* Upper Saddle River: Prentice Hall, 1995.

Bader, Lois, and Verna Hildebrand. "An Exploratory Study of Three- to Five-Year-Old's Responses on the Bader Reading and Language Inventory to Determine Development Stages of Emerging Literacy." *Early*

Child Development and Care 77, August 1992, 83–95.

Butler, Dorothy. *Babies Need Books.* New York: Atheneum, 1980.

Cianciolo, Patricia Jean, ed. *Picture Books for Children.* Chicago: American Library Association, 1981.

De Regniers, Beatrice, et al., eds. *Poems Children Will Sit Still For.* New York: Scholastic Book Services, 1969.

Friedberg, Joan. "Helping Today's Toddlers Become Tomorrow's Readers." *Young Children* 44:2, January 1989, 13–16.

Harris, Violet J. "Multicultural Curriculum: African American Children's Literature." *Young Children* 46:2, January 1991, 37–44.

Harsh, Ann. "Teach Mathematics With Children's Literature." *Young Children* 42:6, September 1987, 24–29.

International Reading Association. "Literacy Development and Pre-First Grade." *Young Children* 41:4, May 1986, 10–13.

Jalango, Mary Renck. *Young Children and Picture Books: Literacy from Infancy to Six.* Washington, DC: NAEYC, 1991.

MacCarry, Bert. "Helping Preschool Child Care Staff and Parents Do More With Stories and Related Activities." *Young Children* 44:2, January 1989, 17–21.

Mills, Heidi, and Jean Ann Clyde. "Children's Success as Readers and Writers." *Young Children* 46:2, January 1991, 54–59.

NAEYC. "NAEYC Position Statement Responding to Linguistic and Cultural Diversity—Recommendations for Effective Early Childhood Education." *Young Children* 51:2, 4–12.

Raines, Shirley C., and Robert J. Canady. *The Whole Language Kindergarten.* New York: Teacher's College Press, 1990.

Schickedanz, Judith A. *More Than the ABCs: The Early Stages of Reading and Writing.* Washington, DC: NAEYC, 1986.

Schmidt, Velma, and Earldene McNeill. *Cultural Awareness: A Resource Bibliography.* Washington, DC: NAEYC, 1978.

Smith, Charles A. "Nurturing Kindness Through Storytelling." *Young Children* 41:6, September 1985, 48–51.

Strickland, Dorothy S., and Lesley Morrow, eds. *Emerging Literacy: Young Children Learn to Read and Write.* Washington, DC: NAEYC, 1994.

Teale, William H., and Miriam G. Martinez. "Getting on the Right Road to Reading: Bringing Books and Young Children Together in the Classroom." *Young Children* 44:1, November 1988, 10–15.

Walker-Dalhouse, Doris. "Beginning Reading and the African American Child at Risk." *Young Children* 49:1, November 1993, 24–28.

Wolter, Deborah L. "Whole Group Story Reading?" *Young Children* 48:1, November 1992, 72–75.

CHAPTER 15

Dramatic Play Activities

Garden City, Kansas Community College

Objectives

✔ Relate developmental tasks to dramatic play activities.
✔ Explain why children like dramatic play activities.
✔ Explain how careful observation of dramatic play helps teachers understand children.
✔ Identify, describe, and evaluate dramatic play activities for early childhood schools.

"How much are the eggs?" asked four-year-old Nancy of four-year-old Jim, who ran the "store."

Jim stood behind the toy cash register expectantly. "Two dollars," he replied.

Nancy started away with the egg container. "No, you didn't pay me," Jim said. He altered his voice slightly and continued, "Pretend to pay me." Nancy complied.

Jim busily arranged the empty food boxes and egg trays on the shelves. He turned all the cash registers away except one. He said, "You know why I have to use this big register all alone? Because my helpers aren't here today."

Jim tried to talk Nancy into buying more items. He said, "These are my secret sauce. These are my secret peaches." Nancy chose an assortment and paid him. "Thank you," said Jim, giving her the change. He wanted to do some more business, but Nancy left the store.

"Let's pretend it's ten more days from now," Jim called over the divider that separated "store" from "house." It worked. Nancy returned and took some more groceries.

"Hey, you didn't give me any money and I didn't give you any money." Nancy was leaving and made no move to come back. Jim put his hand out in front of him and pretended to get the money. Then he closed up shop and went to the housekeeping area to join Nancy.

Nancy started out for the "store." Hating to see her go, Jim said, "No, the store closes at four o'clock and it's four o'clock now."

Nancy said, "But, I'm going to the other store," and left.

"Oh," said Jim, "I wonder where wife has gone now."

DRAMATIC PLAY: DEFINED

Scenes like the one played by Jim and Nancy are common among young children. From their front-row seats teachers and parents are privileged to attend children's first performances as they step out on life's stage. No written lines are needed. Few props are called for. The child can be alone or with others when feelings and ideas—real and imagined—spill out in **spontaneous role-playing** called **dramatic play**, also called **symbolic play**.

Dramatic play is the champagne of the under-six set. It gives the sparkle to home, school, or wherever children gather. Children are actors without stage fright. They perform as expertly to an empty barn as to a full house. They say what they feel and feel what they say. They unashamedly use erroneous conceptions and unintentional puns. Creativity abounds. Children ride a plank "horse," eat sand "cakes," and drink water "beer" without apology for their lack of realism. If adults have sensitive ears, eyes, and hearts, they may be moved from deepest anguish to poetic ecstasy or be entertained by rollicking slapstick. Write items down immediately if you want to remember some of children's choice comments.

Vygotsky's work helps shed light on dramatic play as it does on language and cognitive development. The social aspects of child development are particularly interesting to Vygotsky. Berk explains, "according to Vygotsky, play supports the emergence of two complementary capacities: (a) the ability to separate thought from actions and objects, and (b) the capacity to renounce impulsive action in favor of deliberate, self-regulatory activity. That is, where there is an imaginary situation, there are rules. A child cannot behave in an imaginary situation without rules."[1]

VALUES OF DRAMATIC PLAY

Contributing to All Developmental Tasks

All areas of a child's growth can be stimulated by dramatic play. Briefly, dramatic play contributes to development of the cognitive, physical, creative, social, and emotional components of the child's being. Language development enhances dramatic play.

---

[1]Laura E. Berk, "Vygotsky's Theory: The Importance of Make-Believe Play," *Young Children* 50:1 (November 1994), 30–39. Berk cites L. Vygotsky, "The Role of Play in Development," in *Mind in Society*, eds. M. Cole, V. John-Steiner, and E. Souberman, pp. 92–104 (Cambridge, MA: Harvard University Press, 1978). Original in Russian published in 1933.

Cognitive Development

Children's dramatic roles expand as their world expands. They integrate concepts from every area into the imaginative play that develops. They wonder, question, and experiment. This active role helps develop the depth needed to make concepts their own. While selecting roles and props, children learn to make choices. They make decisions beginning with whether or not to join an activity. Language skills, so crucial to concept information, are called for and practiced in dramatic play. The example in the introduction to this chapter illustrates how Jim used language to keep the play going and how each child's mental images of previous experience contributed to the play. The use of simple props—cash register, shelves, and grocery boxes—and Nancy saying she was "going to the other store," show the children's use of mental pictures of ideas and objects.

As children mature, cognitive development shows increasing use of symbols or mental pictures. Some people call dramatic play *symbolic play* because children use internalized mental pictures (symbols) of the objects, space, people, and interactions they play out. Others label this play **pretend play** and emphasize the imaginative aspects of the play. Whatever the label, children **role-play** the people and, at times, the animals in their lives.

Parents and teachers may, occasionally, see themselves in children's symbolic play. However, like a good screen actor, the role the child plays may convey not only the basic information of the character but the child's personal feelings about the character as well.

Symbolic play begins early; for example, when a toddler puts a miniature baby bottle to a doll's mouth. Roles increase in depth and breadth with additional experience and are most extensive between ages three and six. Older children typically play roles in more depth and detail than younger children, and may carry a theme over day after day. Their increased cognitive skills—memory, reasoning, and language—help sustain the theme.

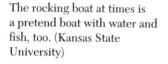

The rocking boat at times is a pretend boat with water and fish, too. (Kansas State University)

For example, in one group following a number of public funerals that many children had witnessed on television, the children repeatedly played "funeral." They used a red wagon as the hearse and carried each other as the "dead person" to a nearby ditch that had been dug by a maintenance crew in preparation for a repair project. The ditch was called the "grave." Most children wanted a turn at being "dead" and made their body limp for the children who cooperated to throw each one into the "grave" after a rough ride around the yard, lying in the red wagon. After staying still for some minutes in the "grave," they asked permission from the hearse drivers to get out of the grave.

Although it is likely that none of the families had encouraged the children to watch the funerals, many children had observed considerable detail. There was confusion because of the flashback scenes showing the individuals alive. These replays were difficult to explain because children, being preoperational thinkers, seem to believe that what is shown on television is real and in the present. Adults helped some to talk about other experiences with death—dead pets or relatives. The children's spontaneous choice of a theme for their symbolic play seemed to help the children deal with their cognitive confusion over death.

Thus, teachers and parents can watch children's symbolic play for evidence of cognitive growth—an increasing ability to handle ideas abstractly. Because it takes a period of time for this symbolization to develop, considerable time and openness should be allowed for free play every day. Even though the teachers may propose a theme for the play, they should be open to the children's changing that theme to suit themselves or even totally disregarding the teacher's plan in favor of something with personal meaning for them, such as the funeral play in the example.

Physical Development

It is a rare child who needs encouragement to exercise. Given space, equipment, and a friend or two, activity involving exercise naturally occurs. Many dramatic roles require fast, rugged action. Good health and physical stamina are fostered.

Dolls of many sizes are stimuli for dramatic play. (University of Illinois)

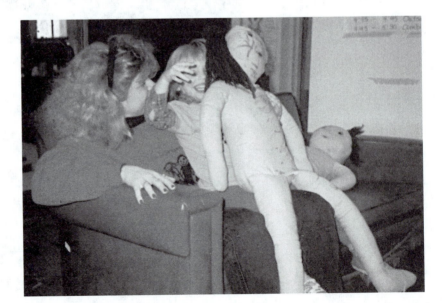

See Chapter 9 for ways to facilitate dramatic play on the play yard.

Creative Development

Original thoughts, words, and deeds spill out effortlessly in dramatic play. "Pretend to pay me," said Jim. "Pretend I'm a gorilla," says a petite blond, and for a while she is a gorilla. Children on these untrod paths find new (to them) ways to do things, new things to do, and new uses for old objects—all creative discoveries.

Emotional Development

The full range of feelings is expressed and experienced as the child plays with others in dramatic play. The child knows joy and sorrow, affection and rejection, anger and pleasure, satisfaction and dissatisfaction. The child learns to know what it means to have feelings.

"If we want to get closer to the truth we must look deeper into the reasons for our behavior," wrote Virginia Axline, a child psychologist. Therapists such as Axline use the technique of play therapy, which includes spontaneous dramatic play, for discovering the source of a child's emotional disturbance. Axline explains, "We are seeking understanding, believing that understanding will lead us to the threshold of more effective ways of helping the person to develop and utilize his capacities more constructively."[2]

Social Development

In dramatic play the child develops a concept of his or her own gender role. Numerous social roles are tried out and increase the depth of understanding of many other roles. The child begins integrating the rules of society. Often one hears a child admonish friends who forget the rules. A conscience is developing.

In Chapter 3 the stages of social play were discussed in relation to children of different ages.

During dramatic play you may observe a toddler pretending to give the doll a bottle while playing alone. That is *solitary play*. Later, as a three-year-old the child may feed the doll while playing side by side with another child in an episode of *parallel play*. The children do the same thing with the same equipment at about the same time. Finally, at ages four and five the plot will thicken as *cooperative play* is used to integrate fathers, siblings, and others in a network of baby care, housework, and perhaps even a fire with a fire truck arriving with full siren to add excitement. The latter play is possible when children have extensive language or symbolic thinking skills. They become increasingly creative and spontaneous in their dramatic play. You will see examples of these stages of dramatic play as you move from one age group to another. There will be some overlap because the divisions are not sharp.

Leadership develops within dramatic play groups. Usually older children lead younger, more immature children because of their improved language skills and more extensive ideas. Sustained attention span is noticeable as children play roles that have meaning for them.

Fostering Positive Social Play Behavior

Positive social play is highly valued in early childhood classrooms. This type of play is often labeled **prosocial**. Prosocial play is a child's spontaneous action for helping another person, cooperating with others, showing interest in others, and being able to take the perspective of another. Prosocial behavior may include altruism. In prosocial behavior the child wishes to help the other child and may or may not think there will be a reward. Altruism is often observed in a child who expresses sympathy for another who is crying.

An example of prosocial behavior was observed by a mother of a prospective kindergartner, Olivia. The just-turned-five-year-old was accompanying her mother as they visited a kindergarten that the mother was considering for her daughter for the fall. The two were admitted to Mrs. K's room while the children were having

---

[2]Virginia M. Axline, *Dibs: In Search of Self* (Boston: Houghton Mifflin, 1964), pp. 8–9. Dibs was first observed by nursery school teachers who after a period of concern called in the psychologist for consultation. This is a report of the author's work with Dibs in play therapy. It is such a moving account that teachers everywhere should read it.

Blocks of many types are used
in high-quality dramatic play.
(V. Hildebrand, photographer)

small-group time with several children seated around the various small tables. Kindergartner Karen noticed Olivia's entry. She went to Olivia and asked her to sit at her table. She introduced herself, smiled at Olivia, and offered her a sheet of paper and the use of her box of crayons. Olivia was very touched by Karen's warmth. She remembered it throughout the summer, and whenever anyone asked her about going to kindergarten in the fall, she always remembered to tell them about Karen. "I met a girl at my kindergarten. I already have a friend," she said.

Karen was acting prosocially. Was Karen naturally prosocial, or had adults helped her become prosocial? How can parents and teachers help children? Could the teacher have prepared Karen to be prosocial?

Free play time offers children many opportunities for prosocial behavior. During peer interaction a child's prosocial behavior receives positive response while negative behavior receives negative reinforcement. During peer interaction a child who is a good negotiator often facilitates play. When teacher-structured activities occur there are fewer instances of prosocial behavior.[3]

Theoretical Explanations

During play with other children, children learn morals, gender roles, and social roles. Early childhood is a period of importance for this learn-

---

[3]Dwight L. Rogers and Dorene D. Ross, "Encouraging Positive Social Interaction Among Young Children," *Young Children* 41:3 (March 1986), 12–17.

STRATEGIES FOR INCREASING PROSOCIAL BEHAVIOR

Teachers can plan together with parents to increase prosocial behavior by using the following strategies.

1. *Keep groups at recommended size for age with a minimum of two teachers.* That is, twelve two-year-olds, fourteen three-year-olds, eighteen four-year-olds, twenty five-year-olds. Appropriate size groups and adult-child ratios should mean that there are enough adults available to observe children closely and facilitate prosocial behavior.

2. *Allow a minimum of 50–70 minutes in one block for free play time.* About this much time is needed for cooperative play to develop among children where prosocial behaviors typically occur.

3. *Verbalize the need for cooperative and helpful behavior toward fellow students.* Put your prestige on the line for these values.

4. *Reinforce positively a child using prosocial behavior.* Say, "I really feel good when you help Marty when he is hurt." Reinforce the specific child to let him or her know that you approved. Make the statement quietly to avoid making others feel competitive.

5. *Plan and carry out prosocial minidramas.* For example, encourage children to play out welcoming a new child to the room (like Olivia in the preceding example). See if children can take the perspective of the new child. (Evidence shows that bilingual children soon recognize to whom they can speak their native tongue. If they can take the perspective of another, then surely some other children can also.)

6. *Use problem-solving techniques to promote prosocial behavior.* For example, use "I" messages, talk-it-overs, and negotiation to let children express their feelings.

7. *Plan stories, songs, poems, and the like to reinforce cooperating and helpfulness between children at school.*

8. *Talk individually and briefly in groups about behavior that hurts good feelings between children.* Because children are egocentric, they seldom believe these "bad guys" could be them, but try it anyway and see what happens.

9. *Use photos and other illustrations in the room to illustrate people working together cooperatively.*

10. *Talk over your prosocial strategies with parents and encourage their help.* Car-pooling and visits at home between children often facilitate friendships among children.

ing. By using different theories you can gain different perspectives on play, especially dramatic play. For example, the psychoanalytic theorists like Freud and Erikson believe young children have sexual fantasies, that they have guilt feelings that result from some inner feelings and thoughts. Children eventually develop a superego, which contributes to the development of moral codes.

The behaviorists believe that moral codes and social roles are learned because of the way par-ents and others reward children for appropriate behavior or punish them for inappropriate behavior. Social learning theorists, on the other hand, believe that these learnings come as children observe those around them. Parents are important models in early childhood. Children are imitating their parents and other significant persons, according to social learning theory. Cognitive theorists focus on the child's ability to reason. Of course, children in early education programs are often too egocentric to understand another person's point of view. Most children must be in their fourth or fifth year before they understand right and wrong, and know that they can't change their sex by putting on clothes of the opposite gender.

Each of these approaches adds a dimension to understanding dramatic play. A fascinating study is to record an episode of children's play, then analyze it according to several of the theoretical approaches. None gives a complete answer; thus professionals will continue to puzzle over the meanings of children's behavior. It is wise to avoid hard-and-fast conclusions from a few samples of children's dramatic play.

Satisfying the Child

What are satisfactions that children derive from dramatic play? In the first place, they have a good time. Having fun is a strong motivator for young children. If they can have fun, they will willingly go along with most other goals the adult has for them.

In the second place, they make friends. They can choose companions and be chosen. Friendships grow out of a mutuality of interests and needs. When children are old enough for early childhood schools, companions their own age become increasingly important. Most children are drawn to other children of their own age.

Third, each has an opportunity to learn. Children are anxious to learn. They see their friends doing something and want to try it. They imitate their actions and their speech. Imitation is a great teacher. Children don't always tackle what is easy. Dramatic play encourages them to do better, climb higher, and become smarter than before. Dramatic play offers children an informal opportunity to pit themselves against new ideas and against their peers.

Fourth, by trying out various roles the child comes to understand himself or herself better. A role repeated frequently can be considered to have special significance for the child. Keeping notes helps teachers know the repeated themes.

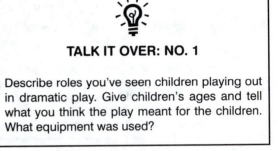

TALK IT OVER: NO. 1

Describe roles you've seen children playing out in dramatic play. Give children's ages and tell what you think the play meant for the children. What equipment was used?

Fifth, dramatic play offers the children the opportunity to release the natural abundance of energy each possesses. Children thrive on action. While awake, most are busily on the move. Freedom to keep moving and talking, which is allowed during dramatic play, permits the child to play as that energy level dictates.

Observing to Understand Children

Teachers and parents, too, seek ways to understand children and thus to promote their development more effectively. Dramatic play, whether it occurs at home or at school, can give insights into the behavior of children. Whereas most children enrolled in early childhood schools do not have deep-seated emotional problems that require play therapy, they may nevertheless have problems that could make them candidates for therapy should those problems continue unresolved. Teachers may have occasion to recommend therapy for a child after observing him or her for some time at school.[4]

Teachers should observe children's dramatic play carefully. Through a system of periodic observation and note taking, teachers develop evidence for decisions. Some teachers use self-sticking blank labels to write short notes on, then quickly transfer the note to a child's file, complete with date.

What can teachers learn from such observations? They will note the recurring themes and

---

[4]Ibid., Chapter 1.

Old telephones contribute to children role-playing the adults around them. Each classroom should have several phones. (University of Vermont)

the roles the child plays. They will know if a certain child seldom participates in dramatic play. Notes will show what he or she does instead. If a child is thought of as typically happy or cross or hostile, the teacher notes whether one type of incident or a particular group situation invites this typical behavior.

In a typical classroom certain children will require more adult guidance than others. Observing helps the teacher determine at what point guidance is called for with such children. For example, a child may strike out each time the teacher asks him or her to wait for attention. By observing this pattern in operation, the adults can make a concerted effort to satisfy needs for attention in some satisfactory way before the child acts out. Observation will reveal certain children who never cause trouble. What are they doing? Notes often point out children who seem hungry or ill or who lack physical stamina.

The teacher seeking answers will observe and listen. What questions do the children ask? What concepts are they using? What misconceptions do they have? Who are the leaders? What characteristics do the leaders have in common? Do some children enter groups easily? What techniques do they use? The answer to these questions may give the teacher a clue as to how to help a child who has difficulty entering groups.

The teacher looks at all behavior, not just negative or troublesome behavior. The positive relationships observed will build confidence that all children can learn to relate to their friends and use their blossoming intellects creatively.

Helping a Child Solve Personal Problems

The teacher's focus will be on recurring themes in a child's relationships instead of on isolated incidents. A few examples of teachers' actions follow.

The teacher helps build up the child's feelings of self-confidence—a positive self-concept. If children reveal that they feel little and helpless, the teacher seeks ways to help them feel bigger and stronger. If they reveal that they feel left out, ways are sought to help them feel included and wanted. If one reveals that big brothers are bossing him or her around, the teacher can accept his or her bossing in school, protecting only those children who can't protect themselves. If a child teases, the teacher notes whom and when the child teases and searches to understand why teasing seems satisfying.

A child may reveal certain fears through dramatic play or that family relationships are difficult. The teacher helps get feelings out in the open. The child can talk to the teacher and play out feelings with puppets or small figures. The teacher may read a story that initiates a discussion of the problem. Or, an endeavor to help the child through the parents is made.

It is not uncommon to observe a young child playing the role of the opposite gender during dramatic play. That is, a boy selects women's clothing or a girl selects men's clothing for dramatic roles. Much of this play is natural curiosity about each of those roles. The teacher, through close observation, can attempt to determine the significance of the behavior. Is the child merely trying out a role? How frequently does the play occur? Why does the child seem to prefer the role? What is the child's place in the total group? Does the role reversal give him or her unusual attention from adults and children? What is the home situation? Do the parents accept the child's real gender role?

The teacher's role when dealing with children who frequently play the role of the opposite gender is first to be certain that the dress-up closet contains many interesting men's as well as women's clothing. Helpers are advised to avoid giving undue attention to a child who dresses in this manner and to seek to show attention at other times. One can talk to individual children and the group about their various "pretend" roles to help them differentiate real from pretend.

Consulting Parents

Teachers have an obligation to alert parents to a child's problems. Teachers are not doctors or therapists and should avoid giving the impression they are. Observations should be made carefully, then thought be given about how to present the observation to parents. Naturally parents are very protective of their child and also very sensitive about their own parenting. If blamed, they can be expected to react negatively and defensively. Thus teachers need to learn how to state observations of problem behavior in a tentative manner as "this is what we've seen at school." Parents can be encouraged to do their own observations or to discuss behavior they may have noticed already. Things to try can be suggested.

If a child has difficulty relating to others, the teacher may encourage the parents to provide a companion for him or her. Children who ride together in car pools often have their plans for the day made when they get to school, so teachers may suggest a car pool to parents whose child is on the outside of the social groups. The teacher may suggest that they regularly invite one of the classmates home for a visit. The teacher may carefully pair this child with a child whose similar interests make him or her a prospective friend.

The teacher who observes that a child seems consistently tired or listless confers with the parents and may suggest a medical examination. If the child appears hungry, the teacher offers a snack early and checks with the parents to learn about mealtimes at home.

Teachers can watch for physical complications. For example, if children breathe through the mouth and are unusually loud in their eating, they may have enlarged tonsils and adenoids. Need for corrective shoes may be revealed as children are observed running across a wide expanse. The teacher encourages the parents to consult a specialist when such problems are observed.

Referrals to Outside Professionals

After doing some careful observations over time, the teacher will have consulted the school's internal professional sources for advice on a child's problem. Teachers should be frank to admit when problems are beyond their training and experience, or when they lack time for dealing with a child with special problems. When referring parents to outside professionals, the teacher should check the agency or clinic beforehand to be certain that the service parents might be seeking is available. It is difficult for parents to go from agency to agency and tell their child's problem. Then the teacher and parents should meet in a private conference where each can understand the other's concern and where a plan of action for the benefit of the child can be developed. The teacher can offer to follow through with a plan a therapist helps design that can appropriately be carried out in an early childhood program.

PLANNING FOR DRAMATIC PLAY

In planning for dramatic play, the teacher takes into consideration the group of children and the developmental tasks confronting each one. The teacher considers their age and their previous experiences at home, at school, and in the community. First plans are tentative. The plans are firmed up as the teacher gets better acquainted with the group. He or she encourages spontaneous themes to develop and willingly discards ideas that seem insignificant at a given time or for a given group. Plans include introducing numerous concepts and reinforcing learning through dramatic play. Frequently the teacher selects the specific ideas from the questions the children initiate, realizing that children will only be able to represent roles that they have observed. For example, children who have never been to a restaurant won't know how a waiter acts. Most could play McDonald's drive-through, however.

A rich, coordinated program is planned to open new vistas that children can incorporate into their dramatic play. Special visitors, trips, movies, pictures, books, and science discoveries are included in the curriculum plan. The plan, however, is more of a housecoat than a straitjacket.

Teacher's Role

The teacher must be a friendly, open, spontaneous, and creative person with many strengths that keep her or his personality on an even keel, even when emergencies arise. Deep personal regard for each child, which is conveyed openly and often, helps the children feel at ease in the teacher's presence.

Teachers must support dramatic play continuously if its values are to be realized. Just because the children are playing happily is no reason for the teacher to complete office tasks or make a trip to the principal's office. Measures that prevent problems are more effective than mopping-up procedures. When the class is operating smoothly is the best time to record the positive examples that will sustain the teacher in moments of discouragement. Moreover, activities should be enriched and extended at every opportunity. The teacher who keeps close to the children, observing and listening to them, can more meaningfully plan the highly motivating, worthwhile program that each child deserves.

Atmosphere

The teacher establishes an atmosphere conducive to meaningful creative dramatic play. There is an air of freedom that the children sense. They seem to be like the old slave who got his freedom after the Civil War. Someone asked him if he wasn't as well off under slavery. He was reminded that he had the same master, the same food, and the same bed. He replied, "Yes, except there is a looseness about this freedom that I like."

There is a "looseness" in the early childhood school that allows for spontaneous, impromptu,

About an hour of free play time is needed for children to build dramatic play structures and finally use them in their roles. (Oregon State University)

original, and different things to take place. There is a steady hum of talking, laughing, and learning as the children work individually and in small groups.

Time

Time is required for dramatic play to develop and for themes to be carried to satisfying conclusions. If the daily schedule is interspersed with many teacher-instigated activities, the children may find little opportunity to develop an idea before the teacher calls them to another circle. In such classrooms dramatic play soon withers.

In most schools dramatic play takes place during indoor and outdoor self-selected activity periods. If such play is to flourish, a minimum of 30 minutes, but preferably about 50 minutes, will be needed for the self-selected activity period. The teacher keeps the schedule flexible. For example, if the children have worked hard on getting a "train" ready for an imaginary trip, the teacher allows them to take at least one ride before announcing that it is cleanup time. On the other

hand, if the train trip is over and the children seem at loose ends for a new activity, the teacher may decide that it is a good time to clean up even though the clock doesn't quite say so. The teacher quietly warns the children when a transition is approaching, thus encouraging them to bring their activities to a close.

Allowing children to enter the playroom or yard and immediately start their dramatic play facilitates imaginative play. As a few children enter they are attracted to the areas that are available and proceed to get started. While traveling to school they will make plans for what they will do. The hour of free play begins easily, and teachers can greet each child individually and talk over where each might like to play.

This suggestion goes counter to some teachers' preference for having a group time at the beginning of the day, then letting children decide where they want to play. Such decision making may be useful for some purposes; however, it often deters the very spontaneity that is desired for dramatic play to develop to its fullest. Upon arrival children are frequently more physically ready for action than for sitting in a group time. You often get crowding in one center or must disallow a child's choice because too many children have already chosen a learning center. Children frequently cannot confer with their friends to see where they are going to play, thus eliminating an important element of choice. An initial group time does not serve many child care centers where children arrive on an irregular schedule. For some ages, having the whole group together is developmentally inappropriate. Teachers should evaluate their practices in light of total goals for the children.

Space

Adequate space is a requirement for dramatic play. Children need space to move around. Several areas of the room and yard can provide opportunities for dramatic play. Such areas are the work tables, the housekeeping area, the block area, the music area, the literature area, the woodworking area, and the outdoor area, which includes spaces for climbing, digging, riding, and using sand and other materials typically kept indoors. Having several areas available provides room for alternative activities should congestion occur in one location. See Chapters 4 and 9 for suggestions for the use of space.

Limits

Limits are defined, discussed, and maintained without punishment or harshness. Only those limits necessary to protect children, the learning environment, and property are set. Limits help children feel secure. Dramatic play should not become a free-for-all.

SUGGESTED PROPS FOR DRAMATIC PLAY THEMES

The following materials and equipment are suggested for enriching and extending the roles chil-

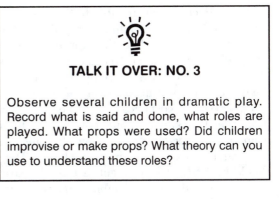

TALK IT OVER: NO. 3

Observe several children in dramatic play. Record what is said and done, what roles are played. What props were used? Did children improvise or make props? What theory can you use to understand these roles?

dren play. Props are placed where they will be noticed by the children. They are stored so that the children can find them readily and are kept orderly to suggest constructive creative play.

Dress-up

Both men's and women's clothing should be available. Castoff clothing makes good "dress-ups." Rummage sales are good sources of these materials. Children seem to be attracted to texture, so clothing articles of velveteen, satin, or fur are favorites. The crinoline petticoats of a bygone era are considered extremely elegant, especially when worn as "wedding dresses." Hats, purses, shoes, boots, and costume jewelry are also popular items.

Big brother's shirts, sport coats, Scout uniforms, vests, boots, and shoes are a better size for young children than are dad's. Hats for some community helpers—firefighters, police officers, bus drivers—can be purchased from school supply catalogs. Farmer and cowboy hats are available in variety stores. The metal hat of the lineman is popular and can be purchased in hardware stores. Painter's hats are often free at paint stores.

Long circle skirts encourage role-playing and creative dancing. A group would enjoy a number of these, which can be made by a teacher, parent, or professional. A simple elastic-filled waistband pattern that fits the largest child is used, then an ankle-length circle skirt is cut to fit the waist (the waist-to-ankle distance being the radius of the circle). A zipper should be placed in the front to make self-dressing easier. You can alter women's old skirts for self-dressing by putting elastic in the waistband or sewing Velcro on the opening.

Other popular costumes that can be made by a professional or skilled volunteer are clown, drum major, bunny, doctor, and nurse outfits. Children like bright colors in their dress-up clothes. They should be made of lightweight material because children wear them over clothing and easily get overheated.

Dress-ups should be stored so that they present a suggestive array from which children can choose and so that clothes stay in good condition. If clothes are stuffed into a trunk or a box, a chaotic disorder results that is not part of constructive learning. An open cupboard built at the children's level using regular coat hangers is one type of storage. Pegs may also be used. In most cases, some adult help will be necessary at cleanup time. Dress-up clothing should be laundered regularly. A good-quality, full-length mirror is indispensable in the dress-up area. Avoid Halloween-type clothing because it often contributes to overstimulation of the children.

Housekeeping

The housekeeping area or playhouse is perhaps the most common dramatic play area. This seems logical because the first roles the child assumes are family roles. Household routines and relationships affect young children very directly. They become alert to the people and the activities of the home. In the following example, roles are carefully self or peer assigned and played.

Five-year-olds are playing in the housekeeping area. They begin building another room along the playroom wall outside the housekeeping area. They use chairs to enclose their room. They move a number of toys into the "new house." The

Playing "baby" holds fascination for young children. They take turns playing the parent and baby roles. (U.S. Army Child Development Services, Baumholder, Germany)

three girls wear dress-up clothing. Susie is the mother, Ruth the baby, and Cindy a small child. Mark is the father. Baby says to Mother, "Pretend you came in and saw a baby." Mother pats Baby on the head and then says, "Now, Baby, you can get up. Your daddy is coming home." Father enters. Mother says, "Honey, will you put this toy in the box over there?" Father does as requested. The small child enters and starts to go out again. Mother commands, "Come back. Come back. Here, take this," giving the small child a toy. She then says, "Now you sit there and play until time to eat."

Furnishing the housekeeping area can be quite simple or very elegant, depending on ideas and financing. Staff and parents who have ingenuity and skill with tools can furnish the area at little cost. Old tables can be cut down, cupboards can be made with wood and cardboard boxes. Stove grills can be painted on one end of a box. The cushion from a car's backseat can be purchased at a salvage yard and used as an upholstered sofa or a child-size bed.

Durable dolls of various sizes and colors should be available. Dolls with molded hair are more durable and withstand the countless baths better than those with hair. Doll clothes should be made so that children can manage the buttons and zippers. Slip-on pants and skirts can be made with elastic belts and are good for those children who are interested in undressing and dressing dolls.

Other furnishings are small dishes, pots and pans, silverware, several telephones, mop, broom, and carpet sweeper. A doll carriage, a bed, and a small rocker are popular. A small chest of drawers for the doll clothes is important. A few food tins, cereal boxes, and a milk carton or two can be added.

The children can be very helpful in putting the materials away each day. However, the teacher should check before their arrival to be sure the area is clean and tidy. Materials should be washed as needed and dangerous broken pieces disposed of or repaired. To make the area inviting or to stimulate its use, the teacher may place a doll in a high chair and set out the baby food. Little parents take over from there.

If children want to use water or playdough in the housekeeping area, the teacher must establish limits. These materials do add to the realism. However, if the teacher finds the mess excessive, the children can be asked to use water and playdough elsewhere and to "just pretend" in the playhouse.

The housekeeping area should be rearranged occasionally to stimulate the play. Changing the location in the room may bring it to the attention of a child who hasn't played there before. For example, when the housekeeping area is close to the large block area, the two areas may supplement each other, and the children will move back and forth between a block structure and the housekeeping area. Some of the housekeeping equipment may be moved to equip a block house or may be moved outdoors to help extend the role-playing to the yard. In a study where the block and housekeeping areas were joined, researchers found an enhancement of social and play experiences, particularly of girls and younger children.[5]

Beauty Shop and Barbershop

The following materials invite beauty shop and barbershop play: a long mirror or several smaller ones, curlers, combs, a safety razor without the blade, whipped soap flakes for "shaving cream," and an old electric shaver. Large "hairdryers" can be made from round commercial ice cream cartons obtained at an ice cream parlor or supermarket. The carton is taped to a yardstick, then taped to the back of a small chair and set against the wall for support. Don't forget a stack of magazines or books nearby!

After beauty and barbershop play, dip the tools in disinfectant. Avoid this play altogether if the children have infections on the scalp.

---

[5]Cheryl A. Kinsman and Laura E. Berk, "Joining the Block and Housekeeping Areas: Changes in Play and Social Behavior," *Young Children* 35:1 (November 1979), 74.

Children may play many roles with a bare suggestion of realistic props, just as they do with realistic equipment. (Cloud County Community College, Concordia, Kansas)

Restaurant

During various cooking projects—making pancakes, hamburgers, or pizzas—the housekeeping areas can become a restaurant or a drive-in. Menus can be posted. Tablecloths can be made out of bright cloth. A cash register operator handles the money. Boys like Jim may like the play. He announced that he was the "cook" and this was his "restaurant." He methodically took orders. He indicated several times that a cook's role was acceptable for a boy in a restaurant but not in a house. The teacher took the opportunity during this role-playing to discuss with Jim that some men do cook at home. This was an effort to broaden his view of social roles.

Store

With a few shelves built from planks and blocks, a cash register, paper sacks, pencils, and note pads, children will enter into store play. A collection of grocery cartons and cans suggests a grocery store. The hats from the dress-up areas change it to a hat store. Shoes make it a shoe store. Play is enriched by trips to a supermarket or a department store.

Office

An old typewriter (provided free by some business machine companies), computer, telephones, tables, and chairs will be sufficient furniture for the office. The typewriter is a very popular piece of equipment and probably should have a permanent place in the classroom because of its importance to modern living. A microcomputer in the classroom may offer a similar opportunity for role-playing.

It is interesting to note children's concepts of an office. In one group where even a number of the children's mothers had offices, the children first used such equipment for a "doctor's office." They altered the teacher's initial arrangement by bringing in a bed from the housekeeping area. They searched for the stethoscopes. After several days of playing doctor, they thought of using the space as the parent's office. However, the roles they played were themselves. They indicated that crayons and paper had to be available. Drawing seems to be the child's pastime when he or she visits a parent's office. One mother with an office in her home recalls her two daughters dressed up in their "business clothes," carrying their "business suitcases" packed full of important manuscripts and books. They would go outside to the garage to get their "cars" (and often a doll in a stroller), then drive around the house to the office door to make their deliveries or pick up "jobs."

Post Office

Post-office play naturally follows the mailing of a letter to a friend or the posting of valentines. A schoolbag can be the mail carrier's satchel. A cardboard box can be painted to resemble the mailboxes the children see along the street. A collection of old holiday cards and inexpensive envelopes for the children to address provide mail.

A letter can be mailed to each child to prove that the postal system works. But if you give children stamps to put on their letters, many will lick off the glue, so be prepared with the glue bottle or glue stick to help finish the job. The newer self-adhesive stamps will minimize this problem. A visit to the post office and a talk with the postal clerk will add realism to the play.

Miniatures

Small figures of people, animals, cars, and trucks also contribute to dramatic play. Children are the manipulators of the scene, moving the figures around and speaking for them. Small blocks and construction toys may supplement the play. A model house of a size suitable for the people figures prompts domestic dramas.

Block Area

Both boys and girls will develop a variety of dramatic play themes in the block area. Using the large hollow blocks, children design space in which they function as actors. After one group built a room using these blocks, they all got inside and completely closed themselves in by placing a wheeled cart with a wire mesh side in front of the door. One boy said, "We are all in jail." His friends replied, "I knew we shouldn't have robbed."

During a period of reruns of "The Lone Ranger" on television, five-year-olds began building "horses" out of the large blocks. They stood three blocks upright, then stacked three lengthwise on top of the first three. They made a "neck" and a "head" with smaller blocks and finished their "Hi Ho Silver" with a tail of colored plastic scribble-sticks tucked into a crevice of the blocks in the appropriate place. They mounted their horses and called, "I'll meet you at Ransom Canyon." (Ransom Canyon was a local picnic spot.)

The large hollow blocks and packing boxes are free of detail and therefore allow the imagination free reign. They are very strong and will hold numerous children at play. See Chapter 12 for other details regarding block play.

Auxiliary toys enhance block play. A mounted steering wheel suggests the building of a car, a bus, a train, or an airplane. Models of domestic animals suggest a farm and wild animals a zoo. Cars, trucks, and trains encourage road building. Housekeeping toys, especially telephones, are popular in the block area.

In the following example economic information is combined with building, the children with the broader experience leading the way. Later on during a discussion the teacher could let Bill explain more about his ideas.

Four boys finished building a tunnel through which they could drive their cars, trains, and trucks. Everyone was lined up to make the grand entrance into the tunnel. Bill said, "We forgot one thing." "What's that?" Jack asked. Bill replied, "We forgot to put someone at the start to collect money from everyone." Jeff responded, "What?" Bill explained, "Yes, to help pay for building the tunnel." Jack hurried to the art table to get paper to make money.

Firefighters

A trip to the fire station, a fire in the neighborhood, or even a fire engine screaming past the school will often stimulate firefighter play.

With a little help children can make their own firefighter's hat. Using two sheets of a double-

FIGURE 15–1

Children can make a newspaper firefighter's hat, color or paint it if desired, then play the role of firefighter indoors or out.

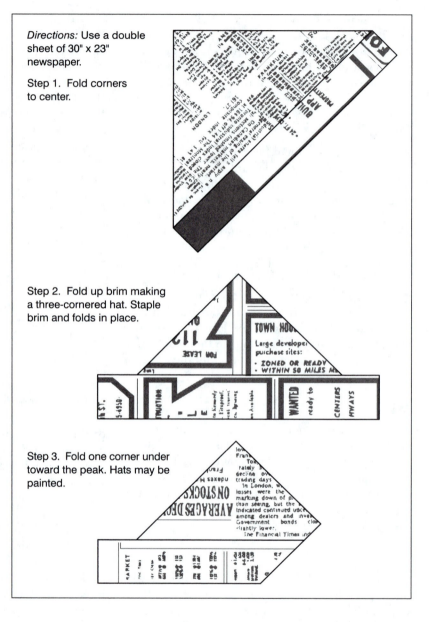

Directions: Use a double sheet of 30" x 23" newspaper.

Step 1. Fold corners to center.

Step 2. Fold up brim making a three-cornered hat. Staple brim and folds in place.

Step 3. Fold one corner under toward the peak. Hats may be painted.

paged newspaper (30-by-23 inches), fold along the original lengthwise fold. Bring the upper right and upper left corners together at the center line as you would to make the usual three-cornered hat. (See Figure 15–1.) About 3 inches remain to turn up for the brim on each side. Staple the brim to the hat body. Turn in one corner to the center peak and staple it in place. This leaves the other long corner to go down the back. These hats may be painted.

The newspaper hats or commercial plastic firefighter's hats team up with hoses, ladders, and red wagons when the children play out their helping roles, complete with sound effects.

Gas Station

Wheel toy "cars," of course, need gasoline. A large hollow block can become the gas pump if a piece of garden hose is attached to it. A plastic nozzle with a squeeze-type handle that comes with cleaning liquid can be attached to the hose. During warm weather the children can carry out a car-wash idea by washing the wheel toys. A few screwdrivers and pairs of pliers will foster mechanics play. Visits to a gas station, a garage, or a car wash will interest the young drivers.

Television

A window cut in a large cardboard box can serve as a TV screen. A few cereal boxes will encourage TV commercials. Puppets and musical instruments may invite performances. A few chairs or cushions can be arranged for the audience. A trip to a television studio will foster this play.

Camping

Camping is a popular family experience. A small tent erected in the yard will provide the children many opportunities for camp-related play. A sheet can be draped over equipment when no tent is available. Suitcases and fishing poles might be added.

Fishing

The children can simulate fishing by tying string to a stick. Magnets can be tied to the end of the string. If paper clips are attached to paper or plastic fish or to the Creepy Crawlers made with liquid plastic kits, the children will enjoy catching these fish. With this same setup, the children can "fish" numbers, colors, or the lotto cards out of a box. The paper clips should be securely attached to avoid a safety problem with very young children.

Farm

Farm play is popular in rural neighborhoods. For city children, concepts learned on a trip to the farm can be reinforced through dramatic play. Models of domestic animals and farm machinery are available. Barns can be constructed out of boxes. Hay bales can be added to the yard to roll around, to walk on, and to hide behind.

For young cowboys and cowgirls an old saddle mounted on a wooden sawhorse makes exciting riding. Because guns do not contribute positively to the goals for the child's development, the school does not provide such accessories. In fact, teachers usually have rules against using any toy as a gun, and guns that are brought to school are kept in the teacher's office for safekeeping and are not allowed to be used at school.

Construction

Construction play is fostered when road graders, bulldozers, trucks, and shovels are provided. Digging can take place in the sandbox or other digging area. Construction and road building are particularly popular when children can see construction taking place in their neighborhood. Children like to get inside large cardboard boxes that have been opened at both ends. They roll around the yard and may be called "bulldozers" by young workers.

Transportation

Youngsters' imaginations can transform ordinary packing boxes into a train. One plank across another becomes an airplane. A boat or the skeleton of an old car can be placed in the yard for the little drivers. These should be kept well painted to avoid a junkyard appearance in the yard. Traffic signs can be added to extend the play.

Space Exploration

Space exploration intrigues even the youngest. A large refrigerator carton can become the spaceship that blasts off after the countdown. With the teacher's help, opaque plastic milk jugs can be cut to resemble space helmets, and large paper grocery bags can be made into temporary space suits by cutting out holes for the head and arms.

Superheroes

Children eventually will start to play superheroes. The heroes chosen are often the ones being currently popularized on television. You may wonder how to handle this play. Many teachers feel that permitting superhero play allows outside forces to invade their school—interfering with more worthwhile plans for children.

Children may come to school with costumes—even realistic weapons! Weapons use is not allowed. These toys are stored in the teacher's desk until returned at going-home time. The costumes may be more problematic. Allowing costumes encourages others to invest in them—a use of funds that might better be spent for more appropriate toys. Some teachers let the child wear the costume briefly, then store it in a locker until taken home. One solution is that children only wear the school's costumes, which can consist of hats for firefighters, police, construction workers, farmers, cowboys, doctors, nurses, and the various other items stored in the dramatic play corner.

It is important to reflect on which children select superhero play and why. We should try to allow a child appropriate places to be powerful. However, we cannot allow the play to become violent and hurt others. These are times for teachers to observe and discuss with children, with parents, and among themselves to arrive at a policy. An article by Kostelnik, Whiren, and Stein has proven helpful to teachers. These teachers suggest the following ten ways to manage superhero play:

- help children recognize humane characteristics of superheroes
- discuss real heroes and heroines
- talk about the pretend world of acting
- limit the place and time for superhero play
- explore related concepts
- help children develop goals for superheroes
- help children de-escalate rough-and-tumble play

- make it clear that aggression is unacceptable
- give children control over their lives
- praise children's attempts at mastery.[6]

A discussion with parents in an early orientation meeting can help forestall some costumes being worn to school. An early stated policy helps parents keep from feeling they have to buy them. At the same meeting or at individual conferences you can clarify a policy about Halloween costumes, which frequently is "no costumes," due to children being frightened by the strange "people."

Conclusions

Dramatic play is the spontaneous, imaginative role-playing taking place in schools for young children during the self-selected activity period.

Dramatic play is a valuable activity because it contributes to the child's growth in all developmental areas, it provides adults an opportunity to gain insight into children's inner thoughts and feelings, and it affords teachers the opportunity to help children with some of the problems they might be having.

Children find dramatic play satisfying because they can have fun with their friends in meaningful, energy-releasing activities. Creativity is encouraged, and children enjoy learning about themselves by playing out numerous roles.

Planning is required to reap the benefits possible from dramatic play. An atmosphere of freedom is established by a teacher who is alert, warm, and responsive. Time and space are required and necessary limits must be set. An interesting array of materials and equipment will stimulate a variety of dramatic play themes.

Applications

1. Discuss the "Talk It Over" items found in the chapter.
2. Write an activity plan for a dramatic play activity for a few children using information and the sample plan (Figure 6–2) in Chapter

---

[6]Marjorie Kostelnik, Alice Whiren, and Laura Stein, "Living with He-Man: Managing Superhero Fantasy Play," *Young Children* 41:4 (May 1986), 3–9.

6. Secure approval, carry out the plan, and evaluate the results from the children's point of view and your viewpoint. Prepare a report and hand it in along with your approved plan.

3. Evaluate your total participation performance on your evaluation form developed in Chapter 1.

4. Add ideas and plans for dramatic play activities to your Resource File.

Study Questions

1. Define *dramatic play, symbolic play,* and *prosocial behavior.*
2. Explain how dramatic play contributes to children's development.
3. Explain why children find dramatic play satisfying.
4. Explain how observation of dramatic play can help teachers understand children. What theories are helpful? Does any theory tell the whole story?
5. Describe ways teachers can go about helping children with personal problems that are revealed through dramatic play.
6. State some precautions to be taken when preparing to discuss a child's problems with his or her parents.
7. Describe planning for dramatic play, especially the teacher's role, time and space allocation, and setting limits on behavior.
8. Describe five typical dramatic play themes and the appropriate props for each.

Videotapes

Curriculum for Preschool and Kindergarten
    16 minutes

Dr. Lilian Katz discusses appropriate curriculum for four- and five-year-olds. NAEYC Media, 1509 16th St. NW, Washington, DC 20036-1426, 1-800-424-2460.

Additional Readings

Berk, Laura E. "Vygotsky's Theory: The Importance of Make-Believe Play." *Young Children* 50:1, November 1994, 30–39.

Bredekamp, Sue, ed. *Accreditation Criteria and Procedures of the National Academy of Early Childhood Programs.* Washington, DC: NAEYC, 1984.

————. *Developmentally Appropriate Practice in Early Childhood Programs Serving Children from Birth Through Age 8.* Washington, DC: NAEYC, 1987.

Brown, Mac H., Rosemary Althouse, and Carol Anfin. "Guided Dramatization: Fostering Social Development in Children With Disabilities." *Young Children* 48:2, January 1993, 68–71.

Goffin, Stacie G. "Cooperative Behaviors: They Need Our Support." *Young Children* 42:2, January 1987, 75–81.

Hildebrand, Verna. *Guiding Young Children.* Upper Saddle River, NJ: Merrill/Prentice Hall, 1994.

Hirsch, Elizabeth S. *The Block Book.* Washington, DC: NAEYC, 1984.

Kostelnik, Marjorie, Laura Stein, Alice Whiren, and Anne Soderman. *Guiding Children's Social Development.* Cincinnati, OH: South-Western, 1988.

Kostelnik, Marjorie, Alice Whiren, and Laura Stein. "Living with He-Man: Managing Superhero Play." *Young Children* 41:4, May 1986, 3–9.

Myhre, Susan M. "Enhancing Your Dramatic Play Area Through the Use of Prop Boxes." *Young Children* 48:5, July 1993, 6–11.

Peters, D. L., J. T. Neisworth, and T. D. Yawkey. *Early Childhood Education: From Theory to Practice.* Monterey, CA: Brooks/Cole, 1985.

Rogers, Dwight L., and Dorene Doerre Ross. "Encouraging Positive Social Interaction Among Young Children." *Young Children* 41:3, March 1986, 12–17.

Schiamberg, Lawrence. *Child and Adolescent Development.* New York: Macmillan, 1988.

Trawick-Smith, Jeffrey. "Play Leadership and Following Behavior of Young Children." *Young Children* 43:5, July 1988, 51–59.

CHAPTER 16

Creative Music Activities

Texas Woman's University

Objectives

✔ Explain why children enjoy music activities in the early childhood school.

✔ Relate creative music activities to developmental tasks.

✔ Identify teachers' resources for increasing their abilities to plan and carry out music activities with young children.

✔ Identify, describe, and evaluate musical and movement activities for early childhood schools.

Jennie Jenkins

Will you wear red,
O my dear, o my dear?
O will you wear red,
Jennie Jenkins?
I won't wear red,
It's the color of my head,
I'll buy me a fol-de-rol-dy
Til-dy-tol-dy seek-a-double roll
Jennie Jenkins roll. (1)[1]

---

[1]Each song is given a number the first time it is mentioned. By referring to "Sources of Songs" at the end of the chapter, the reader can locate a book containing the music for each song.

T hus sang the kindergarten teacher introducing a new song. As the chorus ended,
the children clapped and called, "Sing it
again, teacher, sing it again." The teacher knew
then that they liked the song and continued with
other verses, using black, brown, blue, and green
in place of red. The children picked up the
rhythm and began clapping. They caught the
repeat and chimed in on "roll Jennie Jenkins
roll." The teacher sang a verse using "pink," they
rhymed it with "stink" and laughed hilariously!

"Jennie Jenkins" became a favorite. The song
would go on and on for as many verses as there
were children present. They felt each must have
a chance to choose a color before the teacher was
permitted to terminate the song. Children liked
to stump the teacher by choosing such variations
as "aqua" and "striped" that were hard to rhyme.

ENJOYING MUSIC: THE MAJOR GOAL

Why was "Jennie Jenkins" a children's favorite?
In the first place it has a catchy rhythm, a toe-
tapping tempo that stays with you for a long time.
It has a familiar element—colors—that each
child got a turn to name. "Jennie Jenkins" also
has freshness, a surprise of nonsense words that
especially tickle the funny bones of five-year-
olds. But most of all, the children simply enjoyed
the song—the most important reason for singing
it in kindergarten.

Children are natural musicians. Their feeling
for music begins early. Baby's first movements
are rhythmical—two feet kicking, two hands
waving. The infant experiments with different
tones while crying and babbling—long before the
ability to speak develops.

Singing and dancing are creative arts. The
emphasis in the school for young children is on
the child's enjoyment of musical expression
rather than on any particular outcome. Though
the teacher may start with words or a tune that is
well known, creativity is encouraged by permitting the children to interpret the music in their

Music can start in one-to-one experiences with a single
child. (Michigan State University)

own way, responding with new rhythms and
words. This same emphasis on the process rather
than on the product is suggested for all areas of
learning.

Children can be musically creative, and teachers and parents should get as much fun out of
their original tunes and dances as they do out of
their original utterances. No one says a child lacks
talent when sentences aren't adultlike, so is it fair
to say the child lacks talent when tunes aren't the
same as those of adults? Children do make many
original compositions that are a result of experimenting with sounds, rhythm, and singing. Adults
can simply say, "I liked your song."

Music can occur at any time of day. It happens
at work time, cleanup time, outdoor time, and at
dressing and undressing time. Children compose
songs, chants, and dances. In an atmosphere of
freedom and trust the child will express moods in
spontaneous music.

The goal is to introduce music to children so
that their lives will be richer. Music gives them
another medium through which they can express

their thoughts and feelings. Enjoyment is the first requirement. Any demand for perfection has no place at this young age. Care must be taken so music is not subverted, that is, used to upgrade deficiencies or learn concepts in a way that robs the child of an enjoyment of music.

Of course, there were some secondary values offered by "Jennie Jenkins" and other songs. By practicing the feel of words on the speech and hearing organs, children had a chance to say and hear words, rhymes, and sounds. They learned by rote, challenging their memory. Color concepts were introduced. Taking turns was required and practiced. Each of these values is important, but none is important enough for the teacher to sing the song if it does not bring joy to the children.

PLANNING MUSIC EXPERIENCES

Goals

Planning is required if children are to enjoy music, have a medium for expressing their thoughts and feelings, and lead richer lives because of their introduction to music. Just as is true of other areas of the curriculum, achieving the desired goals requires meaningful music experiences that will not result from haphazard teaching. Music for these years is an action art—as opposed to a spectator art or a performing art. The young children should have an opportunity to become personally involved in music, moving, trying various expressions, using no patterns, and receiving neither coercion nor criticism.

Supporting Developmental Tasks

Most of the developmental tasks of early childhood (see Chapter 2) are supported through creative music activities—independence, motor and language practice, social relations, following directions, remembering, and learning concepts including self-concept and body awareness.

Planning musical activities logically focuses on the children's developmental level and their prior experiences. Even the youngest infants are delighted with music. Singing to them readily gets their attention and often stops them from crying. Toddlers eagerly respond to rhythm records and like to march around a table and fall down at the end of the song.

Resources

The teacher must discover what the children know and how they feel about music. The resources can be surveyed, that is, the teacher's personal musical skills and knowledge and also those of the school, the families, and the community. The teacher remains open to ideas that encourage creativity in the children. Planning requires sitting down regularly to evaluate what is being done and to decide on new experiences to provide in the future.

Search for Ideas

Teachers must search constantly for ideas for music experiences. Those teachers with a music background have many advantages, of course, because they can play or sing a new song or play an accompaniment for dancing without much effort. But teachers without formal music training can also "have music wherever they go." To these latter teachers much of the following will be most relevant, for there are ways for teachers to compensate for lack of formal music training. Some of the best musical experiences for children are provided in groups in which the teacher's formal training in music is almost nonexistent. The secret lies in opening up the teacher's creativity and overcoming a lack of self-confidence.

Most adults know many songs that can be used with young children. The way to find out whether this statement is true of you is to make a list of songs you know. Start humming to yourself right now. Remember those old nursery songs your parents or grandparents sang? Or the camp songs for Scouts? How about hymns? Folk tunes? School songs? Popular songs? There you have six categories for your list. Add to it daily. Turn through songbooks, listen to records. You'll find a tape recorder useful for learning new song mate-

The Autoharp makes a nice addition to singing time. The teacher has small flannel figures to help children know the next figure to sing about. Later on they will think of their own animals and verses. (Georgia Southern College)

rial from parents or other teachers. Before you know it, you'll have a much larger repertoire than you might believe was possible.

Get used to singing out on those songs on your list. Work at remembering tunes. Try picking up the tune in the middle of a song. Share a song that you know but have never seen in print with members of your class. Or maybe you remember a tune to which classmates can supply words.

You have songs on your list that you think aren't appropriate for young children. But wait. If you've remembered the tune for many years, it must have special holding power. Could you use the tune and adapt words to it?

An example of an adapted song is the old hymn, "Jacob's Ladder" (2). Using that tune and part of the words you can sing

> John is climbing up the ladder,
> John is climbing up the ladder,
> John is climbing up the ladder,
>   Reaching up so high.

TALK IT OVER: NO. 1

Before reading further, write down the titles of songs you've sung since childhood. Add others as you read on. Share your list with your classmates and add to your own list as you recognize songs they know that you also know.

Of course, once you start this, several children may want you to sing them up the jungle gym. You can also give John advice—musically—such as

> John is holding very tight,
> John is holding very tight,
> John is holding very tight,
>   As he climbs a way up high.

Have you heard the song "Goodnight, Irene" (3) that folk singers have sung for years? You could sing it at rest time merely by inserting each child's name where "Irene" appears in the song. Or you could use it outdoors when you want to help a child.

> Come here, Millicent,
> Come here, Millicent,
> Come here, Millicent,
> Come here, Millicent,
> I want to tie your bow.

Teachers should feel at complete liberty to adapt any song to their needs. Creativity is the word. It's fun for the teacher and the children will love it, too. For example, here's the way "Old Roger Is Dead" (4) was adapted:

We Came to Our School

> We came to our school and we
> painted with paints,
> Painted with paints, painted with paints.

TALK IT OVER: NO. 2

Hum a tune that comes to mind. Think of a task at school. Now, put the tune and phrases common to the task together. Try it several times to your own work, then try it with children. Is it fun?

> We came to our school and
> we painted with paints.
> It was so much fun!

The teacher points to a child as the last phrase is sung, and the child comes up with the next activity phrase, for example, we climbed on the jungle gym, we played in the dollhouse, we built with the blocks, and so on.

A visiting musician provides a delightful opportunity for children to learn about an instrument and a musician and to sing a familiar song or two. (Oakwood College, Alabama)

Use Recordings to Learn Songs

Children's records and tapes can be used to help teachers learn new material to teach. By listening to the recording and writing down the words, you can learn quickly. You might like to take the recording home and sing as you get supper ready or do your homework. Of course, you could simply use the recording, having the children sing along with it. However, a recording often interferes with adapting songs to individual children or with adapting a song to the special needs of a group—such as giving them time to stand up or to laugh about the words. You might not like the pitch or the tempo of the recording. Having to operate the player may also interfere with spontaneity. But the biggest drawback yet may be that the recording is a crutch that teachers rely on when they could very well go it alone. Recordings can interfere with creativity—both yours and the children's. Thus, be brave—sing the song without.

Of course, recordings have an important place in the classroom. After you've learned a song from one, put it out on the listening shelf; you'll get a response like this one from Emily, who heard "Do-Re-Mi" (5) from *The Sound of Music*. She was overjoyed. She ran to Susie, her teacher, and pulled her to the music corner, "That's the song you taught us! We know that song. Teacher, I found our song. Listen!"

Children like to hear their favorite over and over. A familiar song is like an old friend that it's nice to run into. Therefore, teachers need not worry about using song material that some other teacher might use later on. Children will enjoy the song later if they like it now.

Trust Your Ability

Teachers should apply the principle of enjoyment to themselves as well as to the children. They should never try to teach a song or use a recording they don't enjoy. In the first place, there is such an abundance of good material, why do it? Second, the children will sense a teacher's lukewarm attitude, so they won't enjoy it either.

Many adults lack faith in their musical ability. Perhaps this is because the modern world is flooded with music via recordings, concerts, and television. It's probably because they have never been encouraged to think of themselves as musical. But even when you think you can't carry a tune you can still help children find joy in music. Children are uncritical and readily respond to a teacher's effort. Their response will be rewarding and encouraging. With repeated successes the teacher's confidence grows.

A common concern for students is, "But I have to sing in front of my supervising teacher!" What they may not realize is that the teacher went through the same conflicts when in training and is likely to be the least critical of all. The demonstration teacher knows that children will respond with joy to music if adequate opportunities are being planned for them—even when the leader has stage fright.

Some nonmusician teachers feel embarrassed because they don't play an instrument. However, most songs that are suitable for young children can be sung without the piano. Rhythms too are possible without the piano.

Using Instruments

When the piano is used for children's singing, it often overshadows the children's voices, so that neither they nor the teacher can hear them. Children may get lazy or become distracted by

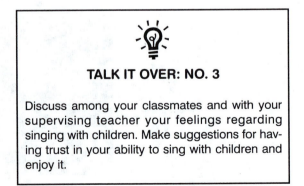

TALK IT OVER: NO. 3

Discuss among your classmates and with your supervising teacher your feelings regarding singing with children. Make suggestions for having trust in your ability to sing with children and enjoy it.

watching the pianist. Unskilled pianists are often slaves to the printed music and become flustered over deviations. Often they cannot watch the children and play; therefore a barrier exists between the teacher and the children. However, a mirror attached to the piano enables the teacher partially to overcome this barrier. Also, unless the pianist can transpose, the song may be played in a key that is suitable to neither the teacher nor the children.

On the other hand, an accompanist who can play by ear or one who follows the children rather than leads can be a great help at music time. Unfortunately, this talent is rare. Teachers therefore can plan to sing unaccompanied or try the chording instruments that will be discussed.

The guitar makes a delightful accompaniment for children's songs. Its simple chords need not overshadow the children's voices. Even though it is large, the children will want to have a chance to strum and test the tones resulting from changing the finger position on the strings. Many books of children's songs have chords marked that are suitable for piano, guitar, or Autoharp. The teacher needs only to play a few chords because it is best to keep the harmonies simple. In some songs only one chord is required for the entire song. See Figure 16–1 for the chords commonly used in children's songs.

A baritone ukulele is a melodious instrument that teachers find relatively easy to learn to play. Children call it a "guitar" because its size is about the same proportion to them that a guitar is to an adult. In areas where western and folk music are popular, this instrument will contribute to role-playing as well as to music. Because the baritone uke strings are tuned the same as the highest four strings of the guitar, any music showing guitar chords can be played (see Figure 16–1).

An Autoharp is a popular instrument for schoolrooms. It is held on the lap or in the arms; therefore it easily goes to singing time either indoors or out. The Autoharp has preset chords, so the player has only to push the lever to play

FIGURE 16–1
Guitar chords.

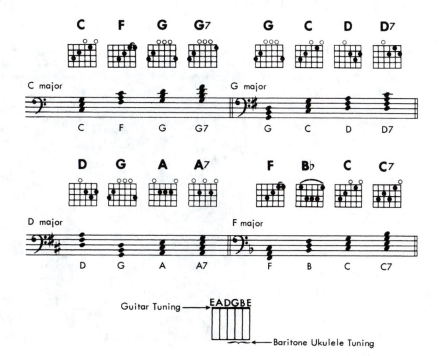

the desired chord. A fifteen-chord Autoharp offers the teacher the most variations. When the teacher wishes to use the Autoharp during singing time, it is well to have it out during self-selected activity periods. Children will get their turn for experimenting. If they feel satisfied, the teacher can say at singing time, "It is my turn now to use the Autoharp." The Autoharp, like any instrument, should be kept tuned. If necessary, the teacher may ask a music store or a musician to tune the Autoharp. Guitar and piano chords can be played on the Autoharp.

Singing

Singing can occur spontaneously in both children and teachers. Singing also occurs through the systematic introduction of songs at a regular group time.

New Songs

Though repetition is necessary for learning, variety is the spice of life in schools for young children as elsewhere. Because every song the teacher presents will not appeal equally to all children, the teacher provides variety in hopes of touching every child. It's important to bring new material to them every week; then no one song gets overworked until someone cries, "Not that again!" Because it takes several hearings before children will be able to sing a song, they should have a number of songs in various stages of learning.

The teacher keeps up a constant search for new songs. Some songs can relate to concepts being developed with the children. For example, as each season is studied, a number of songs are found that reinforce those concepts, let children practice the new vocabulary, and encourage them to express their feelings about the season. At the same time, songs related to their other interests are included, as well as nonsense songs and old favorite nursery songs.

One place to discover song material is to listen to the children. They often sing a song from home, television, or recordings that would be fun for the group. Children's records and songbooks will offer many suggestions. The nonmusician who needs help learning new songs can find songs in books and then locate them on records.

Experimenting and listening to their own music is fascinating to children. An important rule is to respect the piano as a fine instrument. (Bethany Weekday School, Houston)

Students and teachers often teach each other songs. Teachers make notes of songs they hear. Simply writing the words down helps them remember songs. The words help locate the song in a book or on a record.

New songs may be introduced as a story, or they may first be sung at the art or science table in the presence of only a few children. Because songs can accurately describe concepts, they may be used in this way. Having sung the song in a small group, children may want to hear it again during singing time.

If you are a student teacher, you will want to learn to manage the singing time without your teacher's help. Managing the children and handling discipline will be up to you. If the teacher feels required to step in to help you, it will be difficult for you to regain the children's attention. Therefore you must go to singing time with the confidence that your planning has been sufficient to carry you through.

Planning is very significant. It may look so easy and natural when your teacher leads singing—but she or he plans, too. Your control of the group begins as you plan, long before you sit before the group. Make a list of songs that the children might request—those the teacher has taught them. Do you know all the words? If not, write them down and learn them. Make a list of the songs you expect to teach. On index cards type the words to new songs and note the tune if the words are adapted from something familiar. Or, type words on the computer and cut out the words to fit your file cards. Notes will help you keep from forgetting. They will offer suggestions when you feel "blank." Forgetting is easy when you have had many things to consider, watch for, and remember, as teachers do at singing time.

Sit with the children on the floor or on a small chair. The piano stool is too far away for an intimate singing time to develop.

Look at each child as you sing. Smile so they know you enjoy singing with them. Shift quickly from a familiar song to a fingerplay to a new song. Pick up cues from the children so that you move

with the group instead of pushing against what they want to do. More than anything, have fun singing with the group and you'll find the children listening, singing, and responding. Discipline will be no problem.

Teaching a New Song

Sing a new song straight through at normal speed—just as you hope the children will learn to sing it. Let them catch the song's flavor. Don't exaggerate any part. If the song is short, sing it several times so the children become familiar with the ideas and the repeats. Don't ask them if they want to hear it again, for someone will surely say "No." Just sing. By the time it has been sung this way several times, the children will be chiming in. Don't wear it out, though, and don't dissect it—singing it a line at a time. This destroys the whole effect of the song. The next day repeat the same procedure. This time you can specifically invite the children to help you sing. By the third day many of your group will be beginning to sing. You will be able to tell whether they are going to like the song. If they fail to respond after three or four days, this indicates that the song apparently isn't for them at this time. Save that song until later. A song worth singing doesn't need to be pushed onto children.

Choice of Songs

Children are attracted by action songs. Such songs give them a way to participate with their hands and sometimes their whole bodies. The actions will attract some children who may do the actions long before they sing many of the words. Clapping can accompany some songs that don't suggest other actions.

Content of Songs

Elements of familiarity are important in songs. The teacher searches for songs about things the children know, such as children, animals, bugs, snow, wind, space flight, and so on. However, the teacher does not explain a song word for word but lets most of the song's meaning come to the children as they sing and as they experience their

ACTION SONGS

Eency Weency Spider (6)

Eency weency spider went up the water spout,
Down came the rain and washed the spider out,
Out came the sun and dried up all the rain,
And the eency weency spider went up the spout again.

(*Actions:* Use fingers to imitate spider going up. Wiggle fingers to give rain effect, encircle face with hands for the sun, and make the spider climb again.)

Where Is Thumbkin?
(Tune: "Frère Jacques," or "Are You Sleeping?") (7)

	Actions
Where is Thumbkin?	(Hands behind back.)
Where is Thumbkin?	
Here I am.	(Bring hands out, thumbs extended.)
Here I am.	(One thumb bows to other.)
Howdy-do dy day sir?	(Other thumb bows in return.)
Very well I thank you,	(Return behind child.)
Run away, run away.	

Other verses: Pointer, middle, ring finger, and little finger. (The last two are difficult for small children to extend, but they like to try.)

The Wheels on the Bus
(Tune: "Mulberry Bush") (8)

	Actions
The wheels on the bus (car)	(Children roll hands around each other.)
Go round and round,	
Round and round,	
Round and round,	
The wheels on the bus	
Go round and round	
All over town.	
Other verses:	(Short claps.)
Money goes clink	(Fingers go back and forth.)
Wipers go swish	(Pretend to honk.)
Horn goes beep	(Pretend to cry.)
Babies go waa	

If You're Happy and You Know It (9)

If you're happy and you know it,
Clap your hands (clap clap).
If you're happy and you know it,
Clap your hands (clap clap).
If you're happy and you know it,
Then your smile will surely show it.
If you're happy and you know it,
Clap your hands (clap clap).

Other verses: Pat your head (pat pat); Toot your horn (toot toot); Touch your nose (tap tap).

---

world. If a song has a catchy melody in a suitable range, children will sing it with gusto even if they do not understand it entirely. Their renditions of hymns and patriotic songs offer humorous examples of this fact. The range from middle C to D, a ninth above, is appropriate for kindergarten, with middle C to A being better for young children who are learning to sing.

Concepts the children are learning can be the subjects of songs, but teachers should keep in mind that children must also enjoy the songs. By singing a new word, children receive a kinesthetic or sensory experience in the speech and hearing organs from which other understandings can grow. Of course, a counting song combined with pointing to objects—fingers or children— will help a child learn numbers. The teacher sings "Mary Wore a Red Dress" (10); Mary stands up, and Alonzo sees her red dress and his color concepts are improved. If the children enjoy singing the ABCs to the tune of "Twinkle Twinkle Little Star" (11), there's no harm done and they get the kinesthetic experience necessary for beginning to know the alphabet. Teachers dealing with children of all languages can use songs to help build vocabulary and provide ear training.

Songs that call for children's individual participation have strong appeal. Teachers will need as many of this type of songs as they can find. They should feel perfectly comfortable adapting songs to the needs of their groups. Sometimes the child's name is used, sometimes he or she gets to select the animal or activity that goes into the verse. In the song "Where Oh Where?" on page 352, the child's name and shirt color are designated.

"What Shall We Do When We All Go Out?" (17) can be sung with each child suggesting a different outdoor activity. After a few days this song can become a cue song—like a closing hymn in a house of worship—that tells the children that outdoor time has come.

When "The Farmer in the Dell" (18) is altered to say "The Farmer Has a _____," each child can select a different animal or machine for the farmer. The children may eventually become quite imaginative, selecting such animals as deer, dolphins, or dodo birds. Their suggestions are usually indications of their imaginations, not their lack of concepts. Such jokes are signs of their increasing maturity.

Other songs calling for individual contributions are "When I Was a Young Maid" (19), which

SONGS ADAPTED TO TEACH CONCEPTS

Color Song
(Tune: "Pawpaw Patch") (12)

Children wearing red, please stand up.
Children wearing red, please stand up.
Children wearing red, please stand up.
So we can see your colors.

Note: The song continues designating the colors the children know, introducing new colors, and at the same time letting each child stand at least once.

Do You Know?
(Tune: "Muffin Man") (13)

Do you know the firefighters,
   the firefighters,
   the firefighters?
Do you know the firefighters
   who drive a big red truck?
Oh, yes we know the firefighters,
   the firefighters,
   the firefighters.
Oh, yes we know the firefighters
   who drive the big red truck.

Other verses: Police officers—police car
           Mail carriers—red, white, and blue jeep
           Garbage collector—gray truck

Counting Song
This Old Man (14)

	Actions
This old man he played one,	(1 finger up.)
He played nick-nack on my thumb;	(Tap thumb.)
Nick-nack, paddy wack,	(Clap.)
Give my dog a bone,	
This old man came rolling home.	(Roll hands over each other.)
2—on my shoe	(Tap shoe.)
3—on my knee	(Tap knee.)
4—on my door	(Knock on floor.)
5—on my side	(Tap ribs.)
6—on my sticks	(Tap fingers.)
7—up in heaven	(Tap reaching high.)
8—on my pate	(Tap forehead.)
9—on my spine	(Tap backbone.)
10—once again.	(Applause.)

Old MacDonald's Farm (15)
(Tune: Traditional)

Old MacDonald had a farm,
E–I–E–I–O
And on this farm he had a duck,
E–I–E–I–O
With a quack quack here,
And a quack quack there,
Here a quack, there a quack,
Everywhere a quack quack,
Old MacDonald had a farm
E–I–E–I–O.

Other verses: Let the children select the other farm animals to sing about.

Up in a Space Capsule
(Tune: "Up in a Balloon") (16)

Up in a capsule, boys (girls),
Up in a capsule,
Flying 'round the little stars
And way out to the moon.
Up in a capsule, boys (girls),
Up in a capsule,
Won't we have a jolly time,
Up in a capsule!

Parts of My Face
(Tune: "Ten Little Indians") (14)

Eyes, ears, nose, and mouth;
Eyes, ears, nose, and mouth;
Eyes, ears, nose, and mouth;
Belong to my face.

Note: The children touch each part as they sing.

Ojos, Orejas, Nariz, Boca
(Tune: "Ten Little Indians") (14)

Ojos, Orejas, nariz, boca;
Ojos, Orejas, nariz, boca;
Ojos, Orejas, nariz, boca;
Son parte de me cara.

Diez Gatitos (Ten Little Kittens)
(Tune: "Ten Little Indians") (14)

Uno, dos, tres gatitos,
Cuatro, cinco, seis gatitos,
Siete, ocho, nueve gatitos,
Diez gatitos son.

Note: Insert *niñitos*—children, *politos*—chicks, *perritos*—puppies, etc.

¿*Dónde Está Juanito?*
(Tune: "Pawpaw Patch") (12)

¿Dónde, dónde, está Juanito?
¿Dónde, dónde, está Juanito?
¿Dónde, dónde, está Juanito?
¿Él está allí?
¿Dónde, dónde, está Maria?
¿Dónde, dónde, está Maria?
¿Dónde, dónde, está Maria?
¿Ella está allí?

Note: Insert each child's name. Use *él* for boys and *ella* for girls.

Vamos a la Escuela
(Tune: "Pawpaw Patch") (12)

Vamos, vamos a la escuela,
Vamos, vamos a la escuela,
Vamos, vamos a la escuela,
A la escuela hoy.

Note: Add verses with activities such as

a *pintar*—to paint
a *jugar*—to play
a *leer*—to read
a *cortar*—to cut
a *dormir*—to sleep

Spanish versions of songs are given above. You can use them when teaching Spanish or working with Spanish-speaking children.

Where Oh Where?
(Tune: "Pawpaw Patch") (12)

Where oh where is dear little *Jimmy*?
Where oh where is dear little Jimmy?
Where oh where is dear little Jimmy?
Way over there with the *blue shirt* on.

Note: When the teacher must sing everybody's name, try putting several together—Where oh where are Peter, James, and John?

calls for occupations and tools, and "Monkey See Monkey Do" (20), in which the child suggests a motion for others to make.

Teachers should know lullabies as well as rousing songs. A quiet song is worth a thousand shushes, just as are the quiet fingerplays suggested in Chapter 12. A quiet song can help restore order out of chaos. The teacher can start a song like "My Pigeon's House" (35) in an I'm-telling-a-secret voice, singing to two or three children who are sitting near, then scan the group with active eyes, encouraging others to listen and join the singing. The teacher nods and smiles to children who begin listening. The songs work their miracle as one child after another relaxes and begins to listen and sing.

Soothing Songs

Kumbaya (21)

Mary's listening, Kumbaya,
Mary's listening, Kumbaya,
Mary's listening, Kumbaya,
Oh, Oh, Kumbaya.

Hush, Little Baby (22)

(Tune: Traditional)

Hush, little baby, don't say a word,
Mommy's going to buy you a mocking bird.
If that mocking bird won't sing,
Mommy's going to buy you a diamond ring.

If that diamond ring turns to brass
Mommy's going to buy you a looking glass.
If that looking glass gets broke,
Mommy's going to buy you a billy goat.

If that billy goat won't pull,
Mommy's going to buy you a cart and bull.
If that cart and bull turn over,
Mommy's going to buy you a dog
named Rover.

If that dog named Rover won't bark,
Mommy's going to buy you a mule
and cart.
If that mule and cart fall down,
You're still the sweetest little boy in town.

Guidance can be sung instead of spoken and is often more effective as a result. Each teacher will have favorite tunes that readily come to mind and can be used with guidance phrases such as "Barry, walk around the puddle" or "Time to go indoors." Cleanup time can be lots more fun if everyone bursts into song as materials are put away. They can sing "Pickin' up blocks, put them on the shelf," instead of "Pickin' up pawpaws" (12). "Here We Go Round the Mulberry Bush" (8) readily becomes a cleanup song when it's time to put things away.

Cleanup Time

(Tune: "Here We Go Round the Mulberry
Bush") (8)

This is the way we stack the blocks,
Stack the blocks, stack the blocks,
This is the way we stack the blocks,
When it's time for cleanup time.

Other verses: Wash the easel, wash the
paint brushes, or wipe the tables.

The late four-year-olds and five-year-olds will enjoy songs with cumulative verses. "The Twelve Days of Christmas" (23) is a familiar example. For such long songs the teacher can prepare drawings to illustrate each verse so the children can "read" as they sing. Drawings help them learn more quickly and help the teacher too. The following are songs of this type: "Had a Little Rooster" (24), "I Bought Me a Cat" (25), and "I Know an Old Lady" (26).

The use of sad songs is often discussed by teachers. Some believe that sadness should never be a part of a song for young children. Others believe that a sad song may help the child learn about feelings. They feel that a child may use a sad song to express inner sadness. The song may help bring concerns out where they can be dealt with. "Old Roger Is Dead" (4) and "Go Tell Aunt Rhodie" (27) are considered sad by some teachers.

Of course, a child's reaction to a song will depend on the way it is sung. Songs that seem sad to adults may not seem sad to children. Whether a teacher uses sad songs should be up to the individual because one of the requirements in choosing songs is that the teacher enjoy the music presented to children. If a sad song has special meaning for a teacher, she or he should be free to try it with the children. They may sense that feeling and appreciate the song too.

Allowing children to select songs during singing time is important because it makes the period more their own. No harm can come from singing "Jingle Bells" (28) in June, so a seasonal choice should be honored as would any other. A teacher must, however, decide from moment to moment how much to lead and how much to follow the children. Occasionally, one child wants the same song every day, and others don't get a turn to choose. If the entire music period is regularly left in the children's hands, stagnation will set in very soon. The teacher's skill and tact are required to balance the offering of a new song with the familiar songs the children enjoy. Good balance results from planning and from being sensitive to children's moods. The teacher can learn to sense the children's moods and follow the leads they give. The length of the music period will vary from day to day depending on the children's response.

The following are examples of leads that a teacher might follow: If a child kicks his or her heels, perhaps the teacher can think of a song in which kicking might be an appropriate sound effect. If the children lie down as though sleeping, try to think of a sleeping song. If a child should pretend to play the guitar, can the teacher think of a song that could work this in? If the

children have been sitting for quite a while, can the choice be a song that would get them up for a stretch, then get them to sit back down so that a story could follow? By following the children's leads, the teacher can make the singing experience fun, relaxing, and creative, yet organized enough so that it is pleasant for everyone.

When teachers establish an atmosphere of freedom and use music creatively throughout their teaching, it won't be long before the children will be bursting out in song wherever they play. Both their tunes and their words may be original. If the teacher can capture some of these compositions in notes and sing them back to the child, they will show that the accomplishments are appreciated.

Carol was heard responding to the question, "Do you need a push?" She sang:

> I can push myself so high
> I can just fly
> Into the sky.

Another sang:

> Hooray for today!
> I can play all day!

Exuberance for life showed when yet another sang:

> I love these snowy days!
> It's fun today!

Young children's spontaneity and zest for living are pleasurable to behold.

Creative Movement

Children are naturally rhythmical in their movements. Swinging, jumping, swaying, whirling, tapping, and running are rhythmic movements familiar to any teacher of young children. Movement is important to children. From the smallest wiggling finger to the largest leaps, the child

---

TALK IT OVER: NO. 4

Describe creative movement activities you've seen children do. State children's ages, the music used, and outcomes.

---

loves to be in motion. The teacher's role is to establish the atmosphere of freedom that lets the children express their feelings, and there will be rhythm.

Many interesting rhythms are noted during activities that may not be thought of as rhythmical, such as cutting, painting, or rocking in the rocking chair or the rocking boat. Teachers may help children recognize these rhythms. They might develop a chant to go with one of them, like

> Pound, pound, pound, pound, pound
> on the clay.
> Pound, pound, pound, pound, pound
> it down.

Spontaneous dancing often results when classical music is played on the tape or record player. The children will enjoy wearing long skirts for whirling and twirling to the music. Long streamers of colored fabric or paper or colored scarves will prompt a gentle flowing rhythmic expression. The following compositions lend themselves nicely to children's interpretive movements:

Hungarian Dance No. 1 by Brahms

"March of Toreadors" by Bizet

Sousa marches

"Waltz of the Flowers" and "Dance of the Sugar Plum Fairy" from the *Nutcracker* by Tchaikovsky

Movement can also be accompanied by a piano, a tom-tom, a tambourine, or clapping.

Children need space so their movement does not interfere with that of others. However, once children are spread out in the room or the yard, they have difficulty hearing the teacher's suggestions and comments. Teachers know that shouted guidance is ineffective. The teacher can solve the problem by developing a signal so children will know when it's time for them to come together. The signal could be one loud "bang" on the tom-tom or three taps. The teacher can call them to a "secret huddle" to talk over the plans for the next activity. The huddle will help keep the children's attention.

Children can be encouraged to use their imaginations to suggest movements to make. They can name birds or animals to imitate. They can imitate machines—large like a bulldozer and small like the mixer at home. Sound effects go with rhythms, of course. This is rarely a quiet time of day.

Children can be encouraged to use their space by jumping their highest or crawling their lowest. They can experiment with different ways to move through space—walk, run, hop, jog, leap, twirl, skate, slide, creep, glide, gallop, skip, and BLAST OFF! The teacher can pick up the rhythm of a particular child and tap it out on the tom-tom. "Jason, your rhythm pattern is tap, tap-tap, tap, tap." The teacher may say, "That was a HIGH leap, Jennifer." "What a smooth glide you have, Dennis!" A child who wouldn't participate in dancing may happily jump on a jumping board or a mattress. The teacher can recognize movement by tapping out the rhythm or singing a song to its beat.

A teacher may crumple a plastic shopping bag in the children's presence. They watch it unfold, then they pretend to be a crumpled-up plastic bag. Many exhibit lovely, unusual movement. With older children, who won't mind if balloons break, setting several balloons loose in the room may stimulate skipping, leaping, and running to keep the balloons floating through the air.

If the children seem overactive during planned rhythm experiences, they may need to be more active otherwise or they may already be overtired. Children can be rested by doing small movement with eye, tongue, finger, head, and nose as they relax on the floor.

There should be no desire to get every child doing the same thing. Take care to recognize each child's unique contribution. Children will be freer without their shoes. Be sure to plan for taking shoes off, their storage, and how you'll get them back on without creating chaos.

Teachers can use children's creative imitations to help at transition time. "Hop like bunnies to get your coats" or "Now on quiet feet like a mouse, let's go to the video room."

Listening Activities

The opportunity to listen is important for growth in music appreciation. Listening is also important for language development. Many of the opportunities offered through music make important contributions to language. Acuity is tested. Memory is developed through listening activities.

Records and Cassette Tapes

An area of the room can be furnished with recordings and a record or cassette player that the children are allowed to operate. Dancing, marching, and the playing of instruments may occur spontaneously. The children should also be able to listen uninterruptedly to a musical selection or a story. Attention spans are often quite long when children are listening to music voluntarily during the self-selected activity period.

Children can be taught rules for caring for the recordings and the equipment. A rack should be available for holding records and tapes so the children can learn to place them in the rack rather than on chairs and tables. A small selection should be available and changed frequently. Many teachers have success with tape recording songs they wish to teach children. Some children can handle the tape player themselves.

Sound

Many experiments with sound are related to music. Glass juice bottles can be tuned. Colored water in different amounts is added to eight bottles until the notes of the scale can be played by tapping each bottle with a wooden mallet. The advantage of tuning bottles instead of drinking glasses is that lids can be placed on the bottles to prevent evaporation when not in use. Sound experiments also result from putting on and taking off the lids.

Vibrations cause sound. Vibrations can be felt in one's own throat, and some children discover this themselves. Children can feel instruments vibrate simply by placing a hand on the instrument. A shoe box can be strung with rubber bands of different widths and tautness, which are plucked to create various effects. Children can relate the experiment to the guitar, the Autoharp, and the piano. During such a study children will enjoy a trip to hear a harpist. Other stringed instruments may be brought into the school for listening and experimenting. Piano tuning is interesting for children to watch. Also, many listening experiences will be carried on by children as they play the piano. Rules should be established so that the piano is treated with the respect due a musical instrument.

Special Events

A trip to a school music room can help children learn about the sounds made by various instruments. They will like a close-up view. They like to go to band practices and watch the musicians up close.

Frequently delightful music experiences can be provided by the parents and siblings of the children in a class. For example, a father who was an evangelist singer came to sing. He made up songs, using each child's name. Another father brought his banjo. After a number or two he had each child use a hollow block for a drum—what rhythm resulted!

One child's brother played the trombone, another a steel guitar. A sister twirled. Another

Earphones provide the opportunity to listen to music without interfering with other children's activity. (University of South Carolina)

sister came with her friend. Wearing a striking Spanish dress, the sister danced the exotic Spanish flamenco. The friend made a striking contrast with a slow, graceful dance in a pastel ballet dress and slippers. A mother who played the lead in the community production of *The Sound of Music* taught children to sing "Do-Re-Mi" (5).

By singing songs from their countries, foreign students can help children learn about peoples of other lands. At the same time foreign students learn about American children.

Many opportunities such as those suggested will develop children's listening skills. Children also practice appropriate behavior as a member of an audience. However, each guest was advised ahead of time about ways to include the children in the presentation. The children thus became part of each experience. The involvement of family members is especially important to a child.

Rhythm Instruments

Rhythm instruments can be used creatively. They are placed in the music center so that the children will use them alone, accompany themselves in singing, or tap out a rhythm as a record plays. The children may organize their own band. When they do, the teacher will notice that they keep excellent time to the marching rhythm. A few recordings of good marches such as those of college marching bands will be sufficient stimulation.

Gone are the days of sitting everyone in a row to hold an instrument until time comes to tap just so. Rigid adult structure curtails creativity. When children organize a marching band, the teacher's role need only be to place a table or a collection of chairs in the center of the room to guide the direction of the march. Children think of a march tempo as "parade" music, so marching is important. If there is an insufficient number of the favorite instruments, the teacher may get agreement on a signal that tells the children when to exchange instruments. If the teacher plays the piano for the marchers, the rhythm should be clear and strong. Then the children can keep time.

Children have a number of opportunities to see marching bands on television. Attending a parade or visiting a marching band practice will create interest. If a child's sibling plays a band instrument, she or he can be invited to play. A twirler will interest children, too. Parents should be alerted about forthcoming public parades.

Several good-quality tom-toms, bongo drums, and maracas invite individual and small-group experimentation with primitive rhythms.

Musical Guessing Games

The teacher asks, "What tune is this?" after humming or playing a tune on the piano. The children guess. The children, too, can have turns humming tunes for others to guess.

Using the tom-tom, the teacher can tap out the children's names. First, start by choosing two children to stand up, then say, "Whose name am I tapping?" The teacher can plan ahead, selecting children whose names have contrasting beats.

Some teachers record each child as he or she sings or talks, then brings the tape for the children to hear as a group. This gives the children another guessing game requiring listening to distinguish whose voice is being played.

Singing Games

Some of the group games used with older children must be adapted if they are to be used with kindergarten children. Many are totally unsuited to prekindergarten children. Too many rules, too many specific directions, and competition make them too complicated. Even the traditional manner of playing "The Farmer in the Dell" (18) is too complicated. Young children don't understand not being chosen. Some teachers improvise verses until each child is in the circle. Another alternative is to divide the group into several circles with an adult in each; then the game can be played in more or less the traditional manner. If all the groups are in the same room, they can still sing together.

The game of musical chairs is popular with elementary school children but is not recommended for younger children because a child cannot understand being left out. In this game sufficient chairs are available minus one. The group marches around until the music stops, then everyone runs for a chair. However, if at this point the child who is left out gets to choose a rhythm instrument and becomes part of the band, the child's concern about not having a chair is somewhat removed. Better yet, just do the game with enough chairs for everyone. Children will still enjoy the game.

Games requiring children to hold hands and move in a circle are also too structured. Often, however, it is just as well to let children stand where they will and move in their own circle. Late four- and five-year-olds will enjoy "Did You Ever See a Lassie?" (29), "Monkey See Monkey Do" (20), "Mulberry Bush" (8), "Round and Round the Village" (30), and "Punchinello" (31). Younger children may like "Ring Around the Rosy" (32), "Sally Go Round the Moon" (33), and "London Bridge" (34) if the teacher lets them move where they want to.

Singing games may be used to substitute in part for outdoor exercise when a sudden storm prevents going out. Children much prefer going outdoors; therefore, singing games should be used for this purpose only occasionally. Tumbling and rhythms offer energy release in a similar manner.

ROLE OF PARENTS IN A CHILD'S MUSICAL EDUCATION

Numerous times in the previous sections suggestions have been made for involving families directly in the music program of the school. Not only does a richer program result when families are involved, but each child whose parent participates gets a special boost. Parents make a significant contribution and feel more comfortable at school when they are invited to demonstrate some special skill to the children. By coming they gain a better understanding of their child and the school.

Teachers can keep parents informed about what their children are doing in music at school. As experiences are planned with the children's developmental level in mind, the teacher should be able to provide helpful suggestions for parents. Parents may seek guidance as to the appropriateness of piano, dancing, or voice lessons. The teacher should become familiar with the music programs offered in the community in order to guide parents.

Teachers can watch for musical events in the community that families can attend to add to their enjoyment of music. Examples are a children's theater musical or a symphony concert planned especially for children. The teacher can see that parents have this information, including information on admission charges. Children enjoy attending parades to see the musicians and hear the music.

Music at Home

Teachers may also encourage the parents' enjoyment of music with their own children. Words to children's songs can be sent home. Then when the child is singing, the parents can refer to the song sheet and grasp more clearly just what the child is singing about. Perhaps they can even sing along. In a parents' meeting they may wish to sing some of the songs. Teachers can explain their purposes and demonstrate techniques for working with children.

Parents may seek guidance about the type of record or tape player and recordings to buy. Teachers can be more helpful if they visit shops and have an idea of what is available locally. Sometimes a teacher can guide the choice that is offered by conferring with the owner of a local music store. Public libraries have recordings and videos to lend, just as they have books. Parents may need this information, because some may not be aware of their availability for children's listening.

It is important for children to have their own songbooks. This is true even though no one in the family plays an instrument. Because children's songbooks are often beautifully illustrated,

children can "read" their favorite songs by recognizing the pictures. Children will turn through the book and sing to themselves. Teachers can provide parents with names of appropriate songbooks. Some are available in libraries. Many families report having songfests with their children. Others say that bedtime singing sometimes takes the place of bedtime stories.

Presenting Programs

In some schools one traditional way of communicating with the home is to have the children present a program for the parents. However, caution is advised! If the tradition seems harmful or totally developmentally inappropriate for the children, the teacher has a professional obligation to ask for changes in the format. The preparation for and the performance of the program should not be harmful in any way to even one child. No child should feel that he or she is being exhibited, left out, or embarrassed. The program should have educational benefit to children.

The children and the teacher can plan a simple program. They can decide together what things they would like to share with the parents. The program should be short, only 10 to 15 minutes. It should never be rehearsed until no fun remains in the numbers. (Sadly enough, overrehearsed programs are common at Christmastime.) No child should be allowed to star. This keeps competition from developing among children and parents. Memorized lines should be avoided.

An acceptable program topic would be "a day in school," for example, showing the singing and rhythm time as customarily carried on in the classroom. By seeing such a program, parents learn about the school's goals and techniques. There is room for the children's natural spontaneity to occur. The children will be at ease because the format is familiar.

Conclusions

Music in the early childhood school takes specific planning, just as is required by other parts of the curriculum. Planning is required if the children are to enjoy music, have another medium for expressing their thoughts and feelings, and lead richer lives because of their introduction to music.

The children's developmental levels and their previous experience are taken into consideration in the planning of music activities.

Teachers without formal music training can provide a good music program if they make a special effort to overcome any feelings of inadequacy. They will seek variety in the materials they present. They will watch the children for cues and leads in order to appreciate their creativity and adapt the program to their needs. Teachers will freely adapt material to suit the children. They will plan music for quiet and active moods. They will plan music to support the concepts that the children are developing, but the enjoyment of music will have priority. Teachers will involve the parents in the children's music experiences whenever possible.

Applications

1. Do the "Talk It Over" items found in the chapter.
2. Write an activity plan for a music or movement activity for a few children using information and the sample plan (Figure 6–2) in Chapter 6. Secure approval, carry out the plan, and evaluate the results from the children's point of view and your viewpoint. Prepare a report and hand it in along with your approved plan.
3. Evaluate your total participation performance on your evaluation form developed in Chapter 1.
4. Add ideas and plans for music and movement activities to your Resource File.

Study Questions

1. State and explain the major goal for providing music for young children.
2. Describe places for teachers to look for ideas to use as musical experiences for children.

3. Explain how to teach children a new song.
4. Give examples of ways the teacher's creativity can be used during musical activities.
5. Give examples of ways children's creativity can be encouraged during musical activities.
6. According to studies, the best place to pitch a song for young children is between _____ and _____.
7. List and describe ways parents can become involved in musical activities for their children.

Videotapes

Learning Can Be Fun
    57 minutes

Ella Jenkins demonstrates how she sings and uses music to promote learning. You can do it, too. NAEYC Media, 1509 16th St. NW, Washington, DC 20036-1426, 1-800-424-2460.

Music Across the Curriculum
    20 minutes

Thomas Moore gives examples of music in an early childhood classroom and benefits of integrating music in the classroom. NAEYC Media, 1509 16th St. NW, Washington, DC 20036-1426, 1-800-424-2460.

Sources of Songs Mentioned

Note: Each song was given a number in the text to correspond to the following numbered sources in which the songs can be found. Use the library and library loan to help secure books unavailable locally.

1. "Jennie Jenkins," in *Exploring Music: Kindergarten*, E. Boardman and B. Landis, pp. 66–67.
2. "Jacob's Ladder," in *Sing and Strum*, Alice M. Snyder, p. 20.
3. "Goodnight, Irene," in *The Weaver's Song Book*, Ronnie Gilbert, ed., p. 34.
4. "Old Roger Is Dead," in *Songs to Grow On*, Beatrice Landeck, p. 112.

5. "Do-Re-Mi," in *The Sound of Music Vocal Selections*, Richard Rodgers and Oscar Hammerstein, pp. 16–21.

6. "Eency Weency Spider," in *American Folk Songs for Children*, Ruth Crawford Seeger, p. 126.

7. "Frère Jacques," in *The New Golden Song Book*, Norman Lloyd, p. 83.

8. "Mulberry Bush," in *The New Golden Song Book*, Norman Lloyd, p. 44.

9. "If You're Happy and You Know It," in *This Is Music, Book I*, William Sur, Adeline McCall, William R. Fischer, and Mary R. Tolbert, p. 16.

10. "Mary Wore a Red Dress," in *Songs to Grow On*, Beatrice Landeck, p. 12.

11. "Twinkle Twinkle Little Star," in *The New Golden Song Book*, Norman Lloyd, p. 16.

12. "Pawpaw Patch," in *Songs to Grow On*, Beatrice Landeck, p. 116.

13. "Muffin Man," in *The New Golden Song Book*, Norman Lloyd, p. 35.

14. "This Old Man," in *Music: A Way of Life for the Young Child*, K. M. Bayless and M. Ramsey, p. 161.

15. "Old MacDonald's Farm," in *The New Golden Song Book*, Norman Lloyd, p. 20.

16. "Up in a Balloon," in *More Songs to Grow On*, Beatrice Landeck, p. 12.

17. "What Shall We Do When We All Go Out?" in *American Folk Songs for Children*, Ruth Crawford Seeger, p. 59.

18. "The Farmer in the Dell," in *The New Golden Song Book*, Norman Lloyd, p. 36.

19. "When I Was a Young Maid," in *American Folk Songs for Children*, Ruth Crawford Seeger, p. 168.

20. "Monkey See Monkey Do," in *Train to the Zoo*, Children's Record Guild Recording No. 1001.

21. "Kumbaya," in *The Weaver's Song Book*, Ronnie Gilbert, ed., p. 156.

22. "Hush, Little Baby," in *The Weaver's Song Book*, Ronnie Gilbert, ed., p. 24.

23. "Twelve Days of Christmas," in *This Is Music, Book 4*, William R. Sur et al., pp. 174–175.

24. "Had a Little Rooster," in *More Songs to Grow On*, Beatrice Landeck, p. 34.

25. "I Bought Me a Cat," in *Songs to Grow On*, Beatrice Landeck, p. 76.

26. "I Know an Old Lady," in *I Know an Old Lady*, Rose Bonne and Allan Mills, p. 1.

27. "Go Tell Aunt Rhodie," in *The Weaver's Song Book*, Ronnie Gilbert, ed., p. 99.

28. "Jingle Bells," in *The New Golden Song Book*, Norman Lloyd, p. 56.

29. "Did You Ever See a Lassie?" in *The New Golden Song Book*, Norman Lloyd, p. 38.

30. "Round and Round the Village," in *The New Golden Song Book*, Norman Lloyd, p. 37.

31. "Punchinello," in *More Songs to Grow On*, Beatrice Landeck, p. 96.

32. "Ring Around the Rosy," in *The New Golden Song Book*, Norman Lloyd, p. 39.

33. "Sally Go Round the Moon," in *American Singer: No. 1*, John W. Beattie, p. 184.

34. "London Bridge," in *Fifty Songs for Children*, Mary Nancy Graham, p. 2.

35. "My Pigeon's House," in *Fireside Book of Folk Songs*, Margaret Bradford Boni, ed. (New York: Simon and Schuster, 1947), pp. 112–113. (The tune is a German folk song, "Muss I Denn.")

Music Books

Arnoff, F. W. *Move with Music: Songs and Activities for Young Children.* New York: Turning Wheel Press, 1982.

Bayless, K. M., and M. E. Ramsey. *Music: A Way of Life for the Young Child.* Upper Saddle River, NJ: Merrill/Prentice Hall, 1988.

Beall, Pam C., and Susan H. Nip. *Wee Sing and Play.* Los Angeles: Price Stern, 1981.

———. *Wee Sing.* Los Angeles: Price Stern, 1982.

———. *Wee Sing Silly Songs.* Los Angeles: Price Stern, 1982.

Beethoven, Jane, et al. *World of Music.* Morristown, NJ: Silver Burdett and Ginn, 1989.

Curry, W. L. *Songs for Children*. Philadelphia: Westminster Press, 1978.

Farina, A. M. *Developmental Games and Rhythms of Children*. Springfield, IL: Charles C. Thomas, 1981.

Glazer, Tom. *Tom Glazer's Treasury of Songs for Children*. Ft. Lauderdale, FL: J. R. Publishing, 1980.

———. *Music for Ones and Twos: Songs and Games for the Very Young*. New York: Doubleday, 1983.

Nelson, Esther. *Everybody Sing & Dance*. New York: Instructor Books, 1989.

Weikart, Phyllis. *Round the Circle: Key Experiences in Movement for Children Age 3 to 5*. Morristown, NJ: Silver Burdett and Ginn, 1989.

———. *Teaching Movement and Dance: A Sequential Approach to Rhythmic Movement*. Morristown, NJ: Silver Burdett and Ginn, 1989.

Zeitlin, P. A. *A Song Is a Rainbow: Music Movement and Rhythm Instruments in the Nursery School and Kindergarten*. Glenview, IL: Scott, Foresman, 1982.

Records and Tapes

Each of the following companies and many others have tapes and records to assist teachers with children's singing and movement activities. Teachers should listen to tapes and records before purchasing or using them to be assured of the quality of presentation and the appropriateness of the records or tapes for a specific group of children. Write for current lists and prices to

Ella Jenkins Records
1844 North Mohawk St.
Chicago, IL 60614

Miss Jackie Music
10001 El Monte
Overland Park, KS 66207

Richard Alan Productions
2208 W. 68th St.
Minneapolis, MN 55423

Silver Burdett and Ginn
250 James St.
Morristown, NJ 07632

Smithsonian Folkways Records
One Camp St.
Cambridge, MA 02140

Thomas Moore Records
4600 Park Rd., Suite 1000
Charlotte, NC 28209

Youngheart Records
2413½ Hyperion Ave.
Los Angeles, CA 90027

Additional Readings

Andress, Barbara. *Music Experiences in Early Childhood*. New York: Holt, Rinehart & Winston, 1980.

———. "From Research to Practice: Preschool Children and Their Movement Responses to Music." *Young Children* 47:1, November 1991, 22–27.

Bayless, Kathleen M., and M. E. Ramsey. *Music: A Way of Life for the Young Child*. Upper Saddle River, NJ: Merrill/Prentice Hall, 1988.

Buchoff, Rita. "Joyful Voices: Facilitating Language Growth Through the Rhythmic Response to Chants." *Young Children* 49:4, May 1994, 26–30.

Chenfield, M. B. *Creative Activities for Young Children*. New York: Harcourt Brace Jovanovich, 1983.

Jalango, M. R., "Using Recorded Music With Young Children: A Guide for Nonmusicians." *Young Children* 51:5, July 1996, 6–14.

Jalango, M. R., and M. Collins. "Singing with Young Children! Folk Singing for Nonmusicians." *Young Children* 40:2, January 1985, 17–22.

National Dance Association. *Music, Dance, Drama and All the Arts*. Washington, DC: NAEYC, 1992.

Sullivan, Molly. *Feeling Strong, Feeling Free: Movement Exploration for Young Children*. Washington, DC: NAEYC, 1991.

Williams, V. B. *Music for Everyone*. New York: Greenwillow, 1984.

Wiseman, A. *Making Musical Things: Improvised Instruments*. New York: Charles Scribner's Sons, 1979.

Wolf, Jan. "Let's Sing it Again: Creating Music with Young Children." *Young Children* 47:2, January 1992, 56–60.

———. "Singing with Children Is a Cinch." *Young Children* 49:4, May 1994, 20–25.

CHAPTER 17

Field Trips and Special Visitors

Bethany Weekday School, Houston

Objectives

✔ Explain how field trips and visitors are part of the cumulative curricular plan of the school for young children.

✔ Identify the values to children that come from taking field trips or having special visitors.

✔ Identify and explain the steps required in adequate planning for field trips and special visitors.

✔ Identify and describe a variety of field trips and special visitors appropriate for the early childhood school.

Our Fall Trip

Once upon a time nineteen children went to the woods. It is called the Arboretum Park. We took the Sugar Bush Trail, or path, or road. We saw a squirrel. He was eating bread.

We saw cows with long horns. We saw prairie dogs and deer—reindeer.

We fed the raccoon. They eat with their claws. They have a face that looks like a mask.

We found two caterpillars.

We jumped in a big pile of leaves under a tree. We made the pile. That was fun.

*We saw the ducks. We fed them
bread. Did you see three swans?
Except one of them was a white
duck.*

We saw buffalo—two buffaloes.

*We ate some bread, peanut but-
ter, and Koolaid.*

*We came back to our school. We
had fun.*

The four-year-old children dictated this
story to the teacher following a fall field
trip to a wooded wildlife park. Such field
trips take the child to an observation that cannot
readily be brought into the classroom. Field trips
and special visitors are educational methods used
to provide children firsthand information, observation, and study. As children discuss and dictate
stories about their new experience, opportunities
are presented for clarifying concepts and expanding knowledge.

Catherine Landreth, a child psychologist and
recognized leader in the field of early childhood
education, reminds teachers that the young child
is a "laboratory rather than a lecture student."
She says teaching young children requires providing materials and activities in such a way that
children learn from their own experience.[1] Landreth, of course, stresses the use of developmentally appropriate practice. She means that children learn most by having opportunities to see
for themselves, to touch, to taste, to smell, to
hear, and then to talk about their experiences.
Their concepts are broadened through firsthand
experience. Field trips and the special visitors
invited to the school offer the children experi-

ences that help them understand more fully the
life going on around them, the books that are
read to them, and the books they will later learn
to read. Pictures, films, recordings, poems, and
songs will also have more meaning following
firsthand experiences.

PLANNING FIELD TRIPS

Five considerations are weighed by the teacher
in the decision to use the field trip method for a
group of young children. These considerations
are (1) the educational goals for the group, (2) the
suitability of the available field trips, (3) the time
required, (4) the costs involved, and (5) the dangers involved.

Cumulative planning, as described in Chapter
11, utilizes a number of basic themes that run
through the entire curriculum. Learning activities are offered for each theme in varying
amounts in an effort to help children link new
information with that previously known. Field
trips and special visitors help children receive
more authentic educational experiences than if
only classroom activities are used. Frequently
field trips are a capstone experience following a
buildup of information and exploration within the
classroom. Many field trips can also be a spring-
board to other learning activities in the days and
weeks following, which is part of the spiraling
effect of cumulative planning.

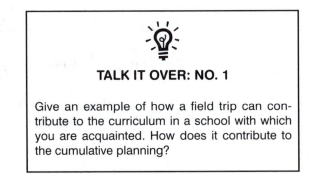

TALK IT OVER: NO. 1

Give an example of how a field trip can contribute to the curriculum in a school with which
you are acquainted. How does it contribute to
the cumulative planning?

---

[1]Catherine Landreth, *Preschool Learning and Teaching* (New
York: Harper & Row, 1972), p. 161.

One type of field trip is to see a crop in various stages from planting to harvesting. (V. Hildebrand, photographer)

Educational Goals for Field Trips

Before the field trip educational goals should be well established. A field trip can be used to stimulate interest in a subject as well as to extend information. It can also be fun and add variety to the school program. Although the latter purposes are valued, most teachers would agree that the first two are the more important purposes of field trips.

The teacher will have some tentative goals based upon knowledge of and experience with children of the age of those in the class. However, the teacher's decision on specific field trips must be made after a period of assessing the needs of a particular group of children. The teacher will want to know: What experiences have they had previously at home and school? What questions are they asking? What interests them? What do they talk about? What books do they select? From such study the teacher can decide what information needs extending and what interests should be stimulated.

The field trip ideas mentioned in this chapter should be considered only as examples to help you think about your own community resources. You should select only those that meet the criteria for educational goals and for suitability for your group of children at a given time.

Suitability of Available Field Trips

Teachers will continuously survey their community for ideas for worthwhile field trips and special events. The interest and cooperation of the parents of the children should be enlisted in order to provide a rich curriculum. For example, one group visits the television studio because a child's mother works there and helps arrange the visit. Another group goes to the police station because a child's father works there. Parents can assist on buses, drive cars, and act as guides.

There will be differences among groups, so there is a fallacy in saying, "Kindergartners always go to the fire station." In some schools every child goes on every trip, regardless of age or previous experience. Can this practice be justified?

Attending school may be a sufficiently new, strange, and stimulating adventure for two- and three-year-olds. Teachers must determine whether it is best to delay field trips until the children are at ease in the school setting. A trip may undermine security just when the children are beginning to feel comfortable away from home. Tammy is an example. Usually a confident, happy three-year-old, she wondered, "Will my Daddy find me here?" during a walk less than a block from the school. She verbalized a concern that many of the others may have felt.

Field trips for the youngest children should be simple and close to school. Teachers may explore

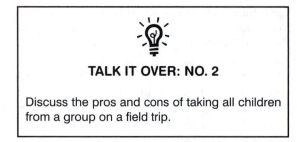

TALK IT OVER: NO. 2

Discuss the pros and cons of taking all children from a group on a field trip.

the possibility of taking only a few of the children, leaving behind those who aren't ready for field trip experiences. Such a plan, of course, requires activities, helpers, and perhaps some explanations for those who remain.

Field trips usually serve their purposes best for those late four-year-olds and kindergarten children who are confident with the teacher and in the school situation and are fully ready for broadening adventures. This age is ready for more things to look at, to talk about, to think about, and to use creatively in their schoolwork.

Communities offer many more resources for field trips than teachers sometimes recognize. The field trip suggestions that follow are listed because they are known to have been successful for some groups. The list is not exhaustive, and teachers should use it to help them find resources in their communities. There is no set list of experiences every child should have. Therefore the teacher should develop the curriculum that makes sense for a particular group at this time.

Costs Involved

Many field trips are free. Some may require admission fees. Transportation is a cost even though it may be borne by a school district or by a number of parents who drive their private cars. A total cost should be calculated if there are numerous fees. Careful determination should be made as

to whether the trip is the best use of the resources. For example, if a train trip is calculated to cost one hundred dollars for fifteen children, would this be the best use of one hundred dollars?

Time Required

The time required to plan and carry through the field trip should be considered from the standpoint of the children, the teachers, and other adults who may be requested to assist. Time is a valuable resource and should be used wisely. The teacher must ask, "Is the time required for this trip the best use of everybody's time?"

Danger Involved

There are added dangers associated with taking children away from school, whether by bus, by car, or on foot. No concerned teacher assumes the responsibility for a group of children without giving some thought to possible accidents. The school's legal liability in case of accident is one consideration. Another is the need to provide seatbelts for each person in each car, according to regulations. Liability insurance for private automobiles is another. However, insurance is a hollow consolation to a teacher if an accident does occur. Parents should feel that utmost care for children's safety is planned. Trips that are planned haphazardly often do not give safety sufficient attention.

TALK IT OVER: NO. 3

Discuss the dangers involved in taking children on field trips. Summarize precautions to take to avoid these dangers.

FIELD TRIP SUGGESTIONS

Animals

Farm—sheep, cattle, horses, pigs, turkeys, chickens
County fair—animal exhibits
Dairy at milking time
Rodeo horses
Ducks in pond
Zoo
Hatchery—fish/chicken
Fish/Pet store

Fish/Aquarium
Fishing boats
Wildlife exhibit
Bird sanctuary
Pets—in pet shop or in child's home
Veterinary hospital
Museum—animal and bird exhibits

Growing Things

Botanical garden
Christmas tree farm/Nursery
Flower garden
Nature walks—four seasons
Pumpkin farm

Orchard—fruit/nuts
Park
Woods
Farm—wheat, corn, oats,
Farm—cotton/flax

Community Services and Workers

Art gallery
Artist's studio
Athletic center—gym, pool, steam room
Bakery
Barbershop
Beauty shop
Bowling alley
Cabinet shop
Car wash
Children's houses
Computer laboratory
Concert
County fair
Dairy bottling plant
Department store windows
Dormitory room
Doughnut/Bagel shop
Fire station
Flour mill
Garage mechanic
Grocery
Grain elevator/storage

Health clinic
Home economics classroom
Ice cream parlor
Ice or roller skating rink
Library
Lunchroom kitchen
Museum—old fashioned house, doll collection, native American houses, historical exhibits
Office
Parade
Police station
Post office
Potter's studio
Puppet show
School—kindergarten for four-year-olds, first grade for kindergarten children
Science classroom
Swimming pool
Teacher's house
Television studio

Transportation and Machines

Airport	Elevator
Train ride	Escalator
Train station	Streetcar ride
Exhibited train	Car dealer's showroom
Model train collection	Bus ride
Construction site	Museum—machine exhibit
Street repair	Museum—space exhibit
Farm machinery show	Boat ride

Other

Museum—dinosaur, geology exhibit, Christmas trees, children's art	Planetarium
	Seashore
Science classroom—skeleton, insect collections, botanical collections	Ecology walk—litter pickup

Preparation for Field Trips

Five stages of field trip planning are outlined here that, if considered carefully, should ensure the enrichment of the children's experience that the teacher seeks. These are

1. the teacher's preparation,
2. the children's preparation,
3. the field trip,
4. follow-up activities, and
5. posttrip activities.

These stages can be applied with modifications to special events brought into the school by a visitor or the teacher.

Teacher's Preparation

The teacher becomes fully informed about the subject of the trip that has been chosen. The teacher goes to the site ahead of time to see specifically what there is for the children to learn and what things may need to be pointed out to the children. As inexperienced observers, they may miss important points unless helped in their observation. The teacher will plan for parking, note any hazards that might endanger the children's safety, and recruit additional adult helpers if needed. Videos are often taken by a parent, the teacher, or a helper. These can be used for additional learning and recall later on.

Guides The teacher talks with the guide, helping the person to appreciate the level of learning of the children. Many adults have little idea what will interest children. For example, at a bus station, when children were anxious to get aboard a bus, the guide tried to inform them how to get a refund on a ticket. Needless to say, the children's attention wandered! A teacher can decide how to help the guide if he or she fails to show the things that are important, or if the talk is above the children's level. Having developed rapport prior to the actual event, it is easy to say, "Mr. Arthur, could we see those baby calves? I know the children would enjoy those." Or after a complicated explanation, one might say, "What Mr. Arthur means is that those calves get some special food to see how they will grow."

Day of Week Choosing the right day of the week for the trip is an important decision. Several things must be considered. First, what immediate preparation will the teacher give the children and how many days will that take? What kinds of follow-up activities are expected to result, such as dramatic play, art activities, rhythm responses, and science experiments? The teacher knows that through reliving the experience, the children work out some of their concepts, roles, and feelings. If plans call for a great deal of this type of follow-up, it is best to schedule the trip early in the week so that there will be maximum carryover into the school activity. The amount of carryover will be greatly reduced if a weekend intervenes, and will be almost nonexistent if a vacation follows the trip. For example, children play firefighters for days after a trip to the fire station. They wear their self-made firefighters' hats, carry ladders on little red wagons, and put out fires in their "houses" made of packing boxes and wooden planks.

Time of Day Where in the daily schedule is the best place for the trip? This is an important consideration. The date and time must be convenient for the host or owner of the place to be visited. The teacher considers the energy demands of the trip on the children. An active trip such as a walk on the seashore or on a farm would logically follow a quiet interlude at school rather than a period of outdoor play. A trip to hear a harpist play and accompany the children's singing logically follows a period of active play. Children's bodies will then be ready for the behavior that the situation demands. Active and quiet play have good balance in a program that meets children's needs. Some readjustment in the routine activities will be necessary to fit the trip into the schedule.

The teacher plans for sufficient time for the total trip, including leeway for any emergency. In addition, a bonus experience may occur on any trip. For example, on a walk to the museum a cement mixer was observed dumping its load of cement. What a tragedy if the schedule would not permit even a little peek!

Rules An important part of the teacher's preparation is to think through rules for walking and riding during field trips. Walking trips will come first, while the teacher is still learning about the group. One way is to appoint a pair of leaders and call them "engines" and "cabooses." They should all practice certain signals so that the leaders will know when to stop and when to go. Learning that "red light" means stop is more fun than just having the teacher call "stop." "Green light" permits them to proceed. The meaning of traffic lights should be understood and practice sessions held in the classroom to help the children learn their meaning.

When crossing streets, the teacher may ask the child who has been designated the "engine" to stop the "train" at some landmark they see on the other side. The teacher then remains in the middle of the street until all children have crossed.

Transportation Transportation is often essential for field trips. In public schools teachers can usually depend on buses with qualified drivers. This is a real advantage. In other schools parents may be asked to drive several children. Care must be taken not to overload a car, thereby interfering with safe driving. Every passenger must have a seatbelt. Only insured cars should be taken on trips.

Thought should be given to deciding which children ride together. Two children who are noted for being hard to handle should be separated. When a parent is driving, her or his child should be allowed to ride in that car. It is essential to have an extra adult accompany each driver. The drivers should be given a list of the children who ride in their car and their phone numbers to use in any emergency. Also, the address and phone number of the destination and detailed instructions for getting there should be written out for each driver. To depend on one car following another in city traffic with a car full of children is hazardous. Drivers can lose each other and may end up not knowing where to go.

Permission Some schools require a signed permission slip from parents for each trip. These forms are often difficult for teachers to collect from the children because they are easily misplaced or forgotten. Other schools ask parents to sign a permission slip that covers all trips throughout the year, which can be taken care of during the child's enrollment. Teachers should also clarify with the school's legal adviser the problem of liability in case of accident.

Inform Parents   Teachers should inform parents of all planned trips. Not only will parents then be able to dress the child appropriately, but they can more intelligently supplement the teacher's goals if they don't have to guess what is taking place. That is, parents can ask questions to draw out the child's information about and reactions to the trip, answer their child's questions, and arrange family trips that further supplement the school's efforts.

Children's Preparation

Preparing the children for the field trip is essential for maximum learning. Preparation for a field trip may cover several months, with the trip serving as a capstone, or in some cases the trip may appropriately be initiated after a few days' discussion, with most of the learning to come after the event.

Through pictures, stories, records, role-playing, and discussions, the children can become aware of the details they can expect to find on field trips. A firefighter expressed amazement at the vocabulary of a group of kindergartners. If they didn't readily find a tool, they asked the firefighters where it was. They used the correct name. These children had learned about the firefighters' tools during the week prior to the trip. Sometimes there are exceptions or differences in what the child sees in a picture book and what will be found on the trip. The teacher can warn the children of these exceptions ahead of time and help avoid disappointment. For example, new fire stations may not have the traditional firehouse pole. This is a source of disappointment to children who are expecting it.

Stories, songs, and poems may be used to help children learn about a subject they will be seeing on a field trip. Books make excellent resource material for both preparation and follow-up activities.

Role-playing helps children learn more about the trip. It will help them feel self-assured in a strange place. Prior to a train trip one group

arranged chairs as they expected their train seats to be arranged. Young artists designed tickets and took turns being the conductor who punched their tickets. They talked about the differences between their upcoming trip of 15 miles and one they might take with their parents, for which they might need luggage, sleep on the train, spend more on tickets, and not return for several days. Reassurance was necessary for a child or two who wondered when they were going to return. The children pretended to see the parents' cars waiting at the station as the train pulled in. Their make-believe ride included what they were seeing from their train window. It made them better watchers as the real train rolled along a few days later.

The Field Trip

When the day of the field trip finally arrives, all should be in readiness, including the enthusiasm of the children. Teachers should make efforts to keep talk in a low key to avoid overstimulation. The teacher gathers the group around for a brief review of what they are going to see. Next, talk turns to how they are expected to behave—"quiet in the museum" or "quiet in the egg-laying barn." Perhaps they have to think about how quiet quiet is and why it is necessary.

Toileting cannot be forgotten when one is dealing with young children. After specifically reminding the children to go to the bathroom before leaving the building, the teacher will check on children who are known to have difficulties. Also, it is helpful if adults carry small packages of tissues. Drinks, too, are another consideration. On warm days a picnic jug of water and some paper cups are essential. A sack of cookies will add a festive air to the excursion.

On walking trips the teacher makes assignments for engines and cabooses according to the practiced routine. When the children clamor for this responsibility, the teacher may keep a list to be sure to pass the favor around.

For trips by car the teacher makes car assignments by giving each driver a list of the children who will ride in her or his car. It must be made clear that the same children should always ride in the same car throughout the trip. The teacher discusses with the children the need to sit down in the car and tells the children in the presence of the drivers that if they stand up, the driver will stop the car beside the road until all are sitting down again. Seatbelts must be used. The children's safety has highest priority.

The teacher checks last-minute details. Drivers are advised where to park and what to do until all arrive. Drivers are asked to act as guides for the children in their car, to ask questions of children that will help the children notice details, to listen to the children's comments, and to answer their questions. All drivers should be encouraged to be alert to "their" children's whereabouts and safety. Unless the teacher specifically requests it, outsiders may be hesitant to assume this helpful role. Occasionally the teacher may hold a briefing for the guides in order to coordinate the trip more effectively.

When the group arrives, they wait for the guide who will show them the things they came to see. The children are given lots of time to look, find details, and relate what they are seeing to what they have studied. After a while the adults can point out things they feel the children have missed. A relaxed, nonrushed atmosphere is important. If unexpected learning opportunities arise, the teacher should be happy to take time to observe these, too.

The children should wear their name tags. Name tags aid assistants who do not know all of the children's names. They could help police should a child get lost. They help the host of the field trip relate to individual children by calling them by name.

The Follow-up

The follow-up occurs during the ensuing days and helps the children develop further in their learning. The children may use new concepts in the self-selected activity period. Science materials, blocks, books, pictures, dress-up clothes, records, and art materials may all be used. Sometimes the teacher brings out a new or stored piece of equipment to stimulate dramatic play. A steering wheel, for example, contributes to transportation themes.

Creative art activities may result from the trip. After visiting the prairie dog town, Cindy drew

Safety is a concern of all adults involved in any field trip. Avoid saying, "Be careful." Just watch children closely. (Bethany Weekday School, Houston)

her version of what she had seen. The mounds were as big as mountains, each topped with a family of the animals, just as they were seen. Between the mounds were trees the same height as the mounds, giving the observer the idea that Cindy found the mounds more important than the trees as she viewed the scene. Making a firefighter's hat, stringing a Native American necklace, or modeling a caveman's house from clay may result, depending on the stimulus from the trip. Immediate freedom to use crayons, chalk, clay, and paints for interpreting the trip in the children's own way is important.

The stimulation of language expressed is a prime value of a field trip. Generalizing in their own words from their own experience promotes the children's learning. Every opportunity should be taken to encourage the children to talk about what they saw. Discussing what they saw, how they felt, and how it sounded and smelled is thoroughly enjoyed by the children and helps them remember. Frequently teachers are afraid of free open discussion because they fear it will get too loud and out of hand. Having a few pet fingerplays, songs, or poems in mind to use as attention-getters helps draw young talkers back to the fold. Verbal self-expression is very important for all children, but especially for those children who haven't had much to talk about before. Thus teachers should hesitate before squelching children's language expressions.

Written expression can result too. A dictated letter to the individual who so kindly permitted the visit is one type of expression. Making a poem and dictating a story are others. The opening story in this chapter is an example of a story dictated by children. Other examples are offered in Chapter 14.

Posttrip Activities

Posttrip activities provide for the children's continued learning after the original emphasis passes and the class goes on to other subjects. This step can continue from the time of the trip to the end of the year. The teacher can place a book on the library shelf, read a story that will cause the chil-

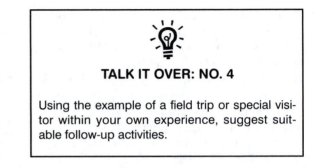

TALK IT OVER: NO. 4

Using the example of a field trip or special visitor within your own experience, suggest suitable follow-up activities.

dren to recall their trip, or play a video that reminds them about it. They like to reread their own story or letter of thanks. When these stories are sent home, the parents too can carry on posttrip activities. Communication with parents enables them to add family experiences that build on the foundation the school initiates.

SPECIAL VISITORS INVITED TO THE SCHOOL

Because of the complications surrounding field trips, it is often more desirable to bring special visitors to the children. The visitor should be one who can help extend the children's information and stimulate their interest. The children should be carefully prepared for these events. Many of the steps suggested for field trips are applicable here.

Following is a list of some suggested special visitors who might be invited to the school:

Mail carrier	Magician
Police officer	Nurse
Highway trooper	Rock collector
Musician	Insect collector
Baton twirler	Parent and baby
Dancer	Custodian
Firefighter with truck	Rope twirler
Forest ranger	Foreign visitor
Clown	Photographer
Artist	Veterinarian
Santa Claus	Weaver
Storyteller	

A Japanese teacher visited the four-year-olds. She told them about children in her school in Japan and let them try on kimonos made especially for young children. (Michigan State University)

The daily schedule may need to be adjusted so that the children will be ready for the type of behavior the event requires. Some visitors can function well during the self-selected activity period. They can talk to small groups of children, letting them come and go from their discussion or exhibit. This works for visitors with musical instruments and for those with various collections. The children who are most interested will stay a long time; those with less interest will spend their time elsewhere.

If the visitor will be working with the group as a whole, then special plans should be made so that the children are ready for the listening behavior usually required. The teacher might want a period of vigorous outdoor play to precede the event, for example. Transition times should be given special thought. A visitor may cause overstimulation of the children. At the same time the teacher will be distracted by being responsible for a guest. The situation is just right for chaos to develop.

An assistant might be designated to meet the guest. Special songs can be prepared to use in case of delay. Activities can be planned that relax the children rather than add to their excitement.

When the visitor is a child's parent, the child too should get to be in the limelight, introducing the parent, sitting close by, and helping in any way. The parent should know that giving her or his child this bit of recognition is part of the plan. Otherwise the parent may be embarrassed at what seems to be quite possessive behavior on the child's part. Children definitely enjoy having their parent to show off and to show around.

Visitors from various countries of the world enjoy the opportunity to talk with children in an early childhood center. Perhaps they have a native garment to wear or show, or songs, dances, food, or stories to share with children. Occasionally a foreign student participates over a period of time until children realize how much like everyone else that person is. The bridge to the world community has been opened for children in such a group. A world globe is very helpful to aid in the discussion with a foreign visitor. Teachers must study to become knowledgeable about the visitor's culture.

Children are particularly interested in their own photos. A visiting photographer set up a camera so children could shoot their own photo with a bulb-operated shutter. Teachers or parents can film with a video camera, recording many experiences the children enjoy. (Michigan State University)

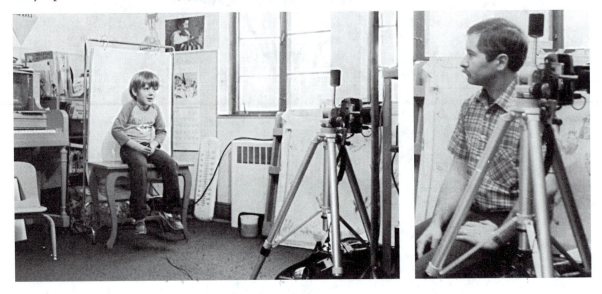

Visitors should be helped to understand the interests of the children. For example, musicians welcome suggestions of songs the children know. Visitors like to know how much the teacher expects the children to become involved. For example, a ballet dancer can simply perform a dance or can lead the children in their own ballet, which, of course, makes the event much more meaningful for the children. The teacher should be alert to help where needed to be sure that the visitor also has a pleasant experience.

Special visitors also deserve children's thank-yous. The following is how one group said thanks to a young mother who brought her baby for them to see.

Conclusions

Field trips and special visitors are appropriate methods to use with young children. In some instances children are better off remaining at school than being taken on field trips prematurely.

For these methods to give maximum educational benefit, these considerations should be weighed: the educational goals for the group, the suitability of available field trips, the time required, the costs, and the dangers involved. Teachers should make adequate preparation, prepare the

Dear Mrs. Smith,

Thank you for letting us see the baby. Thank you for telling us how he eats the cereal. Thank you for letting us see him drink his apple juice. Thank you for putting on the bib.

Thank you for letting us see his toes. Thank you for letting us see his hair—his little black fur. Thank you for letting us see his shoes or his slippers—his bootsies!

Thank you for coming.

Please come again. Thank you. Thank you. Thank you.

Love,
The Kindergarten Kids

A piñata is the center of many Hispanic celebrations. Here a visitor helps the children strike the piñata. (University of New Mexico)

children, and consider details of the special event, the follow-up, and the posttrip activities.

Applications

1. Discuss the "Talk It Over" items found in the chapter.
2. Write an activity plan for a field trip or a special visitor using information in the chapter. Secure approval and carry out the plan. Evaluate the results from the children's point of view and your viewpoint. Prepare a report and hand it in along with your approved plan.
3. Evaluate your total participation performance on your evaluation form developed in Chapter 1.
4. Add ideas and plans for field trips and special visitors to your Resource File.

Study Questions

1. Using an example from your experience, show how a field trip or special visitor is part of a cumulative plan.
2. State and discuss factors determining whether the teacher should consider using the field trip method of teaching.
3. State and discuss the steps for planning high-quality field trips or planning for special visitors in the school.
4. Identify dangers in taking field trips and list the steps teachers should take to minimize dangers.
5. Discuss the advantages and disadvantages of inviting a visitor to school rather than taking a field trip to that person's place of work.

Additional Readings

Forman, George, and David S. Kuschner. *The Child's Construction of Knowledge: Piaget for Teaching Children.* Washington, DC: NAEYC, 1984.

Peters, Donald L., John T. Neisworth, and Thomas D. Yawkey. *Early Childhood Education: From Theory to Practice.* Monterey, CA: Brooks/Cole, 1985.

CHAPTER 18

Food Activities, Meals, and Snacks

Oregon State University

Objectives

✔ Identify nutrition information that young children can appropriately learn.

✔ Describe guides for presenting nutrition and food information to young children.

✔ State the goals for mealtimes in early childhood schools and explain ways to fulfill each goal.

✔ State procedures for providing snacks in early childhood schools.

✔ Describe and evaluate food activities for early childhood schools.

"We're having jelly today," sang the teacher while passing out the food for snack.

"Oh, good, I'm having jelly in my belly," sang Robert, a sturdy five-year-old, matching the teacher's song.

Robert was sitting next to Betty, his regular snack time friend. The menu didn't please Betty so much. "I don't want any bread," she said. The teacher said perhaps someone else would like it then. Betty repeated, "I don't want any bread."

Robert's hearing acuity was good, and his reaction time was evident in the haste and skill he displayed in slipping a napkin over both of Betty's pieces of bread and jelly and pulling them toward his place.

His snack time friend asked him if he wanted her glass of milk as well. He replied as he pointed to his own and rhymed his answer, "Never fear. I've got some right here." He drank three glasses of milk and ate his own and Betty's sandwich. He left one scraggly crust after inspecting it carefully to be sure there was no hint of jelly still adhering to it.

Robert was a well-nourished and peppy five-year-old who thoroughly enjoyed food. Betty was thin and listless, rejecting many foods that other children enjoyed. How can their early childhood teacher help them establish habits that will guide their eating and nutrition in the years to come?

A CHILD'S NUTRITION: WHOSE RESPONSIBILITY?

A child's body is his or her closest environment. Adequate nutrition is basic to life, growth, and learning. According to nutrition researchers, malnutrition and undernutrition can irreversibly affect a child's brain development.[1]

Parents have the primary responsibility for the kind and quantity of food available to their children. When children are placed in a full-day or part-day early childhood center, the staff assumes a portion of the parents' responsibility. (Quality of food is written into regulations of child care facilities.) Homes and child care facilities keep a given supply of food on hand, and young children cannot secure more or other foods except those supplied. Children at the preprimary age are not responsible for their food supply and are not able to be responsible for the quality of their nutrition.

---

[1]For information on the effects of malnutrition on brain development see Laura E. Berk, *Child Development* (Boston: Allyn and Bacon, 1991), pp. 195–204.

Time for one-to-one interaction allows the teacher to apply Vygotsky's scaffolding as the child learns to make an omelet. (McQueen Preschool, Howard University)

As children mature, they begin to exercise some autonomy in the choices they make within the existing food supply. They may refuse certain foods and request others. Children reach this stage just when their growth rate is slowing down. Parents may worry and often make serious efforts to get children to eat. Food advertisers, particularly on television, capitalize on parents' insecurity. For example, young children are believed by advertisers to be influential in getting their parents to buy certain foods. Certainly the firms believe advertising pays off. At the same time, there are no equally high-prestige or action-packed ads extolling the virtues of a truly healthful diet. Perhaps teachers and parents need to mount a "hard sell" campaign for nutritious foods. It would pay off handsomely if the outcome is healthier human beings.

One important avenue for influencing children's nutritional status is to work with their parents. Some suggestions about how to accomplish this are found in Chapter 20. The present chapter focuses on ways that teachers of young children can initiate learning regarding food and nutrition, and work toward the long-range goal of having children *select nutritionally balanced diets independently.* Note the goal statement carefully. In the early years, if parents and teachers are doing their jobs adequately, the child has only nutritious foods from which to choose. The child begins to have opportunities to make food selections from among all sorts of choices during the early years and beyond. If habits of choosing nutritious foods are developed early, the chances of sustaining those habits later are greater. Teachers and parents need to realize that choice of food often depends on social or peer pressure and practice as well as on rational nutritional information, especially during school-age years.

opportunity to plan food-related experiences as part of their daily educational program. Mealtimes are expected to conform to nutritional requirements as specified in regulations. Food choices should be well balanced, clean, colorful, and served in a pleasant atmosphere that encourages children to eat and to look forward to mealtime. Meals and snacks are essential for refueling and maintaining children's bodies. Children also rest as they eat, which is important.

Food and cooking experiences provided within the curriculum have been encouraged because of the children's high interest level. They enjoy helping with food preparation, eating foods, and talking about food. Children's curiosity and interest in school may be stimulated through food experiences when other activities fail. Parents report hearing more about the food and cooking projects than about many other school activities. The cognitive or mental learning that occurs during food activities has been emphasized, especially contributions to vocabulary and concept building. Children can classify food by color, size, or texture. They can classify food according to source—plant or animal. They can decide what part of the plant they are eating—seed, root, leaf, stem, or flower.

In most food experiences nutritional information is overlooked. Perhaps most teachers assume that if food experiences are provided, children will automatically learn a few nutrition concepts. It seems likely that this assumption is in error.

The intent of this chapter is to encourage teachers to exploit every food experience for its contribution to nutrition education. As teachers, with prestige among children and parents, you can state your high regard for the nutritional qualities of milk, meat, cereals, vegetables, and fruits and get your message across to children as effectively as TV ad writers—if you try.

OPPORTUNITIES FOR FOOD AND NUTRITION EDUCATION

Full-day schools serve meals and snacks, part-day programs serve snacks, and both have ample

GUIDES FOR FOOD AND NUTRITION PROGRAM PLANNING

Five major guides for planning food and nutrition experiences for young children in early child-

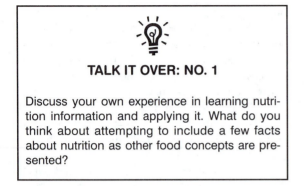

hood centers are to personalize, simplify, dramatize, regularize, and mobilize. Details of these guides will now be discussed.

Personalize

The teacher makes the subjects of food and nutrition come alive for each child personally. Remember, it is individual nutrition that counts.

1. Through questioning and observation, the teacher finds out how advanced children are in their knowledge of foods and nutrition. What are the sources of foods that the children know? Meal or snack time is a good time for informal discussion. For example, one child, Cindy, reported to her kindergarten teacher, "My dentist told me never never drink any more pop or my teeth would all drop out."
2. Through observing the children and talking with parents, the teacher learns the typical foods eaten by each child. Any ethnic groups with differing food patterns should be noted. Capitalizing on these food variations while planning specific projects may be a useful approach.
3. The teacher should find out if any families make their livings in fishing, farming, food processing, or the grocery or restaurant business. With this information, those families' children can be recognized as "authorities" or resource persons. The teacher may also be able to involve the parents as hosts for a field trip or in some school activity.
4. The teacher should weigh and measure the children and record the figures. A chart can be made for recording their growth during the year. With data provided by parents, the chart could begin with birth. When adding to the chart from time to time, the teacher could tell the children that nutritious food helps them grow and stay healthy.
5. The children may bring pictures of favorite foods from home or find them in the school's magazine collection. The teacher could help them make a poster illustrating the basic food groups.
6. The teacher could have children play a game called "I tasted something new, its name was _____, it tasted like _____."
7. Parents can be invited to a meal or snack or to help with a cooking project. Having one's parents at school is very important to children.
8. Each child is given an opportunity daily to have a hands-on experience with food and to relate that food to nutrition information.
9. Each child learns to wash hands carefully before eating and before food-handling events.
10. After each food event the children take a note home—a reminder to tell their parents about the activity.

Food experiences and nutrition information can form the basis for a sound science education. All the sciences can be emphasized—biological, physical, and social sciences.

Children need numerous firsthand experiences with real food. These experiences will teach more about food and nutrition than a lot of pictures or lectures. It is better to have fewer experiences and have them with real food than it is to have many experiences with pictures, models, or drawings on pages to color in. The opportunity to use all senses, to see, touch, taste, smell—yes, and even to hear some foods—makes lasting impressions on children. Remember that young children are here-and-now learners. (Review Chapter 11 for learning stages.) In the course of planned and incidental experiences the teacher can ask the following questions:

- What do you see? (color, shape, size, kind)
- How does it smell? (strong, spicy, fragrant, repulsive)
- How does it feel? (rough, smooth, slimy, hot, cold)
- How does it sound? (loud, soft, crackly, crunchy)
- How does it taste? (sweet, sour, salty, spicy, bitter)

No Blind Tasting: For Safety's Sake

Children should never be asked to taste food while blindfolded. In the first place, young children dislike blindfolds and many refuse to participate when they see blindfolds are called for. More importantly, parents and society want chil-dren instinctively and rationally to refuse to taste or eat any item unless they think about it and their senses tell them that the item is harmless or good for them. For this reason a blind tasting of items that are not known or seen to come out of an appropriate container is poor educational strategy. Caution is always the way of the wise. Most adults would refuse to play some of the food-guessing games children are sometimes asked to play. Many children have been harmed fatally by tasting a substance out of curiosity. Pre-cautionary instincts should be encouraged in early childhood programs.

Simplify

Simplifying food and nutrition concepts to meet the cognitive level of young children is essential and challenging. Young children have been eat-ing all their lives, so they are quite well acquainted with some foods. However, they may not yet know or eat a variety of foods. Thinking about how food relates to their health, energy,

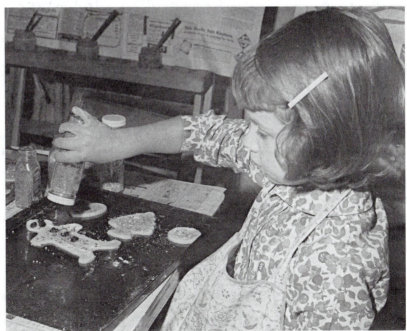

Decorating cookies you've cut out yourself requires lots of time and concentration. (Texas Tech University)

growth, and general well-being will probably be quite new to them. Teachers can check on children's ability to generalize by asking, "Why is milk good for you?"

Nutrition information is very complex and abstract. Nutrients are not something children can see, hold, or weigh, for example. Recalling Piaget's stages of cognitive development from Chapter 11 reminds one how simplified nutrition information must be if we are to hope that children can grasp and use it. The United States Department of Agriculture's nutritionists have designated five food groups to help unspecialized adults with choosing their food. By eating selections daily from each group the expectation is that necessary and sufficient nutrients will be obtained. These five food groups are outlined in Figure 18-1. Excellent and reliable information is also available from your county or state Cooperative Extension Service or from the local National Dairy Council office. Consult the phone book for the nearest office. Both have materials for schoolagers, which will be useful if simplified for younger children.[2]

After labeling the chalkboard with the five food groups by taping representative pictures above five columns, the cook, dietitian, or teacher, with the cooperation of the children, can plan a week's menus for meals or snacks in the center. Children can help classify the foods and help make a "balanced" menu. A picture menu poster can be arranged for the classroom using cutout foods. The foods may be discussed as they are eaten the following week. Take at least five days to cover the groups and restate frequently at meal- or snack time.

As children eat the foods, the teachers can help them verbalize statements as they eat, for example: "Meat is good for me; it helps me grow blood and muscle." "Apples are good for me; they are nice and crunchy for my teeth." "Eggs help my muscles and blood grow." "Vegetables give me energy to run and play." "Carrots are good for me; they make my eyes bright."

Children can feel their own muscles and bones to help in understanding those concepts. They can generalize that it will take lots of food to grow taller. Usually children like to talk about when they've seen blood and how it looked on that occasion. They can be told, "Eating meat helps us grow more blood." After a mirror has been set up and the children have been given apple slices, they can talk about their teeth and jaws and how they move when they chew firm foods like apples. Of course, good chewing is essential to good nutrition. After such tasting it is interesting to see the pictures children draw of themselves. Also, with this focus you may notice children who need dental care for cavities or alignment. Suggest a visit to a dentist to the child's parents.

Dramatize

The enthusiasm and involvement of the teachers and parents will inspire interest in food and nutrition among children. Teachers can brainstorm among themselves, searching for creative ways to increase the appeal of nutritious food and to increase nutrition information and its meaningfulness to children. The various food and cooking projects that will be outlined later in the chapter will help dramatize the learning. Field trips, suggested in Chapter 17, may serve either to stimulate some area of study or become capstone experiences; for example, perhaps after months of intermittent projects related to the milk food group, the children can go to a dairy processing plant to see milk bottling or ice cream and cheese making.

To dramatize, the teacher and children can decorate the classroom with pictures of food, gardens, farms, restaurants, or supermarkets, depending on the current focus. Books can be

---

[2]A useful booklet, *Fun with Good Foods,* was developed by the U.S. Department of Agriculture's Food and Nutrition Service. It is available from the Government Printing Office, Washington, DC 20402. For an in-depth look at integrating nutrition education in classrooms see Shirley Oliver and Katherine Musgrave, *Nutrition: A Teacher Sourcebook of Integrated Activities* (Boston: Allyn and Bacon, 1984).

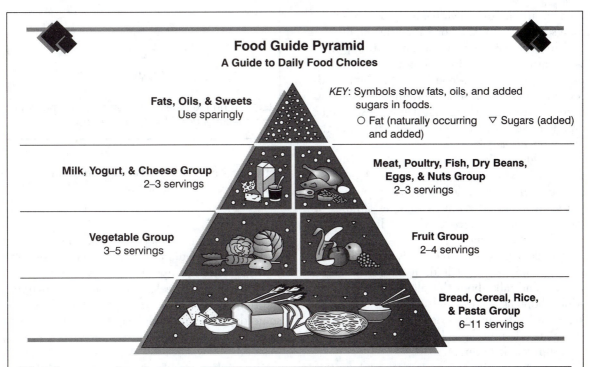

What Counts as One Serving?

Bread, Cereals, Rice, and Pasta
- 1 slice of bread
- ½ cup cooked cereal, rice, or pasta
- 1 ounce ready-to-eat cereal

Vegetables
- ½ cup chopped raw or cooked vegetables
- 1 cup leafy raw vegetables
- ¾ cup vegetable juice

Fruits
- 1 medium whole fruit or melon wedge
- ½ cup chopped, cooked, or canned fruit
- ¼ cup dried fruit
- ¾ cup fruit juice

Milk, Yogurt, and Cheese
- 1 cup milk or yogurt
- 1½-ounces ripened cheese
- 2 ounces process cheese

How Many Servings Do You Need Each Day?

Food Group	Women and some older adults	Children, teen girls, active women, most men	Teen boys and active men
Bread	6	9	11
Vegetable	3	4	5
Fruit	2	3	4
Milk	2–3*	2–3*	2–3*
Meat	2, for a total of 5 ounces	2, for a total of 6 ounces	3, for a total of 7 ounces

*Women who are pregnant or breastfeeding, teenagers, and young adults to age 24 need 3 servings of the milk group.

Meat, Poultry, Fish, Dry Beans, Eggs, and Nuts
- 2½ to 3 ounces cooked lean meat, poultry, or fish (An average hamburger is about 3 ounces.)
- The following equal 1 ounce of lean meat:
  ½ cup cooked dry beans
  1 egg
  2 tablespoons peanut butter

Source: United States Department of Agriculture Nutrition Service

made available for individual and group reading. Songs, fingerplays, and poems can be taught.

Children can play supermarket if supplied with cartons or cans from foods. They can sort out the "good-for-you-foods" and the "not-good-for-you-foods." Food-related dramatic play concerning farming, fishing, gardening, restaurants, and housekeeping can be carried on in either the classroom or play yard.

For older children puppets or flannel-board figures can be made and used to develop a play focusing on foods. If desirable, the play or puppet show could be given to younger siblings or parents, perhaps at a covered-dish dinner sometime during the term.

A large supermarket picture is available from school supply houses. Children can study such a picture and talk about the places they've been while shopping with parents. Or, after a trip to a supermarket to buy groceries for a food project at school, children could all help draw or paint their own supermarket mural.

Dramatic nutrition experiments such as this one can be carried out with kindergarten groups. Two white rats were brought into the classroom and housed in separate cages. One rat received the food from the children's lunchroom—vegetables, fruit, bread, meat, and milk—while the other received a cola and candy diet. After three weeks the children could readily see that "Whitey," who had been fed the cola and candy diet was smaller, had rough hair, and was quarrelsome. The rats were weighed each week and a chart was made to show their gains in weight. These kindergartners perceived the effects of feeding only cola and candy to a rat. "Poor Whitey, he needs some good food," they concluded. How well did they relate the experiment to themselves? Though they were often told that if they ate only cola and candy they'd stay small, the children's ability to relate the nutrition of rats to themselves was disappointing at the close of the experiment. Later on they recalled having had the rats at school, but their ability to relate well the outcome of the experiment to them-

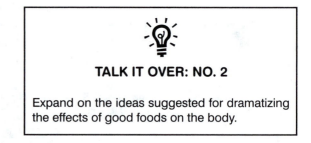

TALK IT OVER: NO. 2

Expand on the ideas suggested for dramatizing the effects of good foods on the body.

selves was still lacking. Perhaps additional effort could overcome this difficulty.

Regularize

Food and cooking projects can become a regular part of the curriculum, occurring once or twice a week in some groups. Every day the children have a nutrition break (snack), and that may be the only emphasis on food on certain days. On some days the emphasis may be extensive, with one or more food-related activities being planned.

When planning a food experience for children, the teacher thinks first of the goals stated earlier. Which ones can be achieved through the project? Experiences may be selected on the basis of the food guide pyramid, giving children firsthand information on a food or two from each of the five food groups. Foods with high sugar and fat content are avoided. Most American children eat excessive amounts of sweets. Never prepare deep-fat fried foods. These are extremely dangerous to make with young children, due to the very high temperature of the oil. Fried foods are difficult for children to digest and, therefore, are to be avoided.

All needed ingredients and utensils should be organized. A picture recipe can be posted for children to "read." When doing a new project, the wise teacher tries it out first at home and notes possible problems that may occur as the children do it.

Allow children to eat their food products as soon after preparing them as possible for most effective learning. When serving foods to chil-

A few children involved at once is best for food preparation projects. This enables the teacher to be sure of cleanliness, safety, and extending children's learning. (Kansas State University)

dren, keep in mind that children like mild-flavored and mild-temperature foods best. They typically let their soup get cool and their ice cream get mushy.

As the children eat their food products, the teacher should remember to discuss the food. Naming, labeling, and restating the procedures used will help children remember. Helping them think of adjectives to describe the appearance and the taste of the foods adds to their vocabulary. Review the food group the food belongs to. Reminding them to tell their parents about the project further strengthens their learning and helps tie the home and the school together.

Food activities can seldom constitute the whole program. Like any good thing they can be overdone. In one group one child demanded on the fifth day of a study about apples, "Do we *have* to talk about apples again today?" Apparently the study of apples was interfering with the child's other strong interests. Such reactions may occur when teachers talk too much rather than providing an action project. The cumulative plan that was described in Chapter 11 is very effective in planning for food and nutrition education. Advo-

cating emphasis throughout the year, the cumulative plan helps children build their concepts and experiences little by little.

Mobilize

The teacher will mobilize available resources—human and nonhuman—to get food and nutrition concepts across to children. Actually, the first resource is the teacher who becomes informed and serves as a model who practices the kind of food habits she or he wishes children to develop. The teacher has tremendous influence on the children in the class because children want to be like the teacher. If a positive approach is used when talking about nutritious food, children will be enthusiastic about these foods. If the teacher enjoys and is willing to taste a wide variety of foods, children will be more inclined to do so.

Parents are a fine resource. They can help by trying out at home foods that are prepared at school. A class newsletter with recipes aids in getting this home activity under way. Parents may also be invited to school to make a dish for the class to try, for instance, Danish pastry from a family whose origins are in Denmark, tortillas from a parent whose roots are Mexican, or a rice dish made by a family with Asian roots. Parents are willing to contribute to the class if teachers invite them and give them personal support and guidance while they make their contributions.

Various other visitors can be helpful as well. Perhaps a member of 4-H or Scouts could give a food preparation demonstration in class. A home economics student could also present a demonstration. A dental hygienist can be invited to discuss how food helps children maintain good teeth. A National Dairy Council spokesperson may speak or send films, booklets, or pictures.

There are many books, pictures, movies, and filmstrips that might be utilized. The teacher should be sure to preview these to see if they can be easily explained to young children. Field trips mentioned earlier may be arranged through parents, interested friends, or local businesses.

The kitchen might be considered the chemical laboratory of the school for young children. It may be the regular school kitchen, with a small table in one corner where an adult and a few children prepare their foods. Some schools have elaborately furnished child-size kitchens. A table or two in the classroom can also become the food preparation center. A hot plate and utensils can be brought in on a tray and removed when the project is completed. The latter arrangement is probably the most common. Teachers frequently bring equipment from home. In public schools with lunchrooms or home economics classrooms, teachers often can use school equipment. Lacking cooking facilities, children's parents can be enlisted to take food home to bake after it is mixed by the children. Numerous possibilities exist. Each teacher explores the options and makes the arrangements to provide opportunities for the children to explore the world of food.

The teacher and the assistants discuss beforehand what their roles will be during the food preparation project. For example, will the assistants help with the food? Or will they carry on other activities? If so, which ones? If it is neces-

A child's measure of independence comes with serving oneself at mealtime. (Kansas State University)

sary to take food or children outside the room, who is to go? Will each child's product be labeled, or will it be placed in a common pan? What if a child wants to put the product in the locker or take it home? Who cleans up after the project?

LONG-RANGE GOALS FOR CHILDREN'S EXPERIENCES WITH FOOD

By providing experiences with food, the teacher helps young children build on the following long-range goals little by little. Children eventually learn these ten goals through their participation in food projects.

1. They need foods from all five food groups in order to grow, run, and learn.
2. It is fun and interesting to try new foods.
3. Foods have names, physical characteristics, and flavors.
4. Plants and animals grown on farms or living in the water are primary sources of food.
5. The supermarket supplies some food products that are ready to eat and others that are ready to prepare.
6. Preparation of food includes such processes as heating, cooling, freezing, beating, and grinding.
7. Cooking tools, equipment, and processes have names.
8. The scientific method of observing, relating, interpreting, and generalizing can be related to food.
9. Safety and cleanliness are important in the kitchen.
10. Both men and women like to prepare food and eat.

As specific food projects are now described, these ten goals will serve as general guides. More specific short-range goals will be needed as each food project is developed.

Learning the Sources of Foods

As far as most children know, the grocery store is the source of food. The children may help the teacher buy food there occasionally. Money concepts develop as they discuss the cost and the number of coins required to pay for a purchase.

Teachers can use visual aids, field trips, or a garden to help the children further their understanding of the primary sources of most foods.

Interest is guaranteed if the children have picked the apples for applesauce or the pumpkin for pumpkin custard, or if they have watched the cows being milked for the milk in ice cream. Garden products, too, will be pronounced "delicious" after they have been cared for by the children. The teacher can discuss the subject of primary

sources by asking, "Where is this food grown?" or "What happens to it before the grocer gets it?"

Because families today buy so many foods already prepared, even adults almost forget how a food is grown or how it appears in its primary state. The chance to plant, care for, pick, clean, cook, and then eat a food crop is experienced by fewer and fewer people as the society becomes increasingly more urban. A garden helps children understand that some food is first a growing plant. Occasionally a window box can be used for growing plants.

If it is not feasible to grow the plants (and teachers could never grow all of them), it may be possible to visit gardens and farms to see plants growing. Teachers can ask local citizens or vendors at a farmer's market for suggestions of local primary sources. The children might go to see such crops as wheat, corn, potatoes, fruit, pumpkins, or beans. Sometimes they may be allowed to pick a sample to take back to school.

A trip to the milking parlor of a dairy will help the children learn the source of their most common food—milk. A trip to the bottling and ice cream plants will add further to their information.

Because commercial egg producers generally won't admit visitors to egg-laying pens (because they excite the hens, who may stop laying), children may never see a hen lay an egg. A student teacher was telling the children that hens lay eggs, when one inquisitive child wanted to know, "How does the egg get out?" The student hadn't anticipated this question and was searching for a way to explain it when a knowledgeable five-year-old saved the day. The boy squatted henlike, then jumped around and squawked! It was real enough for everybody, and the discussion continued.

Pictures may be the only resource for teaching the primary source of many foods. Care should be taken to secure accurate information. One teacher was heard talking about pineapples growing on trees—certainly incorrect information for children to learn.

It is not easy for a child to understand how a cute little squealy pig relates to the breakfast bacon. Some children like animals so much that they really don't want to think about killing them to eat. Even a college student said, "How could you kill a chicken that you had known personally?" The children can be told the sources of meat, but the teacher need not speak of the butchering process unless the children ask. If asked, give a factual answer.

Many interesting food-related experiences can develop around the ocean and lakes with regard to the fish we eat. Children often like to talk about and play at going fishing.

Learning to Taste Fresh Foods

Many foods children eat are canned, bottled, or frozen. Teachers can look for ways to show children food in its fresh state.

Trays of fresh food can be arranged so that the children will taste various foods. Vegetables or fruits can be diced, and the children can serve themselves with toothpicks. An example of the whole food should be reserved so that the children can relate physical qualities—color, shape, size, and weight—to flavor and internal characteristics as they eat. Avoid introducing too many new items in one project. It confuses children. Repeat the project with new foods to taste on other days.

Orange juice is a familiar food. However, many families buy it frozen, bottled, or canned. Squeezing their own oranges and drinking the juice will delight children. Allow one orange per child. Provide several squeezers. Allow children to drink the juice as soon as it is squeezed. Have them talk about the taste, color, and consistency. Tell the children, "Juice is good for your skin and gums." Lemons can be squeezed for lemonade. Fruits such as apples, grapes, and cherries are sometimes heated to extract the juice. The children can help with this process too if reasonable precautions are taken with the hot liquids.

Children will enjoy cutting apples, bananas, celery, carrots, tomatoes, peppers, and cucumbers for their snack. To prevent discoloration, the teacher should remember to keep apples,

bananas, pears, and peaches in citrus juices or in a solution made of ascorbic acid (available in the freezer supply section of the grocery store) mixed in a little water or syrup. Fruits can be served alone or in a fruit cup. Celery stuffed with cream cheese or peanut butter is popular.

Learning How the Consistency of Food Changes

The children learn that through various processes in the kitchen—heating, cooling, freezing, grinding, beating—the food is made ready to eat. Children can observe some of the changes that take place. They can talk about the machines used. Remember all food preparation projects start with washing hands with soap—a rule to learn!

Peanut Butter

Peanut butter, a longtime favorite, can be made from peanuts ground in a blender. The children can shell the peanuts and place them in the blender. After the peanuts are ground, add jelly or honey to give a consistency that will spread. Serve a spoonful to each child, provide a plastic knife, and pass the crackers. Watch them spread the peanut butter and eat!

Gelatin

When making gelatin dessert, the children can see the effect of the hot water on the granules. Then they note the change to a solid after chilling. If gelatin is mixed at the beginning of the day, cooled with ice water or ice cubes, poured into individual paper cups, and cooled in the refrigerator, it is possible to have it ready to serve for snack $1\frac{1}{2}$ hours later. For variation, set the gelatin outdoors on a cold day. The children will conclude that "it's cold as a refrigerator outdoors."

Ice Cream

Making homemade ice cream teaches children that ice cream really does contain all the good foods that their parents say it does. They can actually see the milk, eggs, sugar, and flavoring go into the ice cream as it is being made. Either an electric or a hand-turned freezer can be used—and the children will help! It takes about a half hour or more of turning the handle. The proof is in the eating. M-m-m good! For a variation, one group used snow in place of the ice. Remember you'll need to add rock salt to ice to make it freeze—about 1 cup salt to 8 cups of ice cubes or chipped ice. Two gallon jugs of water frozen then chopped make enough ice for freezing 1 gallon of ice cream.

Butter

Making butter gives the children yet another chance to see a change take place before their eyes. Use 1 pint of whipping cream for fifteen to eighteen children. Pour 1 cup of whipping cream into each of two quart jars and tighten the lids. The children pass the jars around the table, shaking and counting off five shakes per child. The cream becomes whipped, then begins to separate into buttermilk and globules of butter. When sufficiently churned, the butter collects together. The buttermilk can be poured into small paper cups so that everyone can have a taste. The butter can be served on individual serving plates. Give the child a small plastic knife and watch as the butter goes on the crackers. Even children who say they hate butter will like both butter and buttermilk if it is presented to them with "Let's see how it tastes," instead of "Who wants some buttermilk?" or "Would you like some buttermilk?" Because whipping cream is sweet, the buttermilk tastes only slightly different from other milk.

Apples

Apples can be cooked to make applesauce. The children will observe the changing of the hard apples into the mushy sauce and the effect of sugar on the tart apple. Leaving the skin on the apple makes it easier for the children to do more of the project. Allow one apple per child. It is convenient to use the special apple cutter that cuts the apple into eight sections and cores it all in one operation. The children can accomplish this operation with a minimum of help. If cooking is done in the room, the tantalizing aroma will attract other cooks. Stir the cooked apples, add sugar and a bit of cinnamon, and serve for snack. The children will surely go home and ask to repeat this project!

Popcorn

Popcorn is a favorite of children. The addition of heat to popcorn kernels produces such an aro-

Snack time is both a time to rest and refuel and a time to talk to the teacher about activities of the day. (Michigan State University)

matic odor that people in other parts of the building will drop into the classroom. An electric popper or skillet is handy for this project. Follow the usual safety precautions. Some teachers avoid popcorn because children may choke on it. Infants and toddlers should not be given popcorn, and other children should sit quietly while eating it.

Eggs

Eggs change consistency when heated. They can be boiled or scrambled. If shells are needed for dyeing, the inside of the egg can be blown out and scrambled. To blow out the egg, first use a paring knife to tap a hole about $\frac{1}{4}$ inch in diameter in each end of the shell, then BLOW. Adults will help prepare the egg for blowing. Let each child blow an egg into a single cup. If bits of shell break off, the shell can more easily be retrieved. The children can help beat the eggs, adding seasoning and 1 tablespoon of milk per egg. The children can take turns stirring the egg in the electric skillet and watching the coagulation occur as the cooking process progresses. Serve for snack or lunch. Arrange timing to serve warm.

Breads

Breads of many varieties can be made in the classroom. The children learn more if they are made from "scratch" than when they are made from mixes. Actually breads have only a few ingredients. Recipes can be posted near the cooking table. What could be more fun than mixing, cooking, then eating your very own pancake? Pancakes can be served with jelly or powdered sugar. Biscuits, muffins, tortillas, and banana bread are other suggestions. Yeast bread can be made, but the project may require two days.

Baked Goods

Cookies, cakes, and gingerbread can be made with various mixes. However, mixes simplify the process so much that understanding of the total ingredients required is reduced. Cookies and cakes may be made for a special day. Sometimes at the close of school a group makes a single birthday cake for all the children who have summer birthdays. The group sings "Happy Birthday" to each child!

Directions follow for making special sugar cookies in the classroom. By noting the concern for details in this outline, the teacher may be helped with planning other projects.

Main Dishes

Main dishes for the lunch menu or a more substantial snack can also be made by children. Try canned soups, cheese sandwiches, tuna sandwiches, or cinnamon toast.

No child will pass up a vegetable soup after helping to cook the soup bone one day, chopping the vegetables the next, and watching "our soup" simmer to completion the next. By that time everyone will literally have had a finger in the soup and surely will pronounce it "good." Some teachers like to call the soup "stone soup" and relate the familiar children's story to this experience.

Hamburgers, broiled hot dog bits, or pizza can be made. An electric skillet with temperature control is safest for hamburgers. The children can cut the hot dogs and watch with the teacher as they broil. The children can make pizzas by patting out canned biscuits and covering them with mildly seasoned pizza sauce and cheese. The pizzas are then baked.

Jelly

Children can help make jelly using the noncook method. The recipe for "freezer jelly" is found on the pectin box. Sugar is stirred into fresh, canned, or reconstituted frozen juice. The teacher boils the pectin for 1 minute with $\frac{3}{4}$ cup of water. Then children can help stir as pectin is added to the juice and sugar. The jelly sets in a day or so. Children delight in using their "own" jelly and in spreading their own sandwiches with plastic picnic knives. It is a messy job, so teachers should prepare the table with a clean sheet of wide paper. Children will get jelly from ear to ear, too, so a washup must follow the snack

MAKING SUGAR COOKIES WITH YOUNG CHILDREN

1. Use a sugar cookie recipe suitable for rolled cookies. Add a little more flour than is needed if an adult were going to roll them. The recipe will make fewer cookies than it states because the children will not roll them very thin.

2. The children can help put the ingredients together. Mixing may be done the day before the cookies are baked, or the teacher can have the refrigerated cookie dough ready when the children arrive. The time element will be the deciding factor. The rolling, cutting, and baking are usually enough for a half-day group to do.

3. Divide the dough into balls—enough for each child to make three or four cookies. Make a few extras in case of an accident.

4. Have the supplies on a tray—several rolling pins, flour, sifter, spatulas, cookie cutters, colored sugars, raisins, and plenty of cookie sheets.

5. Use a low table so that the children can stand to work. Cover the table with clean tea towels. Pull them tight and tack the edges or secure then with masking tape. Sift flour on the area where each child will roll the dough.

6. Be sure each child washes his or her hands just before coming to help. Supervise the hand washing, or hands may not be clean enough for food handling.

7. The children will be inclined to push down hard on the rolling pin, so tell them, "Let the rolling pin do the work." You may need to stand behind each child, helping each barely press the rolling pin down.

8. When the dough is rolled enough to cut, be ready with this statement, "Let me tell you a cook's secret." Then show each how to fit several cookie cutters on the dough before cutting any. Children are inclined to cut one cookie out of the middle and then have to reroll the dough. Help the child place the cookies on a greased cookie sheet.

9. The cookie decorator's table is set up nearby. It is another low table and should be covered with paper or a cloth for catching the sugar. The children can sit to decorate cookies. Colored sugar is provided in shakers. Raisins and red hots are also popular. The children spend a long time here getting just the right effect. When a child adds so much sugar that it might burn and stick to the pan, the cookies may need to be transferred to a fresh baking sheet.

10. One adult is required to supervise the oven as soon as a pan of cookies is ready. Set a timer because cookies bake quickly. Children enjoy peeking in the oven, so let them take turns as cookie watchers.

11. It is generally best to avoid keeping track of which cookie is whose. Some get broken or burned, so if they are mixed up no one is disappointed with the finished product.

12. Of course, the proof of a cookie is in the eating. As soon as the children are through rolling their cookies and sufficient cookies are out of the oven, it is time to bring out the milk for the pleasurable moment of eating their own cookies.

period. The recipe makes enough jelly for a sandwich for each in a class of fifteen.

Learning About Safety and Cleanliness

Children learn safety concepts along with other concepts during cooking projects. It is best to choose cooking projects that offer a minimum of danger to the children. Nearly any project involving heat or the use of knives requires adult supervision at all times. Locate electric cords out of traffic lanes so that the children won't trip over them. Foods just out of the oven or just off the stove are extremely hot. Take care that the children are not burned. Provide a cutting board for each child and reasonably sharp knives. Take time to show the children safety measures for cutting and for handing tools to each other. Keep the working groups to three or four children. Have sufficient adults to ensure safety.

Cleanliness of children's hands and of utensils can both be taught during food activities. Planning is required to get a child's hands washed with soap just before he or she is ready to handle the food. If the child washes before the activity is ready and turns to play with toys, it is obvious that the hands are no longer clean and should be washed again. All this washing will confuse the children who, of course, can't see the "invisible" germs on their hands. Go ahead and tell them that germs exist. It's the beginning of understanding.

Learning About Gender Roles

All activities are available to all children without regard to their gender. Food activities are of great interest to boys. Teachers may have to dispel the notion that preparing food is only for girls. Many fathers cook and barbecue. Interestingly, the majority of professional chefs are men.

MEALTIME IN THE SCHOOL FOR YOUNG CHILDREN

A visit to a school lunchroom is often a revelation to parents, especially if they can observe out of sight of their child. Parents make comments like the following: "He eats so well!" "I didn't know she could pour milk!" "Doesn't J.D. ask you to feed him?" The child may eat quite differently in a group of children and when guided by a skilled teacher.

When children are old enough for school, they may have recently entered an eating stage that frustrates their parents. The infant grows rapidly, so food consumption is high. At age three the growth curve has leveled out and food needs are

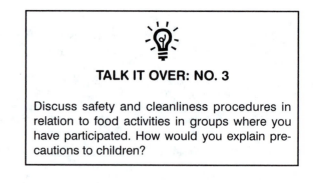

TALK IT OVER: NO. 3

Discuss safety and cleanliness procedures in relation to food activities in groups where you have participated. How would you explain precautions to children?

reduced.[3] About this same time children reach a stage where they want to assert their independence. They say "No" frequently and may refuse to eat foods they have been eating all along. Parents with a child of this age may get into the habit of bribing, cajoling, threatening, then finally feeding the child, just to get some food eaten. When entering an early childhood school, a child brings along home experience with food. However, the presence of other children eating without help gives him or her more mature models to emulate.

Goals for Mealtime

During mealtime the teacher wants the child

- to eat a well-balanced diet,
- to enjoy mealtime,
- to taste and ultimately enjoy eating a wide variety of food,
- to learn to eat independently,
- to sit at the table and develop acceptable table manners.

A balanced diet will be planned by the nutritionist. Each food, including the dessert, is calculated to make a contribution to the child's essential nutrients. For this reason, dessert is not used

---

[3]Corinne H. Robinson and Marilyn R. Lawler, *Normal and Therapeutic Nutrition* (New York: Macmillan, 1982), pp. 370–371.

as a reward for a clean plate. When school meals differ from home meals in both type of food and type of service, there is considerable adjustment for the child to make. The teacher understands that the children will need time to become accustomed to school food.

Food can be pretty as well as tasty. Plan variety in the color, texture, and shape of food. Tables and service should be orderly and attractive. Family style is the usual method of serving, with each table of five or six children having the dishes of food served by an adult at the table.

Children enjoy assuming some responsibility for meal service. Even three-year-olds can help set the table. Four- and five-year-olds will vie for the honor, and the teacher may need to keep a list of the helpers to be sure they all get turns. The children can also assist in cleaning up the tables following the meal. This training is good for all children but may be especially beneficial to children whose home routines appear inadequate.

Every effort should be made to arrange the setting so that it is pleasant, satisfying, and relaxing for both children and adults. The children should be seated on comfortable-height chairs that enable their feet to touch the floor. The youngest may need bibs. You can make self-help bibs by attaching a piece of elastic to a washcloth for the child to slip over the head.

Each child should have a special seat. Sometimes a teacher fosters a friendship by pairing a child who needs a friend with a potential friend during lunch. Although socializing is permitted at mealtime, the primary goal is to eat. The teacher may also wisely plan to seat the children who need special help near an adult, to disperse children who tend to be behavior problems, and to place independent eaters where they can be imitated by more dependent children. A seating arrangement that allows teachers to relax and get some nourishment too is important, because they may be required to spend several more hours that day being responsive to children's needs.

Eating family style with an adult at each table makes it easier for children's individual needs to be met. (University of Illinois)

Breakfast is served to children who arrive early in full-day schools, in Head Start groups, and in many kindergartens since the federal nutrition program has been instituted. Some children may want to eat immediately on arrival, whereas others may prefer to play awhile and then have their breakfast. Breakfast is usually more informal than lunch. One teacher takes care of the eaters and another supervises those who are playing.

Most teachers have observed that when children have a quiet time just prior to lunch, they eat better. Children can do their toileting and washing and then gather around the teacher for quiet stories and songs. The period should not be rushed. It is not the best time to demand the most responsible behavior, because the children who are tired and hungry are more prone to anger.[4] When conflicts are common, teachers may wish to schedule lunch somewhat earlier, provide a more substantial midmorning snack, or plan a less taxing morning program.

An orderly transition to the lunch tables from the story circle helps retain the quiet atmosphere. The teacher can say, "Children who sit with Mrs. D., creep like little hungry mice to your lunch table."

The teacher serves the food, adjusting the amount to an estimation of each child's appetite for a certain food. Many foods will be served in teaspoon-sized servings, especially foods that are new or less popular. The teacher assumes that each child will taste the food. When the teacher knows the child well, it is possible to gauge more accurately the portions, and a clean plate will occur more often. Enjoyment of food is more important than a clean plate, however. "There are three peak periods for the development of obesity in children: late infancy, early childhood around six, and adolescence," according to nutrition researchers. "Obesity interferes with both

health and psychological functioning."[5] Teachers and parents are cautioned by nutritionists about requiring a clean plate, as that may mean urging the child to overeat.

The teacher's small servings permit the child to ask for seconds and to serve him- or herself. Children enjoy this measure of independence. When they want more milk, the teacher will pour the amount appropriate for the glass in a small pitcher and permit the child to pour his or her own milk. If the small pitcher contains more than a glassful, the child may overfill the glass. Children will drink numerous servings when they get to do the replenishing.

The teacher realizes that children generally like foods lukewarm. They may let soups cool and ice cream melt before eating.

A typical serving arrangement allows children to take their dirty plates and silverware to a serving cart and return with their desserts when they have finished the main course. This gives them a chance to move a bit when they have been sitting for a time. They like this measure of confidence that they can walk without spilling their dessert.

Guidance During Mealtime[6]

If the child is actively participating in the school program and is in good health physically and emotionally, he or she will eat what is needed to restore energy and to grow. Guidance during the meal will be related to the goals stated earlier. Every effort is made to help the child grow in independence. Teachers should not fall into a pattern of bribing, cajoling, or feeding children.

Even a three-year-old senses that the teacher can't spoon-feed five or six children (the number generally served at one table). The child simply imitates the others and goes about the business of

---

[4]Catherine Landreth, *Early Childhood: Behavior and Learning* (New York: Alfred A. Knopf, 1967), p. 142.

[5]Myron Winick, "Childhood Obesity," *Nutrition Today* 9:3 (May/June 1974), 9–10. C. Robinson and M. R. Lawler, op. cit., pp. 368–369, support this view.
[6]For more information see Chapter 9, "Guiding Children's Eating Behavior," in *Guiding Young Children* by Verna Hildebrand (Upper Saddle River, NJ: Merrill/Prentice Hall, 1994).

```
      ╲│╱
     ─ 💡 ─
      ╱│╲
       ≡

TALK IT OVER: NO. 4

Discuss the effect on the child of having par-
ents and teachers understand that children pre-
fer foods lukewarm—neither hot nor cold.
```

eating. The teacher quietly praises the child and smiles. The child pours milk, cuts beans, and goes to the serving cart for dessert.

Children's meals at home may be come-and-go affairs, so they may think they can eat a little now and a little later even at school. The teacher can simply say, "If you are finished eating, put your plate on the cart. If you are hungry, sit at the table and eat." The teacher will give the child the choice, and after the decision, both teacher and pupil will live by it. A few days of finding food served at a regular time will help the child realize the necessity of eating at the designated time and place.

The teacher guides the child quietly in brief, positive statements, letting the child know what should be done. The teacher makes statements like: "Use your toast stick," to the child using fingers to get food on a fork; "A spoon will work better," to a child eating apple sauce with a fork; "Hold your glass up straight," to a child whose milk is about to spill; "Swallow before you talk," to the child who is talking with a full mouth; or "Keep your food on your plate," to the child who litters the tablecloth.

The teacher uses demonstrations, perhaps showing the child how to grip the fork for eating or cutting. She or he guides the child's hand to help. For example, while saying, "Point the spoon toward you," the teacher may guide the child's hand to make the tip turn toward the child's mouth.

Children generally feel upset about spills. Children are sometimes scolded harshly at home

and may expect the same treatment at school. When the teacher occasionally spills something, the children may feel a new sense of comradeship. Spills do occur. They are taken in stride. Extra silverware and napkins are kept close by to replace dropped items. A sponge, dustpan, and broom are available in the serving area. When accidents are frequent, a slight change in arrangement might help avoid them. For example, if the table is cluttered, it may help to place serving dishes on a side table within reach. Teachers will prevent some spills if they are alert to remind a child to place the glass back away from the edge of the table.

When the child has finished eating, he or she takes the plate and glass to the serving cart and leaves the dining area. A designated adult takes over for the next steps. It is important that children who remain at the lunch tables are not neglected because of all the adults becoming involved with the children who have finished eating. A routine should be established so that children know what to do next. Generally they go to the bathroom to wash and for toileting needs, then either prepare for going home or for taking a nap, depending on the type of school.

In full-day programs, the nap room is generally readied while the children eat. As children finish lunch, they prepare immediately for naps, to take advantage of the quieting effect of eating.

Snack Time

Midmorning and midafternoon snacks serve several purposes for young children. A snack provides time to rest and food to restore energy. It provides an informal, social conversation time good for summing up the day's activities. Snack may be a fairly organized time of day or it may be informal. In groups that remain at school for lunch, the teacher may plan an early snack to avoid interfering with lunch appetites. Some children are slow starters. They eat very light breakfasts but then are famished by snack time. They eat so much snack that they aren't hungry for an early lunch. If snack is served in an informal come-when-you're-hungry arrangement during the first hour of school, it meets the needs of such children. In groups who take a midday nap at school, it may be customary to allow a few children at a time to eat their midafternoon snack as soon as they wake up. This plan offers the teacher time to talk with a few children individually while others are still napping.

In other groups teachers may like to hold a quiet time immediately following the self-selected activity period, then follow this with a group snack time when everyone eats together. In this way the half-day group accomplishes some of the goals that are achieved with a lunch program. No one plan is "best." The important rule is to make a good plan for a particular group of children.

The numerous suggestions for cooking projects and experiences with food offered in the first part of this chapter will contribute most if the children work together preparing the food, eat it together, and talk about it, thereby reinforcing the learning.

Of course, the children do not prepare every snack. The fare offered should be varied. There surely is no need for children to say, "Not that again!" in disparaging voices when they see the snack tray. Interesting food, attractively arranged and enthusiastically presented, will encourage the children to enjoy eating. They will be not only feeding themselves but learning about food as well.

Children can be designated "helpers" with snack. Perhaps one can serve the beverage, another place the napkins, another take the responsibility for helping serve the food. A poster showing a paper cup, a plate, and a napkin can be used to designate helpers—the names being removable and rotated during the weeks.

It is helpful to arrange in advance individual servings of food and drink at each child's place to eliminate prolonged waiting for the refreshments. For example, a glass of juice, a napkin holding three cookies, a dish of fruit, or a cup-cake liner holding a serving of raisins can be set out on a tray from which the helpers can distribute the servings around the table before the children arrive at their places.

Imagine the impatience felt by the children who waited for one frustrated little girl to count out three cookies to each child in a class of twenty-five youngsters. Not only did they want three cookies, but they didn't want any broken ones. Several children could have been designated to help. The broken cookies should have been made into crumbs and used for some special dessert, as they were undesirable in the broken form.

Guidance suggestions made for serving lunch also apply to snack time. The children remove their glasses and napkins when they are finished, placing them on a tray for removal to the kitchen.

COMMUNICATING WITH PARENTS

Close coordination of the school and the home feeding programs may avoid unnecessary confusion for the child.[7] Parents can be invited to observe snack or lunchtime occasionally so that they will understand the experience their child is having. They should understand the goals the teacher has for a child of this age and the techniques used to foster those goals. Lunch menus can be sent home regularly.

Informing parents when there have been special projects that the children may ask them to duplicate at home helps the parents carry through the learning begun in the school. Metheny et al. found that 34 percent of the children in their study requested their mothers to

---

[7]Reva T. Frankle, Miriam F. Senhouse, and Catherine Cowell, "Project Head Start: A Challenge in Creativity in Community Nutrition," *Journal of Home Economics* 59:1 (January 1967), 24–27. The authors give numerous practical tips for helping children learn to eat nutritious foods and make suggestions for working with parents to improve nutrition in the home.

prepare food they had eaten at school.[8] Recipes can be exchanged. Occasionally the teacher may visit the home to demonstrate how to prepare a food that the child has liked at school. When the teacher and the parent develop rapport on such domestic interests as recipes, it may strengthen the communication between the family and the school.

Parents may enjoy contributing an item for snack or lunch. Some local sanitary codes forbid it, however, the school policy will be stated by the teacher. Parents are asked to inform the teacher ahead of time so that school food projects won't overshadow the parents' contribution. Duplications can then be avoided and parents' choice of a contribution can be guided so that it is appropriate in kind and amount. A typical occasion is a birthday or a holiday. A simple celebration at school is far easier on child and parent than giving a party at home. Teachers typically plan something festive for each child's birthday.

In one kindergarten the teacher left the snack completely up to the parents. If they wanted their child to have a snack, they had to send it to school. What happened in practice was that a group of disadvantaged children regularly sat through the snack period and watched their more well-to-do classmates sip from cans of juice and eat cookies. It is hard to understand how a thinking, feeling teacher could permit such a cruel situation in a class. If the advantaged parents had realized what was happening, they surely would have been willing to contribute to a snack fund to be used to purchase a snack for all the children. In fairness, what is available for one should be available to all.

Conclusions

Adequate nutrition is essential to life and learning. While the parents and teachers are responsi-

ble for the young child's nutrition, the early childhood center is a good place for that child to learn food habits that will help ensure optimal nutritional status in the years ahead. There are numerous opportunities for early childhood teachers to provide food and nutrition education. Efforts must be personalized, simplified, dramatized, regularized, and mobilized. The teacher mobilizes and utilizes various community resources in order to provide the needed experiences. Numerous food experiences were suggested along with some pointers on mealtime and snack time.

Applications

1. Discuss the "Talk It Over" items found in the chapter.
2. Write an activity plan for a food activity for a few children using information and the sample plan (Figure 6–2) in Chapter 6. Secure approval, carry out the plan, and evaluate the results from the children's point of view and your viewpoint. Prepare a report and hand it in along with your approved plan.
3. Evaluate your total participation performance on your evaluation form developed in Chapter 1.
4. Add ideas and plans for food experiences to your Resource File.

Study Questions

1. Give an explanation of why nutrition education is more parent education than child education.
2. Identify and explain each of the five guides for planning food and nutrition activities for young children.
3. State and give examples of each of the ten long-range goals for children's experiences with food.
4. Explain in what ways experiences with food are science experiences.
5. State and discuss the goals for mealtime in full-day schools.

---

[8]Norma Y. Metheny, Fern E. Hunt, Mary B. Patton, and Helene Heye, "The Diets of Preschool Children," *Journal of Home Economics* 54:4 (April 1962), 306.

6. State and discuss the goals for providing snacks in part-day schools.
7. State several ways teachers can involve parents in the food activities of the school.

Videotapes

Establishing Healthful Habits

Thelma Harms and Debby Cryer show how to encourage good nutrition, sleep patterns, and other habits that promote wellness at home and in child care. They suggest solutions to health threats for infants in daycare settings. DC/TATS MEDIA. Frank Porter Graham Child Development Center, University of North Carolina at Chapel Hill CB8040, 300 NCNB Plaza, Chapel Hill, NC 27599-8040.

Additional Readings

Birch, Leann L., Susan L. Johnson, and Jennifer A. Fisher. "Children's Eating: The Development of Food-Acceptance Patterns." *Young Children* 50:2, January 1995, 71–78.

Bredekamp, Sue, ed. *Developmentally Appropriate Practice in Early Childhood Programs Serving Children from Birth Through Age 8.* Washington, DC: NAEYC, 1987.

———. *Accreditation Criteria and Procedures of the National Academy of Early Childhood Programs.* Washington, DC: NAEYC, 1991.

Church, Marilyn. "Nutrition: A Vital Part of the Curriculum." *Young Children* 35:1, November 1979, 61–65.

Cosgrove, Maryellen Smith. "Cooking in the Classroom: The Doorway to Nutrition." *Young Children* 46:3, March 1991, 43–46.

Enders, Jeannette B., and Robert E. Rockwell. *Food, Nutrition, and the Young Child.* Upper Saddle River, NJ: Merrill/Prentice Hall, 1990.

Herr, Judith, and Winifred Morse. "Food for Thought: Nutrition Education for Young Children." *Young Children* 38:1, November 1982, 3–11.

Hildebrand, Verna. *Guiding Young Children.* Upper Saddle River, NJ: Merrill/Prentice Hall, 1994.

Hildebrand, V., and P. Hearron. *Management of Child Development Centers.* Upper Saddle River, NJ: Merrill/Prentice Hall, 1997.

Klefstad, Jill. "Cooking in the Kindergarten." *Young Children* 50:6, September 1995, 32–33.

Oliver, Shirley D., and Katherine O. Musgrave. *Nutrition: A Sourcebook of Integrated Activities.* Boston: Allyn and Bacon, 1984.

Robinson, Corinne H., and Marilyn R. Lawler. *Normal and Therapeutic Nutrition.* New York: Macmillan, 1982.

Rogers, Cosby S., and Sandra S. Morris. "Reducing Sugar in Children's Diets." *Young Children* 41:5, July 1986, 11–16.

Wanamaker, Nancy, K. Hearn, and S. Richarz. *More Than Graham Crackers: Nutrition Education and Food Preparation with Young Children.* Washington, DC: NAEYC, 1979.

Wishon, Phillip, R. Bower, and B. Eller. "Childhood Obesity: Prevention and Treatment." *Young Children* 39:1, November 1983, 21–27.

CHAPTER 19

Managing an Early Childhood Group

Garden City, Kansas Community College

Objectives

✔ Identify and define the managerial tasks of teachers.
✔ Explain the need for setting aside planning and preparation time.
✔ Define and explain a cumulative plan for the curriculum.
✔ Differentiate between technical and social decisions.

"We need to talk about Jerry's progress," said Darlene, holding her open planning book.

"I'd like for us to keep our transportation theme another week. The children's play is developing a lot of depth," said Roger as he settled down for their weekly planning session.

arlene and Roger are meeting to map out the details of their next week's program for their class of four-year-olds. They are taking advantage of the planning time allotted to them while their aide and a substitute teacher manage their room. They are paid for this two-hour block of planning and preparation time because their school is NAEYC accredited. Paid planning time is an important criterion in the NAEYC Center Accreditation Project.[1]

TEACHERS AS MANAGERS

You, like Roger and Darlene, are moving into the role of managing a group of children. Managers make two major types of decisions:

[1]Sue Bredekamp, ed., *Accreditation Criteria and Procedures of the National Academy of Early Childhood Programs* (Washington, DC: NAEYC, 1991), p. 22.

1. **technical decisions** like what activities will contribute to children's language development and
2. **social decisions** like what strategies would be best for helping Jerry get along with other children.

Technical decisions typically apply to things. Social decisions apply to people. It is easier to get hard evidence for technical decisions, whereas for social decisions we need experience, technical information, and wisdom.

You will arrive at the point of taking charge of a group of children after successfully completing several steps in your early childhood teacher education program. Your practice teaching assignment may be your first experience in assuming leadership of others and being "in charge." Before long, there you'll be, a full-fledged teacher and really in charge! You should

Sibling relationships are maintained in multiple age groups. (Ishen Li, photographer)

FIGURE 19–1
Teacher's puzzle.

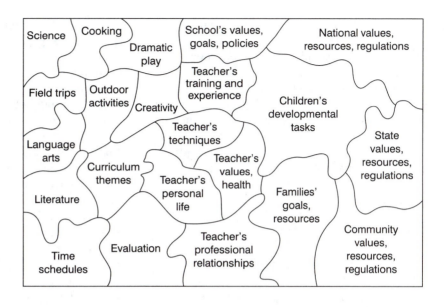

feel ready to put the teacher's puzzle (Figure 19–1) together.

As a teacher you will be the manager of the group and classroom to which you are assigned. The mountain of decisions will be yours. Administrators like to hire well-qualified teachers and to assume they are ready to take charge. The more capably you handle your assignment, the less the principal or school administrator is likely to become involved. You'll be more autonomous. Although you and your co-teacher have some autonomy, however, you still must be prepared to work cooperatively with the administration, the other staff, the parents, and, of course, the children.

It is recommended that you, as a new teacher, look for a mentor with whom you can confer. Early childhood teachers frequently find themselves one of a few, or sometimes even the only early childhood teacher in a school. Thus, for professional stimulation you must make friends and develop links with teachers of older children. An experienced teacher can be a great help to a new teacher just learning the ropes. Teachers who are changing school systems should make contacts with other teachers who can be a source

of information that typically does not come through memos from the administration.

MANAGEMENT TASKS

Management requires five major tasks. In this book the primary focus is on the managerial tasks of teachers who are in charge of groups of children. In another book this author has discussed the managerial tasks of managers, directors, and principals.[2] The following five managerial tasks apply to schools and to many types of agencies that you might manage.

1. **Planning** is defined as a systematic formulation of a program of action for achieving goals.
2. **Organizing** is defined as systematically assembling and utilizing temporal, material, and spatial resources for carrying out a plan of action.

---

[2]V. Hildebrand and P. Hearron, *Management of Child Development Centers* (Upper Saddle River, NJ: Merrill/Prentice Hall, 1997).

3. **Staffing** is defined as selecting, assigning, utilizing, and evaluating the human resources needed for carrying out a plan of action.
4. **Leading** is defined as setting the pace toward present goals and formulating future goals.
5. **Monitoring and controlling** are defined as being alert to the performance of self and others in relation to established standards and making decisions and carrying out adjustments needed for meeting standards.

TALK IT OVER: NO. 1

Review each of the managerial tasks and relate each to the many tasks of teachers. Discuss with your classmates.

PLANNING PROGRAMS FOR YOUNG CHILDREN

Planning the early childhood program requires orchestrating all the distinct components as discussed throughout this book. **Planning** is a systematic formulation of a program of action for achieving goals. Planning requires giving attention to the various relationships and proportions, and achieving a program that can be expected to meet the needs of each child optimally. Just as an artist creates a unique painting by balancing component ideas, feelings, colors, and textures harmoniously, teachers likewise integrate all components. Teachers plan in depth and in detail in order to use human and nonhuman resources advantageously and to carry out a unique program in unique ways for a unique group of unique children. Teaching is a cluster of creative tasks.

Planning is the behind-the-scenes work that ensures a humanistic, person-centered, develop-

Name tags help assistants relate personally to each child. Be sure name tags are ready each day for children to select their own—a good literacy project. (Kansas State University)

mental program responsive to children's needs and interests. Many details of plans appear on written charts, while other details are in the teachers' heads and ready for use at a moment's notice. The less experience the teachers have, the more written planning is essential to be sure that it is adequately done. Shared planning is essential for full cooperation when working with several adults. Evaluating goes hand in hand with planning and is discussed later in this chapter.

Factors That Influence Planning

If a teacher were asked, "What is your major consideration when planning the program for your group of children?" the probable reply would be, "The children." This is, of course, as it should be. However, there are a number of other factors that teachers must also take into consideration. Some forces are national in scope, some are statewide, some are professional, and others originate in the community, the school, and the particular families of children. The planning task is somewhat like a puzzle, like Figure 19–1.

Impact of the Federal Government

The democratic form of government of the United States influences teachers as they educate children to live in a democracy. In an authoritarian country the child is educated to function in that system. An example of national influence is the Supreme Court decision forbidding racial segregation in public schools. Also, the program of federal aid to education stimulated communities to initiate Head Start and other programs. Many research projects and child care centers were assisted through federal funds.

The federal government has passed legislation mandating education for all Handicapped Children (1975) and services and accommodation for Americans with Disabilities (1990). Project Head Start began integrating disabled children in the early years. Thus for over twenty years this profession and many others have been making efforts to comply with this complex set of requirements. Many teachers and directors have made outstanding efforts to become knowledgeable about how to teach and serve children with disabilities. All the concepts of child development are helpful to teachers and parents as they adapt activities and environments for disabled children. For the most part teachers are still learning how to make adjustments for these children and are working valiantly at the tasks.

Private schools are indirectly affected by federal action. For example, the standards established in federal Head Start guidelines regarding the teacher-pupil ratio give parents, teachers, and administrators in for-profit and nonprofit schools a standard they did not have previously.

Impact of State Governments

State governments have an impact on the teacher who plans for a group of children. States generally hold the power to set and enforce minimum standards, grant licenses to schools, and grant certificates to teachers. Most states provide state aid to public schools providing kindergartens. To receive financial aid, the schools are required to meet certain standards for curriculum, qualifications of teachers, and minimum number of days in a school year. State legislation may set some standards concerning facilities, children's medical examinations, or the number and ages of children admitted to classes. Check with the licensing agency in your state. Read through the licensing regulations to appreciate rules your manager is required to follow.

Influence of the Community

The community influences the program planning. In a public school, authority is vested in an elected board of community citizens that acts through a school administrator. Also, a city commission may hire the director of a community child care center or the director of the community action program. Nonprofit agencies, churches, or universities have special objectives that affect the teacher's planning. Local government agencies may also be responsible for enforcing certain fire and health regulations. Teachers must be aware of regulations as they plan.

Influence of the School Administration

The school itself establishes policies for all the classrooms in a system. School administrations control the funds that are spent for supplies, new equipment, janitorial help, and paid assistants. School traditions, such as admission policies or parent participation, will influence planning. Some coordination of programs is required when several classes use the same equipment and play yard. Ideally, the teacher will be called to take part in decisions affecting her or his area of specialization.

Influence of the Parents

Early childhood schools are considered a vital part of the country's family support system. Leadership is needed to build this link with the parents of children in early childhood schools.

Parents of children in a group can influence a teacher's planning. They know something of the impact the teaching is having on their child. When open communication exists between the teachers and the parents, the school gets valuable feedback regarding the positive and negative aspects of a program. The teacher's attitude toward parents can make the difference in parents' vital concern for or apathy toward school matters. If teachers listen to parents and actively involve them in school, parents can have a positive influence. Parents can also be a source of relentless pressure if their interests are consistently ignored. Head Start parents have been effective advocates for their children, saving the program from politicians several times.

In a study completed by the author on "Value Orientations for Nursery School Programs,"[3] parents rated individuality and socialization as their two most preferred value orientations for nursery school programs, when given a choice of nine orientations depicted through nine short stories. The nine value orientations were socialization,

intellect, morality, aesthetics, authority, health, freedom, individuality, and economics. The economic value story was generally rated last.

A teacher must be aware of and attempt to open discussion with parents regarding their value orientations. If parents expect a type of program that is completely unacceptable to the teacher, then the two parties will have to work out some accommodation, or the teacher may decide to teach in another environment. No one value is "right," nor is it entirely unrelated to the other values, but there must be some meeting of minds between teachers and parents or the children's early education experience may suffer.

Influence of the Teacher and the Profession

Classrooms have unique characteristics because teachers are different. Teachers have different professional education and experience. Each teacher associates with other teachers to a different extent. Programs bear the mark of a teacher's philosophy, education, personality, creativity, health, and values. The teacher's personal life away from the school will have an impact on the class, just as the satisfactions gained from teaching will affect personal life.

The standards of the early childhood professions will influence the teacher throughout her or his educational experience and as a practitioner. The more the teachers are involved professionally, the more they are likely to be aware of current developments in the profession. Thus they will be able to choose from the best of current thinking and research regarding child development and early childhood education and incorporate this information into their programs for children and their parents.

The NAEYC is currently influential in setting and improving standards for programs. Through NAEYC's National Academy of Early Childhood Programs, an early childhood school can become accredited. For a center to become accredited means that the school meets the standards for high quality that were derived by consensus of a large group of professional early childhood edu-

---

[3]For a summary of the study see Chapter 24 of *Guiding Young Children* by V. Hildebrand (Upper Saddle River, NJ: Merrill/Prentice Hall, 1994), and idem, *Reading Improvement* 12:3 (Fall 1975), 168–173.

TALK IT OVER: NO. 2

Discuss the community conditions and the local, state, and Federal requirements that are influencing your planning for children.

cators from across the United States. Accreditation is a coveted designation that parents and the public are beginning to recognize as symbolic of high quality.[4]

Influence of Children

Last, but not least, the children influence the program. The school is there for them. Goals for children and characteristics of children in various age groups are discussed in Chapters 2 and 3. Teachers will spend a career searching for ways to help children reach their highest potentials. Knowing them and their families will be a significant part of the task. Each experienced teacher has become aware of the unique characteristics of each group before the school year is many weeks old. The inclusion policies related to children with disabilities creates the need for new learning and new policies.[5]

ADEQUATE PLANNING REQUIRES TIME

Time is required for planning. A program that meets accreditation standards happens by design, not by chance. There is a common fallacy that to

After planning to have a planting project, you'll need to prepare containers, seeds, a place to work, and a place in the sun for the seeds to grow. (G. Hildreth, photographer)

[4]Information about accreditation can be secured by writing the NAEYC, 1509 16th St. NW, Washington, DC 20036-1426, or calling 1-800-424-2460. The National Academy of Early Childhood Programs can be reached at the same address. The standards are presented in S. Bredekamp, ed., *Accreditation Criteria and Procedures of the National Academy of Early Childhood Programs* (Washington, DC: NAEYC, 1991).
[5]See Chapters 2 and 13 in *Knowing and Servicing Diverse Families* by V. Hildebrand et al. (Upper Saddle River, NJ: Merrill/Prentice Hall, 1996.)

teach young children, one has only to drop into the classroom and set out a few toys. Planning time is so important that the NAEYC accreditation standards require that the staff be allowed paid time for planning. Not only must the teacher and staff take time to read, study, generate ideas, and make plans, but they must also prepare materials before the children arrive at school. Obviously the full-day teacher who plans for fifty-two weeks each year has a more extensive planning task than the teacher of a part-day program that meets only three days per week during the winter months. However, both teachers must have plans in place.

When teachers interview for new positions they should inquire about paid planning time. Many schools make no provision in the teacher's schedule for planning or evaluating. Not infrequently, teachers are paid only for the hours they spend in actual contact with children. They are not paid for time in planning and evaluation conferences. Teachers are even scheduled for as many as ten contact hours daily, with no time away from children that could be used for planning. This is a short-sighted view on the part of administrations. If teachers are to do the creative job that should be expected, they should be compensated for the planning that is basic to that job. If one cause could be singled out as the root of current criticism regarding the lack of significant learning in schools for young children, the absence of planning would surely be that cause.

Student teachers, too, may unrealistically assume that their "required hours" are merely the children's class hours. However, for students to make the most of their opportunity to learn with an experienced teacher at their side, they must be willing to attend the necessary planning conferences as well as to search for and prepare resource materials outside the children's class hours. Because the dual role of teaching and studying is heavy, students are well advised to lighten their other obligations during student-teaching assignments.

An outgrowth of conferring is the esprit de corps that can develop when the teachers, aides, students, volunteers, and parent-helpers meet to plan for the children. The group has a common interest—young children. They have a particular interest—a particular group of children. Their commitment to their teaching roles will be strengthened if they can participate and share their thinking with colleagues. Discussions of values shared and not shared are properly aired with some workable agreement being reached. Part of each person's job satisfaction is derived from friendships and from appreciation for each other. Such appreciation can grow through conferring.

A teacher takes time to extend a child's learning by using fingers to help the child count. (Kansas State University)

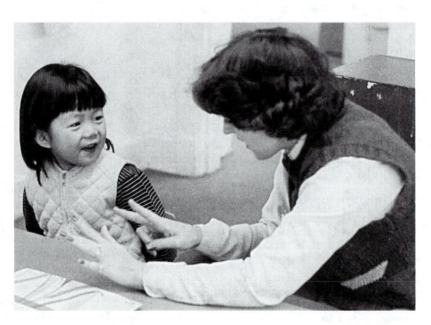

AGENDA FOR PLANNING CONFERENCES

An agenda is helpful for any productive meeting. Using the five managerial tasks mentioned earlier, one can make an agenda form or check sheet, leaving room for additions. Some items will be more time-consuming at one time than at another. When staff members receive agendas early, they can come prepared with appropriate information.

Agenda for Conference

I. Planning tasks
    A. Set goals
    B. Decide on themes
    C. Decide on specific activities
II. Organizing tasks
    A. Setting schedules
    B. Preparing resources
    C. Arranging facility
III. Staffing tasks
    A. Assigning staff
    B. Communication
    C. Personal concerns
IV. Leading tasks
    A. Innovations
    B. Professional opportunities
V. Monitoring and controlling
    A. What's happening
    B. Each child's needs, etc.
    C. Parental needs
    D. Adjustments needed

Setting Goals

Goals have been emphasized throughout the book. It is believed that without a goal or destination it is impossible to chart the best route to any place. The Fifteen-Point Program Guidelines shown in Table 19–1 provide general goals. The developmental tasks upon which those guidelines are based may be reviewed in Chapter 2. From these come *developmental goals* for individual children.

Developmental goals are based on research telling parents and professionals how children typically grow and develop. Using these goals the teacher plans experiences that will enhance one or more areas of the child's or children's development. The integration of development has been pointed out throughout this text along with ways that specific areas of the curriculum can be expected to enhance development. As teachers get better acquainted with children, their plans can be tailored to specific needs and interests of particular children. For example, seeing Louise's interest in airplanes, the teacher initiates a study of flying that culminates in a trip to the airport. Or, noting several children with articulation problems, the teacher plans some language games that are fun for all the children and particularly helpful to those few children.

Remember to use the Bloom *Taxonomy of Educational Objectives* as a guide for developing levels of difficulty in goals and objectives. These levels were presented in Chapter 6.

In particular cases it may be helpful to make individual plans for a child and write specific **behavioral objectives**. Behavioral objectives are carefully worded statements that describe the behavior expected from the child and the criterion or degree of performance expected. Not all educators recommend behavioral objectives, however; some believe they lead to rigidities that are unnecessary. It has been observed that a serious problem arises when students are preparing to be teachers and are still learning the range of behaviors to expect from young children as they become involved with a particular activity or medium. Students may write behavioral objectives that sound logical on paper, but the children behave in other ways—often more interesting, unusual, and sometimes more advanced than the students anticipated in the objective. Although a planned activity was a resounding success for the child or children, the teacher-in-training may feel that she or he has failed and certainly must check "did not accomplish objectives" on an evaluation. It is not a failure, however, because early childhood students and teachers need a wealth of experience observing children using materials

Table 19–1

Fifteen-Point Program Guidelines.

A fifteen-point guide for planning an effective program for children is outlined below. Teachers may also use the guides as a check list for evaluating their programs.

1. *A good program is planned from the point of view of the whole child in the immediate environment.* Whether the child is from a small or a large family, from the city or the country, from an advantaged or a disadvantaged home, ongoing experiences are the basis for all planning. The child is observed then guided through sequential steps to new heights of accomplishment.

2. *A good program values the child's healthy, happy, responsive, secure approach to living.* The teacher expects the children to respond fully and learn appropriately for their age. An important goal is for them to learn to love school and learning, teachers, and other children. Developing a self-confidence that says, "Whatever there is to do, I can do it," is very important.

3. *A good program provides for the emotional growth of the child.* It accepts the child as he or she moves from the protected, individualized home experience to a group experience. Every effort is made to give a feeling of security in the new setting—this goal being paramount for some time, depending on the child's need. Parents are helped and guided during this transition period.

4. *A good program balances active and quiet activities.* Within large time blocks the child has freedom to select the type of activity preferred. The teacher's schedule balances routines and learning experiences in logical sequences of events. Both extremes of prolonged sitting and prolonged physical exertion are avoided. Tensions build up during enforced sitting, and fatigue contributes to lack of inner control that interferes with maximum learning.

5. *A good program provides appropriate opportunities for children to grow in self-direction and independence.* It provides an opportunity for them to learn to make choices through experience. Each child gains in self-understanding.

6. *A good program establishes and maintains limits on behavior for the protection of individuals, the group, and the learning environment.* By helping a child learn the reasons for various rules, the teacher encourages self-discipline.

7. *A good program is challenging to children's intellectual powers.* They are encouraged to think, reason, remember, experiment, and generalize. The laboratory rather than the lecture method is used almost exclusively.

8. *A good program provides media of self-expression.* Creativity is valued, fostered, and recognized in every learning center. Art, literature, and music are part of every day's activity.

9. *A good program encourages children's verbal expressions.* To learn words and sentence structure, children must have an opportunity to talk. Being quiet is not necessarily valued.

Table 19–1
continued

10. *A good program provides opportunities for social development.* The child learns through experience to share, take turns, and interact with individuals and groups. He or she learns to choose friends and to be chosen. Yet the program also allows time to be alone if desired.

11. *A good program encourages children to learn about and care for their bodies.* A routine of washing, eating, resting, and eliminating is established. Safety training has priority, both to protect children and to teach them to protect themselves.

12. *A good program provides opportunities for each child to use the whole body in a daily period of outdoor activity.* When bad weather prevents going outdoors, adequate provision is made for gross motor activities in semisheltered or indoor areas.

13. *A good program is action packed.* It is frequently noisy compared to traditional upper-age classes. The reasons action, noise, and talking are permitted may have to be explained to administrators and others so that programs for children are not curtailed unnecessarily. Carpeting, draping, or other soundproofing should be provided in classrooms to cut down the noise level.

14. *A good program is fun for children.* Learning themes and materials are selected that especially attract young children. Their needs and interests determine the choice of learning experiences in most cases. When a theme or a concept lacks appeal, others replace it.

15. *A good program considers the interests and needs of the parents as well as the children.* The parents are helped to feel and be important to their child's growth and development. They are counseled directly and indirectly so that they will make significant contributions to the child's growth and development. Positive help is provided to individuals and groups to foster this principle. Referrals are made to appropriate agencies when the teacher recognizes a need for help she or he cannot provide.

and learning before they are ready to write prescriptive behavioral objectives. Also needed is very specific information about one child or group of children, which most students do not have. A therapist might write detailed objectives for a child with some developmental difficulty. For that child behavioral objectives may be warranted.

There are also **group goals** to consider. As a social group the children and teachers expect to be living together for several hours daily over a considerable period of months. There is rarely sufficient adult help for every child to be treated as though the group did not matter. Goals for developing this group cooperation are important from the beginning. You are soon rewarded when you hear children saying, "This is *my* Children's Center." They are gaining their first sense of community outside their family.

Deciding on Themes and Activities

Using a **cumulative plan** as discussed in Chapter 11 is the recommended approach. This approach

A "What dissolves?" activity requires a tray, some bowls, water, and a few objects. Children will do the rest. (Metropolitan State College, Denver)

utilizes a trusted principle of learning—*one learns by relating new information with previously learned information.* You recognize this principle because you use it when you explain something new to someone by relating the new thing to something familiar. Six basic themes for a cumulative plan were suggested in Chapter 11 and are repeated here:

1. the child—his or her name, gender, health, safety, and relationship to the family, the school, the community, and the world;
2. the community—its people, its workers, its institutions, and its traditions, including festivals;
3. the world of plants—especially those the child sees every day and those that provide food;
4. the world of animals—especially those the child sees every day and those that provide food;
5. the world of machines—including vehicles and other large and small machines;
6. the physical forces in the world.

Cumulative Plan

One way to handle cumulative planning is to list the six themes on six separate sheets of paper. List possible subthemes or goals under each basic theme. For example, under the theme The Child, you might list:

- to state his or her own name and to respond when name is called
- to locate and use the bathroom appropriately
- to put belongings in designated locker
- to separate easily from parent (may take several days)
- to play safely in the room and yard
- to adjust comfortably to the teachers and children

Each of these goals is high on teachers' agendas for the first weeks of school. Each goal has cognitive, social, language, physical, and emotional connotations. Until these goals are accomplished for each child, other themes will likely get little attention.

Other themes will be integrated with The Child theme, with the child's needs remaining primary. Perhaps the teacher uses a subtheme called Rabbits from the World of Animals theme. Stories and songs about rabbits can be highlighted as a rabbit comes to visit at the school for a few days. Pictures of rabbits are displayed on the bulletin board. Rabbit puzzles and a stuffed rabbit or two are available to use. (This is just one of many animals the children will see and talk about during the ensuing months.)

At learning centers other basic themes may be highlighted, even as rabbits are the major focus. Knowledge of the children's interests and their readiness for more activity will be the teachers' guide.

The Six Basic Themes serve as the key ideas, with aspects of each basic theme being introduced through subthemes. Thus the spiral of the cumulative plan progresses forward—from simple to increasingly complex. Stimulation for returning to a subtheme comes from the children as you observe children and listen to them expressing their interests and ideas.

Children typically have lots of interests; however, they may need help in freeing up their ideas and expressing them. They will become free when they begin to know that you will follow through on a topic if they suggest an interest in it.

A brief example of the use of a cumulative plan using the World of Animals theme follows. The teacher asks children, "Do you remember what animal we visited last week? What was it called?" The children answer the teacher, "An elephant," and several minutes of conversation follow as children tell what they recall about the trip to see the elephant.

"Yes, an elephant," confirms the teacher. "Is this animal that is visiting us today an elephant?"

"No!" laugh the children. They spend several lively minutes guessing and naming. They talk about the animal's characteristics and how they differ from the elephant's. The teacher agrees with one child who says the animal is a guinea pig, and further information is given about that animal. The children are very interested in the conversation, and they do most of the talking. In future weeks other animals will be discussed in a similar manner. Memory will be stimulated as the children become personally involved.

Decide which theme should come first for your particular group or for individuals within the group. Remember that appropriate planning requires providing a **continuum of difficulty**, from simple to complex, within your classroom. The goal is to serve the needs of the children who are just being introduced to a concept or skill, the ones at the other end of the continuum who need advanced challenges to be able to continue to grow, and all those in between.

Your on-the-spot assessment of each individual is what the concept **developmentally appropriate** is all about. This concept is being discussed throughout the profession. Developmentally appropriate means an activity is (1) appropriate to the age group, and (2) appropriate to the individuals within the specific classroom who are of that age group.[6]

Resource Unit Plan

Another planning approach is the **resource unit plan**, wherein one concept may be presented for a number of days or weeks, then dropped, and another concept selected. Such plans create programs that often seem choppy and unrelated. Also, the spontaneous interests of the children are often ignored.

A unit is apt to become too long for small children, as illustrated in the following example. A four-year-old asked her mother, "Why does Mrs. T. talk about food every day?" A study of the food groups had been carried on in great detail. Although the children probably had some interest in food, the unit had become too much lecture and not enough laboratory to hold the four-year-old's interest.

---

[6]Sue Bredekamp, ed., *Developmentally Appropriate Practice in Early Childhood Programs Serving Children from Birth Through Age 8*, (Washington, DC: NAEYC, 1987).

With a resource unit plan, a unit on community helpers might be taught in a single week. Thus children with varied interests aren't given enough opportunity to explore their interests before some topics are terminated for the year and new topics started.

In a cumulative plan, on the other hand, community helpers is a concept that is discussed from time to time. For example, throughout the year many people, including the parents of the children, are recognized for their contribution to the community.

In some schools the entire program focuses on holidays, following the same emphasis every year. Of course, holidays are one aspect of the child's community. However, it must be quite boring for children to hop from Halloween to Thanksgiving to Christmas and so on, for all the years of their elementary school. Surely more child-oriented themes, with incidental activities related to holidays where they are appropriate, would be more interesting and educational over the years. Teachers should build their curriculum around a broad concept of what the children want and need to know—which goes far beyond the few holidays of the school year. With a cumulative plan, the temptation to jump from one holiday to another for major themes is avoided. Also avoided is the overstimulation that often occurs around holiday time.

Activities

Specific learning activities have been detailed throughout Part 2 of this book. The choices can

be noted on a Daily Plan of Activities form such as shown in Figure 19–2. See Chapter 6 for suggestions about planning specific activities. A form such as that in Figure 19–3 can show the week at a glance. When interesting learning opportunities arise unexpectedly, the plans are flexible enough to incorporate them. However, advanced planning helps ensure a program with educational goals for children.

ORGANIZING TIME, MATERIALS, AND SPACE

Organizing means systematically assembling and utilizing temporal, material, and spatial resources for carrying out a plan of action.

Setting Schedules

Scheduling means designating events for a fixed future time. Both long-term and short-term scheduling are needed. In scheduling, the teacher looks ahead to the whole year, to a convenient period of weeks, to the week, and to the day.

The **daily schedule** or sequence of events is established in the first planning session. If it fits the group well, this routine may remain in effect for a number of months with only minor variations. Scheduling was discussed in Chapter 4. Changing the schedule often creates uncertainty for young children that teachers must anticipate. Regular routine helps children know what comes next.

Three to six large time blocks are suggested for the schedule or sequence of events. Chapter 4 discusses the number of time blocks and the amount of time contained in each. Briefly, decisions depend upon

- the goals for the group,
- the special needs of the group,
- the time of day the children arrive,
- how long the children stay at school,
- what happens at home before the children come to school each day,
- the season of the year.

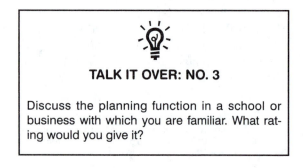

TALK IT OVER: NO. 3

Discuss the planning function in a school or business with which you are familiar. What rating would you give it?

FIGURE 19–2
Daily plan of activities.

DAILY PLAN OF ACTIVITIES

Date _____

Activity   *Who Is Responsible?*

Things to remember:

Art projects:

Science projects:

Dramatic play:

Literature–language area:

Music area:

Group time:

Outdoor activity:

Transition:

Snack menu:

Diary:

To schedule long-range plans it is helpful to arrange a calendar of the entire school year in such a way that the total year can be seen. Some suitable commercial calendars are available, but a teacher can make one with a large sheet of paper. A space for notes with each date provides a ready reference for checking progress toward goals.

On the calendar the teacher blocks out the number of school days. From the administration calendar school vacations, holidays, and other days that have significance for planning are marked. Teachers usually write in children's birthdays. Many entries can be indicated in pencil so that they can be shifted as events dictate. Events that are regular occurrences can be placed on the calendar. For example, an end-of-school picnic or the kindergarten visit to the first grade can be noted tentatively at the beginning of school. Community events, such as a community parade that typically occurs when the chil-

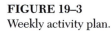

FIGURE 19–3
Weekly activity plan.

WEEKLY ACTIVITY PLAN					
Week of _____	Mon.	Tues.	Wed.	Thurs.	Fri.
Art:					
Science:					
Dramatic play:					
Lit.–Lang:					
Music area:					
Group time:					
Outdoor act.:					
Transition:					
Snack:					
Trips:					
Planning notes:					

Themes
The child learns about clarification:

1. Self	3. Animals	5. Machines
2. Other people	4. Plants	6. Physical forces

dren can watch, are set months in advance and can be placed on the planning calendar. The teacher's diary can provide other tentative dates, such as when to plan a spring nature walk.

Periodic planning may mean a month, six weeks, a quarter, or a semester—whatever is a convenient administrative time unit in a particular school. For example, in a university laboratory school where plans involve the schedule of university students, the students' schedule also becomes the period for planning for the children. If student teachers typically assume certain levels of responsibility at different points during the term, these dates are marked on the planning calendar.

Preparing Resources

Resource materials are necessary for teaching each theme. The teacher will develop files of materials and ideas for teaching numerous concepts. By developing many materials, a teacher will have sufficient ideas to use in developing teaching plans to fit a particular group of children. The file will offer a collection from which to choose just the right poem or song for a group. One need never panic because of a shortage of material.

A resource file is assembled over time. If the teacher has a good filing system, newly discovered material is easily preserved. When needed, the material will be easily located. The file is suggested as a project for this course.

One filing system uses manila folders with a different color tab for each of the six themes. The colored tabs are bought where office supplies are sold. For example, all animal folders are labeled with a pink label. The file may contain only two

FIGURE 19–4
Resource file cover page.

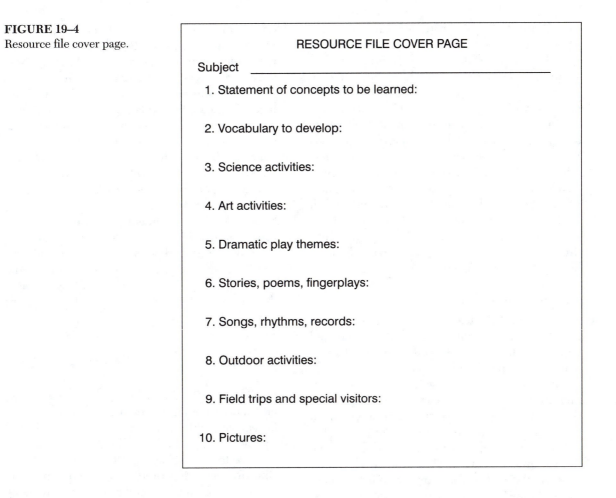

RESOURCE FILE COVER PAGE

Subject _____

1. Statement of concepts to be learned:

2. Vocabulary to develop:

3. Science activities:

4. Art activities:

5. Dramatic play themes:

6. Stories, poems, fingerplays:

7. Songs, rhythms, records:

8. Outdoor activities:

9. Field trips and special visitors:

10. Pictures:

folders at first: (1) domestic birds and animals and (2) wild birds and animals. However, as the file grows, the teacher will divide the material until there is a file for each animal of interest. Figure 19–4 is the suggested cover page for each folder; it can serve as the teacher's summary of the materials the file contains. As indicated in the figure, each folder can contain (1) a statement of concepts to be developed; (2) vocabulary to develop; (3) science experiments that teach concepts; (4) art ideas; (5) dramatic play ideas; (6) stories, poems, and fingerplays; (7) songs, rhythms, and records; (8) outdoor activities; (9) field trips or special visitors; and (10) pictures.

Throughout this textbook there are suggested resources for teaching ideas. As you read the chapters you are invited to use your creativity to invent new activities as you read about those invented by other teachers. Consult the Additional Readings sections for worthwhile resources.

Commercially printed or computerized kits of teaching materials that encourage each child in every class to join in lockstep education should be avoided. Both the children's and the teacher's creativity are seriously jeopardized when the plan becomes more important than the children. Packaged materials can help teachers, but teachers should feel a definite responsibility for screening materials and adapting them to each group of children. Constance Kamii, who has spent many years researching how children learn to understand concepts of number, writes critically of workbook exercises. "These workbook exercises are undesirable because they preclude any possibility for the child to move the objects to make a set. Besides, such an exercise easily elicits the kind of thinking that yields the right answer for the wrong reason. Such children may or may not have the slightest idea about which set has more. If they do not know how to tell this difference, the exercise is useless because children do not learn to make quantitative judgments by drawing lines on paper."[7]

Arranging the Facility

Another task of the teachers' planning conference is to consider the effectiveness of, and needed changes in, the facility. The effective use of space and its cleanliness and attractiveness should be given attention. Details regarding room arrangement were discussed in Chapter 4 under "Setting the Stage." As teachers start a new group of young children, they find it important to keep the room arrangement the same for awhile to give the children security in their new environment. However, after they are comfortable in school they will enjoy variety. Some weeks the housekeeping area and music areas can change places. A little shifting may create interest for a child who seems not to have noticed an area before.

New objects on shelves and on bulletin boards can give the children plenty to look for and talk about as they arrive each day. Children's art, neatly and colorfully arranged, should be changed regularly. Many teachers display a few of their own artifacts to brighten the room.

Beauty should be part of the environment. A tacky, unpainted look can change overnight if a

civic group with a do-good bent lends a hand. Parents can be enlisted to help. Student groups may enjoy assisting the teacher to improve the attractiveness of a classroom. Teachers should seek such sources of assistance when maintenance funds are inadequate.

Cleanliness and order should be important to the teachers. The children can help with getting materials back in their proper places each day. However, a continuous effort is required of the staff to be sure that finger marks are washed off furnishings and walls, that wilted flowers are tossed out, that broken equipment is sent out for repair, and that general order is maintained in the room, yard, and storage areas. The janitorial staff needs cooperation from the teachers and children. They often are afraid to toss out anything even if it looks useless. A standard list helps them do their tasks.

STAFFING

Staffing is defined as selecting, assigning, utilizing, and evaluating the human resources needed for carrying out a plan of action. The teacher or co-teachers in an early childhood classroom may not hire the individuals, but they will be responsible for orienting them and at times training them for working with children. Wisely utilizing human resources helps both the children and the teachers. It is also very satisfying to see adults learn to be highly qualified teachers of young children, so learn to praise small steps.

A teaching team of a minimum of two adults per group has been the rule in prekindergarten classes for decades. Kindergarten teachers unfortunately have often been expected to manage alone. However, Head Start recommends two adults per fifteen children. Today most teachers are able to involve others in their programs. Many have paid aides; others have community volunteers, high school and university students who assist in various capacities, and parents who volunteer or serve as part of a cooperative plan. It is

---

[7]Constance Kamii, *Number in Preschool and Kindergarten* (Washington, DC: NAEYC, 1982), p. 38.

up to both the teacher and the assistants to make the most meaningful use of all the available help.

The teacher will want the best learning situation for the children. Assistants extend in numerous ways the efforts the teacher can make for the children. It is desirable for each assistant to make a contribution to the children's learning and to have a satisfying experience with the children.

Conferences before each day of school are essential for those adults who work directly with the children. Such conferences are more important than ever when individuals have missed the weekly planning sessions. All will feel much more comfortable knowing the goals for the day—for the group and for individuals. Helpers must be advised of unusual circumstances that confront certain children, such as Debbie's mother going to the hospital or Tony's father leaving for a trip.

Safety requirements dictate that all areas of the room or yard where children are playing be staffed by adults. It seems more effective from the point of children's learning that each adult be assigned responsibility for a specific area of the room or yard. For example, if the adult's assignment is in the language arts area, such a plan makes it acceptable for that adult to remain in the language arts area with a child even though it appears that chaos is reigning in the block room. One can assume that a competent adult is in charge in the block room and will send out an SOS if assistance is needed.

An alternative plan is to let everyone move where "needed." In such a plan, however, teachers may never sit down and take time to extend the learning of children. They feel responsible for other parts of the school—particularly the trouble spots. When they hear chaos in the block room, they are likely to flock there. As a result, less troublesome children who remain absorbed in some task may be slighted, or some area needing the watchful eye of an adult may be left unattended.

Of course, when no children are at work in a learning center, the adult should feel free to observe or assist in other areas until children again show interest in that center. It is possible also to take advantage of the lull to reorganize the center, to bring out some fresh materials, or even to clean it up if a transition time is approaching.

Space is provided in the Daily Plan sheet (Figure 19–2) for noting the assignment of assistants. Some teachers also write the daily plan on a chalkboard so that all helpers can see at a glance who is taking responsibility for a given area. Such posting avoids duplication of effort or concern that no one has an area covered.

If at all possible, the assistants should be involved in the weekly planning. They need to believe they know what is going on. It is a very uncomfortable feeling when a youngster says, or implies, "I've been here longer than you have, I know the rules," as one child was heard to say to an assistant.

In planning sessions, assignments should be discussed to ensure that all members of the teaching team, male and female, share equally all tasks such as giving affection, disciplining, housekeeping, toileting, and playground teaching. Remember, all members of a team are serving as models for the children they teach.

Assignments may be agreed upon in weekly planning conferences. Each individual may assume the responsibility for bringing in the materials needed to enhance the learning in a particular area of responsibility. Regular teachers can assume responsibility in areas offering new learning situations, whereas others take the areas that offer experiences more familiar to the children and for which guidance is more predictable.

In some centers teachers divide activities into categories, agree to assume responsibility for a given category for a two-week period, then rotate to another category of activities for the next two weeks. Under such an agreement meetings to coordinate plans can be shorter.

Of course, in all groups teachers and assistants should be learning along with the children. It is often necessary for a teacher or assistant to participate in an activity even though she or he lacks experience. For example, a person with little confidence in music should be encouraged to volunteer to work in the music area. Other adults can give support until that person gains the confidence needed to carry on as leader. All assistants should make their preferences and talents known so that their capabilities can be utilized in the best possible way for the good of the children.

As the teacher in charge in a group, you will become the person responsible for directing and evaluating a number of employees and, in some instances, students. This task will be discussed under the heading, "Monitoring and Controlling."

Leading the Team

Leading means setting the pace toward present goals and formulating future goals. It requires a clear view of present goals and a vision of future goals. Teachers must think of themselves as leaders. You have an opportunity to lead within your group, school, community, nation, and world. There have been many innovations in early childhood education in recent history. Foresighted people envisioned Head Start and the NAEYC Center Accreditation Project. There will always be room for new ideas.

Communicating with other early childhood professionals will stimulate new ideas. Knowing the needs of children everywhere will stimulate others. A challenging professional life will be the best medicine for preventing "burnout," a condi-

tion that is said to occur in early childhood workers quite frequently.

There are thousands of ways to innovate in your group of children and with your adult assistants. You can ask, "Is there a part of the program, the yard, or our personal relationships that could stand improving?" Work on one of those. Value your co-workers and learn to encourage and enjoy their growth in working with children. Bring in some elementary-age children or some elderly folks as school visitors and find out what happens. Your creativity will be contagious as you try new things and encourage others to innovate, too.

Early childhood educators as a group seem cautious about money. However, don't dampen an idea just because it costs money. If the idea is a good one, think of how funding might be achieved. No one will remember you for the pennies saved, but they will remember you if you spearheaded the play yard renovation or a concert series to benefit children who need scholarships. Ideas are the hallmark of leaders. Be sure to value your own and those of others.

Encourage parents and your staff to participate in community programs that are fun for children. Encourage professional participation—program appearances and professional writing—of your staff and colleagues. Through a wide professional participation you let people know about your high-quality work, and you may be able to influence positively the lives of many other children in the community through your efforts.

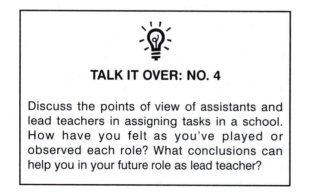

TALK IT OVER: NO. 4

Discuss the points of view of assistants and lead teachers in assigning tasks in a school. How have you felt as you've played or observed each role? What conclusions can help you in your future role as lead teacher?

MONITORING AND CONTROLLING

Monitoring and controlling are defined as being alert to the performance of self and others in relation to established standards, and making decisions and carrying out adjustments needed for meeting standards. These terms are used because they seem more dynamic than the typically used word—evaluation.

The early childhood education profession is particularly concerned about high quality; therefore, it is of critical importance that teachers perform these functions well. Continuous monitoring should take place from moment to moment and from day to day. If something is unsafe or unsanitary, it must be corrected immediately; that's where control comes in. If something is being taught poorly and more preparation would help, then preparation must be undertaken. If learning activities are too easy or too hard, adjustments must be readily forthcoming. If teachers and their assistants are doing the on-the-spot monitoring that is essential, then any outside evaluator will not be frightening to the staff.

Children tell teachers and parents by their actions when things are going fine. Adults should listen to children if they are unhappy, reject others, or refuse to participate. An experienced teacher can tell by the hum of the classroom if things are going well or not, much as an experienced mechanic knows if a motor is having problems. Parents' reports regarding their child's feelings about school should be listened to seriously and investigated for accuracy. Any parent who quietly removes a child from a program should be called by the teacher or administrator to learn why.

Overall Program Evaluation

Overall program evaluation must be based on program goals. The Fifteen-Point Program Guidelines (Table 19–1) used to establish goals can be used to develop a program evaluation sheet. A one-to-five rating scale is suggested, with five as highly satisfactory. Besides teachers doing an internal evaluation, parents can be very helpful. They can receive the same evaluation sheet and return it with their comments. Or, it can be presented in a parent meeting with ample opportunity provided for parents to make comments and ask questions. It is particularly imperative that teachers evaluate and seek outside evaluation of their programs, rather than do nothing or leave the impression that they believe that

perfection has been achieved. Programs can always be improved. By taking the initiative in evaluation, teachers are less likely to be pushed into an uncomfortable defensive position by parents or others. Use forms such as Table 19–2 for regular evaluations by parents and volunteers.

Checking Curricular Offerings

General evaluation can begin by checking the daily plans against the diary of actual events. This provides a picture of what there was available to learn. Even a short diary written at the bottom or on the back of a daily plan sheet will provide information for evaluation. To be realistic, a diary generally must be brief; otherwise, teachers won't have time to keep it.

A regular check of daily and weekly plans and diaries against the fifteen-point guides discussed earlier in this chapter will provide information on where a program is adequate and inadequate. By summarizing the daily plans the teacher can see at a glance how much variety has been offered the group. For example, if the diary shows that a few art projects were repeated frequently, efforts to bring in some new ones or add something new to the old ones can be made.

Knowing what has been offered does not tell the teacher what individual children have learned. Teachers also must make an effort to know how individual children are progressing. It is like knowing the menu at the cafeteria; one must watch the diners to see what they choose and what they actually eat to judge how well nourished they might be.

Observing Each Child

Teachers must consciously observe each child. It helps to use an attendance checklist and watch a child briefly at least once a week. Without a checklist it is easy to overlook a child or two—particularly a quiet child. Monitoring children's skills, for example, motor or language skills, helps teachers know children better. Keeping a folder on each child makes filing a sample of work or an anecdote easy.

Table 19–2
Program Evaluation.

Observer _____Date _____

Teacher _____Center_____Age range_____to ____

Program Guidelines (See Chapter 19 for details)	Fair	Good	Excellent
THE PROGRAM I OBSERVED			
1. Was planned from the point of view of the whole child in the immediate environment.			
2. Valued the child's healthy, happy, responding, secure approach to living.			
3. Provided for the emotional growth of the child.			
4. Balanced active and quiet activities.			
5. Provided appropriate opportunities for children to grow in self-direction and independence.			
6. Established and maintained limits on behavior for protection of individuals, groups, and the learning environment.			
7. Challenged children's intellectual powers.			
8. Provided media of self-expression.			
9. Encouraged children's verbal expressions.			
10. Provided opportunities for social development.			
11. Helped children learn to understand their bodies.			
12. Provided opportunities for each child to play outdoors each day.			
13. Provided opportunities for vigorous large motor action.			
14. Was fun for the children.			
15. Considered the interests and needs of parents as well as children.			

Remarks:

_____

_____

_____

Chapter 15 gives numerous suggestions regarding the teacher's observation notes and their value. Through routinely observing each child and recording evidence of progress toward educational goals, teachers can begin to assess a child's progress. Notes will help teachers in conferences with staff and parents. Recommenda-tions should be made on the basis of sufficient evidence collected over time.

Staff Conferences

It is helpful for teachers to get together to discuss individual children, to gain the benefit of the perceptions of others regarding each child. An outsider may be asked to observe and take notes on certain children to add more objective insight into the handling of behavior and learning problems. University student observers can contribute to such conferences. Students gain from learning to relate theory to practice. Planning and evaluating go hand in hand, as we discussed under planning in this chapter. Your goal should be to recognize objectivity and subjectivity in people's evaluations. Objectivity is the goal, of course.

As a measure of children's progress teachers begin collecting samples of the child's work at the beginning of the year. This collection enables the child, the parents, and the teacher to assess or evaluate the child's progress over time. The materials should all be dated. A variety of expressions of the child's learning should be collected because some children may be stronger in one area than in another. You may want to take photos of some items that cannot be kept—say a block structure or food preparation project. Children also like to have a say in what goes in their portfolio, just as you would want to decide about your portfolio.

Seriously, you should begin planning what would make a good representation of your own work, your creativity, and your best scholarship over your college years. You very likely will be encouraged to build a portfolio at some time. What would you like to include? What do you think might be important to an employer? a scholarship committee? a graduate school admissions officer?

Testing Children

A serious problem with nearly any evaluation is its subjective nature. For that reason those desiring more objective measures turn to tests. Tests taken at the beginning of a term are compared to those taken at the end. This is called pre- and posttesting. It would be helpful if there were more reliable testing materials to measure the growth that takes place in young children during the years they are in prekindergarten and kindergarten. Regardless of numerous inadequacies, pre- and posttesting is being done increasingly in schools across the country. Perhaps eventually, with improvement, more confidence can be placed in the results of such measures.

There are some problems encountered in the testing of young children. In the first place, the children are too young for the more easily administered pencil-and-paper tests that are common in upper-age groups. When pencil-and-paper tests are used with kindergartners, the teacher cannot be sure that the children completely understand the directions. The children may copy from their neighbor, making their test an inaccurate measure.

Individual testing is time-consuming and rarely done on any scale and it has drawbacks, too. A teacher seldom has time to test all the children. Outside testers must know tests; they must have considerable knowledge of children generally and be willing to take time to get acquainted with individuals before starting to test. Testers may play with some children several hours before the children are ready to be tested. Removing a child from the classroom to a testing room may cause anxiety and reduce motivation because the child would rather be back in the room with friends.

Tests generally tend to be oriented toward white middle-class society and therefore may be seriously unfair to others. Even so, the I.Q. score obtained from tests given at a young age has very low predictive value, according to data from the longitudinal study by Bayley.[8] Frost and Rowland predict that "the I.Q. will be abandoned as false and unworthy—especially as educators realize that it is a sample of behavior taken at a specific time under limiting conditions. Educators will cease to attribute to the I.Q. the power to predict or determine the progress of a child; actually, the

---

[8]Nancy Bayley, "On the Growth of Intelligence," *American Psychologist* 10:12 (December 1955), 805–818.

I.Q. never had such power, but it was used in a perverted way."[9]

The I.Q. tests have been criticized because they were developed with a white middle-class bias that makes them grossly unfair to children from other cultural orientations. Adrian Dove, a black sociologist, attempted to point this out with what has become known as the "Chitling Test."[10] This is a test for whites that uses black English. In a humorous fashion, Dove has shown how cultural bias influences one's score on a test. Therefore, until testing can eliminate such bias, one should not take its results too seriously.[11]

If teachers expect to use test results, they should be aware of the shortcomings of the tests. They should know how to interpret the results. Psychologists generally agree that it is unwise to give parents number scores from tests because they use them incorrectly, remember them inaccurately, and may use them for their own aggrandizement.

Two examples illustrate even teachers' confusion with test scores. A parent was told, "Betty didn't do well on her math test." The mother thought of the "S" mark (satisfactory) the teacher had put on the report grade and asked, "What did she make on her test?" The teacher replied, "Only fifty percent." On further investigation, the mother, who was more knowledgeable than most, found that the teacher meant that the child ranked at "the 50th percentile" on math, as compared to ranking at the "76th percentile" on her reading. The meaning of the percentile score was that Betty, when compared to all other children taking that test, scored in the middle of the group on mathematical reasoning and in the top one-fourth in reading.

Another teacher interpreted a score of 56 on a reading-readiness test to mean that the child had an I.Q. of 56. The mother naturally reacted with considerable alarm to this report. She had worked as an aide in a school for retarded children and had heard I.Q. scores bandied about. She had a vague notion of how scores were applied. When, after many worry-filled days, she talked to someone more informed, she learned that the teacher had confused percentile rank with I.Q. score.

Standardized testing was the topic for a major position statement by the NAEYC in 1987. People were found to be using tests to place children inappropriately, according to members who were most familiar with young children's characteristic behavior. Many tests are unsuitable for young children and many testers are inexperienced with young children, not knowing how to talk to—let alone test—a child to obtain valid information. In general, tests done at a young age have very little predictability for the child's future performance. Parents should know they can ask for additional opinions about placing a child in special education.[12]

Certainly, if tests are to be used, they should be administered expertly, interpreted correctly, and used in conjunction with other information, especially when recommendations regarding a child's future are being made.

Teachers must feel an obligation to report to parents on their child's progress. Several methods of doing this are discussed in Chapter 20.

Monitoring Self and Other Adults

As the lead teacher, you will likely be responsible for monitoring the staff and volunteers within your classroom. Each employee should have a job description that states quite precisely what the employee is to do and the standards expected. Students, likewise, should have a description in hand as to what their performance

---

[9]Joe L. Frost and G. Thomas Rowland, *Curricula for the Seventies* (Boston: Houghton Mifflin, 1969), p. 435.

[10]"Taking the Chitling Test," *Annual Editions Readings in Human Development '73-'74* (Guilford, CT: Dushkin, 1973), p. 298.

[11]Psychologist Laura E. Berk discusses the research on testing children's intelligence and helps the reader recognize the biases that have often entered into assessment of intelligence. See "Intelligence: A Psychometric Perspective" in *Child Development* (Allyn and Bacon, 1991), pp. 297–340.

[12]NAEYC developed a "Position Statement on Standardized Testing of Young Children 3 through 8 Years of Age." It is available by calling NAEYC (1-800-424-2460) and asking for the brochure "Standardized Testing."

should be. These descriptions can then be used when monitoring their job performance. It is best to meet with the staff individually to communicate your assessment of their performance. In individual conferences you can point out things they do well and suggest ways they can make improvements. You probably will report to a higher level of administration your findings and your suggestions. It is important to write down observations and evaluations. People working with children are given a special trust. If they break that trust, then they must be removed from working with the children. You will also be evaluated by your administrator. Your staff may be called on to assist with your evaluation.

Monitoring and controlling are required to ensure parents and the community that the early childhood education programs are serving children and families in positive ways. Further, they are needed to ensure everyone that only persons with integrity and good will are working with children. In recent years there has been considerable discussion regarding various levels of child abuse that have been discovered in a few centers. The allegations are frightening enough to everyone of good will that from now on they will be doubly alert to any undesirable behavior on any employee's part. Society expects this vigilance from anyone who plays any role in a young child's education.

A useful study of research related to the nationwide occurrence of child abuse in child care centers was completed by Finkelhor et al. The researchers recommended that parents have open access to the centers and that they must be alert to changes in the behavior of and in the complaints of their children. They recommended removal of partitions and stalls that create private areas where children can be isolated and suggest that managers may need to establish better controls over who takes children into the toilet areas and when this is done.[13]

---

[13]David Finkelhor, Linda M. Williams, Michael Kalinowski, and Nanci Burns, *Sexual Abuse in Day Care: A National Study* (Durham, NH: Family Research Laboratory, University of New Hampshire, 1988), pp. 1–16.

Conclusions

Early childhood education teachers perform many managerial functions as they work with children and staff members in their classrooms and play yards. These functions are planning, organizing, staffing, leading, and monitoring and controlling.

Planning and the other managerial functions require lots of time and should not be slighted if high-quality programs are the goal. The NAEYC accreditation criteria require that staff be given paid planning time. Staff members must meet periodically to set goals, decide on themes, plan specific activities, set schedules, prepare resources, arrange the facility, assess children's progress, communicate as a staff, monitor the quality, and change the performance if it isn't high in quality.

Outcomes for children and parents should be analyzed. The total curricular offerings should be analyzed for quality. The task of monitoring the staff is partially a responsibility of the lead teacher and of the school's administrator. The latter should be quickly informed of serious deviations by staff in performance standards.

Applications

1. Discuss the "Talk It Over" items found in the chapter.
2. Make a weekly curriculum plan for the group where you have been participating. Use the same number of children and staff. Plan assignments for staff, assuming the same skills as the present staff. Write a narrative explaining how you went about your decision making. Tell how your program is a cumulative plan, building on what children have been learning.
3. Evaluate your own performance on the evaluation form designed in Chapter 1.
4. Add your weekly curriculum plan to your Resource File.

Study Questions

1. Identify, define, and explain each of the five managerial tasks as it is applied to early childhood schools and teachers.

2. Identify the various influences on curricular planning.
3. Explain the need for paid planning time.
4. Explain the difference between social and technical decisions.
5. Explain a cumulative plan and a resource unit plan.
6. Explain Constance Kamii's criticism of workbook exercises for learning about numbers.
7. Identify the problems with using standardized tests with young children.

Additional Readings

Blakley, Barbara, et al. *Activities for School-Age Child Care.* Washington, DC: NAEYC, 1991.

Bredekamp, Sue, ed. *Developmentally Appropriate Practice in Early Childhood Programs Serving Children from Birth Through Age 8.* Washington, DC: NAEYC, 1987.

————. *Accreditation Criteria and Procedures of the National Academy of Early Childhood Programs.* Washington, DC: NAEYC, 1991.

Christie, James F., and Francis Wardle. "How Much Time Is Needed for Play?" *Young Children* 47:3, March 1993, 28–32.

Elster, Charles A. "'I Guess They Do Listen': Young Children's Emergent Readings After Adult Read-Alouds." *Young Children* 49:3, March 1994, 27–32.

Essa, Eva L., and Colleen L. Murray. "Young Children's Understanding and Experience With Death." *Young Children* 49:4, May 1994, 74–81.

Helm, Jeanne. "Family Theme Bags: An Innovative Approach to Family Involvement in the School." *Young Children* 49:4, May 1994, 48–52.

Hildebrand, Verna. *Fundamentos de Educación infantil: Jardín de niños y preprimaria.* Mexico, DF: Editorial Limusa, 1992.

————. *Guiding Young Children.* Upper Saddle River, NJ: Merrill/Prentice Hall, 1994.

Hildebrand, Verna, and Patricia Hearron. *Management of Child Development Centers.* Upper Saddle River, NJ: Merrill/Prentice Hall, 1997.

Hildebrand, V., Lillian Aotaki Phenice, Mary McPhail Gray, and Rebecca Peña Hines. *Knowing and Serving Diverse Families.* Upper Saddle River, NJ: Merrill/Prentice Hall, 1996.

Jordan, Nicola H. "Sexual Abuse Prevention Programs in Early Childhood Education." *Young Children* 48:6, September 1993, 76–79.

NAEYC. "Guidelines for Appropriate Curriculum Content and Assessment in Programs Serving Children Ages 3 Through 8." *Young Children* 46:3, March 1991, 21–38.

Parette, Howard P., Nancy S. Dunn, and Debra R. Hoge. "Low-Cost Communication Devices for Children with Disabilities and Their Family Members." *Young Children* 50:6, September 1995, 75–81.

Peters, D. L., J. T. Neisworth, and T. D. Yawkey. *Early Childhood Education: From Theory to Practice.* Monterey, CA: Brooks/Cole, 1985.

Rose, Deborah F., and Barbara J. Smith. "Preschool Mainstreaming: Attitude Barriers and Strategies for Addressing Them." *Young Children* 48:4, May 1993, 59–62.

Schiller, Marjorie. "An Emergent Art Curriculum That Fosters Understanding." *Young Children* 50:3, March 1995, 33–38.

Sciarra, Dorothy, and Anne G. Dorsey. *Developing and Administering a Child Development Center.* Albany, NY: Delmar, 1990.

Taylor, Judy. "How I Learned to Look at a First-Grader's Writing Progress Instead of His Deficiencies." *Young Children* 51:2, January 1996, 38–42.

Thornton, Jane R. "Team Teaching: A Relationship Based on Trust and Communication." *Young Children* 45:5, July 1990, 40–43.

Vartuli, Sue, and Brenda Fyfe. "Teachers Need Developmentally Appropriate Practices Too." *Young Children* 48:4, May 1993, 36–42.

Williams, Richard P., and Judith K. Davis. "Leap Sprightly Into Literacy." *Young Children* 49:4, May 1994, 37–41.

PART 3

Professional Considerations

Chapter 20   **Teacher-Parent Relations**

Chapter 21   **The World's Children**

Chapter 22   **The Profession—Past, Present, and Future**

CHAPTER 20

Teacher-Parent Relations

Pennsylvania State University

Objectives

✔ Explain in what ways all early childhood schools are part of a family support system.

✔ Explain the place of strong, positive, and personal teacher-parent relationships in high-quality early childhood programs.

✔ Identify and describe ways teachers and parents can be in contact throughout the child's early education.

✔ Describe steps to take in planning for conferences with parents.

"Families are fundamental to the lifeblood and strength of our world. They are nurturers, caregivers, role models, teachers, counselors and those who instill values. In recognition of this vital link that connects us, the United States joins with other members of the United Nations in proclaiming 1994 as the International Year of the Family."

President Bill Clinton (December 1993)

As a teacher you will nurture and protect your relationship with each and every parent. The International Year of the Family gave the country and world an opportunity to celebrate families. Your program is a vital part of the support system for families in this country. You make it possible for parents to succeed both in their parenting and in their work roles. As James Hymes, Jr., says, "We have to end the separation of home and school. Too much is at stake to let the foolish lack of communication persist. The left hand must know what the right is doing; the two hands must work together."[1]

A SUPPORT SYSTEM FOR FAMILIES

A high-quality early childhood school can be a tremendous support system for today's families. The school can supplement the time, energy, skills, and ideas that parents have, enabling parents to manage their children more effectively. An attitude of service must be part of the total early childhood program. Children cannot be educated apart from their families and have a high-quality program. Teachers and every early childhood staff member must realize how significant their service is to the well-being of both children and families.

High-quality early childhood schools can make it possible for dedicated parents to survive the hectic pace they lead in today's world—especially including a mother or father who plays the parenting role alone. Virtually all parents have great hopes for their children and are eager to work with the school in any way that will benefit their children. A few parents may need help in learning to relate to the school and teachers; thus teachers must devise strategies for getting them actively involved.

The teacher's warmth expressed for the child in the mother's presence gives the mother a clue as to why her daughter enjoys her early childhood school. (V. Hildebrand, photographer)

In a book, *Knowing and Serving Diverse Families*,[2] this author and three colleagues have developed details of working with families of many diversities. You might like to use information from those chapters as you work with families. Accepting the diversity of families and your own diversity are beginnings. Efforts that lead toward empowerment of each parent are very essential.

Parents also have their concerns about relating to teachers. They hope the teacher and child will like each other. They hope that the teacher

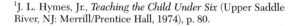

[1]J. L. Hymes, Jr., *Teaching the Child Under Six* (Upper Saddle River, NJ: Merrill/Prentice Hall, 1974), p. 80.

[2]V. Hildebrand, L. A. Phenice, M. M. Gray, and R. P. Hines, *Knowing and Serving Diverse Families*, (Upper Saddle River, NJ: Merrill/Prentice Hall, 1996.)

knows the subject matter and how to get it across to children. Parents worry when problems come up. Will the teacher react to a discussion of a child's failure by taking offense? Will the teacher blame the parents? Will they appear to be asking for special favors for their child if they seek help?

Teachers find that some parents have a very accepting leave-it-to-the-experts attitude. Such parents believe, and teach their children, that "the teacher knows best." They rarely criticize the school. Should the child have trouble, such parents usually feel it is deserved.

Parents who have had little formal education are more likely to be tolerant, or accepting, of the school. They hesitate to go to school even to enroll a child. They have experienced many rebuffs in their lives and may have failed in school. By avoiding school, they protect themselves from being hurt further. They have real and imagined reasons for not taking advantage of a teacher's overtures toward them.

On the other hand, some parents expect to be involved in educational matters. They are concerned lest their child be unprepared for the future. If they disagree with the goals or the methods of the school, they say so. Highly educated parents will make more demands for their children, yet they may be so busy in their business or professional lives that very little time is given to school matters. For instance, some parents say that their days are filled with meetings and that they would rather stay at home with their family in the evening than hire a baby-sitter in order to go out to a parents' meeting.

Plans for relating to children's parents, like plans for educating children, must be based on knowledge of the families concerned. This chapter will focus on relations between parents and teacher more than on parent education because of the belief that the teacher's first task is to relate to parents. Education may follow. However, the teacher may derive more education than the parent. Ideally, a meaningful two-way dialogue will develop and be of substantial benefit to the teacher, the parents, and the child.

TALK IT OVER: NO. 1

Recall your own school years, or your child's if you are now a parent. What were your parents' and teachers' attitudes toward each other? Can you learn anything from these experiences?

VALUES OF TEACHER-PARENT RELATIONSHIPS

Each teacher wishes to build the most relevant program for each child. By getting to know each child's parents and home situation, the teacher can more accurately assess the experiences the child has had before coming to school. Using this background the teacher builds stepping-stones to new experiences.

Reporting to parents on a child's school experience initiates exchanges with parents from which teachers gain valuable feedback regarding programs.

By knowing parents, the teachers can better encourage parental efforts on behalf of a child's education. Through various techniques teachers can help parents use the hours at home with the child to further education.

As teachers and parents get acquainted, they will learn of each other's educational goals and values. Ideally, this relationship will lessen any conflict between the two that might arise and cause confusion in the child's mind.

Even some highly educated parents have little knowledge of or appreciation for little children. Teachers can help all parents develop the understanding necessary for enjoying their children more fully.

The parent-cooperative nursery schools and kindergartens have a long and positive influence on parents. In addition to the objectives for the

An open welcome for parents makes this mother feel comfortable sitting with her young child before rushing home at the end of the day. (University of New Mexico)

growth and development of the children, the cooperatives have objectives for both parents' growth. Parents often mention the changes in themselves that have occurred as a result of having their child in the cooperative nursery school or kindergarten. For example, you hear parents commenting, "I didn't know anything about little kids; I had never been around any but my own, until I came to the co-op." "I was scared. I was afraid I'd do something that would harm the children!" "I got a lot out of talking with the other parents." "My husband and I made friends in the co-op who have been our best friends for years."

Parents in cooperatives learn about child development, about teaching children, about curriculum, about supplies and equipment, and about financing the operation. Such ideas usually elude parents who choose other types of schools for their children. For many, the financial savings offered by the co-op make the difference

between school and no school for their children. Cooperatives encourage a heavy dose of self-education for parents by offering them books to browse through and discussion groups and workshops in which they can share their most recent thoughts concerning their child's development.

From its beginning, Project Head Start encouraged teachers to know and work with parents. Many community resources have been coordinated through the school to improve the living situation of the Head Start children and their families. Today's full-day schools are making creative efforts to communicate with the parents of the children they serve.

Teachers add to their own understanding of children, parents, and families by making the effort to develop good relationships. Even though each family is unique, as are the individuals in it, each experience improves the teacher's ability to relate to other families in the future.

FAMILY CHARACTERISTICS AND LIFESTYLES

As you begin to meet and work with parents, avoid generalizing that all parents come from homes like yours. In Chapter 1, statistics are presented to show the changes in families in recent years, especially the increasing number of working women who have young children and also the increasing number of single-parent families. Many parents of young children are older, having waited later for their first births. The country is more pluralistic at the present time, with families from many cultural and language groups living and working side by side with families whose ancestors colonized America.

In addition, we have many families mixed by race, ethnicity, age, social and economic class, religion, cultural heritage, sexual orientation, and handicapping conditions. We have parents who began their family life at very young ages as teen parents and grandparents who are in their thirties rather than stereotypically aged. Other children in your prekindergarten may have siblings who are adults, making the child-sibling relationship entirely different from one where children are a few years apart. The NAEYC has published a 1996 position statement recommending work with families of many diversities.

Some fathers are serving as primary caregivers in their intact marriages, whereas other fathers have sole custody of young children. You may encounter grandparents and foster parents who are parenting a child in your group.

In short, in your teaching experience you will know young children who are a part of families living widely varied lifestyles. You will often learn intimate information about families that you need to know to work effectively with the young child. This information *must* be kept confidential. Your role will be to treat families equally, with respect, and with the belief that they all want the best for their children. All parents should be helped to support their children's early education.

You will need to extend the hand of friendship, to counsel parents, and to plan parent involvement efforts with families living in these varied groups. Your own racial, religious, ethnic, or lifestyle characteristics should not get in your way of doing an effective job with parents. To improve your own preparation for this work, you should seek out courses in family relationships and sociology to help you broaden your perspective on families. Such courses would make excellent choices in graduate work you might do in the years ahead to keep up-to-date in your field and, as might be required, to maintain your teaching certificate.

PARENTS' PRESENCE DURING BEGINNING DAYS

Early childhood schools have differing procedures for introducing new children to a group. Most prefer to introduce only a few children at a time. This procedure gives the teacher time to relate to each child and leaves plenty of space for a parent to stay with a child until both the teacher and the parent feel the child is confident enough to remain for a period of time without support. Parents without jobs or without other children at home may prolong this introductory period longer than the child needs, unless the teacher is able to help parents in the separation process. Some feel guilty, thinking that "good" parents take care of children at home when they can. Or a parent may be reluctant to leave the child with a stranger. Therefore it is essential for the teachers to communicate a regard for the parent and the child and reassure them that they can handle the situation. Teachers can, of course, assure a parent that they will call if any need arises.

Debbie is an example of a three-year-old who was reluctant to enter a three-year-old group. A number of weeks were needed before she felt secure in the school. Her previous social experience had always included her mother. In fact, the parents had taken her many places but had never left her alone, even to stay with her grandmother. Intellectually, Debbie's mother wanted Debbie to go to school, but psychologically she hesitated to leave her. The process was not rushed. Some days the mother stayed all morning. Sometimes she left for an hour, then returned to take Debbie home. Debbie could easily have become a nursery school dropout if the teachers had displayed less confidence in themselves, in the child, or in the mother. Eventually they were rewarded for their patience when Debbie stood at the school door shouting, "Let me in!" with a smile of confidence lighting her face.

Teachers in full-day centers will seldom have the time to let a child adjust as Debbie was able to do. They must use every technique available to help the child feel secure. Part of the problem is an outgrowth of the hurry-scurry felt in households when families are getting ready to go to work. Parents have mixed feelings as they rush their child off to the child care center and themselves off to work. Employed parents leave many tasks undone, which may lead to guilt feelings.

Sometimes the teacher's role is to help the parents make parting easier for the child. If the parent has time to stay during the introductory phase, he or she should do so. If the parent is required to leave because of a job, he or she should go. If the parent says "It is time to leave," and then lingers if the child cries, this teaches the child that crying will keep a parent longer. Parting may be difficult for both child and parent; but an off-again-on-again leave taking only complicates the matter for all.

Some parents may want to sneak out and leave the child at school. However, it is far better for the long-run adjustment if the child waves a tearful good-bye as he or she is held in the teacher's arms than for the child to discover suddenly that the parent is gone. You can learn how it's done by observing your experienced teacher.

Kindergarten children often need a gradual introduction to school. If this is their first school experience, they may experience anxiety, but usu-

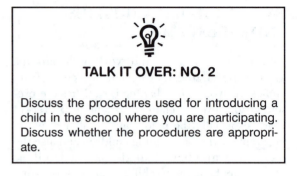

TALK IT OVER: NO. 2

Discuss the procedures used for introducing a child in the school where you are participating. Discuss whether the procedures are appropriate.

ally not of the duration felt by a younger child. Short days, staggered schedules, or many assistants may help the kindergarten teacher as a new group is introduced to the new environment.

TYPES OF CONTACTS BETWEEN PARENTS AND TEACHERS

Initial Meeting

Parents may base their first opinions concerning the teacher on very little information. Perhaps they notice the teacher at a parent meeting. They may ask other parents about personal qualities, teaching ability, and whether their child liked the teacher. They gain some idea of the teacher's patience as their questions are answered during a telephone call. Because teachers have a professional obligation to the public, they should be consistently patient, fair, and friendly with parents wherever they meet them.

Home Visit

The home visits made prior to the opening of school can be one of the teacher's most important activities of the entire year. Arranging introductions on the family's home premises gives the family a chance to feel more at ease. The focus is on the family and their concerns. If the introduction occurs at school, the focus becomes almost entirely school-centered. The goal for the first visit is to learn from the parents about their child and the home environment.

You may learn on a home visit that the child has an opportunity to ride horseback. Such information helps teachers relate more effectively with children and with their parents. (V. Watson, photographer)

This section refers to "parents" in the belief that both parents should be equally invited. Yet one knows that it is often impossible to find both parents at home, especially at the times the teacher has to make home visits. There are also homes with only one parent. Think through how you are going to extend an invitation to both parents, if there are two, but be accepting if the second parent cannot be home or if there is no second parent.

The teacher makes an efficient visiting schedule by grouping children according to their neighborhoods and making telephone calls to arrange a convenient time for a short visit. If the visits are scheduled every half hour or so, there is little time to allow for getting mixed up on directions or waiting while the baby's diaper is changed. The home visit can be presented as a routine event and as an opportunity for the child to get to know the teacher before entering school. Cooperation is usually excellent. Short visits are better than longer ones at this stage.

For an icebreaker a teacher can show the child and parents a packet of snapshots of former classes of children busily at work at school. Pictures always interest children and help them get over some of their shyness. A toy or a book can substitute for pictures. As the child looks at the pictures or plays with the toy, the parents and the teacher can talk over a few details.

The teacher can provide the parents with a school policy statement for later reading and, within school policy guidelines, a list of children's names and addresses, a field trip permission blank, health forms, a brief informational questionnaire, and forms for any research data needed. The teacher explains when the forms are to be returned and why they are needed, and assures parents that personal documents are confidential.

The teacher discusses with parents their role on the first day of school and seeks their estimate of how much support they feel the child will need. Because the first days are so crucial to the child's attitude toward school, it seems worthwhile to ask the parents to stay with the child if necessary. It is rarely necessary for a five-year-old, especially if the home visit has been thoughtfully done. With younger children it may or may not be necessary for the parent to stay. Sometimes the teacher's role is one of helping the parent permit the child to become independent. Sometimes the parent may be more concerned than the child about the new experience.

One of the values of a short visit early in the year is that, as yet, there are no problems to discuss. The parent or child won't worry that a teacher comes with bad tidings. The parent may welcome the chance to forewarn the teacher of a possible problem area and will be grateful for the opportunity to discuss it. Parents, teacher, and child can visit without feeling that others are waiting for their turn or that others are listening—as they might be at the school or at a parents' meeting. Young children are reassured when they later say to their teacher, "You know where I live." They feel real security in this knowledge and believe that in any emergency the teacher could find their house—and she or he sometimes may have to!

The home visit can help the teacher assess the child's psychological position in the home. Sibling competition or favoritism may be noticed as interaction is observed between family members. If the child appears to be overprotected, this may become apparent. Parents may volunteer information on a problem area or special need as the child wanders out of the room.

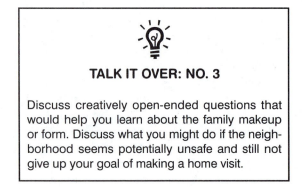

TALK IT OVER: NO. 3

Discuss creatively open-ended questions that would help you learn about the family makeup or form. Discuss what you might do if the neighborhood seems potentially unsafe and still not give up your goal of making a home visit.

Home visits often give information about family activities, interests, or hobbies. This information may also provide ideas for involving a family in class activities. For example, if Johnny brings out his daddy's banjo, the teacher can remember to ask Mr. Smith to play his banjo at school when the class is studying vibrations or stringed instruments. Questions such as "What did you do this summer?" can help a teacher include the child in future class discussions. For example, a teacher learned that shy Ronnie had flown by jet to visit his grandmother. Ronnie then became the class's jet expert when flying was mentioned.

A classroom storybook featuring the children themselves can begin to take shape during home visits. The teacher carries a camera and uses this opportunity to photograph each child. Looking for siblings, pets, or toys to include in the photo brings about informal visiting that adds further to the rapport among all present. See the chapter on literature for more discussion about this storybook. The pictures may also be placed on lockers to help children identify their personal space.

When ending the home visit the teacher can tell the parents, "Please call me at school or at home any time a question comes up that concerns the school and your child. We want to work together to make a good year for Jenny." Usually they quickly respond with the counterpart of that statement, "You call us too if anything comes up or if we can help." If they do not so respond, the teacher can add, "And I'll want to feel free to call you if I have any questions." In addition, parents are extended an open invitation to visit during the school year at any time, for a minute or all day.

Parents may have some anxiety concerning their lack of nice furnishings, but a wise teacher does not concentrate on these things or appear to notice. The goal is to build a relationship with people with whom one expects to work at least a year. The human element interests the teacher more than the quality of sofas. After this informative get-acquainted visit, they'll know each other the next time they meet.

Throughout the year the teacher can realize tremendous value from this brief home visit. In the first place, the teacher can more easily remember the child's name and face after having had some time to talk to the child individually. Calling Sara by name, perhaps asking about a pet or a baby sister, can make her feel more at home those first days at school. Following this procedure, teachers find fewer children who cry on opening day. In addition, during the visit the teacher gains some feeling of the psychological climate surrounding the child. For example, one may sense quite accurately the competition between siblings or the laissez-faire attitudes of parents through firsthand observation.

If the teacher can put parents at ease during the initial home visit, they will look forward to other contacts. Home visits are as unique as families. Teachers should relax, enjoy these new friends, and not feel any compulsion to teach but only to learn. Additional home visits are planned as needed.

When home visits are not feasible before school begins, they should be planned as quickly as possible after the opening of school. On visits later in the year, parents will expect the teacher to tell them about their child. Visits or conferences that are held when there are problems that must be discussed are far more difficult than the initial meeting. They, too, require thoughtful preparation. However, when initial meetings have built a feeling of confidence and respect between teacher and parent, then the relationship can withstand a discussion about a child's problem.

Teachers should take notes on all visits and conferences. These can be written out in full form after the session and filed for future reference. This should be done as soon after the visit as possible to ensure total recall.

In groups that operate year-round, home visits are still very desirable. A newly enrolled child's home visit can be made soon after registration has taken place. The teacher probably does not need to do several a day as might be necessary when school starts in the fall and all children

begin at the same time. The same concerns apply to these home visits as they do to those made in late summer or early fall.

School Visits

Some teachers arrange their first meeting with a child and parent in the school setting. This plan brings the focus more quickly to the school, its equipment, and its procedures. The meeting should be private, with an effort made to learn about the child and the family. Both parents and children will feel more at ease if they have had a chance to look over the school setting when no other children are there.

Some schools conduct a spring meeting of kindergarten and prekindergarten children who will be enrolling in the fall. These are usually called sometimes "kindergarten roundup." The goals for these meetings should be well thought out. Then plans should be made to fulfill the goals.

One goal is for the school to make contact with parents of kindergarten-age children to get enrollment estimates in order to plan for fall. From the child's point of view, a goal should be to initiate or build on the excitement of entering school. However, some schools are eliminating this excitement by conducting screening procedures (tests). These can create anxiety not only in the child, but in the parents as well. Tests and their validity were discussed toward the end of Chapter 19.

Children should not be subjected to tests by strangers in a crowded, unfamiliar place that, indeed, reminds one of a cattle roundup where the calves are milling around, bawling, and getting their shots. Shots have been given to children at some kindergarten roundups, too! Would you wonder that the children resisted coming back to school? Plans should be made for a few children at a time to visit the classroom with their parents and meet the teacher. Current kindergarten children can show the newcomers around. Visiting children should be allowed some

Fathers picking up their young child or participating in a cooperative often find the child showing off favorite places. (Utah State University)

qualified managers even more open to visitors. Many valuable mini-visits that working parents make would be eliminated if prior arrangements were required.

A parent's presence during a visit or on the day a parent-cooperator participates may cause some difficulties in the handling of that parent's child. Children sometimes exhibit dependent behavior that is not characteristic of them. It is natural for a child to want to be near his or her parent. It may be difficult for a child to share a parent, as is necessary in parent-cooperatives. If the parent reacts by admonishing the child to "run and play," the child may feel rejected. It is best to work *with* this feeling of possessiveness rather than *against* it. During a parent's visit, for example, the teacher can encourage the child to give the parent a guided tour. The parent is encouraged to follow and sit near the child until the excitement wears off.

If other children do not seem to understand why the visitor's child gets special attention, a simple explanation such as the following may be all that is necessary: "You know how you like to be near your mother when she comes? That's how Jim feels today."

Parents' Contribution to Program

When teachers become well acquainted with parents, they may learn that certain parents have talents that would interest the children if shared at school. Many parents are musicians or have some musical talents that are delightful when shared with children. For example, a guitar-playing parent singing school songs really brightens the children's day. Some talents may be unusual, like the harpist mother who plays with the city symphony and who gave the children a musical treat that the teachers could never have provided themselves. Other suggestions have been made in various chapters.

time to play with interesting toys and find the bathroom. Parents should be given suggestions for summer activities that would best prepare children for the opening of school in the fall. Screening, if it must be done, should be done elsewhere by others, and not interfere with the positive goals for introducing children to school.

Parents should always feel welcome at school. They should be invited to attend for a moment or an entire period, at their convenience. They should be able to arrive unannounced. The school program can continue on a routine basis with no alteration because of the visitor.

When parents are told that they should call before visiting school, they may feel unwelcome or worry that children are mistreated when visitors aren't present. The occurrence of sex abuse of children in a few child care centers has made

In addition, parents may work where children could visit. A father, for example, helped arrange a visit to a TV studio where he worked. A police officer parent may enjoy stopping by the school to give children a lesson in safety on the streets. Perhaps the children could even visit the police station. Such contributions are very valuable and help bridge the gap between home and school.

Parents from various ethnic groups can make worthwhile contributions by sharing music, stories, or costumes. Or they might be invited to help supervise a cooking project teaching about a traditional food. Thus, a Chicano parent might help with tamales or a German parent might help with German potato salad.

When a parent brings a special exhibit, or in other ways helps with the program, that parent's child should be involved in the plans for the day. The child can help his or her parent get materials ready or share the "secret" of a special event that will surprise the other children. Parents should be aware that one of the values of their participation in special events is the recognition their child receives. Plans should be made for the child to be a helper or to get a front-row seat. The child's pride in the parent's participation should be recognized as a legitimate feeling on the child's part.

Casual Visits

Many casual visits between teacher and parents take place as children are delivered and picked up at school. Teachers should develop a system for sharing information when the child is picked up. Some schools have a note-pocket under each child's name, which is attached to the door. Then it is handy for the teacher to slip a brief note in the pocket, which the parent remembers to look for each day.

Other visits may occur in the supermarket or at social events. At such times the teacher can report pleasurable moments the child has had in school. Parents may report an unusual family event that aids the teacher when working with the child during the day. The teacher must focus attention on the children and the other parents who are coming and going, leaving little time for

discussing difficulties a child might be having. However, an appointment for a conference can be arranged, or the teacher may ask the parent to call when it is convenient to talk.

Telephone Conversations

It is a rare parent who would abuse the teacher's invitation, "Call me whenever there is any problem that concerns your child and school. If I can be of help I want to be." The "on-call" attitude of professional teachers separates them from nine-to-five workers. Teachers know that children sometimes go home confused or with real or imagined slights. They may leave a dearest treasure at school. A call to the teacher can straighten things out so that the family's evening goes smoother. Parents should feel it is all right to call the teacher at home.

Some parents in our mobile society live far away from family or friends with whom they might discuss their children. A call to the teacher may help that parent think through some difficulty. Teachers can encourage friendships between parents, which will help alleviate the loneliness of a parent in a new locale.

Regular Conferences

When parent conferences are the rule rather than the exception, parents will approach teachers with less anxiety. With this procedure all children—not just those with adjustment problems—receive the benefit of thinking and help from those two very important influences in their lives—home and school.

Purpose

The teacher's purpose for arranging the private conference is to learn the parent's impressions of the program, to gain a better understanding of the effect of the program on the child, to get more information about the child, to encourage parents' understanding and support of the program, and to make plans for the child—especially concerning possible difficulties.

Most parents will feel some obligation to attend conferences. The conferences should not be threatening to the parent. Discussion is kept to the stated purposes unless parents indicate other things they wish to discuss. If parents miss conferences, teachers should follow through with calls and appointments for a special conference, rather than despair that parents aren't interested in their children.

Parents will be anxious to know how the child does in school and how he or she relates to other children and the teachers. They may want some indication and reassurance that the child is a good learner. They may be concerned with reading or writing.

The following letter is an example of an invitation to a conference that parents might receive:

Dear Parents,

Now that we have completed two months of school, I'd like us to get together so we can talk about how your child has been getting along since school started. Private conferences are being arranged with each child's parents. This conference and others will be used in place of formal report cards.

Your conference is scheduled for next week <u>Nov. 2 at 2:30 p.m.</u> in my office—106 Wilson School. If this hour is inconvenient, you may trade with another family or call me (345–9996) for a better time.

Volunteers will supervise your children in the classroom during our conference. As you recall, to enable teachers to hold conferences, there is no school during the afternoons next week.

Please do not alarm your child about this conference. You can say, "Your teacher and I are going to talk about what you like at school. What shall I say?"

Of course, both parents are invited to the conference when it is possible for you both to attend.

Sincerely,
Mrs. Verna Hildebrand
Teacher

Note the content of the letter. The date, hour, and place of the conference are stated clearly. The letter suggests some flexibility by letting parents exchange times or call for a change in schedule. The purpose of the conference is stated, as is the fact that all parents are involved. Baby-sitting has been arranged that will help parents solve one problem they always have when the child is not in school and when they may have other young children. Also of importance is the advice regarding interpreting the conference to the child. Having worked to develop rapport with a child, the teacher would hope that the parents would not say something like, "Your teacher is going to tell me how bad you've been."

A face-to-face conference is much more satisfactory for reporting a child's progress to parents than is a written form. Many schools are allowing released time for such conferences today. By meeting parents in a conference, the teacher can help them think through possible alternative solutions to problems. In a written report the parents' reaction to information could be negative instead of the desired positive result for the child.

For example, one kindergarten teacher checked "lacks social skills" on the report card of Charley, a quiet, withdrawn child. Had the teacher mentioned this problem to his parents, their defensive reaction might have been noticed and remedies suggested that would have helped the child improve his social skills. However, the report card merely went home to the parents, who reacted by punishing the child. They kept him in the house every night after school instead of allowing Charley to play in the courtyard with his friends from the neighborhood. Surely the parents reacted in the worst possible way to the teacher's good intention. For the child's best interests it would have been better to have discussed the problem with his parents, including suggestions for helping the child.

Preparation

Teachers should make thoughtful preparations for conferences. They should collect some samples of a child's work and make notes on participation in school. When there are problems that must be discussed, the teacher should think about possible solutions ahead of time in order to be able to make suggestions for discussion. Without suggestions for alleviating a difficulty, some problems may better remain undisclosed. The teacher may find the conference more helpful for learning from the parent about the child and the impact of the program than it is for reporting. Conferring with parents requires different skills than teaching children, and teachers should spend some time developing those skills.

If you are using a collection of the child's work—a portfolio—to illustrate progress, then these materials should be organized and dated as they are placed in the folder. The portfolio is considered a helpful form of evaluation by many teachers.

Procedure

When the teacher has called the conference, the discussion starts something like, "Now that we've had a few weeks of school, I thought it would be helpful for us to talk together. How do you feel things are going for Jack?" This question is usually easy for parents. They talk about things the child likes. The teacher can then ask, "How about things that have bothered Jack—things he didn't like? Do you think he's getting too tired?" By inviting negative reactions, the teacher lets the parents know that suggestions as well as praise are in order.

Nearly all parents enjoy talking about their child to someone who wants to listen. During the first conference the teacher would hope to convince parents of deep interest in the child, an awareness of what the child has been doing at school, and also sincere respect for the child and parents.

Facing Problems

Most parents are grateful to teachers who bring their child's problems to their attention. Difficulties can develop without being noticed by parents. Parents often praise a teacher for helping

them work through a problem. Common, too, is criticism of teachers who wait until difficulties are full-blown before mentioning them. The teacher's solution is usually not to ignore the child's troubles but to think through possible meanings, causes, and solutions before calling parents in for a conference. If parents and teacher know each other through many pleasant instances and mutual trust has developed, each can weather discussion of a child's difficulty without personal threat unless one of them has deep-seated problems.

Teachers should avoid making a premature diagnosis of the cause of a child's behavior. One mother was completely surprised when her child's teacher telephoned and asked whether she and her husband were having marital difficulty. The mother replied, "No, why?" Then the teacher explained that their daughter was acting strangely, so she "just wondered." Months later the mother was still wondering what the child did or said that prompted the teacher to ask. Certainly, if the couple had been having problems, this was hardly an appropriate approach.

Avoid Blaming Parents

While talking with parents, it is of greatest importance to avoid arousing their defensive feelings. Such feelings are stirred if the child is criticized. There are ways of stating a concern regarding a child's behavior without fixing blame or being angry or annoyed. When too forcefully confronted with a child's problem behavior, the

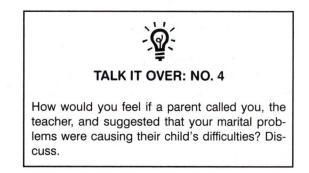

TALK IT OVER: NO. 4

How would you feel if a parent called you, the teacher, and suggested that your marital problems were causing their child's difficulties? Discuss.

defensive parent may deny that the child behaves that way at home and suggest that the behavior must be the product of the school situation. Then comes the teacher's turn to be defensive. Sometimes the teacher may better say, after citing examples, "These are the things we see. Do you have any indication as to why Amy feels this way at school?" Not having to defend themselves, parents may volunteer the information that they are having similar problems at home.

Parents may say, "I know I'm to blame," to which the teacher can say, "Rather than fix a blame, let's think together about things we might try to remedy the situation. Now, here at school we've tried [enumerate a few examples]. Is there something like that you might try at home?" Such a discussion suggests possible solutions for examination. Parents can realize that problems have various solutions, and they can try one that fits their situation.

Parents often have the feeling that teachers just couldn't know how it is to be in parental shoes. As teachers grow in experience and draw on the experience of others, they may help parents realize that other parents before them have solved similar problems. Of course, teachers avoid using names or current classes for examples.

Teachers should be humble; it is extremely difficult really to know the family situation. There is very little that is clear-cut. An outsider should recognize uncertainties when giving advice. Parents' self-confidence must be protected and bolstered. If the conference is to be of any help to the child, the parents must have hope for succeeding as parents.

When parents request a conference, they are often ready to deal with some problem they face with the child. Again the teacher's role is more that of a listener and a suggester of alternatives than a giver of answers. The teacher should be willing to refer parents to other professionals whose training, experience, and available time leave them better equipped to cope with people who have problems.

A file of referral agencies should be on every teacher's desk. When teachers decide to make a referral, they should make some preliminary contacts with the agency in order to be able to give precise information to parents. Parents need to know where to go, when to go, what it will cost, and something about the personnel and procedure used. If the teacher knows the professionals in the agency by name and can personally endorse their qualifications, parents are more likely to follow through with the referral. Parents are understandably reluctant to face new people with their personal problems.

The teacher has the professional obligation to protect the confidentiality of personal information the parent reveals. Any notes the teacher makes should be kept private. Therefore information that is available to students and parent volunteers necessarily omits certain personal facts. Of course, parents should be able to see their child's file at any time.

Occasionally in conferences and casual visits one parent seeks information about or is critical of other parents. The teacher must use diplomacy while turning the discussion back to that parent's own situation. Parents occasionally ask university student helpers about other children; students, too, must learn to handle such comments and avoid discussions that might be construed as gossip. Any information about the children should be discussed in a professional manner and in a professional setting.

Group Meetings for Parents

Getting parents together at meetings is one method of communicating with them. Meetings early in the year may help parents get acquainted with each other. The teacher may use the meeting to discuss goals for the children and outline the ways the school expects to meet these goals. As a student these are valuable opportunities for you.

The needs and interests of parents will determine how many organized meetings are planned. The teacher may leave this decision up to the

Early childhood parent cooperative programs can help parents learn how to invest their energy in their children's education, for example, in La Libertad, Nicaragua's Parent Cooperative. (V. Hildebrand, photographer)

group. The teacher may encourage them to organize their own group, elect a chairperson, or appoint a committee to plan future programs. The more the parents are part of the planning process, the more interest they will have in attending meetings. Involvement of both fathers and mothers is important. An effort must be made to adjust meeting hours so parents working outside the home are not excluded.

Some schools plan workshop programs that involve the parents in learning about school activities. For example, the parents may meet, mix finger paints and playdough, then use the materials to further their understandings of the creative experiences their child is having at school. Some groups plan programs using films or speakers to stimulate their exchange of ideas. They may prefer small-group discussions in which the focus is on their specific child-rearing problems.

Occasionally the topics parents suggest for meetings seem far removed from the child in the school. For example, parents may suggest meetings on meal planning, sewing, fashion, hairdressing, or even jewelry making. In the long run, these meetings may be helpful in developing rapport between home and school. Even when the teacher is unable to be a resource person for such topics, the group can be helped to locate someone who can. Through meeting the personal needs of parents, the child's needs are often served. If the parents are given a positive experience in the school, there will be a good chance that their interest will eventually focus more directly on the child.

Once a meeting has been planned, the teacher can help advertise it. Several notices can be sent home encouraging parents' attendance. First notices will encourage parents in advance to reserve that date on their calendars. On the day of the meeting another notice can remind them. Through personal contacts, interest and enthusiasm can be aroused for the meeting. A committee of parents can contact others to encourage participation and offer transportation. Through such personal contacts parents will feel that they are wanted in the group.

Name tags help parents get acquainted and can help to break down formality because people can more readily use each other's names. It may help to put "Estelle Jones—Anna's Mother" on the name tag so that other parents can associate the mother with a name they may have heard their child mention from day to day. It is a common joke among parents that they lose their identity once their child goes to school. Because young children rarely know each other's last names, they refer to adults as Anna's mother or Bettie's daddy.

Better attendance at meetings results when baby-sitting is arranged. Transportation may also be a problem for some parents. Some schools hold meetings during the child's school hours. Extra volunteers supervise a children's program while the teacher and parents meet in another part of the building. A space may be arranged for infants and toddlers, or little ones may accompany parents to the meeting. This latter practice may cause some distractions because of the needs of the children. Proper toys for the babies should be available.

Evening meetings may not be well attended because of baby-sitting problems. When children must be brought to meetings, their bedtimes are delayed. Some teachers hold potluck suppers and early evening meetings so that parents can return home for their children's usual bedtime.

Some groups use gimmicks to attract parents to meetings. These may be door prizes, recognition for the child's classroom, or performances by the children. Although gimmicks might be used occasionally to attract parents who cannot seem to be interested in other ways, their long-range value is questionable. Likewise, the threat that the child will be deprived of a place in the school if the parents do not participate is also questionable. A better way of attracting parents to meetings is through the personal interest of the teacher and other parents. When personal contacts are adequately made, a friendly atmosphere prevails, and if parents feel the program meets their needs, they are likely to make an effort to participate. The teacher's first meetings and first contacts set the stage for parents' participation. Well-planned, relevant programs are essential for good attendance.

Each chapter of Part 2 of this book has suggested ways of involving parents in that particular area of the curriculum. Each curriculum area offers numerous possibilities for parents' meetings.

Parenting Education Courses

There are a number of specially designed courses to use in parent education. Often these are designed to help parents establish communication with their children. In recent years, to help parents take charge in their parenting tasks, courses have been offered using funding from child-abuse-prevention and drug-abuse-prevention sources. Teachers of young children are often instructors of these courses, as are psychologists, social workers, and mental health consultants. A number of churches offer parent education classes as part of their family outreach programs. Aside from learning some fruitful ways to deal with their own youngsters of various ages, the parents gain deeper understanding from sharing their problems with parents who have similar concerns. Some courses are licensed and require a licensed instructor, who charges a certain fee for presenting the course for parents in the community.

The family life specialists in the Cooperative Extension Services, located at your land-grant state university, or the specialist in your local Family and Consumer Sciences (formerly home economics) Cooperative Extension office can give advice regarding parenting education programs that are available locally. You can discuss with these professionals the possibilities of becoming a family life educator. The following texts are examples of books used for some of the special courses.

> *Active Parenting* by Michael Popkin (New York: Harper & Row, 1987).
>
> *Nurturing Program for Parents and Children 4 to 12 Years: Parent Handbook* by Stephen J. Bavolek and Christine Comstock (Eau Claire, WI: Family Development Resources, 1985).
>
> *Parent Effectiveness Training: P.E.T.* by Thomas Gordon (New York: Peter H. Wyden, 1970).
>
> *The Parent's Handbook: Systematic Training for Effective Parenting (STEP)* by Don Dinkmeyer (New York: Random House, 1990).

Printed Communication for Parents

Teachers usually rely on duplicated letters to inform parents of school affairs. A brief letter written in an interesting, warm style will encourage parents to read it and to feel that it was written especially for them. Underline dates that are to be remembered.

Through letters the teacher can support other community agencies and their programs for families. The exact hours of a public health clinic might be important to some parents. Information on the hours the public library is open and when the children's story hour is held is helpful to parents and encourages library use. Parents can be reminded about musical events, art shows, exhibits, and lectures that are relevant to the many facets of the educational development of parents and children.

To emphasize to the child and to the parents that these letters are important, the teacher gives them special care. They are sealed in envelopes marked with each child's name. The name helps the teacher keep track of undelivered letters. The letter can be attached to the child's coat with a safety pin. Children enjoy the responsibility of serving as "mail carriers" between their teacher and their homes.

Booklets and Newsletters

The manager and staff of each school and center should prepare for public distribution a statement of their program philosophy and operating procedures. This statement can be mailed or handed to parents when they inquire about enrolling their child in the center.

Once the child is enrolled parents appreciate receiving short communications from time to time. Even the youngest enjoy being responsible for being mail carriers and seeing that the envelope is delivered to their parents.

One form of written communication parents really appreciate is a newsletter or booklet of class-related materials prepared by the teacher, duplicated, and sent home to parents. Some teachers prepare communications once a month, others two or three times a year. The content varies, but the following materials have proved popular with parents:

- the names, phone numbers, and addresses of the children in the group
- recipes for finger paint, playdough, and paste
- recipes for food projects enjoyed by the children
- words to songs and fingerplays the children are learning
- stories and letters the children have dictated at school
- toy-buying guides, including suggestions for appropriate gift items
- suggested activities for the children's winter or summer vacation
- examples of correct ways to learn manuscript writing
- suggested books for children
- suggestions for parent reading on the various school activities, family life, or sex education

Attractive covers can be made for booklets from construction paper. One teacher helps the children place their handprints in white paint on the colored paper. Older children can make a drawing or cut out a magazine picture for their booklet. Collage designs can be made by the children to cover their parents' booklet.

A booklet like this makes a nice gift for the children to give to their parents. The children feel the materials are theirs. They like to take the booklets home to share with the whole family. Such an educational device stimulates additional learning and often involves the whole family.

EXPERIENCES FOR STUDENTS AND BEGINNING TEACHERS

Students often wonder how they can go about gaining the experience that enables them to feel comfortable in situations with parents. There are, of course, numerous courses in counseling, family relations, and parent education that will help the student. One practical suggestion is for students to use every opportunity just to talk to people who have children. Knowing families from many walks of life also contributes to understanding. A good opportunity for the student is to volunteer for baby-sitting to get acquainted with parents and to observe how they relate to their children. As students go home for vacations, they can listen to their relatives and encourage both the eldest and the youngest parent to talk about the concerns and pleasures of child rearing. Every parent whom the student has the opportunity to know will provide experience that will help in developing better teacher-parent relations when the student becomes the teacher.

COUNSELING HELP

Teachers often ask where they can get help in learning the counseling skills they need. Indeed, this is a good place to use some of the graduate credit hours you will take from time to time to keep up with your profession. An introductory course in counseling can be quite helpful for providing basic information about counseling principles. You will soon apply the principles to practical situations with parents. Conferences and inservice workshops can also be a source of this information. Encourage your administrator to arrange such sessions to underscore your desire to work comfortably with parents.

EXPLAINING THE NEED FOR PARENT WORK

The process of accreditation of early childhood schools by the NAEYC includes criteria on staff-parent interaction. The information and activities contained in this chapter would prepare a school for accreditation on this item.[3]

Very often the steps that have been outlined here for parent-teacher relations are carried on by teachers in addition to a full day of working with children. If a teacher has fifty or sixty children in two kindergarten classes, it is easy to see why she or he might be unable to carry through all the suggestions made here. However, the situation will never improve unless the teacher discusses the problem with the administrator, who can lighten the class load, grant released time, or hire an assistant so that the teacher can have some time for parent work. Teachers must take a nothing-ventured-nothing-gained attitude while continuing to do the best they can for the children in their groups.

A better plan is for the teacher to work half days with children, using the other half day for planning and for work with parents. This arrangement strengthens the program on two important fronts.

Special parent-educators are hired in some schools to coordinate parent programs for several

---

[3]Sue Bredekamp, ed., *Accreditation Criteria and Procedures of the National Academy of Early Childhood Programs* (Washington, DC: NAEYC, 1991), pp. 15–17.

teachers. They can readily organize parent meetings, meet with committees, and support leadership training that can be the outgrowth of a good program. However, even with a specialist in parent education the teacher will still need to maintain the relationships with parents that have been discussed in this chapter. The work of any specialist should be incorporated into the planning for the class; therefore communication between the teacher and the parent-educator is essential.

Conclusions

Teacher-parent relationships are of utmost importance in the education of the young child. When the school and home are closely united, the child will more likely be able to reach fullest potential.

Teachers will take the leadership in initiating contacts with parents. They will maintain an open, friendly approach to parents, yet remain professional at all times.

The teacher will value relationships with parents as a teaching experience and, perhaps even more important, as a learning experience with respect to the child and parents.

Plans for the parents, like plans for the children, will be made after their needs and interests have been determined. The teacher may initiate some meetings but leave others up to the leaders of the group.

Teachers should be prepared to explain to the administrators of their schools the importance of developing relationships with parents. Teachers should seek recognition that their work with parents on a one-to-one basis as well as on a group basis makes an important contribution to each child's education.

Communication with parents in a number of ways is stipulated in the criteria for accreditation for high-quality early childhood programs by the NAEYC.

Applications

1. Discuss the "Talk It Over" items found in the chapter.

2. Write a plan for a parent activity. Secure approval, carry out the plan if feasible, and evaluate the results from the parents' viewpoints and your viewpoint. Prepare a report and hand it in along with your approved plan.
3. Evaluate your total participation performance on your evaluation form developed in Chapter 1.
4. Add ideas and plans for parent activities to your Resource File.

Study Questions

1. Discuss the ways early childhood schools are part of a family support system.
2. State concerns parents may have as they begin relating to a school and teachers.
3. Discuss the value of good teacher-parent relationships in terms of the child.
4. Discuss the procedure for introducing a child gradually to the school.
5. List and discuss the various types of contacts teachers and parents could have.
6. Discuss details of planning a conference with a child's parents.

Videotapes

Harmonizing the Worlds of Home and Child Care
   30 minutes

Thelma Harms and Debby Cryer examine ways that parents and caregivers can deal with the demands of home and child care so that the child feels support and continuity in both settings. They explore ways to reduce family stress through effective home and child care communication and cooperation. DC/TATS MEDIA, Frank Porter Graham Child Development Center, University of North Carolina at Chapel Hill CB8040, 300 NCNB Plaza, Chapel Hill, NC 27599-8040.

Mister Rogers Talks With Parents
   43 minutes

TV's Mr. Rogers discusses some of the pressures on children today and gives a brief visit to "The Neighborhood." NAEYC Media, 1509 16th St. NW, Washington, DC 20036-1426, 1-800-424-2460.

Whole Language Learning
    20 minutes

Classroom examples of whole-language learning show teacher and parent roles in whole-language activities. NAEYC Media, 1509 16th St NW, Washington, DC 20036-1426, 1-800-424-2460.

Additional Readings

Bavolek, Stephen J., and Christine Comstock. *Nurturing Program for Parents and Children 4 to 12 Years: Parent Handbook.* Eau Claire, WI: Family Development Resources, 1985.

Berger, Eugenia H. *Parents as Partners in Education.* Upper Saddle River, NJ: Merrill/Prentice Hall, 1987.

Bigner, Jerry. *Parent-Child Relations.* New York: Macmillan, 1989.

Bjorklund, Gail, and Christine Burger. "Making Conferences Work for Parents, Teachers, and Children." *Young Children* 42:2, January 1987, 26–31.

Briggs, Beverly A., and Connor M. Walters. "Single-Father Families: Implications for Early Childhood Educators." *Young Children* 40:3, March 1985, 23–27.

Bundy, Blakely F. "Fostering Communication Between Parents and Preschools." *Young Children* 46:2, January 1991, 12–18.

Clay, James W. "Working with Lesbian and Gay Parents and Their Children." *Young Children* 45:3, March 1990, 31–35.

Comer, J. P. *Maggie's American Dream: The Life and Times of a Black Family.* New York: Penguin, 1988.

Dinkmeyer, Don. *The Parent's Handbook: Systematic Training for Effective Parenting (STEP).* New York: Random House, 1990.

Fong, Yun Lee. "Asian Parents as Partners." *Young Children* 50:3, March 1995, 4–9.

Foster, Suzanne M. "Successful Parent Meetings." *Young Children* 50:1, November 1994, 78–80.

Fox, Robert, R. C. Anderson, T. A. Fox, and M. A. Rodriguez. "STAR Parenting: A Model for Helping Parents Effectively Deal with Behavioral Difficulties." *Young Children* 46:6, September 1991, 54–60.

Friedberg, Joan B. "Helping Today's Toddlers Become Tomorrow's Readers: A Pilot Parent Participation Project Offered Through a Pittsburgh Health Agency." *Young Children* 44:2, January 1989, 13–16.

Furman, Robert A. "Helping Children Cope with Stress and Deal with Feelings." *Young Children* 50:2, January 1995, 33–41.

Gordon, Thomas. *P.E.T.: Parent Effectiveness Training.* New York: David McKay, 1975.

Greenberg, Polly. "Parents as Partners in Young Children's Development and Education." *Young Children* 44:4, May 1989, 61–75.

Halpern, Robert. "Major Social and Demographic Trends Affecting Young Families: Implications for Early Childhood Care and Education." *Young Children* 42:6, September 1987, 34–40.

Hildebrand, V., and P. Hearron. *Management of Child Development Centers.* Upper Saddle River, NJ: Merrill/Prentice Hall, 1997.

Hildebrand, V., L. A. Phenice, M. M. Gray, and R. P. Hines. *Knowing and Serving Diverse Families.* Upper Saddle River, NJ: Merrill/Prentice Hall, 1996.

Holcomb, Betty. "How Families Are Changing . . . For the Better." *Working Mother*, July 1994, 29–36.

Karnes, M. B., and L. J. Johnson. "Training for Staff, Parents, and Volunteers Working with Gifted Young Children, Especially Those with Disabilities and from Low-Income Homes." *Young Children* 44:3, March 1989, 49–56.

Koopmans-Dayton, Jill D., and John F. Feldhusen. "A Resource Guide for Parents of Gifted Preschoolers." *Gifted Child Today.* November/December 1987, 2–7. Reprinted in

McKee, J., and Karen M. Paciorek. *Annual Editions Early Childhood Education 89/90.* Guilford, CT: Dushkin, 1989, 141–145.

MacCarry, Bert. "Helping Preschool Child Care Staff and Parents Do More with Stories and Related Activities." *Young Children* 44:2, January 1989, 17–21.

McBride, Brent A. "Interaction, Accessibility, and Responsibility. A View of Father Involvement and How to Encourage It." *Young Children* 44:5, July 1989, 13–19.

McCoy, Ellen. "Childhood Through the Ages." *Parents,* January 1981, 60–65.

Morgan, Elizabeth. "Talking with Parents When Concerns Come Up." *Young Children* 44:2, January 1989, 52–56.

NAEYC. "The Effects of Group Size, Ratios, and Staff Training on Child Care Quality." *Young Children* 48:2, January 1993, 65–67.

———. "NAEYC Position Statement Responding to Linguistic and Cultural Diversity—Recommendations for Effective Early Childhood Education." *Young Children* 51:2, January 1996, 4–12.

Phillips, C. B. "Nurturing Diversity for Today's Children and Tomorrow's Leaders." *Young Children* 43:2, January 1988, 42–47.

Popkin, Michael. *Active Parenting: Teaching Cooperation, Courage, and Responsibility.* New York: Harper and Row, 1987.

Powell, Douglas R. "Home Visiting in the Early Years: Policy and Program Design Decisions." *Young Children* 45:6, September 1990, 65–73.

———. *Families and Early Childhood Programs.* Washington, DC: NAEYC, 1991.

Ramsey, Patricia G. "Growing Up With the Contradictions of Race and Class." *Young Children* 50:6, September 1995, 18–22.

Swick, K. J. *Parent Involvement: Strategies for Early Childhood Education.* Champaign, IL: Stipes, 1981.

CHAPTER 21

The World's Children

V. Hildebrand, photographer

Objectives

✔ Identify the common characteristics and needs of children around the world.

✔ Identify the mutual concerns of the world's early childhood educators.

✔ Relate international observations of children and early childhood programs to multicultural education of teachers.

The right

1. *to affection, love, and understanding;*
2. *to adequate nutrition and medical care;*
3. *to free education;*
4. *to full opportunity for play and recreation;*
5. *to a name and nationality;*
6. *to special care, if handicapped;*
7. *to be among the first to receive relief in times of disaster;*
8. *to learn to be a useful member of society and to develop individual abilities;*
9. *to be brought up in a spirit of peace and universal brotherhood;*
10. *to enjoy these rights, regardless of race, color, sex, religion, national, or social origin.*

United Nations Declaration of the Rights of the Child

The Convention on the Rights of the Child was passed on November 20, 1989, by the United Nations (UN) General Assembly. It was a historic day for children's rights. The rights mentioned in the opening ten points of this chapter are only a few of the fifty-four articles that resolve to improve the lives of all children throughout the world. As the *New York Times* reported,

> "For children, this is the Magna Carta," James P. Grant, executive director of the United Nations Children's Fund, or UNICEF, said. "To get one common doctrine is a near miracle in its own right. It creates a new international norm."
>
> The United Nations Secretary General, Javier Pérez de Cuéllar, said the convention was "as visionary as it is timely." The President of the General Assembly, Joseph N. Garba of Nigeria, said, "The rights of the child have now gone from a declaratory statement of purpose into what will become a binding piece of legislation."[1]

The **Declaration of the Rights of the Child** was originally passed November 20, 1959, and reaffirmed in 1979 during the International Year of the Child. The passage in 1989 of the more powerful **Convention on the Rights of the Child** is heralded as a major positive step by people interested in the general welfare of the world's children.

As is noted in Chapter 22, the United States adopted the Children's Charter in 1930. Many of the same concerns appear in both the Children's Charter and the United Nations' declaration. By the year 2000, with the help of dedicated teachers and parents around the world, great progress can be made on many of these problems crucial to the well-being of children wherever they may reside on our spaceship known as the planet Earth.

---

[1]*New York Times*, "U.N. Assembly Approves Doctrine to Guard Children's Rights" (November 21, 1989), p. 9. For specific details see Kerstin Bäckström, "Convention on the Rights of the Child," *International Journal of Early Childhood* 21:2 (December 1989), 35–44.

GLOBAL INTERDEPENDENCE

World problems in the news today are now about as close to home as local problems were a century ago. There is a rapidly growing recognition of the interdependence of the welfare of the children of the world and that basic human rights extend to children regardless of the region of the world in which they are born. The spherical spaceship Earth, inhabited by children and parents, is like an apartment house. What happens on one side of the global house affects children on the other side and vice versa. There is no place to hide from repercussions. This is true whether we speak of problems concerning environmental contamination, economics, conservation of resources, or the health and well-being of people.

- With respect to environmental contamination, radioactivity from atomic explosions in one area spreads rapidly and poisons the atmosphere of the entire planet.
- With respect to economics, inflation or depression in one area soon extends damaging effects around the world.
- With respect to conservation of resources, the world shortage of petroleum requires global conservation so all areas of the world and future generations may enjoy some of this scarce natural resource. Even population growth must now be studied concerning its impact on scarce natural resources and on environmental pollution.
- With respect to health and well-being, contagious diseases, if unchecked, will spread around the world to the detriment to all.

INTERNATIONAL YEAR OF THE FAMILY AND THE FOURTH WORLD'S WOMEN'S CONFERENCE

Two international conferences during recent years have highlighted children's needs at least in

Nicaraguan children and parents participate in a village parent-cooperative prekindergarten program. (V. Hildebrand, photographer)

part. The year 1994 was designated the **International Year of the Family** by the United Nations. Delegates from around the world met in Malta in an initial meeting to agree on goals for the year. Delegates returned to their countries to carry on their work to improve the situations for families.

The second important meeting was the Fourth World's Women's Conference held in Beijing, China, in 1995. Many of the issues discussed will impact children throughout the world. Over 40,000 delegates (mostly women) attended. During ten days there were over twenty-five hundred workshops on ten major topics, plus plenary sessions. Education for female children was highlighted because girls are the neglected gender in many countries. Health, education, jobs, rights, and violence of many types were also discussed.

Both conferences had a goal of educating the delegates about the needs of families and about women and women's many concerns. Agendas for delegates to pursue when they returned to their home countries were developed. Having a world forum gives the leaders of countries opportuni-

ties to learn from each other and to return home with increased energy and enthusiasm. Early childhood educators were represented in both conferences and were able to benefit from interacting with leaders from many disciplines and organizations. One truly sees the ecology of childhood in the program.

It was clear that each country had sent its best and brightest. Observing delegates of many cultures interacting and making decisions proves that one's culture is not a barrier to good communication. The United Nations published documents related to both of these meetings. (To request information write United Nations, One United Nations Plaza, Division of Public Affairs, New York, NY 10017.)

MULTICULTURAL UNDERSTANDING

Many of today's early childhood teachers are attempting to gain greater knowledge of the world's families and of world affairs in order to teach children more effectively for the century ahead. A current trend attracting the attention and support of many educators is the development and introduction of multicultural information, global perspectives, and aspects of global interdependence into the curriculum for each age group.

Within most countries of the world, educators are recognizing and beginning to value cultural pluralism—the richness and diversity of their populations. Children and their cultures can properly remain unique with basic human rights extended to all individuals. Although previous policies and socialization may have pressed for almost complete denial of ancestral roots, families now are increasingly free to choose to retain and cherish their roots. There is a growing belief that families can be free to maintain links with their ancestral culture and still prepare to function well in modern society. (Of course, over many thousands of years each family probably experienced many ancestral cultures.) A modern progressive society does not need identical human beings. Only a recognition of a common humanity is needed to promote the general welfare; that is, unity can coexist harmoniously with diversity. Intelligent application of all areas of knowledge can make the world safe for differences and enrich society at the same time. One can simultaneously be a citizen of a local, state, national, and international community and enjoy to a still greater extent the benefits of diversity, unity, and progressive change for the improved welfare of all.

To be able to teach more intelligently about cultures other than one's own, teachers are making efforts to expand their horizons by study and travel and by cultivating friendships with families from various cultural groups. For instance, opportunities are increasing for educational travel for students and teachers. Some scholarships are available. Many students spend a term or two in overseas programs operated by their own or foreign universities. Some early child-

hood students have taken the opportunity to do their student teaching in overseas locations. Students participate in activities abroad, such as the American Friend's Service Committee's volunteer work, various student exchange programs, and the Peace Corps, thus gaining valuable educational experience with families in cultures different from their own.

Students from countries around the world are enrolled on most university campuses and are delighted to share their cultural heritage and insights with students of their host country. These foreign students are often pleased to visit early childhood programs and to help provide cross-cultural experiences for young children—a significant educational contribution to world understanding. On some campuses international centers or organizations facilitate the interaction between students from the United States and those students from other countries. These centers may also collect and disseminate information to teachers and to teachers-in-training about various cultures—perhaps through a library, an organized lecture series, films, cultural nights, and the like. On some campuses International Houses provide a multicultural meeting and living environment and sponsor sessions for learning about various cultures, including excellent opportunities to learn and practice many languages.

Remember that foreign students can contribute to your children's program. Students of most every major country will have information about children and families, so invitations can be broadly given. Perhaps they have pictures or artifacts to show. For an activity, you can use the globe to help the children chart a trip from the United States to the student's home country.

Remember, too, that you can contribute to the college student's learning about children and families in the United States. There probably are some students who never get an invitation to an American home, and so they miss learning about how we live, except for what they see in sit-coms—and you realize how misleading these can be! So, if you can find a way to invite foreign students one or two at a time into your dormitories, apartments, and homes for simple occasions that give them a more realistic picture of how Americans live, you'll be making a great contribution to their learning. At the same time you'll further your own learning. Who knows when you may end up as their guest in their country in the future! Wouldn't it be nice to be invited to their home?

Studying families that differ from your's begins at home. Many of the cultures you experience at home have roots in other continents. To start gaining information on families and their diversities, review chapters in *Knowing and Serving Diverse Families*.[2]

Teachers will find that as their sensitivity and understanding of other cultures increases, so does their effectiveness in communicating with others and teaching others about various cultures. Cultural sensitivity is also gained and practiced as one interacts with minority groups at home and need not be thought of as dealing only with overseas cultures.

CHILD GROWTH AND DEVELOPMENT ACROSS CULTURES

Children the world around have a common biological heritage. They develop in the same sequences, going through the same life cycle. With minor variation, children walk and talk about the same time and follow the same stages of logical reasoning. Children are all playful, though what they play with depends on their culture. Children are all born into families where they receive primary care, are taught skills, and are socialized and educated in the ways of the culture.[3]

---

[2]V. Hildebrand, L. A. Phenice, M. M. Gray, and R. P. Hines, *Knowing and Serving Diverse Families* (Upper Saddle River, NJ: Merrill/Prentice Hall, 1996.)
[3]Kurt Fischer and Arlyne Lazerson, *Human Development* (New York: W. H. Freeman, 1984), pp. 12–16.

TALK IT OVER: NO. 1

Discuss the opportunities you have had to know someone from another culture. Share with your class what you learned from each other.

According to Werner, who analyzed many studies of physical growth done on five continents, "When we compare the physical growth curves of middle- or upper-class children from developing countries with those from U.S. and European longitudinal studies, we cannot help but be impressed with the similarity of growth patterns of normal children from different parts of the world. Longitudinal comparisons among economically favored children of different ethnic backgrounds indicate that differences in height and weight are relatively small—at best about 3 percent for height and about 6 percent for weight. . . . In contrast, differences between these well-off children and those from the same ethnic stock who live in the poorest urban and rural regions of the developing world approximate 12 percent in height and 30 percent in weight. Differences in physical growth of preschool children associated with social class are much greater than those that can be attributed to ethnic factors."[4] Thus, the Werner analysis indicates children grow in much the same way around the world if malnutrition and disease are not present as pre- or postnatal factors affecting development.

In studying languages among children in many different language groups, Slobin says, "Children in all nations seem to learn their native languages in much the same way. Despite the

---

[4]Emmy Elizabeth Werner, *Cross-Cultural Child Development* (Monterey, CA: Brooks/Cole, 1979), p. 34.

diversity of tongues, there are linguistic universals that seem to rest upon the developmental universals of the human mind. Every language is learnable by children of preschool age, and it is becoming apparent that little children have some definite ideas about how a language is structured and what it can be used for."[5]

Children have individual differences, too. These derive from their genetic makeup, their family, culture, and social class.

EARLY CHILDHOOD EDUCATION AROUND THE WORLD

Early childhood educators around the world share a common concern for young children. Many professionals are united through the *Organisation Mondiale Pour L'Education Prescolaire* (OMEP). In English, OMEP translates to the World Organization for Early Childhood Education. Linked to the United Nations as a nongovernmental organization, OMEP frequently lends its expertise on international issues affecting children and families. OMEP meets every three years in a study session for international early childhood scholars. It publishes a journal, *The International Journal of Early Childhood* (for address, see Chapter 1).

Some programs for young children's care and education began in Europe in the 1800s, as is indicated in Chapter 22. Prominent leaders were Robert Owen in England, Frederich Froebel in Germany, the McMillan sisters in England, and Maria Montessori in Italy. Today evidence of those early roots can be found in early childhood programs in various countries. For example, some teachers will indicate that they follow the philosophy of Montessori or Froebel.

The early childhood programs highlighted in this chapter are those where I have visited and

---

[5]Dan I. Slobin, "They Learn the Same Way All Around the World," *Psychology Today*, July 1972, reprinted in Anne Kilbride, ed., *Readings in Human Development* 76–77 (Guilford, CT: Dushkin, 1976), p. 272.

> ### ☀ TALK IT OVER: NO. 2
>
> What advantages do you see in early childhood educators from around the world communicating through meetings and publications?

continuously monitored to keep up with the changes occurring in those countries since the visit. As you have an opportunity for international travel, you too can visit young children in their schools and play yards.

Doing your homework is essential in order to make the most of what time and opportunity you have. The goal for this chapter is to stimulate your interest in what early childhood educators around the world are doing and to encourage you to read about and eventually visit some of the programs.

Avoiding overgeneralization about what you've seen on a visit is a necessary precaution, according to Dr. Leah Adams, who is the chair of the U.S. National Committee for OMEP. Getting acquainted with many OMEP members at conferences and in visits to their countries helps one learn what Dr. Adams means by "avoiding overgeneralizing." As she explains, "People in every culture tend to think that their way of doing things is the best and the most natural."[6]

Of course, professionals abroad must coordinate many factors as they develop their early childhood education programs, just as we do here. The value of seeing their work for yourself, rather than only reading reports and government documents, is that you apply a reality check to what you read, either before you observe or after you return home. You should go with the attitude that there is more you can learn, rather than sim-

---

[6]Adams, Leah, "A Global Collage of Impressions: Preschools Abroad," *Day Care & Early Education*, Spring 1991, 4–7.

ply comparing their work with yours. This principle applies to visiting other centers at home as well as abroad.

Canada

Canadian early childhood education programs are very similar to U.S. programs. This is not surprising because the Canadian and U.S. early childhood movements have similar historical roots. Many Canadian teachers and administrators have received part of their education in the United States and some U.S. citizens have ventured north to take teaching and leadership positions. English language professional literature provides another common dimension. Canadian and U.S. citizens also often participate in the same professional conferences due to geographical proximity.

Based on discussions with Canadian early childhood educators and on observations in a number of programs, it is clear that parents on both sides of the border are making similar demands for child care and for similar reasons. Both governments are debating policy issues

Infant in an infant care center at the University of British Columbia, Vancouver, Canada. (V. Hildebrand, photographer)

Mount St. Vincent's College, Halifax, Nova Scotia. (V. Hildebrand, photographer)

concerning expanded child care to serve the needs of children and their families. Of prominent concern to Canadian kindergarten and early elementary educators is the issue of education in both French and English—and especially at what age it is most effective to initiate instruction in the second language.

Another concern is educational opportunities for children in remote sections of the vast country. In addition, Canadian immigration policies permit many people from the developing world to enter the country. Meeting the needs of children from these groups for language and other assistance is a challenge to early childhood teachers.

England

In England, "facilities for informal education and play for children aged two to five are provided free in public sector nursery schools and nursery classes in public sector primary schools. Classes for young children are also available in a few independent schools and a large number of 'preschool play groups' organized by voluntary organizations or by groups of parents. Apart from children only just under five, the proportion of children aged two to four who attend public sector schools remains low (the supply of places being inadequate to meet the demand for them) though attendance, and particularly part-time attendance, has been increasing very rapidly in recent years. Compulsory education begins at five when children in England and Wales go to infant schools or departments."[7]

England's early childhood professionals point out the multiethnic character of their early childhood programs. Children whose parents came from the far corners of the former British empire intermingle in the centers. According to Janeway, the Margaret Thatcher government cut funding to early childhood centers, in spite of a large

increase in demand for the services. The cutbacks created a major problem for teachers of young children as waiting lists doubled.[8]

Australia

Australia's system of early childhood programs receives excellent backing from their federal government. To an American observer, the Australian government's tangible support seems generous, accustomed as we are in the United States to leaders who are not very supportive of early education. Facilities are relatively new and modern and most open into the yard where children can play much of the year in their mild climate. Australia's kindergarten association has given leadership to the early childhood movement for a long time.

---

[8]Elizabeth Janeway, "Child Care Inc.," *World Monitor*, October 1988, 68–73.

Australian child care centers have modern buildings that blend indoor and outdoor play spaces. (V. Hildebrand, photographer)

---

[7]*Education in Britain*, British Information Services, London, 1976, p. 5.

Prekindergartens are available as part of the public schools. Special Commonwealth Government funding has helped promote an expansion of early childhood facilities for the minority aboriginal children. Aboriginal adults are being encouraged to become teachers in order to improve schooling for aboriginal children. A system of "distance education" furnishes activities through the radio and postal service for young children in Australia's outback.[9]

New Zealand

New Zealand's early childhood education is well advanced and follows a Western form for the most part. Three models prevail: kindergartens, play centers, and family preschools. In 1986 the

Department of Education assumed responsibility for early childhood education, thereby eliminating a troublesome dichotomy that had existed when child care was administered by the Social Welfare Department. Play centers enroll the children and involve the parents as helpers, similar to American cooperative nursery schools. Funding for early childhood programs is said to be a partnership between voluntary bodies and the government.

New Zealand has a high level of education nationwide. They are presently making efforts to help their minority Maori population retain their native language through bilingual education. They have organized Maori programs, called Nga Kohanga Reo (Maori Language Nests), where 10 percent of all of New Zealand's children in early childhood centers attend. Visiting in New Zealand centers was similar to visiting in any well-run program in England or America.

---

[9]Gillian Beddington, "Meeting the Needs of Isolated Children," *International Journal of Early Childhood* 21:30, August 1978, 13–17.

New Zealand children's programs are strong and have a long history. (V. Hildebrand, photographer)

New Zealand, like other societies, is also experiencing an increase in mothers with young children joining the work force. The need for more governmental support for child care was emphasized in the prime minister's speech in 1985 when he promised that the government would help fill the gap.[10]

Asia

Japan

Japan's educational system is extremely competitive, beginning in the early childhood years, according to several educational authorities. Families compete for places in the best schools, which then track the children into lifetime jobs and connections upon graduation. A common practice is to group boys and girls together in nursery school and kindergarten, then segregate them in elementary and secondary schools.

Japanese teachers report that children especially enjoy art materials in brilliant colors. Creative drawings are commonly seen in the schools. Visiting in a kindergarten in the city of Kyoto, Japan, I was immediately impressed by the extensive display of children's creative drawings and paintings. The lively children made many efforts to communicate although the language barriers were formidable. They sang "Happy Birthday" in English and several English advertising jingles they'd learned from television. Even though they were not able to speak English and I could not speak Japanese, communication did take place through singing and body language. I watched them use puzzles, blocks, and picture books. The class moved outdoors and demonstrated their routines of marching in various formations on the playground.

In a Tokyo kindergarten, children were observed doing creative movement in response to music and children listened attentively to a story. Classrooms were attractive and well equipped.

China

The Chinese government has taken considerable responsibility for providing nurseries and child care centers for infants and young children. Many of these facilities are attached to the factories where members of a child's family work. It is easy for the mother to drop by the nursery to nurse the infant, for instance. Most mothers do work outside the home; however, some infants remain in the care of their grandparents rather than attending a child care center. This arrangement gives grandparents a useful occupation, which is important in the Chinese culture.

There is a lot of singing in the schools. In one center I walked through various rooms, each occupied by two or three adults with a group of children. The children were standing by their seats and singing while the teacher played on an electric organ.

As you may know, the Chinese government mandates a one-child-per-family policy to hold down the population numbers and ensure that sufficient food will be available for the people. Chinese parents and teachers are concerned about the child in the one-child family. Vaughan, reflecting on her visit, reports that many said they didn't want the only children to be spoiled like "little princes and princesses." However, because they have only one child, teachers reported that parents are taking strong interest in the education their one child receives and are alert to the child's receiving a fair share of attention.

Vaughan observed that Chinese children are expected to be socially responsible at a young age, helping a peer with a coat or cleaning up a work space. They fulfill these expectations without any problem. Discipline is somewhat harsh by American standards; teachers draw attention to a child's behavior or a product when it does not represent good work. Vaughan felt the children accepted this criticism very well.[11]

[10]Ann B. Smith, "Recent Developments in Early Childhood 'Educare' in New Zealand," *International Journal of Early Childhood* 19:2 (December 1987), 33–43.

[11]Vaughan, JoAn. "Early Childhood Education in China," *Childhood Education,* Summer 1993, pp. 196–200.

Japanese early education is co-educational and relaxed, in sharp contrast with their elementary and secondary schools. (Top) A Tokyo prekindergarten engaged in making a large mural with free-hand drawings. (Bottom) A Kyoto prekindergarten sings jingles in English, backed by a display of creative artwork. (V. Hildebrand, photographer)

Many Chinese children attend child care near their parents' work sites. Singing and dancing are significant parts of the children's programs. (V. Hildebrand, photographer)

A Chinese mother on the Peking University campus cares for her only child. (V. Hildebrand, photographer)

The healthy appearance of the children was also impressive. A woman colleague who spent three months in China and who had opportunities to visit many homes mentioned that small children were handled a great deal, being passed around a room of adults, jostled on numerous knees, and spoken to frequently. It should be remembered that the press of population is ever present in China, on the streets, in child care centers, and in homes where many people occupy a small space. Sharing limited space is a part of socialization from the beginning.

India

When visiting schools in India one is continuously reminded that India has a great many children to educate. A very high birth rate exists, despite efforts to encourage spacing children to reduce family size in order to have healthier children with more opportunity for well-being throughout their lives. The high birth rate swells the number needing schooling, and classroom spaces are scarce. Consequently, competition is keen for available spaces in schools. Wealthy people's children attend tuition-based schools. Few poor children receive the benefits of early educa-

(Top) In India early education has a long tradition. In Calcutta the school is operated by the Sisters of Loretto. (Bottom) In Delhi the school is part of Lady Erwin College. (V. Hildebrand, photographer)

A resident school in Kenya where families of orphaned children are kept together. (V. Hildebrand, photographer)

tion. However, it was heartening to see one group of small children, who literally lived on the Bombay streets, being taught by a religious group after each child was given a cup of milk and a banana for breakfast.

Testing is common in India at every educational level and is used as a means for excluding children. As a result, parents pressure teachers to push children to undertake formal school activities that help them pass test items, regardless of the child's motivation, readiness, or interest. One teacher reported screening two-year-olds to determine which children could pass a test to qualify for a toddler school.

Indian early childhood educators report success in the rural villages with a program for poor children. Indian women are often found working in the fields, leaving young children to be cared for by a school-age child. The government program sends a trained child care worker to help mothers improve children's nutrition and plan some learning activities for them. The work resembles Head Start programs in some respects. The child care workers learn to improvise with the very limited resources found in the countryside. The child care workers' reports help the government plan further services for these rural families.

Africa

In parts of Africa, for example, in Liberia and Kenya where I visited, many children from upper-income families are enrolled in private prekindergarten and kindergarten programs in the major cities. Social agency personnel expressed to me the need for more child care centers for children of low-income families. Some observers pointed out that the use of child labor is so prevalent in some poorer families that compulsory school attendance laws are unpopular. When children are required to attend school, parents lose needed labor on the farms or in vending operations.

In Kenya in East Africa the separation between preprimary education and child care was pointed out by educators. Child care is primarily a caretaker function in the domain of a welfare or social agency, whereas preprimary education is primarily an educational function in the domain of an educational agency. This separation is common in many parts of the world, including the United States. While visiting a resi-

Children in a rural village in Liberia are taught by home economics students from a nearby college. They sing short finger-play-type songs. (V. Hildebrand, photographer)

A make-believe gas pump is part of a colorful array of toys in the early childhood school at Pretoria's University of South Africa. (V. Hildebrand, photographer)

Outdoor play at an early childhood program near the University of Transkei, South Africa. (V. Hildebrand, photographer)

dential school for orphaned children in Nairobi, I learned the children lived in family groups with a house parent. Siblings stayed together and helped each other. In another school, care was being provided for handicapped children. Young children suffering with the effects of polio were observed here—a startling reminder of a generation or so ago when epidemics of this dread disease were common in all countries. With internationally coordinated public health and immunization programs, many feared diseases threatening children and families can probably be eliminated worldwide.

The director of the home economics program at the Liberian agricultural college arranged for me to visit a village where several of her students were helping with family and child care programs. Upon my arrival the college students and the group of young children they had organized and worked with proceeded to sing a variety of delightful songs they had learned.

In the Liberian capital city of Monrovia a child care center for children of working mothers was visited. The need for more child care centers providing good child care for the children of working mothers was evident from a discussion with parents and personnel—a need often expressed the world around.

In South Africa a European-style early childhood education program is provided to children of whites, whose standard of living is said to be among the highest in the world. Black children, before legal apartheid policies finally ended, were given few educational opportunities. Black people were required to live in separate townships away from white people. Black fathers are often migrant workers and typically live in workers' housing away from their families. Black working mothers who serve the white households as live-in domestics are also separated from their children, leaving them in the care of others.

South African early childhood teachers participate in a national organization and hold a yearly conference where they set goals for improving early education. This organization admits people of all races. Several universities have strong programs for preparing teachers of young children. I had the opportunity to meet with these teachers at a conference.

In Johannesburg, a university professor who was committed to breaking down the racial barriers arranged for children from a black school to join a group from a white school to play together in an attractive church yard. Her theory was simple: These children and their teachers did not have any occasions where they could meet naturally and learn to enjoy each others' company.

It was a pleasant demonstration of a flexible acceptance of each other when children and adults were brought together on a common interest basis. The children seemed to be saying, "What's the big deal? We're having fun!" The teachers were more restrained than the children, but still spoke with each other. (For some it may have been a first encounter with an equal peer of the opposite race.) Perhaps this sort of program could be adapted in American communities where segregation occurs due to the housing patterns of families.

Latin America

Visiting early childhood centers in Central America, Panama, and Puerto Rico, I noticed a number of similarities that developing areas face. The large population of infants and school-age children is immediately evident. One learns that, though not many middle- and upper-class mothers are employed outside the home, some are sending their children to private preprimary schools. Others leave children at home in the care of maids. There are only a few child care centers organized especially for children of typical working mothers. These child care centers require some public financial support.

A variety of private schools is available. In the capital cities where embassy personnel and business people from various countries live, one may find excellent private schools teaching in one or more languages in addition to Spanish. The

Puerto Rican children participate in a Head Start program similar to that for stateside children. (V. Hildebrand, photographer)

A Panamanian Child Care Center accepts prekindergarten and elementary-age children for after-school care. (V. Hildebrand, photographer)

upper-class local children and children from the international community often attend these schools, benefiting from the multilanguage approach used. About half of the program is taught in the local language and the other half in another language.

In Puerto Rico many children have benefited from Project Head Start, according to teachers, directors, and involved faculty from the University of Puerto Rico with whom I visited. Head Start teachers throughout the island receive training similar to the training and support that stateside Head Start teachers receive. The Head Start centers provide typical early childhood educational experiences led by dedicated teachers. The children were involved with books, blocks, and dramatic play, for example.

In South America the large number of young children puts a strain on educational resources, just as in Central America. The wealthier people's children attend private early childhood schools. Many public schools do not offer kindergarten. Child care centers are available only in larger cities and, according to administrators, demand far exceeds supply of spaces. One attractive child care center in Santiago, Chile, was located in the middle of a municipal park, affording wonderful shade and a swimming pool nearby. Santiago requires companies and agencies hiring more than nineteen women to provide child care for the women's young children. The children were bussed between the center of the city where their mothers worked and the child care center in the park each morning and evening.

When we visited Nicaragua the country was becoming stabilized after the long and divisive Contra-Sandinista War. As part of a Sister-Cities project, we stayed in a small village over half a day's drive from Managua. Many adults and teens in the village were illiterate, having missed schooling altogether.

We planned and started a parent-cooperative prekindergarten with the goal of showing the parents—mostly mothers—what they might do with their children to help them get a start on

At an El Salvador kindergarten children patiently await the opening of school on the first day of school. (V. Hildebrand, photographer)

their education. In preparation we had brought with us a suitcase of supplies: Spanish editions of Little Golden Books, number cards, crayons, paper, scissors, pencils, and foam balls. It was heartening to see how interested the children were in the simple materials. They listened with rapt attention to the stories and "read" the books over and over during play time. Most had never held a colored picture book before. Singing and musical games also were popular activities.

One mother of eight children, whose children had never been to school, brought her three youngest children. She participated two days, then requested that her older daughter be

Guatemalan children in a child care center in the central city sing songs while awaiting their lunch. (V. Hildebrand, photographer)

Mexicans are expanding their early childhood programs. (V. Hildebrand, photographer)

The Honduran children in this kindergarten are learning both Spanish and English. (V. Hildebrand, photographer)

Costa Rica offers a range of early childhood programs from a private school, as pictured, to a public child care center. (V. Hildebrand, photographer)

Children of women city
employees in an attractive
child care center located in a
city park in Santiago, Chile.
(V. Hildebrand, photographer)

Tracking the rolling ball was
interesting to children in the
cooperative prekindergarten in
La Libertad, Nicaragua.
(V. Hildebrand, photographer)

A La Paz, Bolivia, child care center in a new facility. (V. Hildebrand, photographer)

A Cusco, Peru, orphanage cares for homeless children. Older children assist with younger ones. (V. Hildebrand, photographer)

allowed to help in the parent role in her place. This mother was a seamstress and needed to be back at her sewing machine. The mother was reassured that her children were intelligent by the progress the younger children made. Her eldest children were being tutored separately with the hope that they could soon enter school.

The children's parents met to plan ways they could carry on the cooperative prekindergarten when we Americans returned home. The books and supplies were left for them to use and local materials were assembled.

In Managua, the capital city, a university-operated child care center was visited. Here

Children in a Quito, Ecuador, prekindergarten sponsored by the YMCA. (V. Hildebrand, photographer)

were brightly painted furnishings and a number of resources for both children and teachers. This center presented a stark contrast to the one in the village.

Russia and the Czech Republic

The former Soviet Union was one of four countries often cited as examples of major governmental commitment to support and extend child care to children. (The other three are the People's Republic of China, Israel, and Cuba.) Each of these countries places early childhood education in high regard and believes that the child care programs they provide for young children are important for the health and education of these youngest citizens and for developing national strengths. In Russia, however, many children do not attend child care programs. Though mothers typically work outside the home, much child care is provided by grandparents if they are nearby.

Under the move toward more capitalism in the former Soviet Union, it is reported that some private schools have been organized with more flexible curricula. Children are allowed to learn foreign languages and all are allowed to create artwork. Previously, art expression was expected to have a political theme and was often allowed among only exceptionally talented children. Today's teachers feel more free in their interaction with others and are very interested in sharing with and learning from the West.

Visiting a public school early childhood program in the Czech Republic was of particular interest because of their previous domination by Russia. The author was impressed with the colorful furnishings and the variety of activities from which the children could select.

Reggio Emilia, Italy

One of the early childhood schools that is attracting American attention recently is the early childhood school system that has been developed since World War II in the city of Reggio Emilia, Italy. The school's approach was introduced in Chapter 10 on Creative Art Activities. Reggio Emilia was described by the director and founder through what he had to say about cre-

Prekindergarten children in a Chomutov, Czech Republic, government-sponsored program. (V. Hildebrand, photographer)

Prekindergarten children play roles on a make-believe truck in Kazakhstan, Russia. (J. Hildebrand, photographer)

ativity. The school fosters the many and various expressions of children's creativity using a number of theorists as inspiration, such as Bruner, Vygotsky, Guilford, Piaget, Maslow, and others.

Visitors to Reggio Emilia are especially impressed with the ability of the teaching staff to take time to hear the children's discussions and to help them make connections. Children do lots of interpretive works in short- and long-term projects. Teachers make many transcripts of children's expressions in order to do further studies and gain more depth of understanding of each child.

Many exhibits and videos of Reggio Emilia have been shown at conferences and around the United States to help people learn about this approach to early education. Professionals have organized tours to observe in the Italian school. The reader is directed to various articles in education journals that have appeared on Reggio Emilia and to the book *The Hundred Languages of Children*,[12] which helps give the reader insights into the school and its philosophy.

Conclusions

The numerous similarities among children around the world are indeed the most striking discovery of study and travel with related observing. By comparison the differences among the world's children are few. Children grow, learn, laugh, love, and cry much the same the world around. Differences in income levels of parents apparently account for more differences among the world's children than does culture or nationality. The basic needs of the children are universal.

The children of today will become the world's leaders of tomorrow. Throughout the world *all* of these precious human resources must be activated and nurtured to solve serious world problems. The bright eyes of children around the world give us all hope for the future. May we all contribute to their health, safety, and education through our actions, ideas, and support. May the children's bright beacons of love, laughter, and learning shine more brightly around the world throughout the years ahead and light the way to a more just, peaceful, and happy planetary home.

Applications

1. Discuss the "Talk It Over" items in the chapter.
2. Do some library reading on early childhood education in the international arena. See the Additional Readings section for suggestions, or use an encyclopedia or the *Reader's Guide*. Follow up a reference to a country of interest to you. (Key words are *Child Care, Education: Preschool*.)
3. Add ideas on multicultural activities to your Resource File.
4. Evaluate your participation on your evaluation form and discuss your performance with your teacher. Secure a written evaluation for your final record.

Study Questions

1. What is the *UN Declaration of the Rights of the Child?* What does it say? When was it written? When was it used for the International Year of the Child?
2. What happened during the International Year of the Child?
3. Discuss global interdependence and its relationship to children and families.
4. Identify ways to increase your multicultural understanding.
5. In what ways do all children have a common heritage?
6. What is the name of an international organization for early childhood educators? What does it do?
7. Write some generalizations regarding the state of early childhood education after reading the descriptions of early education in the various countries.

---

[12]Carolyn Edwards, Lilia Gandini, and George Forman, eds., *The Hundred Languages of Children: The Reggio Emilia Approach to Early Childhood Education* (Norwood, NJ: Ablex, 1993.)

Videotapes

Culture and Education of Young Children
    10 minutes

A discussion with Carol Phillips on how programs can show respect for our cultural diversity and use this richness to enhance children's learning. NAEYC Media, 1509 16th St. NW, Washington, DC 20036-1426, 1-800-424-2460.

Additional Readings

Danforth, Nick. "Let's Not Forget About the Men." *Choices: The Human Development Magazine* 4:1, August 1995, 33–34.

Evans, Judith, and Robert G. Myers. "A Call to Action: Improving the Situation of Children Worldwide." In *Early Childhood Education 95/96*, eds. Karen Paciorek and Joyce Munro. Guilford, CT: Dushkin, 1995.

Goduka, Ivy, and Verna Hildebrand. "Childhood in South Africa: Separate and Unequal." *Early Child Development and Care* 28:4, August 1987, 373–386.

Hildebrand, Verna. "Families and Child Care: A Global Ecosystem Perspective." In *Child Nurturance*, vol. 2, ed. M. Kostelnik et al. New York: Plenum Press, 1982, 239–263.

———. "Linking Families and Early Childhood Education: A Global Perspective." *International Journal of Early Childhood* 17:1, 1985, 14–19.

Ishigaki, Emiko Hannah. "Lower Birthrate and Children's Rights: The Present Condition of the Japanese Family." *International Journal of Early Childhood* 27:2, 1995, 16–21.

Janeway, Elizabeth. "Child Care, Inc.: Corporate America Learns from Other Countries as It Awakens to the Need to Help Working Parents." *World Monitor*, October 1988, 68–73.

Laosa, Luis M. "Socialization, Education, and Continuity: The Importance of Sociocultural Context." In *Issues and Advocacy in Early Education*, eds. Mary Jensen and Zelda Chevalier. Boston: Allyn and Bacon, 1990, 306–311.

Olmstead, Patricia P., and David P. Weikart, eds. *How Nations Serve Young Children: Profiles of Child Care and Education in 14 Countries.* Ypsilanti, MI: High/Scope Press, 1989.

Phenice, Lillian, and Verna Hildebrand. "Multicultural Education: A Pathway to Global Harmony." *Day Care and Early Education* 16:2, Winter 1988, 15–17.

Sohoni, Neera. "The Invisible Girl." *Choices: The Human Development Magazine* 4:2, August 1995, 7–10.

Tobin, Joseph J., David Y. H. Wu, and Dana H. Davidson. *Preschool in Three Cultures: Japan, China, and the United States.* New Haven, CT: Yale University Press, 1989.

Topolnicki, Denise M. "The World's 5 Best Ideas." In *Early Childhood Education 95/96*, eds. Karen Paciorek and Joyce Munro. Guilford, CT: Dushkin, 1995, 80–84.

United Nations Children's Fund. *The State of the World's Children 1996.* New York: Oxford University Press for UNICEF, 1996.

CHAPTER 22

The Profession— Past, Present, and Future

Savannah, Georgia, Early Childhood Program

Objectives

✔ Identify significant periods in the history of early childhood education.

✔ Identify individuals who were leaders of the early childhood education movement.

✔ Identify historical and current trends and issues in the early childhood education movement.

"I teach in a full-day kindergarten," volunteered Joan, a teacher from Georgia.

"I'm the lead teacher in a four-year-old public school program in Michigan. My children are designated 'at-risk of failure,'" said Don.

Don and Joan are teachers who were attending a workshop on curricular innovations at the annual meeting of the National Association for the Education of Young Children (NAEYC). They are active in their profession. They depend on workshops such as this to keep them up-to-date and enthusiastic about their teaching.

The early childhood profession has an interesting history dating back to the early Greek philosophers. This chapter highlights a few early leaders, the early American roots of the profession, the current policy issues affecting children's programs, and the trends affecting the future of the profession. The reader is encouraged to pursue additional sources on topics of particular interest.

EUROPEAN ROOTS

For those who might be inclined to think that early childhood education has only recently been instituted, it is well to note that the early Greeks—specifically, Socrates (469–399 B.C.), Plato (425–347 B.C.), and Aristotle (384–322 B.C.)—spoke out regarding the education of the child.

During the Industrial Revolution of the eighteenth and nineteenth centuries, European philosophers wrote about educating the young child. In Rousseau's mind (1712–1778) the best education for the child in the later part of the eighteenth century was the education that least hampered the development of the pupil's natural ways.[1] Pestalozzi, a Swiss (1746–1827), was influenced by Rousseau. Especially concerned with education of the poor, he developed a home for paupers and a school for refugees. He felt that schooling should directly involve the child and suggested methods appealing to the senses.[2]

---

[1] Jean Jacques Rousseau, *Emile*, trans. Barbara Foxley (London: J. M. Dent & Sons, 1911), p. 50.
[2] Johann Heinrich Pestalozzi, *How Gertrude Teaches Her Children*, trans. Lucy E. Holland and Francis C. Turner (London: Allen and Unwin, 1894), pp. 200–201.

Teachers keep learning while they work, sharing with other teachers and increasing their expertise. Here a South African teacher prepares for an after-school meeting of local teachers. (V. Hildebrand, photographer)

Many ideas from the eighteenth-century philosophers are still in practice today.

The era of nursery school–kindergarten education that heavily influenced the American movement occurred in early nineteenth-century Europe. Mothers and older siblings were going off to work, leaving small children uncared for. The first institution for the children of working mothers was founded in Germany in 1802.[3]

Friedrich Froebel (1782–1852), a German philosopher, believed that educating children was similar to cultivating plants, and so he coined the term **kindergarten**, meaning "garden of children." He founded the first kindergarten in 1837.[4] Froebel's philosophy was naturalistic; that is, he felt that children should be allowed to play, but that teachers could arrange play for them that developed their minds, bodies, and senses. Froebel had become convinced through work with older boys that their problems were rooted in their earlier experiences. In 1817 he admitted boys as young as three years to his school. Froebel's writings later provided the philosophy for the kindergarten movement in the United States and other countries. Teachers traveled to Germany for special training.[5]

Another historic early childhood education movement occurred in Scotland in 1816, when Robert Owen, a socialist, established an infant school. In France in 1833 Jean Frederic Oberlin founded a nursery school. **Crèches** were organized in Vienna, Austria, in 1847, in Spain in 1855, and in Russia in 1864.[6]

The McMillan sisters, Rachel and Margaret, organized the first English nursery school in London between 1908 and 1910. The McMillans' school and their writings were inspirations for American schools.[7]

Dr. Maria Montessori, founder of schools bearing her name, was born in Italy in 1870 and

[3]*The Encyclopedia Americana*, 1967, s.v. "nursery schools."
[4]Ilse Forest, *Preschool Education: A Historical and Critical Study* (New York: Macmillan, 1927), pp. 154–183; Friedrich Froebel, *Pedagogics of the Kindergarten* (New York: Appleton, 1917), pp. 1–33. See also Friedrich Froebel, *Mother Play and Nursery Songs*, trans. Elizabeth Peabody (Boston: Lothrop and Shepard, 1878).

[5]*The Encyclopedia Americana*, 1967, s.v. "nursery schools."
[6]Ibid.
[7]Margaret McMillan, *The Nursery School* (New York: Dutton, 1921), p. 22.

To be on conference programs just offer your services. You'll be glad you did. (Eastfield Community College, Texas)

died in 1952. She was trained before 1900 as a medical doctor and psychologist. Her major work centered around training feebleminded children in an Italian slum housing project. Her teaching stressed cleanliness and self-help. She designed numerous tasks and believed that children should learn these tasks in a designated sequence. She appears to have been quite successful in getting children to learn.

Montessori schools using Montessori methods and materials continued to be established throughout the world. Some of these schools seem to hold a semi-mystic faith in Montessori's ideas. Surely Dr. Montessori would make some changes if she were alive today. She was a woman ahead of her time. Probably such a creative woman would use any scientific knowledge and experience available and update her methods accordingly.[8]

Nearly all early childhood schools today emphasize the idea of self-help and the development of independence—both stressed in Montessori schools. Children generally help care for their room. "Self-correcting" materials similar to Montessori's have been adapted for general use. In most schools children are allowed to use learning materials in as many creative ways as the mind can suggest. However, in a strict Montessori school, there is only one correct way to use a learning material.[9] To be an authentic Montessori teacher one must complete training in a Montessori teacher education program, which probably will be in addition to the education required for licensing in a given state. Unfortunately, some Montessori schools are not authentic, but only use the name, which is not considered protected by copyright laws. Thus, the trademark of high quality, which being a Montessori school usually signifies, cannot be guaranteed.

EARLY AMERICAN ROOTS

"Nursery for the Children of Poor Women in the City of New York" was the lengthy title given the first child care program in the United States in 1854. Wage-earning women left their children (ages six weeks to six years) there for as long as twelve hours a day.[10] Thus child care centers began for the children of poor, destitute, often immigrant mothers. The center took "custody" of the child while the mother worked in a factory or elsewhere. The term "custodial child care" has over the years become associated with low quality. Placing one's child in child care was also considered a last resort. Social workers are said to have encouraged women to stay at home to care for their children, even in cases when their husband's job did not pay enough to sustain the family.

In the meantime, nursery schools and kindergartens were being organized for children of the more elite and affluent. Thus evolved a two-level standard of quality, one for poor children, another for the well-off. Problems with this dichotomy are still with the profession today, as are arguments about whether mothers should leave their children in a center while they go out to work.

The first American kindergarten was founded in Wisconsin in 1856 by Mrs. Carl Schurz, who had been a student of Froebel. The kindergarten was taught in German. (Mrs. Schurz's husband, an editor and later a senator, was a leader of the German element against slavery.) The first kindergarten for English-speaking children was organized in Massachusetts by Elizabeth Peabody in 1860. These first kindergartens were organized under private auspices. In 1873 the first public-supported kindergarten was established in Saint Louis. Patty Hill of Teachers College, Columbia University, and Alice Temple of the University of Chicago were early American leaders in nursery-kindergarten education.[11]

---

[8]*Montessori in Perspective*, Publication No. 406 (Washington, DC: NAEYC, 1966).

[9]Lois Barklay Murphy, "Multiple Factors in Learning in the Day Care Center," *Childhood Education* 45:6 (February 1969), 317.

[10]*The Encyclopedia Americana*, 1967, s.v. "nursery schools."

[11]Forest, op. cit., pp. 170–182. For additional insight on early leaders see Agnes Snyder, *Dauntless Women in Early Childhood Education: 1856–1931* (Washington, DC: Association for Childhood Education International, 1972).

Maria Montessori developed materials in the early 1900s that are still used in Montessori schools today. (Montessori School, East Lansing, Michigan)

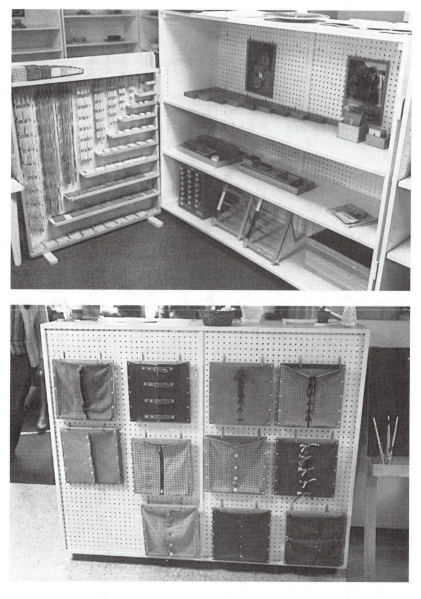

Lizzie Merrill-Palmer, in her will of 1916, provided funds for establishing a center in Detroit to train girls for motherhood.[12] Today the Merrill-Palmer Institute enrolls both men and women and contributes outstanding leadership to studies of children and families. It is now operating under the auspices of Wayne State University in Detroit.

The Laura Spelman Rockefeller Memorial provided for increased emphasis in child-centered research when in the 1920s it was used

---

[12]Forest, op. cit., p. 297.

to sponsor child study centers at a number of major universities. The University of California, the University of Minnesota, Columbia University, and Yale University were four involved in the program.[13] Early research supported the idea that nursery schools contribute to the child's physical progress as well as to his or her ability to respond to intelligence tests. Children who had behavior problems seemed to be helped when attending nursery school. Nursery schools were looked upon as a supplement to the home and not a replacement of it. In the years between 1920 and 1930 the number of nursery schools in the United States grew from 3 to 262.[14]

The first White House Conference concerning children was called by President Theodore Roosevelt in 1909. Since then, conferences have been convened by each president at the beginning of each decade. Out of the first conference came the recommendation for and subsequent organization of the Children's Bureau, which was first housed in the Department of Commerce and Labor. It is now housed in the Department of Health and Human Services.

The final meeting of the 1930 White House Conference was reported in the *New York Times*, November 20, 1930: "Dr. F. J. Kelly of University of Chicago summarized the needs of the child in a machine age, expressed opposition to lock-step education and supported the statement that the cardinal principle in education should be the development of each child to his or her highest level of attainment because 'the danger of a dead level of mediocrity is more grave in a democracy than in any other form of government.'"[15]

Also reported in the *New York Times* was a classic document that came out of the 1930 Conference. It was *The Children's Charter*, reproduced here so that the reader can see that many of the problems of 1930 are with us today—especially when one thinks of the world as the community and of our increasing concern for the world's children.

In fact, in 1995, a group of professionals reaffirmed the principles stated in this 1930 Children's Charter and published an updated version in *Young Children*. They reported the endorsement of fourteen prominent national child related organizations.[16]

THE GREAT DEPRESSION ERA

The Great Depression of the 1930s was felt by children, families, and teachers. The Federal Emergency Relief Administration organized schools for young children. In 1934–1935 there were 75,000 children benefiting from a program designed more to put teachers to work than to educate children. The number decreased when conditions improved, but in 1942 there were still 944 nursery schools operating for 38,735 children. Kindergartens slowed their pace of growth soon after 1930, after sixty years of progress toward acceptance as a public school service. From an enrollment of 15,000 in 1888, to 725,000 in 1930, enrollment dropped during the depression to 600,000 in 1934.[17]

WORLD WAR II ERA

Child care facilities received a major boost during World War II because women were needed to work in production plants in place of men who had joined the military. The Lanham Act of 1942

[13]Mary Dabney Davis, *Nursery Schools: Their Development and Current Practices in the United States*, U.S. Office of Education Bulletin No. 9, 1932 (Washington, DC: Government Printing Office, 1933), pp. 1–10.

[14]Gertrude E. Chittenden, Margaret Nesbitt, and Betsy Williams, "The Nursery School in American Education Today," *Education Digest* (January 1949), 46–51.

[15]"19 Point Program of Child Aid Carried," *New York Times*, November 23, 1930, p. 20. (©1930 by the New York Times Company.)

[16]NAEYC, "Reaffirming a National Commitment to Children," *Young Children* 50:3 (March 1995), 61–63.

[17]Bess Goodykoontz, Mary Dabney Davis, and Hazel F. Gabbard, "Recent History and Present Status of Education for Young Children," *Early Childhood Education (46th Yearbook), Part 2, National Society for the Study of Education* (Chicago: University of Chicago Press, 1947), pp. 45–46.

provided funds for the day care of young children and for the extended day care of school-age children. These schools were held in quickly built "temporary" buildings. The facilities were in many cases a vast improvement in design and convenience over the renovated buildings that commonly housed nursery schools. The direct relationship with the public school system was also a step forward. The U.S. Office of Education and the U.S. Children's Bureau were designated to assume responsibility for the program. Children were the secondary concern of the planners of Lanham Act nursery schools, however; the war effort's need for women workers was of primary importance.

The child care centers connected with war-industry plants are said to be examples of the first corporate child care centers. According to Zinsser, the Kaiser Centers on the West Coast served 3,800 children from 1943 to 1945. They operated 24 hours a day 365 days a year. Lois Meek Stolz, a pioneer in early childhood development, was consulting director of the Kaiser Centers and James Hymes, Jr., was on-site director. (Both individuals made significant professional contributions throughout the postwar years.) Buildings were especially designed to meet children's needs. A comprehensive service of health care for children was provided, with immunizations being given in the attached clinics. The teachers' pay was more than any teacher had ever known. Kaiser knew their salary had to be high enough to keep them from quitting child care to go to work in the factory. Kaiser Centers were funded indirectly by the federal government.[18]

In 1945, at the close of the war era, there were over 50,000 children enrolled in almost 1,500 child care centers, and there were 18,000 receiving extended day care. Kindergartens enrolled 700,877 in 1944.

Sigmund Freud's (1856–1939) theory of human motivation[19] began having an impact on early childhood education. For example, play therapy and dramatic play in the prekindergarten and kindergarten contributed to the understanding of a child's inner feelings. The importance of the parent–child relationship and the significance of the early years, much emphasized by Freud and others, began to guide the early childhood programs.

THE EARLY POST–WORLD WAR II ERA

The post–World War II era witnessed a return to normality as far as the nation's young children were concerned; that is, federal funds for operating child care centers were no longer available. States were allowed to continue operation of their Lanham Act child care centers, but most states permitted them to close. However, women did not all go back to the cookstove after World War II. They either needed or wanted to remain in the labor force. The need for child care facilities continued and continues today.

It is of interest to note that the 1950 White House Conference dealt with the components of a healthy personality for children and youth. Mental health was finally receiving attention after being neglected for so long. In the 1960 White House Conference there was a recommendation for increased public kindergartens and day-care facilities. In 1959 the Office of Education reported that 70 percent of the public elementary schools maintained kindergartens and 5 percent maintained nursery schools.[20] Private and cooperative schools increased during this time. The population shift to the suburbs, improved standards of living, smaller families,

[18]Carolyn Zinsser, "The Best Day Care There Ever Was," *Working Mother*, October 1984, 76–78. Reprinted in Judy McKee and Karen Paciorek, eds., *Early Childhood Education 89/90* (Guilford, CT: Dushkin, 1989), pp. 6–8.

[19]Sigmund Freud, *The Basic Writing of Sigmund Freud*, trans. and ed. A. S. Brill (New York: Random House, 1938).
[20]S. E. Dean, *Elementary School Administration and Organization*, U.S. Office of Education, Bulletin No. 11 (Washington, DC: U.S. Government Printing Office, 1960), p. 19.

CHILDREN'S CHARTER

1. Every child is entitled to be understood, and all dealings with him should be based on the fullest understanding of the child.

2. Every prospective mother should have suitable information, medical supervision during the prenatal period, competent care at confinement. Every mother should have post-natal medical supervision for herself and child.

3. Every child should receive periodical health examinations before and during the school period, including adolescence, by the family physician or the school or other public physicians and such examinations by specialists and such hospital care as its special needs may require.

4. Every child should have regular dental examination and care.

Measures for Protection

5. Every child should have instruction in the schools in health and in safety from accidents, and every teacher should be trained in health programs.

6. Every child should be protected from communicable diseases to which it might be exposed at home or at play, and protected from impure milk and food.

7. Every child should have proper sleeping rooms, diet, hours of sleep and play, and parents should receive expert information as to the needs of children of various ages as to these questions.

8. Every child should attend a school which has proper seating, lighting, ventilation, and sanitation. For younger children, kindergartens and nursery schools should be provided to supplement home care.

9. The school should be so organized as to discover and develop the special abilities of each child, and should assist in vocational guidance, for children, like men, succeed by the use of their strongest qualities and special interests.

10. Every child should have some form of religious, moral, and character training.

11. Every child has a right to play with adequate facilities therefor.

12. With the expanding domain of the community's responsibilities for children, there should be proper provision for and supervision of recreation and entertainment.

Provision for the Handicapped

13. Every child should be protected against labor that stunts growth, either physical or mental, that limits education, that deprives children of the rights of comradeship, of joy and play.

14. Every child who is blind, deaf, crippled or otherwise physically handicapped should be given expert study and corrective treatment where there is the possibility of relief, and appropriate development or training. Children with subnormal or abnormal mental conditions should receive adequate study, protection, training and care. Where the child does not have these services, due to inadequate income of the family, then such services must be provided to him by the community. Obviously, the primary necessity in protection and development of children where poverty is an element in the problem is an adequate standard of living and security for the family within such groups.

15. Every waif and orphan in need must be supported.

16. Every child is entitled to the feeling that he has a home. The extension of services in the community should supplement and not supplant parents.

17. Children who habitually fail to meet normal standards of human behavior should be provided special care under the guidance of the school, the community health, or welfare center or other agency for continued supervision, or, if necessary, control.

18. The rural child should have satisfactory schooling, health, protection and welfare facilities.

Coordinated Organization

19. In order that these minimum protections of the health and welfare of children may be everywhere available, there should be a district, county or community organization for health education and welfare, with full-time officials, coordinating with a statewide program which will be responsible to a nationwide service of general information, statistics and scientific research. This should include:

    a. Trained full-time public health officials and public health nurses, sanitary inspection and laboratory workers.

    b. Available hospital beds.

    c. Full-time public welfare services for the relief and aid of children in special need from poverty or misfortune, for the protection of children from abuse, neglect, exploitation or moral hazard.

    d. The development of voluntary organization of children for purposes of instruction, health, and recreation through private effort and benefaction. When possible, existing agencies should be coordinated.

Source: Gertrude E. Chittenden, Margaret Nesbitt, and Betsy Williams, "The Nursery School in American Education Today," *Education Digest* (January 1949), 46–51.

apartment housing, increased mobility, and the increased level of parental education are frequently cited sociological factors contributing to the interest of parents in early education for their children.

Research at Yale by Dr. Arnold Gesell provided normative data to which parents and teachers could compare a child's growth.[21] During the 1930s and 1940s Gesell utilized the new moving-picture techniques to record young children's behavior. He published ages and stages of development, which he saw as flexible but parents often took as rigid. Gesell's work is still used today with adaptations based on later information.

During the postwar decades Dr. Benjamin Spock's book *Baby and Child Care* sold millions of copies in a pocket edition.[22] Parents of young children needed the reassurance of a more experienced hand, and Spock substituted for the older generation's grandma next door.

The United Nations (UN), which was organized in 1945, contributed to better communication between the peoples of the world. Several specialized agencies within the UN deal with the health and well-being of children and families. These are the World Health Organization (WHO); the Food and Agriculture Organization (FAO); the United Nations Educational, Scientific, and Cultural Organization (UNESCO); and the United Nations Children's Fund (UNICEF).[23] In 1948 the *Organisation Mondiale Pour L'Education Prescolaire* (OMEP), or World

---

[21]Arnold Gesell and F. L. Ilg, *Infant and the Child in the Culture of Today* (New York: Harper & Row, 1943).

[22]Benjamin Spock, *Baby and Child Care* (New York: Pocket Books, Simon & Schuster, 1953).

[23]*United Nation's Visitor's Guide* (New York: United Nations.)

Organization for Early Childhood Education, was founded for the purpose of uniting those who care about children the world around. The OMEP address is at the end of Chapter 1 for those interested in contacting the U.S. branch of this international organization.

THE WAR ON POVERTY ERA: 1960S

The War on Poverty was begun in the 1960s. The accelerated migration of rural Americans to the cities to work, the need for more technically trained workers, the rising school dropout rate, and the growing unrest among minorities woke the nation to some festering ills in its midst. The war in Vietnam contributed to inflation and required resources that might have been used domestically.

The Economic Opportunity Act was passed in March 1964 and on April 11, 1965, the Elementary and Secondary School Act became law.[24] Finally, after long years of debate, federal aid to education was granted. Federal aid was expected to equalize the educational opportunities between the country's rich and poor states, just as state aid helped to equalize opportunities within a state. For decades district financing has helped to equalize educational opportunities among families of a district.

Head Start programs for disadvantaged children under age six became one of the more popular programs in President Lyndon Johnson's War on Poverty. The program was heralded with great expectation in many quarters. Education for young children was given professional leadership and funds. Leaders were saying that Head Start is a program for educating children, not an employment program for the poor. If this attitude did, in fact, guide the leadership, it represents the first time that the needs of children were given top priority in an emergency program.

However, the Head Start program maintains a strong commitment to involve local parents and school dropouts.

Margaret Rasmussen, editor of *Childhood Education,* reported in September 1965 that the first summer of Head Start had involved 536,108 children, 39,463 professionals, 44,589 paid neighborhood residents, 54,996 neighborhood volunteers, and 40,187 other volunteers throughout the nation.[25] By the end of 1979 over 6 million children had been enrolled in the Head Start program since its beginning.[26]

Early Head Start planners held out for trained, qualified teachers and a low pupil–teacher ratio—two paid teachers for fifteen disadvantaged children, plus volunteer helpers. Short courses were established by universities across the country to train teachers, assistant teachers, and aides for the programs. In 1969, 3,600 paraprofessionals were trained in 150 colleges.[27]

The Head Start program also included the Parent and Child Center, which "represented the drawing together of all those resources—family, community, and professional—which contribute to the child's total development. It linked professional skills of persons in nutrition, health, education, psychology, social work, and recreation. It recognized that both paid and volunteer nonprofessionals can make important contributions. Finally the concept emphasized that the family is fundamental to the child's development. Parents should play an important role in developing policies; they should work in the Centers and participate in the programs."[28]

---

[24]J. William Rioux, "New Opportunities: Economic Opportunity Act and Elementary and Secondary Education Act of 1965," *Childhood Education* 42:1 (September 1965), 9–11.

[25]Margaret Rasmussen, "Over the Editor's Desk," *Childhood Education* 42:1 (September 1965), 65.

[26]Office of Children, Youth, and Families (Washington, DC: Department of Health, Education, and Welfare, 1979).

[27]Harriette Merhill, "Highlighting the National Conference on the Paraprofessional, Career Advancement, and Pupil Learning," *Childhood Education* 45:7 (March 1969), 369k.

[28]Dale L. Johnson, Todd Walker, and Gloria G. Rodriquez, "Teaching Low-Income Mothers to Teach Their Children," *Early Childhood Research Quarterly* 11:1 (January 1996), 5–10.

EARLY CHILDHOOD EDUCATION: THE 1970s TO THE LATE 1990s

Increasing enrollments occurred during the 1970s in early childhood programs even as birth rates dropped. More people enrolled their children in programs, especially full-day child care programs. The full-day programs increased in number, while the number of part-day nursery schools appeared to decline. This decline reflected several factors. First, the number of families in which both parents work or that are headed by one parent increased, and the parents tended to choose full-day child care centers or family day care over two- or three-hour programs. Second, in some states the designation "nursery school" required a certified teacher, whereas the child care designation did not. Therefore, in an effort to economize, some centers hired less-qualified persons and relabeled and relicensed their center as a child care center.

Third, during the 1970s a number of states increased their commitment to support kindergartens in the public schools, thereby increasing the total number of five-year-olds enrolled. Some states instituted prekindergarten programs within the public schools. In addition, even though the number of children was relatively small, the provision of programs for handicapped young children added to the growth in total numbers. The number of franchise or private child-care-for-profit schools increased in the 1970s.

Teacher preparation programs grew rapidly in the late 1960s and early 1970s. Head Start and rising numbers of child care centers required more personnel. Four-year colleges, community colleges, and vocational–technical schools all experienced an increase in enrollment in child care–early childhood education curricula. The Child Development Associate program (CDA) was proposed by Dr. Edward Zigler in the 1970s when he was head of the Office of Child Devel-

Researchers share findings that will help teachers. (V. Hildebrand, photographer)

opment in the Department of Health, Education, and Welfare. The CDA was designed to enhance the skills of child care workers outside the formal education system and provide a career ladder for them. The program met with numerous setbacks but finally published the list of competencies candidates were to achieve, and by 1975 the first candidate was certified. The program faced uncertainties in funding. By September 1984, 28 states and the District of Columbia accepted the CDA in state child care licensing requirements.[29]

Head Start today requires a CDA credential as the minimum preparation for teachers working in that program. Information on the CDA is available from the Council for Early Childhood Professional Recognition, 1341 G St. NW, Suite 400, Washington, DC 20005, 1-800-424-4310.

As noted in Chapter 1, Head Start has continued to be funded through all presidential administrations. Presently the funding has reached $3.5 billion. When comparing initial appropriations with today's funding, the real value of the amount is severely reduced due to inflation during the late 1970s and 1980s. Enrollment for 1995 totaled 752,000 with a total of 13 million children benefiting since 1965, according to the Office of Human Development Services, Department of Health and Human Services (formerly called the Department of Health, Education, and Welfare), the agency that administers Head Start. The average cost for a year of Head Start for one child was $4,343 in 1994. There was evidence that only about 50 percent of the eligible children, according to poverty level guidelines, were able to be served by Head Start. Thirteen percent were handicapped. Racial and ethnic composition of Head Start in 1994 was as follows:

Native Americans	4 percent
Hispanic	24 percent
Black	36 percent
White	33 percent
Asian	3 percent[30]

---

[29]*Competence: News of the CDA Community* 2:1 (Fall 1984), p. 7.

[30]*Fact Sheet on Head Start.* Washington, DC: Department of Health and Human Services, 1995.

Marketing has become the byword. Here a community college leader gives information about her program at a conference. (San Antonio College, Texas)

Meeting with students to guide, inspire, and evaluate is an important role for teachers who become involved at any level of teacher education. (Edna, Texas, High School)

Drive for Federal Support for Child Care

As the 1970s arrived hopes were high for passage at the federal level of a comprehensive child development program—including funding for child care and work with parents. A bill passed both houses of Congress only to be vetoed by President Richard M. Nixon in 1971. In years following 1971 bills were introduced repeatedly but failed to gain sufficient support. Some federal matching funds for child care were returned to the states through the Social Security Act as amended in 1975.

During the 1980s federal dollars to match state dollars for child care diminished because of efforts to cut the deficit, balance the budget, and fulfill President Reagan's desire to keep the government out of the affairs of the family. Yet there was even greater demand for high-quality child care as growing numbers of mothers returned to the work force while their children were young (see data in Chapter 1).

ABC Bill

In the late 1980s the Act for Better Child Care (ABC Bill) was written by a coalition of sixty-five groups interested in federal funding for child care. The bill received hearings during the last year of the Reagan administration, then was reintroduced in the new Congress (1989) at the beginning of President George Bush's administration. The advocates tried to keep three elements in the bill—affordability, availability, and high quality. The ABC Bill failed to secure a compromise between the two houses of Congress and President Bush as the first year of the Congress closed in November 1989.

In 1988 the U.S. Department of Labor calculated that, including Head Start, the U.S. government was already spending $6.9 billion on child care.[31] In a study requested by a Senate committee, the average cost per child per year at a NAEYC-accredited center was reported to be $4,070 plus in-kind donations, making a total cost of $4,660.[32]

---

[31]*Child Care: A Workforce Issue*, Report of the Secretary's Task Force (Washington, DC: Department of Labor, April 1988), p. 2.
[32]Government Accounting Office, *Early Childhood Education: Information on Costs and Services at High-Quality Centers* (Washington, DC: Government Accounting Office, July 1989), p. 2.

Finally in 1990 the Congress passed and President George Bush signed the Child Care and Development Block Grant Bill. Funding started at $731 million in 1991 with $925 million for 1992 and for 1993. In 1995 and 1996 under a different Congress and President Bill Clinton, $934.6 million was proposed for 1996 and such funds as needed for 1997 through 2000. Head Start was slated to receive $3.4 billion. A great deal of political pressure was generated by Congress to cut taxes and balance the budget. President Clinton vowed to keep the investment in children's education at all costs.

In a sudden flurry of legislative activity just before the Congressional summer recess of 1996, and just before the two major political party conventions, the Congress passed and sent to President Clinton a welfare reform bill.[33] The president signed the Welfare Reform Act on August 22, 1996, giving states the responsibility to administer welfare. Welfare recipients thus were given notice that before too long, they will be required to go to work. Child care professionals had realized for some time that if these sweeping changes in welfare passed, the need for child care would increase.

Kindergarten

The enrollment of five-year-olds in public school kindergartens became virtually complete in the 1980s, with many schools moving to full days for kindergarten, equal to the elementary school day. Thus, rather than teaching two groups, teachers' loads were adjusted to keeping the same group of children all day. As a result, teachers had time to work much more effectively with individual children. The reduction in the number of children taught by one teacher also brought a reduction in the number of parents to whom kindergarten teachers were responsible, enabling them to know parents better.

---

[33]Dana Milbank, "Welfare Law's Work Rules Worry States," *The Wall Street Journal*, August 5, 1996, pp. A2, A14.

Many states began funding programs in the public schools for four-year-old children "at risk of failure." Some states included only at-risk children in an effort to contain costs, even though many policymakers recommend including all four-year-olds. However, as in Head Start, poor children were again being segregated from their middle-class peers who might have modeled some of the desirable "hidden curriculum" available in the middle-class families from whence they came. In the meantime, middle- and upper-class children were participating in tuition-based early childhood schools and child care centers to a much larger degree than did children of less-affluent or less-educated parents.

STANDARDS FOR CHILD CARE

Custodial care for children is thought by some to be a relic of the past. However, at nearly every meeting of social service personnel and others who are in daily contact with child care services, horror stories are heard concerning children who are being poorly and unsafely housed in centers, poorly fed, inadequately educated, and even mistreated. The minimal standards imposed by most states do not protect all children. In fact, the licensing regulations that control child care centers are so minimal that children sometimes suffer.

Recognizing the need for improved standards for child care licensing, the U.S. Office of Child Development held forums on the subject. With the help of representatives from licensing agencies of the fifty states and some cities, and from national and state organizations with interests in child care, a model for state licensing was prepared. *Guides for Day Care Licensing* was designed for use by states and cities to improve their regulatory functions.

In 1974 when it was proposed that the Federal Interagency Day Care Requirements be attached to some federal child care legislation, a storm of controversy arose—particularly over the staff–child ratio. Congress suspended implementation of the adult–child ratio requirements because the mandated ratios exceeded the ratio requirements in most states and were believed to be too costly. The recommended ratio was one adult to ten children of nursery school age.[34]

Today, well-educated parents are pressing teachers in early childhood schools to raise the standards of full-day child care programs. They want stability of staff so constant shifts in assignments and staff shortages do not interfere with the quality of the program. Most are willing to pay what is required during their child's early childhood years. These parents want assurances that their child is in a good school; then they can concentrate on their careers.

THE NATIONAL ASSOCIATION FOR THE EDUCATION OF YOUNG CHILDREN (NAEYC)

By now you've read many references to NAEYC and have likely been encouraged to join by your instructors or co-teachers. Membership has become an important professional statement among all persons interested in young children's development, care, and education. This organization has a "big tent" policy, which means that anyone can join who is interested in young children. As large organizations go, the dues are very reasonable. The association includes professionals and nonprofessionals alike. Beginning child development students planning to become teachers, teachers, administrators, researchers, parents, and grandparents are welcome and all will find a stimulating group of people interested in children with whom to associate.

The NAEYC is nearing 100,000 members as it reaches toward the twenty-first century. This is phenomenal growth over a few decades and represents one measure of the dynamic quality of the organization. It has kept dues affordable and

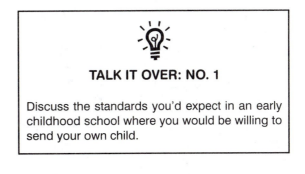

TALK IT OVER: NO. 1

Discuss the standards you'd expect in an early childhood school where you would be willing to send your own child.

provides members many services for the one membership fee, including memberships in their local, state, and regional associations.

The NAEYC was originally called the National Association of Nursery Education (NANE), which was organized in 1926. The members of NANE carried on valiantly during World War II giving leadership to the Lanham Act war-industry child care centers mentioned earlier. In 1944 the *NANE Bulletin* became the journal called *Young Children*. In the late 1960s with the new momentum coming from Project Head Start, the association changed to the present name and the governing board was restructured to include people from the many constituent groups who were entering the early childhood professions. This multifarious board has been the hallmark of the highly diversified and large growth in membership—and key to the NAEYC's national clout today. The organization has stayed true to its local grass-roots—to-state—to-national emphasis that has strengthened early childhood education in every locale.

Many local, state, regional, and national meetings serve as in-service education for the NAEYC members and others every year. People are so enthusiastic about what they learn that they book their travel months ahead. Only cities with the largest numbers of hotels can host the annual fall national meeting, which attracts some 25,000 attendees.

Work-alike groups and focus groups hold preconference meetings at the same time and same city as NAEYC's annual meeting. Meetings are conducted for such groups as the National Asso-

---

[34]Richard Ruopp et al., *Children at the Center: Final Report of the National Day Care Study, Vol. 1* (Washington, DC: Department of Health, Education, and Welfare, 1979), pp. xxxvi–xxxix.

ciation for Early Childhood Teacher Educators, National Head Start Association, Parent Cooperative Preschools International, Coalition for Campus Child Care, National Association of Early Childhood Specialists in State Departments of Education, Military Child Care, World Association of Early Childhood, and many others. These meetings give individuals opportunities to learn from colleagues from across the country who are doing similar tasks. Leadership opportunities arise. At most meetings exhibitors display the latest materials that parents, teachers, and caregivers are seeking.

The reader is well advised to take advantage of the benefits of NAEYC membership with its many services, which include its excellent journal and published materials, its Center Accreditation Project, and its structure for encouraging participation and growth in every member in every locale. If you have a local group be sure to attend, join, and participate. If you have no local affiliate group, why not organize one? NAEYC's address is located in Chapter 1 along with their toll-free phone number for easy access to information.

NAEYC Center Accreditation Project

With the federal government apparently out of the picture of helping to set standards, the NAEYC and others looked for alternative routes to ensure higher quality in all forms of child care and early education. The Center Accreditation Project was initiated by the NAEYC. The criteria for high quality were arrived at by consensus of a large number of professionals. The staff–child ratios were the same as those of the Department of Health, Education, and Welfare rules. The resulting criteria were field-tested in four sites across the country. By November 1984 the project was ready to begin.

Accreditation was described in Chapter 1 of this book. In brief, a center is expected to work for accreditation and, when it is granted, will be able to advertise that it meets the standards of excellence.[35] A campaign of public information regarding the values to children and families of having a center that is of high quality should accompany each accreditation project.

By November 1995, 4,300 centers across the country had been accredited in ten years and 8,000 were in various stages of becoming accredited. Accreditation produced an excitement among parents and professionals as dimensions of high quality were recognized. The accreditation process is voluntary, largely internal, and an excellent tool for improving communication within centers. When asked to study "accredited centers," the U.S. General Accounting Office recognized NAEYC center accreditation as a measure of high quality.[36]

Monitoring education is considered by many to be as important as monitoring restaurants—a practice that has been accepted for years. As services previously carried on in the home are moved out of the home into the commercial arena, governments must move to protect consumers. Early childhood services are consumer services as surely as food, health, or dry cleaning services and, therefore, should be monitored by the local, state, and national government.

THE WOMEN'S MOVEMENT

The women's movement increased its momentum throughout the country during the years from 1965 to 1996, and women pressed for increased and improved child care services. No women's meeting was complete without at least one workshop on the need for child care, and the need was usually dramatized by provision of

---

[35]*Accreditation Criteria and Procedures of the National Academy of Early Childhood Programs* (Washington, DC: NAEYC, 1991.)

[36]For a detailed summary of ten years of NAEYC accreditation see Sue Bredekamp and Barbara Willer, eds., *NAEYC Accreditation: A Decade of Learning and the Years Ahead* (Washington, DC: NAEYC, 1996). Or, see Sue Bredekamp and Stephanie Glowacki, "The First Decade of NAEYC Accreditation: Growth and Impact on the Field," *Young Children* 51:3 (March 1996), 38–44.

TALK IT OVER: NO. 2

Discuss the procedure for having a school accredited. Report on schools that are accredited in your community or state.

child care for the children of the women in attendance. Through such organizations as the National Organization for Women (NOW), the National Women's Political Caucus, and the Women's Equity Action League (WEAL), women were raising their voices for equal access to education, jobs, and the political arena. Full-day early childhood education would enable many women to pursue their goals and to provide their children more than custodial care.

Child care, however, is a family issue more than just a woman's issue. Fathers are taking increased interest in their children. Some fathers are the primary caregivers in their intact families.[37] Also, since the 1970s society has become aware of many fathers who, for various reasons, are rearing children alone. They too need child care.

Contrasted with the poor women who first used child care centers in 1854, many of the mothers and fathers today are very well educated. Most want their children to be in a high-quality school that gives them an education along with food, shelter, and nurturing while the parents work. These are the parents who in an earlier era probably would have enrolled their children in a nursery school because of its educational component.

Part-day early childhood education programs simply do not adequately meet the needs of most modern parents, however. Some are single parents without backup support to cover the hours

when part-day schools are not in session. Others are career parents who must work a full day and need full-day care for their children. If they drop to part-time work or stay home altogether, their careers and income to support family needs would suffer a decided setback. Many persons who care about children continue to hope that high-quality, full-day early education will be provided someday by communities because children need it, rather than simply because adults need their children cared for.

There was a campaign for a law in the 1980s to require employers to provide job-protected maternity leave. One version of the bill in the Congress also included paternity leave for fathers of newborns and leave for family members to care for older children and elderly parents. Finally, in 1993 the Family and Medical Leave Act was passed that included most of the desired features. With a guaranteed maternity leave, child care needs will likely continue to increase as women who formerly would have lost their jobs now have a right to return to work. To date few fathers have used their rights under the act. Individuals' jobs are protected; however, they may not get paid while on leave. Employers must provide twelve workweeks of leave, but this includes any the employer gave previously.

The American tragedy of the late 1990s is that the teachers teaching in the child care programs are paid so poorly that they cannot afford the very child care for their own children that they are providing for others (rather like working for a major car manufacturer but only being able to afford a bicycle). Most early childhood teachers have few or no benefits for health or retirement. The best paying jobs for early childhood teachers are in the public schools where union contracts are in operation. Thus, compensation becomes a major concern of the profession today.

RESEARCH FINDINGS

Research findings have focused on children's learning, on the outcome of early childhood edu-

---

[37]See Kyle Pruett, *The Nurturing Father* (New York: Warner Books, 1987).

cation experiences, and on parent involvement. Some research was initiated in the 1960s during the early days of Head Start.

An example of long-term outcomes is given in a report of the Ypsilanti Perry Preschool Project directed by David Weikart and Lawrence Schweinhart. This longitudinal study followed 123 low-income children until age twenty-seven. The participants were divided into one group who had a high-quality preschool experience that included visits in the home with the child's mother each week and a second group who had no preschool experience but entered the same Ypsilanti, Michigan, schools.

The more favorable outcomes with respect to seven variables of those disadvantaged children who had the preschool experience compared to those without the preschool experience are presented in Table 22–1. According to the researchers, "The return on initial investment was equal to three-and-a-half times the cost of two years of preschool and seven times the cost of one year of preschool. The economic benefits obtained by the end of high school were sufficient to justify public investment in one year of preschool education for disadvantaged children."[38] These conclu-

sions are still valid according to the researchers' report for the subjects at age twenty-seven.[39]

Head Start has maintained a research component throughout its history. A *Review of Head Start Research Since 1970* published in 1983 showed gains in many of the program areas of both direct services to children, that is, in social and medical services to these children, and to services to their parents.[40]

In the 1993 document *Creating a 21st Century Head Start,* an advisory committee appointed by the head of the Department of Health and Human Services suggested changes for the future in Head Start. At that date the program served children of families earning below $14,350 for a family of four in 1990 dollars. It is important to know that only about half of the eligible children are served by Head Start. Even though the funding has increased over the years, so, too, has the number of children needing services. (The reader should recall that the 1990s was a period of "tax revolt" at both the state and federal levels. Agencies had to show savings and evidence of goal achievement in any tax-funded program.)

---

[38]For more detailed information see David P. Weikart et al., *Changed Lives: The Effects of the Perry Preschool Program on Youths Through Age 19* (Ypsilanti, MI: High/Scope Foundation, 1984).

[39]L. J. Schweinhart and D. P. Weikart, "Success by Empowerment: The High-Scope Preschool Study Through Age 27," *Young Children* 49:1 (November 1993), 54–58.

[40]Ruth Hubbell, *A Review of Head Start Research Since 1970* (Washington, DC: U.S. Government Printing Office, 1983), pp. 1–71.

Table 22–1
Outcomes from Preschool Experience.

At Age 19	Preschool	No Preschool
1. Graduated from high school	67%	49%
2. Enrolled in postsecondary education	38%	21%
3. Employed at age 19	50%	32%
4. Receiving welfare assistance	18%	32%
5. Teenage pregnancy rate	64 per 100	117 per 100
6. Detention/arrest rate	31%	51%
7. Classified at some time as mentally retarded	15%	35%

Source: Adapted from Weikart et al., see footnote 39.

```
    ⛆

TALK IT OVER: NO. 3

Discuss the research findings and suggest
ways such information could be helpful to a
teacher explaining or defending a high-quality
early childhood program.
```

The typical Head Start program has always included work with parents and is known as a "two-generation" program. The newer effort is to do more with the parents in order to stabilize the family life of the child.

Head Start became a full-day program in recent years for families needing child care. This extension of time attending a center enabled both parents to be employed or to gain schooling for future employment.

The suggested plan increases emphasis on the **Even Start** model assisting parents to become literate, earn their GED certificate, and learn how to assist their children in both health and literacy development.

A portion of the program is delivered in children's homes long before they are old enough for a group situation. Important social and medical services will be linked through Head Start to families in collaboration with other federal, state, and local funding sources.[41]

HANDICAPPED YOUNG CHILDREN

The Education for the Handicapped Act (Public Law 94-142) was passed in 1975. This act facili-

tated the placement of young special needs children into appropriate services and programs, and provides for free public education for all disabled children from age three. Some state programs for the child with special needs started at birth, while others started at age three. Teachers with knowledge and skills in child development and early childhood education were in demand and were especially helpful in mainstreaming children into the regular classroom, even as they gained understanding of particular special needs.

Head Start mandated inclusion of some special needs children in the program. In 1989, 13.3 percent of the children in Head Start were mildly or moderately disabled.[42] All early childhood educators made efforts to adapt their programs to enable young special needs children to participate.[43]

In 1986, the Ninety-Ninth Congress passed new legislation that increased federal monetary assistance to states and local educational agencies to enable them to provide free appropriate public education to all disabled children aged six through seventeen. At that time only twenty-seven states were still serving special needs children starting at age three. Many parents and specialists felt that age three is too late for services to begin for these youngsters. Thus, the Congress also passed P.L. 99-457 to authorize additional federal assistance to states for the development and delivery of educational and related services to all disabled children from birth to school age. Additional support was given to deaf education in P.L. 99-371.

In 1990 the Americans with Disabilities Act[44] was passed, which applies to adults as well as to children. This legislation was considered a great leap forward for all people with disabilities.

---

[41]See *Creating a 21st Century Head Start* (Washington, DC: U.S. Department of Health and Human Services, December 1993). Also see Raymond C. Collins, "Head Start: Steps Toward a Two-Generation Program Strategy," *Young Children* 48:2 (January 1993), 25–33 and 72–73.

[42]*Fact Sheet on Head Start*, op. cit, p. 3.
[43]For a useful guide to adapting ideas for use with young handicappers, see *Mainstreaming: Ideas for Teaching Young Children* by Judith Souweine, Sheila Crimmins, and Carolyn Mazel (Washington, DC: NAEYC, 1981).
[44]*The Guide to American Law* (New York: West Publishers, 1992).

Increasingly, disabled children are entering regular classes in a process known as inclusion. Inclusion, as the name implies, is a process of integration. Another word used to identify these disabled individuals is "challenged." As you see, this field is replete with terminology that changes every few years. Everyone is concerned with labels, especially negative labels. Today many teachers have been learning how to work with children with "special needs"—a specialty in itself. The important thing to remember is that these children—whether called handicapped, disabled, or challenged—need programs, teachers, and caregivers, and they have parents who need lots of support.

Part of the effort for many administrators and teachers is to convince all parents that the disabled students are not taking the teachers' effort away from their more able children. These able children are learning compassion and the ability to be helpful much as they would if classes contained much younger children who needed assistance. Parents of disabled children often articulate their appreciation for the exciting advancement their children make when given role models with advanced skills to emulate.

As students preparing for careers in the early childhood profession you are encouraged to seek publications about the disabilities you are seeing and to read and ask questions, thus beginning your search for ways to be helpful to disabled children and responsive to their parents. In some instances a special tutor may accompany a child. You may need to relate to that tutor as well as to the child. You might become such a tutor as a volunteer or a paid helper. Some students link a career in early childhood with one in special education whereas others take a few courses to introduce themselves to the area. You will certainly be well ahead of many of your colleagues who finished their college preparation before the 1990 law was passed if you make an effort to become knowledgeable about special needs children. This area of study is now a very essential part of your education.

FUTURE TRENDS FOR EARLY CHILDHOOD EDUCATION

As we move rapidly toward the twenty-first century, what trends are on the horizon?

As of this writing, we have the Child Care and Development Block Grant Bill that will be further extended to cover the children of teenage mothers and other women on the public assistance rolls. Legislators almost everywhere are adamant about getting the women into the work force or into education to prepare them for work so they can support themselves and get off public assistance. There is an irony in this fervor because many of these advocates are philosophically against women in the work force, especially when they have young children. If women are forced to put children in child care, then society must ensure high-quality care.

There is evidence in some states that a great number of additional child care facilities will be needed for all the children of these eligible women if the mothers actually do get into education programs or jobs. Increasing numbers of teachers and caregivers will be needed for these centers.

With the passage of the Family and Medical Leave Act new mothers may take longer leaves from their jobs after giving birth and the fathers too may take time off to help care for a newborn. This may make available a few places in centers while families care for infants at home. So far the use of the right is not a trend, however. Most women do not get wages, only job protection, while on leave.

The corporate child care center will grow in popularity and draw employees toward a company with this service. If a suitable infant care center is available the families may not take the full time allowed for unpaid maternity leave. Employees of corporate child care centers tend to be paid better than community center staff because they are classified as technicians and thus get pay comparable to other technicians in the corporation.

Wages and health and retirement benefits for staff members in child care centers must be addressed in the near future. The service orientation and the nonprofit nature of many centers make the public expect them to provide child care at a minimum cost. Yet many of the parents they serve are very affluent and would be willing to pay far more. It is very incongruent for a teacher or caregiver to work for minimum wage caring for another professional's child to enable that professional to work at a job that could pay more than twenty times more. Perhaps centers should use a sliding scale to determine fees that would cover costs of better wages and benefits for staff.

Before- and after-school programs have been provided in connection with most elementary schools, as was predicted earlier. Now there may be a trend developing for child-family service centers to develop where many services are available, especially for late afternoons. Children's lessons in sports, music, dance, drama, and so on could become available around the school buildings—cutting down on car-pooling and on children being left alone in their houses after school while busy parents are earning a living.

The NAEYC accreditation program will become an accepted standard for all centers and those without accreditation will scramble to get on board. Nearly all parents want "the best" for their children. When parents work hard and can afford high-quality they will be willing to pay for it.

If the so-called taxpayers revolt continues, less state and federal funding for child care is likely in the future. This makes it essential for parents to be able and willing to pay for the care their child needs. The market may demand that centers and schools provide innovative services, and the facilities may need to use marketing strategies so they can advertise these services to attract customers.

Public media can be used to explain the meaning of high-quality in children's services, how it is recognized in the service parents subscribe to, and what it means to children's future skills and abilities. Parent education will be essential for parents. Some innovative methods may use the technology industry—the Internet, video, and the like—to release parents from physically attending meetings after a long day of work away from their children.

The physical safety of children in centers and schools will be of serious concern and all staff members should be trained to cope with serious tragic emergencies. After the bombing in Oklahoma of the federal building that housed a child care center, no teacher should ever take lightly the heavy responsibility of caring for other people's children.

The early childhood profession has moved rapidly to make families and co-workers of all diversities welcome. We've become models for other organizations that want to become more inclusive. Our attitude of acceptance, empowerment, and growth will be useful to others. However, there is still much to do, so your help will be needed.

Professionals will see the need for more advanced education and swamp the graduate schools for entrance. High-quality schools and centers will make staying there in a career more feasible. The complexity of children's growth and development and their related education, care, health, and recreation will all be exciting to a career-oriented staff member who is not just marking time until something better comes along. New types of child and family services can be expected to evolve as teachers grow increasingly serious about their lifetime efforts.

Conclusions

Between Socrates and Head Start there are over two thousand years of ideas and experience contributing to the education of young children today. Yet, in a sense, early childhood education is still a young profession, with many ideas to be tested and evaluated.

Growth in early childhood education has resulted from recognized crises. The plight of women workers who needed a safe place to leave their children stimulated initial programs as the

Industrial Revolution proceeded to gain momentum. The economic depression of the 1930s and later World War II led to a major expansion of early childhood education in the United States. In the first instance, the need was for jobs for numerous unemployed people; in the second, the need was for child care for the children of women working in war industries. However, in the United States no period equals the 1970s through the 1990s for interest in the education of young children. Since 1965 large numbers of children have been enrolled in Head Start, and many professionals, volunteers, and parents have become involved. Kindergarten is now universal. Child care, especially infant and toddler care, was the big growth area in the 1980s.

The new century will be one for fine-tuning the early childhood programs as more and more centers become accredited. As professionals work in concert, the real winners are young children, their parents, and societal progress.

In a real sense, whether people will survive and thrive on this planet depends upon the development of the full constructive potential of *all* children—children who will be capable of building a harmonious world community. Thus early childhood education becomes a relevant and vital movement with which to be associated if one wishes to help solve significant interrelated local, national, and global problems.

Applications

1. Discuss the "Talk It Over" items found in the chapter.
2. Use the library to learn more about the development of the early childhood education profession. Select one or more references from the Additional Readings section or from citations in the footnotes. Summarize your findings and discuss with your class.
3. Add ideas or information about the past, present, and future of the early childhood profession to your Resource File.
4. Report on a professional meeting you have attended.

Study Questions

1. Identify significant periods in early childhood education history.
2. Identify significant individuals and their contributions to early childhood education over the years.
3. Discuss advances in early childhood education in the United States since 1965.
4. State conclusions from cited research on early education concerning children's cognitive development, personal relations, language development, and parental involvement.
5. Explain how the women's movement for economic and political participation and for equality has affected early childhood education.
6. Explain how the people involved in early childhood education have become increasingly professional since 1965.
7. State ways that increased professionalization of early childhood education helps children and families.

Videotapes

Salaries, Working Conditions, and the Teacher Shortage
    17 minutes

Marcy Whitebook and Jim Morin discuss the complex issues contributing to the crisis in recruitment and retention of qualified staff. A new advocacy tool. NAEYC Media, 1509 16th St. NW, Washington, DC 20036-1426, 1-800-424-2460.

Celebrating Early Childhood Teachers
    22 minutes

An upbeat view of the role of the early childhood professional with a serious side concerning the problems in retaining qualified staff. NAEYC Media, 1509 16th St. NW, Washington, DC 20036-1426, 1-800-424-2460.

Additional Readings

Baldwin, Wendy H., and Christine W. Nord. *Delayed Childbearing in the U.S.: Facts and*

Fictions. Washington, DC: Population Reference Bureau, 1984.

Blakley, B., et al. *Activities for School-Age Child Care.* Washington, DC: NAEYC, 1988.

Blank, Helen. "Improving Child Care Quality and Supply: The Impact of the Child Care and Development Block Grant." *Young Children* 48:6, September 1993, 32–34.

Bredekamp, Sue. "What Do Early Childhood Professionals Need to Know and Be Able to Do?" *Young Children* 50:2, January 1995, 67–69.

Collins, Raymond C. "Head Start: Steps Toward a Two-Generation Program Strategy." *Young Children* 48:2, January 1993, 25–33, 72–73.

Fisher, Dorothy C. *The Montessori Manual.* Cambridge, MA: Robert-Bentley, 1973.

Goffin, Stacie G., and Joan Lombardi. *Speaking Out: Early Childhood Advocacy.* Washington, DC: NAEYC, 1988.

Greenberg, Polly. "Before the Beginning: A Participant's View." *Young Children* 45:6, September 1990, 41–52.

———. "Making the Most of It: Expanding Professional Horizons." *Young Children* 48:1, November 1992, 58–61.

Grotberg, Edith, ed. *200 Years of Children.* Washington, DC: Department of Health, Education, and Welfare, 1977.

Hildebrand, V., and P. Hearron. *Management of Child Development Centers.* Upper Saddle River, NJ: Merrill/Prentice Hall, 1997.

Hymes, James L., Jr. *Twenty Years in Review: A Look at 1971–1990.* Washington, DC: NAEYC, 1991.

Janeway, Elizabeth. "Child Care, Inc.: Corporate America Learns from Other Countries as It Awakens to the Need to Help Working Parents." *World Monitor,* October 1988, 68–73.

Langlois, Jane. *Serving Children Then and Now: An Oral History of Early Childhood Education and Day Care in Metropolitan Detroit.* Detroit, MI: Wayne State University, 1989.

Lombardi, Joan. "Head Start: The Nation's Pride, a Nation's Challenge." *Young Children* 45:6, September 1990, 22–29.

Montessori, Maria. *The Montessori Method.* Cambridge, MA: Robert-Bentley, 1965.

NAEYC. "NAEYC Position Statement: A Conceptual Framework for Early Childhood Professional Development." *Young Children* 49:3, March 1994, 68–77.

Osborn, D. Keith. *Early Childhood Education in Historical Perspective.* Athens, GA: Education Associates, 1980.

Powell, Douglas R. *Families and Early Childhood Programs.* Washington, DC: NAEYC, 1988.

Schorr, L. B. *Within Our Reach: Breaking the Cycle of Disadvantage.* New York: Doubleday, 1988.

Schweinhart, Lawrence J., and David P. Weikart. "Success by Empowerment: The High-Scope Perry Preschool Study Through Age 27." *Young Children* 49:1, November 1993, 54–58.

Snyder, Agnes. *Dauntless Women in Early Childhood Education.* Washington, DC: Association for Childhood Education International, 1972.

Washington, Valora, and Ura Jean Oyemade Bailey. *Project Head Start: Models and Strategies for the Twenty-First Century.* Hamden, CT: Garland, 1995.

Wolery, Mark, and Jan S. Wilbers, eds. *Including Children with Special Needs in Early Childhood Programs.* Washington, DC: NAEYC, 1995.

Wyman, Andrea. "The Earliest Early Childhood Teachers: Women Teachers of American's Dame Schools." *Young Children* 50:2, January 1995, 29–32.

Glossary

Accommodation In Piaget's theory of intelligence, the process of modifying existing schema in order to account for the novel properties of objects or events.

Accreditation The recognition by the NAEYC of a high-quality program in a voluntary initiative by the early childhood school or center.

Affective guidance A method of acknowledging a child's feelings while influencing the child's behavior.

Altruism A variation of prosocial behavior in which the child expects no external reward.

Anecdotal record Recording details of a single instance of behavior.

Assimilation In Piaget's theory, the incorporation of the novel aspects of objects or events into existing schemata or structures of intelligence.

Attachment A primary social bond that develops between the infant and caregiver.

Autonomy The ability of the human being to determine her or his own behavior.

Babbling Infant vocalizations that occur at approximately three or four months, combining a consonant and vowel sound (kaka, dada).

Behavior Any human action or reaction in relation to internal, external, or self-generated stimulation.

Behavioral objectives Statements of the behavior the teacher expects the child to be able to perform during an activity.

Behaviorism A psychological theory that emphasizes that an organism's behavior is largely the result of the learning produced by external factors such as reinforcement.

Bilingual Understanding and speaking more than one language.

Bloom Taxonomy of Educational Objectives A system for classifying educational objectives in a hierarchy.

Bonding Part of the attachment system that develops during the newborn period.

Caldecott Medal Recognition for the best children's picture book of the year, named for an early children's book illustrator, Randolph Caldecott.

Case study An intensive study of one individual.

Centering In Piaget's theory, being focused on one perception or characteristic of an object and unable to perceive any others.

Child care center A center that provides care of children to supplement parental care.

Child Development Associate (CDA) A credential earned by individuals who work in child care centers and learn on the job.

Children's Charter A 1930 document stating the needs of children, which was the outcome of the White House Conference on Children in 1930.

Cognitive development Changes throughout the life span in thinking, organizing perceptions, and problem solving. Knowing, mental or intellectual development.

Collage An art product made with bits of paper, string, and other items. *Collage* is French for *gluing*.

Concrete operations Third stage in Piaget's developmental stages, applying to ages approximately 7 to 11 years. Child uses logical thought processes as applied to real objects or experiences.

Conservation A Piagetian concept meaning that when the form of an object or liquid is shifted into a new position, the substance, weight, length, area, and number remain the same.

Cooperative Extension A service in the land-grant universities and their related outlets in most counties within each state for providing research information from the universities to the people.

Cooperative nursery A nursery school or kindergarten operated by parents who assist the qualified teacher whom they hire.

Cooperative play A stage of play wherein children make plans, agree to roles, and spontaneously handle the problems that arise. Usually occurs in children after age 3.

Cumulative plan   A way to organize the presentation of ideas to children, moving from the simple to the complex.

Day care   Care for children in the absence of parents. Called *child care* in this text.

Decentering   In Piaget's theory, being able to focus on several characteristics of an object or situation.

Decoding   The process of converting messages from spoken or written symbols into understandable language. Reading or comprehending the speech of others.

Dependence   The reliance on other people for assistance, nurturance, or comfort.

Developmental philosophy   One that follows children's developmental sequences.

Developmental task   Refers to particular learning that tends to occur at a given stage of life that individuals must successfully negotiate to meet cultural requirements of the next stage.

Development change   Change that is orderly, sequential, grows out of previous stage, is adaptive and permanent.

Diary records   Writing down what a child does in minute detail as the child behaves.

D'Nealian manuscript   A form of printing with slanted letters made continuously and ending in a curved line to facilitate learning cursive writing later on.

Dramatic play   Spontaneous symbolic play wherein the child uses his or her imagination or pretends to symbolize events, people, or things.

Drop-in center   A child care center that accepts children for a short period on an occasional basis.

Educational objectives   Goals for educating someone.

Egocentric thinking   Characterized by the child focusing on the environment only from the perspective of his or her own limited experience.

Employer-sponsored center   Child care center funded wholly or partially by an employer for employees' children.

Encoding   The process of using spoken or written symbols to designate objects or ideas. Speaking and writing.

Evaluation   Looking at the results of an action and deciding how close the action was to the standard expected.

Extended day care   Before- or after-school care of children, sometimes termed "latchkey" care, *latchkey* referring to the key school-age children often carry on a string hung around their necks to let themselves into their empty houses after school.

Eye-hand coordination   Small motor skills in hands, indicates relationship between perceptual (seeing) and motor response.

Family   The group of interacting individuals responsible over time for the support, care, nurturing, and socialization of children and other family members.

Family day care homes   Child care centers wherein care of children takes place in the home of the child care provider, usually along with the provider's own children. Accommodates school-age children in addition to infants and young children. Have various levels of regulation, depending on state laws.

Field trip   An excursion away from the school to gain firsthand experience.

Fine-motor coordination   Skills with the hands for manipulating objects.

Finger painting   Using the fingers and hands as the painting tools to manipulate a colored pastelike medium.

Fingerplays   Short poems and verses accompanied by finger motions that represent some of the words.

Flopsy doodle   A yarn object made to throw and catch.

Food pyramid   A model for a well rounded healthful diet.

Formal operations   In Piaget's theory, the highest level, the ability to think abstractly.

Gender   Refers to a set of qualities and behaviors expected from a female or male by society. A person's gender behavior is believed to be affected by social or cultural expectations that come from the idea that certain qualities and therefore certain roles are "natural" for men or women. These roles are learned, change over time, and vary widely within and among cultures.

Handedness   The child's unconscious preference to use the left or right hand, based on brain lateralization.

Head Start   The early education system developed for disadvantaged young children (3- to 5-year-olds), originated during President Lyndon Johnson's War on Poverty and continuing to the present day. Designed to help disadvantaged children develop skills needed to be successful in school.

Home Start   A federal program connected with Head Start that takes some early education experiences into the homes of young disadvantaged children.

Home visits   Visits by the teacher to a child's home.

Hospital schools   Schools typically organized for ill children in a hospital playroom.

Intellectual operations   Cognition, memory, convergent, divergent, and evaluative thinking.

Kindergarten   An early childhood school usually for 5-year-olds.

Laboratory schools   Schools usually connected with a college or technical school that enroll children with whom students practice their teaching techniques and learn about child development. Often sites for research studies on children.

Language development   The progressive growth of oral, aural, writing, and reading symbol systems.

Lanham Act Nursery Schools   Federally funded child care centers attached to defense plants for the care of women workers' children during World War II.

Latchkey programs   Refers to extended-day or before- and after-school child care programs for young elementary-age children whose parents work. Term derived from the key to the child's home carried by many on a string tied around the neck.

Learning center   A space for 4 to 6 children set up within a playroom or yard with materials for hands-on exploration or discovery learning.

Locomotor skills   Motor skills used to move the body through space, walking, running, skipping, jumping, galloping, etc.

Manipulative toys   Small toys used to challenge small motor practice with the hands.

Manuscript writing   A style of printing using straight lines and circles. In use for over 100 years.

Masturbation   Self-stimulation of the genital organs.

Merrill-Palmer Institute   An endowed school in Detroit, noted for research and teaching in early child development. Now part of Wayne State University.

Montessori schools   Named for Dr. Maria Montessori, an Italian physician who developed an educational system for retarded children in Rome. The system was later adopted by educators in various parts of the world. Toys used were self-correct-

ing, in that the child recognized when the response was accurate.

Multicultural activities   Inclusive system helping children appreciate the contributions from peoples of many cultural groups.

National Academy of Early Childhood Programs   The division within NAEYC responsible for the accreditation of centers and schools.

National Association for the Education of Young Children (NAEYC)   The largest professional organization devoted to young children's growth, development, and education.

Normative   Based on averages or established norms.

OMEP   *See* World Association for Early Childhood.

Parallel play   Children playing side by side with similar toys with minimum interaction.

Parent cooperatives   Early childhood schools owned and operated by parents who assist the paid professional teacher in teaching.

Parent Effectiveness Training (PET)   A system of parent education developed by Thomas Gordon.

Piaget, Jean   Swiss psychologist who studied development of children's language and logical reasoning.

Pictorial stage   When child combines basic shapes and lines to represent familiar objects in drawing or painting.

Portfolio   A collection of work usually done over time. Being used in education as a means to track progressive development and to evaluate or assess the level of performance of the individual, child or adult.

Preoperational thought   Second level in Piaget's theory, ages 2 to 7, moves from functioning in a sensorimotor mode to functioning in a symbolic mode, being able to internally represent objects and ideas in thinking.

Prereading   Literacy activities engaged in by children in years before formal reading begins.

Prosocial behavior   Activity intended to help or assist other people.

Receptive listening   Behavior required to learn from hearing a book read or other instructional activity of a teacher.

Reinforcement   From Behaviorist theory, showing that when stimuli are applied following a response, the response will increase or decrease. Positive reinforcement will increase response, whereas negative reinforcement will decrease response.

Reversibility   In Piaget's theory, ability to reorganize thoughts, restore or reverse mental processes. Child knows the amount of water is the same even when it is poured from tall to short glass.

Rights of the Child   A United Nations document designating rights for all children.

Scaffolding   What Vygotsky, the Russian psychologist, means by talking with the child—helping each gain new understanding step by step. Talking with and leading the child at each step of learning until the child understands enough at that level to form a "scaffold" from which to step to the next new height of learning. Language is very important in this social interaction for learning.

Science activities   All biological, physical, and social science activities found in the early childhood school.

Self-concept   The individual's understanding of being a person, a boy or girl, of being loved.

Self-correcting   Equipment such as a puzzle that allows the child to correct a mistake when he or she notices that the pieces do not fit. Self-correcting toys are part of the Montessori system of education.

Self-efficacy   The individual's belief in his or her ability to perform a task. Individual's measure of effectiveness.

Self-esteem   The individual's belief in him- or herself.

Self-selected activity   An activity wherein children are free to choose from the array prepared for them.

Sensorimotor stage   The first stage in Piaget's hierarchy of development, characterized by perceiving input through the senses and acting on the perception motorically.

Seriation   Arranging objects according to ascending or descending sizes or gradations.

Sex role   Generally refers to biology and anatomy. People are said to be of the male sex or female sex as determined by (1) external sex organs, (2) internal sex organs, and (3) secondary sexual development at puberty—breasts, beards, and the like.

Show-and-tell   A time when the child shows something brought from home and tells the audience or other children about the object. A language experience.

Sibling   Brother or sister.

Social class   Differentiation of people based on income, occupation, or education.

Solitary play   When a child plays alone. At the infant age the child plays alone because of limited social skills for interacting. At older ages solitary play usually means the child has a long attention span and a depth of interest in completing something he or she has started.

Structured activities   Those activities arranged by adults with limits set, making outcomes somewhat more predictable.

Symbolic play   Period of play from age 2 to 6, wherein the child uses symbols to depict objects or people in spontaneous pretend play.

Synchrony   Coordinated responsive action between parent and infant, with the adult responding to cues from the infant. Part of bonding or attachment process.

Syntax   The rule structure of language, organization of words into meaningful sentences.

Teacher certification   A license or credential earned after one has completed a prescribed set of courses and experience. Usually established by state law.

Telegraphic speech   Two-word phrases in infant speech.

Theory   An organized set of ideas that purport to explain phenomena. Theory parts must be carefully defined. Theory is tested by many, with results published in the public domain.

Transitions   The period when shifts take place between major blocks of activities. Transitions require planning to avoid chaos.

Unit plan   A collection of learning activities focused on a single concept, usually carried on in a classroom over time.

Value   A concept of the desirable.

Vygotsky, Lev   A Russian researcher, a peer of Piaget's, who believed that social interaction was important to children's learning.

White House Conference on Children   Meetings held every ten years since 1909 to discuss children's development, health, and education. In 1980 it was called the White House Conference on Families.

World Association for Early Childhood (OMEP)   An international professional society devoted to young children, with branches in various countries, including the United States. Concerned with children's growth, development, and education.

Young Children   Journal of the NAEYC.

Name Index

Abbott, C. F., 62
Adams, L., 458
Alexander, N. P., 29
Allen, K. E., 62
Althouse, R., 337
Andress, B., 362
Anfin, C., 337
Atkins, C., 62, 278
Attwood, M. E., 167
Axline, V. M., 321

Bader, L., 314
Bailey, U. J. O., 503
Balaban, N., 62
Baldwin, W., 502
Bandura, A., 141, 144, 256, 284
Banville, T., 203, 259
Baratz, J. C., 271
Barbour, N., 278
Bavolek, S. J., 448, 450
Bayless, K. M., 362
Bayley, N., 425
Bayman, A. G., 278
Beddington, G., 461
Bergan, J. R., 211–212
Berger, E. H., 450
Berk, L. E., 62, 110, 136, 203, 207, 232, 236, 257, 259, 271, 275, 278, 280, 318, 331, 337, 425
Berne, E., 212
Betz, C., 97
Beyer, E., 110
Biber, B., 45
Bigner, J., 450
Birch, L. L., 400
Bjorklund, G., 450
Blakley, B., 428, 503
Blank, H., 45, 503
Blaszczynski, B., 120–121, 134–135

Bloom, B. S., 102–103, 236
Borden, E. J., 232
Bower, R., 158, 400
Bowman, B., 110
Brand, S., 29
Branta, C., 167
Brazelton, T. B., 29, 45, 62, 118, 123, 141
Bredekamp, S., 45, 60, 62, 66, 80, 87, 114, 167, 337, 400, 404, 409, 415, 450, 496, 503
Briggs, B. S., 450
Brittain, W. L., 171, 174–175, 179, 182, 198
Brock, D. R., 278
Brown, M. H., 337
Buchoff, R., 362
Bundy, B. F., 450
Bullock, J. R., 62
Bruner, J., 171
Burns, M. S., 253
Burns, N., 428
Butler, D., 315

Caldecott, R., 289
Caldwell, B. M., 29, 32–33, 123
Caltron, C. E., 94
Canady, R. J., 315
Caplan, F., 46
Caplan, T., 46
Cartwright, S., 198, 253
Caruso, D. A., 123
Casey, M. B., 29
Castle, K., 29, 123
Cazdon, C. B., 278
Charlesworth, R., 232
Chenfleld, M. B., 362
Chevalier, Z., 487
Chittenden, G. E., 486

Christie, J., 427
Chukovsky, K., 256, 278
Church, M., 400
Cianciolo, P., 315
Clay, J. W., 450
Clements, D. H., 251, 253
Clifford, R. M., 198
Clinton, W. J., 431, 494
Clyde, J. A., 315
Cohen, S., 232
Cole, E., 198
Cole, M., 318
Collins, M., 63, 362
Collins, R. C., 503
Colman, M., 45
Comer, J. P., 450
Comstock, C., 450
Cooper, C. R., 278
Corbin, C., 167
Cosgrove, M. S., 400
Cowell, C., 398
Cratty, B. J., 167
Crinklaw-Kiser, D., 278
Cryer, D., 62, 198, 400, 450
Cullinan, B. E., 275
Cummins, S. 499
Curry, N. E., 45

Danforth, N., 478
Daniels, J., 97
Da Ros, D., 141
Davis, J. K., 428
Davis, M. D., 486
de la Roche, E., 198
De Regniers, B., 315
Dean, S. E., 487
Derman-Sparks, L., 303
DeVries, R., 232, 242, 253
Dinkmeyer, D., 97, 447, 450

Dittman, L., 123, 141
Dobie, J. F., 96
Dodd, E. L., 278
Dorsey, A. G., 428
Dove, A., 425
Downs, M. P., 257
Driekurs, R., 97
Driscoll, A., 98
Duckworth, E., 207
Dumtschin, J. U., 278
Dunn, N. S., 427
Dyson, A. H., 278

Edwards, C., 170, 477
Edwards, J., 278
Edwards, L., 198
Eheart, B. K., 123, 141
Elicker, J., 97, 124
Elkind, D., 29, 62, 250
Eller, B., 400
Elster, C. A., 427
Enders, J. B., 400
Erikson, E., 115, 323
Esbensen, S. B., 167
Essa, E. L., 427
Evans, J., 478

Faurve, M., 62
Feeney, S., 62, 198
Feldhusen, J. F., 450
Fenton, G. M., 222
Finkelhor, D., 427
Fisch, L., 256
Fischer, K., 457
Fisher, D. C., 503
Fisher, J. A., 400
Flemming, B. M., 232
Fogel, A., 63
Fong, Y. L., 450
Ford, S. A., 46
Forest, I., 483, 485
Forman, G., 198, 232, 253, 377
Foster, S. M., 450
Fox, R. C., 450
Fox, T. A., 450
Frankle, R. T., 400
French, L., 141
Freud, S., 323, 487
Friedberg, J., 315, 450

Froebel, F., 483
Froschl, M., 62
Frost, J. L., 167, 425
Furman, R. A., 450
Fyfe, B., 428

Gabbard, H. F., 486
Gage, J., 63
Galin, D., 173, 259
Galvin, E. S., 80
Gandini, L., 170
Garcia, E. E., 278
Gardner, H., 171
Garel, M. B., 249–250
Garner, A. P., 253
Gartreil, D., 29
Genishi. C., 278
George, F., 278
Gerber, M., 123
Gesell, A., 489
Glowacki, S., 496
Goduka, I., 478
Gold, S., 62
Goffin, S. G., 97, 232, 337, 503
Goin, L., 253
Goodnow, J., 178, 198
Goodwin, L. D., 198, 249–250
Goodwin, W., 249–250
Goodykoontz, B., 486
Gordon, T., 94, 447, 450
Gowen, J., 141
Gray, M. M., 50, 91, 216, 409, 427,
    432, 457
Greenberg, P., 46, 124, 450, 503
Grotberg, E., 503
Guilford, J. P., 171, 204, 236–237

Hale, J. F., 63
Hanline, M. F., 63
Harlan, J. D., 232
Harms, T., 62, 167, 198, 400, 450
Harris, V. J., 315
Harsh, A., 315
Haubenstricker, J., 145–156
Havighurst, R. J., 36–39, 236
Hayes, L., 198, 278
Hearn, K., 400
Hearron, P., 29, 68, 400, 405, 428,
    450, 503

Hemenway, W., 257
Henniger, M. L., 110
Hershey, G. L., 243
Heye, H., 399
Hildebrand, V., 29, 46, 63, 68, 80,
    91, 216, 278, 303, 337, 428, 450,
    457, 478
Hill, P., 485
Hilliard, A. G., 45
Hillman, C., 29, 63
Hines, R. P., 50, 91, 216, 278, 291,
    303, 409, 428, 450, 457
Hirsch, E. S., 244, 253, 337
Hitz, R., 97
Hoge, D. R., 428
Holcomb, B., 450
Holt, B., 232
Honig, A. S., 29, 63, 97, 114, 123,
    141, 278
Hubbell, R., 498
Hughes, F. P., 124
Hunt, F. E., 399
Hymes, J. L., Jr., 29, 86, 89, 94, 487,
    503

Ilg, F. L., 489
Ishigaki, E. H., 478

Jaggar, A. M., 275
Jalongo, M. R., 80, 124, 141, 315,
    362
Jan, T. D., 253
Janeway, E., 478, 503
Javenick, E., 63
Jenkins, E., 362
Johnson, C. N., 45
Johnson, D. L., 490
Johnson, L. J., 450
Johnson, S. L., 400
Jones, E., 45
Jordan, N. H., 428
Juliebo, M., 278

Kalinowski, M., 425
Kamii, C., 206–207, 232, 239, 242,
    253, 420
Karnes, M. B., 450
Katz, L., 62, 198, 337
Kendall, E. D., 94

Khatena, J., 198
Kitano, M. K., 232
Kinsman, C. A., 331
Klefstad, J., 400
Kontos, S., 284
Koopmans-Dayton, J. D., 450
Kostelnik, M., 29, 92, 110, 336
Kuschner, D. S., 232, 253, 377

Lally, J. R., 124
Landreth, C., 262, 366, 396
Langlois, J., 503
Languis, M., 173
Laosa, L. M., 478
Larrick, N., 288
Lasky, L., 97
Lawler, M. R., 394
Lazerson, A., 457
Leavitt, R. L., 123
Leithead, M., 253
Levine, J., 46
Lewin, K., 171
Lilenthal, J. W., 37–39
Lind, K. K., 232
Lippman, M., 29
Lombardi, J., 503
Lovell, P., 167
Lowenfeld, V., 171, 174, 182
Lueck, P., 167
Lugo, J. 0., 243

MacCarry, B., 315, 451
Maker, C. J., 63
Malaguzzi, L., 170
Manfredi/Petitt, L. A., 63
Manning, G., 278
Manning, M., 278
Marshall, H. H., 97
Martinez, M. G., 315
Maslow, A., 171
Mason, J., 284–285
Mazel, C., 499
McBride, B. A., 46, 451
McCloskey, R., 225
McCoy, E., 451
McKee, J., 487
McMillan, M., 483
McNeil, E., 315
Meddin, B. J., 63

Melson, C. F., 63
Merhill, H., 490
Metheny, N. Y., 399
Meyerhoff, M. K., 80
Milbank, D., 494
Milisen, R., 276
Miller, C. S., 97
Mills, H., 232, 315
Montessori, M., 240–241, 484–485,
  503
Moran, J. D. III, 84
Moravcik, E., 198
Morency, A., 276
Morgan, E., 451
Morin, J., 502
Morris, S. L., 46
Morris, S. S., 400
Morrison, G., 278
Morrow, L. S., 278, 315
Morse, W., 400
Moustakas, C., 44
Mukerji, R., 97
Munro, J., 478
Murphy, D. T., 46
Murphy, L. B., 484
Murray, C. L., 428
Musgrave, K. 0., 384, 400
Myers, R. C., 478
Myhre, S. M., 337

National Black Child Development
  Institute, 29
Nastasi, B. K., 251, 253
Neisworth, J. T., 337, 377, 428
Nelson, A. B., 63
Nixon, R. M., 493
New, R., 198
Nord, C. W., 502
Nourot, P. M., 63
Nurss, J. R., 278

Oliver, S. D., 384, 400
Olmstead, P. P., 478
Orrstein, R., 199
Osborn, D. K., 204, 253, 503
Osborn, J. D., 204, 253

Paciorek, K. M., 63, 451, 487
Palmer, L. M., 485

Patton, M. B., 399
Peabody, E., 484
Pellegrini, A. D., 63
Perlmutter, J. C., 63
Perry, G., 97
Pestalozzi, J. H., 492–493
Peters, D. L., 337, 377, 428
Phenice, L., 50, 91, 216, 409, 428,
  450, 457, 478
Phillips, C. B., 63, 110, 451
Phillips, D., 29
Piaget, J., 117–118, 171, 204–207,
  236–239
Pizzo, P. D., 124, 141
Poest, C. A., 167
Popkin, M., 451
Powell, D. R., 29, 451, 503
Prescott, E., 45, 167
Pruett, K., 497

Raines, S. C., 315
Ramsey, M. E., 362, 451
Rasmussen, M., 490
Reifel, S., 199, 253
Reinsberg, J., 124
Richarz, S., 400
Riley, S. S., 232
Rioux, J. W., 490
Rivkin, M., 80, 98
Robinson, C. H., 394, 400
Rockwell, R. E., 400
Rodriquez, G. G., 490
Rogers, C., 171
Rogers, C. S., 29, 46, 400
Rogers, D. D., 322, 337
Rogers, D. L., 98, 322, 337
Rogers, J. A., 63
Rose, D. F., 428
Rosen, A. L., 63
Ross, D. D., 98
Ross, H. W., 124
Rothenberg, M., 63
Rousseau, J. J., 482
Rowland, G. T., 425
Ruopp, R., 495

Sanchez, G. I., 271
Sanders, T., 173
Sawyers, J. K., 29, 46, 84

Schaefer, C., 198
Schiamberg, L., 63, 115, 118, 131, 138, 141, 167, 337
Schickedanz, J. A., 315
Schiller, M., 428
Schirrmacher, R., 199
Schmidt, V., 315
Schon, I., 278
Schorr, L. B., 503
Schurz, C., 484
Schweinhart, L. J., 63, 498
Sciarra, D., 428
Seefeldt, C., 63, 177, 199
Seefeldt, V., 145–156
Senhouse, M. F., 398
Sheldon, A., 278
Sholtys, K. C., 278
Skeen, P., 253
Slobin, D. I., 458
Smith, A. B., 462
Smith, B. J., 428
Smith, C. A., 315
Smith, J. K., 278
Smith, N. R., 199
Smith, R., 232
Snyder, A., 503
Soderman, A., 63, 92, 337
Sohoni, N., 478
Soto, L. D., 51, 63
Souweine, J., 499
Spock, B., 63, 489
Sprung, B., 232
Stein, L., 92, 336–337
Stern, V. W., 276
Stonehouse, A., 141
Strickland, D., 275, 315
Sullivan, M., 156, 363
Sulzby, E., 46
Surr, J., 29

Swaminathan, S., 251, 253
Swick, K. J., 451

Taylor, J., 428
Teale, W. H., 315
Tegano, D. W., 84
Templin, M. C., 276
Theillheimer, R., 46
Thorne, B., 46
Thornton, J. R., 428
Thurber, D. N., 267
Tinney, S., 63
Tipps. S., 173
Tobin, J. J., 478
Topolnicki, D. M., 478
Torrance, E. P., 171, 199, 268
Trawick-Smith, J., 337
Tryon, C., 37–39

Van Horn, J. L., 63
Van Riper, C., 276
Vartuli, S., 428
Veen, L. C., 124
Vygotsky, L., 106–108, 110, 124, 207, 236, 238, 318, 337

Wagman, A., 260, 271, 276
Walker-Dalhouse, D., 315
Walker, T., 490
Walling, L., 159
Walters, C. M., 450
Walton, S., 278
Wardle, F., 63, 167, 428
Washington, V., 503
Weber-Schwartz, N., 97
Weikart, D. P., 478, 498, 503
Weiner, P., 276
Weiser, M., 80, 124, 141
Wellhousen, K., 302

West, J., 63
Wheat, R., 110
Whiren, A., 92, 336, 337
White, B., 124
White, B. P., 141
Whitebook, M., 29
Wilbers, J. S., 503
Willer, B., 496
Williams, J. R., 167
Williams, L. M., 29, 427
Williams, R. P., 428
Williams, V. B., 363
Wilson, L. G., 124, 141
Wilson, S., 46
Winick, M., 158, 396
Winsler, A., 110, 232
Wiseman, A., 363
Wishon, P., 158, 400
Witt, D., 167
Wolery, M., 503
Wolf, A. D., 199
Wolf, J., 363
Wolfson, E., 63
Wolter, D. L., 315
Wood, C. F., 97
Wood, D., 278
Wong, A., 141
Wortham, S. C., 167
Wu, D. Y. H., 478
Wyman, A., 503

Yawkey, T. D., 377, 428

Zan, B., 232
Ziemer, M., 232
Zigler., E., 491
Zill, N., 63
Zimmerman, B., 211–212
Zinsser, C., 487

Subject Index

ABC Bill, 494
Abuse, sexual, 427–429
Accreditation, 19, 65–66, 404, 409, 415, 448, 496
Activities
  art, 169–199
  dramatic play, 217–337
  field trips, 364–377
  food, 378–400
  language, 254–278
  literature, 280–315
  motor, 143–167
  music, 338–363
  perceptual, 234–253
  planning, 100–110, 209–210, 402–425
  science, 201–232, 234–253, 364–376, 378–400
Administration, 402–428
Adult educator, 95, 196–197, 420, 451
Aerobics, 143
African schools, 466–467, 482
Age characteristics, 50–63, 394
  art, 179
  five-year-olds, 321
  four-year-olds, 321
  infants, 321
  three-year-olds, 321
  toddlers, 127–141, 321
American Association of Family and Consumer Sciences, 28
Anecdotal record, 20–22
Animals, 223–226
Ant farm, 226
Aprons, 188
Art activities, 169–199
Articulation, 275–276, 319, 411
Assignments. *See* Staff

Association for Childhood Education International, 28
Attachment, 115, 122
Attendance chart, 214–215
Attention span, 128, 286, 291
Autoharp, 345–346
Autonomy, 131–133
Australian school, 460

Balls, 149–150
Baritone ukelele, 345
Bases for goals, 32–35
Basic food groups, 385
Bathroom, 70, 216
Behavioral objectives, 411
Bilingual education, 259, 271–275
Black English, 275
Blocks, 244–246, 333
Bloom Taxonomy of Educational Objectives, 102–103, 236, 411
Bolivian schools, 452, 474
Bonding, 115–117
Books, children's, 280–315
  illustrations, 289
  infant's, 291
  toddler's, 291
Box art, 194
Brain development, 172–174, 238–253, 256–257
Breakfast, 396

Caldecott Medal, 289
Canadian schools, 459, 473
Carpentry, 163
Catching, 149–150
Chalk, 190–191
Chemistry, 229
Child care centers, 16, 494

Child Development Associate (CDA), 19, 491
Childhood Education, 28
Children, age characteristics, 52–58
  socio-cultural characteristics, 50–52
  special needs, 58–59
  toddlers, 127–141
Children's Charter, 454, 488–489
Children's needs, 34
Children Today, 28
Chile's school, 473
Chinese child care center, 464
Chords, music, 345
Church sponsored schools, 16
Classification, Piaget, 204–206
Clay, modeling, 194
Coloring books, 174
Computer, 235, 249–252
Concrete operations, Piaget, 204–206
Conference, parents, 358, 441–444
Conservation, Piaget, 204, 240
Controlling, 422–424
Cooking experiences, 388–393
Cooperative extension, 216
Cooperative nursery, 17, 433–434, 496
Cooperative play, 55–56, 244–248, 258
Coordination, 234–253
Corporate centers, 16
Costa Rican school, 472
Council for Exceptional Children, 28
Crayons, 190
Creativity, 170–174, 238, 244, 321
Cultural differences, 189, 259, 272–275, 289, 297, 409, 432–433, 457–458
Cultural experiences, 455–458

Cumulative planning, 209–210,
327–329, 364–377, 414–416
Cutting skills, 192

Daily schedule, 73–76, 416–417
Dairy Council, 216
Death, discussion of, 320
Decisions, of manager, 402–428
Declaration of Rights of the Child,
454, 488–489
Developmental
philosophy, 34–40
stages, art, 178–180
general, 36–40
motor skills, 138–139, 143–167,
178–180, 243–253
tasks, 36–40
Developmentally appropriate, 37,
129–130, 321, 404–409, 415
Diary records, 20
Directions
for evaluation performance, 25–27
for observers, 20
for participants, 22–25, 261–275
Disabled, 152, 499
Discipline. *See* Guidance
Dramatic play, 267, 316–337
blocks, 244–246, 333
contribution to development,
318–327
outdoors, 161–162, 333–335
themes for, 316–337
Drawing, 190–191
Drop-in-center, 17
Duty chart, 218

Eating, 70, 378–400
Ecuador schools, 475
Educational objectives. *See* Goals
El Salvador schools, 470
Employer-sponsored center, 16
England schools, 460
Enrollments, in early childhood
school, 7–10
Evaluating, 422–426
activity, 109, 197
children, 145–155
college students, 25–27
total program, 422–426

Exceptional Children, 28
Excursions, 268, 364–377
Exercise, 143–167, 320, 358, 396
Extension, cooperative, 216, 385, 446
Eye-hand coordination, 178–180,
234–253

Facility, 416–418
Family. *See* Parents
comments, art, 180
language, 257–258, 265, 272
variations, 51–52
Family day care, 16
Family, international conference,
454–455
Family Relationships, 28
Field trips, 219–220, 268
Films and videotapes
The Adventure Begins: Preschool
and Technology, 252
Block Play: Constructing Realities,
253
Building Self-Confidence, 96
Building Quality Child Care:
Independence, 96
Career Encounters: ECE, 27
Caring for Our Children, 123
Celebrating Early Childhood
Teacher, 28, 502
A Classroom with Blocks, 253
Culture and Education of Young
Children, 110, 478
Curriculum for Preschool and
Kindergarten, 62, 337
Developmentally Appropriate
Practice: Birth Through Age 5,
62, 141
Discipline: Appropriate Guidance
of Young Children, 96
Establishing Healthful Habits, 400
Fundamental Object Control
Skills, 167
Fundamental Locomotor Skills, 167
Harmonizing the Worlds of Home
and School, 449
How Young Children Learn to
Think, 231
Infant Curriculum: Great Explo-
rations, 123

Kids Construction Video, 231
Learning Can Be Fun, 360
Listening and Talking, 277
Meeting Special Needs, 62
Mister Rogers Talks with Parents,
449
Music Across the Curriculum, 360
Nurturing Community, 28
Reading and Young Children, 314
Relating to Others, 96
Role of the Teacher, 96
Salaries, Working Conditions, and
the Teacher Shortage, 502
A Secure Beginning, 123
Seeing Infants with New Eyes, 123
Sensory Play: Constructing Reali-
ties, 232
Sharing Books with Young Chil-
dren, 314
Sharing Nature with Young Chil-
dren, 232
Thinking and Creativity, 198
Toddler Curriculum: Making Con-
nections, 141
Training System for Caregivers, 123
Using the Early Childhood Class-
room Observation, 62
What Is Quality Child Care?, 28
Whole-Language Learning, 277, 450
Fingerpainting, art, 185–190
Fingerplays, 300, 307–313
Firefighter's hats, 334
Five-year-olds, 179
Flopsy doodle, 150
Food experiences, 378–400
Foreign language, 271–276, 458
Four-year-olds, art, 179

Games, language, 264
mathematical, 238–243
musical, 358
Gender, 214, 394
Gifted Child Quarterly, 28
Global education, 220–221, 452–478
Gluing, cutting, 193
Goals
art education, 174–181
cognitive, 203–204, 234–253
developmental, 13–15

dramatic play, 246, 318–326
early childhood education, 31–46, 101, 412–413, 424
field trips, 219–220, 276, 364–377, 389
food experiences, 381, 388–394
guidance, 178–181, 246
language, 136–137, 260–264
literature, 282–288
mealtime, 394–399
music activity, 340–341
outdoor activity, 143–167
parent involvement, 140, 179, 180, 358–359, 398–399, 431–450
perceptual-motor, 234–253
science, 200–232
total program, 4, 31–46, 101, 412–413, 424
Goodenough Draw-A-Man test, 176
Grammar, 261–263
Grouping children, 415
Guatemalan schools, 471
Guidance, 82–98, 131–136, 164–166, 178–181, 246, 261–263, 396–398
Guidelines, 412–413, 424
Guitar chords, 345

Handicapped child's schooling, 18, 152, 499
Head Start, 12, 18–19, 407, 408, 420, 490–499
Health measures, 79, 139, 380–381
Hearing, 256–257, 276
High school preschools, 15
History of profession, 480–499
Home visits, 60, 441–444
Honduran school, 472
Hospital schools, 18
Humor, children's, 291, 294, 299

Imagination, 170–172, 245–246, 256, 354
India's schools, 465
Infants, 52, 113–124
Instructions
  for observers, 20–22
  for participants, 22–25, 158–166, 196–197

International Journal of Early Childhood, 19, 28, 496
International Year of the Family, 454–455
International women's conference, 454–455
Invented spelling, 267, 270
IQ tests, 425–426

Japanese schools, 463
Journal of Early Childhood Teacher Educators, 28
Journals, professional, 28–29

Kenyan schools, 466
Kicking stages, 147, 152
Kindergarten, 15–18, 56, 174–175, 484

Laboratory schools, 15
Language arts, 254–278
  records, tapes, 264–265
  show and tell, 269–271
Language development, 136–137, 254–278
  articulation, 275–276
  bilingual, 272–275
  field trips, 374, 389
  general discussion, 254–278
  infants, 117–119, 260
  toddlers, 136–137, 260–261
Lanham Act nursery schools, 486–487
Latin American schools, 468–475
Learning centers, 41, 69, 178–196, 234–253, 416–420
Legislation, child care, 494
Liberian schol, 467
Literacy, emerging, 136, 266–267, 280–315, 406
Literature, 280–315
Locker space, 69, 416–420
Locomotor skills, 138–139, 143–167
Lunch, 394–397

Machines and tools, 227
Magazines, children's, 232
Magnets, 227
Managers, of schools, 402–428
Manipulative toys, 243–244, 246

Manuscript writing, 177, 266–267
Mathematics activities, 206–207, 238–243
Mealtime, 378–400
Mental development
  art, 172–175
  outdoors, 155–164
  perceptual-motor, 234–253
  science, 201–232, 388–400
Merrill-Palmer Institute, 485
Mexican school, 471
Modeling clay, 194–195
Montessori school, 241, 484–485
Motor skills, 138–139, 143–167, 234–253
Multicultural, activities, 271–275, 302–303, 452–478
  books, 298, 302
  differences, 216–217, 432
Music activity
  books, 361
  chords, 345
  games, 358
  goals, 340
  involving parents, 358–359, 424
  listening, 356, 358
  movement, 354–356
  records, 362
  singing, 346–354

Name tags, 78
National Association of Early Childhood Teacher Educators, 28, 496
National Association for the Education of Young Children (NAEYC), 482, 495
  accreditation, 65–66
  organization, 66, 495
  position statements, 59, 258
National Association for Gifted Children, 28
National Council on Family Relations, 28
New Zealand schools, 461
Nicaraguan schools, 455, 473

Obesity, 4, 396
Objectives. *See* Goals
Observer instructions, 20–22

OMEP (World Association), 19, 28, 458, 496

Organizations, professional, 19, 28, 496

Organizing play centers, 40–44, 65–80, 234–253

Outdoor learning activity, 143–167, 219–221, 337

Painting, 182–190

Panama schools, 469

Parallel play, 134–135, 321

Parent Child Development Center, 490

Parent conference, 441–444
  meetings, 441

Parent cooperatives, 17, 433–434, 473

Parental needs, 33–34, 163–164

Parent Effectiveness Training (PET), 441–444

Parent involvement, 424
  in art activity, 180–181
  in field trips, 371–372
  in food experiences, 398–399
  in home visit, 436–439
  in music, 358–359
  in reading/literature, 265, 305–307

Participation instructions, 22–25, 261–263

Perceptual skills, 234–253

Personal message, 83, 92

Perry Preschool Project, 498

Peru school, 474

Philosophy, developmental, 102–103, 136, 235–243, 415

Photos
  Australian Child Care Center, 460
  Baylor University, 30, 48
  Bethany Weekday School, 182, 346, 364, 373
  Children's Center, Denver, 6, 52, 67, 102, 105, 157, 168, 208, 224
  Chile's school, 473
  Chinese Children's school, 464
  Cloud County Community College, 70, 118, 132, 332
  Cusco, Peru, 474
  East Field (Texas) Community College, 483

Edna, Texas High School, 493

Garden City (Kansas) Community College, 316, 402

Guatemalan child care center, 471

Honduran child care center, 472

Howard University, 82, 238, 380

India's schools, 465

Kadena Air Force Base, 119

Kansas State University, 1, 4, 34, 41, 53, 55, 75, 84, 90, 107, 109, 128, 142, 173, 251, 264, 280, 290, 319, 387, 388, 406, 410

Kenyan orphanage, 466

Kyoto, Japan kindergarten, 463

La Paz, Bolivia center, 452, 274

Liberian village school, 467

Metropolitan State College, 240, 414

Mexican kindergarten, 471

Michigan State University, 5, 20, 36, 40, 144, 191, 211, 262, 283, 340, 375, 376, 391

Michigan State University Motor Skills Program, 147–149, 154–156

Montessori School, 485

Mt. St. Vincent's College, 88, 459

National Institute of Education, 236, 247

New Zealand Children's Center, 461

Nicaragua, parent coop, 440, 450

Oakwood College, 343

Oregon State University, 186, 242, 245, 328, 378

Panamanian child care center, 469

Pennsylvania State University, 32, 131

Puerto Rican Head Start, 469

Quito, Ecuador school, 475

Russian school, 476

San Antonio College, 43

Santiago, Chile child care center, 473

Savannah, Georgia pre-k, 295, 480

South African schools, 467, 482

South East Oakland Vocational Technical Center, 48, 100, 170, 200, 298

Texas Tech University, 383

Texas Woman's University, 338

Toy-Eiwa School, Tokyo, 463

University Costa Rica, 472

University Illinois, 64, 66, 85, 108, 157, 228, 320, 395

University New Mexico, 42, 377, 434

University S. Carolina, 259, 337

University Vermont, 325

U.S. Army/Germany, 122, 254, 330

Utah State University, 440

Photographers
  Hildebrand, C., 138, 282
  Hildebrand, V., 50, 56, 112, 115, 330, 432, 445
  Hildreth, G., 409
  Hines, R., 129, 202
  Kertez, F., 180, 234
  Kim, Y., 116
  Kosobayshi, M., 57
  Kummerow, M., 140
  Li, I., 130, 404
  Masud, S., 126
  Page, J., 203
  Russell, S., 14, 239
  Schiamberg, L., 286
  Watson, V., 437

Piaget's stages, 239–241

Planning, 64–80, 100–110, 129–140, 402–428. *See also* each chapter for planning details

Play, 34, 40–44, 316–337

Playdough, 194–195

Playground activity, 143–167, 246

Poetry, 291–295

Premath, 238–243

Prereading, 136, 175–176, 265, 280–315

Printing, 175, 266–267

Professional
  history, 480–499
  journals & organizations, 28

Pronunciation, 276

Prosocial, support for, 131–136, 321, 321–323
  sharing, 165, 269–271

Puerto Rico school, 469

Punishment, 88

Puppets, 297
Puzzles, 236–238, 248–249

Questioning, 212, 237–238

Ranger Rick's Nature Magazine, 232
Ratios, staff-child, 60, 134–135
Reading, pre-, 175–176, 280–315
Records, 362
Reggio Emilia, Italy schools,
    476–477
Rights of the child, 453–454,
    488–489
Russian school, 476

Safety, 164–166, 368, 393–394, 421
Sand, 162
Scheduling, 71–77, 163–164, 409,
    416–420
Science activities, 155–158,
    200–232, 237–253, 364–377,
    378–400
Scissors, 192
Sculptures, 194
Second language, 272–275
Self-selected activity, 178–182,
    234–253, 304–305, 327–336
Self-sufficiency (self-efficacy),
    131–133
Sensorimotor stage, Piaget,
    204–207, 235
Seriation, 240–241
Sexual abuse, 214–216, 427
Sharing, 135–136, 165, 244–246,
    269–271
Show and tell, 269–271
Silly putty, 194
Singing, 137
Six-year-olds, 299
Size of groups, 130
Small motor skills, 175–176,
    234–253
Snacktime, 397–398
Social play, 244–246, 321–324
Songs, 341–343

South African school, 467, 482
Spanish
    first language, 273–275
    songs, 346–354
Speaking. *See* Language
Special children, 152, 271–275
Special visitors, 374–376
Staff assignments, 77–78, 164–165,
    181–182, 261–263, 420–422
Stages, art
    cognitive, 102–103, 204–207,
        235–243, 411
    motor-skill, 131–133, 234–253
    social play, 134–135, 244–246,
        321–324
Standards
    accreditation, 19, 404, 409, 448,
        496
Statistics, of ECE, 7–12
Stories, presentation, 295–300
Structured activities, 42–44,
    234–253
Swings, 162
Symbolic play, 246–247, 267–268,
    316–337

Teacher
    for infants, 112–124
    for toddlers, 126–141
Teacher certification
    infants, 113–123
    qualities, 86–87
Teaching style, 42–44, 84–87,
    196–197
Testing children, 425–426
Themes, curriculum, 130, 213–231,
    329–336, 413–414
Theory, theorists, 132
    Axline, V., 321
    Bandura, A., 132, 144, 256
    Bloom, B., 102–103, 236, 411
    Development, 35–37
    Erickson, E., 323
    Eye-hand coordination, 234–253
    Freud, S., 323

Guilford, J. P., 204, 237
Pestalozzi, J. H., 482
Piaget, J., 117–118, 204–207, 235,
    238–243
Play, 44, 143–167, 322–324
Rousseau, J. J., 482
Vygotsky, L., 106–108, 136, 207,
    238, 318
Thinking types, 204
Time block plan, 72–76, 416–417
Three-year-olds, 53–55
Throwing, 138–139, 151, 154
Toileting, 25, 59, 139
Transition times, 95, 300, 396
Trends, in ECE, 7–11
Trips. *See* Field trips
Two-year-olds, 127–141
Types of schools, 15–18

Ukelele, 345
United Nations, 453–455, 489

Values, 33, 144, 236–239, 433
Verbal guidance, 178–181, 196, 246,
    396–397
Videotapes. *See* Films
Visitor's, contribution, 374–375
Vocabulary, 254–278
Voice, 90–92, 261
Vygotsky's theory, 59, 106–108, 207,
    238, 322

"War on Poverty" period, 490
Weather, 76–77, 221, 227
White House Conferences, 487
Women's Fourth World Conference,
    454–455, 496–497
World Association for Early Child-
    hood, 32–33, 458, 496
Writing, pre-, 176–177, 265–267

Young Children, 28, 495
Your Big Back Yard, 232